INTRODUCTION TO BIBLICAL HEBREW

INTRODUCTION TO BIBLICAL HEBREW

Thomas O. Lambdin
HARVARD UNIVERSITY

Darton, Longman and Todd, London

First published in Great Britain in 1973 by
Darton, Longman & Todd Limited
85 Gloucester Road, London SW7 4SU

Printed in Great Britain by
Fletcher & Son Ltd, Norwich

ISBN 0 232 51202 7

PREFACE

This textbook is designed for a full year's course in elementary Biblical Hebrew at the college level. In its choice of vocabulary and grammar it is essentially an introduction to the prose, not the poetical language. While my aim has been to include only what I consider necessary for the grammatically intelligent reading of the texts on which the work is based, experienced teachers may nevertheless wish to expand or condense one portion or another according to the needs of their own courses and the problems of their particular students. By keeping the grammatical discussion at a relatively unsophisticated level I have tried to make the book as serviceable as possible to those who want to study the language without a teacher.

Although the present work clearly falls within the category of traditional grammars, there are several features in the presentation which require a brief comment. The generous use of transliteration is meant to serve three purposes: to enable the student to perceive Hebrew as a language, and not an exercise in decipherment; to remove the customary initial obstacle, wherein the student was required to master innumerable pages of rather abstract phonological and orthographic details before learning even a sentence of the language; and to facilitate the memorization of the paradigms, where the essential features are, in my opinion, set in greater relief than in the conventional script. The morphology of the verb is presented in a way that best exploits the underlying similarities of the various forms, regardless of the root type; this permits the introduction of the most common verbs at an appropriately early point in the grammar and also allows the discussions of the derived "conjugations" to be unhampered by restriction to examples from sound roots. As much space as possible has been given to the systematic treatment of noun morphology and to the verb with object suffixes; the simplification of this material attempted in many elementary grammars is actually a disservice to the student. When he turns to his first page of unsimplified reading, he finds that what he should have learned systematically must instead be learned at random, inefficiently and with no little difficulty. And finally, special attention has been given to an orderly presentation of prose syntax, beginning with a characterization of the various types of individual clauses and proceeding to sequences of interrelated clauses.

In the initial stages of preparing this book I was greatly aided in the selection of vocabulary by George M. Landes' *A Student's Vocabulary of Biblical Hebrew* (New York, 1961), furnished to me in page proof at that time by the author, to whom I now wish to acknowledge my thanks. In the nearly ten years since that time the innumerable suggestions and corrections submitted by my students and colleagues working with various drafts of the book have been of enormous help in improving the quality of the finished product. I am especially grateful, however, to Dr. Avi Hurwitz, now at the Hebrew University, for his great kindness in giving an earlier draft of this book a thorough and critical reading and in providing me with many corrections. The errors that remain are of course due to my own oversight.

The setting of pointed Hebrew with a special sign marking stress always proves to be a difficult job, even in this age of technological marvels. I wish to thank the publisher and the printer for their unstinting efforts to ensure correctness in this regard.

Cambridge, Mass. THOMAS O. LAMBDIN
May 1971

CONTENTS

INTRODUCTION

The Hebrew Bible (Christian Old Testament) is a collection of writings whose composition spans most of the millennium from c. 1200 B.C. to c. 200 B.C. Because a spoken language does not remain constant over so long a period of time, we must recognize Biblical Hebrew as a form of the spoken language standardized at a particular time and perpetuated thereafter as a fixed literary medium. It is generally assumed that Biblical Hebrew, to the extent that it is linguistically homogeneous, is a close approximation to the language of the monarchic periods preceding the Babylonian Exile (thus, before 587 B.C.), during which a major portion of biblical literature was compiled and composed. The sparse inscriptional material of the ninth to seventh centuries B.C. corroborates this view, but does not permit us to establish more precise limits. In the post-exilic period spoken Hebrew came under the strong influence of other languages, especially Aramaic, but also Persian and, later, Greek. The literary language of biblical writings during this time remained relatively free of this influence, which shows up more clearly in post-biblical sources such as the Rabbinic Hebrew of the Mishna and other traditional works lying beyond the scope of this grammar. Exactly when Hebrew ceased to be a spoken language is difficult, if not impossible, to determine, but in all probability its demise was concurrent with the devastation of Judaea in the Jewish revolts against Roman rule in the first two centuries A.D.

Hebrew is a member of the extensive Semitic language family, whose principal divisions are as follows:

(1) Northeast Semitic: Babylonian and Assyrian (Akkadian);
(2) Southeast Semitic: Ancient South Arabic and the related modern languages of South Arabia and Ethiopia;
(3) Southwest Semitic: Classical Arabic and the host of related modern Arabic dialects;
(4) Northwest Semitic, comprising
 (a) Aramaic
 (b) Canaanite (Ugaritic, Phoenician, Hebrew)

Our knowledge of Biblical Hebrew is directly dependent on Jewish oral tradition and thus on the state of that tradition during and following the various dispersions of the Jews from Palestine. This dependence arises from the peculiarly deficient orthography in which the biblical text was written: it is essentially vowelless, or at most, vocalically ambiguous (see below, §8). The actual pronunciation of the language was handed down orally, and as the Jews left or were expelled from Palestine and formed new communities in Babylonia, Egypt, and eventually throughout most of the civilized world, the traditional reading of biblical texts diverged gradually from whatever norm might have existed prior to these dispersions. The written consonantal text itself achieved a final authoritative form around the end of the first century A.D. This text was successfully promulgated among all the Jewish communities, so that texts postdating this time do not differ from one another in any important particulars. Prior to the fixing of an authoritative text, however, the situation was quite different, and the reader is referred to the bibliography (Appendix E) for the names of a few works that will introduce him to the complex problems of ancient texts and versions.

Modern printed versions of the Hebrew Bible derive from several essentially similar sources, all reflecting the grammatical activity of Jewish scholars (or Masoretes, traditionalists) in Tiberias, who during the 9th and 10th centuries A.D. perfected a system of vowel notation and added it to the received consonantal text. Because the vowel system reflected in this notation is not exactly the same as that of the tradition used in other locales, we must recognize that Hebrew grammar, as based on the vocalized Tiberian Masoretic text, is no more or less authentic than that which would derive from other traditions: it is simply the best preserved and has received, by universal adoption, the stamp of authority. A treatment of the fragmentary evidence of the non-Tiberian traditions lies beyond the scope of an elementary grammar. The standard Masoretic text is also known as the Ben Asher text, after the family name of the Tiberian scholars identified with the final editing. The *Biblia Hebraica* (3rd edition, Stuttgart, 1937) used by most modern students and scholars is based on the copy of a Ben Asher manuscript now in Leningrad and dating from 1008/9 A.D. Most other printed Hebrew Bibles are based ultimately on the text of the Second Rabbinic Bible (Venice, 1524–25); the manuscript sources of this work have not been fully identified, but it does not differ substantially from the text of the *Biblia Hebraica*. A new and comprehensive edition of the Hebrew Bible is in progress in Israel; it will utilize the partially destroyed Aleppo Codex, which is convincingly claimed as an authentic manuscript of the Ben Asher family.

A limited number of variant readings are indicated marginally in the Masoretic text. These are commonly referred to as *kəṯîḇ-qərē*, i.e. one word is written (*kəṯîḇ*) in the consonant text itself but another, as indicated in the margin, is to be read (*qərē*).

SOUNDS AND SPELLING

[*Note: The material in this section has been presented as a unit for ready reference. After studying § § 1–3 the reader should begin Lesson 1 (p. 3). The reading of further paragraphs will be indicated as required.*]

1. The Sounds of Biblical Hebrew.

As stated in the Introduction, we cannot determine absolutely the sounds of Biblical Hebrew in the period during which the literary language was fixed. The pronunciation used in this book has been chosen to preserve as faithfully as possible the consonantal and vocalic distinctions recognized by the Masoretes, but, at the same time, to do the least violence to what we know of the earlier pronunciation. A uniform system of transliteration has been adopted which attempts to represent the Hebrew orthography simply and accurately.

a. Consonants

Type	*Transliteration*	*Pronunciation**
Labial	b	[b] as in bait
	p	[p] as in pay
	m	[m] as in main
	w	[w] as in well
Labio-dental	ḇ	[v] as in vase
	p̄	[f] as in face
Interdental	ṯ	[θ] as in thin
	ḏ	[δ] as in this
Dental or alveolar	t	[t] as in time
	d	[d] as in door
	s }	[s] as in sing
	ś }	
	z	[z] as in zone

* Square brackets enclose currently used phonetic symbols as a guide to those who are familiar with them. Do not confuse these with the transliteration.

	n	[n] as in noon
Prepalatal	š	[ʃ] as in show
	y	[y] as in yes
Palatal	k	[k] as in king
	g, ḡ	[g] as in go
	ḵ	[x] as in German Bach
Velar	q	[q]

There is no exact English equivalent of this sound. It is a type of [k], but with the contact between the tongue and the roof of the mouth as far back as possible.

Guttural	ʼ	[ˀ] the glottal stop
	h	[h] as in house
	ʻ	[ˤ] no Eng. equivalent
	ḥ	[H] no Eng. equivalent

The glottal stop [ˀ] is used in English, but not as a regular part of its sound system. It is made by a complete stoppage of breath in the throat and may be heard in certain Eastern pronunciations of words like *bottle* and *battle*, in which the glottal stop replaces the normal *t*, thus [bɑˀl], [bæˀl]. The sound [H] is an *h*-sound, but with strong constriction between the base of the tongue and the back of the throat, thus with a much sharper friction than ordinary *h*. The [ˤ] is similarly produced, but with the additional feature of voicing. Most modern readers of Biblical Hebrew do not use these two sounds, replacing them with [x] and [ˀ] respectively. Those making such a simplification should be careful not to confuse these four sounds in spelling.

The four sounds which we shall call gutturals throughout this book are more precisely described as laryngeals and pharyngealized laryngeals, but because the modern terminology is often inconsistently applied, we find no compelling reason to abandon the more traditional designation.

Liquids	r	[r] as in rope
	l	[l] as in line
Modified Dental	ṭ	[t] as in time
	ṣ	[ts] as in hits

The pronunciation indicated for *ṭ* and *ṣ* is a standard modern substitution for the original sounds, whose true nature can only be conjectured as [t] and [s] accompanied by constriction in the throat (pharyngealization or glottalization), thus producing a tenser, duller sound.

b. Vowels

It is customary in treating Hebrew vowels to speak of length as well as quality. Though this distinction is probably valid for the earlier pronunciation, it is doubtful whether vowel quantity played any important part in the original Masoretic system. The diacritical marks used in our transcription are thus to be taken as devices reflecting the Hebrew spelling and not necessarily as markers of real length.

î, ī	[i] as in mach*i*ne	û, ū	[u] as in m*oo*d
i	[ɪ] as in *i*t	u	[ʊ] as in b*oo*k
ê, ē	[e] as in th*ey*	ô, ō	[o] as in n*o*te
e, ệ	[ɛ] as in b*e*t	o	[ɔ] as in b*ou*ght
a	[ɑ] as in f*a*ther or [a] as in th*a*t	ə	[ə] as in *a*bove, and very brief in duration
ā, â	[ɑ] as in f*a*ther or [ɔ] as in b*ou*ght		

Some distinction between the two vowels *a* and *ā* should be made, since they must always be clearly distinguished in spelling. The choice is left to the reader: either [a] as opposed to [ɑ] or [ɑ] as opposed to [ɔ].

In addition to the vowels listed above there are three others (*ă ĕ ŏ*) which, together with *ə*, are known as reduced vowels. They are of very brief duration but with the same quality as the corresponding full vowel: *ă* is a very short *a*, *ĕ* a very short *e*, and *ŏ* a very short *o*.

The following diphthongal combinations of vowel + *y* or *w* occur frequently at the ends of words:

îw	the vowel *î* + a very short [ŭ]. Also pronounced as [iv], as in English *eve*.
ēw, êw	*ē*/*ê* + [ŭ]. Also [ev], as in *save*.
āw, âw	*ā* + [ŭ] like the *ou* of *house*, or as [ɑw] or [ɑv]
aw	*a* + [ŭ], or as [ɑv] or [av]
āy	[ɑy] like the *y* of *sky*; or [ɔy], similar to the *oy* of *toy*.
ay	[ɑy] or [ay]
ôy, ōy	[oy], similar to the *owy* of *showy*, but without the *w*.
ûy, ūy	[uy] somewhat like the *uey* of *gluey*.

For descriptive purposes we shall refer to the vowels according to the following classification, without prejudice to the actual length of the vowels involved:

(1) unchangeable long: *î ê ô û* and sometimes *ō*
(2) changeable long: *ē ā ō*
(3) short: *i e a o u*
(4) reduced: *ə ă ĕ ŏ*

2. Syllabification.

With very few exceptions a syllable must begin with a single consonant followed at least by one vowel. This rule alone will suffice for the accurate division of a word into syllables. Consider the following examples:

miḏbār (wilderness): *miḏ-bār*	pronounced	[mɪδ'bɑr]
'āḇîw (his father): *'ā-ḇîw*		['ɑ'viw]
dəḇārîm (words): *də-ḇā-rîm*		[dəvɑ'rim]
mimménnî (from me): *mim-mén-nî*		[mɪm'mɛnni]
gibbôrîm (warriors): *gib-bô-rîm*		[gɪbbo'rim]
yišlāḥḗnî (he will send me): *yiš-lā-ḥḗ-nî*		[yɪʃlɑ'ʜeni]
malkəḵā (your king): *mal-kə-ḵā*		[mɑlkə'xɑ]
malḵêḵem (your kings): *mal-ḵê-ḵem*		[mɑlxe'xɛm]

In none of these examples is any other division of syllables possible without violating the basic rule.

Syllables are of two types: *open* and *closed*. An open syllable is one which ends in a vowel; a closed syllable ends in a consonant. Syllables containing a diphthong may be considered as closed, taking the *y* or *w* as a consonant. The distinction is irrelevant in this case.

When determining syllabification note that a doubled consonant, such as *–bb–* or *–mm–*, is always to be divided in the middle. This does not mean that there is any perceptible pause between the syllables in pronunciation: a doubled consonant is simply held longer than a single one. Contrast the long *n* of English *meanness* with the normal short *n* of *any*. Examples are

libbəḵā (your heart): *lib-bə-ḵā*	[lɪbbə'xɑ]
mimməḵā (from you): *mim-mə-ḵā*	[mɪmmə'xɑ]
haššāmáyim (the heavens): *haš-šā-má-yim*	[hɑʃʃɑ'mɑyɪm]

3. Stress.

Words are stressed on the last syllable (ultima) or on the next to last (penultima). The former is more frequent.

ultimate stress: *dāḇār* (word); *dəḇārîm* (words); *nāḇî'* (prophet)
penultimate stress: *méleḵ* (king); *láylāh* (night); *nəḥṓšeṯ* (bronze)

Only penultimate stress will be marked in this book.

The stressed syllable is often referred to as the *tonic* syllable, and the two preceding it as the *pretonic* and *propretonic* respectively.

4. The consonants known as the begadkepat.

Two sets of six sounds each are closely related to one another, both in sound and distribution. These are the six stops *b, g, d, k, p, t* on the one hand and their spirantized counterparts *ḇ, ḡ, ḏ, ḵ, p̄,* and *ṯ* on the other. Although no rule can be given for the choice between the sounds of one set and those of the other without important exceptions, the following observations will provide a safe guide for the majority of occurrences.

(a) Of the two sets, only the stops occur doubled. Thus we find *-bb-* (as in *habbáyiṯ*, the house), *-dd-* (*haddéleṯ*, the door), *-kk-* (*hakkəlî*, the vessel), etc., but never *-ḇḇ-*, *-ḡḡ-*, *-ḏḏ-*, etc.

(b) The stops *b, g, d, k, p, t* occur (excluding the doubling just mentioned) only at the beginning of a syllable when immediately preceded by another consonant:

malkî (my king): *mal-kî*

but *méleḵ* (king): *mé-leḵ*.

Elsewhere one finds the spirantized counterpart, which, by a simple process of elimination, occurs (a) mainly at the close of a syllable, or (b) at the beginning of a syllable when the preceding sound is a vowel. Contrast, for example, the *b* of *miḏbār* (*miḏ-bār*) and the *ḇ* of *nāḇîʼ* (*nā-ḇîʼ*).*

When a word begins with one of these sounds, it usually has the stop when it occurs in isolation (thus: *báyiṯ*, a house), but when some element ending in a vowel is prefixed, the stop is automatically replaced by the corresponding spirant. Be sure the following examples are clear:

báyiṯ	a house	but	*kəḇáyiṯ*	like a house
kəlî	a vessel		*ûḵəlî*	and a vessel
déleṯ	a door		*ləḏéleṯ*	to a door.

In a sentence the mere fact that the preceding word ends in a vowel is enough to warrant the spirant; thus,

bānû ḇáyiṯ they built a house

not *bānû báyiṯ*.

There are, however, many exceptions to this, depending on the degree of grammatical relationship between the words in question.

It is best, at least hypothetically, to regard the stop *g* and the spirant *ḡ* as two distinct sounds, although no modern tradition except the Yemenite has preserved the difference.

5. Vowel Reduction.

Many of the changes that characterize Hebrew inflections follow distinct and predictable patterns, of which the most consistent is that of vowel reduction.

(a) *Propretonic reduction*. The vowels *ā* and *ē* are regularly reduced to *ə* in open *propretonic* syllables. That is, when in the course of inflection the

* Note that our statement does not preclude the possibility of a spirant occurring at the beginning of a syllable preceded by another consonant: *malḵêḵem* (your kings).

accent is shifted so as to place these two vowels in propretonic position, the replacement just mentioned is made. For example, when the plural ending *-îm* is added to the stem of the noun *nāḇîʾ* (prophet), the accent is on the ending, leaving the *ā* in propretonic position.

Thus,	*nāḇîʾ* + *îm*	→	**nā-ḇî-ʾîm*	→	*nəḇîʾîm*
Similarly with *ē*:	*lēḇāḇ* + *ôṯ*	→	**lē-ḇā-ḇôṯ*	→	*ləḇāḇôṯ*
Other examples are	*māqôm* + *ôṯ*	→	**mā-qô-môṯ*	→	*məqômôṯ*
	zāqēn + *îm*	→	**zā-qē-nîm*	→	*zəqēnîm*

This type of reduction is regularly found in the inflection of nouns and adjectives, but is less common among verbs other than those with object suffixes.

(b) *Pretonic reduction.* A second reduction pattern, often conflicting with the above, involves reduction of *ā* or *ē* in a *pretonic* open syllable. In noun inflections this is true mainly for those words whose first syllable (propretonic) is unchangeable (i.e. contains one of the unchangeable long vowels or is a closed syllable) and whose pretonic syllable would contain *ē*:

šōp̄ēṭ + *îm* → *šōp̄əṭîm*

Pretonic reduction is very frequent in verbs, regardless of the vowel:

yiḵtōḇ + *û*	→	*yiḵtəḇû*	(they will write)
yittēn + *û*	→	*yittənû*	(they will give)
yišmaʿ + *û*	→	*yišməʿû*	(they will hear).

Attention has been called to these two reduction patterns since one or the other figures in most of the inflections to be studied. Unfortunately, however, it is not always possible to predict accurately which pattern will be followed, so that each paradigm should be carefully analyzed.

THE RULE OF SHEWA. A sequence of two syllables each with *ə* (shewa) is not tolerated by Hebrew structure. When such a sequence would arise in the course of inflection or when combining various words and elements, the following replacement is made:

consonant + *ə* + cons. + *ə* → cons. + i + cons.

Thus: *lə* (to) + *nəḇîʾî* (my prophet) → *linḇîʾî* (not *lənəḇîʾî*).

6. Special Features of the Guttural Consonants and R.

(a) The gutturals and *r* do not occur doubled.

(b) The gutturals are never followed immediately by *ə*.

These two characteristics account for certain regular deviations from an expected norm. For example, since the definite article before non-gutturals is *ha* + doubling of the following consonant, we should expect the article to be somewhat different before words beginning with a guttural or *r*. We shall see in the lessons that *hā-* occurs in some cases, *ha-* (without doubling) in others. Whenever a long vowel (*ā ē ō*) occurs before a guttural or *r* and corresponds formally to a short vowel before a doubled non-guttural, the vowel is said to be long by *compensatory lengthening*, i.e. to compensate for the non-doubling of the guttural. When a short vowel (*a i u o*) occurs before a guttural in similar situations, the guttural is said to be *virtually doubled*.

As for the second feature listed above, the presence of a guttural means a substitution of *ă* (less commonly of *ĕ* or *ŏ*) for an expected *ə*. This is illustrated by

ḥāḵām (wise person) + *îm* → *ḥăḵāmîm* (not *ḥəḵāmîm*)
ḥāzāq (strong person) + *îm* → *ḥăzāqîm* (not *ḥəzāqîm*).

It is convenient to think of *ă*, *ĕ*, and *ŏ* as varieties of *ə* to be used after gutturals and to see that a word like *ḥălôm* (dream) has essentially the same vowel pattern as *bəḵôr* (first-born).

When a word ends with ʿ , *ḥ*, or *h* (when this is not a vowel letter, see §8), a preceding *î ē û ô* is followed by a non-syllabic glide element *a*. Thus,

sûs (horse) but *lûaḥ* (tablet)
kōṯēḇ (writing) but *šōlēaḥ* (sending)
gāḏôl (big) but *gāḇôah* (high).

THE RULE OF SHEWA as applied to sequences involving gutturals:
cons. + *ə* + guttural + *ă* → cons. + *a* + gutt. + *ă*
E.g. *bə* (in) + *ḥălômî* (my dream) → *baḥălômî*
Similarly with *ĕ* and *ŏ*. Another sequence arising from vowel reduction is illustrated by *ḥāḵām* + *ê* (which requires double reduction) → **ḥăḵəmê* → *ḥaḵmê*.
I.e. gutt. + *ă* + cons. + *ə* → gutt. + *a* + cons.
N.B. Rules given in the grammar to account for the peculiarities of gutturals do not apply to *r* unless so stated.

7. The Hebrew Alphabet.

The alphabet used in writing all the traditional texts of the Old Testament is more properly Aramaic than Hebrew. The situation is summarized by the table on the following page.

Sometime during the first half of the second millennium B.C. the alphabet was invented in the Syro-Palestinian area. This alphabet was a new creation, not directly based on any other system of writing then in use, but it seems to have been most clearly influenced by certain features of Egyptian hieroglyphic writing, especially in the lack of symbols to represent vowels.

The most prolific branch of the alphabet was the Phoenician, attested in

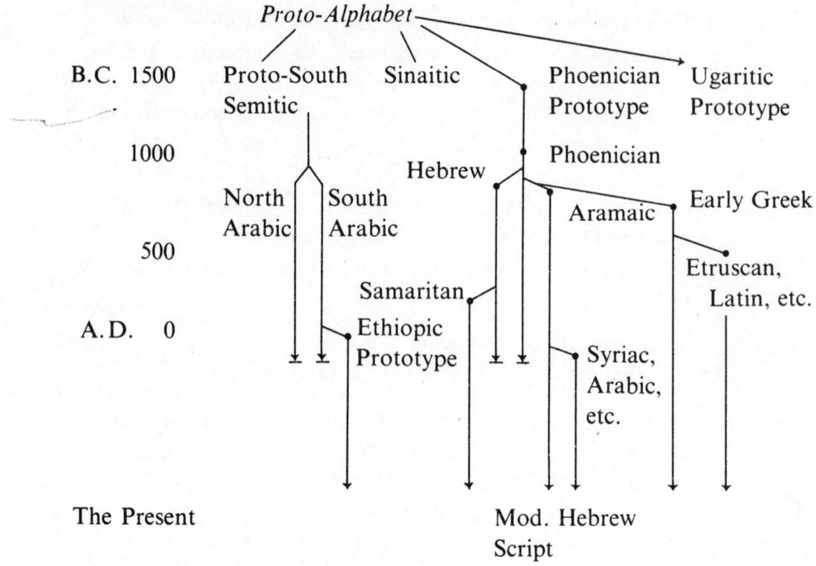

inscriptions from about the eleventh century onward. The Hebrews borrowed their script from the Phoenicians in the tenth century B.C., and this new "Hebrew" script, subsequently diverging from the parent Phoenician, was used in various types of inscriptions down to the beginning of the Christian Era. With the exception, however, of the manuscript traditions of the Samaritan sect, which still employs a form of this genuinely Hebrew script, the old script was replaced, especially in manuscript uses, by a cursive form of the Old Aramaic script, itself a daughter of the parent Phoenician of nearly the same age as the Hebrew.

It is this Aramaic manuscript hand which is already employed in Hebrew papyri and parchments of the second and first centuries B.C. and is attested as the normal alphabet for writing Hebrew from that time until the present.

THE HEBREW ALPHABET

NAME	LETTER	OUR TRANSCRIPTION	PHONETIC VALUE
'ā́lep̄	א	'	glottal stop or *zero*
bêṯ	בּ	b	[b]
	ב	ḇ	[v]
gîmel	גּ	g	[g]
	ג	ḡ	[g]
dā́leṯ	דּ	d	[d]
	ד	ḏ	[δ]
hē	ה	h	[h] or *zero*

NAME	LETTER	OUR TRANSCRIPTION	PHONETIC VALUE
wāw	ו	w	[w] or *zero*
záyin	ז	z	[z]
ḥēṯ	ח	ḥ	[ʜ]
ṭēṯ	ט	ṭ	[t]
yōḏ	י	y	[y] or *zero*
kap̄	כּ ךּ	k	[k]
	כ ך	ḵ	[x]
lā́meḏ	ל	l	[l]
mēm	מ ם	m	[m]
nûn	נ ן	n	[n]
sā́meḵ	ס	s	[s]
ʿáyin	ע	ʿ	[ʕ]
pēh	פּ ףּ	p	[p]
	פ ף	p̄	[f]
ṣāḏēh	צ ץ	ṣ	[ts]
qōp̄	ק	q	[q]
rēš	ר	r	[r]
śîn	שׂ	ś	[s]
šîn	שׁ	š	[ʃ]
tāw	תּ	t	[t]
	ת	ṯ	[θ]

8. Some Features of Hebrew Orthography (Spelling).

a. Hebrew is written from right to left.

b. Five of the letters have a special form used only at the end of a word: ך *k*, ם *m*, ן *n*, ף *p*, ץ *ṣ*.

c. In the earliest Hebrew and Phoenician inscriptions (10th cent. B.C.) no vowels were indicated in the writing. Thus the words *méleḵ* (king), *mōlēḵ* (ruling), *mālaḵ* (he ruled), *malkāh* (queen), *māləḵû* (they ruled), etc., would all be written simply as מלך *mlk*. From the ninth to the sixth centuries (i.e. pre-Exilic period, before the fall of Jerusalem in 587 B.C. and the Babylonian Exile) the consonants י *y*, ו *w*, and ה *h* were used at the end of a word to indicate final vowels:

ו *w* = *û* e.g. מלכו *māləḵû*, they ruled
י *y* = *î* e.g. מלכי *malkî*, my king
ה *h* = any other final vowel e.g. מלכה *malkāh*, queen.

In the post-Exilic period י and ו were used as vowel indicators also inside a word, and values slightly different from those just cited were acquired:

ו *w* = *û* or *ô*
י y = *ê*, *ḛ*, or *î*

The letter ה *h* was still used only at the end of a word as a vowel letter representing any vowel other than those just mentioned. The three letters ,י ,ו, and ה in their function as vowel indicators are called *matres lectionis* (literally, mothers of reading), following traditional Hebrew grammatical terminology.

d. The MT in general reflects this stage of orthographic development. There are, however, some inconsistencies and irregularities to be noted:

(1) י and ו are sometimes missing when we should otherwise have expected them. The shorter spelling is called defective and the longer, full.

Full		*Defective*		
יקום	*yāqûm*	יקם	*yāqūm*	he will arise
ירים	*yārîm*	ירם	*yārīm*	he will raise
גדול	*gāḏôl*	גדל	*gāḏōl*	big

Note that the only distinction between the vowels transcribed by *û*, *ū*; *î*, *ī*; and *ô*, *ō* is that the former of each pair is represented in the script by a *mater lectionis* while the latter is not.

(2) A final *ā* is not always indicated by ה: לְךָ *ləḵā* (to you) תִּכְתֹּבְנָ *tiḵtōḇnā* (they shall write).

(3) א is unpronounced in many instances, but is always an integral part of the spelling: ראשׁ *rōš* (head), מצא *māṣā*(') (he found). It does not, however, belong to the category of *matres lectionis* discussed above since its appearance is limited mainly to words whose roots occur elsewhere in the language with the א retained in pronunciation. We have generally indicated quiescent א in our transliteration. Sometimes, for the sake of clarity, we have added the ' in parentheses, as in *māṣā*(') above.

Points (2) and (3) will be mentioned later in the section dealing with the grammatical forms in which these irregularities are commonly found.

9. The Daghesh

The Masoretes employed a dot or point within a letter to indicate

(a) that the consonant in question is doubled:

המּלך *hammélek̲* the king

(b) that, in the case of the ambiguous letters ב ג ד כ פ ת, the one with the point is the stop; the one without, the spirant:

בּ	*b* or *bb*	ב	*ḇ*
גּ	*g* or *gg*	ג	*ḡ*
דּ	*d* or *dd*	ד	*ḏ*

(c) that a final ה is not to be taken as a vowel letter but as a morphologically significant consonant. Contrast

מלכה	*malkā(h)*	a queen	[ה is a *mater* for final -*ā*]
מלכהּ	*malkāh*	her king	[הּ is part of the suffix meaning "her"]
בנה	*bānāh*	he built	[ה is a *mater*]
גבהּ	*gāḇōᵃh*	high	[הּ is a root consonant, pronounced in this case]*

When the point indicates doubling, it is called *daghesh forte* (strong daghesh). When it indicates stop instead of spirant, it is called *daghesh lene* (weak d.). In a final הּ it is known as *mappîq*.

The only use of daghesh where there is a possible source of confusion is in the *bəḡaḏkəp̄aṯ* letters. Technically we should expect two dagheshes when these represent doubled consonants, one to show the doubling (*d. forte*) and one to show *b* not *ḇ*. But since the spirant values for these six letters do not occur doubled, a second dot is superfluous and never written.

10. The Vowel Points.

Following their traditional pronunciation, the Masoretes added vowel points to the Hebrew text (see the Introduction). Because these points were superimposed on a text that already had a crude system for indicating vocalization, i.e. the *matres lectionis,* a large number of combinations were created (and hence the apparent complexity of our transliteration). The following table shows the form of the vowel signs and their position in relation to the consonants (here ב *b* and ח *ḥ*):

Name of Sign	Plain		With *mater* י *y*		With *mater* ו *w*		With *mater* ה *h* (final only)	
pátaḥ	בַ	*ba*	—		—		—	—
qāmeṣ	בָ	*bā* or *bo*	בָי	*bâ* (rare)	—	—	בָה	*bāh*
hîreq	בִ	*bi* (or *bī*)	בִי	*bî*	—	—	—	—
ṣērê	בֵ	*bē*	בֵי	*bê*	—	—	בֵה	*bēh*
səḡōl	בֶ	*be*	בֶי	*bệ*	—	—	בֶה	*beh*
ḥōlem	בֹ	*bō*	—	—	בוֹ	*bô*	בֹה	*bōh*(rare)
qibbûṣ	בֻ	*bu*	—	—	בוּ	*bû*	—	—

And the reduced vowels:

בְ	*bə*	חֲ	*ḥă*	חֱ	*ḥĕ*	חֳ	*ḥŏ*

Remarks:

(1) In the case of defective writings, where *î* or *û* is meant but there is no *y* or *w* in the text, the vowel signs for *i* and *u* are used. The vowel וּ (בּ) is

* It is doubtful that every הּ with *mappîq* is to be given a consonantal value [h]. The distinction between מלכה (queen) and מלכהּ (her king) was probably a graphic and not a phonological one.

called *šûreq*. Note that the reduced vowels *ă ĕ ŏ* are represented by a combination of the sign for *ə* and that of the corresponding non-reduced vowel. The names of the reduced vowels are *šəwā* (our Shewa), *ḥāṭēp̄ páṯaḥ*, *ḥāṭēp̄ səḡōl*, and *ḥāṭēp̄ qắmeṣ* respectively.

(2) The distinction between ◌ָ = *ā* (*qắmeṣ*) and ◌ָ = *o* (*qắmeṣ ḥāṭûp̄*) is usually clear: ◌ָ = *o* in a closed, unaccented syllable (e.g. שָׁמְרִי *šomrî*; יָשְׁמַד *yošmaḏ*), but ◌ָ = *ā* elsewhere. There is ambiguity when a following consonant is pointed with ◌ְ: should, e.g., מָלְכוּ be read *māləḵû* or *molḵû*? To resolve this ambiguity, a metheg is used (see §11).

(3) When a consonant closes a syllable (except at the end of a word), the Masoretes placed beneath it the Shewa sign: מַלְכִּי *mal-kî* (my king). For the beginning student this constitutes one of the biggest problems in reading Hebrew: when does the sign ◌ְ represent the vowel ə and when does it represent nothing (i.e. end of a syllable)? The answer to this question is not simple; in fact there are several schools of thought on the subject among the traditional Hebrew grammarians. Since it is completely immaterial to the understanding of the language and to translation, we shall not enter into the dispute, but rather adopt the following simple conventions:

(a) When two Shewa signs occur under consecutive consonants (except at the end of a word), the first represents zero and the second *ə*:

יִשְׁמְרוּ *yišmərû* (not *yišəmrû* or *yišəmərû*).

(b) When a preceding syllable has any one of the long vowels (*û/ū*, *ô/ō*, *î/ī*, *ê/ē*, *ệ*, *ā*), the Shewa sign represents *ə*:

הוּקְמוּ *hûqəmû* they were established
בֹּרְכוּ *bōrəḵû* they were blessed
יְשִׂימְךָ *yəśîməḵā* he will place you
יֵרְדוּ *yērəḏû* they will go down
שָׁתְתָה *šāṯəṯāh* she drank (see §11)

But after any other vowel it represents zero:

שִׁמְךָ *šimḵā* your name
מַלְכֵי *malḵê* kings
יִשְׁמָרְךָ *yišmorḵā* he will watch you

But under the first of two identical consonants the Shewa sign always represents the vowel *ə*, regardless of the type of vowel in the preceding syllable:

צִלְלֵי *ṣilalê* shadows (not *sillê*).

(c) The Shewa sign under the first consonant of a word always represents *ə*:

בְּיָדוֹ *bəyāḏô* in his hand

[The various forms of the number two (fem.) are the only exceptions:

שְׁתַּיִם *štáyim* שְׁתֵּי *štê*]

(4) The glide vowel *a* (see §6) is represented by ַ placed under the final guttural but pronounced before it: שְׁמֹעַ *šəmōª*‘; שָׂמֵחַ *śāmēªḥ*. It is traditionally called *páṯaḥ furtivum*.

(5) The vowel sign *ḥôlem* may coincide with one of the dots differentiating *śîn* and *šîn*; printed texts may vary. E.g. נָשֹׂא *nāśō*’ (to lift); בֹשׁ *bōš* (ashamed).

(6) The coincidence of a mater ִי *y* and a consonantal י *y* is frequent:

נָכְרִיָּה *noḵrîyāh* (could also be transcribed as *nokriyyāh*)

(7) The consonant ךְ at the end of a word always has a shewa sign if it has no other vowel; thus לָךְ *lāḵ* (to you f.) but לְךָ *ləḵā* (to you m.).

(8) In the rather rare situation where a final syllable of a word closes with two consonants, e.g. *wayyēḇk* (and he wept), the sign shewa is placed under both: וַיֵּבְךְּ.

11. Metheg.

The metheg is a short perpendicular stroke placed under a consonant and to the left of the vowel sign (if any). It serves several purposes in the orthography, of which the following are the most important:

(1) Since the vowels *ā* and *ē* are regularly replaced by *ə* in open syllables two or more places before the main stress, their appearance in such positions may be regarded as anomalous. They are usually marked with metheg:

אָֽנֹכִי *’ānōḵî* I

בֵּֽרַכְתַּנִי *bēraḵtánî* you blessed me

(2) In fact, any long vowel occurring two or more syllables before the main stress may be so marked, although manuscripts are inconsistent in this. Compare

הוֹשַׁע *hôša*‘ save!

הֽוֹשִׁיעֵנִי *hôšî‘ênî* save me!

This usage is particularly important with the vowel ָ, which is a short vowel *o* [ɔ] in closed, unaccented syllables and a long vowel *ā* elsewhere. The metheg is used with ָ = *ā* in any doubtful position to ensure the correct reading:

יְבָֽרְכֵנִי *yəḇārəḵênî* he will bless me (not *yəḇorḵênî*).

[Another device used in a word like the one just given to ensure correct reading is to point with ֳ instead of ְ:

יְבָרֲכֵנִי *yəḇārăḵênî*

This is an irregular use of *ă* for *ə*, since the consonant under which it appears need not be a guttural.]

(3) Short vowels before the main stress usually occur in closed syllables. Whenever the contrary occurs, the vowel may be marked with metheg:

תַּֽעֲמֹד *ta'ămōḏ* she will stand

אָֽהֳלוֹ *'ohŏlô* his tent.

This last example, with ָֽ = *o*, would seem to cancel out the usefulness of metheg for distinguishing between the two values of ָ mentioned above. Actually, this is not often so, since ָֽ = *ā* is very rarely followed by ֳ *ŏ* in the next syllable, but rather by ֲ ă: e.g. בָּֽחֲרוּ *bāḥărû* (they chose).

(4) Metheg with a short vowel in what appears to be a closed syllable indicates that the normal doubling of the following consonant has been given up: הַֽמְרַגְּלִים *hamraggəlîm* (the spies) for הַמְּרַגְּלִים *hammaraggəlîm*. In this book metheg will be used consistently only with ָ to mark the distinction between the o and ā values of the sign. Thus

אָֽכְלָה *'āḵəlāh* she ate

אָכְלָה *'oḵlāh* food

It is also employed sporadically to alert the reader to a syllabic division that might otherwise escape his notice.

INTRODUCTION TO BIBLICAL HEBREW

LESSON 1

[Read §§1–3 of the section "Sounds and Spelling," pp. xv-xviii]

12. The Noun: Gender.

Nearly all Hebrew nouns belong to one of two grammatical categories called gender: masculine and feminine. Nouns denoting animate beings usually have grammatical gender corresponding to natural gender (sex), but there is otherwise no clear correlation between gender and meaning. For example הַר *har* (mountain) is masculine, while גִּבְעָה *giḇʿāh* (hill) is feminine.

There are some formal indications of gender: nouns ending in *-ā́h*, *-eṯ*, and *-aṯ* are nearly always feminine, such as

מַלְכָּה	*malkā́h*	queen	דַּ֫עַת	*dáʿaṯ*	knowledge
בַּת	*baṯ*	daughter	תִּפְאֶ֫רֶת	*tip̄ʾéreṯ*	glory

Nouns without these endings are usually masculine, but there are important exceptions, such as

אֶ֫בֶן	*ʾéḇen*	stone (fem.)
עִיר	*ʿîr*	city (fem.)
אֶ֫רֶץ	*ʾéreṣ*	earth (fem.)

Gender should therefore be learned for each noun, since it cannot be deduced safely from form or meaning. In the vocabularies of the lessons all nouns ending in *-ā́h*, *-eṯ*, and *-aṯ* are to be taken as feminine and all others as masculine unless there is a remark to the contrary. Typical listing will be

אִשָּׁה	*'iššāh*	woman	אֶרֶץ	*'éreṣ*	earth (f.)
דָּבָר	*dāḇār*	word	דֶּרֶךְ	*déreḵ*	way (m. or f.)

The last entry means that *déreḵ* may be used as either masculine or feminine; such words constitute a very small class.

13. Number.

Three categories of number are distinguished in Hebrew: singular, dual, and plural. The dual and plural are marked by special endings, but the singular is not:

Singular		Dual		Plural		
יָד	*yāḏ*	יָדַיִם	*yāḏáyim*	יָדוֹת	*yāḏôṯ*	hand
יוֹם	*yôm*	יוֹמַיִם	*yômáyim*	יָמִים	*yāmîm*	day
בֵּן	*bēn*	——		בָּנִים	*bānîm*	son
בַּת	*baṯ*	——		בָּנוֹת	*bānôṯ*	daughter

The dual is very restricted in use, being found mainly with the paired parts of the body and with set expressions of time or number, like "200," "twice," and "two years." For details, see below, §92.

The plural is indicated by the endings *-îm* and *-ôṯ* (or *-ōṯ*). Unfortunately, the plural is not always formed by simply adding one of these endings to the singular stem. In a very large number of nouns changes take place in the form of the stem:

מֶלֶךְ	*méleḵ*	king	plural:	מְלָכִים	*məlāḵîm*
אִישׁ	*'îš*	man		אֲנָשִׁים	*'ănāšîm*
יוֹם	*yôm*	day		יָמִים	*yāmîm*

The only general observation to be made concerning the plural endings is that most feminine nouns have plurals in *-ôṯ* and most masculine nouns in *-îm*. That this is only approximately true is clear from the following interesting exceptions:

אָב	*'āḇ*	father	plural:	אָבוֹת	*'āḇôṯ*	(masculine)
אִשָּׁה	*'iššāh*	woman		נָשִׁים	*nāšîm*	(feminine)

Note that a noun does not change its gender, regardless of the ending it has in the plural. During the next few lessons we shall take up the most important types of nouns and their plural forms. For use in the exercises the plural forms of a few very frequent (and often quite irregular) nouns will be introduced in the vocabulary before their general type has been studied in detail. It is advisable to learn these as they occur.

14. The Definite Article.

The definite article of Hebrew corresponds closely to the definite article of English in usage and meaning. The basic form of the article is *ha-* plus the doubling of the following consonant. It is prefixed directly to the noun it determines:

בַּ֫יִת	*báyiṯ*	a house	מֶ֫לֶךְ	*méleḵ*	a king
הַבַּ֫יִת	*habbáyiṯ*	the house	הַמֶּ֫לֶךְ	*hamméleḵ*	the king
נַ֫עַר	*ná'ar*	a youth			
הַנַּ֫עַר	*hanná'ar*	the youth			

There is no indefinite article; *báyiṯ* may be translated as "house" or "a house." The noun with a definite article is used also to express the vocative: הַמֶּ֫לֶךְ *hamméleḵ* O king!

15. Prepositions.

From a purely formal point of view there are three types of prepositions in Hebrew:

a. Those joined directly to the following word and written as part of it. These are בְּ *bə* (in), לְ *lə* (to), and כְּ *kə* (like).

מֶ֫לֶךְ	*méleḵ*	a king	לְמֶ֫לֶךְ	*ləméleḵ*	to a king
בְּמֶ֫לֶךְ	*bəméleḵ*	in a king	כְּמֶ֫לֶךְ	*kəméleḵ*	like a king

When a noun is determined by the definite article, these three prepositions combine with the article into a single syllable having the same vowel of the article:

הַמֶּ֫לֶךְ	*hamméleḵ*	the king	לַמֶּ֫לֶךְ	*lamméleḵ*	to the king
בַּמֶּ֫לֶךְ	*bamméleḵ*	in the king	כַּמֶּ֫לֶךְ	*kamméleḵ*	like the king

b. Those joined (usually) to the following word with a short stroke called *maqqēp̄*. Among these are אֶל־ *'el-* (to, towards), עַל־ *'al-* (on, upon), and מִן־ *min-* (from):

עַל־הַבַּ֫יִת	*'al-habbáyiṯ*	on the house
אֶל־הַבַּ֫יִת	*'el-habbáyiṯ*	to the house
מִן־הַבַּ֫יִת	*min-habbáyiṯ*	from the house

The *maqqēp̄* indicates that these words are proclitic, i.e. have no stress of their own, but are pronounced as the first syllable of the whole group taken as a single word.

c. The third and largest group consists of prepositions written as separate words:

אֵ֫צֶל הַבַּ֫יִת *'ēṣel habbáyiṯ* near the house

נֶ֫גֶד הָעָם *néḡeḏ hā'ām* before the people
לִפְנֵי הַמֶּ֫לֶךְ *lip̄nê hamméleḵ* in the presence of the king

Many combinations of these types exist and will be noted in the vocabularies. Prepositions in the third group may on occasion be united with the following word with *maqqēp̄*. This optional proclitic pronunciation is dictated by rather complicated accentual rules which cannot be treated here. The reader should follow the example of the exercises, which will emphasize the more common usage.

16. Sentences with Adverbial Predicates.

A juxtaposed noun and prepositional phrase (or local adverb) constitute a predication in Hebrew.

הַנַּ֫עַר בַּבַּ֫יִת *hanná'ar babbáyiṯ* The young man (is) in the house.

Such sentences contain no overt correspondent of the English verb "to be" and gain their tense from the context in which they occur. The isolated sentences of the exercises are best translated with the English present tense. The normal word order is subject (i.e. noun)—predicate (i.e. prepositional phrase or adverb), but an interrogative adverb, such as *'ayyēh* (where?), always stands first in the sentence:

אַיֵּה הַנַּ֫עַר *'ayyēh hanná'ar* Where is the young man?

17. Vocabulary 1.

NOUNS:	נַ֫עַר	*ná'ar*	young man, boy, lad; also used in the sense of "attendant, servant"
	זָקֵן	*zāqēn*	old man, elder (of a city)
	בַּ֫יִת	*báyiṯ*	house
	נָהָר	*nāhār*	river
	שָׂדֶה	*śāḏeh*	field
	דֶּ֫רֶךְ	*déreḵ*	road, way (m. or f.)
PREPOSITIONS:	עַל־	*'al-*	on, upon, against, concerning, because of, over
	בְּ	*bə*	(see §15a) in, with (in the sense "by means of")
	אֵ֫צֶל	*'ēṣel*	near, beside, by
ADVERBS:	שָׁם	*šām*	there, in that place
	אַיֵּה	*'ayyēh*	where? in what place?
CONJUNCTION:	וְ	*wə*	and [prefixed directly to the following word: *wəhanná'ar*, and the young man]

Exercises:

(a) Divide each of the following words into syllables:

שְׁמָעֻ֫נִי	*šəmā'ênî*	מִכּוֹכְבֵי	*mikkôḵəḇê*
וַיְדַבְּרוּ	*wayḏabbərû*	דְּבָרָיו	*dəḇārâw*

בִּקַּשְׁתִּ֫יךָ	*biqqaštîḵā*	שְׁלֹשִׁים	*šəlōšîm*
יִתְּנֵ֫הוּ	*yittənḗhû*	יָשְׁמְדוּ	*yošmədû*
בָּרֲכֵ֫נִי	*bārăḵḗnî*	שְׂדוֹתֵיכֶם	*śəḏôṯêḵem*
הִגַּדְתַּ֫נִי	*higgaḏtánî*	יַעַמְדוּ	*ya'amḏû*
וַיָּ֫מָת	*wayyā́moṯ*	זִקְנֵיהֶם	*ziqnêhem*

(b) Give the Hebrew for the following orally:

1. a house, the house, in the house, near the house
2. a field, in a field, in the field
3. a road, on a road, on the road
4. Where is the boy? — the old man? — the house?
5. The boy (old man, house) is there.
6. the old man and the boy; the house and the field.

(c) Translate:

1. 'ayyēh hanná'ar? hanná'ar babbáyiṯ.	1 אַיֵּה הַנַּ֫עַר. הַנַּ֫עַר בַּבַּ֫יִת.
2. 'ayyēh hazzāqēn? hazzāqēn šām.	2 אַיֵּה הַזָּקֵן. הַזָּקֵן שָׁם.
3. 'ayyēh habbáyiṯ? habbáyiṯ 'ḗṣel hannāhār.	3 אַיֵּה הַבַּ֫יִת. הַבַּ֫יִת אֵ֫צֶל הַנָּהָר.
4. haśśāḏeh 'ḗṣel hannāhār.	4 הַשָּׂדֶה אֵ֫צֶל הַנָּהָר.
5. hanná'ar wəhazzāqēn baśśāḏeh.	5 הַנַּ֫עַר וְהַזָּקֵן בַּשָּׂדֶה.
6. 'ayyēh hazzāqēn? hazzāqēn 'al-hadderek.	6 אַיֵּה הַזָּקֵן. הַזָּקֵן עַל־הַדֶּ֫רֶךְ.

(d) Write the following in Hebrew:

1. The house and the field are near the river.
2. The young man is on the road.
3. Where are the boy and the old man?
4. The boy is in the field.
5. The river is near the house.

LESSON 2

[*Read §§4–6 of the section "Sounds and Spelling," pp. xviii-xxi*]

18. The Definite Article (cont.).

Before words beginning with a guttural consonant (א ʾ, ע ʿ, ה *h*, ח *ḥ*) or ר *r* the definite article has a form slightly different from that given in the preceding lesson.

a. Before א ʾ and ר *r* the article is הָ *hā-*

אִישׁ	*ʾîš*	a man	הָאִישׁ	*hāʾîš*	the man
רָעָב	*rāʿāḇ*	a famine	הָרָעָב	*hārāʿāḇ*	the famine

b. Before ע ʿ the article is normally הָ *hā-*, but if the ʿ is followed by an unaccented *ā*, the article is הֶ *he-*

עִיר	*ʿîr*	a city	הָעִיר	*hāʿîr*	the city
עָרִים	*ʿārîm*	cities	הֶעָרִים	*heʿārîm*	the cities
עָפָר	*ʿāpār*	dust	הֶעָפָר	*heʿāpār*	the dust

c. Before ה *h* and ח *ḥ* the article is normally הַ *ha-* (no doubling). But if ה *h* is followed by an unaccented *ā*, or if ח *ḥ* is followed by an accented or unaccented *ā*, the article is הֶ *he-*

הֵיכָל	*hêḵāl*	a palace	הַהֵיכָל	*hahêḵāl*	the palace
חֶ֫רֶב	*ḥéreḇ*	a sword	הַחֶ֫רֶב	*haḥéreḇ*	the sword
חָכָם	*ḥāḵām*	a wise man	הֶחָכָם	*heḥāḵām*	the wise man
הָרִים	*hārîm*	mountains	הֶהָרִים	*hehārîm*	the mountains

As noted in §15a the prepositions בְּ *bə*, לְ *lə*, and כְּ *kə* are joined immediately to the noun they govern, and before a noun with the definite article the consonant of the prepositon replaces the *h* of the article. The vowel of the article, chosen according to the rules just given, is in no way altered by this change:

הָאִישׁ	*hā'îš*	the man	לָאִישׁ	*lā'îš*	to the man
הֶהָרִים	*hehārîm*	the mountains	בֶּהָרִים	*behārîm*	in the mountains

19. Noun Plurals.

Consider the following sets of nouns:

a.	בְּכוֹר	*bəḵôr*	plural:	בְּכוֹרִים	*bəḵôrîm*	first-born
	חֲלוֹם	*ḥălôm*		חֲלוֹמוֹת	*ḥălômôṯ*	dream
b.	דָּבָר	*dāḇār*		דְּבָרִים	*dəḇārîm*	word
	זָקֵן	*zāqēn*		זְקֵנִים	*zəqēnîm*	old man
	מָקוֹם	*māqôm*		מְקוֹמוֹת	*məqômôṯ*	place

In the first set (a) the stems of the singular and plural are identical, but in the second set (b) the *ā* of the first syllable is reduced to *ə* in accordance with the principle given in §5. Note that in group (a) the vowel of the first syllable is already *ə* (or an equivalent) in the singular, so that there can be no further reduction in the plural.

A second, very frequent, type of two-syllable noun is represented by

מֶלֶךְ	*méleḵ*	plural:	מְלָכִים	*məlāḵîm*	king
זֶבַח	*zéḇaḥ*		זְבָחִים	*zəḇāḥîm*	sacrifice
סֵפֶר	*sēp̄er*		סְפָרִים	*səp̄ārîm*	book
נַעַר	*náʻar*		נְעָרִים	*nəʻārîm*	young man
עֶבֶד	*ʻéḇeḏ*		עֲבָדִים	*ʻăḇāḏîm*	servant

The singular form of these nouns is characterized by penultimate stress. All such nouns have the same pattern in the plural, as illustrated above. Note that the vowel of the singular is not significant for the vocalization of the plural form. Why is there an *ă* in the first syllable of עֲבָדִים *ʻăḇāḏîm*?

20. Vocabulary 2.

NOUNS:	אִישׁ	*'îš*	(pl. irreg. אֲנָשִׁים *'ănāšîm*) man, husband
	אִשָּׁה	*'iššāh*	(pl. irreg. נָשִׁים *nāšîm*) woman, wife
	בָּתִּים	*bāttîm*	the irreg. pl. of בַּיִת *báyiṯ*, house
	יֶלֶד	*yéleḏ*	(pl. *-îm*) boy, child
	הֵיכָל	*hêḵāl*	palace, temple
	מֶלֶךְ	*méleḵ*	(pl. *-îm*) king, ruler
	סֵפֶר	*sēp̄er*	(pl. *-îm*) book

	עֶבֶד	*ʿéḇeḏ*	(pl. *-îm*) servant, slave
	עִיר	*ʿîr*	(pl. irreg. עָרִים *ʿārîm*) city (f.)
PRONOUNS:	הוּא	*hûʾ*	he, it (ref. to masc. noun)
	הִיא	*hîʾ*	she, it (ref. to fem. noun)
	מִי	*mî*	who? (no gender distinction)
ADVERBS:	פֹּה	*pōh*	here, in this place
	אֵיפֹה	*ʾêp̄ōh*	where? (a synonym of אַיֵּה *ʾayyēh*)

Exercises:

(a) Prefix the preposition לְ *lə-* (to) to the following nouns and pronounce the resulting combination (§4):

כֹּהֵן	*kōhēn*	(priest)	בָּבֶל	*bāḇel*	(Babylon)
כֶּרֶם	*kérem*	(vineyard)	בּוֹר	*bôr*	(pit)
כֶּלֶב	*kéleḇ*	(dog)	בָּקָר	*bāqār*	(cattle)
תּוֹרָה	*tôrāh*	(law)	גֵּר	*gēr*	(sojourner)
פָּרָשׁ	*pārāš*	(horseman)	פֶּסֶל	*pésel*	(idol)
דַּמֶּשֶׂק	*damméśeq*	(Damascus)	דֶּרֶךְ	*déreḵ*	(way)
דּוֹר	*dôr*	(generation)	גּוֹרָל	*gôrāl*	(lot)
פֶּגֶר	*péḡer*	(corpse)	פִּיךָ	*pîḵā*	(your mouth)

(b) Add the plural ending as indicated to each of the following nouns in accordance with the rules given in §§5–6.

גְּבוּל	*gəḇûl*	(*-îm*)	boundary	עָנָן	*ʿānān*	(*-îm*)	cloud
רְחוֹב	*rəḥôḇ*	(*-ôṯ*)	street	נָהָר	*nāhār*	(*-ôṯ*)	river
צָבָא	*ṣāḇāʾ*	(*-ôṯ*)	army	שָׁכֵן	*šāḵēn*	(*-îm*)	neighbor
קָהָל	*qāhāl*	(*-îm*)	assembly	חָצֵר	*ḥāṣēr*	(*-ôṯ*)	courtyard

(c) Give the proper form of the article for the following nouns:

הָדָר	*hāḏār*	splendor	אֲדָמָה	*ʾăḏāmāh*	ground
עָפָר	*ʿāp̄ār*	dust	חָלָב	*ḥālāḇ*	milk
אָדָם	*ʾāḏām*	mankind	חָכְמָה	*ḥoḵmāh*	wisdom
רִיב	*rîḇ*	quarrel	הֵיכָל	*hêḵāl*	

(d) Form the plurals of the following nouns, using the ending indicated:

פֶּגֶר	*péḡer*	(*-îm*)	corpse	עֶבֶד	*ʿéḇeḏ*	(*-îm*)	
שֶׁקֶל	*šéqel*	(*-îm*)	shekel	מֶלֶךְ	*méleḵ*	(*-îm*)	
קֶבֶר	*qéḇer*	(*-îm*)	grave	דָּבָר	*dāḇār*	(*-îm*)	
יֶלֶד	*yéleḏ*	(*-îm*)		זָקֵן	*zāqēn*	(*-îm*)	
עֶצֶם	*ʿéṣem*	(*-ôṯ*)	bone	דֶּרֶךְ	*déreḵ*	(*-îm*)	
אֶבֶן	*ʾéḇen*	(*-îm*)	stone	נֶפֶשׁ	*népeš*	(*-ôṯ*)	soul
נַעַר	*náʿar*	(*-îm*)		חֶדֶר	*ḥéḏer*	(*-îm*)	room
נָהָר	*nāhār*	(*-ôṯ*)		חֶרֶב	*ḥéreḇ*	(*-ôṯ*)	sword

(e) Give the Hebrew for the following orally:

1. man, men, the men, in the men
2. woman, women, the women, in the women
3. king, kings, on the kings
4. elder, elders, on the elders
5. house, houses, near the houses
6. book, books, in the books
7. city, cities, in the cities

(f) Translate:

1. hā'ănāšîm bā'îr.	1 הָאֲנָשִׁים בָּעִיר.
2. hannāšîm babbáyiṯ.	2 הַנָּשִׁים בַּבַּ֫יִת.
3. hammélek̲ wəhā'ăb̲āḏîm bahêk̲āl.	3 הַמֶּ֫לֶךְ וְהָעֲבָדִים בַּהֵיכָל.
4. hassəpārîm babbáyiṯ.	4 הַסְּפָרִים בַּבַּ֫יִת.
5. 'ayyēh hannə'ārîm? hannə'ārîm baśśāḏeh.	5 אַיֵּה הַנְּעָרִים. הַנְּעָרִים בַּשָּׂדֶה.
6. 'êpōh habbāttîm? habbāttîm bā'îr.	6 אֵיפֹה הַבָּתִּים. הַבָּתִּים בָּעִיר.
7. 'êpōh hannəhārôṯ? hannəhārôṯ šām.	7 אֵיפֹה הַנְּהָרוֹת. הַנְּהָרוֹת שָׁם.
8. he'ārîm šām wəhaddérek̲ pōh.	8 הֶעָרִים שָׁם וְהַדֶּ֫רֶךְ פֹּה.

(g) Write in Hebrew:

1. The men and the women are in the city.
2. The king is in the palace.
3. The women are here.
4. Where are the young men and the servants?
5. The books are in the city.
6. The cities are near the rivers.

LESSON 3

21. The Definite Article (concluded).

When a word begins with the syllables *yə-* or *mə-*, the definite article is usually הַ *ha-* without the doubling:

יְלָדִים	*yəlāḏîm*	הַיְלָדִים	*haylāḏîm*	the boys
יְאֹר	*yə'ōr*	הַיְאֹר	*hay'ōr*	the river, the Nile
מְרַגְּלִים	*məraggəlîm*	הַמְרַגְּלִים	*hamraggəlîm*	the spies

Note that in these words the prefixing of the article occasions the loss of a syllable in pronunciation: *hay-lā-ḏîm*, not *ha-yə-lā-ḏîm*. Exceptions to the preceding rule occur when the second syllable of the noun begins with ע ʻ or ה *h*:

יְהוּדִים	*yəhûḏîm*	הַיְּהוּדִים	*hayyəhûḏîm*	the Jews, Judaites

Several words have a slightly different form with the article. The following are the most important:

אֶרֶץ	*'éreṣ*	הָאָרֶץ	*hā'ā́reṣ*	earth, land
הַר	*har*	הָהָר	*hāhār*	mountain
עַם	*ʻam*	הָעָם	*hāʻām*	people, nation
גַּן	*gan*	הַגָּן	*haggān*	garden
פַּר	*par*	הַפָּר	*happār*	steer, ox
חַג	*ḥag*	הֶחָג	*heḥāg*	feast, festival
אֲרוֹן	*'ărôn*	הָאָרוֹן	*hā'ārôn*	box, chest, ark

Note that in הָהָר *hāhār* the form of the article does not follow the rule given in the preceding lesson.

22. Adjectives.

Adjectives agree in number and gender with the noun they modify. Unlike the noun, where gender need not be related to form, the distinction between masculine and feminine in the adjective is clearly and uniformly marked:

	SINGULAR		PLURAL	
masc.	טוֹב	*ṭôḇ* (good)	טוֹבִים	*ṭôḇîm*
fem.	טוֹבָה	*ṭôḇāh*	טוֹבוֹת	*ṭôḇôṯ*

Adjectives of two syllables with *ā* in the first syllable show a change in the stem before the endings of the fem. sing. and of the plural. The *ā* is replaced by *ə* (as described in §5 above):

גָּדוֹל	*gāḏôl*	גְּדוֹלִים	*gəḏôlîm*	חָכָם	*ḥāḵām*	חֲכָמִים	*ḥăḵāmîm*
גְּדוֹלָה	*gəḏôlāh*	גְּדוֹלוֹת	*gəḏôlôṯ*	חֲכָמָה	*ḥăḵāmāh*	חֲכָמוֹת	*ḥăḵāmôṯ*

The forms of קָטֹן *qāṭōn* (small) are unusual in that there is a different stem before the endings:

קָטֹן	*qāṭōn*	קְטַנִּים	*qəṭannîm*
קְטַנָּה	*qəṭannāh*	קְטַנּוֹת	*qəṭannôṯ*

Monosyllabic adjectives, a relatively small group, show the following typical forms. The principles underlying the change in the stem will be discussed in a later lesson:

רַב	*raḇ*	רַבָּה	*rabbāh*	רַבִּים	*rabbîm*	רַבּוֹת	*rabbôṯ*	much, many ✓
מַר	*mar*	מָרָה	*mārāh*	מָרִים	*mārîm*	מָרוֹת	*mārôṯ*	bitter ✓
רַע	*ra'*	רָעָה	*rā'āh*	רָעִים	*rā'îm*	רָעוֹת	*rā'ôṯ*	evil ✓
עַז	*'az*	עַזָּה	*'azzāh*	עַזִּים	*'azzîm*	עַזּוֹת	*'azzôṯ*	strong
חַי	*ḥay*	חַיָּה	*ḥayyāh*	חַיִּים	*ḥayyîm*	חַיּוֹת	*ḥayyôṯ*	living
דַּל	*dal*	דַּלָּה	*dallāh*	דַּלִּים	*dallîm*	דַּלּוֹת	*dallôṯ*	poor

Adjectives ending in *-eh* have the following forms:

יָפֶה	*yāp̄eh*	יָפָה	*yāp̄āh*	יָפִים	*yāp̄îm*	יָפוֹת	*yāp̄ôṯ*	beautiful
קָשֶׁה	*qāšeh*	קָשָׁה	*qāšāh*	קָשִׁים	*qāšîm*	קָשׁוֹת	*qāšôṯ*	hard, difficult

Other types of adjectives will be commented upon as they occur.

23. The Use of Adjectives.

Adjectives occur in two functions, attributive and predicative. By attributive is meant an adjective which forms a phrase with the noun it modifies, and this phrase as a whole has a single function in the sentence. For example, in I read a good book, good modifies book and the phrase a good book is the object of the verb read. The attributive adjective in Hebrew follows its noun and agrees with it in number, gender, and definiteness.

אִישׁ טוֹב	*'îš ṭôḇ*	a good man
הָאִישׁ הַטּוֹב	*hā'îš haṭṭôḇ*	the good man
אֲנָשִׁים טוֹבִים	*'ănāšîm ṭôḇîm*	good men
הָאֲנָשִׁים הַטּוֹבִים	*hā'ănāšîm haṭṭôḇîm*	the good men
אִשָּׁה טוֹבָה	*'iššāh ṭôḇāh*	a good woman
הָאִשָּׁה הַטּוֹבָה	*hā'iššāh haṭṭôḇāh*	the good woman
נָשִׁים טוֹבוֹת	*nāšîm ṭôḇôṯ*	good women
הַנָּשִׁים הַטּוֹבוֹת	*hannāšîm haṭṭôḇôṯ*	the good women
עִיר גְּדוֹלָה	*'îr gəḏôlāh*	a great city (f.)
הָעִיר הַגְּדוֹלָה	*hā'îr haggəḏôlāh*	the great city
עָרִים גְּדוֹלוֹת	*'ārîm gəḏôlôṯ*	great cities
הֶעָרִים הַגְּדוֹלוֹת	*he'ārîm haggəḏôlôṯ*	the great cities

Note that the adjective agrees with the gender of the preceding noun and not with its ending.

A juxtaposed noun and articleless adjective usually constitute a predication, the adjective being taken as the predicate and the noun as the subject. In the predicate function the adjective may stand before or after its noun subject. There is agreement in number and gender, but the predicate adjective does not, by definition, have the definite article:

טוֹב הָאִישׁ	*ṭôḇ hā'îš*	The man is good.
הָאִישׁ טוֹב	*hā'îš ṭôḇ*	
טוֹבָה הָאִשָּׁה	*ṭôḇāh hā'iššāh*	The woman is good.
הָאִשָּׁה טוֹבָה	*hā'iššāh ṭôḇāh*	
טוֹבִים הָאֲנָשִׁים	*ṭôḇîm hā'ănāšîm*	The men are good.
טוֹבוֹת הַנָּשִׁים	*ṭôḇôṯ hannāšîm*	The women are good.

A series of adjectives may occur in either function:

הָעִיר הַגְּדוֹלָה וְהַטּוֹבָה *hā'îr haggəḏôlāh wəhaṭṭôḇāh* the great and good city
הָעִיר גְּדוֹלָה וְטוֹבָה *hā'îr gəḏôlāh wəṭôḇāh* The city is great and good.

An adjective may be modified by a prepositional phrase in the predicate usage:

טוֹבָה הָעִיר לָעָם *ṭôḇāh hā'îr lā'ām* The city is good for the people.

When a subject noun is indefinite, there is a chance of ambiguity:

חָכְמָה טוֹבָה good wisdom or Wisdom is good.

This is uncommon and can usually be resolved from the context.

Adjectives may be used as nouns (i.e. in noun functions) in two ways: (1) the adjective, usually with the definite article, may mean "the one who is...," as הֶחָכָם *heḥāḵām* the wise one, the wise man; (2) both the masc. and fem. singular forms of some adjectives may be used as abstract nouns, "that which is...," as הָרַע *hāra'* or הָרָעָה *hārā'āh*, evil, wickedness.

24. Vocabulary 3.

NOUNS: דָּבָר *dāḇār* (pl. *-îm*) word, matter, thing, affair
רָעָב *rā'āḇ* famine
אֶרֶץ *'éreṣ* (pl. *-ôṯ*) land, earth (f.)
הַר *har* mountain
עַם *'am* people, nation
גַּן *gan* garden

ADJECTIVES: טוֹב *ṭôḇ* good
גָּדוֹל *gāḏôl* great, big
קָטֹן *qāṭōn* small, little, unimportant
יָפֶה *yāpeh* beautiful, handsome
רַע *ra'* evil, bad, wicked

ADVERBS: מְאֹד *mə'ōḏ* much, very (follows the adjective it modifies, as in טוֹב מְאֹד *ṭôḇ mə'ōḏ*, very good)

Exercises:

(a) Give all four forms (masc., fem.; sing., pl.) of the following adjectives:

קָדוֹשׁ	*qāḏôš*	holy	כָּבֵד	*kāḇēḏ*	heavy
רָחוֹק	*rāḥôq*	distant	צָמֵא	*ṣāmē'*	thirsty
קָרוֹב	*qārôḇ*	near	שָׁלֵם	*šālēm*	whole, sound

(b) Give the Hebrew for the following orally:

1. the good man, the small man, the evil man
2. the large city, the small city, the evil city
3. the beautiful woman, the small woman, the good woman
4. a good boy, a big city, a small field, a large house
5. in the city, in the large city, near the large city
6. in the great palace, near the large river
7. cities, the cities, in the cities, in the great cities
8. men, the men, the evil men, in the evil men
9. women, the women, concerning the evil women
10. land, the land, the great land

(c) Translate:

1. hā'iššāh rā'āh mə'ōḏ. — 1 הָאִשָּׁה רָעָה מְאֹד.
2. hû' yāp̄eh. — 2 הוּא יָפֶה.

3. hāʾîš wəhāʾiššāh yāpîm məʾōḏ.   הָאִישׁ וְהָאִשָּׁה יָפִים מְאֹד. 3

4. ʾayyēh hāʾănāšîm haṭṭôḇîm?   אַיֵּה הָאֲנָשִׁים הַטּוֹבִים. 4
    hāʾănāšîm haṭṭôḇîm bāʿîr   הָאֲנָשִׁים הַטּוֹבִים בָּעִיר הַקְּטַנָּה.
    haqqəṭannāh.

5. ʾêpōh hannáʿar hārāʿ?   אֵיפֹה הַנַּעַר הָרָע. 5
    hûʾ babbáyiṯ haggāḏôl.   הוּא בַּבַּיִת הַגָּדוֹל.

6. ʾayyēh hammélek?   אַיֵּה הַמֶּלֶךְ. 6
    hûʾ bahêkāl haggāḏôl.   הוּא בַּהֵיכָל הַגָּדוֹל.

7. mî ṭôḇ? ṭôḇāh hāʾiššāh hayyāpāh.   מִי טוֹב. טוֹבָה הָאִשָּׁה הַיָּפָה. 7

8. haddāḇār ṭôḇ məʾōḏ.   הַדָּבָר טוֹב מְאֹד. 8

9. gāḏôl hārāʿāḇ bāʿîr.   גָּדוֹל הָרָעָב בָּעִיר. 9

10. hāʿăḇāḏîm rāʿîm məʾōḏ.   הָעֲבָדִים רָעִים מְאֹד. 10

11. hazzəqēnîm ʾéṣel habbáyiṯ.   הַזְּקֵנִים אֵצֶל הַבַּיִת. 11

12. heʿārîm haqqəṭannôṯ ʾéṣel hannāhār   הֶעָרִים הַקְּטַנּוֹת אֵצֶל הַנָּהָר 12
    haggāḏôl.   הַגָּדוֹל.

(d) Write in Hebrew:

1. The women are very beautiful.
2. The city is very large.
3. The house is near a small field.
4. The men and the women are on the road.
5. The large houses are in the city.
6. The women are wicked.
7. The matter is unimportant (lit. small).
8. The small garden is near the road.

LESSON 4

[*Read* § 7 *in the section "Sounds and Spelling," pp. xxi-xxiii*]

25. Noun Plurals (cont.).

Nouns of two syllables whose first syllable is either closed or contains an unchangeable long vowel and whose second syllable has either *ā* or *ē* form their plurals in two ways: the first syllable remains unchanged, but in the second *ē* is reduced to *ə*, while *ā* is generally retained. The following nouns illustrate most of the important types:

(a) with a closed first syllable:

מִשְׁפָּט	*mišpāṭ*	pl. מִשְׁפָּטִים	*mišpāṭîm*	judgment
מַלְאָךְ	*mal'āḵ*	מַלְאָכִים	*mal'āḵîm*	messenger
מִזְבֵּחַ	*mizbēᵃḥ*	מִזְבְּחוֹת	*mizbəḥôṯ*	altar

(b) with an unchangeable long vowel in the first syllable:

אֹיֵב	*'ōyēḇ*	אֹיְבִים	*'ōyəḇîm*	enemy
כֹּהֵן	*kōhēn*	כֹּהֲנִים	*kōhănîm*	priest
כּוֹכָב	*kôḵāḇ*	כּוֹכָבִים	*kôḵāḇîm*	star
הֵיכָל	*hêḵāl*	הֵיכָלִים	*hêḵālîm*	temple

A special situation is encountered in a few words such as

עִוֵּר	*'iwwēr*	עִוְרִים	*'iwrîm*	blind (adj.)
כִּסֵּא	*kissē'*	כִּסְאוֹת	*kis'ôṯ*	throne

in which the doubled consonant of the singular is simplified in the plural with the resulting loss of a syllable: not *'iwwərîm, kissə'ôṯ*. Such irregularities will always be noted in the vocabularies.

26. The Active Participle.

All verb forms and most nouns in Hebrew can be analyzed into at least two parts: a root and a formative vowel pattern. In the group of words

בָּרוּךְ	*bārûḵ*	blessed (adj.)
מְבָרֵךְ	*məḇārēḵ*	blessing (verb)
בֹּרַךְ	*bōraḵ*	he was blessed
בֵּרֵךְ	*bērēḵ*	he blessed
בְּרָכָה	*bərāḵāh*	blessing (noun)

the sequence of consonants *BRK* carries the basic notion of "bless." Such a sequence is called the root of the forms given above. Note that the root is a grammatical abstraction from the given words and not *vice versa*; that is, because a root has no existence apart from its incorporation into words, it leads to misunderstanding the nature of language to say that the words are derived from the root.

The pattern of vowels associated with a given word may or may not have a specific meaning of its own. For example, from the words *méleḵ* (king), *malkāh* (queen), *malḵûṯ* (kingdom), *mālaḵ* (he ruled), *homlaḵ* (he was made to rule), etc., we may certainly abstract a root *MLK* having to do with kings and ruling. Nevertheless, we cannot find any but the most meager support for taking the word *méleḵ* as the root *MLK* plus a meaningful formant pattern *e-e* (as one who does what the root specifies). The vowel pattern *e-e* is not a normal one for the formation of agent nouns. But consider the following set of words:

כֹּתֵב	*kōṯēḇ*	writing	הֹלֵךְ	*hōlēḵ*	walking, going
יֹשֵׁב	*yōšēḇ*	sitting	יֹרֵד	*yōrēḏ*	descending

The vowel pattern *ō-ē* is a regular one for the formation of the active participle with roots of the triconsonantal type illustrated. Thus, while it is always analytically legitimate to isolate roots and formative patterns, one must exercise caution about assigning specific meaning to the latter.

We shall begin our study of the Hebrew verb with the participial form mentioned above. The participle is in nearly all respects an adjective so far as its syntax and inflection are concerned:

masc.	יֹשֵׁב	*yōšēḇ*	יֹשְׁבִים	*yōšəḇîm*	sitting
fem.	יֹשֶׁבֶת	*yōšéḇeṯ*	יֹשְׁבוֹת	*yōšəḇôṯ*	

The first vowel is unchangeably long; the vowel of the second syllable is *ē* and therefore changeable. Note the feminine singular form with *-eṯ* and a corresponding change in the vowel of the final stem syllable; the form יֹשְׁבָה *yōšəḇāh* is also found, but less frequently.

The participle may be used attributively,

הָאִישׁ הַכֹּתֵב *hā'îš hakkōṯēḇ* the writing man or the man who is writing

or predicatively,

הָאִישׁ כֹּתֵב *hā'îš kōṯēḇ* The man is writing.

These differ in no way from the adjectival syntax of the preceding lesson.

The participle, both as an attribute and as a predicate, usually indicates a continuing action, one in progress, and is best translated with the English progressive tenses. Tense, as in the adjectival sentences of the preceding lesson, must be gained from the context. The participial sentences in the exercises should be translated in the present tense or in the immediate future (he is going to..., he is about to...):

הָאִישׁ נֹתֵן לֶחֶם לַדַּלָּה *hā'îš nōṯēn léḥem laddallāh*
The man is giving (is going to give) bread to the poor woman.

27. The Object Marker אֶת־ *'eṯ-*.

When the direct object of a verb is a definite noun (i.e. has the definite article) or is a proper name, it is usually preceded by the object marker אֶת־ *'eṯ-* (or, without *maqqēp̄*, אֵת *'ēṯ*):

הָאִישׁ שֹׁמֵר אֶת־הַתּוֹרָה *hā'îš šōmēr 'eṯ-hattôrāh*
The man is observing the Law.

הָעָם אֹהֵב אֶת־דָּוִד *hā'ām 'ōhēḇ 'eṯ-Dāwīḏ*
The people love David.

But if the object is indefinite, it is not marked:

הָאִישׁ כֹּתֵב דָּבָר *hā'îš kōṯēḇ dāḇār*
The man is writing a word.

אֶת may be repeated before each member of a compound object:

הָאֲנָשִׁים שֹׁמְרִים אֶת־הַתּוֹרָה וְאֶת־הַמִּצְוֹת *hā'ănāšîm šōmərîm 'eṯ-hattôrāh wə'eṯ-hammiṣwōṯ*
The men are observing the Law and the commandments.

28. Vocabulary 4.

NOUNS: שֹׁפֵט *šōpēṭ* (pl. *-îm*) judge
מַלְאָךְ *mal'āḵ* (pl. *-îm*) messenger, angel
כִּסֵּא *kissē'* (pl. irreg. כִּסְאוֹת *kis'ôṯ*) throne

VERBS: כֹּתֵב *kōṯēḇ* writing

אֹכֵל *'ōḵēl* eating
נֹתֵן *nōṯēn* giving, setting, placing
הֹלֵךְ *hōlēḵ* going, walking
יֹשֵׁב *yōšēḇ* sitting, dwelling, inhabiting

PREPOSITIONS: אֵת *'ēṯ* or אֶת־ *'eṯ-* direct object marker (see §27)
לְ *lə-* to, for (in dative sense); as
אֶל־ *'el-* to, toward (motion or traversing of space usually implied, but often synonymous with לְ *lə-*)
בְּעֵינֵי *bə'ênê* in the eyes of, in the opinion of, as far as — is concerned

Exercises:

(a) Form the plurals of the following nouns:

סֹפֵר *sōpēr* (-*îm*) scribe	גַּנָּב *gannāḇ* (-*îm*) thief
מוֹעֵד *mô'ēḏ* (-*îm*) appointed time	שֻׁלְחָן *šulḥān* (-*ôṯ*) table
מִשְׁכָּן *miškān* (-*îm*) tabernacle	מִקְדָּשׁ *miqdāš* (-*îm*) sanctuary

(b) Give the Hebrew for the following orally:

1. the judge is sitting
2. the king is writing
3. the boy is going
4. the woman is giving
5. the messenger is going
6. the man is giving
7. the slave is eating
8. the woman is going

(c) Pluralize each of the items in the preceding exercise. E.g. the judges are sitting, etc.

(d) Transform the items of exercise (b) into noun + modifier, as "the judge who is sitting," etc.

(e) Translate:

1. haššōpēṭ nōṯēn 'eṯ-hasséper lā'îš. — 1 הַשֹּׁפֵט נֹתֵן אֶת־הַסֵּפֶר לָאִישׁ.
2. hā'iššāh yōšébeṯ wə'ōḵéleṯ babbáyiṯ. — 2 הָאִשָּׁה יֹשֶׁבֶת וְאֹכֶלֶת בַּבָּיִת.
3. hā'ănāšîm hōləḵîm 'el-hahêḵāl haggāḏôl. — 3 הָאֲנָשִׁים הֹלְכִים אֶל־הַהֵיכָל הַגָּדוֹל.
4. hammélek yōšēḇ wəḵōṯēḇ bassēper. — 4 הַמֶּלֶךְ יֹשֵׁב וְכֹתֵב בַּסֵּפֶר.
5. hammal'āḵîm hōləḵîm 'el-hahêḵāl. — 5 הַמַּלְאָכִים הֹלְכִים אֶל־הַהֵיכָל.
6. ra' haddāḇār bə'ênê hā'ām. — 6 רַע הַדָּבָר בְּעֵינֵי הָעָם.
7. hannə'ārîm hōləḵîm 'el-hannāhār. — 7 הַנְּעָרִים הֹלְכִים אֶל־הַנָּהָר.
8. hammélek yōšēḇ 'al-hakkissē' bahêḵāl. — 8 הַמֶּלֶךְ יֹשֵׁב עַל־הַכִּסֵּא בַּהֵיכָל.
9. hā'ām yōšēḇ bā'áreṣ haggəḏôlāh. — 9 הָעָם יֹשֵׁב בָּאָרֶץ הַגְּדוֹלָה.
10. hā'îš wəhā'iššāh yōšəḇîm bā'îr hārā'āh. — 10 הָאִישׁ וְהָאִשָּׁה יֹשְׁבִים בָּעִיר הָרָעָה.
11. haššōpəṭîm hōləḵîm 'el-hannāhār. — 11 הַשֹּׁפְטִים הֹלְכִים אֶל־הַנָּהָר.

12. haylāḏîm yōšəḇîm ’éṣel hannāhār haqqāṭōn. — 12 הילדים ישבים אצל הנהר הקטן.
13. hû’ kōṯēḇ ’eṯ-haddəḇārîm ‘al-hassḗp̄er. — 13 הוא כתב את־הדברים על־הספר.
14. ’ēp̄ōh yōšəḇôṯ hannāšîm? — 14 איפה ישבות הנשים.
15. ṭôḇîm hā‘ăḇāḏîm bə‘ênê hammélek̲. — 15 טובים העבדים בעיני המלך.

(f) Write in Hebrew:

1. The boys are going to the city.
2. The slaves are sitting near the small houses.
3. The boy is giving the book to the man.
4. The man and the woman are living in the garden.
5. The men are giving the small field and the garden to the king.
6. The people are dwelling in a good land.

LESSON 5

[*Read* §§*8–9 in the section "Sounds and Spelling," pp. xxiii-xxv*]

29. The Prepositions בְּ *bə-*, **לְ** *lə-*, **and כְּ** *kə-*.

The form of these three prepositions is determined by the first consonant or syllable of the word to which they are prefixed:

a. If the noun begins with the syllable יְ *yə*, the anticipated forms **bəyə*, **ləyə*, and **kəyə* are replaced by *bî*, *lî*, and *kî*:

יְרוּשָׁלַ͏ִם	*yərûšāláim*	Jerusalem
בִּירוּשָׁלַ͏ִם	*bîrûšāláim*	in Jerusalem
לִירוּשָׁלַ͏ִם	*lîrûšāláim*	to Jerusalem
כִּירוּשָׁלַ͏ִם	*kîrûšāláim*	like Jerusalem

b. If the noun begins with any other consonant followed by *ə*, the prepositions have the vowel *i*:

שְׁמוּאֵל	*šəmû'ēl*	Samuel
בִּשְׁמוּאֵל	*bišmû'ēl*	in Samuel
לִשְׁמוּאֵל	*lišmû'ēl*	to Samuel
כִּשְׁמוּאֵל	*kišmû'ēl*	like Samuel

Note that the *ə* of the noun is dropped in pronunciation: *biš-mû-'ēl*, not *bi-šə-mû-'ēl.*

c. If the noun begins with a guttural followed by a reduced vowel (*ă*, *ĕ*, or *ŏ*), the prepositions have the corresponding full short vowel:

חֲלוֹם	*ḥălôm*	a dream	אֱמֶת	*'ĕméṯ*	truth
בַּחֲלוֹם	*baḥălôm*	in a dream	בֶּאֱמֶת	*be'ĕméṯ*	in truth
לַחֲלוֹם	*laḥălôm*	to a dream	לֶאֱמֶת	*le'ĕméṯ*	to truth
כַּחֲלוֹם	*kaḥălôm*	like a dream	כֶּאֱמֶת	*ke'ĕméṯ*	like truth
אֳנִיָּה	*'ŏnîyāh*	a ship			
בָּאֳנִיָּה	*bo'ŏnîyāh*	in a ship, etc.			

d. Before words stressed on the first syllable (thus mainly monosyllabic words) the prepositions are optionally vocalized with *ā*. Instances of this rather restricted form will be noted as they occur.

e. As we have stated previously, these three prepositions combine with the definite article, which loses its initial ה *h*. The vowel of the article remains unchanged.

f. Aside from the special circumstances given in the preceding paragraphs, the prepositions occur simply as בְּ *bə-*, לְ *lə-*, and כְּ *kə-*:

בְּעִיר	*bə'îr*	in a city
כְּמֶלֶךְ	*kəméleḵ*	like a king
לְאִישׁ	*lə'îš*	to a man.

30. The Preposition מִן *min.*

a. Before the definite article this preposition may have either the form מֵ *mē-*, which is joined directly to the following word, or מִן *min-*, which is usually joined to the following word with *maqqēp̄*:

from the king	*min-hamméleḵ*	מִן־הַמֶּלֶךְ
or	*mēhamméleḵ.*	מֵהַמֶּלֶךְ

b. Before nouns beginning with a guttural or *r*, the preposition takes the form מֵ *mē-*, joined directly:

עִיר	*'îr*	a city	מֵעִיר	*mē'îr*	from a city
רֹאשׁ	*rō(')š*	a head	מֵרֹאשׁ	*mērō(')š*	from a head

c. Before all other nouns the form is מִ *mi* + the doubling of the first consonant:

מֶלֶךְ *méleḵ* a king מִמֶּלֶךְ *mimméleḵ* from a king.

The sequence *miyyə-* is commonly contracted to *mî-,* as in

מִיהוּדָה *mîhûḏāh* (for **miyyəhûḏāh*) from Judah.

31. The Comparative.

The adjective is not altered in form to express the comparative. Instead, the preposition מִן *min* is used before the noun which is the basis of comparison.

הָאִישׁ חָכָם מֵהַנַּעַר *hā'îš ḥāḵām mēhanná'ar*
The man is wiser than the boy.

Other sentence orders are possible and not unusual:

יָפָה הָאִשָּׁה מֵהַנַּעֲרָה *yāpāh hā'iššāh mēhanna'ărāh*
The woman is more beautiful than the girl.

The same construction may be translated "too . . . for:"

קָשָׁה הָעֲבוֹדָה מֵהָאִישׁ *qāšāh hā'ăḇôḏāh mēhā'îš*
The work is *too* hard *for* the man.

The choice between the comparative and "too" translations depends on which makes the better sense.

32. The Relative Word אֲשֶׁר *'ăšer.*

Unlike English, the prepositional phrase in Hebrew does not commonly stand next to a noun as a modifier. Thus, while we may speak of *the book on the table* or *the fountain in the park*, where *on the table* and *in the park* modify *book* and *fountain* respectively, in Hebrew such modification is more frequently introduced by the word אֲשֶׁר *'ăšer*, which is usually the equivalent of the English relative pronouns *who*, *which*, and *that*.

הָאִישׁ אֲשֶׁר בָּעִיר	*hā'îš 'ăšer bā'îr*	the man in the city, or the man who is in the city
הָעָם אֲשֶׁר בָּאָרֶץ	*hā'ām 'ăšer bā'āreṣ*	the people in the land, or the people which is in the land.

The word אֲשֶׁר *'ăšer* is not affected by the gender or number of the antecedent:

הָאִשָּׁה אֲשֶׁר בַּהֵיכָל *hā'iššāh 'ăšer bahêḵāl* the woman in the temple.

אֲשֶׁר *'ăšer* is not commonly employed before adjectives or participles. Thus, English *the man who is wise* is simply הָאִישׁ הֶחָכָם *hā'îš heḥāḵām*, or הֶחָכָם *heḥāḵām* alone. *The man who is sitting* is הָאִישׁ הַיֹּשֵׁב *hā'îš hayyōšēḇ*. The participle may be used alone, even without the definite article, as an equivalent of English *one who, anyone who, whoever, he who*:

הֹלֵךְ בֶּאֱמֶת *hōlēḵ be'ĕmét* he who (or whoever) walks in truth.

33. Vocabulary 5.

NOUNS:	זָהָב	*zāhāḇ*	gold
	חָכְמָה	*ḥoḵmāh*	wisdom
	כֶּסֶף	*késep̄*	silver, money
	עֲבוֹדָה	*'ăḇôḏāh*	work, task, servitude (cf. *'éḇeḏ*)
	עֵצָה	*'ēṣāh*	counsel, advice

ADJECTIVES: יָקָר *yāqār* precious
יָשָׁר *yāšār* just, upright
צַדִּיק *ṣaddîq* righteous
קָשֶׁה *qāšeh* difficult, hard, harsh
רָשָׁע *rāšā'* evil, bad, criminal

PROPER NAMES: דָּוִד *Dāwīḏ* David
שְׁמוּאֵל *šəmû'ēl* Samuel
יְרוּשָׁלַםִ *Yərûšāláim* Jerusalem [Note that in the Hebrew spelling the second ׳ is missing. This spelling may point to an early dialectal variant pronunciation *Yərûšālêm*]

OTHER: מִן *min-* (prep.) from; also used partitively: מֵהָאֲנָשִׁים *mēhā'ănāšîm*, some of the men.
אֲשֶׁר *'ăšer* (rel. pronoun) who, which, that

Exercises:

(a) Prefix the preposition בְּ *bə-* to the following words, first without the article, then with it. Example: *késep̄*, *bəḵésep̄*, *bakkésep̄*.

מְלָכִים *məlāḵîm*	יְלָדִים *yəlāḏîm*	חֲדָרִים *ḥăḏārîm*	(rooms)
עֲבָדִים *'ăḇāḏîm*	דְּרָכִים *dərāḵîm*	אֲדָמָה *'ăḏāmāh*	(ground)
עָרִים *'ārîm*	נְעָרִים *nə'ārîm*	אֳנִיָּה *'ŏnîyāh*	(ship)

(b) Give the Hebrew for the following orally. Use the adjective in the masculine singular form.

1. better than the boy
2. larger than the house
3. larger than the river
4. smaller than a field
5. worse than the men
6. more precious than gold
7. more just than the king

(c) Give the Hebrew for the following orally. Then transform them into phrases using *'ăšer*. Example:

The city is in the land → the city which is in the land
hā'îr bā'āreṣ → *hā'îr 'ăšer bā'āreṣ*

1. The boy is in the large field.
2. The words are in the book.
3. The woman is on the road.
4. The gold is in the temple.
5. The silver is in the house.

(d) Translate:

1. yəqārāh ḥoḵmāh mizzāhāḇ. — 1 יְקָרָה חָכְמָה מִזָּהָב.
2. qāšāh hā'ăḇôḏāh mēhā'ănāšîm. — 2 קָשָׁה הָעֲבוֹדָה מֵהָאֲנָשִׁים.

3. yəšārîm hā‘ăḇāḏîm mēhamməlāḵîm.	3 יְשָׁרִים הָעֲבָדִים מֵהַמְּלָכִים.
4. Dāwīḏ yāšār mə’ōḏ.	4 דָּוִד יָשָׁר מְאֹד.
5. hû’ nōṯēn ḥoḵmāh lammélek̲ hayyōšēḇ ‘al-hakkissē’.	5 הוּא נֹתֵן חָכְמָה לַמֶּלֶךְ הַיֹּשֵׁב עַל־הַכִּסֵּא.
6. rā‘îm haddəḇārîm ’ăšer bassēp̄er.	6 רָעִים הַדְּבָרִים אֲשֶׁר בַּסֵּפֶר.
7. ṭôḇāh ḥoḵmāh mikkésep̄.	7 טוֹבָה חָכְמָה מִכֶּסֶף.
8. yəšārîm hā’ănāšîm.	8 יְשָׁרִים הָאֲנָשִׁים.
9. Dāwīḏ wəhā’ănāšîm yōšəḇîm bîrûšāláim.	9 דָּוִד וְהָאֲנָשִׁים יֹשְׁבִים בִּירוּשָׁלִַם.
10. mî ṣaddîq miššəmû’ēl?	10 מִי צַדִּיק מִשְּׁמוּאֵל.
11. hā‘ēṣāh rā‘āh mə’ōḏ.	11 הָעֵצָה רָעָה מְאֹד.
12. ’ayyēh hayšārîm wəhaṣṣaddîqîm?	12 אַיֵּה הַיְשָׁרִים וְהַצַּדִּיקִים.

(e) Write in Hebrew:

1. The king is giving the gold and the silver to the men who are in the palace.
2. Wisdom is more precious than silver.
3. The messengers in Jerusalem are very bad.
4. Samuel and David are just and righteous.
5. The task is too difficult for the boy.
6. The field is larger than the garden near the house.
7. The judges are more evil than the kings.

LESSON 6

[*Read* § *10 in the section "Sounds and Spelling," pp. xxv-xxvii*]

34. Noun Plurals (cont.).

There are, in general, two types of monosyllabic nouns in terms of changes in the plural stem: (a) those with no change, and (b) those having a doubling of the final consonant:

(a)	שִׁיר	*šîr*	שִׁירִים	*šîrîm*	song
	סוּס	*sûs*	סוּסִים	*sûsîm*	horse
	אוֹת	*'ôṯ*	אוֹתוֹת	*'ôṯôṯ*	sign
	דָּם	*dām*	דָּמִים	*dāmîm*	blood
	עֵץ	*'ēṣ*	עֵצִים	*'ēṣîm*	tree
(b)	עַם	*'am*	עַמִּים	*'ammîm*	people
	חֵץ	*ḥēṣ*	חִצִּים	*ḥiṣṣîm*	arrow
	חֹק	*ḥōq*	חֻקִּים	*ḥuqqîm*	statute

Note the following particulars:

(1) Nouns with the stem vowels *û*, *î*, *ô*, and usually *ā* do not alter the stem before the plural ending.

(2) Nouns with stem vowel *ē* behave in one of two ways:

(a) the stem is unchanged, as in *'ēṣ* – *'ēṣîm*

(b) the final stem consonant is doubled and *ē* is replaced by *i*, as in *ḥēṣ* – *ḥiṣṣîm*.

(3) Nouns with *a* are similar to the above:

(a) When the final stem consonant is a guttural or *r*, the stem vowel is "lengthened" to *ā*, as in *har* – *hārîm*.

(b) Otherwise the final stem consonant is doubled and the stem vowel remains the same, as in *'am* – *'ammîm*.

(4) Nouns with the stem vowel *ō* usually follow the pattern of *ḥōq* – *ḥuqqîm*. Often, however, *ō* is a defective writing for *ô*, so that care must be taken not to confuse the type *ḥōq* with that of *'ôṯ* in group (a).

Because of irregularities and minor unpredictable deviations, the plurals will be given with the singulars in the vocabularies. The following nouns are irregular in that the plural stems do not conform to the types just enumerated:

ראשׁ	*rō(')š*	head	plural:	רָאשִׁים	*rā(')šîm*
יוֹם	*yôm*	day		יָמִים	*yāmîm*
בֵּן	*bēn*	son		בָּנִים	*bānîm*
עִיר	*'îr*	city		עָרִים	*'ārîm*
אִישׁ	*'îš*	man		אֲנָשִׁים	*'ănāšîm*

35. Participles (cont.).

When the second or third consonant of a verbal root is a guttural (א ', ע ', ה *h*, ח *ḥ*) the forms of the participle are slightly modified. When the second consonant is a guttural, we find *ă* for *ə* in the plural stem:

צֹעֵק	*ṣō'ēq*	צֹעֲקִים	*ṣō'ăqîm*	crying out
צֹעֶקֶת	*ṣō'éqeṯ*	צֹעֲקוֹת	*ṣō'ăqôṯ*	

When the third consonant is an ע ' or ח *ḥ*, the feminine singular has *a* instead of *e* in the last two syllables:

בֹּרֵחַ	*bōrēªḥ*	בֹּרְחִים	*bōrəḥîm*	fleeing
בֹּרַחַת	*bōráḥaṯ*	בֹּרְחוֹת	*bōrəḥôṯ*	

When the third consonant is א ', which is not pronounced when it would close a syllable, the fem. sing. has *ē*:

קֹרֵא	*qōrē'*	קֹרְאִים	*qōrə'îm*	calling
קֹרֵאת	*qōrē(')ṯ*	קֹרְאוֹת	*qōrə'ôṯ*	

36. Vocabulary 6.

NOUNS: קוֹל *qôl* (pl. *-ôṯ*) voice, sound; *bəqôl gāḏôl*: aloud, in a loud voice
עֵץ *'ēṣ* (pl. *'ēṣîm*) tree, wood
כֶּרֶם *kérem* (pl. *-îm*) vineyard
VERBS: צֹעֵק *ṣō'ēq* crying out (in distress)
שֹׁלֵחַ *šōlēªḥ* sending
נֹטֵעַ *nōṭēª'* planting
יֹצֵא *yōṣē'* going forth, leaving

OTHER: תַּחַת *táḥat* (prep.) under; instead of
כִּי *kî* (conj.) because, since, for; that
רַב *rab̲* (adj.) much, many, numerous (forms in § 22)

Exercises:

(a) Give the Hebrew for the following orally:

1. The old man is going forth.
2. The woman is planting.
3. The judge is sending.
4. The people is crying out.
5. The servant is going forth.

(b) Pluralize each of the sentences in (a).

(c) Translate:

1. hā'ănāšîm nōṭə'îm 'ēṣîm rabbîm 'al-hāhār.	הָאֲנָשִׁים נֹטְעִים עֵצִים רַבִּים עַל־הָהָר. 1
2. hanná'ar yōšēb̲ táḥat̲ hā'ēṣ 'ăšer baggān.	הַנַּעַר יֹשֵׁב תַּחַת הָעֵץ אֲשֶׁר בַּגָּן. 2
3. gəd̲ôlîm hā'ēṣîm 'ăšer behārîm mēhā'ēṣîm 'ăšer 'ḗṣel hannāhār.	גְּדוֹלִים הָעֵצִים אֲשֶׁר בֶּהָרִים מֵהָעֵצִים אֲשֶׁר אֵצֶל הַנָּהָר. 3
4. 'ammîm rabbîm yōšəb̲îm bā'ā́reṣ kî hā'ā́reṣ ṭôb̲āh mə'ōd̲.	עַמִּים רַבִּים יֹשְׁבִים בָּאָרֶץ כִּי הָאָרֶץ טוֹבָה מְאֹד. 4
5. hā'ām ṣō'ăqîm bəqôl gād̲ôl kî qāšāh mə'ōd̲ hā'ăb̲ôd̲āh.	הָעָם צֹעֲקִים בְּקוֹל גָּדוֹל כִּי קָשָׁה מְאֹד הָעֲבוֹדָה. 5
6. mî yōṣē' min-hā'îr hārā'āh?	מִי יֹצֵא מִן־הָעִיר הָרָעָה. 6
7. rā'îm haddəb̲ārîm bə'ênê hammélek̲ hayyāšār.	רָעִים הַדְּבָרִים בְּעֵינֵי הַמֶּלֶךְ הַיָּשָׁר. 7
8. hā'iššāh yōṣē(')t̲ mēhabbáyit̲.	הָאִשָּׁה יֹצֵאת מֵהַבַּיִת. 8
9. hā'ăb̲ād̲îm nōṭə'îm kérem qāṭōn 'ḗṣel haśśād̲eh.	הָעֲבָדִים נֹטְעִים כֶּרֶם קָטֹן אֵצֶל הַשָּׂדֶה. 9

(d) Write in Hebrew:

1. The king is sending the messengers to the judge who is in the city.
2. The people are going out of Jerusalem because the famine is very great.
3. Who is crying out in the house?
4. The vineyard and the garden are near the house.
5. He is sitting under a large tree.
6. The men are good, but the servants are bad.
7. The servants are better than the messengers.

LESSON 7

[*Read* § *11 of the section "Sounds and Spelling," pp. xxvii-xxviii*]

37. Predication of Existence.

In order to state that something exists, Hebrew employs the word יֵשׁ *yēš*, commonly translated "there is (are)."

יֵשׁ אִישׁ	*yēš 'îš*	There is a man.
יֵשׁ אִשָּׁה	*yēš 'iššāh*	There is a woman.
יֵשׁ אֲנָשִׁים	*yēš 'ănāšîm*	There are men.

There is no change in the word for number or gender of the object predicated. The negative expression, for non-existence, is אֵין *'ên*:

אֵין אִישׁ	*'ên 'îš*	There is no man.
אֵין אִשָּׁה	*'ên 'iššāh*	There is no woman.

This sentence type figures largely in expressing possession:

אֵין לָאִישׁ כֶּסֶף	*'ên lā'îš késep̄*	The man has no silver.
יֵשׁ אִישׁ לָאִשָּׁה	*yēš 'îš lā'iššāh*	The woman has a husband.

In the preceding lessons we dealt with sentences having an adverbial predicate. All of the examples used, both in the lesson and in the exercises, had definite nouns as subjects. When one constructs a similar sentence with an indefinite subject, such as "A man is in the house," we find that this is virtually equivalent to the existential sentence "There is a man in the house."

Thus, the sentences expressing existence and those having adverbial predicates are sometimes identical:

subj. definite	הָאִישׁ בַּבַּ֫יִת	*hāʼîš babbáyiṯ*	The man is...
subj. indef.	יֵשׁ אִישׁ בַּבַּ֫יִת	*yēš ʼîš babbáyiṯ*	A man is ... There is a man...
	אֵין אִישׁ בַּבַּ֫יִת	*ʼên ʼîš babbáyiṯ*	No man is... There is no man...

38. The Prepositions בְּ *bə*-, לְ *lə*-, and אֶת־ *ʼeṯ*- with Pronominal Suffixes.

When a personal pronoun is the object of a preposition, it is appended as a suffix directly to the preposition:

לִי	*lî*	to me	לָ֫נוּ	*lā́nû*	to us
לְךָ	*ləḵā*	to you (m. s.)	לָכֶם	*lāḵém*	to you (m. pl.)
לָךְ	*lāḵ*	to you (f. s.)	[לָכֶן	*lāḵén*	to you (f. pl.)]
לוֹ	*lô*	to him	לָהֶם	*lāhém*	to them (m. pl.)
לָהּ	*lāh*	to her	לָהֶן	*lāhén*	to them (f. pl.)

Here, as elsewhere in the language, a distinction between genders is made in the second person as well as in the third. There are thus four Hebrew pronouns corresponding to English "you."

The preposition בְּ *bə* with suffixes is exactly like the above. An alternate form בָּם *bām* for בָּהֶם *bāhém* is also used.

The pronouns as objects of the verb may occur as suffixes on the object marker, as follows:

אֹתִי	*ʼōṯî*	me	אֹתָ֫נוּ	*ʼōṯā́nû*	us
אֹתְךָ	*ʼōṯəḵā*	you (m. s.)	אֶתְכֶם	*ʼeṯḵem*	you (m. pl.)
אֹתָךְ	*ʼōṯāḵ*	you (f. s.)	[אֶתְכֶן	*ʼeṯḵen*	you (f. pl.)]
אֹתוֹ	*ʼōṯô*	him	אֹתָם	*ʼōṯām*	them (m. pl.)
אֹתָהּ	*ʼōṯāh*	her	אֹתָן	*ʼōṯān*	them (f. pl.)

The 3rd pers. pl. forms also occur as אֶתְהֶם *ʼeṯhem* and אֶתְהֶן *ʼeṯhen*.

Some examples of usage:

הָאִישׁ נֹתֵן לָ֫נוּ לֶ֫חֶם	*hāʼîš nōṯēn lā́nû léḥem* The man is giving (to) us bread.
אֵין לִי כֶּ֫סֶף	*ʼên lî ḵésep̄* I have no silver.
יֵשׁ לָהֶם מֶ֫לֶךְ	*yēš lāhem méleḵ* They have a king.
הַמֶּ֫לֶךְ שֹׁלֵחַ אֹתָם אֶל־הָעִיר	*hammélek šōlē*^{a}*ḥ ʼōṯām ʼel-hāʻîr* The king is sending them to the city.

39. Vocabulary 7.

NOUNS:	צֹאן	*ṣō(ʾ)n*	(no pl.) a collective term for small cattle (sheep and goats)
	בָּקָר	*bāqār*	(no pl.) a collective term for large cattle (bulls, steers, cows, etc.)
	גָּמָל	*gāmāl*	(pl. irreg. גְּמַלִּים *gəmallîm*) camel
	לֶחֶם	*léḥem*	(no pl.) bread, food
VERBS:	יֹרֵד	*yōrēḏ*	descending, going down
ADJECTIVES:	עָשִׁיר	*ʿāšîr*	rich
	דַּל	*dal*	poor
PARTICLES:	יֵשׁ	*yēš*	there is, there are
	אֵין	*ʾên*	there is not, there are not

Exercises:

(a) Give the Hebrew for the following orally:

1. I have a ____. (house, garden, field, vineyard)
2. She has no ____. (husband, slaves, money, books)
3. We have no ____. (king, judge, city, camels)
4. The man has no wife.
5. They (m. pl.) have ____. (small-cattle, camels, gold, silver)
6. There are no trees on the mountain.
7. There are many houses in the city.
8. There are many messengers here.
9. He is sending us.
10. He is writing to us.
11. He is giving us bread.
12. He is dwelling in it.
13. She is sending them.
14. She is planting it for them.

(b) Translate:

1. ʾên ʾîš yōšēḇ ʿal-hakkissēʾ. — 1 אֵין אִישׁ יֹשֵׁב עַל־הַכִּסֵּא.
2. yēš sḗp̄er šām. — 2 יֵשׁ סֵ֫פֶר שָׁם.
3. ʾên šōp̄ēṭ yāšār bāʿîr. — 3 אֵין שֹׁפֵט יָשָׁר בָּעִיר.
4. hammalʾāḵîm yōrəḏîm mēhāhār kî ʾên lāhem léḥem šām. — 4 הַמַּלְאָכִים יֹרְדִים מֵהָהָר כִּי אֵין לָהֶם לֶ֫חֶם שָׁם.
5. hāʿăšîrîm nōṯənîm léḥem laddallîm hayyōšəḇîm šām. — 5 הָעֲשִׁירִים נֹתְנִים לֶ֫חֶם לַדַּלִּים הַיֹּשְׁבִים שָׁם.
6. hāʾănāšîm yōṣəʾîm min-hāʿîr wəhōləḵîm ʾel-hāhār. — 6 הָאֲנָשִׁים יֹצְאִים מִן־הָעִיר וְהֹלְכִים אֶל־הָהָר.
7. hannāšîm yōṣəʾôṯ mēhāʿîr wəyōrəḏôṯ ʾel-hannāhār. — 7 הַנָּשִׁים יֹצְאוֹת מֵהָעִיר וְיֹרְדוֹת אֶל־הַנָּהָר.

8. yēš lā́nû báyiṯ gāḏôl wəḡan qāṭōn.

9. mî hā'ănāšîm hahōləḵîm 'el-hā'îr?

10. haylāḏîm yōšəḇîm wə'ōḵəlîm bakkérem.

11. hû' 'āšîr mə'ōḏ; yēš lô ḵésep̄ wəzāhāḇ.

8 יֵ֣שׁ לָ֫נוּ בַּ֫יִת גָּדוֹל וְגַן קָטֹן.

9 מִי הָאֲנָשִׁים הַהֹלְכִים אֶל־הָעִיר.

10 הַיְלָדִים יֹשְׁבִים וְאֹכְלִים בַּכֶּ֫רֶם.

11 הוּא עָשִׁיר מְאֹד. יֵשׁ לוֹ כֶּ֫סֶף וְזָהָב.

(c) Write in Hebrew:

1. The king has no city and he has no land.
2. Where are the young men sitting and eating?
3. The rich have bread but the poor have no bread.
4. The poor are crying out because they have no food.
5. The judges are sending the books to the king, for there are many good things in them.
6. The king is sending me to the judge because he has a difficult problem (= thing).
7. There are many camels here.

LESSON 8

40. The Demonstrative Adjectives and Pronouns.

	SINGULAR			PLURAL		
masc.	זֶה	*zeh*	this	אֵ֫לֶּה	*'ḗlleh*	these
fem.	זֹאת	*zō(')ṯ*	this			
masc.	הוּא	*hû'*	that	הֵם	*hēm*	those
fem.	הִיא	*hî'*	that	הֵ֫נָּה	*hḗnnāh*	those

These words have a usage parallel to that of the adjective.

הָאִישׁ הַזֶּה	*hā'îš hazzeh*	this man
הָאִשָּׁה הַזֹּאת	*hā'iššāh hazzō(')ṯ*	this woman
הָאֲנָשִׁים הָאֵ֫לֶּה	*hā'ănāšîm hā'ḗlleh*	these men
הַנָּשִׁים הָאֵ֫לֶּה	*hannāšîm hā'ḗlleh*	these women
הָאִישׁ הַהוּא	*hā'îš hahû'*	that man
הָאִשָּׁה הַהִיא	*hā'iššāh hahî'*	that woman
הָאֲנָשִׁים הָהֵם	*hā'ănāšîm hāhēm*	those men
הַנָּשִׁים הָהֵ֫נָּה	*hannāšîm hāhḗnnāh*	those women

The demonstrative stands last in a series of adjectives:

הָאִישׁ הַטּוֹב הַזֶּה	*hā'îš haṭṭôḇ hazzeh*	this good man
הָאִשָּׁה הַטּוֹבָה הַזֹּאת	*hā'iššāh haṭṭôḇāh hazzō(')ṯ*	this good woman

The form without the article has the status of a pronoun (compare the use of the predicate adjective):

זֶה הָאִישׁ	*zeh hā'îš*	This is the man.
זאת הָאִשָּׁה	*zō(')ṯ hā'iššāh*	This is the woman.
אֵלֶּה הַדְּבָרִים	*'élleh haddəḇārîm*	These are the words.

Note that agreement in number and gender is present, as with the adjective.

41. Participles (cont.).

masc.	בֹּנֶה	*bōneh*	בֹּנִים	*bōnîm*
fem.	בֹּנָה	*bōnāh*	בֹּנוֹת	*bōnôṯ*
	(בֹּנִיָּה	*bōnîyāh*)		

The final ה *h* of the form בֹּנֶה *bōneh* is a *mater lectionis* for the final vowel and is not a third root consonant. The root in this class of verbs must be considered as variable in form, sometimes *BN-*, sometimes *BNY*. Note that the feminine has two forms in the singular; either may be used, but *bōnîyāh* is quite rare.

42. Vocabulary 8.

NOUNS:	בִּינָה	*bînāh*	understanding, perceptiveness
	צֶדֶק	*ṣéḏeq*	righteousness (cf. *ṣaddîq*)
	אֵשׁ	*'ēš*	(no. pl.) fire (f.)
	נָבִיא	*nāḇî'*	(pl. *-îm*) prophet
VERBS:	בֹּנֶה	*bōneh*	building
	עֹלֶה	*'ōleh*	ascending, going up
	נֹפֵל	*nōpēl*	falling

Exercises:

(a) Give the Hebrew for the following orally:

1. this famine
2. these houses
3. that city
4. this money
5. that task
6. this advice
7. these cities
8. these mountains
9. those peoples

(b) Transform the phrases of (a) into sentences according to the model:

this famine → This is the famine.

(c) Translate:

1. dal hannāḇî' hazzeh wə'ên lô léḥem. — 1 דַּל הַנָּבִיא הַזֶּה וְאֵין לוֹ לֶחֶם.
2. hā'ănāšîm hā'élleh 'ōlîm 'el-hehārîm. — 2 הָאֲנָשִׁים הָאֵלֶּה עֹלִים אֶל־הֶהָרִים.
3. hannəḇî'îm hayšārîm hōləḵîm bəṣéḏeq. — 3 הַנְּבִיאִים הַיְשָׁרִים הֹלְכִים בְּצֶדֶק.

4. bînāh wəḥoḵmāh ṭôḇôṯ mizzāhāḇ.	4 בִּינָה וְחָכְמָה טוֹבוֹת מִזָּהָב.
5. hā'ēš nōp̄éleṯ 'al-habbáyiṯ 'ăšer 'ḗṣel hahêḵāl.	5 הָאֵשׁ נֹפֶלֶת עַל־הַבַּיִת אֲשֶׁר אֵצֶל הַהֵיכָל.
6. hā'ănāšîm bōnîm báyiṯ gāḏôl bā'îr hahî'.	6 הָאֲנָשִׁים בֹּנִים בַּיִת גָּדוֹל בָּעִיר הַהִיא.
7. rā'îm hā'ām kî 'ên lāhem bînāh.	7 רָעִים הָעָם כִּי אֵין לָהֶם בִּינָה.
8. hû' šōlēaḥ lā́nû nāḇî' ṣaddîq.	8 הוּא שֹׁלֵחַ לָנוּ נָבִיא צַדִּיק.
9. 'ên méleḵ bîrûšāláim.	9 אֵין מֶלֶךְ בִּירוּשָׁלַםִ.

(d) Write in Hebrew:

1. These camels are mine (lit. to me) and those camels are yours.
2. You have no understanding.
3. He is going up to the cattle which are in the mountains.
4. She is falling.
5. The boys are building a small house near the garden.
6. The people are dwelling in this land because it is great and beautiful.
7. He is placing (lit. giving) fire upon that wicked city.

LESSON 9

43. The Perfect of כָּתַב *kāṯaḇ*.

There are two full verbal inflections for person, number, and gender for each Hebrew verb. The first, called the perfect, is formed by adding subject suffixes to a relatively fixed stem, as illustrated by

כָּתַב	*kāṯaḇ*	he wrote
כָּתַ֫בְתִּי	*kāṯáḇtî*	I wrote.

The second, called the imperfect, uses a different stem and has person, number, and gender marked by both prefixes and suffixes, as in

יִכְתֹּב	*yiḵtōḇ*	he will write
תִּכְתֹּ֫בְנָה	*tiḵtṓḇnāh*	they (fem. pl.) will write.

We shall begin our study of the verb with the perfect, the full inflection of which is as follows:

כָּתַב	*kāṯaḇ*	he wrote	כָּתְבוּ	*kāṯəḇû*	they wrote
כָּתְבָה	*kāṯəḇāh*	she wrote			
כָּתַ֫בְתָּ	*kāṯáḇtā*	you (m. s.) wrote	כְּתַבְתֶּם	*kəṯaḇtem*	you (m. pl.) wrote
כָּתַבְתְּ	*kāṯaḇt*	you (f. s.) wrote	כְּתַבְתֶּן	*kəṯaḇten*	you (f. pl.) wrote
כָּתַ֫בְתִּי	*kāṯáḇtî*	I wrote	כָּתַ֫בְנוּ	*kāṯáḇnû*	we wrote

The following particulars should be noted:

(**1**) The traditional arrangement of a verbal paradigm in Hebrew begins with the third person and proceeds to the first.

(**2**) In the perfect, there is a distinction in form for gender in the second and third persons of the singular and the second person plural. The others, including the first person singular and plural and the third person plural, do not reflect the gender of the subject.

(**3**) The endings given in the paradigm above are standard for nearly all the verbs in the language. Many variations will be seen to occur in the stems of various verb types, but the endings themselves remain fairly constant. The 2nd pers. masc. sing. also appears with a final *mater lectionis*: כָּתַ֫בְתָּה *kāṯáḇtāh*.

(**4**) The stem of the verb *kāṯaḇ* changes in accordance with the shape of the suffix added:

(a) Before the unstressed endings *-tā*, *-t*, *-tî*, and *-nû* the stem remains the same as in the third person masculine singular.

(b) The addition of the endings *-āh* and *-û*, both stressed and consisting of a vowel, opens the final syllable of the stem. Before these endings the second stem vowel is regularly replaced by (reduced to) *ə*.

(c) The endings *-tem* and *-ten* are always stressed. Because they begin with a consonant the second stem syllable remains closed and unchanged. The first stem vowel, if in an open syllable as in the paradigm under study, is reduced to *ə*.

(**5**) When the final root consonant is the same as that which begins the suffix, only one letter is written, but with daghesh *forte*; thus, from כָּרַת (he cut) we have כָּרַ֫תִּי *kārátti* (I cut), and from שָׁכַן (he settled), שָׁכַ֫נּוּ *šākánnû* (we settled).

Verbs whose roots contain a guttural consonant, or whose roots have other phonological peculiarities, such as that of *bōneh*, deviate from the paradigm given above and will be dealt with in the following lessons. Verbs whose roots have no phonological peculiarities are sometimes referred to as "sound" or "regular" triliteral verbs.

44. The Meaning of the Perfect.

We shall see in the course of this book that the translation value of Hebrew tenses is very largely dependent on the kind of sentence or clause in which the verb is used. In the isolated sentences of the following exercises there are only two or three values possible for the translation of the perfect:

(**1**) With all verbs, regardless of their meanings, the Hebrew perfect may be translated as the English simple past (I wrote) or the present perfect (I have written).

(**2**) With verbs signifying perception, or the attitude or disposition of the subject toward an object, rather than a direct action performed on the object, the perfect may be translated by the general present tense:

אָהַ֫בְתִּי *'āhábtî* I love (or, as above, I loved, have loved)
יָדַ֫עְתִּי *yāḏá'tî* I know (or, I knew, have known).

(**3**) With verbs signifying the mental or physical state of the subject, and which consequently do not occur with a direct object, the perfect may be translated by the English present of the verb "to be" + an adjective:

זָקַ֫נְתִּי *zāqántî* I am old (or I have become old, I grew old)

(**4**) Rarely in prose, but rather frequently in poetry and proverbial expressions, the perfect is used to denote habitual activity with no specific tense value. Such uses are translated by the English general present (I write).

45. Word Order in the Verbal Sentence.

The verb usually stands first, then the subject, object, and various adverbial elements in that order.

זָכַר הָאִישׁ אֶת־הַדְּבָרִים *zāḵar hā'îš 'eṯ-haddəḇārîm*
The man remembered the words.
כָּתַב הָאִישׁ אֶת־הַדָּבָר בַּסֵּ֫פֶר *kāṯaḇ hā'îš 'eṯ-haddāḇār basséper.*
The man wrote the word in the book.

It is by no means unusual to find the subject or some other element before the verb, but such sentence order is often conditioned by interclause relationships (taken up below) or by emphasis on the element which is placed first.

The verb agrees in person, number, and gender with its subject. Pronominal subjects are inherent in the verb form itself.

זָכַר אֶת־הַדְּבָרִים *zāḵar 'eṯ-haddəḇārîm*
He remembered the words.
זָֽכְרָה אֶת־הַדְּבָרִים *zāḵərāh 'eṯ-haddəḇārîm*
She remembered the words.
זָֽכְרָה הָאִשָּׁה אֶת־הַדְּבָרִים *zāḵərāh hā'iššāh 'eṯ-haddəḇārîm*
The woman remembered the words.

The particle אֶת־ *'eṯ-* is used before definite objects, as previously explained.

The perfect is negated with לֹא *lō'*, which is always placed immediately before the verb:

לֹא זָכַ֫רְתִּי אֶת־הַדָּבָר *lō' zāḵártî 'eṯ-haddāḇār*
I did not remember the word.

The indirect object, always marked by the preposition *lə-*, tends to precede the direct object when the former is pronominal and the latter nominal:

נָתַן לוֹ אֶת־הָאִשָּׁה	*nāṯan lô 'eṯ-hā'iššāh* He gave him the woman.

Otherwise, direct object + indirect object may be considered the normal order:

נָתַן אֹתָהּ לוֹ לְאִשָּׁה	*nāṯan 'ōṯāh lô lə'iššāh* He gave her to him as a wife.
נָתַן אֶת־הָאִשָּׁה לָאִישׁ	*nāṯan 'eṯ-hā'iššāh lā'îš* He gave the woman to the man.

46. The Forms of the Conjunction וְ *wə*-.

Like the prepositions *bə*-, *lə*-, and *kə*, the conjunction וְ *wə*- (and) differs in form before various word beginnings:

(a) Before a labial consonant ב *b*, פ *p*, or מ *m*, its form is וּ *û*-:

בַּ֫יִת	*báyiṯ*	a house	וּבַ֫יִת	*ûḇáyiṯ*	and a house
פֹּה	*pōh*	here	וּפֹה	*ûpōh*	and here
מַ֫יִם	*máyim*	water	וּמַ֫יִם	*ûmáyim*	and water

(b) Before a word beginning with יְ *yə*-, the conjunction and the first syllable of the word contract to וִי *wî*-:

יְהוּדָה	*yəhûḏāh*	Judah	וִיהוּדָה	*wîhûḏāh*	and Judah
יְדַעְתֶּם	*yəḏa'tem*	you knew	וִידַעְתֶּם	*wîḏa'tem*	and you knew

(c) Before a word beginning with any consonant (except י *y*) + *ə*, the form is וּ *û*-:

שְׁמוּאֵל	*šəmû'ēl*	Samuel	וּשְׁמוּאֵל	*ûš(ə)mû'ēl*	and Samuel

(d) Before a guttural + *ă*, *ĕ*, or *ŏ*, the conjunction is respectively וַ *wa*-, וֶ *we*-, or וָ *wo*-:

אֲרָצוֹת	*'ărāṣôṯ*	lands	וַאֲרָצוֹת	*wa'ărāṣôṯ*	and lands
אֱדֹם	*'ĕḏōm*	Edom	וֶאֱדֹם	*we'ĕḏōm*	and Edom
אֳנִי	*'ŏnî*	a fleet	וָאֳנִי	*wo'ŏnî*	and a fleet

47. Vocabulary 9.

NOUNS:	יוֹם	*yôm* (pl. irreg. יָמִים *yāmîm*) day; note הַיּוֹם *hayyôm*, today.	
	לַ֫יְלָה	*láylāh* (pl. rare) night [Note position of stress; masculine.]	
	מָקוֹם	*māqôm* (pl. -*ôṯ*) place, locale	
	שָׁמַ֫יִם	*šāmáyim* (pl.) heaven(s), sky	
VERBS:	יָלַד	*yālaḏ*	to bear, give birth to
	קָבַץ	*qāḇaṣ*	to gather

	זָכַר	*zāḵar*	to remember
ADJECTIVE:	אֶחָד	*'eḥāḏ*	one (fem. irreg. אַחַת *'aḥaṯ*); אֶחָד מִן *'eḥāḏ min* one of
PREPOSITIONS:	בֵּין	*bên*	between; "between A and B" may be expressed as *bên A ûḇên B* or *bên A wəB.*
	בְּתוֹךְ	*bəṯôḵ*	in the midst of
	מִתּוֹךְ	*mittôḵ*	from the midst of
ADVERBS:	גַּם	*gam*	also, even, too [Placed directly before the word it modifies, as in *gam-hammélek*, the king too, even the king.]
	לֹא	*lō'*	no, not; general negative placed before the word it negates

Exercises:

(a) Give orally the full paradigm of the perfect for each of the following verbs: זָכַר יָשַׁב יָרַד

(b) Write out the following phrases in Hebrew with special attention to the form of the conjunction "and":

(1) gold and silver
(2) wisdom and understanding
(3) advice and work
(4) small cattle and large cattle
(5) servants and camels; camels and servants
(6) a great and rich man
(7) a poor and unimportant woman
(8) one man and one woman

(c) Translate:

1. yāšaḇ hā'îš bên-hannāhār ûḇên-haśśāḏeh. — יָשַׁב הָאִישׁ בֵּין־הַנָּהָר וּבֵין־הַשָּׂדֶה.
2. qāḇaṣ hannāḇî' 'eṯ-hā'ām 'éṣel hahêḵāl haggāḏôl. — קָבַץ הַנָּבִיא אֶת־הָעָם אֵצֶל הַהֵיכָל הַגָּדוֹל.
3. bayyôm hahû' nāpəlāh 'ēš min-haššāmáyim. — בַּיּוֹם הַהוּא נָפְלָה אֵשׁ מִן־הַשָּׁמָיִם.
4. hāləḵû hā'ām 'el-haššōpēṭ hayyāšār wəlō' hāləḵû 'el-hannāḇî' hārāšā'. — הָלְכוּ הָעָם אֶל־הַשֹּׁפֵט הַיָּשָׁר וְלֹא הָלְכוּ אֶל־הַנָּבִיא הָרָשָׁע.
5. mî hannəḇî'îm hahōləḵîm 'el-hā'îr? — מִי הַנְּבִיאִים הַהֹלְכִים אֶל־הָעִיר.
6. balláylāh hahû' yārədû hā'ănāšîm mēhehārîm. — בַּלַּיְלָה הַהוּא יָרְדוּ הָאֲנָשִׁים מֵהֶהָרִים.

7. yāšáḇnû bəṯôḵ hā'îr wəlō' hāláḵnû min-hammāqôm hahû'.	יָשַׁ֫בְנוּ בְּתוֹךְ הָעִיר וְלֹא הָלַ֫כְנוּ מִן־הַמָּקוֹם הַהוּא׃ 7
8. yālədāh hā'iššāh yəlāḏîm rabbîm wəyāp̄îm.	יָלְדָה הָאִשָּׁה יְלָדִים רַבִּים וְיָפִים׃ 8
9. ləmî qāḇáṣtā 'eṯ-hakkésep̄ wə'eṯ-hazzāhāḇ?	לְמִי קָבַ֫צְתָּ אֶת־הַכֶּ֫סֶף וְאֶת־הַזָּהָב׃ 9
10. lō' nāp̄al 'eḥāḏ mēhannə'ārîm.	לֹא נָפַל אֶחָד מֵהַנְּעָרִים׃ 10

(d) Write in Hebrew:

1. He gave wisdom and understanding to the prophets.
2. They sent the gold and the silver to the men in the temple.
3. This work is very hard because we have no understanding.
4. Today the men are building a house in the city.
5. Where did they write those words?
6. I remember that he gave me the book.
7. There is evil in this place.
8. One of the women is leaving the city.

LESSON 10

48. The Perfect of Verbs with Guttural Root Consonants.

The presence of guttural consonants in the root of a verb occasions slight modifications in the inflection of the perfect. All of these are simple and predictable variations, with the exception of roots whose third consonant is א (hereafter designated simply as verbs III-*Aleph*),* whose inflection will be considered separately from those given here.

3 m. s.	עָמַד	*ʿāmaḏ*	בָּחַר	*bāḥar*	שָׁמַע	*šāmaʿ*
3 f. s.	עָמְדָה	*ʿāməḏāh*	בָּחֲרָה	*bāḥărāh*	שָׁמְעָה	*šāməʿāh*
2 m. s.	עָמַ֫דְתָּ	*ʿāmáḏtā*	בָּחַ֫רְתָּ	*bāḥártā*	שָׁמַ֫עְתָּ	*šāmáʿtā*
2 f. s.	עָמַ֫דְתְּ	*ʿāmaḏt*	בָּחַ֫רְתְּ	*bāḥart*	שָׁמַ֫עַתְּ	(*šāmaʿt*)
1 s.	עָמַ֫דְתִּי	*ʿāmáḏtî*	בָּחַ֫רְתִּי	*bāḥártî*	שָׁמַ֫עְתִּי	*šāmáʿtî*
3 pl.	עָמְדוּ	*ʿāməḏû*	בָּחֲרוּ	*bāḥărû*	שָׁמְעוּ	*šāməʿû*
2 m. pl.	עֲמַדְתֶּם	*ʿămaḏtem*	בְּחַרְתֶּם	*bəḥartem*	שְׁמַעְתֶּם	*šəmaʿtem*
2 f. pl.	עֲמַדְתֶּן	*ʿămaḏten*	בְּחַרְתֶּן	*bəḥarten*	שְׁמַעְתֶּן	*šəmaʿten*
1 pl.	עָמַ֫דְנוּ	*ʿāmáḏnû*	בָּחַ֫רְנוּ	*bāḥárnû*	שָׁמַ֫עְנוּ	*šāmáʿnû*

In verbs I-gutt. (i.e. whose first root consonant is a guttural) the only variation from the standard paradigm is the replacement of *ă* for *ə* in the 2nd pers. pl. forms. This replacement should by now be familiar to the reader

* Most Hebrew grammars employ the letters פ, ע, and ל to designate the first, second, and third root consonants respectively. Thus, our III-*Aleph* corresponds to the more usual designation *Lamedh-Aleph*.

from previous examples. The same is true for verbs II-gutt., where we find *ă* for *ə* in the forms *bāḥărāh* and *bāḥărû*.

The only form in the paradigm of *šāma‘* (III-gutt.) that requires comment is שָׁמַ֫עַתְּ, which, as it stands, is anomalous. It is likely that such spellings were meant by the punctators to show an option: we should read either שָׁמַ֫עַת *šāmá‘at̲*, ignoring the daghesh, or שָׁמַ֫עְתְּ *šāma‘t*, ignoring the second *a*.

49. The Perfect of נָתַן nāt̲an.

This verb has a peculiarity in its inflection: the second *n* of the stem is always assimilated to the initial consonant of the subject suffixes. Note carefully the following forms; the daghesh is *forte*, indicating doubling.

נָתַן	*nāt̲an*	he gave	נָתְנוּ	*nāt̲ənû*	they gave
נָתְנָה	*nāt̲ənāh*	she gave			
נָתַ֫תָּה	*nāt̲áttā*	you (m. s.) gave	נְתַתֶּם	*nət̲attem*	you (m. pl.) gave
נָתַתְּ	*nāt̲att*	you (f. s.) gave	נְתַתֶּן	*nət̲atten*	you (f. pl.) gave
נָתַ֫תִּי	*nāt̲áttî*	I gave	נָתַ֫נּוּ	*nāt̲ánnû*	we gave

50. Noun Plurals (continued).

(a) Dissyllabic nouns with the sequence *-áyi-* show a regular contraction in the plural stem:

זַ֫יִת	*záyit̲*	olive tree	pl.	זֵיתִים	*zêt̲îm*
אַ֫יִל	*’áyil*	ram		אֵילִים	*’êlîm*

The noun בַּ֫יִת *báyit̲* (house) is irregular: בָּתִּים *bāttîm*. Note the *ā* in a closed unaccented syllable; this is virtually unique with this word.

(b) There are many nouns of two syllables whose singular and plural stems are identical. These include nouns both of whose syllables are not susceptible to the changes presented in the preceding sections dealing with the noun. Examples are

אֶבְיוֹן	*’eb̲yôn*	poor	pl.	אֶבְיוֹנִים	*’eb̲yônîm*
גִּבּוֹר	*gibbôr*	warrior		גִּבּוֹרִים	*gibbôrîm*
צַדִּיק	*ṣaddîq*	righteous man		צַדִּיקִים	*ṣaddîqîm*
עַמּוּד	*‘ammûd̲*	column		עַמּוּדִים	*‘ammûd̲îm*

Note that both syllables of such nouns are either closed or contain an unchangeable long vowel.

(c) A small group of nouns ends in *-eh* in the singular. Although this is not a suffix, but an integral part of the root word, it does not occur on the plural stem:

שָׂדֶה *śāḏeh* field pl. שָׂדוֹת *śāḏôṯ*
מַחֲנֶה *maḥăneh* camp מַחֲנוֹת *maḥănôṯ*

Nouns originally participles of verbs III-*Hē* (i.e. whose third root consonant is given as ה) also belong to this class: רֹעֶה *rō'eh*, pl. רֹעִים *rō'îm*, shepherd.

51. Vocabulary 10.

NOUNS: גִּבּוֹר *gibbôr* (pl. *-îm*) warrior, hero, valiant man
גִּבְעָה *giḇ'āh* hill
מַ֫יִם *máyim* water [Like שָׁמַ֫יִם, a plural without a singular]
מַחֲנֶה *maḥăneh* (pl. *-ôṯ*) camp
מִלְחָמָה *milḥāmāh* battle, war
פְּרִי *pərî* fruit

VERBS: בָּחַר *bāḥar* to choose [May take object with אֶת־ *'eṯ-*, but more commonly with בְּ *bə*: בָּחַר בִּי *bāḥar bî* he chose me.]
הָרַג *hārag̱* to kill, slay
יָדַע *yāḏa'* to know
לָקַח *lāqaḥ* to take
עָמַד *'āmaḏ* to stand

PREPOSITION: לִפְנֵי *lip̄nê* before, in front of, in the presence of

Exercises:

(a) Inflect in the perfect: הָלַךְ אָכַל צָעַק שָׁלַח נָטַע

(b) Give the Hebrew for the following orally:

1. They planted many trees.
2. She stood near the houses.
3. You chose me.
4. They did not choose you.
5. I took the money.
6. They killed the young man.
7. You (f. s.) took the water.
8. You (m. pl.) have eaten the bread.
9. We sent the messengers to the judge.

(c) Translate:

1. nāṭə'û hā'ănāšîm kérem gāḏôl 'al-haggiḇ'āh. — 1 נָֽטְעוּ הָאֲנָשִׁים כֶּ֫רֶם גָּדוֹל עַל־הַגִּבְעָה.
2. lō' yāḏá'tî kî hû' hārag̱ 'eṯ-hannāḇî'. — 2 לֹא יָדַ֫עְתִּי כִּי הוּא הָרַג אֶת־הַנָּבִיא.
3. 'āməḏû hā'ăḇāḏîm hārəšā'îm lip̄nê hammélek̲. — 3 עָֽמְדוּ הָעֲבָדִים הָרְשָׁעִים לִפְנֵי הַמֶּ֫לֶךְ.

4.	bāḥártî bəḵā ləméleḵ ‘al-hā‘ām haggāḏôl hazzeh.	בָּחַ֫רְתִּי בְּךָ לְמֶ֫לֶךְ עַל־הָעָם הַגָּדוֹל הַזֶּה.	4
5.	nāp̄əlû gibbôrîm rabbîm bammilhāmāh hahî’.	נָֽפְלוּ גִּבּוֹרִים רַבִּים בַּמִּלְחָמָה הַהִיא.	5
6.	yēš maḥăneh ḇên-hannāhār ûḇên-hehārîm.	יֵשׁ מַחֲנֶה בֵּין־הַנָּהָר וּבֵין־הֶהָרִים.	6
7.	mî šālaḥ ’ōṯəḵā ’el-hammāqôm hazzeh?	מִי שָׁלַח אֹתְךָ אֶל־הַמָּקוֹם הַזֶּה.	7
8.	mî hārag̱ ’eṯ-hā’ănāšîm hā’ḗlleh?	מִי הָרַג אֶת־הָאֲנָשִׁים הָאֵ֫לֶּה.	8
9.	lāqəḥāh hā’iššāh mēhappərî wənāṯənāh ’ōṯô lā’îš.	לָֽקְחָה הָאִשָּׁה מֵהַפְּרִי וְנָֽתְנָה אֹתוֹ לָאִישׁ.	9
10.	bāḥărû hā‘ām ’eṯ-Dāwīḏ lāhem ləméleḵ.	בָּֽחֲרוּ הָעָם אֶת־דָּוִד לָהֶם לְמֶ֫לֶךְ.	10

(d) Write in Hebrew:

1. He planted a tree in the midst of this garden.
2. They cried out in a loud voice because of this hard work.
3. They chose for them(selves) a land and dwelt there.
4. The men took the gold and silver from the temple. They also slew the prophets who (were) there.
5. She knew that those words (were) very bad.
6. One of the young men fell in that battle.
7. They gave me bread and water, but I did not give them the money.

LESSON 11

52. The Perfect of Verbs III-Aleph: מָצָא māsā'.

מָצָא	*māṣā(')*	he found	מָֽצְאוּ	*māṣə'û*	they found
מָֽצְאָה	*māṣə'āh*	she found			
מָצָ֫אתָ	*māṣā́(')ṯā*	you (m. s.) found	מְצָאתֶם	*məṣā(')ṯem*	you (m. pl.) found
מָצָ֫את	*māṣā́(')ṯ*	you (f. s.) found	מְצָאתֶן	*məṣā(')ṯen*	you (f. pl.) found
מָצָ֫אתִי	*māṣā́(')ṯî*	I found	מָצָ֫אנוּ	*māṣā́(')nû*	we found

In verbs III-*Aleph* the second syllable of the stem in the perfect has *ā* instead of *a* in those forms to which a suffix beginning with a consonant is added. In other words, whenever א originally closed a syllable, it was lost and the lengthening of the vowel took place as a consequence. The ʾ is preserved when it begins the syllable, as in *māṣə'āh* and *māṣə'û*. Remember, however, that the א is always found in the spelling, even when not pronounced. Note too that there is no *daghesh lene* in the ת of the suffixes, since they are now preceded in pronunciation by a vowel instead of a consonant.

53. Noun Plurals (continued).

The majority of feminine nouns in *-āh* show no change in the stem before the plural ending:

שָׁנָה	*šānāh*	year	pl.	שָׁנִים	*šānîm*
תּוֹרָה	*tôrāh*	law		תּוֹרוֹת	*tôrôṯ*
אַמָּה	*'ammāh*	cubit		אַמּוֹת	*'ammôṯ*
בְּרָכָה	*bərāḵāh*	blessing		בְּרָכוֹת	*bərāḵôṯ*

בְּהֵמָה	*bəhēmāh*	beast	בְּהֵמוֹת	*bəhēmôṯ*
תְּבוּאָה	*təḇû'āh*	product	תְּבוּאוֹת	*təḇû'ôṯ*
תְּפִלָּה	*təp̄illāh*	prayer	תְּפִלּוֹת	*təp̄illôṯ*
מִשְׁפָּחָה	*mišpāḥāh*	family	מִשְׁפָּחוֹת	*mišpāḥôṯ*

But nouns of the general pattern *CvCCāh*,* like מַלְכָּה *malkāh* (queen), where the two contiguous consonants are different (thus not *'ammāh* above), have a different plural stem:

מַלְכָּה	*malkāh*	queen	pl.	מְלָכוֹת	*məlāḵôṯ*	[Note the ā.]
גִּבְעָה	*giḇ'āh*	hill		גְּבָעוֹת	*gəḇā'ôṯ*	
חֶרְפָּה	*ḥerpāh*	reproach		חֲרָפוֹת	*ḥărāp̄ôṯ*	

But note מִצְוָה *miṣwāh*, pl. מִצְוֹת *miṣwōṯ*, where the מ is a prefix and not part of the root.

54. Interrogative הֲ hă-.

Any sentence may be converted into a question by prefixing a form of the particle הֲ *hă-* to the first word:

הֲשָׁלַח הָאִישׁ	*hăšālaḥ hā'îš* ...	Did the man send ...?
הֲטוֹבָה הָאָרֶץ	*hăṭôḇāh hā'āreṣ*	Is the land good?

Before gutturals the form is normally הַ *ha-*:

הַעֹמֵד הָאִישׁ	*ha'ōmēḏ hā'îš*	Is the man standing?

But if the guttural is followed by *ā* or *o*, the form used is הֶ *he-*:

הֶאָכַלְתָּ	*he'āḵáltā*	Have you eaten?

Before non-guttural consonants followed by *ə* the form is also הַ *ha-*:

הַכְתַבְתֶּם	*haḵ(ə)ṯaḇtem*	Did you write?

Rarely one encounters the same doubling of the following consonant that we met in the definite article:

הַכְּתַבְתֶּם	*hakkəṯaḇtem*	Did you write?

55. More on אֲשֶׁר 'ăšer.

We saw above (§32) that אֲשֶׁר *'ăšer* indicates that a following phrase modifies as a unit the preceding word. This is true also for clauses, as the following examples show:

* C = consonant; v = a, i, e, o.

הַכֹּהֵן אֲשֶׁר כָּתַב אֶת־הַדָּבָר *hakkōhēn 'ăšer kāṯaḇ 'eṯ-haddāḇār*
the priest *who* wrote the word

הַמַּלְאָךְ אֲשֶׁר שָׁלַח הַמֶּלֶךְ *hammal'āḵ 'ăšer šālaḥ hamméleḵ*
the messenger *whom* the king sent

56. Vocabulary 11.

NOUNS: שֶׁמֶשׁ *šémeš* sun
יָרֵחַ *yārēaḥ* moon
כּוֹכָב *kôḵāḇ* (pl. *-îm*) star
עָנָן *'ānān* cloud
בְּרָכָה *bərāḵāh* (pl. *-ôṯ*) blessing
שָׁנָה *šānāh* (pl. *-îm*) year
תּוֹרָה *tôrāh* (pl. *-ôṯ*) law, The Law

VERBS: מָצָא *māṣā'* to find
בָּרָא *bārā'* to create
קָרָא *qārā'* to call, name; to summon; to declare, read aloud [+ *'el*: to call unto (someone); + *lə*: to summon (someone)]
אָמַר *'āmar* to say, speak

CONJUNCTION: לֵאמֹר *lē(')mōr* introduces a direct quotation after verbs of saying; it has no translation value in English)

Exercises:

(a) Form the plurals of the following nouns, as described in §53:

צָרָה	*ṣārāh* (*-ôṯ*) distress	עֵצָה	*'ēṣāh* (*-ôṯ*) counsel
עוֹלָה	*'ôlāh* (*-ôṯ*) burnt-offering	חֻקָּה	*ḥuqqāh* (*-ôṯ*) statute
מִנְחָה	*minḥāh* (*-ôṯ*) gift, offering	שִׂמְלָה	*śimlāh* (*-ôṯ*) cloak
עֶגְלָה	*'eglāh* (*-ôṯ*) heifer	עֲרָבָה	*'ărāḇāh* (*-ôṯ*) desert, steppe
קְלָלָה	*qəlālāh* (*-ôṯ*) curse	בְּתוּלָה	*bəṯûlāh* (*-ôṯ*) virgin
מְסִלָּה	*məsillāh* (*-ôṯ*) highway	מְגִלָּה	*məḡillāh* (*-ôṯ*) scroll
מַמְלָכָה	*mamlāḵāh* (*-ôṯ*) kingdom		

(b) Give the Hebrew for the following orally. Then convert each into a question by prefixing the appropriate form of הֲ *hă-*:

1. He stood before the king.
2. They slew the warriors in the battle.
3. You (m. pl.) knew that the city (was) on a hill.
4. I took the fruit.
5. You chose us.
6. We have no water.
7. The rich man has large cattle and camels.

8. You went down to the river.
9. You (m. sing.) ate the bread.

(c) Translate:

1 אֵ֫לֶּה הַדְּבָרִים אֲשֶׁר כָּתַב הַנָּבִיא בַּסֵּ֫פֶר הַהוּא.
2 הָֽלְכוּ אֶל־הָעִיר וְלֹא מָֽצְאוּ אֶת־הַיֶּ֫לֶד הַקָּטֹן.
3 הַשֶּׁ֫מֶשׁ בַּשָּׁמַ֫יִם וְגַם־הַיָּרֵחַ שָׁם, הַשֶּׁ֫מֶשׁ בַּיּוֹם וְהַיָּרֵחַ בַּלַּ֫יְלָה.
4 גַּם־בַּלַּ֫יְלָה יֵשׁ כּוֹכָבִים רַבִּים וְיָפִים.
5 בַּשָּׁנָה הַהִיא נָֽפְלוּ גִּבּוֹרִים רַבִּים.
6 שָׁלַח עָנָן גָּדוֹל אֲשֶׁר עָמַד לִפְנֵי הָעָם.
7 אָמַר לוֹ הַמֶּ֫לֶךְ לֵאמֹר הֲשָׁלַ֫חְתָּ אֶת־הָאִישׁ אֶל־הָהָר.
8 מִי בָרָא אֶת־הָאָ֫רֶץ וּמִי בָרָא אֶת־הַשָּׁמַ֫יִם.
9 טוֹבָה הַתּוֹרָה וְטוֹבִים הַדְּבָרִים אֲשֶׁר בָּהּ.
10 יָצָא קוֹל מִתּוֹךְ הֶעָנָן.
11 הַיְצָאתֶם מֵהָעִיר הָרָעָה.
12 קָרָא הַנָּבִיא אֶל־הָעָם בְּקוֹל גָּדוֹל לֵאמֹר רָעִים מְאֹד הַדְּבָרִים אֲשֶׁר אֲמַרְתֶּם.

(d) Write in Hebrew:

1. He created the sun, the moon, and the stars.
2. Did you find the book in the house?
3. Did he say to them that (*kî*) the law is just?
4. This blessing is for us and for those who dwell in the midst of this people.
5. The cloud stood over the earth.
6. Where did he find the small cattle?
7. The king summoned the prophet, but the prophet did not go to the palace.
8. Have you (m. pl.) remembered this law and the words which I have written in it for you?

LESSON 12

57. The Perfect of Verbs III-Hē: בָּנָה bānāh.

בָּנָה	*bānāh*	he built	בָּנוּ	*bānû*	they built
בָּנְתָה	*bānəṯāh*	she built			
בָּנִיתָ	*bānîṯā*	you (m. s.) built	בְּנִיתֶם	*bənîṯem*	you (m. pl.) built
בָּנִית	*bānîṯ*	you (f. s.) built	בְּנִיתֶן	*bənîṯen*	you (f. pl.) built
בָּנִיתִי	*bānîṯî*	I built	בָּנִינוּ	*bānînû*	we built

Note that the stem vowel in the first syllable behaves quite normally. The stem itself is variable (*bānāh*, *bānəṯ-*, *bānî-*, *bənî-*, *bān-*), and we must again point out that the ה of the 3rd masc. sing. is not a real root consonant but a *mater lectionis* for the final vowel. It is convenient, however, to follow traditional grammar and to speak of this class of verbs as III-*Hē*.

When a verb III-*Hē* is also I-gutt., the regular substitution of *ă* for *ə* is found in the 2nd pers. pl. forms:

עֲלִיתֶם	*'ălîṯem*	you (m. pl.) went up
עֲלִיתֶן	*'ălîṯen*	you (f. pl.) went up

The verb הָיָה *hāyāh* (to be) is inflected regularly as a member of this class; only the 2nd pers. pl. shows a slight peculiarity, with *ĕ* for *ă*:

הֱיִיתֶם	*hĕyîṯem*	you (m. pl.) were

58. Directive ה ָ -āh.

The suffix *-āh* added to a noun indicates motion toward. It occurs on both proper nouns and common nouns, the latter with or without the article.

This ending is never stressed and may thus be distinguished from the feminine ending *-āh*. Because directive *-āh* cannot be added to all nouns, each form is best learned individually, without a lengthy analysis of the minor changes that take place in the stem. The following list contains the most important of the words using this suffix:

אֶרֶץ	*'éreṣ*	land, earth	אַרְצָה	*'árṣāh*	to the earth, to the land, onto the ground
בַּיִת	*báyiṯ*	house	הַבַּיְתָה / בַּיְתָה	*habbáyṯāh* / *báyṯāh*	to the house, home
הַר	*har*	mountain	הָהָרָה / הֶרָה	*hāhā́rāh* / *hérāh*	to the mountain, mountainward
מִדְבָּר	*miḏbār*	wilderness	מִדְבָּרָה	*miḏbā́rāh*	toward the wilderness
עִיר	*'îr*	city	הָעִירָה	*hā'îrāh*	toward the city
שָׁמַיִם	*šāmáyim*	heaven	הַשָּׁמַיְמָה	*haššāmáymāh*	heavenward
מִצְרַיִם	*miṣráyim*	Egypt	מִצְרַיְמָה	*miṣráymāh*	toward Egypt
יְרוּשָׁלַםִ	*yərûšālá(y)im*	Jerusalem	יְרוּשָׁלַםְָה	*yərûšālá(y)māh*	toward Jerusalem
נֶגֶב	*néḡeḇ*	Negev (the southern part of Palestine; the south in general)	נֶגְבָּה	*néḡbāh*	toward the Negev, southward
שְׁאֹל	*šə'ōl*	Sheol (residence of the dead)	שְׁאֹלָה	*šə'ṓlāh*	to Sheol

Note especially its use on the directional adverbs:

אָנָה *'ā́nāh* whither? to what place (contrast אַיֵּה)
שָׁמָּה *šā́mmāh* thither, to that place (contrast שָׁם)
הֵנָּה *hénnāh* hither, to this place (contrast פֹּה)

Similarly on the terms for the directions:

צָפוֹן	*ṣāpôn*	north	צָפוֹנָה	*ṣāpônāh*	northward
קֶדֶם	*qéḏem*	east	קֵדְמָה	*qéḏmāh*	eastward
תֵּימָן	*têmān*	south	תֵּימָנָה	*têmā́nāh*	southward
יָם	*yām*	sea, west	יָמָּה	*yā́mmāh*	seaward, westward

59. Vocabulary 12.

Special Note: The two most frequent designations of God in the OT are אֱלֹהִים *'ĕlōhîm* and יהוה *Yhwh*.

(1) אֱלֹהִים is a plural word, generally construed as a singular. It may mean "gods" when used as a plural and "God" when used as a singular or a plural, with or without the article.

(2) יהוה is the name of God. For pious or superstitious reasons יהוה was read as אֲדֹנָי *'ăḏōnāy* (lit. my lords, my Lord). Just when this practice began is not certain, but it may predate the Christian Era. The Masoretes indicated this substitution by applying the vowel points of *'ăḏōnāy*, slightly modified, to יהוה, hence יְהוָה. The literal interpretation of this latter form as *Yəhōwāh* = *Jehovah* dates from modern times.

Both of these words behave erratically after the prefixed prepositions: the initial א is lost in pronunciation:

בֵּאלֹהִים	bē(')lōhîm	בַּיהוה	ba(')ḏōnāy
לֵאלֹהִים	lē(')lōhîm	לַיהוה	la(')ḏōnāy
כֵּאלֹהִים	kē(')lōhîm	כַּיהוה	ka(')ḏōnāy

Those who wish to read יהוה as *Yahweh*, the most likely original pronunciation, must remember to repoint these prepositions as *bəYahweh*, *ləYahweh*, etc.

When the name יהוה occurs in conjunction with אֲדֹנָי, the former is read as אֱלֹהִים and pointed יֱהוִה. This is to avoid the repetition in reading *'ăḏōnāy 'ăḏōnāy*.

NOUNS: בְּרִית *bərîṯ* covenant, treaty (f.)
חֵן *ḥēn* grace, favor
יְשׁוּעָה *yəšû'āh* (pl. *-ôṯ*) salvation, deliverance, victory
שִׂמְחָה *śimḥāh* (pl. *-ôṯ*) joy

VERBS: עָשָׂה *'āśāh* to do, make, act, perform, bring about
רָאָה *rā'āh* to see
כָּרַת *kāraṯ* to cut; כָּרַת בְּרִית to make a treaty
נָסַע *nāsa'* to set out, travel, journey

PREPOSITIONS: עִם *'im* with, together with
כְּ *kə* like, as, according to
אֵת *'ēṯ*, אֶת־ *'eṯ-* with, together with

Note the idiom מָצָא חֵן בְּעֵינֵי as in
מָצָא דָוִד חֵן בְּעֵינֵי הַמֶּלֶךְ David found favor with the king.
(or, The king became fond of David.)

Exercises:

(a) Give the Hebrew for the following orally:

1. On that day he made a treaty with the king.
2. The prophet grew fond of the boy.
3. A great sound ascended heavenward.
4. They went up toward-the-city with the people.
5. They built a house in that place.
6. Who did this evil thing?
7. Did you act according to the words which are there?

8. The woman fell to-the-ground.
9. They traveled from the midst of the city toward-the-mountain.
10. Those men also did not remember.

(b) Translate:

1 עָשָׂה הַגִּבּוֹר יְשׁוּעָה גְדוֹלָה לָעָם.
2 אֵין יְשׁוּעָה בֵּאלֹהִים לָאִישׁ הָרַע.
3 הֶעָשִׂיתָ אֶת־הַדָּבָר הַזֶּה.
4 הֲזְכַרְתֶּם אֶת־הַבְּרִית אֲשֶׁר כָּרַת יהוה אֶת־הָעָם.
5 יֵשׁ שִׂמְחָה גְדוֹלָה בִּירוּשָׁלַםִ כִּי יהוה שָׁם.
6 גְּדוֹלָה הָעִיר אֲשֶׁר בָּנִינוּ בָּאָרֶץ הַזֹּאת.
7 רָאִיתִי אֵשׁ יֹרֶדֶת מֵהַשָּׁמַיִם וְנֹפֶלֶת אַרְצָה.
8 נָסַע הַזָּקֵן הָעִירָה.
9 עָשָׂה אֱלֹהִים אֶת־הַשָּׁמַיִם וְאֶת־הָאָרֶץ.
10 עָלְתָה הָאִשָּׁה יְרוּשָׁלַמָה כִּי שָׁם הַשֹּׁפֵט.
11 לֹא זָכַרְתָּ אֶת־הַבְּרִית אֲשֶׁר כָּרַתְנוּ עִם־הָעָם.

(c) Write in Hebrew:

1. Who said to you that the camp is near the river?
2. The man is a just judge.
3. Did you see the moon and the stars?
4. God did not find a righteous man in the evil city.
5. These are the words which we saw in the law.
6. Great and good is the earth which the Lord created.
7. The people came forth from that land in that year.
8. The king was pleased with the woman (lit. the woman found favor etc.).

LESSON 13

60. Sentences with a Nominal Predicate.

One of the simplest of all sentence types in Hebrew is that in which two nouns (or noun phrases) are juxtaposed to indicate a predication:

דָּוִד מֶ֫לֶךְ טוֹב *Dāwīḏ méleḵ ṭôḇ* (1)
David is a good king.

The demonstrative pronouns הוּא *hû'*, הִיא *hî'*, and their plurals are often used in sentences of this type in the following way:

דָּוִד הוּא מֶ֫לֶךְ טוֹב *Dāwīḏ hû' méleḵ ṭôḇ* (2)
דָּוִד מֶ֫לֶךְ טוֹב הוּא *Dāwīḏ méleḵ ṭôḇ hû'* (3)

Although it is probable that the use of the demonstrative pronoun places a greater emphasis on one or another of the sentence elements, it is impossible for us to determine this nuance with any accuracy, since there are no informants available who speak Biblical Hebrew. It is likely that (2) answers the question "Who is a good king?" and that (3) answers "What is David?", while the first type (1) is a neutral statement of fact without a question in mind.

61. The Verb הָיָה hāyāh (to be).

In the preceding lessons we have studied four types of non-verbal sentences:

(1) with adjectival predicate: טוֹב הָאִישׁ *ṭôḇ hā'îš*

(2) with adverbial predicate: הָאִישׁ בַּבַּ֫יִת *hā'îš babbáyiṯ*
(3) with existential predicate: יֵשׁ אִישׁ *yēš 'îš*
(4) with nominal predicate: דָּוִד מֶ֫לֶךְ טוֹב *Dāwīḏ méleḵ ṭôḇ*

None of these has any specific tense value, which must rather depend on the context in which the sentence occurs. All of these sentences, however, may be converted into verbal sentences by using the verb הָיָה *hāyāh*, which in the perfect has the normal tense values of that form:

(1) הָיָה הָאִישׁ טוֹב	*hāyāh hā'îš ṭôḇ*	The man was good.
(2) הָיָה הָאִישׁ בַּבַּ֫יִת	*hāyāh hā'îš babbáyiṯ*	The man was in the house.
(3) הָיָה כֶּ֫סֶף	*hāyāh ḵésep̄*	There was silver.
(4) דָּוִד הָיָה מֶ֫לֶךְ טוֹב	*Dāwīḏ hāyāh méleḵ ṭôḇ*	David was a good king.

Each is negated with לֹא *lō'*. Note that יֵשׁ is replaced by הָיָה in (3) and that a negative existential sentence like אֵין כֶּ֫סֶף becomes לֹא הָיָה כֶּ֫סֶף.

In sentences of the type

הָיָה דָוִד לְמֶ֫לֶךְ טוֹב *hāyāh Dāwīḏ ləméleḵ ṭôḇ*

the preposition adds the nuance of "becoming" to the verb of being. Although such a sentence equates two nominal elements, it is nevertheless of type (2).

Note the following use of לְ:

הָיְתָה שָׂרָה לְאַבְרָהָם לְאִשָּׁה *hāyəṯāh Śārāh lə'Aḇrāhām lə'iššāh*

which may be translated "Sarah became Abraham's wife" or "Sarah became a wife of Abraham's" or "Sarah was Abraham's wife." If we replace לְ with כְּ, the idea is that of "acting in the place or capacity of, but not actually being":

הָיָה הָאִישׁ לַנַּ֫עַר כְּאָב *hāyāh hā'îš lanná'ar kə'āḇ*

The man was like a father to the youth, or
The man became the youth's father, as it were.

Of course הָיָה לְ, as the past tense of יֵשׁ לְ, may be used to translate possession in past time:

הָיָה צֹאן לְאַבְרָהָם *hāyāh ṣō(')n lə'Aḇrāhām* Abraham possessed cattle.

Sentences with a participial predicate, such as הָאִישׁ כֹּתֵב, the man is (was) writing, are seldom converted with הָיָה. Why this is so will become clearer when we have taken up the syntax of Hebrew narrative below.

62. Noun Plurals (concluded).

Feminine nouns ending in *-eṯ*, *-aṯ*, *-āṯ*, *-îṯ*, *-ôṯ*, or *-ûṯ* show much variety in the plural. The words given below are a sufficient sampling of this group, whose forms must be learned singly as they occur. None of these words represents a frequent type.

בַּת	*bat̲*	daughter	pl.	בָּנוֹת	*bānôt̲*
עֵת	*'ēt̲*	time		עִתִּים	*'ittîm*
דֶּ֫לֶת	*délet̲*	door		דְּלָתוֹת	*dəlāt̲ôt̲*
מִשְׁמֶ֫רֶת	*mišméret̲*	office		מִשְׁמָרוֹת	*mišmārôt̲*
חַטָּאת	*ḥaṭṭāt̲*	sin		חַטָּאוֹת	*ḥaṭṭā'ôt̲*
חֲנִית	*ḥănît̲*	spear		חֲנִיתִים	*ḥănît̲îm*
מַלְכוּת	*malk̲ût̲*	kingdom		מַלְכֻיּוֹת	*malk̲ûyôt̲*

63. Vocabulary 13.

NOUNS: חַטָּאת *ḥaṭṭā(')t̲* (pl. חַטָּאוֹת) sin (f.)
חֲלוֹם *ḥălôm* (pl. *-ôt̲*) dream
בַּת *bat̲* (pl. בָּנוֹת) daughter
אֵימָה *'êmāh* fear, terror, dread
שִׁפְחָה *šip̄ḥāh* (pl. *-ôt̲*) maidservant, female slave
אָמָה *'āmāh* (pl. irreg. *'ămāhôt̲* אֲמָהוֹת) maidservant, female slave

VERBS: הָיָה *hāyāh* to be, become (+ לְ)
חָטָא *ḥāṭā'* to sin (against: לְ)
חָלַם *ḥālam* to dream
לָכַד *lāk̲ad̲* to capture, take captive

Exercises:

(a) Give the Hebrew for the following sentences orally:
1. Samuel is a just judge.
2. Jerusalem is a great city.
3. This servant is a righteous man.
4. The sun and moon are in the heavens.
5. The blessing which he spoke is good.
6. The cloud is very large.
7. There are many stars in the sky.
8. He has many daughters.
9. The warriors are in the camp.

(b) Transform the sentences of (a) into past tense with the appropriate form of the verb הָיָה.

(c) Translate:

1 לָֽכְדוּ אֶת־הֶֽעָרִים אֲשֶׁר בָּאָ֫רֶץ הַהִיא וְגַם־אֶת־הָעָם אֲשֶׁר בָּהֶן.
2 בַּלַּ֫יְלָה חָלַ֫מְתִּי חֲלוֹם וְזֶה הַחֲלוֹם אֲשֶׁר חָלַ֫מְתִּי.
3 שָֽׁלְחָה הָאִשָּׁה אֶת־הַשִּׁפְחָה אֶל־הַנָּבִיא.
4 נָֽפְלָה אֵימָה גְדוֹלָה עַל־הָעָם כִּי חָֽטְאוּ לַיהוה.

5 יֵשׁ לִי בָּנוֹת רַבּוֹת וְיָפוֹת.
6 לֹא הָיִינוּ רָעִים בְּעֵינֵי הַנָּבִיא.
7 אֵימָה נֹפֶלֶת עַל־הָאָרֶץ כִּי לָכַדְנוּ אֶת־הֶעָרִים.
8 רַבּוֹת הַחַטָּאוֹת אֲשֶׁר חָטָאתָ לֵאלֹהִים.
9 כָּתַב בַּסֵּפֶר אֶת־הַדְּבָרִים אֲשֶׁר רָאָה בַּחֲלוֹם אֲשֶׁר חָלַם.

(d) Write in Hebrew:

1. We made no treaty with these people.
2. There was no joy in the city that day.
3. We did not find favor in the eyes of the prophet.
4. Where did they find you?
5. These words are a great blessing for the people.
6. The king is a just and righteous man.

LESSON 14

64. The Perfect of קָם qām and בָּא bā'.

The two verbs קָם *qām* (he arose) and בָּא *bā'* (he came) represent a new type of root not mentioned previously. These verbs have essentially biconsonantal roots so far as their verbal inflections are concerned, but because there are sometimes associated with them nouns exhibiting a second form of the same root with *Waw* or *Yodh* in the middle, these roots are classified as II-*Waw* or II-*Yodh* in traditional grammar. They are also spoken of as Hollow Verbs. In the standard lexicon of Biblical Hebrew קָם and בָּא are listed under the roots קוּם and בוֹא respectively. The distinction between roots II-*Waw* and II-*Yodh* will become clear only when certain forms are taken up later; for the present the distinction is immaterial. קָם will be taken as the norm of this class:

קָם	*qām*	he arose	קָ֫מוּ	*qā́mû*	they arose
קָ֫מָה	*qā́māh*	she arose			
קַ֫מְתָּ	*qámtā*	you (m. s.) arose	קַמְתֶּם	*qamtém*	you (m. pl.) arose
קַמְתְּ	*qámt*	you (f. s.) arose	קַמְתֶּן	*qamtén*	you (f. pl.) arose
קַ֫מְתִּי	*qámtî*	I arose	קַ֫מְנוּ	*qámnû*	we arose

Note that the stem vowel is short in all persons other than the 3rd. The length of the stem vowel is almost completely dependent on whether or not the stem syllable is open or closed. Unlike verbs previously learned, the accent remains on the stem in the forms of the 3rd fem. sing. and the 3rd common plural.

Because בָּא has א as its final root consonant, we find the same kind of deviation here as with מָצָא. The full paradigm of this important verb is

בָּא	*bā'*	he came	בָּ֫אוּ	*bā́'û*	they came
בָּ֫אָה	*bā́'āh*	she came			
בָּ֫אתָ	*bā́(')ṯā*	you (m. s.) came	בָּאתֶם	*bā(')ṯem*	you (m. pl.) came
בָּאת	*bā́(')ṯ*	you (f. s.) came	בָּאתֶן	*bā(')ṯen*	you (f. pl.) came
בָּ֫אתִי	*bā́(')ṯî*	I came	בָּ֫אנוּ	*bā́(')nû*	we came

The stem of the participle in these verbs is the same as that of the 3rd masc. sing. perfect:

	Singular		Plural	
masc.	קָם	*qām*	קָמִים	*qāmîm*
fem.	קָמָה	*qāmāh*	קָמוֹת	*qāmôṯ*

Stress is normal in these forms, being on the ultima (final syllable). Note that the fem. sing. part. is distinguished from the 3rd fem. sing. perf. only by the position of the stress: קָ֫מָה *qā́māh* she arose, but קָמָה *qāmā́h* arising. Given a sentence such as

הָאִישׁ קָם *hā'îš qām*,

we may, unless we have the context in which the sentence occurs, translate "the man arose" (perfect) or "the man is arising" (participle). The only criterion that can be applied to an isolated sentence is that the perfect more frequently precedes its subject, while the participle follows it. The above sentence, then, without further information, is *more probably* participial.

65. The Prepositions מִן min and כְּ kə with pronominal suffixes.

מִמֶּ֫נִּי	*mimménnî*	from me	מִמֶּ֫נּוּ	*mimménnû*	from us
מִמְּךָ	*mimməḵā*	from you (m. s.)	מִכֶּם	*mikkem*	from you (m. pl.)
מִמֵּךְ	*mimmēḵ*	from you (f. s.)	מִכֶּן	*mikken*	from you (f. pl.)
מִמֶּ֫נּוּ	*mimménnû*	from him	מֵהֶם	*mēhem*	from them (m. pl.)
מִמֶּ֫נָּה	*mimménnāh*	from her	מֵהֶן	*mēhen*	from them (f. pl.)
			מֵהֵ֫נָּה	*mēhénnāh*	
כָּמוֹנִי	*kāmônî*	like me	כָּמוֹנוּ	*kāmônû*	like us
כָּמוֹךָ	*kāmôḵā*	like you (m. s.)	כָּכֶם	*kāḵem*	like you (m. pl.)
כָּמוֹךְ	*kāmôḵ*	like you (f. s.)	כָּכֶן	*kāḵen*	like you (f. pl.)
כָּמוֹהוּ	*kāmôhû*	like him	כָּהֶם	*kāhem*	like them (m. pl.)
כָּמוֹהָ	*kāmôhā*	like her	כָּהֶן	*kāhen*	like them (f. pl.)

The forms of the suffixed pronouns with these two prepositions are somewhat different from those already studied. Although a comparison is helpful, it is best to learn these forms as a new paradigm.

The forms *kāmônî* etc. may be used in a quasi-pronominal sense "anyone like me" etc.

אֵין כָּמֹוהוּ בָּאָרֶץ *'ên kāmôhû ḇā'āreṣ*
There is no one like him in the land, or
There is not his like (or equal) in the land.

66. כל kōl.

The word כֹּל *kōl* in one form or another corresponds variously to English "each, every, all, the whole." The uninflected form precedes the noun it modifies and may be joined with *maqqēp̄* as כָּל־ *kol-* or stand independently as כֹּל *kōl.* The following examples represent typical usage. Note carefully the constructions translated with "each, every," as opposed to "all."

כָּל־יוֹם	*kol-yôm*	each day, every day
כָּל־הַיּוֹם	*kol-hayyôm*	all the day, the whole day, all day
כָּל־הַיָּמִים	*kol-hayyāmîm*	all the days
כָּל־עִיר	*kol-'îr*	each city, every city
כָּל־הָעִיר	*kol-hā'îr*	all the city, the whole city
כָּל־הֶעָרִים	*kol-he'ārîm*	all the cities.

The expression כָּל־אֲשֶׁר *kol-'ăšer* is used as a compound relative "everything which (or that)." As the object of a verb it is preceded by *'eṯ-*:

נָתַן לוֹ אֶת־כָּל־אֲשֶׁר קָנָה *nāṯan lô 'eṯ-kol-'ăšer qānāh*
He gave him everything that he had acquired.

With an adjective כָּל has an indefinite pronominal sense:

כָּל־חָדָשׁ anything new

67. Vocabulary 14.

NOUNS: כְּלִי *kəlî* (pl. irreg. כֵּלִים) vessel, utensil
עֶרֶב *'éreḇ* evening
שֻׁלְחָן *šulḥān* (pl. *-ôṯ*) table
בֹּקֶר *bốqer* morning

VERBS: קָם *qām* to arise
שָׂם *śām* to put, set, place
בָּא *bā'* to come, enter (may be followed by a noun of place without a preposition)
צָם *ṣām* to fast
גָּר *gār* to sojourn
שָׁתָה *šāṯāh* to drink

OTHER: עַד *'aḏ* (Prep.) to, as far as, by, until
כֹּל *kōl* all, each, every

Exercises:

(a) Give the Hebrew for the following orally:

1. He is better than I.
2. There is none like us.
3. He took the money from us.
4. Have you seen a woman like her?
5. in the whole land which is before the people
6. every joy and every deliverance which I have given to you
7. all the sins which you have sinned
8. each treaty which I have made with the people
9. all the gold and all the silver
10. everything I own (lit. everything which is to me).

(b) Translate:

1 נָפַל הַמֶּ֫לֶךְ אַ֫רְצָה וְלֹא קָם כָּל־הַיּוֹם הַהוּא עַד־הָעֶ֫רֶב.
2 שַׂ֫מְנוּ אֶת־הַכֵּלִים עַל־הַשֻּׁלְחָן, הֲלֹא מְצָאתֶם אֹתָם שָׁם.
3 עָשׂוּ אֶת־הַכֵּלִים מִזָּהָב וּמִכֶּ֫סֶף כִּי הֵם הָיוּ לַהֵיכָל הַגָּדוֹל אֲשֶׁר בִּירוּשָׁלַ֫ם.
4 בָּ֫אוּ הָעָם הָעִ֫ירָה בְּשִׂמְחָה גְדוֹלָה כִּי לָהֶם הָיְתָה יְשׁוּעָה בַּמִּלְחָמָה.
5 צַ֫מְנוּ כָל־הַיּוֹם וְלֹא אָכַ֫לְנוּ לֶ֫חֶם וְלֹא שָׁתִ֫ינוּ מַ֫יִם.
6 אֵ֫לֶּה הָאֲנָשִׁים הַגָּרִים בְּתוֹךְ הָעָם הַזֶּה.
7 אֵיפֹה שַׂ֫מְתָּ אֶת־הַפְּרִי אֲשֶׁר לָקַ֫חְתָּ מֵהָעֵץ.
8 בָּ֫אוּ כָל־הַגִּבּוֹרִים הֵ֫נָּה כִּי יָדְעוּ כִּי פֹה הַמֶּ֫לֶךְ.
9 שָׁ֫תוּ הָאֲנָשִׁים מַ֫יִם וְגַם־אָכְלוּ לֶ֫חֶם.
10 זֶה הָאִישׁ אֲשֶׁר בְּחַרְתֶּם לָכֶם לְמֶ֫לֶךְ.

(c) Write in Hebrew:

1. She did not see the men who were coming on the road toward the city.
2. The righteous are fasting day and night.
3. God has given us a great victory today.
4. He set out for Jerusalem in the evening.
5. The Lord is God, and there is none like Him in the earth and in the heavens.
6. They set a large table before the king.
7. They sat there all that night until morning.
8. Many and great are the sins that we have committed.

LESSON 15

68. The Perfect of סָבַב sāḇaḇ.

The root of this verbal type is peculiar in having identical second and third root consonants. The Perfect is as follows:

סָבַב	*sāḇaḇ*	he went around	סָבֲבוּ	*sāḇăḇû*	they went around
סָבֲבָה	*sāḇăḇāh*	she went around			
סַבּוֹתָ	*sabbôṯā*	you (m. s.) "	סַבּוֹתֶם	*sabbôṯem*	you (m. pl.) "
סַבּוֹת	*sabbôṯ*	you (f. s.) "	סַבּוֹתֶן	*sabbôṯen*	you (f. pl.) "
סַבּוֹתִי	*sabbôṯî*	I went around	סַבּוֹנוּ	*sabbônû*	we went around

Here we find a new feature: before all suffixes beginning with a consonant the stem is *sabbô-*. Otherwise the forms are relatively normal, but note *ă* for *ə*, in accordance with §11 (2).

When the last two root consonants are a guttural or *r*, the forms where we should expect doubling are replaced with ones showing compensatory lengthening.

אָרַר	*'ārar*	he cursed	אָרֲרוּ	*'ārărû*	they cursed
אָרֲרָה	*'ārărāh*	she cursed			
אָרוֹתָ	*'ārôṯā*	you (m. s.) cursed	אָרוֹתֶם	*'ārôṯem*	you (m. pl.) cursed
אָרוֹת	*'ārôṯ*	you (f. s.) cursed	אָרוֹתֶן	*'ārôṯen*	you (f. pl.) cursed
אָרוֹתִי	*'ārôṯî*	I cursed	אָרוֹנוּ	*'ārônû*	we cursed

69. The Prepositions עִם ‘im and אֶת־ ’eṯ with Pronominal Suffixes.

עִמִּי	*‘immî*	with me	עִמָּ֫נוּ	*‘immā́nû*	with us
עִמְּךָ	*‘imməḵā*	with you (m. s.)	עִמָּכֶם	*‘immāḵem*	with you (m. pl.)
עִמָּךְ	*‘immāḵ*	with you (f. s.)	עִמָּכֶן	*‘immāḵen*	with you (f. pl.)
עִמּוֹ	*‘immô*	with him	עִמָּם	*‘immām*	with them (m. pl.)
עִמָּהּ	*‘immāh*	with her	עִמָּן	*‘immān*	with them (f. pl.)

An equally common variant of the 1st pers. sing. is עִמָּדִי *‘immāḏî*, with me; and of עִמָּם *‘immām*: עִמָּהֶם *‘immāhem*, with them.

אִתִּי	*’ittî*	with me	אִתָּ֫נוּ	*’ittā́nû*	with us
אִתְּךָ	*’ittəḵā*	with you (m. s.)	אִתְּכֶם	*’ittəḵém*	with you (m. pl.)
[אִתָּךְ	*’ittāḵ*	with you (f. s.)]	[אִתְּכֶן	*’ittəḵén*	with you (f. pl.)]
אִתּוֹ	*’ittô*	with him	אִתָּם	*’ittām*	with them (m. pl.)
אִתָּהּ	*’ittāh*	with her	[אִתָּן	*’ittān*	with them (f. pl.)]

Note the curious contrast between עִמָּכֶם with *ā* and אִתְּכֶם with *ə*.

70. Final Remarks on אֲשֶׁר.

Since אֲשֶׁר is not normally governed by a preposition in Hebrew, the counterparts of English "to whom," "for whom," and the like must be expressed differently. This is accomplished by using a resumptive pronoun within the relative clause itself, as the following examples will make clear:

the man *to whom* I gave the silver → the man *who* I gave the silver *to him*
הָאִישׁ אֲשֶׁר נָתַתִּי לוֹ אֶת־הַכֶּ֫סֶף *hā’îš ’ăšer nāṯáttî lô ’eṯ-hakkésep̄*
the city *from which* they came → the city *which* they came *from it*
הָעִיר אֲשֶׁר יָצְאוּ מִמֶּ֫נָּה *hā‘îr ’ăšer yāṣə’û mimménnāh*
the man *with whom* they sat → the man *who* they sat *with him*
הָאִישׁ אֲשֶׁר יָשְׁבוּ אִתּוֹ *hā’îš ’ăšer yāšəḇû ’ittô*

If appropriate, the adverbs שָׁם and שָׁ֫מָּה may be used instead of a pronoun:

the city in which he dwelt → the city which he dwelt there
הָעִיר אֲשֶׁר יָשַׁב שָׁם *hā‘îr ’ăšer yāšaḇ šām*
the city to which he went → the city which he went thither
הָעִיר אֲשֶׁר הָלַךְ שָׁ֫מָּה *hā‘îr ’ăšer hālaḵ šā́mmāh*

The resumptive pronoun is optional when אֲשֶׁר refers to the direct object of the verb:

the man whom I sent → the man *who* I sent *him*
הָאִישׁ אֲשֶׁר שָׁלַ֫חְתִּי אֹתוֹ *hā’îš ’ăšer šāláḥtî ’ōṯô*

or simply (and normally)
הָאִישׁ אֲשֶׁר שָׁלַ֫חְתִּי

In this and previous paragraphs (§§32, 55) we have outlined the more or less normative uses of אֲשֶׁר as a close correspondent of the English relative pronouns. Many instances of אֲשֶׁר are met, however, which do not tally with the simple treatment given here. Most of these uses can be dealt with as they are met if two general tendencies are kept in mind:

(1) אֲשֶׁר tends to take on a compound relative meaning "that which." As such, it may stand as a conjunction at the head of a clause with the force "the fact that..." and further may require the translation value of "since, because," or some other English subordinating conjunction. The exhaustive classification of all these independent pronominal and quasi-conjunctional uses is beyond the scope of an elementary grammar.

(2) Because אֲשֶׁר acquires an independent pronominal status ("that which"), it may occasionally be found with a preceding preposition, quite contrary to common usage.

Resulting from these tendencies and *in regular use as conjunctions are*

יַ֫עַן אֲשֶׁר	*yá'an 'ăšer*	because (lit. because of the fact that)
אַחֲרֵי אֲשֶׁר	*'aḥărê 'ăšer*	after
כַּאֲשֶׁר	*ka'ăšer*	as, according as, when

Finally, although most relative clauses are signalled with אֲשֶׁר, it is possible to use a clause to modify a preceding noun with no formal mark of the relationship whatever (the term asyndetic is used to describe this):

Gen. 15:13	בְּאֶ֫רֶץ לֹא לָהֶם	in a land (which is) not theirs
I Sam. 6:9	מִקְרֶה הוּא הָיָה לָ֫נוּ	It was a chance thing (that) happened to us.

This type of relative clause in more frequent in poetry than in prose, and more frequent after an indefinite antecedent than a definite one.

71. Vocabulary 15.

NOUNS:	מִצְוָה	*miṣwāh* (pl. *-ōṯ*)	commandment
	אוֹר	*'ôr* (pl. *-îm*)	light
	חֹשֶׁךְ	*ḥōšeḵ*	darkness
	אֹיֵב	*'ōyēḇ* (pl. *-îm*)	enemy
VERBS:	סָבַב	*sāḇaḇ*	to surround, go around
	אָרַר	*'ārar*	to curse
	עָזַב	*'āzaḇ*	to abandon
	עָבַר	*'āḇar*	to cross (a place); to transgress (a commandment)
	יָרַשׁ	*yāraš*	to inherit
	שָׁכַח	*šāḵaḥ*	to forget
CONJUNCTION:	כַּאֲשֶׁר	*ka'ăšer*	as, according as, when

Exercises:

(a) Give the Hebrew for the following orally:

1. the vessel in which there is water
2. the man whom the king summoned
3. the house in which we found a table
4. the evening in which we ate and drank
5. the people with whom he is sojourning
6. the day during (lit. in) which we fasted
7. the cloud from which fire came forth
8. the year in which many fell in battle
9. the law in which there are blessings and wisdom
10. the heavens in which he created the sun, moon, and stars

(b) Translate:

1 עָבַ֫רְנוּ אֶת־הַמִּצְוֹת אֲשֶׁר שָׂם הַנָּבִיא לִפְנֵי הָעָם.

2 הֶעֱזַבְתָּ אֹתִי וְאֶת־הָעָם אֲשֶׁר אִתִּי.

3 זֹאת הָאָ֫רֶץ אֲשֶׁר יָרַ֫שְׁנוּ כַּאֲשֶׁר אָמַר לָ֫נוּ הָאֱלֹהִים.

4 בַּלַּ֫יְלָה הַהוּא חָלַ֫מְתִּי חֲלוֹם וּבוֹ רָאִ֫יתִי אֶת־הַכּוֹכָבִים אֲשֶׁר בַּשָּׁמַ֫יִם.

5 הָעָם הֹלְכִים בְּחֹ֫שֶׁךְ כִּי אֵין לָהֶם אוֹר.

6 קָרָא אֱלֹהִים לַחֹ֫שֶׁךְ לַ֫יְלָה וְלָאוֹר קָרָא יוֹם.

7 הָאֹיְבִים סָבֲבוּ אֹתִי וְאֵין לִי יְשׁוּעָה מֵיהוה כִּי חָטָ֫אתִי חַטָּאוֹת רַבּוֹת לַיהוה וְהוּא אָרַר אֹתִי
וְאֶת־הָעָם אֲשֶׁר עִמִּי.

8 עָמַ֫דְנוּ עַל־הַגִּבְעָה וּמִשָּׁם רָאִ֫ינוּ כִּי סָבֲבוּ הָאֹיְבִים אֶת־הָעִיר וְהָֽרְגוּ אֶת־כָּל־הָעָם.

9 לָֽכְדוּ אֶת־הָעִיר וְגַם־לָֽקְחוּ אֶת־כָּל־הַכֵּלִים מֵהַהֵיכָל.

10 בַּבֹּ֫קֶר עָבַר אֶת־הַנָּהָר הוּא וְכָל־הָעָם אִתּוֹ כַּמִּצְוָה אֲשֶׁר אָמַר אֱלֹהִים לָהֶם.

(c) Write in Hebrew:

1. Light is better than darkness.
2. Have you forgotten the words which I wrote for you in the book?
3. I have transgressed all the laws and all the commandments which you gave to me.
4. The Lord cursed the evil city and all the wicked people who were in it.
5. There are no enemies in this land.
6. The old man gave me good advice, for he knew that I had not done those evil things.

LESSON 16

72. The Construct Chain.

There is in BH no preposition having the same range of meaning expressed by English "of." The of-relationship, the genitive case of the classical languages, has its correspondent in the construct chain:

קוֹל הַנָּבִיא	*qôl hannāḇî'*	the voice of the prophet
מֶלֶךְ הָאָרֶץ	*mélek̲ hā'āreṣ*	the king of the land

As these examples show, the simple juxtaposition of two nouns serves to mark a modifying relationship. The first noun in such a chain is said to be in the construct state. In more modern terminology, the first noun occurs in a bound form as opposed to the normal or free form (absolute) used elsewhere.

The construct or bound form of a noun is frequently different from the absolute. This difference has arisen mainly because of the stress situation involved: the first noun loses its primary stress and becomes proclitic to the second noun. Loss of stress may be complete, as commonly with בֶּן (note the *maqqēp̄*):

בֶּן־הַמֶּלֶךְ	*ben-hammélek̲*	the son of the king

but more commonly the first noun retains its stress:

מֶלֶךְ הָאָרֶץ	*mélek̲ hā'ā́reṣ*	the king of the land

More important than stress difference, however, is the change in vocalization found in many words:

דְּבַר הַמֶּלֶךְ	*dəḇar hammélek̲*	the word of the king

This will be taken up below.

Only the final noun in a construct chain may have the definite article. The definiteness of the entire expression depends on the second noun: if it is made definite with the article or is a proper name, the first noun is also definite:

קוֹל הַנָּבִיא	*qôl hannāḇî'*	*the* voice of *the* prophet
קוֹל שְׁמוּאֵל	*qôl šəmû'ēl*	*the* voice of Samuel

as contrasted with

קוֹל נָבִיא	*qôl nāḇî'*	*a* voice of *a* prophet

Thus, the nouns of a construct chain will correspond generally to English "the ... of the ..." or "a ... of a ..." In order to express explicitly "a ... of the ...," the preposition לְ is used (often with אֲשֶׁר) with the normal (absolute) form of the noun:

דָּבָר (אֲשֶׁר) לַמֶּלֶךְ	*dāḇār ('ăšer) lammélek̲*	a word of the king
מִזְמוֹר לְדָוִד	*mizmôr ləD̲āwīd̲*	a psalm of David

Either noun of a construct chain may be pluralized. The special forms of the plural construct will be dealt with in Lesson 18. For the present note that דִּבְרֵי *diḇrê* is the construct form of דְּבָרִים:

דְּבַר הַנְּבִיאִים	*dəḇar hannəḇî'îm*	the word of the prophets
דִּבְרֵי הַנָּבִיא	*diḇrê hannāḇî'*	the words of the prophet
דִּבְרֵי הַנְּבִיאִים	*diḇrê hannəḇî'îm*	the words of the prophets

Any adjective modifying either noun must follow the entire chain. Some ambiguity may occur here, but agreement in number and gender or the general context is usually a sufficient guide. Be sure all of the following examples are clear (אֵשֶׁת and נְשֵׁי are the construct forms of אִשָּׁה and נָשִׁים respectively):

דְּבַר הַנָּבִיא הָרַע	the word of the evil prophet
	or, the evil word of the prophet
דִּבְרֵי הַנָּבִיא הָרָעִים	the evil words of the prophet
דְּבַר הַנְּבִיאִים הָרָעִים	the word of the evil prophets
אֵשֶׁת הָאִישׁ הַטּוֹב	the wife of the good man
אֵשֶׁת הָאִישׁ הַטּוֹבָה	the good wife of the man
נְשֵׁי הָאִישׁ הַיָּפוֹת	the beautiful wives of the man
נְשֵׁי הָאֲנָשִׁים הַיָּפִים	the wives of the handsome men

The use of two adjectives, one modifying each noun, is avoided. But two adjectives may modify either noun, as in

דִּבְרֵי הַמֶּלֶךְ הַטּוֹב וְהַיָּשָׁר	the words of the good and just king
דִּבְרֵי הַמֶּלֶךְ הַטּוֹבִים וְהַיְשָׁרִים	the good and just words of the king

The construct chain may be extended to three or more nouns, but examples of four or more are very rare:

אֵשֶׁת בֶּן־הַנָּבִיא	the wife of the son of the prophet

The same rules for definiteness and adjectival modification apply.

Occasionally, and usually with fixed expressions, the first or second noun of a construct chain may be replaced by a longer phrase. The following types are considered anomalous and should not be used in the exercises:

מֶלֶךְ הַשָּׁמַיִם וְהָאָרֶץ	the king of heaven and earth (second noun replaced by noun + noun)
דִּבְרֵי וּמַעֲשֵׂי הַמֶּלֶךְ	the words and deeds of the king (first noun replaced by noun + noun)
שִׂמְחַת בַּקָּצִיר	the joy of (or in) the harvest (preposition used with second noun; possibly a contamination with the verbal idiom *śāmēaḥ bə* to rejoice in)

Active participles may be construed with a following object (1) as verbs

הַשֹּׁמֵר אֶת־הַתּוֹרָה	the one who is (now actually) keeping the law

or (2) in a construct relationship as nouns

שֹׁמֵר הַתּוֹרָה	the one who (in general) keeps the law.

As indicated, there is frequently a difference in meaning: as a verb, the reference is real and particular; as a noun, general and non-particular.

The precise meaning of the construct chain is difficult to define. While a rough translation using "of" or the possessive, as in "the king's son," will often suffice, there are many instances where an adjective or prepositional phrase is better:

לוּחַ אֶבֶן	a stone tablet
לוּחַ הָאֶבֶן	the stone tablet
הַר קֹדֶשׁ	a holy mountain
כְּלִי מַיִם	a vessel for water

The student should keep in mind the fact that in a construct chain the second noun modifies or restricts the first in some way; from this general rule he may proceed to a correct translation as demanded by the context and by proper English usage. Slavish adherence to a single translation pattern should be avoided.

73. The Form of the Construct Singular.

The construct form of a singular noun (exclusive of feminines in *-āh* and a few others) may be derived from the absolute by the application of the following rules:

(1) Unstressed *ē* and *ā* are replaced by *ə*.
(2) *ā* in a final closed syllable is replaced by *a*.
(3) *ē* in a final closed syllable usually remains unchanged, but in a small group of words is replaced by *a*.

Below are listed examples of the most frequent noun types:

Absolute		*Construct*		*Rule applied*
יָד	*yāḏ*	יַד	*yaḏ*	2
מָקוֹם	*māqôm*	מְקוֹם	*məqôm*	1
נָבִיא	*nāḇî'*	נְבִיא	*nəḇî'*	1
כּוֹכָב	*kôḵāḇ*	כּוֹכַב	*kôḵaḇ*	2
הֵיכָל	*hêḵāl*	הֵיכַל	*hêḵal*	2
מִשְׁפָּט	*mišpāṭ*	מִשְׁפַּט	*mišpaṭ*	2
גַּנָּב	*gannāḇ*	גַּנַּב	*gannaḇ*	2
דָּבָר	*dāḇār*	דְּבַר	*dəḇar*	1 and 2
זָקֵן	*zāqēn*	זְקַן	*zəqan*	1 and 3 (with change)
שֹׁפֵט	*šōp̄ēṭ*	שֹׁפֵט	*šōp̄ēṭ*	3 (without change)
לֵבָב	*lēḇāḇ*	לְבַב	*ləḇaḇ*	1 and 2
מֶ֫לֶךְ	*méleḵ*	מֶ֫לֶךְ	*méleḵ*	none
סֵ֫פֶר	*sḗp̄er*	סֵ֫פֶר	*sḗp̄er*	none (the *ē* is stressed)
נַ֫עַר	*náʻar*	נַ֫עַר	*náʻar*	none

74. Vocabulary 16.

NOUNS: אֶ֫בֶן *'éḇen* (pl. *-îm*) stone (f.)
דָּג *dāḡ* (pl. *-îm*) fish [The fem. דָּגָה *dāḡāh* is used as a collective term.]
חֲצִי *ḥăṣî* (no. pl.) half
יָם *yām* (pl. יַמִּים *yammîm*) sea; note יָ֫מָּה *yámmāh* seaward, westward.
לוּחַ *lû^{a}ḥ* (pl. *-ôṯ*) tablet
מְלָאכָה *məlā(')ḵāh* occupation, work
עוֹף *'ôp̄* (coll., no pl.) birds, fowl
עֵ֫שֶׂב *'ḗśeḇ* (coll.) grass, herbage
צֶ֫לֶם *ṣélem* (pl. *-îm*) image, likeness

VERBS: שָׁבַר *šāḇar* to break, smash

שָׁמַע *šāma‘* to hear; + אֶל or לְ to heed, listen to; + בְּ/לְקוֹל to obey.

שָׁבַת *šāḇaṯ* to cease, rest

OTHER: לָ֫מָּה *lā́mmāh* Why? [Before the gutturals א, ה, and ע the form לָמָ֫ה *lāmā́h* is preferred.]

Exercises:

(a) Form the construct singular of the following nouns (all according to rule):

אֹיֵב	אוֹר	אֶרֶץ	אִישׁ
גִּבּוֹר	גָּמָל	גַּן	בֹּקֶר
הַר	הֵיכָל	דָּבָר	דֶּרֶךְ
חֲלוֹם	חֵן	זָהָב	זָקֵן
כֶּסֶף	כִּסֵּא	יוֹם	יֶלֶד
לֶחֶם	כְּלִי	כּוֹכָב	כֶּרֶם
נָהָר	מָקוֹם	מַלְאָךְ	מֶלֶךְ
עִיר	עֶבֶד	סֵפֶר	נָבִיא
עֶרֶב	עָנָן	עֵץ	עַם
קוֹל	פְּרִי	צֹאן	צֶדֶק
	שֻׁלְחָן	שֹׁפֵט	רָעָב

(b) Give orally the Hebrew for the following:

1. a vessel of silver
2. the mountain of the Lord
3. the man's camel
4. the woman's garden
5. the temple of the city
6. the boy's dream
7. the men's silver
8. the servant's voice
9. the light of the stars
10. the child's bread
11. the river of that land

(c) Translate:

(1) פְּרִי הָעֵץ
(2) עֵץ הַגָּן
(3) גַּן הָאִישׁ הַקָּטֹן
(4) אִישׁ הָאִשָּׁה הָרַע
(5) אִישׁ הָאִשָּׁה הָרָעָה
(6) שֹׁפֵט הָעָם הַיָּשָׁר
(7) קוֹל הַנָּבִיא
(8) עֶבֶד הַמֶּלֶךְ הַטּוֹב
(9) אִישׁ הָעִיר הֶעָשִׁיר
(10) רְעַב הַדַּלִּים
(11) עֲנַן הַשָּׁמַיִם הַגָּדוֹל
(12) זְהַב הַהֵיכָל הַיָּקָר

(d) Translate:

(1) לֹא שָׁמְעוּ הָעָם לְקוֹל הַנָּבִיא כִּי הָיוּ רְשָׁעִים מְאֹד.
(2) שָׁבַר הַנָּבִיא אֶת־לוּחַ הָאֶבֶן וְלֹא נָתַן אֹתוֹ לָעָם.
(3) לָ֫מָּה שְׁבַתֶּם מֵהַמְּלָאכָה.
(4) בָּעִיר הָרָעָה רָאִינוּ צֶלֶם גָּדוֹל וְלֹא יָדַעְנוּ מִי הוּא.

(5) הַאֲכַלְתֶּם אֶת־הַדָּגִים אֲשֶׁר נָתַנּוּ לָכֶם.

(6) עוֹף הַשָּׁמַיִם יָפֶה מְאֹד.

(7) יָצָא חֲצִי הַמַּחֲנֶה לַמִּלְחָמָה.

(8) בָּאנוּ הָעִירָה וְלֹא מָצָאנוּ שָׁם אֶת־נְבִיא הָאֱלֹהִים.

(9) שָׂם הַכֹּהֵן אֶת־סֵפֶר הַתּוֹרָה עַל־הַשֻּׁלְחָן.

(10) קַמְתִּי בַבֹּקֶר וְלֹא זָכַרְתִּי אֶת־הַצֶּלֶם אֲשֶׁר רָאִיתִי בַחֲלוֹם אֲשֶׁר חָלַמְתִּי.

(11) זֶה הַמֶּלֶךְ אֲשֶׁר שָׂם הָעָם עַל־הַכִּסֵּא.

(12) בָּאָה הָאִשָּׁה לִפְנֵי הַמֶּלֶךְ וְהַמֶּלֶךְ לֹא שָׁמַע אֶל־קוֹל הָאִשָּׁה.

(13) בַּלַּיְלָה וּבְאוֹר הַיּוֹם הָעָם שֹׁמְעִים אֶל־קוֹל הָאֱלֹהִים וְהֹלְכִים בְּדֶרֶךְ יהוה כַּמִּצְוָה אֲשֶׁר נָתַן לָהֶם.

(e) Write in Hebrew:

1. He crossed the road of the city.
2. Why have you abandoned me to the enemy?
3. Who broke this vessel?
4. He cursed us because we forgot the word of the law.
5. The wicked king took captive the people of Jerusalem.
6. He abandoned me because I sinned against him and did not listen to him.
7. They did not rest until the evening.

LESSON 17

75. The Construct Singular: Minor Types.

(a) The two words אָב and אָח show a suffixed *-î* in the construct, with regular reduction of the stem vowel: אֲבִי *'ăḇî*, אֲחִי *'ăḥî*.

(b) All nouns of the patterns בַּ֫יִת and מָ֫וֶת show a regular contraction in the construct (*ayi* → *ê* and *āwe* → *ô*):

בַּ֫יִת *báyiṯ*	constr.	בֵּית *bêṯ*	
מָ֫וֶת *mắweṯ*		מוֹת *môṯ*	

(c) The construct form of בֵּן is commonly proclitic to the following word as בֶּן־ (with *e*). A similar form occurs for שֵׁם but is much less frequent.

(d) A few nouns outwardly identical to the type זָקֵן (constr. *zəqan*) have an unusual construct form; these include

כָּתֵף *kāṯēp̄*	constr.	כֶּ֫תֶף *kéṯep̄*	shoulder
יָרֵךְ *yārēḵ*		יֶ֫רֶךְ *yéreḵ*	thigh

(e) Nouns ending in *-eh* have construct forms in *-ēh*. Other changes are in accordance with the rules given:

שָׂדֶה *śāḏeh*	constr.	שְׂדֵה *śəḏēh*	
מַחֲנֶה *maḥăneh*		מַחֲנֵה *maḥănēh*	

There are quite a few other apparent exceptions to the basic rules given in

Lesson 16. None of these, however, is frequent enough to represent a type; such individual deviations will be noted in the vocabularies when necessary.

76. The Construct Singular of Feminine Nouns in -āh.

After the replacement of the ending *-āh* by *-aṯ*, these nouns normally conform to the rules given in the preceding lesson.

שָׁנָה	*šānāh*	year	constr.	שְׁנַת	*šənaṯ*	Rule 1
עֵצָה	*ʿēṣāh*	advice		עֲצַת	*ʿăṣaṯ*	Rule 1
מַלְכָּה	*malkāh*	queen		מַלְכַּת	*malkaṯ*	No further change
תְּבוּאָה	*təḇûʾāh*	produce		תְּבוּאַת	*təḇûʾaṯ*	”
תְּפִלָּה	*təp̄illāh*	prayer		תְּפִלַּת	*təp̄illaṯ*	”
בְּרָכָה	*bərāḵāh*	blessing		בִּרְכַּת	*birkaṯ*	Rule 1 and the Rule of Shewa (§5)*
נְבֵלָה	*nəḇēlāh*	corpse		נִבְלַת	*niḇlaṯ*	As above.

These last two examples should be clear: the reduction of *a* to *ə* by Rule 1 would have led to **bərəḵaṯ*, which, by the Rule of Shewa, becomes *birkaṯ*.

Two types of variations from the norm are common:

(1) Most trisyllabic nouns beginning with a closed syllable have penultimately stressed construct forms:

מִלְחָמָה	*milḥāmāh*	war	constr.	מִלְחֶמֶת	*milḥémeṯ*
מִשְׁפָּחָה	*mišpāḥāh*	family		מִשְׁפַּחַת	*mišpáḥaṯ*

(2) Sometimes the expected reduction of *ē* or *ā* to *ə* does not take place. This is by and large unpredictable and will require special note.

בְּרֵכָה	*bərēḵāh*	pond	constr.	בְּרֵכַת	*bərēḵaṯ*
צָרָה	*ṣārāh*	distress		צָרַת	*ṣāraṯ*

Most feminine nouns ending in *-aṯ*, *-eṯ*, *-ûṯ*, *-îṯ*, etc., in the absolute are not susceptible to further change in the construct form. Those that are follow the rules. The construct form of אִשָּׁה is quite irregular: אֵשֶׁת *ʾéšeṯ*.

77. Vocabulary 17.

NOUNS: רָקִיעַ *rāqîᵃʿ* the firmament (apparently considered as a solid barrier by the cosmographers of Genesis)

יַבָּשָׁה *yabbāšāh* dry ground

אָב *ʾāḇ* (pl. *-ôṯ*) father

אָח *ʾāḥ* (pl. irreg. אַחִים *ʾaḥîm*) brother

* Note the reversion of *ḵ* to *k*. This is unusual; one would expect בִּרְכַת without *daghesh lene*.

בֵּן *bēn* (pl. irreg. בָּנִים *bānîm*) son
מַלְכָּה *malkāh* (pl. *-ôṯ*) queen
שֵׁם *šēm* (pl. *-ôṯ*) name

ADJECTIVES: רִאשׁוֹן *rišôn* first (fem. רִאשׁוֹנָה *rišônāh*)
שֵׁנִי *šēnî* second (fem. שֵׁנִית *šēnîṯ*)
שְׁלִישִׁי *šəlîšî* third (fem. שְׁלִישִׁית *šəlîšîṯ*)
רְבִיעִי *rəḇîʿî* fourth (fem. רְבִיעִית *rəḇîʿîṯ*)
חֲמִישִׁי *ḥămîšî* fifth (fem. חֲמִישִׁית *ḥămîšîṯ*)

OTHER: עַל־פְּנֵי *ʿal-pənê* (prep.) on the surface of, up against
כֵּן *kēn* (adv.) thus, so (referring to what has been mentioned)

Exercises:

(a) Translate:

(1) בֵּית הַנָּבִיא
(2) עֲצַת הַמֶּלֶךְ
(3) שְׁנַת הַמִּלְחָמָה הַגְּדוֹלָה
(4) בִּרְכַּת הָאָבוֹת
(5) מַלְכַּת הַשָּׁמַיִם
(6) תּוֹרַת הָאֱלֹהִים
(7) שִׂמְחַת הָעָם הַגְּדוֹלָה
(8) עֲבוֹדַת הָאִישׁ הַקָּשָׁה
(9) יְשׁוּעַת הַגִּבּוֹרִים
(10) גִּבְעַת הָאָרֶץ הַהִיא
(11) בֶּן־הַשֹּׁפֵט
(12) בַּת הָאִישׁ הַדַּל
(13) שֵׁם הָאָרֶץ הַזֹּאת
(14) מַחֲנֵה הָאֹיְבִים

(b) Give orally the Hebrew for the following:

1. The rich man's field
2. the father of the king
3. the third battle of the year
4. the youngest (= small) brother of the prophet
5. the fifth word of the law
6. the blessing of the Lord
7. the wisdom of the king
8. the first house of the city
9. the firmament of the heavens
10. the image of God

(c) Reading: The Creation

[N.B. Genuine BH narrative requires the use of a verb form we shall not study until Lesson 22. The reading selections of Lessons 17 to 22 should therefore be regarded as simply sequences of isolated sentences, related in meaning but not in syntax.]

בַּיּוֹם הָרִאשׁוֹן בָּרָא אֱלֹהִים אֶת־הַשָּׁמַיִם וְאֶת־הָאָרֶץ. הָאָרֶץ הָיְתָה תֹהוּ וָבֹהוּ* וְחֹשֶׁךְ הָיָה עַל־פְּנֵי הַמָּיִם. בָּרָא אֱלֹהִים אֶת־הָאוֹר. קָרָא לָאוֹר יוֹם וְלַחֹשֶׁךְ קָרָא לָיְלָה. כֵּן עָשָׂה אֱלֹהִים בַּיּוֹם הָרִאשׁוֹן.

בַּיּוֹם הַשֵּׁנִי עָשָׂה אֱלֹהִים רָקִיעַ בְּתוֹךְ הַמַּיִם וְהָרָקִיעַ עָמַד בֵּין הַמַּיִם אֲשֶׁר תַּחַת הַשָּׁמַיִם וּבֵין הַמַּיִם אֲשֶׁר עַל־הַשָּׁמַיִם. קָרָא לָרָקִיעַ שָׁמַיִם. כֵּן עָשָׂה בַּיּוֹם הַשֵּׁנִי.

בַּיּוֹם הַשְּׁלִישִׁי קָבַץ אֱלֹהִים אֶת־הַמַּיִם אֲשֶׁר תַּחַת הַשָּׁמַיִם אֶל־מָקוֹם אֶחָד. לַיַּבָּשָׁה קָרָא אֱלֹהִים אֶרֶץ וְלַמַּיִם קָרָא יַמִּים. גַּם־בַּיּוֹם הַשְּׁלִישִׁי בָּרָא אֶת־כָּל־עֵשֶׂב הָאָרֶץ וְאֶת־כָּל־עֵץ.

(d) Write in Hebrew:

1. The house of stone did not fall.
2. The joy of the people is in the law of the Lord.
3. Half of the young men fell in the battle that day.
4. I drank the water from a stone vessel and I ate the food which was on a wooden table.
5. I sojourned with the people of that land (for) many years.
6. In the morning he set out toward-the-west.
7. The name of this king is David.

* *tōhû wāḇōhû:* a designation of the primordial chaos; "formlessness and void" is an acceptable translation for this rather obscure phrase.

LESSON 18

78. The Construct Forms of Plural Nouns in -îm.

In the construct form of nouns having plurals in *-îm*, this ending is replaced by *-ê*. Vowel reductions take place as usual in accordance with the rules given in §73.

Absolute		Construct		Rules applied
יָמִים	*yāmîm*	יְמֵי	*yəmê*	1
בָּנִים	*bānîm*	בְּנֵי	*bənê*	1
חִצִּים	*ḥiṣṣîm*	חִצֵּי	*ḥiṣṣê*	
עַמִּים	*ʿammîm*	עַמֵּי	*ʿammê*	
סוּסִים	*sûsîm*	סוּסֵי	*sûsê*	
זֵיתִים	*zêṯîm*	זֵיתֵי	*zêṯê*	
בְּכוּרִים	*bəḵôrîm*	בְּכוּרֵי	*bəḵôrê*	
גְּבוּלִים	*gəḇûlîm*	גְּבוּלֵי	*gəḇûlê*	
גְּמַלִּים	*gəmallîm*	גְּמַלֵּי	*gəmallê*	
דְּבָרִים	*dəḇārîm*	דִּבְרֵי	*diḇrê*	1 and rule of *ə*
אֲנָשִׁים	*ʾănāšîm*	אַנְשֵׁי	*ʾanšê*	1 and rule of *ə*
זְקֵנִים	*zəqēnîm*	זִקְנֵי	*ziqnê*	1 and rule of *ə*
כֵּלִים	*kēlîm*	כְּלֵי	*kəlê*	1
כּוֹכָבִים	*kôḵāḇîm*	כּוֹכְבֵי	*kôḵəḇê*	1
הֵיכָלִים	*hêḵālîm*	הֵיכְלֵי	*hêḵəlê*	1
מִשְׁפָּטִים	*mišpāṭîm*	מִשְׁפְּטֵי	*mišpəṭê*	1
כֹּהֲנִים	*kōhănîm*	כֹּהֲנֵי	*kōhănê*	

Dissyllabic nouns with penultimate stress (the general type *méleḵ*) must be singled out for particular attention. Although all these nouns have a common *absolute* plural pattern, the *construct* form cannot be obtained by normal rules:

(**a**) Nouns like מֶ֫לֶךְ (with *é*) have *a* or *i* in the stem syllable of the plural construct. The correct vowel must be learned with each word. Following is a list of all words of this group that have been introduced to this point. Hereafter the characteristic vowel of each word will be noted in the vocabularies.

מְלָכִים	מַלְכֵי	*malḵê*
עֲבָדִים	עַבְדֵי	*'aḇḏê*
כְּרָמִים	כַּרְמֵי	*karmê*
יְלָדִים	יַלְדֵי	*yalḏê*
דְּרָכִים	דַּרְכֵי	*darḵê*
אֲבָנִים	אַבְנֵי	*'aḇnê*
נְעָרִים	נַעֲרֵי	*na'ărê*

(**b**) Nouns like סֵ֫פֶר (with *ḗ*) have *i* (sometimes *e*):

סֵ֫פֶר	סְפָרִים	סִפְרֵי	*sip̄rê*	
שֵׁ֫בֶט	שְׁבָטִים	שִׁבְטֵי	*šiḇṭê*	tribes
עֵ֫דֶר	עֲדָרִים	עֶדְרֵי	*'eḏrê*	herds

(**c**) Nouns like שֹׁ֫רֶשׁ (with *ō*) have *o*:

שֹׁ֫רֶשׁ	שֳׁרָשִׁים	שָׁרְשֵׁי	*šoršê*	roots

There are several nouns with irregularities in the plural construct which should be noted here:

רָאשִׁים	*rāšîm*	רָאשֵׁי	*rāšê*	No reduction
עָרִים	*'ārîm*	עָרֵי	*'ārê*	No reduction
הָרִים	*hārîm*	הָרֵי	*hārê*	No reduction

The construct forms of שָׁמַ֫יִם and מַ֫יִם are שְׁמֵי *šəmê* and מֵי *mê* respectively.

79. The Construct Form of Plural Nouns in -ôṯ.

The ending *-ôṯ* remains in the construct form, which is subject to the same rule (1) of reduction already cited. Here again, if nouns of the types *méleḵ*, *sḗp̄er*, *šṓreš* (or *ná'ar*, *zéra'*, *'ṓraḥ*) have plurals in *-ôṯ*, the stem vowel cannot be predicted on the basis of rules.

שֵׁם	שֵׁמוֹת	שְׁמוֹת	*šəmôṯ*	Rule 1
לֵב	לִבּוֹת	לִבּוֹת	*libbôṯ*	
נֶ֫פֶשׁ	נְפָשׁוֹת	נַפְשׁוֹת	*nap̄šôṯ*	Unpredictable
חֶ֫רֶב	חֲרָבוֹת	חַרְבוֹת	*ḥarḇôṯ*	”

אֶרֶץ	אֲרָצוֹת	אַרְצוֹת	*'arṣôṯ*	"
אֹרַח	אֳרָחוֹת	אָרְחוֹת	*'orḥôṯ*	
מָקוֹם	מְקוֹמוֹת	מְקוֹמוֹת	*məqômôṯ*	
בְּרָכָה	בְּרָכוֹת	בִּרְכוֹת	*birḵôṯ*	1 and rule of *ə*
שָׂדֶה	שָׂדוֹת	שְׂדוֹת	*śəḏôṯ*	1

The construct plurals of feminine nouns like גִּבְעָה and מַלְכָּה take the same vowel as the singular: גִּבְעוֹת but מַלְכוֹת.

80. Vocabulary 18.

NOUNS: אָדָם *'āḏām* (1) the proper name Adam; (2) a collective term (no pl.) mankind; (3) a singular noun (no pl.) a man [*'āḏām* characterizes a man as opposed to what is not human, while *'îš* is man as opposed to woman or child.]

אֲדָמָה *'ăḏāmāh* earth, ground, soil, landed property [sometimes synonymous with *'éreṣ*, which retains more of a geographical or political rather than agricultural sense]

בְּהֵמָה *bəhēmāh* (constr. בֶּהֱמַת *behĕmaṯ*) (pl. *-ôṯ*) beast, animal, often used collectively

רֶמֶשׂ *rémeś* (no pl.) a collective term for all creeping things

זָכָר *zāḵār* (pl. *-îm)* a male

נְקֵבָה *nəqēḇāh* a female

שַׁבָּת *šabbāt* (pl. irreg. שַׁבָּתוֹת) sabbath (f.)

ADJECTIVES: שִׁשִּׁי *šiššî* sixth (fem. שִׁשִּׁית *šiššîṯ*)

שְׁבִיעִי *šəḇî'î* seventh (fem. שְׁבִיעִית *šəḇî'îṯ*)

אַחֵר *'aḥēr* other, another (fem. אַחֶרֶת *'aḥéreṯ*; m. pl. אֲחֵרִים *'ăḥērîm*, f. pl. אֲחֵרוֹת *'ăḥērôṯ*)

VERBS: יָצַר *yāṣar* to form, fashion

Note: Three words often confused are

(1) חַי *ḥay*, an adjective whose forms are given in §22; "alive, living"
(2) חַיָּה *ḥayyāh*, a noun (pl. *-ôṯ*), used as a general term for any "living thing or animal."
(3) חַיִּים *ḥayyîm*, a noun used only in the plural form but with the singular meaning "life, lifetime."

Exercises:

(a) Translate the following phrases. Make sure that all construct forms are clearly understood.

(1) אַנְשֵׁי הָעִיר
(2) נְשֵׁי הַמֶּלֶךְ
(3) אֹיְבֵי הָעָם
(4) בָּתֵּי הָעִיר

(5) גִּבְעוֹת הָאָ֫רֶץ
(6) דִּבְרֵי הַסֵּ֫פֶר
(7) הֵיכְלֵי הָעִיר
(8) הָרֵי הָאָ֫רֶץ
(9) מַלְכֵי הָאָ֫רֶץ
(10) כּוֹכְבֵי הַשָּׁמַ֫יִם
(11) בֶּהֱמַת הַשָּׂדֶה
(12) חַיַּת הָאָ֫רֶץ
(13) חַיֵּי הָאִישׁ
(14) אַבְנֵי הָהָר
(15) דְּגֵי הַיָּם
(16) לוּחוֹת הַתּוֹרָה
(17) צַלְמֵי הָאֱלֹהִים
(18) בְּנוֹת הָעָם
(19) דַּרְכֵי הֶהָרִים
(20) בִּרְכוֹת הַנְּבִיאִים
(21) גְּמַלֵּי הֶעָשִׁיר
(22) גִּבּוֹרֵי הָעָם
(23) זִקְנֵי הָעִיר
(24) חֲלוֹמוֹת הַנַּ֫עַר
(25) יַלְדֵי הַנָּשִׁים
(26) יְמֵי הַמְּלָכִים
(27) כְּלֵי הַהֵיכָל
(28) מַלְאֲכֵי הַמֶּ֫לֶךְ

(b) Give first the plural of each noun; then use the construct plural form in the given phrase.

(1) place, the places of the land
(2) camp, the camps of the enemy
(3) commandment, the commandments of the Lord
(4) river, the rivers of the land
(5) prophet, the prophets of that city
(6) book, the books of the prophets
(7) servant, the servants of the king
(8) city, the cities of the land
(9) tree, the trees of the garden
(10) judge, the judges of the people
(11) father, the fathers of the children
(12) son, the sons of the elders

(c) Reading: The Creation (concluded).

בַּיּוֹם הָרְבִיעִי בָּרָא אֱלֹהִים אֶת־הַשֶּׁ֫מֶשׁ וְאֶת־הַיָּרֵחַ. הַשֶּׁ֫מֶשׁ הוּא הָאוֹר הַגָּדוֹל אֲשֶׁר לַיּוֹם וְהַיָּרֵחַ הוּא הָאוֹר הַקָּטֹן אֲשֶׁר לַלַּ֫יְלָה. עָשָׂה גַם־אֶת־הַכּוֹכָבִים וְנָתַן אֹתָם בִּרְקִיעַ הַשָּׁמָ֫יִם.

בַּיּוֹם הַחֲמִישִׁי בָּרָא אֱלֹהִים אֶת־הַדָּגִים אֲשֶׁר בַּיַּמִּים וּבַנְּהָרוֹת וּבְכָל־הַמַּ֫יִם הָאֲחֵרִים אֲשֶׁר עַל־הָאָ֫רֶץ. עָשָׂה אֶת־הָעוֹף אֲשֶׁר עַל־הָאָ֫רֶץ וְעַל־פְּנֵי רְקִיעַ הַשָּׁמָ֫יִם.

בַּיּוֹם הַשִּׁשִּׁי עָשָׂה אֱלֹהִים אֶת־חַיַּת הָאָ֫רֶץ אֶת־כָּל־בְּהֵמָה וְאֶת־כָּל־רֶ֫מֶשׂ. יָצַר אֶת־הָאָדָם מֵהָאֲדָמָה בְּצֶ֫לֶם אֱלֹהִים. זָכָר וּנְקֵבָה בָּרָא אֹתָם.

בַּיּוֹם הַשְּׁבִיעִי שָׁבַת אֱלֹהִים מִכָּל־הַמְּלָאכָה אֲשֶׁר עָשָׂה.
(הַיּוֹם הַשְּׁבִיעִי אֲשֶׁר שָׁבַת אֱלֹהִים בּוֹ הוּא יוֹם הַשַּׁבָּת.)

(d) Write in Hebrew:

1. These are the names of the children of the people who came to Jerusalem.

2. He slew the evil sons of the prophet because they had transgressed the laws of the Lord.
3. He gave money to the first woman, but to the other he gave nothing.
4. Have you seen the stars of the heaven which God placed in the firmament?
5. Where are the tablets of stone which the prophet smashed?
6. The Lord is the salvation of all peoples.

רוּחַ – exterior breath

נֶפֶשׁ (soul) life giving breath
breath in throat

נְשָׁמָה – life breath – in nose
face.

own hand

lofties word some closer to the mind

1 Kings 17:17

1:27

וַיִּבְרָא אֱלֹהִים אֶת־הָאָדָם בְּצַלְמוֹ

בְּצֶלֶם אֱלֹהִים בָּרָא אֹתוֹ

זָכָר וּנְקֵבָה בָּרָא אֹתָם

④

2:7

וַיִּיצֶר יְהוָה אֱלֹהִים אֶת־הָאָדָם עָפָר ③ ② ①

* * * Sham [18]

נַפְשַׁ ② נָאֶצָר וַיִּפַּח ① [18]

הָאֲדָמָה

Amato

פִּי הָאָרֶץ

חַיִּים אַפָּיו נִשְׁמַת

*

וַיְהִי הָאָדָם לְנֶפֶשׁ חַיָּה

man became a living being

LESSON 19

81. The Independent (Subject) Form of the Personal Pronoun.

אֲנִי	*'ănî*	I	אֲנַ֫חְנוּ	*'ănáḥnû*	we
אָנֹכִי	*'ānōḵî*	I			
אַתָּה	*'attāh*	you (m. s.)	אַתֶּם	*'attem*	you (m. pl.)
אַתְּ	*'att*	you (f. s.)	אַתֶּן / אַתֵּ֫נָּה	*'atten, 'attḗnnāh*	you (f. pl.)
הוּא	*hû'*	he, it (m. s.)	הֵם / הֵ֫מָּה	*hēm, hḗmmāh*	they (m. pl.)
הִיא	*hî'*	she, it (f. s.)	הֵ֫נָּה	*hḗnnāh*	they (f. pl.)

Remarks: Both forms of the 1st pers. sing. pronoun are very frequent, with no clear difference in meaning or range. A rare alternate of the 2nd fem. sing. is attested: אַתִּי , with final *î*. נַ֫חְנוּ and אֲנוּ occur as very rare variants of אֲנַ֫חְנוּ. The 2nd pers. fem. pl. forms are too infrequent to determine preferences; אַתֶּן is vocalized אַתֵּן in some texts. In the Pentateuch the 3rd pers. fem. sing. is spelled הִוא, i.e. the masculine form is written but the feminine form is read; the reason for this is obscure. הֵם and הֵ֫מָּה are both frequent, but show slightly different distributions: הֵם dominates in the Pentateuch, while הֵ֫מָּה is commoner in Samuel and several of the poetic books.

The independent forms of the personal pronoun are used mainly as the subjects of sentences, and mostly of non-verbal sentences:

אֲנִי טוֹב	I am good.
אֲנִי הֹלֵךְ	I am walking.
אֲנִי אִישׁ	I am a man.
אֲנִי בַבַּ֫יִת	I am in the house.

They may be used in a variety of disjunctive ways and may stand before the verb in a verbal sentence to give emphasis to the subject. This emphasis need not be strong; it may be merely that the discourse has had a shift in subject, which would not entail any special emphasis in the English translation.

82. The Interrogative Pronouns.

(**a**) מִי *mî* who? Not inflected for number or gender.

מִי עָשָׂה אֶת־הַדָּבָר הַזֶּה Who did this thing?
מִי אַתְּ Who are you?
בַּת מִי אַתְּ Whose daughter are you?
לְמִי נָתַתָּ אֶת־הַכֶּסֶף To whom did you give the money?

(**b**) מַה *mah* what? Not inflected for number or gender.

The form of this word depends on the beginning of the following word, but in a less consistent way than was the case with the definite article or the conjunction *wə*-. The following simplified rule will cover most instances met:

(1) Before א ה ר use מָה *māh*.
(2) Before ח ע use מֶה *meh*.
(3) Elsewhere, before non-guttural consonants, use מַה *mah* plus the doubling of the first consonant of the following word.

Any of these forms may be followed by *maqqēp̄*.
Both מִי and מַה are sometimes followed by a demonstrative pronoun, better left untranslated, as in

מַה זֹּאת עָשִׂיתָ What have you done?
מִי זֶה הוּא Who is he?

83. The Prepositions אֶל, עַל, תַּחַת and אַחֲרֵי with Pronominal Suffixes.

These four prepositions, among others, take a set of pronominal endings quite different from those already studied.

1 c. s.	אֵלַי	*'ēlay*	עָלַי	*'ālay*
2 m. s.	אֵלֶיךָ	*'ēlẹ̄kā*	עָלֶיךָ	*'ālẹ̄kā*
2 f. s.	אֵלַיִךְ	*'ēláyik*	עָלַיִךְ	*'āláyik*
3 m. s.	אֵלָיו	*'ēlâw*	עָלָיו	*'ālâw*
3 f. s.	אֵלֶיהָ	*'ēlẹ̄hā*	עָלֶיהָ	*'ālẹ̄hā*
1 c. pl.	אֵלֵינוּ	*'ēlênû*	עָלֵינוּ	*'ālênû*
2 m. pl.	אֲלֵיכֶם	*'ălêkem*	עֲלֵיכֶם	*'ălêkem*
2 f. pl.	אֲלֵיכֶן	*'ălêken*	עֲלֵיכֶן	*'ălêken*
3 m. pl.	אֲלֵיהֶם	*'ălêhem*	עֲלֵיהֶם	*'ălêhem*
3 f. pl.	אֲלֵיהֶן	*'ălêhen*	עֲלֵיהֶן	*'ălêhen*

1 c. s.	תַּחְתַּי	*taḥtay*	אַחֲרַי	*'aḥăray*
2 m. s.	תַּחְתֶּיךָ	*taḥtêḵā*	אַחֲרֶיךָ	*'aḥărêḵā*
2 f. s.	תַּחְתַּ֫יִךְ	*taḥtáyiḵ*	אַחֲרַ֫יִךְ	*'aḥăráyiḵ*
3 m. s.	תַּחְתָּיו	*taḥtâw*	אַחֲרָיו	*'aḥărâw*
3 f. s.	תַּחְתֶּ֫יהָ	*taḥtêhā*	אַחֲרֶ֫יהָ	*'aḥărêhā*
1 c. pl.	תַּחְתֵּ֫ינוּ	*taḥtênû*	אַחֲרֵ֫ינוּ	*'aḥărênû*
2 m. pl.	תַּחְתֵּיכֶם	*taḥtêḵem*	אַחֲרֵיכֶם	*'aḥărêḵem*
2 f. pl.	תַּחְתֵּיכֶן	*taḥtêken*	אַחֲרֵיכֶן	*'aḥărêḵen*
3 m. pl.	תַּחְתֵּיהֶם	*taḥtêhem*	אַחֲרֵיהֶם	*'aḥărêhem*
3 f. pl.	תַּחְתֵּיהֶן	*taḥtêhen*	אַחֲרֵיהֶן	*'aḥărêhen*

84. Vocabulary 19.

NOUNS: נָחָשׁ *nāḥāš* (pl. *-îm*) snake, serpent
עֵ֫זֶר *'ḗzer* help, assistance
צֵלָע *ṣēlā'* (pl. *-îm* or *-ôṯ*) rib, side; the construct form is irregular: צֶ֫לַע *ṣéla'*
שִׁיר *šîr* (pl. *-îm*) song
בָּשָׂר *bāśār* flesh, meat; כָּל־בָּשָׂר *kol-bāśār* mankind
מָ֫וֶת *mā́weṯ* death

ADJECTIVES: אָרוּר *'ārûr* accursed
נֶחְמָד *neḥmāḏ* pleasant
חָכָם *ḥākām* wise; as noun: a wise man

VERBS: שָׁר *šār* to sing (cf. שִׁיר above)

OTHER: אֶתְמוֹל *'eṯmôl* or תְּמוֹל *təmôl* (adv.) yesterday
אַחֲרֵי *'aḥărê* / אַחַר *'aḥar* (prep.) after, behind; (conj.) + אֲשֶׁר after

Exercises:

(a) Translate:

(1) אֲנַ֫חְנוּ הֹלְכִים הָעִ֫ירָה
(2) הַאַתֶּם עֹלִים יְרוּשָׁלַ֫יְמָה
(3) לָ֫מָּה אַתָּה צֹעֵק
(4) מָה אַתְּ שֹׁתָה וּמָה אַתְּ אֹכֶ֫לֶת
(5) אֲנִי כֹתֵב אֶת־הַדְּבָרִים הָהֵם
(6) הַאַתֶּן גָּרוֹת בְּתוֹךְ הָעָם הַזֶּה
(7) מַה־יָּצַר אֱלֹהִים מֵהָאֲדָמָה
(8) מִי זָכָר וּמִי נְקֵבָה
(9) מַה־יּוֹם הַשַּׁבָּת
(10) אֲנַ֫חְנוּ צָמִים וְהֵם אֹכְלִים
(11) הָהֵם קֹרְאִים אֶל־הַנָּבִיא

(b) Give orally the Hebrew for the following:

1. What is the name of this man?
2. Who is the son of the rich woman?
3. What did he do on the sixth day?
4. What did he call the dry ground?

5. What did you do yesterday?
6. Did you see him yesterday?

(c) Translate:

(1) שָׁמְעוּ הַנְּעָרִים אֶל־קוֹל הַגִּבּוֹר כִּי הוּא הָיָה חָכָם מִכָּל־הָאֲנָשִׁים.
(2) יָפֶה וְנֶחְמָד הַגָּן אֲשֶׁר נָטַעְתָּ בַּמָּקוֹם הַזֶּה.
(3) אֲרוּרִים הָאֲנָשִׁים הָהֵם כִּי חָטְאוּ לַיהוה אֱלֹהִים.
(4) אָכַלְנוּ מִבְּשַׂר הַבָּקָר וּמִמֵּי הַנָּהָר שָׁתִינוּ.
(5) לָמָּה לֹא נָתַתָּ אֶת־חֲצִי הַבָּשָׂר לַדַּלִּים כִּי הָיָה לָהֶם רָעָב.
(6) אַיֵּה שַׂמְתָּ אֶת־הָאֶבֶן הָאַחֶרֶת.
(7) מִי שָׁבַר אֶת־הַכֵּלִים הָאֵלֶּה אֲשֶׁר יָצַרְתִּי אֶתְמוֹל.
(8) אֵלֶּה דִּבְרֵי הַשִּׁיר אֲשֶׁר שָׁר הַמֶּלֶךְ עַל־מוֹת הַגִּבּוֹרִים הַגְּדוֹלִים.
(9) אָכְלָה הַבְּהֵמָה מֵעֵשֶׂב הַשָּׂדֶה.
(10) מָה הַמְּלָאכָה אֲשֶׁר עֲשִׂיתֶם אֶתְמוֹל.
(11) יָשְׁבוּ שָׁם כָּל־יְמֵי חַיֵּי הַנָּבִיא.

(d) Write in Hebrew:

1. God made woman from the rib of the man.
2. Who are the enemies of this people?
3. These are the words concerning the life of the great king.
4. He made the fish of the seas and the birds of the heavens.
5. In whose image (lit. in the image of whom) did God fashion man?
6. What did he place in the firmament of the heavens on the fourth day?

(e) Reading: In the Garden of Eden

קָרָא הָאָדָם שֵׁמוֹת לְכָל־הַבְּהֵמָה וּלְעוֹף הַשָּׁמַיִם וּלְכָל־חַיַּת הַשָּׂדֶה וּלְאָדָם לֹא הָיָה עֵזֶר כְּנֶגְדּוֹ.[1] בָּנָה יהוה אֱלֹהִים אֶת־הַצֵּלָע אֲשֶׁר לָקַח מִן־הָאָדָם לְאִשָּׁה.[2] הָיְתָה הָאִשָּׁה אֶת־הָאִישׁ בַּגָּן.

הַנָּחָשׁ הָיָה עָרוּם[3] מִכָּל־חַיַּת הַשָּׂדֶה אֲשֶׁר עָשָׂה יהוה אֱלֹהִים. שָׁמְעָה הָאִשָּׁה אֶל־קוֹל הַנָּחָשׁ וּמִפְּרִי[4] הָעֵץ אֲשֶׁר בְּתוֹךְ הַגָּן אָכְלָה כִּי רָאֲתָה כִּי טוֹב וְנֶחְמָד הָעֵץ. אָכַל גַּם־הָאָדָם אֶת־הַפְּרִי אֲשֶׁר נָתְנָה לוֹ הָאִשָּׁה.

אָמַר אֱלֹהִים אֶל־הָאָדָם לֵאמֹר הֲמִן־הָעֵץ אֲשֶׁר בְּתוֹךְ־הַגָּן אָכָלְתָּ. אָמַר הָאָדָם לֵאמֹר הָאִשָּׁה אֲשֶׁר נָתַתָּ עִמָּדִי הִיא נָתְנָה לִי מִן־הָעֵץ. אָמַר יהוה אֱלֹהִים לָאִשָּׁה: מַה־זֹּאת עָשִׂית. וְהִיא אָמְרָה לוֹ אֶת־כָּל־אֲשֶׁר אָמַר הַנָּחָשׁ אֵלֶיהָ. אָמַר יהוה אֶל־הַנָּחָשׁ: כִּי עָשִׂיתָ זֹּאת אָרוּר אַתָּה מִכָּל־הַבְּהֵמָה וּמִכָּל־חַיַּת הַשָּׂדֶה. יָצְאוּ הָאָדָם וְהָאִשָּׁה מִן־הַגָּן כִּי חָטְאוּ חַטָּאת לַיהוה אֱלֹהִים.

Notes to Reading:

1. "suitable for him"
2. בָּנָה ... לְ in the sense "to build or make something into something else"
3. "crafty, shrewd"
4. Note the frequent partitive use of מִן: "some of the fruit"

Puel all-together
Suffixes + *constut*

The land of the King
myland
same

LESSON 20

85. The Noun with Pronominal Suffixes. *Singular*

Pronominal possession, such as "my book," "his king," etc., is indicated in Hebrew by suffixation of the pronominal element. The forms of the pronoun attached to the singular noun are more or less the same as those used with the prepositions already studied. The major difficulty lies, as usual, in the alterations of the nominal stem rather than in the endings. Here is the paradigm of סוּס (horse), the stem of which remains unchanged throughout:

[Singular]
A no change O | O

סוּסִי	sûsî	my horse	סוּסֵנוּ	sûsénû	our horse
סוּסְךָ	sûsəkā	your (m. s.) horse	סוּסְכֶם	sûsəkem	your (m. pl.) horse
סוּסֵךְ	sûsēk	your (f. s.) horse	סוּסְכֶן	sûsəken	your (f. pl.) horse
סוּסוֹ	sûsô	his horse	סוּסָם	sûsām	their (m. pl.) horse
סוּסָהּ	sûsāh	her horse	סוּסָן	sûsān	their (f. pl.) horse

Special note should be made of the following points:

(1) The 2nd pers. fem. sing. and the 1st pers. com. pl. always have -ē-. Recall that the prepositions are mixed in this regard, with ā in some cases (bāk, lāk, 'immāk) and ē in others (mimmēk).

(2) The ə of סוּסְךָ sûsəka should be thought of as properly part of the suffix (sûs + əkā) and not part of the noun stem. On the contrary, the ə of סוּסְכֶם sûsəkem and סוּסְכֶן sûsəken should be taken as part of the noun stem (sûsə + kem). The reason for this apparently arbitrary distinction will become clear below.

B.   Let us next look at these same suffixes on a noun like דָּבָר:

דְּבָרִי	*dəḇārî*	דְּבָרֵ֫נוּ	*dəḇārēnû*
דְּבָרְךָ	*dəḇārəḵā*	דְּבַרְכֶם	*dəḇarḵem*
דְּבָרֵךְ	*dəḇārēḵ*	דְּבַרְכֶן	*dəḇarḵen*
דְּבָרוֹ	*dəḇārô*	דְּבָרָם	*dəḇārām*
דְּבָרָהּ	*dəḇārāh*	דְּבָרָן	*dəḇārān*

The shift of the stress from the noun stem to the suffix has produced the same kind of reduction we encountered in the plural and construct forms, namely, *ā* and *ē* in propretonic (two before the main stress) open syllables are replaced by *ə*. The 2nd pers. forms are the only ones that require comment. As suggested above, the *ə* of *-əḵa* is taken as part of the suffix; this leaves the final stem syllable open (*də-ḇā-rə-ḵā*), and the noun stem before this suffix will accordingly have in most cases the same form as the 1st pers. sing. The endings of the 2nd pers. pl., however, are *-ḵem* and *-ḵen* (without *ə*); the final syllable of the noun stem is closed (*də-bar-ḵem*) and the vowel, if possible, is shortened. The noun stem before these two suffixes is most often identical to the construct form. To understand the stem changes, then, the suffixes must be considered as of two kinds: (1) those beginning with a consonant, often called "heavy" (*-ḵem* and *-ḵen*), and (2) those beginning with a vowel (all the rest), often called "light."

Feminine nouns in *-āh* have *-āṯ* before the light suffixes and *-aṯ* before the heavy suffixes:

תּוֹרָתִי	*tôrāṯî* my law etc.	תּוֹרָתֵ֫נוּ	*tôrāṯēnû*
תּוֹרָתְךָ	*tôrāṯəḵā*	תּוֹרַתְכֶם	*tôraṯḵem*
תּוֹרָתֵךְ	*tôrāṯēḵ*	תּוֹרַתְכֶן	*tôraṯḵen*
תּוֹרָתוֹ	*tôrāṯô*	תּוֹרָתָם	*tôrāṯām*
תּוֹרָתָהּ	*tôrāṯāh*	תּוֹרָתָן	*tôrāṯān*

Nouns with penultimate stress, like *méleḵ* and *náʻar*, and certain other irregular types will be treated separately in later lessons. The following table includes most of the remaining common types of singular nouns illustrated with light and heavy suffixes. Be sure that the phonetic changes noted in the comments are clear.

Sing. Abs.	w. suff. 1 s.	w. suff. 2 pl.	Comments
1. Monosyllabic nouns:			
יָד *yāḏ*	יָדִי *yāḏî*	יֶדְכֶם *yeḏḵem*	Irregular; we expect *yaḏḵem*.
עַם *ʻam*	עַמִּי *ʻammî*	עַמְּכֶם *ʻamməḵem*	Cf. pl. stem in *ʻammîm*.
אֵם *'ēm*	אִמִּי *'immî*	אִמְּכֶם *'imməḵem*	Cf. pl. stem in *'immôṯ*.
שִׁיר *šîr*	שִׁירִי *šîrî*	שִׁירְכֶם *šîrəḵem*	

אִישׁ	*'îš*	אִשִׁי	*'îšî*	אִישְׁכֶם	*'îšəḵem*	
עִיר	*'îr*	עִירִי	*'îrî*	עִירְכֶם	*'îrəḵem*	
קוֹל	*qôl*	קוֹלִי	*qôlî*	קוֹלְכֶם	*qôləḵem*	
יוֹם	*yôm*	יוֹמִי	*yômî*	יוֹמְכֶם	*yôməḵem*	
רֹאשׁ	*rō(')š*	רֹאשִׁי	*rō(')šî*	רֹאשְׁכֶם	*rō(')šəḵem*	
סוּס	*sûs*	סוּסִי	*sûsî*	סוּסְכֶם	*sûsəḵem*	

2. Nouns with *-áyi-* and *-ấwe-*:

בַּיִת	*báyiṯ*	בֵּיתִי	*bêṯî*	בֵּיתְכֶם	*bêṯəḵem*	Note *-áyi-* → *-ê-*.
מָוֶת	*mấweṯ*	מוֹתִי	*môṯî*	מוֹתְכֶם	*môṯəḵem*	Note *-ấwe-* → *-ô-*.

3. Dissyllabic nouns:

רְכוּשׁ	*rəḵûš*	רְכוּשִׁי	*rəḵûšî*	רְכוּשְׁכֶם	*rəḵûšəḵem*	
חֲלוֹם	*ḥălôm*	חֲלוֹמִי	*ḥălômî*	חֲלוֹמְכֶם	*ḥălôməḵem*	
דָּבָר	*dāḇār*	דְּבָרִי	*dəḇārî*	דְּבַרְכֶם	*dəḇarḵem*	Propretonic reduction.
זָקֵן	*zāqēn*	זְקֵנִי	*zəqēnî*	זְקַנְכֶם	*zəqanḵem*	Propretonic reduction.
נָבִיא	*nāḇî'*	נְבִיאִי	*nəḇî'î*	נְבִיאֲכֶם	*nəḇî'ăḵem*	Propr. red.; *ă* after gutt.
מָקוֹם	*māqôm*	מְקוֹמִי	*məqômî*	מְקוֹמְכֶם	*məqôməḵem*	Propr. red.
כּוֹכָב	*kôḵāḇ*	כּוֹכָבִי	*kôḵāḇî*	כּוֹכַבְכֶם	*kôḵaḇḵem*	
מִשְׁפָּט	*mišpāṭ*	מִשְׁפָּטִי	*mišpāṭî*	מִשְׁפַּטְכֶם	*mišpaṭḵem*	
אֹיֵב	*'ōyēḇ*	אֹיְבִי	*'ōyəḇî*	אֹיִבְכֶם	*'ōyiḇḵem*	
צַדִּיק	*ṣaddîq*	צַדִּיקִי	*ṣaddîqî*	צַדִּיקְכֶם	*ṣaddîqəḵem*	

4. Feminine nouns in *-āh*:

שָׁנָה	*šānāh*	שְׁנָתִי	*šənāṯî*	שְׁנַתְכֶם	*šənaṯḵem*	Propretonic reduction.
עֵצָה	*'ēṣāh*	עֲצָתִי	*'ăṣāṯî*	עֲצַתְכֶם	*'ăṣaṯḵem*	Propretonic reduction.
תּוֹרָה	*tôrāh*	תּוֹרָתִי	*tôrāṯî*	תּוֹרַתְכֶם	*tôraṯḵem*	
בִּינָה	*bînāh*	בִּינָתִי	*bînāṯî*	בִּינַתְכֶם	*bînaṯḵem*	
חֻקָּה	*ḥuqqāh*	חֻקָּתִי	*ḥuqqāṯî*	חֻקַּתְכֶם	*ḥuqqaṯḵem*	
גִּבְעָה	*giḇ'āh*	גִּבְעָתִי	*giḇ'āṯî*	גִּבְעַתְכֶם	*giḇ'aṯḵem*	
אֲדָמָה	*'ăḏāmāh*	אַדְמָתִי	*'aḏmāṯî*	אַדְמַתְכֶם	*'aḏmaṯḵem*	Propretonic reduction and Rule of Shewa.
בְּרָכָה	*bərāḵāh*	בִּרְכָתִי	*birḵāṯî*	בִּרְכַתְכֶם	*birḵaṯḵem*	Propretonic reduction and Rule of Shewa.
עֲבוֹדָה	*'ăḇôḏāh*	עֲבוֹדָתִי	*'ăḇôḏāṯî*	עֲבוֹדַתְכֶם	*'ăḇôḏaṯḵem*	
תְּפִלָּה	*təp̄illāh*	תְּפִלָּתִי	*təp̄illāṯî*	תְּפִלַּתְכֶם	*təp̄illaṯḵem*	

The suffixes attached to the plural noun have the forms given in the preceding lesson for אֶל and עַל. When a noun plural ends in *-îm*, these suffixes replace the plural ending. They should thus be thought of as a fusion of the plural ending and the pronominal element:

סוּסַי	*sûsay*	my horses etc.	סוּסֵינוּ	*sûsênû*
סוּסֶיךָ	*sûsệḵā*		סוּסֵיכֶם	*sûsêḵem*
סוּסַיִךְ	*sûsáyiḵ*		סוּסֵיכֶן	*sûsêḵen*
סוּסָיו	*sûsâw*		סוּסֵיהֶם	*sûsêhem*
סוּסֶיהָ	*sûsệhā*		סוּסֵיהֶן	*sûsêhen*
דְּבָרַי	*dəḇāray*		דְּבָרֵינוּ	*dəḇārênû*
דְּבָרֶיךָ	*dəḇārệḵā*		דִּבְרֵיכֶם	*diḇrêḵem*
דְּבָרַיִךְ	*dəḇāráyiḵ*		דִּבְרֵיכֶן	*diḇrêḵen*
דְּבָרָיו	*dəḇārâw*		דִּבְרֵיהֶם	*diḇrêhem*
דְּבָרֶיהָ	*dəḇārệhā*		דִּבְרֵיהֶן	*diḇrêhen*

Note the stress difference when the endings of the 2nd pers. and 3rd pers. pl. are added. Here a noun with two changeable vowels will undergo the double reduction met in the plural construct form.

Nouns with plurals in *-ôṯ* add these same suffixes, but directly to the plural ending without replacement.

תּוֹרוֹתַי	*tôrôṯay*	my laws etc.	תּוֹרוֹתֵינוּ	*tôrôṯênû*
תּוֹרוֹתֶיךָ	*tôrôṯệḵā*		תּוֹרוֹתֵיכֶם	*tôrôṯêḵem*
תּוֹרוֹתַיִךְ	*tôrôṯáyiḵ*		תּוֹרוֹתֵיכֶן	*tôrôṯêḵen*
תּוֹרוֹתָיו	*tôrôṯâw*		תּוֹרוֹתֵיהֶם	*tôrôṯêhem*
תּוֹרוֹתֶיהָ	*tôrôṯệhā*		תּוֹרוֹתֵיהֶן	*tôrôṯêhen*
בִּרְכוֹתַי	*birḵôṯay*		בִּרְכוֹתֵינוּ	*birḵôṯênû*
בִּרְכוֹתֶיךָ	*birḵôṯệḵā* etc.		בִּרְכוֹתֵיכֶם	*birḵôṯêḵem* etc.

The suffix *-êhem* is occasionally replaced by *-ām*, as in אֲבוֹתָם for אֲבוֹתֵיהֶם their fathers.

A complete list of noun types, under which all nouns used in this book are classified, will be found in Appendix A. When in doubt about the behavior of a noun stem before the pronominal suffixes the reader should locate the noun in the glossary and refer to the number indicated for the reference list.

The following selection of the most frequent plural types should prove adequate for most purposes:

abs. pl.		w. suff. 1 s.		w. suff. 2 m. pl.		
דָּמִים	*dāmîm*	דָּמַי	*dāmay*	דְּמֵיכֶם	*dəmêḵem*	blood
בָּנִים	*bānîm*	בָּנַי	*bānay*	בְּנֵיכֶם	*bənêḵem*	sons
יָמִים	*yāmîm*	יָמַי	*yāmay*	יְמֵיכֶם	*yəmêḵem*	days
שָׁנִים	*šānîm*	שָׁנַי	*šānay*	שְׁנֵיכֶם	*šənêḵem*	years

נָשִׁים	*nāšîm*	נָשַׁי	*nāšay*	נְשֵׁיכֶם	*nəšêḵem*	wives
עַמִּים	*ʻammîm*	עַמַּי	*ʻammay*	עַמֵּיכֶם	*ʻammêḵem*	peoples
חִצִּים	*ḥiṣṣîm*	חִצַּי	*ḥiṣṣay*	חִצֵּיכֶם	*ḥiṣṣêḵem*	arrows
שִׁירִים	*šîrîm*	שִׁירַי	*šîray*	שִׁירֵיכֶם	*šîrêḵem*	songs
סוּסִים	*sûsîm*	סוּסַי	*sûsay*	סוּסֵיכֶם	*sûsêḵem*	horses
עָרִים	*ʻārîm*	עָרַי	*ʻāray*	עָרֵיכֶם	*ʻārêḵem*	cities
בָּתִּים	*bāttîm*	בָּתַּי	*bāttay*	בָּתֵּיכֶם	*bāttêḵem*	houses
דְּבָרִים	*dəḇārîm*	דְּבָרַי	*dəḇāray*	דִּבְרֵיכֶם	*diḇrêḵem*	words
אֲנָשִׁים	*ʼănāšîm*	אֲנָשַׁי	*ʼănāšay*	אַנְשֵׁיכֶם	*ʼanšêḵem*	men
זְקֵנִים	*zəqēnîm*	זְקֵנַי	*zəqēnay*	זִקְנֵיכֶם	*ziqnêḵem*	elders
נְבִיאִים	*nəḇîʼîm*	נְבִיאַי	*nəḇîʼay*	נְבִיאֵיכֶם	*nəḇîʼêḵem*	prophets
מִשְׁפָּטִים	*mišpāṭîm*	מִשְׁפָּטַי	*mišpāṭay*	מִשְׁפְּטֵיכֶם	*mišpəṭêḵem*	judgements
אֹיְבִים	*ʼōyəḇîm*	אֹיְבַי	*ʼōyəḇay*	אֹיְבֵיכֶם	*ʼōyəḇêḵem*	enemies
בָּנוֹת	*bānôṯ*	בְּנוֹתַי	*bənôṯay*	בְּנוֹתֵיכֶם	*bənôṯêḵem*	daughters
תּוֹרוֹת	*tôrôṯ*	תּוֹרוֹתַי	*tôrôṯay*	תּוֹרוֹתֵיכֶם	*tôrôṯêḵem*	laws
מְלָכוֹת	*məlāḵôṯ*	מַלְכוֹתַי	*malḵôṯay*	מַלְכוֹתֵיכֶם	*malḵôṯêḵem*	queens
גְּבָעוֹת	*gəḇāʻôṯ*	גִּבְעוֹתַי	*giḇʻôṯay*	גִּבְעוֹתֵיכֶם	*giḇʻôṯêḵem*	hills
מִצְוֹת	*miṣwôṯ*	מִצְוֹתַי	*miṣwôṯay*	מִצְוֹתֵיכֶם	*miṣwôṯêḵem*	commandments
בְּרָכוֹת	*bərāḵôṯ*	בִּרְכוֹתַי	*birḵôṯay*	בִּרְכוֹתֵיכֶם	*birḵôṯêḵem*	blessings

Note that *-ôṯ* plurals have the same stem as the construct plural before all the suffixes, while *-îm* plurals have the construct plural stem only before *-ḵem*, *-ḵen*, *-hem*, and *-hen*.

A noun with a pronominal suffix is definite. Therefore

(1) a modifying adjective has the definite article:

סוּסִי הֶחָזָק my strong horse
דְּבָרָיו הַטּוֹבִים his good words

(2) when it is the direct object of a verb, the preposed *'eṯ* is required:

רָאִיתִי אֶת־סוּסוֹ I saw his horse.

But when the noun refers to a part of the body *'eṯ* is frequently omitted:

שָׁלַח יָדוֹ He put forth (lit. sent) his hand.

86. Vocabulary 20.

NOUNS: חוּץ *ḥûṣ* the outside; חוּצָה *ḥûṣāh* and הַחוּצָה *haḥûṣāh* to the outside, outwards; מִחוּץ לְ *miḥûs lə-* on the outside of

חַיִל *ḥáyil* (pl. חֲיָלִים) strength; army; wealth. Very frequent in the phrase גִּבּוֹר חַיִל a warrior, fighter

מִסְפָּר *mispār* number, enumeration; אֵין מִסְפָּר לְ (are) without number, innumerable; from this idiom מִסְפָּר comes to be used alone in the sense of "numerable," i.e. "few" — e.g. אַנְשֵׁי מִסְפָּר a few men (lit. men of number)

מֶרְכָּבָה *merkāḇāh* (pl. מַרְכָּבוֹת) chariot
סוּס *sûs* (pl. *-îm*) horse
פָּרָשׁ *pārāš* (constr. פָּרַשׁ ; pl. פָּרָשִׁים) horseman, rider
צָבָא *ṣāḇā'* (constr. צְבָא ; pl. *-ôṯ*) army, host (of soldiers, angels, celestial bodies). Also in the frequent designations of God as יהוה צְבָאוֹת or אֱלֹהֵי צְבָאוֹת
רוּחַ *rûᵃḥ* (pl. *-ôṯ*) breath, wind, spirit (f.)
צוּר *ṣûr* (pl. *-îm*) rock, cliff; fig. support, defence
קָהָל *qāhāl* assembly, congregation
קִיר *qîr* (pl. *-ôṯ*) wall

ADJECTIVES: חָדָשׁ *ḥāḏāš* new
חָזָק *ḥāzāq* strong, firm, hard

VERBS: רָכַב *rāḵaḇ* to ride

Exercises:

(a) Translate. Be sure you understand why the stems appear as they do.

1 קוֹלְךָ קֹלָהּ
2 זְקֵנֶיהָ זְקַנְכֶם
3 שְׁנָתֵנוּ שָׁנֵינוּ
4 שִׂמְחָתִי שִׂמְחוֹתַי
5 כִּסְאִי כִּסְאוֹ
6 כּוֹכָבֶיהָ כּוֹכְבֵיכֶם
7 אוֹרוֹ אוֹרָיו
8 אַדְמַתְכֶם אַדְמָתָם
9 זְהָבְךָ זְהַבְכֶם
10 חָכְמָתוֹ חָכְמָתָהּ
11 מִצְוֹתֶיךָ מִצְוָתֵךְ
12 יְשׁוּעָתֵנוּ יְשׁוּעַתְכֶם
13 נְהָרָהּ נְהָרוֹתֶיהָ
14 מוֹתִי מוֹתוֹ
15 שֻׁלְחָנְךָ שֻׁלְחָנֵךְ

(b) Give the Hebrew for the following orally:

1. your (m. s.) people, your tree, your birds
2. your (m. pl.) song, your advice, your (small) cattle
3. my places, my camps, my hunger, my commandments
4. my voice, my law, my messengers, my prophet
5. his firmament, his tablet, his throne, his palace
6. his words, his fish (pl.), his camels, his blessings
7. their (f. pl.) enemies, their warriors, their death

(c) Translate:

(1) אֵין מִסְפָּר לְחֵיל הָאֹיֵב. יֵשׁ לָהֶם גִּבּוֹרִים כְּמִסְפַּר כּוֹכְבֵי הַשָּׁמַיִם.
(2) אֵין כָּל־חָדָשׁ תַּחַת הַשָּׁמֶשׁ.

(3) קָם מֶ֫לֶךְ חָדָשׁ עַל־הָאָ֫רֶץ.

(4) חָזָק הוּא מִמֶּ֫נִּי.

(5) אָנֹכִי בָּא אֵלֶ֫יךָ בְּשֵׁם יהוה צְבָאוֹת.

(6) שָׁלַח הַמֶּ֫לֶךְ אֶת־סוּסָיו אֶת־מַרְכְּבוֹתָיו וְאֶת־פָּרָשָׁיו.

(7) שָׁרוּ אֶת־שִׁירָם הֶחָדָשׁ לַיהוה.

(8) רָאִ֫יתִי אֶת־הַשֶּׁ֫מֶשׁ וְאֶת־הַיָּרֵחַ וְאֶת־הַכּוֹכָבִים וְאֶת־כָּל־צְבָא הַשָּׁמָ֫יִם.

(9) אֵ֫לֶּה שְׁמוֹת כָּל־גִּבּוֹרֵי הַחַ֫יִל אֲשֶׁר נָפְלוּ בַּמִּלְחָמָה הַהִיא.

(10) בָּנוּ בַּ֫יִת חָדָשׁ בְּעִירָם.

(11) הָרָעָב הָיָה חָזָק בָּאָ֫רֶץ וְלֹא הָיָה לֶ֫חֶם לָעָם.

(12) אָמַר אֵלָיו הַמַּלְאָךְ: יהוה עִמְּךָ גִּבּוֹר הַחָ֫יִל.

(13) שָׁבְרָה רוּחַ גְּדוֹלָה וַחֲזָקָה אֶת־צוּרֵי הֶהָרִים.

(14) אֲרוּרִים אֲנָשֶׁ֫יךָ כִּי חָטְאוּ בְּעֵינֵי יהוה.

(15) רָאִ֫ינוּ אֶת־הָאֲנָשִׁים רֹכְבִים עַל־סוּסֵיהֶם.

(16) מִי גִּבּוֹר הַחַ֫יִל הָרֹכֵב עַל־הַמֶּרְכָּבָה.

(d) Write in Hebrew:

1. He took a rib from the man and from it he made a woman.
2. The song which they sang was pleasant and good.
3. The enemy is too strong for our warriors.
4. They slew the beast and ate (from) its flesh.
5. This is a new song about horsemen, chariots, and war.
6. There is no help for our congregation.
7. The wall of their great city fell.

LESSON 21

87. Stative Verbs.

In addition to verbs like those already studied there is a much smaller group with *ē* or *ō* in the final stem syllable of the perfect. The majority of these verbs are stative, i.e. they denote the state of the subject rather than describing an action, and are translated in English mainly by adjectives:

כָּבֵד	*kāḇēḏ*	he is heavy, was heavy, has become heavy
זָקֵן	*zāqēn*	he is old, was old, has become old

There are other verbs of the regular *a*-perfect type which belong to this category on the basis of their meaning and which, to judge from other inflectional forms they exhibit, originally belonged to the stative inflectional category as well, but in the course of time have been assimilated to the dominant *a*-perfect type because their meaning shifted from a purely stative one to an action, such as

קָרַב *qāraḇ* he is (was, has become) near; he approached.

Then too, there are verbs with perfects in *ē* which are treated as transitive active, with a direct object, such as

שָׂנֵא *śānē'* he hated.

Formally, there are *ē*-verbs in the uncomplicated triliteral class (כָּבֵד *kāḇēḏ*), in the class III-*Aleph* (מָלֵא *mālē'* to be full), and in the class of Hollow Verbs (מֵת *mēṯ* he died); there are *ō*-verbs in the uncomplicated triliteral class and in the hollow class (בֹּשׁ *bōš* he was ashamed). The inflection of these verbs is given below in parallel columns to facilitate comparison. The most frequent type, that of *kāḇēḏ*, is given in full as a model. The others are given with conjectured forms in parentheses since not all the forms are attested in BH.

to be heavy		to be afraid	
כָּבֵד	*kāḇēḏ*	יָרֵא	*yārē'*
כָּבְדָה	*kāḇədāh*	יָרְאָה	*yārə'āh*
כָּבַדְתָּ	*kāḇáḏtā*	יָרֵאתָ	*yārḗṯā*
כָּבַדְתְּ	*kāḇáḏt*	יָרֵאת	*yārēṯ*
כָּבַדְתִּי	*kāḇáḏtî*	יָרֵאתִי	*yārḗṯî*
כָּבְדוּ	*kāḇəḏû*	יָרְאוּ	*yārə'û*
כְּבַדְתֶּם	*kəḇaḏtem*	יְרֵאתֶם	*yərēṯem*
כְּבַדְתֶּן	*kəḇaḏten*	[יְרֵאתֶן	*yərēṯen*]
כָּבַדְנוּ	*kāḇáḏnû*	יָרֵאנוּ	*yārḗnû*

to die		to be able		to be ashamed	
מֵת	*mēṯ*	יָכֹל	*yāḵōl*	בֹּשׁ	*bōš*
מֵתָה	*mḗṯāh*	יָכְלָה	*yāḵəlāh*	בּוֹשָׁה	*bôšāh*
מַתָּה	*máttā*	יָכֹלְתָּ	*yāḵṓltā*	[בֹּשְׁתָּ	*bṓštā*]
[מַתְּ	*mátt*]	יָכֹלְתְּ	*yāḵṓlt*	בֹּשְׁתְּ	*bṓšt*
מַתִּי	*máttî*	יָכֹלְתִּי	*yāḵṓltî*	בֹּשְׁתִּי	*bṓštî*
מֵתוּ	*mḗṯû*	יָכְלוּ	*yāḵəlû*	בֹּשׁוּ	*bṓšû*
[מַתֶּם	*mattem*]	יְכָלְתֶּם	*yəḵoltem*	[בָּשְׁתֶּם	*boštem*]
[מַתֶּן	*matten*]	יְכָלְתֶּן	*yəḵolten*	[בָּשְׁתֶּן	*bošten*]
מַתְנוּ	*máṯnû*	יָכֹלְנוּ	*yāḵṓlnû*	בֹּשְׁנוּ	*bṓšnû*

Because of their non-action meaning stative verbs rarely appear in a participial form like כֹּתֵב. There is often an adjective associated with each of these verbs, frequently identical in stem form to the 3rd pers. masc. sing. of the perfect, with which it can be easily confused.

Verb			Adjective		
כָּבֵד	*kāḇēḏ*	to be heavy	כָּבֵד	*kāḇēḏ*	heavy
זָקֵן	*zāqēn*	to be old	זָקֵן	*zāqēn*	old
רָעֵב	*rā'ēḇ*	to be hungry	רָעֵב	*rā'ēḇ*	hungry
טָהֵר	*ṭāhēr*	to be pure	טָהוֹר	*ṭāhôr*	pure
קָרַב	*qāraḇ*	to be near	קָרֵב	*qārēḇ*	approaching; קָרוֹב *qārôḇ* near

מֵת	*mēṯ*	to die	מֵת	*mēṯ*	dead
מָלֵא	*mālē'*	to be full	מָלֵא	*mālē'*	full
קָטֹן	*qāṭōn*	to be small	קָטֹן	*qāṭōn*, קָטָן *qāṭān*	small

Only in the masc. sing. is there any formal ambiguity. An isolated sentence such as

זָקֵן הָאִישׁ

may be translated verbally, "The man grew old (was old, has become old)," or adjectivally, "The man (is) old." But when the subject is feminine or plural, the distinction is clear:

זָֽקְנָה הָאִשָּׁה	(verbal) The woman grew old.
זְקֵנָה הָאִשָּׁה	(adjectival) The woman is old.
זָֽקְנוּ הָאֲנָשִׁים	(verbal) The men became old.
זְקֵנִים הָאֲנָשִׁים	(adjectival) The men are old.

There is no ambiguity, of course, when the verbal and adjectival stems are different in form.

Both verbs and adjectives may, because of their meaning, be construed with מִן in a comparative sense:

כָּבֵד הָאִישׁ מִמֶּנִּי The man became more important than I.

Stative verbs from geminate roots (cf. §68) are inflected as follows in the third person:

תַּם	*tam*	תַּ֫מּוּ	*támmû*	to be complete, finished
תַּ֫מָּה	*támmāh*			

The remainder of the inflection is like that of סָבַב.

88. The Nouns אָב, אָח and פֶּה.

These three nouns are similar in having *-î* in the construct singular and before suffixes. Note also the variant form of the suffixes:

abs.	אָב	*'āḇ*	father	אָח	*'āḥ*	brother	פֶּה	*peh* mouth
constr.	אֲבִי	*'ăḇî*		אֲחִי	*'ăḥî*		פִּי	*pî*
	אָבִי	*'āḇî*		אָחִי	*'āḥî*		פִּי	*pî*
	אָבִ֫יךָ	*'āḇîḵā*		אָחִ֫יךָ	*'āḥîḵā*		פִּ֫יךָ	*pîḵā*
	אָבִיךְ	*'āḇîḵ*		אָחִיךְ	*'āḥîḵ*		פִּיךְ	*pîḵ*
	אָבִ֫יהוּ	*'āḇîhû* }		אָחִ֫יהוּ	*'āḥîhû* }		פִּ֫יהוּ	*pîhû* }
	אָבִיו	*'āḇîw* }		אָחִיו	*'āḥîw* }		פִּיו	*pîw* }
	אָבִ֫יהָ	*'āḇîhā*		אָחִ֫יהָ	*'āḥîhā*		פִּ֫יהָ	*pîhā*
	אָבִ֫ינוּ	*'āḇînû*		אָחִ֫ינוּ	*'āḥînû*		פִּ֫ינוּ	*pînû*

אֲבִיכֶם	*'ăḇîḵem*	אֲחִיכֶם	*'ăḥîḵem*	פִּיכֶם	*pîḵem*
אֲבִיכֶן	*'ăḇîḵen*	אֲחִיכֶן	*'ăḥîḵen*	פִּיכֶן	*pîḵen*
אֲבִיהֶם	*'ăḇîhem*	אֲחִיהֶם	*'ăḥîhem*	פִּיהֶם	*pîhem*
אֲבִיהֶן	*'ăḇîhen*	אֲחִיהֶן	*'ăḥîhen*	פִּיהֶן	*pîhen*

The plural forms of אָח are noteworthy:

abs.	אַחִים	*'aḥîm*	אַחַי	*'aḥay*	אַחֵינוּ	*'aḥênû*
constr.	אֲחֵי	*'ăḥê*	אַחֶיךָ	*'aḥêḵā*	אֲחֵיכֶם	*'ăḥêḵem*
			אַחַיִךְ	*'aḥáyiḵ*	אֲחֵיכֶן	*'ăḥêḵen*
			אֶחָיו	*'eḥâw*	אֲחֵיהֶם	*'ăḥêhem*
			אַחֶיהָ	*'aḥêhā*	אֲחֵיהֶן	*'ăḥêhen*

89. Vocabulary 21.

NOUNS: פֶּה *peh* (pl. rare) mouth. Note the prepositional phrases לְפִי, כְּפִי, and עַל־פִּי with the meaning "in proportion to, according to." These may be used as conjunctions with אֲשֶׁר: כְּפִי אֲשֶׁר "according as." Note the phrase פֶּה אֶחָד "unanimity"

יָד *yāḏ* (du. יָדַיִם; pl. *-ôṯ*) hand, side, (fig.) force (f.)

דָּם *dām* (pl. *-îm*) blood

כָּבוֹד *kāḇôḏ* glory, honor, wealth

מִנְחָה *minḥāh* (pl. מְנָחוֹת) offering

VERBS: כָּבֵד *kāḇēḏ* to be heavy, important, serious; adj. כָּבֵד *kāḇēḏ*.

מָלֵא *mālē'* to be full, filled, fulfilled. No preposition is required in Hebrew: מָלְאָה הָאָרֶץ רָעָה The earth was filled *with* wickedness. Adj. מָלֵא *mālē'*, full.

מֵת *mēṯ* to die; adj. מֵת *mēṯ* dead

בּשׁ *bôš* to be ashamed (no corresponding adj.)

שָׁמַר *šāmar* to watch, keep, observe

עָבַד *'āḇaḏ* to serve, work; till (the ground)

חָרָה *ḥārāh* to become angry, used impersonally with לְ: חָרָה לָאִישׁ The man became angry.

רָעָה *rā'āh* to tend (flocks), to shepherd (+ dir. obj. or + בְּ); to graze; רֹעֶה *rō'eh* a shepherd

PROPER NAMES: קַיִן *Qáyin* Cain

הֶבֶל *Hébel* Abel

חַוָּה *Ḥawwāh* Eve

Exercises:

(a) Translate and identify each of the following sentences as verbal or non-verbal. Which are ambiguous?

(1) אָבִיו מֵת

(2) הַכְּלִי מָלֵא דָם

(3) מָלֵא הַהֵיכָל כְּבוֹד יהוה

(4) מֵתוּ הָאֲנָשִׁים

(5) הָאִשָּׁה מֵתָה

(6) כָּבֵד הָרָעָב

(7) בֹּשְׁנוּ כִּי חָטָאנוּ

(8) הָאֲנָשִׁים מֵתִים

(9) כְּבֵדָה הָאֶבֶן מִמֶּנִּי

(10) הַמַּיִם מְלֵאוּ דָגִים

(11) מָלֵאנוּ שִׂמְחָה

(b) Translate:

(1) כְּפִי דְבָרֶיךָ

(2) מִפִּי אָבִיהוּ

(3) דִּבְרֵי פִּיךָ

(4) לְפִי דִבְרֵי אָחִיךָ

(5) כְּפִי אֲשֶׁר אָמַרְתָּ

(6) עִם־אֶחָיו

(7) מִתּוֹךְ אַחַי

(8) אֲחִי אָבִינוּ

(c) Give the Hebrew for the following orally:

1. the law of our fathers
2. the year of the death of our brother
3. The sky is full of clouds.
4. The field was full of chariots and horsemen.
5. The new vessel is full of water.
6. They were ashamed.
7. The heavens are in his hand.

(d) Write in Hebrew:

1. They served the just king many years.
2. The shepherd became angry because the men had killed his brother.
3. We have observed the law which you gave to our fathers and we have not transgressed the commandments which are therein.
4. The man's hand was full of blood.
5. The army sat outside the city, and inside the city the people cried out: "We are (as) dead (men)."
6. This matter is too serious for us.

(e) Reading: Cain and Abel.

יָדַע[1] הָאָדָם אֶת־חַוָּה. יָלְדָה חַוָּה בֵּן לְאִישָׁהּ וְקָרְאָה אֶת־שֵׁם הַיֶּלֶד קָיִן. יָלְדָה גַם־אֶת־הֶבֶל אֲחִי קָיִן. קַיִן הָיָה עֹבֵד אֶת־הָאֲדָמָה וְהֶבֶל הָיָה רֹעֵה צֹאן. הֵבִיא[2] קַיִן מִפְּרִי הָאֲדָמָה מִנְחָה[3] לַיהוה וְהֶבֶל הֵבִיא[2] גַם־הוּא מִבְּכֹרוֹת[4] צֹאנוֹ. הָיְתָה מִנְחַת הֶבֶל טוֹבָה בְּעֵינֵי יהוה וּמִנְחַת קַיִן לֹא הָיְתָה טוֹבָה. חָרָה לְקַיִן מְאֹד. הָרַג קַיִן אֶת־הֶבֶל אָחִיו בַּשָּׂדֶה.

אָמַר יהוה אֶל־קָיִן: אֵי הֶבֶל אָחִיךָ.

אָמַר קַיִן: לֹא יָדַעְתִּי. הֲשֹׁמֵר אָחִי אָנֹכִי.

אָמַר יהוה: מֶה־עָשִׂיתָ. קוֹל דְּמֵי אָחִיךָ צֹעֲקִים[5] אֵלַי מִן־הָאֲדָמָה, וְעַתָּה אָרוּר אַתָּה[6] מִן־הָאֲדָמָה אֲשֶׁר לָקְחָה אֶת־דְּמֵי אָחִיךָ מִיָּדֶךָ.

אָמַר קַיִן אֶל־יהוה: עֲוֹנִי[7] גָדוֹל מִמֶּנִּי.

Notes to the Reading.

1 in a sexual sense
2 "(he) brought"
3 supply "as"
4 "from the first-born of"
5 pl. by attraction to דְּמֵי ; the real subject is קוֹל .
6 repetition for emphasis: "and as for you, you are cursed (or banned)"
7 "my guilt"

LESSON 22

90. The Imperfect.

We come now to the second main inflection of the Hebrew verb, the imperfect. The imperfect, in contrast to the perfect, is primarily a prefixal conjugation, although suffixal elements are also present.

SING.	יִכְתֹּב	*yik̲tōb̲*	he will write
	תִּכְתֹּב	*tik̲tōb̲*	she will write
	תִּכְתֹּב	*tik̲tōb̲*	you (m. s.) will write
	תִּכְתְּבִי	*tik̲təb̲î*	you (f. s.) will write
	אֶכְתֹּב	*'ek̲tōb̲*	I shall write
PLURAL	יִכְתְּבוּ	*yik̲təb̲û*	they (m. pl.) will write*
	תִּכְתֹּבְנָה	*tik̲tṓb̲nāh*	they (f. pl.) will write
	תִּכְתְּבוּ	*tik̲təb̲û*	you (m. pl.) will write
	תִּכְתֹּבְנָה	*tik̲tṓb̲nāh*	you (f. pl.) will write
	נִכְתֹּב	*nik̲tōb̲*	we shall write

Note that the reduction of the stem vowel from *ō* to *ə* is regular before a suffixal element consisting of a vowel. In the plural there is a formal difference in the 3rd pers. pl. (contrast the perfect) between the two genders, but the fem. pl. of the 3rd and 2nd persons are formally the same.

We shall see that in the study of the imperfect it is necessary to make

* A not uncommon variant has the ending *-ûn* with or without the reduction of the stem vowel: יִכְתְּבוּן *yik̲təb̲ûn* or יִכְתֹּבוּן *yik̲tōb̲ûn* they will write.

more subdivisions among the root types than was necessary with the perfect. For example, verbs with נ , א , or י in first root position have forms which diverge considerably from those just given for the sound triliteral verb. Verbs introduced thus far in the vocabularies and inflected exactly like כָּתַב are the following:

יִזְכֹּר זָכַר	*yizkōr*	to remember	יִלְכֹּד לָכַד	*yilkōd̲*	to capture
יִכְרֹת כָּרַת	*yik̲rōt̲*	to cut	יִקְבֹּץ קָבַץ	*yiqbōṣ*	to gather
יִשְׁבֹּר שָׁבַר	*yišbōr*	to break	יִשְׁבֹּת שָׁבַת	*yišbōt̲*	to cease
יִשְׁמֹר שָׁמַר	*yišmōr*	to observe	יִכְתֹּב כָּתַב	*yik̲tōb̲*	to write

91. The Meaning of the Imperfect.

(a) Future: יִכְתֹּב he will write

(b) Habitual or customary action: יִכְתֹּב he writes (as a matter of custom), he used to write (as a matter of custom), or he will write (idem). In this usage tense is not explicit and must be gained from the context in which the verb occurs.

(c) Modal: the imperfect must frequently be translated in one of several modally modified ways, using the English equivalents "may, might, would, could, can, should." Precise directions for this translation are virtually impossible to give, since it is conditioned by the entire syntactic structure in which the verb is imbedded (conditional clause, final clause, etc.). The most important of these syntactic patterns will be considered in later lessons. In an isolated sentence the future or habitual translation is more appropriate.

With the exception of the future usage, where the action described may be quite specific, the imperfect is otherwise used to described action conceived by the speaker as general, non-specific, habitual, potential, or to some degree probable. It is not entirely accurate, however, to describe such action as incomplete or unfinished, as is often done (hence the name imperfect for the form).

The imperfect is negated with לֹא:

לֹא יִכְתֹּב he will not write, does not write, was not accustomed to write, wouldn't write etc.

In poetry the negative אַל־ is also found: אַל יִכְתֹּב.

92. The Dual.

Nouns denoting objects which naturally occur in pairs are frequently used in a dual form, the endings of which are *-áyim*, constr. *-ê*. When suffixes are added to the dual, the resulting form is the same as that of the *-îm* plurals: e.g. יָדַי my (two) hands. Following is a list of the nouns most often encountered in the dual, with a sampling of suffixed forms.

Sing.	*Dual Abs.*	*Constr.*	*With Suffixes*:	
יָד	יָדַיִם	יְדֵי	יָדָיו יָדַיִךְ יָדֶיךָ יָדַי	hand (f.)
רֶגֶל	רַגְלַיִם	רַגְלֵי	רַגְלֵיכֶם רַגְלֶיךָ רַגְלַי	foot (f.)
[מֹתֶן]	מָתְנַיִם	מָתְנֵי		loins (m.)
עַיִן	עֵינַיִם	עֵינֵי	עֵינָיו עֵינַיִךְ עֵינֶיךָ עֵינַי	eye (f.)
אֹזֶן	אָזְנַיִם	אָזְנֵי	אָזְנָיו אָזְנַיִךְ אָזְנֶיךָ אָזְנַי	ear (f.)
כָּנָף	כְּנָפַיִם	כַּנְפֵי	כְּנָפָיו כְּנָפַיִךְ כְּנָפֶיךָ	wing (f.)
קֶרֶן	קְרָנַיִם/קַרְנַיִם	קַרְנֵי	קְרָנָיו/קַרְנָיו	horn (f.)
שֵׁן	שִׁנַּיִם	שִׁנֵּי		teeth (f.) (two rows)

Also the following expressions of time and measurement:

יוֹמַיִם	two days (יוֹם)	עַרְבַּיִם	two evenings (עֶרֶב)
שְׁנָתַיִם	two years (שָׁנָה)	צָהֳרַיִם	noon (not *two* noons)
שְׁבוּעַיִם	two weeks (שָׁבוּעַ)	אַמָּתַיִם	two cubits (אַמָּה)
פַּעֲמַיִם	twice (פַּעַם once)		

Adjectives modifying the dual are found in the plural:

יָדַיִם חֲזָקוֹת (two) strong hands (rem. יָד is feminine)

93. Vocabulary 22.

NOUNS: אֹזֶן *'ōzen* (du. אָזְנַיִם ; pl. *-ôṯ*) ear (f.)
רֶגֶל *régel* (du. רַגְלַיִם ; pl. *-îm*) foot (f.); note the phrase בְּרַגְלֵי "belonging to, in the following of"
קֶבֶר *qéḇer* (pl. *-îm*) grave, sepulchre
עַיִן *'áyin* (du. עֵינַיִם ; pl. *-ôṯ*) eye; spring, well (f.)
צָהֳרַיִם *ṣohŏráyim* (du. only) noon
מִצְרַיִם *miṣráyim* Egypt; מִצְרַיְמָה *miṣráymāh* to Egypt.

VERBS: קָבַר *qāḇar* (imperf. יִקְבֹּר) to bury
מָכַר *māḵar* (imperf. יִמְכֹּר) to sell
שָׂרַף *śārap̄* (imperf. יִשְׂרֹף) to burn
דָּרַשׁ *dāraš* (imperf. יִדְרֹשׁ) to inquire, seek, require

ADVERBS: פַּעֲמַיִם *pa'ămáyim* twice

Exercise:

(a) Translate:

(1) יִשְׂרְפוּ אֶת־הַבַּיִת
(2) נִזְכֹּר אֹתוֹ
(3) יִקְבְּרוּ אֹתָנוּ
(4) תִּמְכֹּרְנָה אֹתָם
(5) אֶדְרֹשׁ כֶּסֶף מִמֶּנּוּ
(6) תִּשְׁמְרִי אֹתִי
(7) תִּמְכְּרוּ אֹתוֹ
(8) תִּכְרְתוּ בְרִית אִתָּנוּ
(9) תִּכְתְּבִי אֵלֵינוּ
(10) יִשְׂרֹף אֹתָהּ

(b) Give the Hebrew for the following orally:

1. My (two) ears have heard.
2. Your (m. s.) (two) eyes have seen.
3. He put forth (= sent) his (two) hands.
4. Her (two) eyes are beautiful.
5. I placed them under my (two) feet.
6. The people who belong to him (lit. are in his feet) are standing.

(c) Translate:

(1) הָיָה יהוה עִם־הַמֶּ֫לֶךְ כִּי אֶת־אֱלֹהֵי אָבִיו דָּרַשׁ וּבְמִצְוֹתָיו הָלַךְ.
(2) יִשְׂרְפוּ אֶת־הָאִשָּׁה הָרָעָה בָּאֵשׁ מִחוּץ לָעִיר.
(3) יִמְכְּרוּ אֶת־אֲחִיהֶם הַקָּטֹן בִּידֵי הָאֲנָשִׁים הַיֹּרְדִים מִצְרַ֫יְמָה.
(4) עָשָׂה הָאִישׁ אֶת־כָּל־מְלֶ֫אכֶת עֲבוֹדַת בֵּית יהוה.
(5) בַּיּוֹם הַהוּא תִּשְׁבֹּת מִכָּל־מְלָאכָה אֲשֶׁר אַתָּה עֹשֶׂה כִּי יוֹם הַשַּׁבָּת הוּא.
(6) אֶדְרשׁ אֶת־יהוה כָּל־יְמֵי חַיַּי כִּי צוּרִי וִישׁוּעָתִי הוּא.
(7) הֲתִמְכְּרוּ אֹתִי בְּיַד אֹיְבַי.
(8) מַה־מְּלֶ֫אכֶת אָחִיךָ.
(9) שָֽׂרְפוּ אֹיְבָיו אֶת־בֵּית יהוה וְאֶת־בֵּית הַמֶּ֫לֶךְ וְאֶת־כָּל־בַּ֫יִת גָּדוֹל שָֽׂרְפוּ בָאֵשׁ.
(10) לַיּוֹם הַהוּא קָֽרְאוּ שַׁבָּת כִּי בוֹ שָׁבַת יהוה מֵהַמְּלָאכָה.

(d) Write in Hebrew:

1. He will break them like a vessel.
2. I shall remember your (m. s.) commandments all the days of my life.
3. They will bury their father in the grave of his fathers.
4. What do my brothers require of (= from) me?
5. The evil sons did not (customarily) remember the words of their old father.
6. Will our enemies capture the city and its people?

LESSON 23

94. Imperfect in a.

Stative verbs of the types כָּבֵד and קָטֹן, as well as all verbs with a guttural consonant in second or third root position, have *a* instead of *ō* in the stem of the imperfect.

יִכְבַּד	*yiḵbaḏ*	יִשְׁמַע	*yišma'*	יִבְחַר	*yiḇḥar*
תִּכְבַּד	*tiḵbaḏ*	תִּשְׁמַע	*tišma'*	תִּבְחַר	*tiḇḥar*
תִּכְבַּד	*tiḵbaḏ*	תִּשְׁמַע	*tišma'*	תִּבְחַר	*tiḇḥar*
תִּכְבְּדִי	*tiḵbəḏî*	תִּשְׁמְעִי	*tišmə'î*	תִּבְחֲרִי	*tiḇḥărî*
אֶכְבַּד	*'eḵbaḏ*	אֶשְׁמַע	*'ešma'*	אֶבְחַר	*'eḇḥar*
יִכְבְּדוּ	*yiḵbəḏû*	יִשְׁמְעוּ	*yišmə'û*	יִבְחֲרוּ	*yiḇḥărû*
תִּכְבַּדְנָה	*tiḵbáḏnāh*	תִּשְׁמַעְנָה	*tišmá'nāh*	תִּבְחַרְנָה	*tiḇḥárnāh*
תִּכְבְּדוּ	*tiḵbəḏû*	תִּשְׁמְעוּ	*tišmə'û*	תִּבְחֲרוּ	*tiḇḥărû*
תִּכְבַּדְנָה	*tiḵbáḏnāh*	תִּשְׁמַעְנָה	*tišmá'nāh*	תִּבְחַרְנָה	*tiḇḥárnāh*
נִכְבַּד	*niḵbaḏ*	נִשְׁמַע	*nišma'*	נִבְחַר	*niḇḥar*

A small group of verbs, exactly like כָּתַב in the perfect, and which are neither stative nor with guttural root consonants, are nevertheless inflected with *a* in the imperfect. The most important of these are:

שָׁכַב	*šāḵaḇ*	יִשְׁכַּב	*yiškaḇ*	to lie down
לָמַד	*lāmaḏ*	יִלְמַד	*yilmaḏ*	to learn
רָכַב	*rāḵaḇ*	יִרְכַּב	*yirkaḇ*	to ride

95. Verbs III-Aleph: the Imperfect.

As in the perfect, the quiescence of **א** at the end of a syllable has led to the lengthening of the stem vowel:

יִקְרָא	*yiqrā'*	יִקְרְאוּ	*yiqrə'û*
תִּקְרָא	*tiqrā'*	תִּקְרֶ֫אנָה	*tiqré(')nāh*
תִּקְרָא	*tiqrā'*	תִּקְרְאוּ	*tiqrə'û*
תִּקְרְאִי	*tiqrə'î*	תִּקְרֶ֫אנָה	*tiqré(')nāh*
אֶקְרָא	*'eqrā'*	נִקְרָא	*niqrā'*

96. The Nouns בֵּן and שֵׁם.

These two nouns are similar in the singular before suffixes in that the stem vowel is reduced to *ə*:

בְּנִי	*bənî*	בְּנֵ֫נוּ	*bənḗnû*	שְׁמִי	*šəmî*	שְׁמֵ֫נוּ	*šəmḗnû*
בִּנְךָ	*binkā*	[בִּנְכֶם	*binkem*]	שִׁמְךָ	*šimkā*	שִׁמְכֶם	*šimkem*
בְּנֵךְ	*bənēk*	[בִּנְכֶן	*binken*]	שְׁמֵךְ	*šəmēk*	[שִׁמְכֶן	*šimken*]
בְּנוֹ	*bənô*	[בְּנָם	*bənām*]	שְׁמוֹ	*šəmô*	שְׁמָם	*šəmām*
בְּנָהּ	*bənāh*	[בְּנָן	*bənān*]	שְׁמָהּ	*šəmāh*	[שְׁמָן	*šəmān*]

Remember that the plural of בֵּן is בָּנִים and that of שֵׁם is שֵׁמוֹת. There is no irregularity in these plural forms before the pronominal suffixes.

97. Vocabulary 23.

NOUNS: רְכוּשׁ *rəkûš* moveable property
כְּנַעֲנִי *kəna'ănî* Canaanite (adj. or noun)
מִזְבֵּחַ *mizbēᵃḥ* (constr. מִזְבַּח; pl. *-ôt*) altar
קֶ֫דֶם *qédem* east; מִקֶּ֫דֶם לְ on the east of

VERBS: שָׁכַב *šākab* (יִשְׁכַּב) to lie down
בָּטַח *bāṭaḥ* (יִבְטַח) to trust, rely
גָּאַל *gā'al* (יִגְאַל) to redeem
שָׂמַח *śāmaḥ* (יִשְׂמַח) to rejoice

ADVERBS: אָז *'āz* then, at that time
מִשָּׁם *miššām* = מִן + שָׁם from there, thence
אָ֫נָה *'ā́nāh* whither? to what place?
מֵאַ֫יִן *mē'áyin* from where? whence?

Proper Names in the Reading:

אַבְרָם *'Abrām* an alternate form of אַבְרָהָם *'Abrāhām*
אוּר כַּשְׂדִּים *'Ur Kaśdîm* Ur of the Chaldaeans, a city in southern Mesopotamia
תֶּ֫רַח *Téraḥ* the father of Abraham

חָרָן *Ḥārān* (1) a son of Terah
(2) a city in northern Mesopotamia

שָׂרַי *Śāray* an alternate form of שָׂרָה *Śārāh*, the wife of Abraham

לוֹט *Lôṭ* Abram's nephew

כְּנַ֫עַן *Kənáʻan* Canaan, a designation of the area later comprising Palestine and Phoenicia.

שְׁכֶם *Šəḵem* Shechem, a city about 40 m. north of Jerusalem

בֵּית־אֵל *Bêṯ-'ēl* Bethel, a city about 15 m. north of Jerusalem

Exercises:

(a) Translate:

(1) אָ֫נָה תִשְׁלַח אֹתִי
(2) אֶל־מִי תִקְרְאוּ
(3) אֵיפֹה תִמְצֶ֫אנָה הַנָּשִׁים לֶ֫חֶם לִבְנֵיהֶן וְלִבְנוֹתֵיהֶן
(4) לָ֫מָּה תִשְׂמַ֫חְנָה בְּנוֹת יְרוּשָׁלַ֫ם
(5) יִבְחֲרוּ לָהֶם בְּמֶ֫לֶךְ
(6) לֹא אֶבְטַח בְּךָ וּבְדִבְרֵי פִ֫יךָ
(7) מִי יִגְאַל אֹתִי מִידֵי אֹיְבַי
(8) מֵאַ֫יִן בָּ֫אתָ בְּנִי
(9) מִקֶּ֫דֶם לָעִיר בָּ֫אתִי אָבִי
(10) אָ֫נָה אַתָּה הֹלֵךְ

(b) Give the Hebrew for the following orally:

1. our sons and our daughters
2. our little brother
3. our names
4. our father and our brother
5. our army and our horsemen
6. our congregation and our people
7. our blood
8. our offering; our offerings

(c) Translate:

(1) יִשְׂמַח כָּל־בֹּטֵחַ בְּךָ כִּי יְשׁוּעַת עַמֵּ֫נוּ אַתָּה.
(2) יִשְׁכְּבוּ הָאֲנָשִׁים שָׁם עַד־הַבֹּ֫קֶר.
(3) טוֹב הָאִישׁ אֲשֶׁר יִבְטַח בְּשֵׁם יהוה.
(4) יִכְבַּד שֵׁם הָאִישׁ הַזֶּה מִשֵּׁם כָּל־אִישׁ יֹשֵׁב בָּאָ֫רֶץ הַזֹּאת.
(5) לֹא יִשְׁמְעוּ בְּנֵי הַזָּקֵן אֶל־קוֹל אֲבִיהֶם כִּי רָעִים הֵם מְאֹד.
(6) יָדַ֫עְתִּי כִּי הוּא יִגְאַל אֶת־עַמִּי.
(7) שָׂמַ֫חְתִּי כַּאֲשֶׁר רָאִ֫יתִי אֶת־כָּל־אֲשֶׁר עָשָׂה לָ֫נוּ יהוה.
(8) מִי יִגְאַל אֹתָ֫נוּ מִיַּד הָאֹיְבִים.
(9) תִּכְבַּד הָעֲבוֹדָה עָלֶ֫יךָ וְתִצְעַק אֵלַי בְּקוֹל גָּדוֹל וְלֹא אֶשְׁמַע לְקוֹלְךָ.
(10) אֶבְחַר מִכֶּם אִישׁ לִי לְנָבִיא.

(d) Write in Hebrew:

1. His enemies will not find him in Egypt.
2. He will create a new heaven (m. pl.) and a new earth.
3. We have seen that his hands are strong and we know that our deliverance is in him.
4. His brothers went in-the-following-of the wicked king.

5. Our eyes have seen the glory of the Lord.
6. The stars of heaven were without number.
7. The heavens were filled with a great light.

(e) Reading: Abraham

יָשְׁבוּ אַבְרָם בֶּן־תֶּרַח וְלוֹט בֶּן־הָרָן בֶּן־תֶּרַח בְּאוּר כַּשְׂדִּים. יָצָא תֶּרַח אֶת־אַבְרָם בְּנוֹ וְאֶת־לוֹט בֶּן־בְּנוֹ וְאֶת־שָׂרַי אֵשֶׁת אַבְרָם לָלֶכֶת[1] אַרְצָה כְּנַעַן.[2] יָשְׁבוּ בְחָרָן וְשָׁם מֵת תֶּרַח אֲבִי אַבְרָם. הָלַךְ אַבְרָם מֵחָרָן כַּאֲשֶׁר אָמַר לוֹ יהוה. לָקַח אַבְרָם אֶת־שָׂרַי וְאֶת־לוֹט בֶּן־אָחִיו אִתּוֹ וְגַם־אֶת־כָּל־הָרְכוּשׁ אֲשֶׁר הָיָה לָהֶם בְּחָרָן.

בָּאוּ אַרְצָה כְּנַעַן. עָבַר אַבְרָם בָּאָרֶץ עַד־מְקוֹם שְׁכֶם. הָיָה הַכְּנַעֲנִי אָז בָּאָרֶץ. אָמַר יהוה אֶל־אַבְרָם בִּשְׁכֶם: אֲנִי נֹתֵן אֶת־הָאָרֶץ הַזֹּאת לְזַרְעֲךָ.[3] בָּנָה אַבְרָם מִזְבֵּחַ לַיהוה שָׁם.

נָסַע מִשָּׁם הָהָרָה[4] מִקֶּדֶם לְבֵית־אֵל. גַּם־שָׁם בָּנָה מִזְבֵּחַ וְקָרָא שָׁם בְּשֵׁם[5] יהוה.

Notes to the Reading:

1. "to go"
2. The directive *-āh* may, as here, appear on the first member of a construct chain: "toward the land of Canaan."
3. "your progeny"
4. See §58
5. קָרָא בְּ "to call *on* the name of"

LESSON 24

98. The Narrative Sequences.

Peculiar to Hebrew among the Semitic languages, the narrative sequences, as we shall call them, involve a complementary use of the two verbal conjugations, the perfect and the imperfect. The translation values given for the perfect (§44) and imperfect (§91) are in no way altered by the following discussion as long as the verb in question does not stand in one of the sequences we shall describe.

(a) The *Perfect + Imperfect* sequence is used mainly for past tense narration and is extremely common throughout the OT. The mark of this sequence is a special form of the conjunction, *wa* + doubling, joining the verbs in the sequence. Such sequences may continue for dozens of clauses, each of which, if it is a part of the main narrative, *begins with the verb* in the imperfect with the conjunction prefixed:

קָם הָאִישׁ וַיִּדְרשׁ...	The man arose and sought...
עָמַד וַיִּקְרָא...	He stood and called...

The subject need not be the same in each clause:

יָשַׁב אֵצֶל הַהֵיכָל וַיִּקְרְאוּ אֵלָיו הָעָם וַיִּשְׁמַע אֶל־קוֹלָם...	He sat down near the temple and the people called to him and he hearkened unto their voice...

The form of the conjunction is illustrated by

וַיִּכְתֹּב	*wayyiḵtōḇ*	and he wrote	וַיִּכְתְּבוּ	*wayyiḵtəḇû*	and they (m.) wrote
וַתִּכְתֹּב	*wattiḵtōḇ*	and she wrote, etc.	וַתִּכְתֹּבְנָה	*wattiḵtṓḇnāh*	and they (f.) wrote, etc.
וָאֶכְתֹּב	*wā'eḵtōḇ*	and I wrote	וַנִּכְתֹּב	*wanniḵtōḇ*	and we wrote

All past tense narrative in which each verb is temporally or logically consequent upon the preceding verb employs this sequence. The imperfects so used take on the tense value of the perfect and are said to be converted. The "perfect" value of the form *wa* + imperfect became so commonplace that it may be employed even without a perfect to begin the sequence:

וַיִּכְתֹּב הָאִישׁ אֶת־הַדְּבָרִים (And) The man wrote the words.

The conjunction used in the narrative sequences is called the *waw*-conversive or the *waw*-consecutive, after its function.

Because every Hebrew narrative, then, contains a series of clauses beginning with "and" plus a verb, it is obviously impossible to translate literally and have acceptable English. The student should make generous use of subordinating constructions, such as adverbial clauses and participial modifiers, in his English translation, taking care only to preserve the proper logical or temporal sequence of the Hebrew.

(b) The *Imperfect + Perfect* sequence is used with all the meanings of the imperfect, whether future or habitual/durative. The conjunction before the perfect is normal and pointed according to the regular rules given in §46.

יִמְצָא אֹתוֹ וְנָתַן לוֹ אֶת־הַכֶּסֶף He will find him and give him the money.
יִשְׂרְפוּ אֶת־הָעִיר וְלָכְדוּ אֶת־הָעָם They will burn the city and take captive the people.

If the first imperfect is used in the habitual sense, this is carried through the sequence:

יִקְרָא אֶל־הַנָּבִיא וְאָמַר: He used to call to the prophet and say:

Note that when a negative clause is inserted in the sequence, the verb is no longer first. The verb of the negative clause is then in its normal, non-converted form:

הָלְכוּ וַיִּקְרְאוּ אֵלָיו וְלֹא שָׁמַע They went and called to him but he did not hear.

After such an interruption the original sequence may be resumed by reverting to the converted forms. This and other complications will be dealt with below.

In the converted perfect the stress is usually shifted to the final syllable in the 1st pers. sing. and the 2nd pers. masc. sing.:

וְכָתַבְתִּי	*wəḵāṯaḇtî*	and I shall write
וְכָתַבְתָּ	*wəḵāṯaḇtā́*	and you shall write

Pointing (vocalization) is unaffected by this shift in stress, which does not take place in all instances, especially the corresponding forms of verbs III-*Aleph* and III-*Hē*.

99. The Segholates.

Nouns with penultimate stress, like מֶ֫לֶךְ, are collectively called segholates because of the presence of the vowel seghol (*e*) in one or both syllables. These nouns revert to an original one-syllable stem in the singular when a suffix is added: מַלְכִּי *malkî* my king. The vowel of the suffixal form, in this instance *a*, is the characteristic vowel of the word and also occurs in the construct plural. The four main types of segholate nouns are represented by

Absolute	Construct	w. suff.	pl. Abs./Constr.	Pl. w. suff.	
(a) מֶ֫לֶךְ	מֶ֫לֶךְ	מַלְכִּי מַלְכְּךָ מַלְכְּכֶם	מְלָכִים מַלְכֵי	מְלָכַי מַלְכֵיהֶם	king
(b) קֶ֫בֶר	קֶ֫בֶר	קִבְרִי קִבְרְךָ קִבְרְכֶם	קְבָרִים קִבְרֵי	קְבָרַי קִבְרֵיכֶם	grave
(c) סֵ֫פֶר	סֵ֫פֶר	סִפְרִי סִפְרְךָ סִפְרְכֶם	סְפָרִים סִפְרֵי	סְפָרַי סִפְרֵיכֶם	book
(d) קֹ֫דֶשׁ	קֹ֫דֶשׁ	קָדְשִׁי קָדְשְׁךָ קָדְשְׁכֶם	קֳדָשִׁים קָדְשֵׁי	קֳדָשַׁי קָדְשֵׁיכֶם	holiness

Nouns with *ē* have a characteristic *i*; those in *ō* have *o*. But those with *e* may have either *a* or *i*, which must accordingly be learned with each noun. Of the nouns of this type which have occurred thus far all have a characteristic *a* (thus צֶ֫לֶם, אֶ֫בֶן, עֶ֫בֶד, מֶ֫לֶךְ, כֶּ֫רֶם, יֶ֫לֶד, כֶּ֫סֶף, חֶ֫סֶד, דֶּ֫רֶךְ, אֶ֫רֶץ) except קֶ֫בֶר and צֶ֫דֶק, which have *i* (קִבְרִי, צִדְקִי).

100. Remarks on Some Prepositions.

(a) The noun פָּנִים (face), found only in the plural (with sing. meaning) forms a part of several important prepositions:

לִפְנֵי	*lip̄nê*	in the presence of, before
מִפְּנֵי	*mippənê*	from the presence of, from before, because of
מִלִּפְנֵי	*millip̄nê*	
עַל־פְּנֵי	*'al-pənê*	on the surface of, up against

When suffixes are added the noun behaves normally (cf. the plural בָּנִים with suffixes):

לְפָנַי	*ləpānay*	before me	לְפָנֵינוּ	*ləpānênû*	before us
לְפָנֶיךָ	*ləpānêkā*	before you etc.	לִפְנֵיכֶם	*lip̄nêkem*	before you etc.

(**b**) Many prepositions, like the preceding, are compounded from a simple preposition plus a noun. Suffixes are attached according to the rule applying to the noun type in question, e.g.

עַל־דְּבַר	*ʿal-dəḇar*	because of	עַל־דְּבָרִי	*ʿal-dəḇārî*	etc.
בְּתוֹךְ	*bəṯôḵ*	in the midst of	בְּתוֹכוֹ	*bəṯôḵô*	in the midst of it
בְּקֶרֶב	*bəqéreḇ*	in the midst of	בְּקִרְבּוֹ	*bəqirbô*	in the midst of it

(**c**) Even the simple prepositions may be compounded with one another for greater clarity. Most of these are self-explanatory:

מֵעַל	*mēʿal*	from on	מִתַּחַת	*mittáḥaṯ*	from under
מֵאֵת	*mēʾēṯ*	from with, from at			

101. Vocabulary 24.

NOUNS: קֶרֶב *qéreḇ* (w. suff. קִרְבִּי) inward part, midst; בְּקֶרֶב (prep.) within

חֶסֶד *ḥéseḏ* (w. suff. חַסְדִּי; pl. *-îm*) kindness; a proper act

מִדְבָּר *miḏbār* (no pl.) wilderness, desert; land for grazing, not necessarily uninhabited, but away from the larger urban centers

פָּנִים *pānîm* (pl. only) face

מַרְאֶה *marʾeh* appearance

מִצְרִי *miṣrî* (pl. מִצְרִים) Egyptian (adj. or noun); fem. מִצְרִית

מִקְנֶה *miqneh* cattle, property

חֲמוֹר *ḥămôr* (pl. *-îm*) donkey, he-ass

אָתוֹן *ʾāṯôn* (pl. *-ôṯ*) donkey, she-ass (f.)

מַגֵּפָה *maggēpāh* (pl. *-ôṯ*) stroke, plague, affliction

נֶגֶב *négeḇ* the Negev, the southern part of Palestine; הַנֶּגְבָּה toward the Negev

אָחוֹת *ʾāḥôṯ* (pl. abs. not attested) sister

כֹּהֵן *kōhēn* (pl. *-îm*) priest

VERBS: נָגַף *nāgap̄* to strike, plague, afflict

OTHER: לְמַעַן *ləmáʿan* (conj.) so that, in order that (+ the imperfect)

בַּעֲבוּר *baʿăḇûr* (prep.) for the sake of, because of

עַל־דְּבַר *ʿal-dəḇar* (prep.) for the sake of, because of

Exercises:

(a) Translate:

(1) הָרְגוּ אֶת־מַלְכֵּנוּ וַיִּקְבְּרוּ אֹתוֹ מִחוּץ לָעִיר.

(2) נָגַף אֱלֹהִים אֶת־הָעָם וַיִּשְׁלַח אֶת־נְבִיאוֹ אֲלֵיהֶם.

(3) לָֽכְדוּ אֶת־רְכוּשׁוֹ וַיִּשְׂרְפוּ אֶת־בֵּיתוֹ.
(4) יִקְרְאוּ אֵלָיו וְלָֽקְחוּ אֹתוֹ וּמָֽכְרוּ אֹתוֹ בִּידֵי אֹיְבָיו.
(5) בָּ֫אוּ אֶל־בֵּית הָאִשָּׁה וַיִּשְׁכְּבוּ שָׁם כָּל־הַלָּ֫יְלָה.
(6) שָׁמַ֫עְנוּ אֶל־קוֹלְךָ וַנִּבְטַח בִּדְבָרֶ֫יךָ.
(7) קָ֫מוּ וַיִּבְחֲרוּ לָהֶם מֶ֫לֶךְ.
(8) בַּצָּהֳרַ֫יִם נִרְכַּב עַל־חֲמוֹרֵ֫ינוּ הַמִּדְבָּ֫רָה.
(9) תִּקְרְאוּ בְקוֹל גָּדוֹל וְסַבּוֹתֶם אֶת־הָעִיר פַּעֲמַ֫יִם.
(10) הֲלֹא שָׁמַ֫עְתָּ בְּאָזְנֶ֫יךָ אֶת־דִּבְרֵי נְבִיאִי.
(11) טוֹבָה אַרְצֵ֫נוּ וְטוֹבִים כְּרָמֵ֫ינוּ.
(12) נִשְׁבֹּר אֶת־צַלְמוֹ.
(13) זָכַ֫רְנוּ אֶת־חַסְדְּךָ אֲשֶׁר עָשִׂיתָ אִתָּ֫נוּ.
(14) הָאֵ֫לֶּה יְלָדֶ֫יךָ.

(b) Give the Hebrew for the following orally:

1. his book, his books
2. his money, his gold
3. his ear, his foot
4. his way, his ways
5. his enemy, his judges

Repeat the preceding with "her" for "his."

(c) Translate:

(1) נָגַף יהוה אֶת־מֶ֫לֶךְ מִצְרַ֫יִם כִּי עָשָׂה אֶת־הָרָע בְּעֵינָיו.
(2) בָּעֶ֫רֶב שָׂ֫מָה הָאִשָּׁה לֶ֫חֶם וּמַ֫יִם לְפָנָיו עַל־הַשֻּׁלְחָן וְלֹא אָכַל וְלֹא שָׁתָה.
(3) בָּ֫אוּ הַבַּ֫יְתָה וַיִּשְׁכְּבוּ שָׁם עַד־הַבֹּ֫קֶר.
(4) לָֽקְחוּ הַכֹּהֲנִים אֶת־הַבָּשָׂר מֵעַל־הַמִּזְבֵּחַ.
(5) קָֽבְרוּ אֶת־אֲבִיהֶם בַּמָּקוֹם אֲשֶׁר קָבַר בּוֹ אֲבִיהֶם אֶת־אָבִ֫יהוּ.
(6) הָֽלְכוּ הָאֲנָשִׁים אֶל־הַהֵיכָל וַיִּקְרְאוּ בְקוֹל גָּדוֹל לִפְנֵי הַמֶּ֫לֶךְ וַיִּשְׁמַע הַמֶּ֫לֶךְ אֶל־קוֹלָם.
(7) אֶשְׁלַח אֶת־הַכֶּ֫סֶף אֵלֶ֫יךָ בַּעֲבוּר בִּנְךָ הַקָּטֹן.
(8) עָשִׂיתָ חֶ֫סֶד עִמָּ֫נוּ וְעִם־עַמֵּ֫נוּ.
(9) לָֽקְחוּ אֶת־אֲחִיהֶם וַיִּמְכְּרוּ אֹתוֹ בִּידֵי הָאֲנָשִׁים הַיֹּרְדִים מִצְרַ֫יְמָה וְהֵם מָֽכְרוּ אֹתוֹ בִּידֵי הַמִּצְרִים.
(10) רָכַב עַל־חֲמוֹרוֹ הָעִ֫ירָה וּבְנוֹ אִתּוֹ.

(d) Write in Hebrew:

1. She became angry and smashed all the vessels which were in the house.
2. He went outside the city to the fields and sought his brothers there and he found them near the river.
3. You have not observed the treaty which you made with us.
4. We are fasting that God may hear our words and give (seq. with "hear") us deliverance from the enemy.
5. He will capture the nations with a strong hand and the wise men of the earth will come in order to hear his words.

(e) Reading: Abraham in Egypt

יָרַד אַבְרָהָם מִצְרַ֫יְמָה כִּי כָבֵד הָרָעָב בְּאֶרֶץ כְּנָ֫עַן. אָמַר אַבְרָהָם לְשָׂרָה כַּאֲשֶׁר בָּ֫אוּ מִצְרַ֫יְמָה:
יָדַ֫עְתִּי כִּי אִשָּׁה יְפַת מַרְאֶה[1] אַתְּ. יִרְאוּ[2] אֹתָךְ הַמִּצְרִים וְאָמְרוּ אֵשֶׁת הָאִישׁ הַהוּא זֹאת וְהָרְגוּ
אֹתִי וְלָקְחוּ אֹתָךְ. אִמְרִי[3] כִּי אֲחוֹתִי אַתְּ לְמַ֫עַן יִיטַב לִי[4] בַּעֲבוּרֵךְ.

כֵּן עָשְׂתָה שָׂרָה כַּאֲשֶׁר בָּ֫אוּ מִצְרַ֫יְמָה. אָמְרָ֫ה אֶל־הַמִּצְרִים כַּדְּבָרִים אֲשֶׁר אָמַר לָהּ אִישָׁהּ.
לָקְחוּ הַמִּצְרִים אֹתָהּ אֶל־בֵּית פַּרְעֹה וְלֹא הָרְגוּ אֶת־אַבְרָהָם. נָתְנוּ לְאַבְרָהָם צֹאן וּבָקָר
וַחֲמוֹרִים וַעֲבָדִים וּשְׁפָחוֹת וַאֲתוֹנוֹת וּגְמַלִּים בַּעֲבוּר שָׂרָה.

נָגַף יהוה אֶת־פַּרְעֹה מַגֵּפוֹת גְּדֹלוֹת[5] עַל־דְּבַר שָׂרָה אֵשֶׁת אַבְרָהָם וַיִּקְרָא פַּרְעֹה לְאַבְרָהָם
לֵאמֹר: מַה־זֹּאת עָשִׂיתָ לִּי. לָמָּה אָמַרְתָּ אֲחוֹתִי הִיא. וַיְשַׁלַּח[6] אֶת־אַבְרָהָם וְאֶת־שָׂרָה וְאֶת־
כָּל־אֲשֶׁר לוֹ. עָלָה אַבְרָהָם מִמִּצְרַ֫יִם הוּא וְשָׂרָה וְכָל־אֲשֶׁר־לוֹ וְלוֹט עִמּוֹ הַנֶּ֫גְבָּה. אַבְרָהָם
כָּבֵד מְאֹד בַּמִּקְנֶה בַּכֶּ֫סֶף וּבַזָּהָב.

Notes to the Reading:

1. Note the adj. in construct with a specifying noun: "beautiful in appearance."
2. "They will see". Note the beginning of an imperfect sequence.
3. "Say" (imperative)
4. "it will go well for me"
5. Note the use, very frequent in Semitic, of a cognate object, "to strike a striking." It is best to translate: "struck the Pharaoh *with* great plagues"
6. "and he expelled"

LESSON 25

102. The Imperative.

The basic stem of the Imperative is always closely related to that of the imperfect and can be deduced from it.

IMPERFECT		IMPERATIVE	
יִכְתֹּב	*yiktōḇ*	כְּתֹב	*kətōḇ*
יִשְׁכַּב	*yiškaḇ*	שְׁכַב	*šəkaḇ*
יִשְׁמַע	*yišmaʻ*	שְׁמַע	*šəmaʻ*
יִבְחַר	*yiḇḥar*	בְּחַר	*bəḥar*
יִקְרָא	*yiqrā'*	קְרָא	*qərā'*

The endings of the imperative are the same as those on the second person forms of the imperfect:

	SING.	PLURAL
masc.	—	*-û*
fem.	*-î*	*-nāh*

But when *-î* and *-û* are added to the stem, it is altered as follows:

כְּתֹב	*kətōḇ*	כִּתְבִי	*kiṯḇî*	כִּתְבוּ	*kiṯḇû*	כְּתֹבְנָה	*kətṓḇnāh*
שְׁכַב	*šəkaḇ*	שִׁכְבִי	*šikḇî*	שִׁכְבוּ	*šikḇû*	שְׁכַבְנָה	*šəkáḇnāh*
שְׁמַע	*šəmaʻ*	שִׁמְעִי	*šimʻî*	שִׁמְעוּ	*šimʻû*	שְׁמַעְנָה	*šəmáʻnāh*
בְּחַר	*bəḥar*	בַּחֲרִי	*baḥărî*(!)	בַּחֲרוּ	*baḥărû*(!)	בְּחַרְנָה	*bəḥárnāh*
קְרָא	*qərā'*	קִרְאִי	*qir'î*	קִרְאוּ	*qir'û*	קְרֶאנָה	*qəré(')nāh*(!)

The suffix *-āh* occurs frequently on the masc. sing. imperative with no striking modification of meaning. The stem usually appears with *o* before this suffix:

כָּתְבָה *koṯḇāh* write! (m. s.)

but verbs with *a*-imperfects often have *i*, as in שִׁכְבָה lie down; שִׁלְחָה send. The negative of the imperative is

(a) אַל + imperfect: for immediate, specific commands, such as "Don't go!" "Don't wait!" etc.

(b) לֹא + imperfect: for durative, non-specific: "you shall not do such-and-such (ever)."

The particle נָא may follow any imperative form, as in

קְרָא נָא   שִׁמְעִי נָא   שְׁלַח נָא

It is frequently joined with *maqqēp̄*, which means that the verb surrenders its primary stress to the particle. The pattern of שְׁמֹר נָא with *maqqēp̄* is

שְׁמָר־נָא *šəmor-nā'*

נָא may also be added to the אַל of the negative imperative:

אַל־נָא תִשְׁלַח Do not send!

This particle may be translated as "please", "I pray," or the like, but is most often best ignored.

103. Verbs I-guttural: Imperfect and Imperative.

The two basic types of imperfect for this class are represented by

(a)	עָבַד	imperf. יַעֲבֹד *ya'ăḇōḏ*	imperat.	עֲבֹד	*'ăḇōḏ*	to serve
(b)	חָזַק	יֶחֱזַק *yeḥĕzaq*		חֲזַק	*ḥăzaq*	to be strong

Verbs with *ō*-imperfects have *a* in the prefixal element (except in 1st pers. sing.); those with *a*-imperfects have *e*. The imperfect in each of these main types has developed a secondary vowel after (under) the guttural root consonant. In inflection the *Rule of Shewa* must apply: thus, expected יַעֲמְדוּ *ya'ămədu* becomes יַעַמְדוּ *ya'amdû* (note retention of *ḏ*), and similarly elsewhere:

יַעֲמֹד	*ya'ămōḏ*	יַעַמְדוּ	*ya'amdû*	יֶחֱזַק	*yeḥĕzaq*	יֶחֶזְקוּ	*yeḥezqû*
תַּעֲמֹד	*ta'ămōḏ*	תַּעֲמֹ֫דְנָה	*ta'ămṓḏnāh*	תֶּחֱזַק	*teḥĕzaq*	תֶּחֱזַ֫קְנָה	*teḥĕzáqnāh*
תַּעֲמֹד	*ta'ămōḏ*	תַּעַמְדוּ	*ta'amdû*	תֶּחֱזַק	*teḥĕzaq*	תֶּחֶזְקוּ	*teḥezqû*
תַּעַמְדִי	*ta'amdî*	תַּעֲמֹ֫דְנָה	*ta'ămṓḏnāh*	תֶּחֶזְקִי	*teḥezqî*	תֶּחֱזַ֫קְנָה	*teḥĕzáqnāh*
אֶעֱמֹד	*'e'ĕmōḏ*	נַעֲמֹד	*na'ămōḏ*	אֶחֱזַק	*'eḥĕzaq*	נֶחֱזַק	*neḥĕzaq*

The inflection of the imperative offers no special problems:

עֲבֹד	*ʿăḇōḏ*	עִבְדִי	*ʿiḇḏî*	עִבְדוּ	*ʿiḇḏû*	עֲבֹ֫דְנָה	*ʿăḇṓḏnāh*
חֲזַק	*ḥăzaq*	חִזְקִי	*ḥizqî*	חִזְקוּ	*ḥizqû*	חֲזַ֫קְנָה	*ḥăzáqnāh*

There are several verbs where no secondary vowel is present. The inflection, except for the vowel of the preformative, follows the regular pattern of יִכְתֹּב or יִכְבַּד. E.g.

יַחְשֹׁב	*yaḥšōḇ*	he will reckon	תֶּהְדַּר	*tehdar*	you will honor
יַחְשְׁבוּ	*yaḥšəḇû*	they will reckon			

The verb חָטָא, both I-gutt. and III-*Aleph*, combines the features of each type:

יֶחֱטָא	*yeḥĕṭā'*	יֶחֶטְאוּ	*yeḥeṭ'û*
תֶּחֱטָא	*teḥĕṭā'*	תֶּחֱטֶ֫אנָה	*teḥĕṭé(')nāh*
תֶּחֱטָא	*teḥĕṭā'*	תֶּחֶטְאוּ	*teḥeṭ'û*
תֶּחֶטְאִי	*teḥeṭ'î*	תֶּחֱטֶ֫אנָה	*teḥĕṭé(')nāh*
אֶחֱטָא	*'eḥĕṭā'*	נֶחֱטָא	*neḥĕṭā'*

104. The Segholates (cont.)

The main types of segholates are slightly modified when gutturals occur in the root.

(a) Guttural in first position: only the type סֵ֫פֶר is affected; the characteristic vowel is *e* instead of *i*:

עֵדֶר	עֵ֫דֶר	עֶדְרִי עֶדְרְךָ עֶדְרְכֶם	עֲדָרִים עֶדְרֵי	עֲדָרַי	flock

(b) Guttural in second root position:

נַעַר	נַ֫עַר	נַעֲרִי נַעַרְךָ נַעַרְכֶם	נְעָרִים נַעֲרֵי	נְעָרַי נַעֲרֵיכֶם	young man
תֹּאַר	תֹּ֫אַר	תָּאֳרִי תָּאָרְךָ תָּאָרְכֶם	no pl. attested		form

Note especially the forms before the heavy suffixes and *-kā*.

(c) Guttural in third root position:

זֶרַע	זֶ֫רַע	זַרְעִי זַרְעֲךָ זַרְעֲכֶם	זְרָעִים זַרְעֵי	זְרָעַי זַרְעֵיכֶם	seed
זֶבַח	זֶ֫בַח	זִבְחִי זִבְחֲךָ זִבְחֲכֶם	זְבָחִים זִבְחֵי	זְבָחַי זִבְחֵיכֶם	sacrifice

אֹ֫רַח	אֹרַח	אָרְחִי	אֳרָחוֹת	אָרְחוֹתַי	way (f.)
		אָרְחֲךָ	אָרְחוֹת	אָרְחוֹתֵיכֶם	
		אָרְחֲכֶם			

105. Vocabulary 25.

NOUNS: צָרָה *ṣārāh* (pl. *-ôṯ*) distress, trouble [The first vowel is not reduced; constr. צָרַת]

גְּבֶ֫רֶת *gəḇéreṯ* (pl. not attested) mistress, lady [With suff. גְּבִרְתִּי]

עֵ֫דֶר *ʿēḏer* (pl. *-îm*) flock, herd

זֶ֫רַע *zéraʿ* (pl. *-îm*) seed, offspring, progeny, descendants

VERBS: יָרֵא *yārēʾ* (§ 87) to be afraid (of מִן or מִפְּנֵי or with simple object construction)

בָּרַח *bāraḥ* (יִבְרַח) to flee

שָׁב *šāḇ* to return, go or come back

הָרָה *hārāh* to conceive, become pregnant

OTHER: אֵי־מִזֶּה *ʾê-mizzeh* (adv.) from what place? from where? [May also be used adjectivally: אֵי־מִזֶּה עִיר from what city?]

פֶּן־ *pen-* (conj.) lest, so that not [followed by imperfect]

כַּיּוֹם *kayyôm* today, this day

נָא *nā(ʾ)* particle used after imperatives, cohortatives, and jussives; see §§ 102, 136.

Exercises:

(a) Translate:

(1) דִּרְשׁוּ אֶת־יהוה
(2) קְבֹץ נָא אֶת־הָעָם לְפָנַי
(3) לִכְדוּ אֶת־עָרֵי אֹיְבֵיכֶם
(4) קְבֹר אֹתָם שָׁם
(5) רִכְבִי אֵלָיו עַל־סוּסֵךְ
(6) אַל־תִּכְרְתוּ בְרִית אִתָּם
(7) אַל־תַּעֲזֹב אֶת־כֹּהֲנֶ֫יךָ
(8) עִבְרוּ אֶת־הַשָּׂדֶה עַד־הַכֶּ֫רֶם
(9) דְּרָשׁ־נָא כַיּוֹם אֶת־דְּבַר יהוה
(10) לֹא תַעַבְרוּ אֶת־מִצְוֹת יהוה
(11) אַל־תַּעַמְדִי שָׁם
(12) שְׁלַ֫חְנָה אֶת־הָאָתוֹן אֵלַי

(b) Give the Hebrew for the following orally:

1. Where is your sister?
2. Do not sin against the Lord.
3. Do not kill those men.
4. Send me my books.
5. Gather the priests and the prophets.
6. Do not cross over toward the Negev.
7. Sell these vessels.
8. Redeem your servant.
9. Send your maidservants to me.
10. Abandon your sinful ways.

(c) Translate:

(1) תִּשְׁמַע אֶל־קוֹלִי וְשַׁבְתָּ הָעִירָה פֶּן־יַהַרְגוּ אֹתְךָ אֹיְבֶיךָ.
(2) תַּעַמְדוּ פֹּה וּשְׁמַעְתֶּם אֶת־דִּבְרֵי גְּבִרְתְּכֶם.
(3) נַעֲבֹר אֶת־הָאָרֶץ וְיָשַׁבְנוּ עַד־הַיָּם.
(4) אֶרְכַּב הָהָרָה וְהָרַגְתִּי אֶת־הָאֲנָשִׁים הָרָעִים הַיֹּשְׁבִים שָׁם.
(5) תִּקְבֹּץ אֶת־הָעָם לְפָנַי וְאָמַרְתִּי אֲלֵיהֶם כַּדְּבָרִים הָאֵלֶּה.
(6) שָׁכַב הַנַּעַר וַיַּחֲלֹם חֲלוֹם.
(7) לֹא תֶחֶטְאוּ לַיהוה אֱלֹהֵיכֶם.

(d) Write in Hebrew:

1. I shall abandon my flock and return to the city.
2. They will serve the Lord all the days of their life.
3. I shall ride to the city on my donkey so that I may sell this property.
4. Because of you they will kill me and take my possessions for them (selves).
5. His sister is beautiful in appearance.
6. At that time the Canaanite dwelt east of this place up to the desert.
7. He is an old man and has no offspring.
8. I am afraid of you and your men.

(e) Reading: Sarah and Hagar

שָׂרָה אֵשֶׁת אַבְרָהָם לֹא יָלְדָה לוֹ וְלָהּ שִׁפְחָה מִצְרִית וּשְׁמָהּ הָגָר.[1] נָתְנָה שָׂרָה אֶת־הָגָר שִׁפְחָתָהּ הַמִּצְרִית לְאַבְרָהָם אִישָׁהּ לוֹ לְאִשָּׁה.[2] בָּא אַבְרָהָם אֶל־הָגָר[3] וְהִיא הָרְתָה.
חָרָה לְשָׂרָה כַּאֲשֶׁר רָאֲתָה כִּי הָרְתָה הָגָר.
יָרְאָה הָגָר מִפְּנֵי שָׂרָה גְּבִרְתָּהּ וַתִּבְרַח הַמִּדְבָּרָה.
מַלְאַךְ יהוה מָצָא אֹתָהּ עַל־עֵין הַמַּיִם[4] בַּמִּדְבָּר. אָמַר הַמַּלְאָךְ: הָגָר שִׁפְחַת שָׂרָה אֵי־מִזֶּה בָּאת וְאָנָה אַתְּ הֹלֶכֶת. אָמְרָה הָגָר: מִפְּנֵי שָׂרָה גְּבִרְתִּי אָנֹכִי בֹּרַחַת. אָמַר לָהּ מַלְאַךְ יהוה: שׁוּבִי[5] אֶל־גְּבִרְתֵּךְ. אֶת־שֵׁם הַבֵּן אֲשֶׁר אַתְּ יֹלֶדֶת תִּקְרְאִי יִשְׁמָעֵאל כִּי שָׁמַע יהוה אֶל־צָרָתֵךְ. שָׁבָה הָגָר אֶל־שָׂרָה גְּבִרְתָּהּ. יָלְדָה הָגָר לְאַבְרָהָם בֵּן וַיִּקְרָא אַבְרָהָם שֵׁם בְּנוֹ אֲשֶׁר יָלְדָה הָגָר יִשְׁמָעֵאל.

Notes to the Reading:

1. Note the series of non-verbal (thus non-consecutive) clauses taking their tense value from the general context.
2. The לוֹ is superfluous in translation, since it simply reinforces לְאַבְרָהָם. It could, however, be retained thus: "...(to act) as a wife for him."
3. בָּא אֶל־ is frequently used of a man approaching a woman for sexual intercourse.
4. The definite article frequently appears where the narrator has a specific object in mind even though it has not been previously mentioned.
5. "return" (imperative)

LESSON 26

106. The Jussive and Cohortative.

The imperfect, with or without slight modifications, may be used in an indirect imperative sense in all persons. For example,

יִשְׁלַח	he will send or let him send
תִּשְׁלַח	you will send or may you send
אֶשְׁלַח	I shall send or let me send

The third person forms, singular and plural, so used are called jussives. In the verbs we have studied thus far these are identical in form to the imperfect. The first person indirect imperative, called the cohortative, is usually marked with a suffix *-āh* on the imperfect:

אֶשְׁלַח	*'ešlaḥ*	I shall send	נִשְׁלַח	*nišlaḥ*	we shall send
אֶשְׁלְחָה	*'ešləḥāh*	let me send	נִשְׁלְחָה	*nišləḥāh*	let us send

Note that the vowel of the imperfect is regularly reduced to *ə* before this suffix. The cohortative form may replace the normal imperfect in a perfect + imperfect narrative sequence with no apparent change in meaning.

107. Sequences involving the Imperative, Jussive, and Cohortative.

In meaning these three form a single paradigm: jussive = 3rd pers., imperative = 2nd pers., cohortative = 1st person. The sequences involving one are usually similar to or the same as sequences involving the others. The following three sequences are the most frequently met:

(a) *Imperative + Imperative.* Imperatives may be simply listed one after the other and joined by the required regular form of the conjunction:

שְׁמַע... וּשְׁלַח... וַעֲמֹד... hear . . . and send . . . and stand . . .

Verbs joined in this way may or may not be consequent on one another.

(b) *Imperative + Perfect.* Explicit consecution is expressed by this sequence, which is the analog of the *imperfect + perfect* narrative sequence:

שְׁמַע וְשָׁלַחְתָּ וְעָמַדְתָּ hear . . . and (then) send . . . and (then) stand . . .

(c) Imperative Jussive Cohortative	+	Imperfect Cohortative	This important sequence

usually has a special translation value, which should be carefully noted. The second clause expresses a purpose or result (Eng. "so that"):

שְׁמַע ... וְאֶשְׁלַח Hear . . . so that I may send
כְּתֹב ... וְאֶשְׁמַע Write . . . so that I may hear
נֵלְכָה... וְיִמְצָא Let us go . . . so that he may find

Note that the conjunction *wə-* has its normal, non-converting form here.

108. Verbs I-Aleph: Imperfect and Related Forms.

Verbs I-*Aleph* fall into two groups in the imperfect:

(a) Five verbs regularly have *ō* in the preformative, with quiescence of the א:

אָכַל	*'āḵal*	יֹאכַל	*yō(')ḵal*	to eat
אָמַר	*'āmar*	יֹאמַר	*yō(')mar*	to say
אָבַד	*'āḇaḏ*	יֹאבַד	*yō(')ḇaḏ*	to perish

The other two, אָפָה (to bake) and אָבָה (to be willing), will be treated under verbs III-*Hē*. The inflection of the imperfect is otherwise normal:

יֹאכַל	*yōḵal*	יֹאכְלוּ	*yōḵəlû*
תֹּאכַל	*tōḵal*	תֹּאכַלְנָה	*tōḵálnāh*
תֹּאכַל	*tōḵal*	תֹּאכְלוּ	*tōḵəlû*
תֹּאכְלִי	*tōḵəlî*	תֹּאכַלְנָה	*tōḵálnāh*
אֹכַל	*'ōḵal*	נֹאכַל	*nōḵal*

Note that only one א is written in the 1st pers. sing.

When preceded by *waw*-conversive the forms יֹאמַר, תֹּאמַר, and נֹאמַר are replaced by forms with *e*, with a retraction of the stress:

וַיֹּאמֶר *wayyṓmer* and he said
וַתֹּאמֶר *wattṓmer* and she (or you, m. s.) said
וַנֹּאמֶר *wannṓmer* and we said

But when these stand at the end of a clause, immediately preceding what is said, the regular form with *a* may be used. Contrast:

וַיֹּאמֶר אֵלָיו: שְׁמַע And he said to him: "Hear."
וַיֹּאמַר: שְׁמַע And he said: "Hear."

(**b**) Other verbs I-*Aleph* resemble the class of I-guttural verbs, e.g.

אָסַר *'āsar* יֶאֱסֹר *ye'ĕsōr* (or יֶאְסֹר *ye'sōr*) to bind

but with *e* in the preformative regardless of the stem vowel. In the inflection the *e* is replaced by *a* when the *Rule of Shewa* is applied. This is in contrast to verbs I-guttural with *e*:

יֶחֱזַק *yeḥĕzaq* but יֶאֱסֹר *ye'ĕsōr*
יֶחֶזְקוּ *yeḥezqû* יַאַסְרוּ *ya'asrú*

A few verbs show conflicting forms due to mixing. Among the most frequently met are אָחַז (to hold), which has imperfect יֶאֱחֹז and יֹאחֵז (note the anomalous *ē*), and אָהַב (to love), whose attested forms are

יֶאֱהַב	*ye'ĕhab̲*		——
תֶּאֱהַב	*te'ĕhab̲*		——
תֶּאֱהַב	*te'ĕhab̲*	תְּאֶהָבוּ	read *tēhăb̲û*
	——		——
אֱהַב אֹהַב	*'ēhab̲* or *'ōhab̲*		——

All regular verbs I-*Aleph*, whether of type (a) or (b), have the same forms in the imperative:

אֱסֹר *'ĕsōr* אִסְרִי *'isrî* אִסְרוּ *'isrû* אֱסֹרְנָה *'ĕsṓrnāh*
אֱמֹר *'ĕmōr* אִמְרִי *'imrî* אִמְרוּ *'imrû* אֱמֹרְנָה *'ĕmṓrnāh*

109. Vocabulary 26.

NOUNS: בֶּגֶד *béged̲* (בִּגְדִי; pl. *-îm*) garment
שַׁעַר *šá'ar* (pl. *-îm*) gate (of a city or large building); also refers to the space inside the city gate used by officials for public meetings.
אָסִיר *'āsîr* (pl. *-îm*) prisoner

VERBS: אָבַד *'āb̲ad̲* (יֹאבַד) to perish, be destroyed, die
אָחַז *'āḥaz* (יֹאחֵז or יֶאֱחֹז) to seize, grasp, take hold of
אָסַר *'āsar* (יֶאֱסֹר) to bind, fetter, take prisoner
אָהַב *'āhab̲* (יֶאֱהַב) to love

קָרַע *qāra‘* (יִקְרַע) to tear, rend
פָּתַח *pāṯaḥ* (יִפְתַּח) to open
סָגַר *sāḡar* (יִסְגֹּר) to close
גָּדַל *gāḏal* (יִגְדַּל) to be/become great; to grow up, reach maturity

Exercises:

(a) Translate:

(1) אֶשְׁכְּבָה
(2) נִדְרְשָׁה
(3) יִזְכֹּר
(4) נִשְׁבְּרָה
(5) אֶשְׁבְּתָה
(6) פְּתַח . . . וּסְגֹר
(7) קִרְאִי . . . וְכִתְבִי
(8) שִׁבְרוּ . . . וּשְׂרַפְתֶּם
(9) שִׁמְעוּ . . . וִידַעְתֶּם
(10) עִמְדוּ . . . וְתִשְׁמְעוּ

(b) Give the Hebrew for the following orally:

1. Let us make a treaty.
2. Let him eat the fish.
3. Let us seize their property.
4. Let him smash the tablets of stone.
5. Let us chose a king for ourselves (= us).
6. May his name become great throughout (= in) the entire land.
7. May they hear our words and know that we are good men.
8. Let me hear the words which the prophet spoke.

(c) Translate:

(1) קָרַע הַמֶּלֶךְ אֶת־בְּגָדָיו וַיֹּאמַר: תֹּאבַד הָעִיר וְאָסְרוּ הָאֹיְבִים אֶת־עַמָּהּ.
(2) בַּבֹּקֶר יִפְתְּחוּ אֶת־שַׁעַר הָעִיר וּבְרַחְתֶּם עִמָּנוּ הָהָרָה פֶּן־יִמְצְאוּ אֶתְכֶם וְהָרְגוּ אֶתְכֶם.
(3) נִשְׁלְחָה אֹתוֹ אֶל־הַמִּלְחָמָה וְיֹאבַד שָׁם.
(4) אִסְרוּ אֹתָם וּלְקַחְתֶּם אֹתָם הַחוּצָה.
(5) סִגְרוּ אֶת־שַׁעַר הָעִיר כִּי בָא הָאֹיֵב עָלֵינוּ.
(6) תֶּאֱהַב אֶת־אִמְּךָ וְאֶת־אָבִיךָ.
(7) יֹאבְדוּ הָרְשָׁעִים כִּי אֵין לָהֶם יְשׁוּעָה.
(8) וַיֹּאמֶר הַנָּבִיא: יוֹם רַע בָּא וְנָגַף אֱלֹהִים אֶתְכֶם וְאֶת־בְּנֵיכֶם כִּי לֹא שְׁמַעְתֶּם אֶל־קוֹל נְבִיאָו וְלֹא שְׁמַרְתֶּם אֶת־מִצְוֹת הַתּוֹרָה.
(9) אֱחֹז אֶת־חֲצִי הַכֶּסֶף לְךָ וְנָתַתָּ לִי אֶת־הַחֲצִי הָאַחֵר.
(10) לֹא תֹאכְלוּ מֵעוֹף הַשָּׁמָיִם.
(11) נֹאמְרָה אֶל־הַמֶּלֶךְ כִּי הָעֲבוֹדָה קָשָׁה מִמֶּנּוּ.
(12) יֹאחֲזוּ אֶת־הַזָּהָב וְנָתְנוּ אֹתוֹ לַאֲחֵרִים.

(d) Write in Hebrew:

1. Let us close the gates and remain (= dwell) in the city until morning.
2. Why did he break the tablets and say that we had sinned against the Lord?

3. Remember (m. pl.) these words lest you sin.
4. He loved the woman because she was beautiful in appearance.
5. They will tear their garments on that day, for the enemy will bind them and they will go with the other prisoners to another country and dwell there (for) many years.

LESSON 27

110. Temporal Clauses and Phrases.

Within a narrative sequence temporal modifiers are very frequently placed before the clause they modify and are introduced by *waw-conversive* + a form of the verb הָיָה. In the past tense narrative this is uniformly וַיְהִי *wayhî* (יְהִי *yəhî* is the imperfect form of הָיָה) and in the future (or habitual/durative) narrative it is וְהָיָה *wəhāyāh*. The temporal clause is then followed by the expected sequential form of the main narrative. Study the following examples carefully (all are to be taken as though imbedded in a narrative):

וַיְהִי בַבֹּקֶר וַיִּשְׁלַח...	and in the morning he sent...
וַיְהִי אַחַרֵי הַדְּבָרִים הָאֵלֶּה וַיִּשְׁמַע קוֹל..	and after these things he heard a voice...
וַיְהִי כַאֲשֶׁר רָאָה אֹתָם וַיִּקְרָא...	and when he saw them he cried out...
וְהָיָה כִּי תִשְׁמְעוּ אֶת־הַדְּבָרִים הָאֵלֶּה תִּזְכַּרְתֶּם...	and whenever you hear these words you shall remember...
וְהָיָה בַבֹּקֶר וִיצָאתֶם...	and in the morning you shall go forth...

Note that either a clause or prepositional phrase may occur in this position. The most frequently met conjunctions are כַּאֲשֶׁר (when, as), and כִּי (when, whenever). Time words such as עֵת , שָׁנָה , יוֹם (time) are common with the preposition בְּ ; also מִקֵּץ (at the end of, after). Rarely a participial clause occurs, requiring the English conjunction "while":

וַיְהִי הֵם עֹמְדִים שָׁם וַיִּשְׁמְעוּ...	and while they were standing there they heard...

111. Feminine Nouns Ending in -eṯ and -aṯ.

These behave much like the segholates in the singular before suffixes:

גְּבֶ֫רֶת	גְּבִרְתִּי	my mistress (cf. קִבְרִי)
דַּ֫עַת	דַּעְתִּי	my knowledge
בֹּ֫שֶׁת	בָּשְׁתִּי	my shame (cf. קָדְשִׁי)

Also to this group belong those nouns with penultimately stressed construct forms:

מִלְחָמָה	constr.	מִלְחֶ֫מֶת	w. suff.	מִלְחַמְתִּי.
מְלָאכָה		מְלֶ֫אכֶת		מְלַאכְתִּי

The noun בַּת has the stem בִּת *bitt-* before the suffixes: בִּתִּי my daughter.

אִשָּׁה before suffixes appears as אִשְׁתִּי, אִשְׁתְּךָ, etc.

The attachment of suffixes to the plural stems of these nouns offers no special problems.

112. Nouns of the Type פְּרִי.

It is difficult to formulate rules for this small class of nouns other than to note the replacement of the final long vowel by a consonantal *y* before the light suffixes in the singular. There is, however, much inconsistency, especially in the formation of the plural. The following sampling of attested forms should enable the student to identify nouns of this class when encountered:

כְּלִי	w. suff.	כֶּלְיְךָ	כְּלִיכֶם	(pl.	כֵּלִים)	vessel
פְּרִי		פִּרְיִי	פֶּרְיְךָ	פִּרְיוֹ פִּרְיֵךְ	פִּרְיָהּ	fruit
			פֶּרְיְכֶם	פִּרְיהֶם	פִּרְיָן	
עֳנִי		עָנְיִי		עָנְיֵךְ		affliction
חֳלִי		חָלְיוֹ		(pl.	חֳלָיִים)	sickness
חֲצִי		חֶצְיוֹ	חֶצְיָם			

113. Vocabulary 27.

NOUNS: זְקוּנִים *zəqûnîm* (pl. only in sing. sense) old age

בְּאֵר *bə'ēr* (pl. *-ôṯ*; constr. pl. בְּאֱרוֹת) well, pit

עֳנִי *'ŏnî* (see § 112) affliction

VERBS: פָּקַד *pāqaḏ* (יִפְקֹד) to keep one's promise or commitment toward; to pay attention to; to visit; to appoint; to pass in review, muster

רַע *ra'* to be bad (cf. תַּם, § 87; root is רעע)

תָּעָה *tā'āh* to wander about lost

כָּלָה *kālāh* to be depleted, finished, at an end

ADVERB: אַחֲרֵי כֵן *'aḥărê kēn* afterwards, after this

Note the idiom: מַה־לָּךְ What is the matter with you?

Exercises:

(a) Translate:

(1) וַיְהִי אַחֲרֵי מוֹת אָבִינוּ וַנַּעֲזֹב אֶת־עִירֵנוּ וַנַּעֲבֹר אֶת־הָאָרֶץ עַד־הַיָּם.
(2) וְהָיָה בַּיּוֹם הַבָּא וְשָׁלַחְתִּי אֶת־אֲמָתִי אֵלֶיךָ כַּאֲשֶׁר אָמַרְתָּ לִי אֶתְמוֹל.
(3) וַיְהִי בַבֹּקֶר וַיִּשְׁכַּח אֶת־הַחֲלוֹם אֲשֶׁר חָלַם בַּלָּיְלָה.
(4) וְהָיָה כִּי תִשְׁמְעוּ אֶל־קוֹל נְבִיאַי וְזָכַרְתִּי אֶתְכֶם כִּי עַמִּי אַתֶּם.
(5) וַיְהִי כַּאֲשֶׁר רָאָה אֶת־בְּאֵר הַמַּיִם וַיִּשְׂמַח.
(6) וַיְהִי כַּאֲשֶׁר שָׁמַע אֶת־קוֹלָהּ וַיִּשְׁלַח אֶת־מַלְאָכוֹ אֵלֶיהָ.
(7) וְהָיָה בַּיּוֹם הַהוּא וְרָעִיתָ אֶת־עֶדְרְךָ פֹּה פֶּן־יַאַסְרוּ אֹיְבֵינוּ אֹתְךָ וְלָקְחוּ אֶת־הָעֵדֶר.
(8) וְהָיָה כִּי אֶקְרָא אֵלֶיךָ וּבָרַחְתָּ מִן־הַמָּקוֹם הַזֶּה וְשַׁבְתָּ הַבַּיְתָה.
(9) וְהָיָה בַּשָּׁנָה הַהִיא וְסָבְבוּ אֹיְבֵיכֶם אֶת־עִירְכֶם כִּי אָרַר יהוה אֶתְכֶם בַּעֲבוּר הַחַטָּאוֹת אֲשֶׁר חֲטָאתֶם לוֹ.
(10) וַיְהִי בַּיּוֹם הַשְּׁבִיעִי וַיִּשְׁבֹּת אֱלֹהִים מִמְּלַאכְתּוֹ.

(b) Translate:

(1) קוֹל עָנְיֵךְ
(2) חֲצִי פִּרְיוֹ
(3) שְׁנַת מִלְחַמְתֵּנוּ
(4) יוֹם מְלַאכְתְּךָ
(5) יְמֵי זְקוּנֶיךָ
(6) דִּבְרֵי גְבִרְתִּי
(7) אֲמָהוֹת וּשְׁפָחוֹת
(8) אֲחוֹת הַכְּנַעֲנִי
(9) רְכוּשׁ הַמִּצְרִים
(10) מִזְבַּח הַהֵיכָל

(c) Write in Hebrew:

1. When they saw him they called to him.
2. When his life came to an end, they buried him in the grave of his fathers.
3. When you cross the river you will see the land which I am about to give (use participle) to you.
4. Afterward they sent men to Egypt, for there was a famine in the land.
5. On that day you will see him standing before you.
6. When she found the tree she ate some of (lit. from) its fruit.
7. In the evening you shall go out of the city and flee toward the mountain.

(d) Reading: Sarah and Hagar (cont.)

יהוה פָּקַד אֶת־שָׂרָה כַּאֲשֶׁר אָמַר. יָלְדָה שָׂרָה לְאַבְרָהָם בֵּן לִזְקֻנָיו וַיִּקְרָא אַבְרָהָם אֶת־שֵׁם בְּנוֹ אֲשֶׁר יָלְדָה לוֹ שָׂרָה יִצְחָק וַיִּגְדַּל הַיֶּלֶד עִם־בֶּן־הָגָר הַמִּצְרִית וַיְהִי כַּאֲשֶׁר רָאֲתָה שָׂרָה אֶת־בֶּן־הָאָמָה עִם־בְּנָהּ יִצְחָק וַתֹּאמֶר לְאַבְרָהָם אִישָׁהּ לֵאמֹר: גָּרֵשׁ[1] אֶת־הָאָמָה הַזֹּאת וְאֶת־בְּנָהּ.

רַע הַדָּבָר מְאֹד בְּעֵינֵי אַבְרָהָם עַל־דְּבַר בְּנוֹ יִשְׁמָעֵאל וַיֹּאמֶר אֱלֹהִים אֶל־אַבְרָהָם: כֹּל־אֲשֶׁר תֹּאמַר אֵלֶיךָ שָׂרָה שְׁמַע בְּקוֹלָהּ כִּי בְיִצְחָק יִקָּרֵא לְךָ[2] זָרַע וְגַם־אֶת־בֶּן־הָאָמָה לְגוֹי גָּדוֹל אֲשִׂימֶנּוּ[3] כִּי זַרְעֲךָ גַּם־הוּא.

וַיְהִי אַחֲרֵי־כֵן וַיְשַׁלַּח[4] אַבְרָהָם אֶת־הָגָר וְאֶת־בְּנָהּ. תְּעֶתָה הָאָמָה בַּמִּדְבָּר וַיְהִי כַּאֲשֶׁר כָּלוּ הַמַּיִם וְהַלֶּחֶם אֲשֶׁר נָתַן לָהּ אַבְרָהָם וַתִּשְׁכַּב עַל־הָאֲדָמָה וַתֵּבְךְּ[5] וַיִּשְׁמַע אֱלֹהִים אֶת־קוֹל הַנַּעַר וַיִּקְרָא מַלְאַךְ אֱלֹהִים אֵלֶיהָ מִן־הַשָּׁמַיִם לֵאמֹר: מַה־לָּךְ הָגָר. אַל־תִּירְאִי[6] כִּי שָׁמַע אֱלֹהִים אֶת־קוֹל הַנַּעַר.

וַיְהִי אַחֲרֵי הַדְּבָרִים הָאֵלֶּה וַתִּמְצָא הָגָר בְּאֵר מַיִם. הָיָה אֱלֹהִים אֶת־הַנַּעַר וַיִּגְדַּל הַנַּעַר בַּמִּדְבָּר עִם־אִמּוֹ.

Notes to the Reading:

1. "drive away" (imperative)
2. "your descendants will be named"
3. "I shall make him into a great nation *(gôy)*"
4. "expelled"
5. "and wept"
6. "fear not!"

SSON 28

114. The Infinitive Construct.

Each Hebrew verb has two forms to which the name infinitive is given. One of these, the infinitive absolute, functions more as an adverb and will be dealt with in a later lesson. The other, the infinitive construct, corresponds more closely to the traditional view of an infinitive. The form of the infinitive construct is more or less uniform for those verb classes whose imperfects we have studied up to this lesson. The vowel of the first syllable is *ə* (or with gutturals *ă* or *ĕ*) and that of the second is *ō*. The infinitive is frequently used with pronominal suffixes, before which the stem is variable.

	Perfect	*Imperfect*	*Imperative*	*Inf. Construct*	*w. suff.*
Sound trilit.	כָּתַב	יִכְתֹּב	כְּתֹב	כְּתֹב	כָּתְבִי
I-guttural	עָמַד	יַעֲמֹד	עֲמֹד	עֲמֹד	עָמְדִי
II-guttural	בָּחַר	יִבְחַר	בְּחַר	בְּחֹר	בָּחֳרִי
III-guttural	שָׁמַע	יִשְׁמַע	שְׁמַע	שְׁמֹעַ	שָׁמְעִי
I-*Aleph*	אָכַל	יֹאכַל	אֱכֹל	אֱכֹל	אָכְלִי
III-*Aleph*	מָצָא	יִמְצָא	מְצָא	מְצֹא	מָצְאִי

Some inconsistency is found among those verbs which have *a*-imperfects but which are neither II/III-guttural; this includes stative verbs like כָּבֵד and the small group represented by יִשְׁכַּב שָׁכַב. These are poorly attested for the infinitive construct, but they usually follow the pattern given above. Occasionally there is a form with *a*, such as שְׁכַב (to lie down), but even here, before suffixes, the normal pattern emerges: שָׁכְבִי *šoḵḇî.*

115. Some Uses of the Infinitive Construct.

The infinitive is by definition a form having both nominal and verbal functions. In the latter role it may have subjects and objects as well as other typically verbal adjuncts. The infinitive, together with its adjuncts, then occupies a nominal function in the total clause. When pronouns form the subject of an infinitive, they are suffixed:

כָּתְבִי	*kot̲b̲î*	my writing	כָּתְבֵנוּ	*kot̲b̲ēnû*
כָּתְבְךָ	*kot̲b̲ək̲ā*	your (m. s.) writing	כָּתְבְכֶם	*kot̲b̲ək̲em*
כְּתָבְךָ	*kət̲ob̲k̲ā*		כָּתְבְכֶן	*kot̲b̲ək̲en*
כָּתְבֵךְ	*kot̲b̲ēk̲*	etc.	כָּתְבָם	*kot̲b̲ām*
כָּתְבוֹ	*kot̲b̲ô*		כָּתְבָן	*kot̲b̲ān*
כָּתְבָהּ	*kot̲b̲āh*			

When the infinitive construct stands before a following noun, that noun may be either the subject or object of the infinitive, although the former is more likely:

כְּתֹב הָאִישׁ the man's writing (i.e. act of writing)
הֲרֹג אִישׁ killing a man
(or) a man's killing

The ambiguity of the second example is grammatical as well as semantic. The infinitive is in construct (hence its name) with its subject, as in the first example, but in the second the word אִישׁ should probably be regarded as an object noun (not construct) when it is the object, especially since it requires אֶת when made definite:

הֲרֹג אִישׁ to kill a man
הֲרֹג אֶת־הָאִישׁ to kill the man

When pronouns are involved with the infinitive construct, the arrangement of subject and object is a little more complicated, but the following examples should make the situation clear:

הָרְגִי אֶת־הָאִישׁ my killing the man
הֲרֹג הָאִישׁ אֹתִי the man's killing me
שָׁמְרִי אֶת־הַתּוֹרָה my observing the law
שָׁמְרִי אֹתוֹ my observing him
שָׁמְרוֹ אֹתִי his observing me
כְּתֹב דָּבָר to write a word
כְּתֹב אֶת־הַדָּבָר to write the word
כָּתְבְךָ אֶת־הַדָּבָר your writing the word

As a unit the infinitival phrase may be

sentence subject: טוֹב שָׁמְרְךָ אֶת־הַתּוֹרָה your observing the law is good or it is good that you observe the law

object of a prep.: עַד־מָצְאֲךָ אֹתוֹ until you find him
object of verb: לֹא יָכֹלְתִּי שְׁמֹעַ I was not able to hear

But the most frequent use of the infinitive construct is with the prepositions ב, כ, and ל:

(a) With ב and כ the infinitive is the equivalent of an adverbial (mostly temporal) clause in English:

כְּשָׁמְעוֹ אֶת־הַדָּבָר when he heard the word
בְּעָמְדִי לְפָנָיו when (or while) I stood before him

Both prepositions are common in this usage, but with certain verbs, especially שָׁמַע and רָאָה, כְּ is by far the preferred preposition. There are reasons, founded in the aspectual nature of these verbs, which govern this choice, but a catalog of uses would serve no purpose in an elementary grammar of this sort.

The infinitive with בְּ or כְּ is very frequent in the construction treated in §110:

וַיְהִי כִּשְׁמֹעַ אַבְרָהָם... and when Abraham heard...
וְהָיָה כְּשָׁמְעֲךָ אֶת־קוֹלִי... and when you hear my voice...

(b) With לְ the inf. construct occurs in a wide variety of complementary and explanatory uses, often with the meaning of purpose, goal, or result:

בָּאוּ...לִשְׁמֹעַ... They came . . . to hear . . .
לֹא יָכְלוּ לִלְכֹּד... They could not capture . . .
תִּשְׁמֹר אֶת־דֶּרֶךְ יהוה לַעֲשׂוֹת You shall observe the way of the Lord
צֶדֶק... by doing (inf. of עָשָׂה) righteousness . . .

(1) הָיָה + לְ + Inf. expresses (a) "to be about to" or (b) "to be compelled to": הָיָה הַשַּׁעַר לִסְגֹּר The gate was about to close.
(2) עַל + noun or pron. + לְ + Inf. expresses obligation or responsibility: עָלַי לִמְצֹא אֹתוֹ I must find him.
(3) אֵין + לְ + Inf. = "it is not possible (permitted) to": אֵין לָבוֹא Entering is forbidden.

The infinitive construct is negated with בִּלְתִּי:

לְבִלְתִּי אֲכֹל אֶת־הַפְּרִי not to eat the fruit
לְבִלְתִּי שְׂרֹף אֶת־הַמְּגִלָּה not to burn the scroll

116. Final Remarks on Some Noun Types.

The only important group of nouns not included in our previous discussions is that comprising nouns ending in *-eh*. Most of these are derived from roots found in verbs III-*Hē* and which in an earlier stage of the language were either III-*Yodh* or III-*Waw*. Subsequent contractions and loss have obscured the origins of these forms, and certain coincidental developments within the language have led to some formal confusion between singular and plural. In the singular these nouns:

(1) may follow regular inflection with complete loss of the *-eh*:

שָׂדֶה field שָׂדִי שָׂדְךָ etc.
מַטֶּה staff מַטְּךָ

(2) may exhibit a partially distinct set of suffixes, especially *-ēhû* in the 3rd pers. sing.

מַעֲשֶׂה deed מַעֲשֵׂהוּ
מִקְנֶה cattle מִקְנֵהוּ

(3) or may have suffixal forms like the *-îm* plurals:

מִקְנַי my cattle מַעֲשַׂי my deed

For nouns having plurals in *-ôṯ*, such as שָׂדֶה and מַחֲנֶה, the occurrence of such forms as שָׂדַי and מַחֲנַי as plurals is suspect. Although these may be listed as plurals in concordances and grammars, many such forms are more likely singulars.

117. Vocabulary 28.

VERBS: יָכֹל *yāḵōl* to be able; (+ לְ) to prevail over
חָפֵץ *ḥāp̄ēṣ* (יַחְפֹּץ) to take delight in; to desire (to do something: + inf.)
חָדַל *ḥāḏal* (יֶחְדַּל) to cease, stop (intr.); to stop (doing something: + inf.)
תַּם *tam* (see §87) to finish, be at an end; to finish (doing something: + inf.)
אָסַף *'āsap̄* (יֶאֱסֹף) to gather

NOUNS: תֹּאַר *tố'ar* form, appearance
מִשְׁתֶּה *mišteh* banquet
אַהֲבָה *'ahăḇāh* love [used as the inf. constr. of אָהַב]
אֵם *'ēm* (w. suff. אִמִּי; pl. *-ôṯ*) mother

Prepositions frequently used before the infinitive construct:

עַד	until	כְּ	when, as
אַחֲרֵי	after	לְמַעַן	so that, so as to
בְּ	when, while	יַעַן	because

Exercises:

(a) Translate:

(1) לְמַעַן שָׁמְרְךָ אֶת־הַתּוֹרָה (2) בְּהָרְגוֹ אֶת־אֹיְבָיו

(3) כִּשְׁלֹחַ הַמֶּלֶךְ אֶת־עֲבָדָיו
(4) כִּשְׁמֹעַ הָאִישׁ אֶת־קוֹלֵנוּ
(5) בְּכָרְתֵנוּ בְרִית
(6) בְּבָרְאוֹ אֶת־הָרֶמֶשׂ
(7) לַהֲרֹג אֶת־כָּל־הַזְּכָרִים
(8) בְּצַעֲקָם אֵלַי
(9) בְּכָתְבְךָ אֶת־דְּבָרָיו
(10) בִּשְׂרֹף אֹיְבֵינוּ אֶת־הָעִיר
(11) בְּקָרְאוֹ שֵׁמוֹת לַחַיּוֹת
(12) בְּקָרְעִי אֶת־בְּגָדַי
(13) יַעַן סָגְרָם אֶת־הַשַּׁעַר
(14) עַד־מָצְאָם אֹתוֹ
(15) לְבִלְתִּי אֱכֹל־אֶת־בַּהֲמוֹת הַשָּׂדֶה
(16) לְבִלְתִּי עֲבֹר אֶת־מִצְוֹתָיו

(b) Give the Hebrew for the following orally:

1. when you forget this law
2. while I stood there
3. after we gathered them
4. when they buried him
5. until they bind us
6. after they lie down
7. not to ride on the horse
8. until you call to us
9. until I break the tablets
10. while he was eating
11. so that he send you to us
12. so that you observe them

(c) Translate:

(1) וְהָיָה בְּבָחֳרָם בּוֹ לְמֶלֶךְ וְיָשַׁב עַל־הַכִּסֵּא.
(2) לָמָּה עָשִׂיתָ הָרַע בְּעֵינַי לְבִלְתִּי שְׁמֹעַ בְּקוֹלִי.
(3) וַיְהִי בְּמָצְאוֹ אֶת־הַיֶּלֶד וַיַּהֲרֹג אֹתוֹ.
(4) וַיְהִי כְּשָׁמְעֵנוּ אֶת־הַקּוֹל וַנִּשְׂמַח.
(5) לֹא יָכֹלְתִּי אֱכֹל אֶת־הַלֶּחֶם הַזֶּה.
(6) חָפְצוּ לַהֲרֹג אֶת־יֹשְׁבֵי הָעִיר וְלֹא יָכְלוּ לִמְצֹא אֹתָם.
(7) וְהָיָה אַחֲרֵי אָסְפוֹ אֶת־הָאֲנָשִׁים אֵלָיו בְּבֵיתוֹ וְעָשָׂה מִשְׁתֶּה גָּדוֹל.
(8) טוֹב אַתָּה כִּי זָכַרְתָּ אֶת־מִצְוֹתַי לְבִלְתִּי חֲטֹא לִי.
(9) וַיְהִי כַּאֲשֶׁר רָאָה אֹתָהּ כִּי יְפַת תֹּאַר וִיפַת מַרְאֶה הִיא מְאֹד וַיֶּאֱהַב אֹתָהּ וַיַּחְפֹּץ אֹתָהּ לוֹ לְאִשָּׁה.
(10) וְהָיָה בִּפְקֹד יהוה אֶת־שָׂרָה וְהָרְתָה וְיָלְדָה בֵּן לְאִישָׁהּ.
(11) מִי יַחְפֹּץ לִגְאֹל אֹתָךְ.
(12) יָצְאוּ מֵהַהֵיכָל לְבִלְתִּי שָׁמְעָם אֶת־דִּבְרֵי הַמֶּלֶךְ הָרָשָׁע.
(13) וַיְהִי אַחֲרֵי חָדְלוּ לִשְׁמֹעַ בְּקוֹל הַנָּבִיא וַיֶּחֶטְאוּ חֲטָאוֹת רַבּוֹת.
(14) תַּמּוּ הָעָם לַעֲבֹר אֶת־הַנָּהָר.
(15) הָיוּ הַשָּׁנִים כְּיָמִים בְּעֵינָיו בְּאַהֲבָתוֹ אֹתָהּ.
(16) וַיְהִי בֶּאֱחֹז הָאִשָּׁה אֶת־בִּגְדוֹ וַיַּעֲזֹב אֶת־בִּגְדוֹ וַיִּבְרַח מִן־הַבָּיִת.

(d) Write in Hebrew:

1. When they killed the prisoners we fled from there and crossed over hither.
2. You have sinned in not loving your father and your mother.
3. They sat in her house until the men opened the gate.
4. We wish to remember both the living and the dead.
5. It is not permitted to eat the flesh of these animals.

6. When he saw (use perf.) the dry ground, he rejoiced, for he knew that the waters had ceased from the face of the earth.
7. We were not able to write, nor were we able to read.

LESSON 29

118. Verbs I-Nun: Imperfect and Related Forms.

The following two verbs are the most typical of this class:

	Perfect	Imperfect	Imperative	Inf. Constr.	w. suff.
ō-imperf.	נָפַל	יִפֹּל	נְפֹל	נְפֹל	נָפְלִי
a-imperf.	נָסַע	יִסַּע	סַע	נְסֹעַ	נָסְעִי

In the imperfect of both types the *nûn* is assimilated to the second root consonant throughout the inflection, which is otherwise quite regular:

יִפֹּל	*yippōl*	יִפְּלוּ	*yippəlû*
תִּפֹּל	*tippōl*	תִּפֹּ֫לְנָה	*tippṓlnāh*
תִּפֹּל	*tippōl*	תִּפְּלוּ	*tippəlû*
תִּפְּלִי	*tippəlî*	תִּפֹּ֫לְנָה	*tippṓlnāh*
אֶפֹּל	*'eppōl*	נִפֹּל	*nippōl*

Verbs with *a*-imperfects have a short imperative, inflected as follows:

סַע	*sa‘*	סְעִי	*sə‘î*	סְעוּ	*sə‘û*	סַ֫עְנָה	*sá‘nāh*
סְעָה	*sə‘āh*						

The infinitive construct of verbs with *a*-imperfects may be of two different types, both of which occur for most of these verbs: (1) a regular form, like נְסֹעַ *nəsō*^{a}*‘*, (2) a short form with the suffix *-t*: סַ֫עַת

Perfect	Imperfect	Imperative	Inf. Construct	w. suff.	
נָגַע	יִגַּע	גַּע	גַּ֫עַת	—	to strike
			נְגֹעַ	נָגְעִי	
נָטַע	יִטַּע	טַע	טַ֫עַת	—	to plant
			נְטֹעַ	—	
—	יִגַּשׁ	גַּשׁ	גֶּ֫שֶׁת	גִּשְׁתִּי	to approach
			—	—	

Special Remarks:

(a) Note that יִגַּשׁ is not used in the perfect.

(b) The forms of נָשָׂא (to raise up), which is also III-*Aleph*, are

נָשָׂא	יִשָּׂא	שָׂא	שְׂאֵת / שֵׂאת	שְׂאֵתִי
			נְשֹׂא	—

(c) The verb נָתַן has an imperfect etc. with *ē*:

נָתַן	יִתֵּן	תֵּן	תֵּת	תִּתִּי

(d) The verb לָקַח behaves as though I-*Nun* in the imperfect etc.:

לָקַח	יִקַּח	קַח	קַ֫חַת	קַחְתִּי

(e) The doubling of the second root consonant of the imperfect is given up in some verbs when followed by *ə*:

יִסְעוּ *yis'û* (they will set out) not יִסְּעוּ *yissə'û*

Below are the full paradigms of נָסַע, נָשָׂא, נָתַן, and לָקַח.

Imperfect:	יִסַּע	יִשָּׂא	יִתֵּן	יִקַּח
	תִּסַּע	תִּשָּׂא	תִּתֵּן	תִּקַּח
	תִּסַּע	תִּשָּׂא	תִּתֵּן	תִּקַּח
	תִּסְעִי	תִּשְׂאִי	תִּתְּנִי	תִּקְחִי
	אֶסַּע	אֶשָּׂא	אֶתֵּן	אֶקַּח
	יִסְעוּ	יִשְׂאוּ	יִתְּנוּ	יִקְחוּ
	תִּסַּ֫עְנָה	תִּשֶּׂ֫אנָה	תִּתֵּ֫נָּה	תִּקַּ֫חְנָה
	תִּסְעוּ	תִּשְׂאוּ	תִּתְּנוּ	תִּקְחוּ
	תִּסַּ֫עְנָה	תִּשֶּׂ֫אנָה	תִּתֵּ֫נָּה	תִּקַּ֫חְנָה
	נִסַּע	נִשָּׂא	נִתֵּן	נִקַּח
Imperative:	סַע	שָׂא	תֵּן	קַח
	סְעִי	שְׂאִי	תְּנִי	קְחִי
	סְעוּ	שְׂאוּ	תְּנוּ	קְחוּ
	סַ֫עְנָה	שֶׂ֫אנָה	תֵּ֫נָּה	קַ֫חְנָה

The preposition לְ appears as לָ before the infinitives with a stressed first syllable unless the infinitive is in construct with a following noun. E.g.

לָטַ֫עַת   לָגֶ֫שֶׁת   לָשֵׂאת   לָקַ֫חַת   לָתֵת

119. Vocabulary 29.

NOUNS: מְגוּרִים *məḡûrîm* (pl. only) the place where one sojourns, residence

כְּתֹ֫נֶת *kəṯṓneṯ*, (pl. *-ôṯ*) tunic

כֻּתֹּ֫נֶת *kuttṓneṯ*

נֵ֫דֶר *néḏer* or נֶ֫דֶר *nḗḏer* (w. suff. נִדְרִי; pl. *-îm*) vow

תּוֹלְדוֹת *tôləḏôṯ* history, genealogy (pl. only)

VERBS: יִגַּשׁ *yiggaš* (perf. not used) to approach [usually with אֶל]

נָדַר *nāḏar* (יִדֹּר) to vow

גָּעַר *gā'ar* (יִגְעַר) to rebuke

שָׂנֵא *śānē'* (יִשְׂנָא) to hate

הַב *haḇ* A defective verb found only in the imperative forms: הָבוּ הָבִי הָבָה הַב give! come now... let's...!

נָשָׂא *nāśā'* (יִשָּׂא) to raise, lift up, carry

ADJECTIVE: צָעִיר *ṣā'îr* small, young

NUMBERS: שְׁנַ֫יִם *šənáyim* (masc.) two; constr. שְׁנֵי *šənê*

שְׁתַּ֫יִם *štáyim* (fem.) two; constr. שְׁתֵּי *štê*

The absolute form of the number "two" may stand before or after the noun it modifies, which is in the plural:

אֲנָשִׁים שְׁנַ֫יִם or שְׁנַ֫יִם אֲנָשִׁים

נָשִׁים שְׁתַּ֫יִם — שְׁתַּ֫יִם נָשִׁים

The construct form is used only before the noun:

שְׁנֵי אֲנָשִׁים — שְׁתֵּי נָשִׁים

PROPER NAMES: רָחֵל *Rāḥēl* Rachel

לֵאָה *Lē'āh* Leah

לָבָן *Lāḇān* Laban

יַעֲקֹב *Ya'ăqōḇ* Jacob

Exercises:

(a) Translate:

(1) תֵּן לִי שְׁנֵי סְפָרִים

(2) קְחִי אֶת־כַּסְפֵּךְ

(3) יִגַּשׁ אֵלַי הָאִישׁ

(4) וַתִּדֹּר הָאִשָּׁה נֶ֫דֶר

(5) אַל־תִּשְׂנְאוּ אֶת־אֲחִיכֶם.

(6) וַיִּגֹּף אֹתָם מַגֵּפוֹת רַבּוֹת וּכְבֵדוֹת

(7) וַיִּקְחוּ אֶת־כְּתָנְתּוֹ וַיִּקְרְעוּ אֹתָהּ

(8) שְׁנַ֫יִם זְקֵנִים הֹלְכִים עַל־הַדָּ֫רֶךְ

(9) גְּשִׁי אֵלַי בִּתִּי

(10) סְעוּ מִצְרַ֫יְמָה

(11) תֵּן לָ֫נוּ עֵ֫זֶר

(12) יִפֹּל אַ֫רְצָה בְּגִשְׁתְּךָ אֵלָיו

(13) טוֹב תִּתְּךָ לִי אֶת־הַכֶּ֫סֶף

(14) שָׂא אֶת־עֵינֶ֫יךָ הַשָּׁמַ֫יְמָה

(b) Give the Hebrew for the following orally:

1. Give (m. pl.) us your help.
2. Kill (m. pl.) the snake.

3. Do not eat (m. pl.) its flesh.
4. Take (m. s.) two stones.
5. Plant (m. s.) the tree here.
6. Approach (f. s.) him.
7. and he struck him
8. and they gave him their sons
9. and I fell to the ground
10. and he traveled toward the wilderness
11. we shall give them food
12. we shall set out in the morning

(c) Translate:

(1) לֹא יָכֹלְתִּי לָשֵׂאת הָאֲבָנִים הָאֵלֶּה כִּי כְבֵדוֹת הֵנָּה מִשְּׂאֵתִי אֹתָן.
(2) לֹא יַחְפֹּץ לָגֶשֶׁת אֵלֶיךָ בְּקָרְאֲךָ אֵלָיו.
(3) אֱסֹף אֶת־הָעָם הֵנָּה פֶּן־יֹאבְדוּ בִּידֵי הָאֹיְבִים.
(4) בָּרַח הָהָרָה לְבִלְתִּי קַחְתָּם אֹתוֹ וְאֶת־מִקְנֵהוּ.
(5) סְגֹר אֶת־שַׁעַר הָעִיר פֶּן־יִגְּשׁוּ הָאֲנָשִׁים וְהָרְגוּ אֹתָנוּ.
(6) וַיִּטְּעוּ שָׁם כֶּרֶם וְעֵצִים רַבִּים.
(7) וַיְהִי בְּגִשְׁתּוֹ אֵלַי וָאֶשָּׂא אֶת־עֵינַי אֵלָיו וָאֹמַר: לָמָּה בָּאתָ אֵלַי בְּנִי.
(8) תָּעֲתָה הָאִשָּׁה עִם־שְׁנֵי בָנֶיהָ וְלֹא יָכְלָה לִמְצֹא לָהֶם מַיִם.
(9) חָפַצְתִּי לִנְסֹעַ אֶתְמוֹל וְלֹא יָכֹלְתִּי לִמְצֹא אֶת־בְּגָדַי וְאֶת־כֻּתָּנְתִּי.
(10) וְהָיָה כְּפִתְחָם אֶת־הַשַּׁעַר וִיצָאתֶם הַחוּצָה.
(11) הָבָה נִשְׁמְעָה בְּקוֹלוֹ כִּי צַדִּיק הוּא בְּעֵינֵינוּ.
(12) קְחוּ אֶת־רְכוּשְׁכֶם וְאֶת־כָּל־אֲשֶׁר־לָכֶם וּנְסַעְתֶּם אֶל־הָאָרֶץ הַהִיא וִישַׁבְתֶּם גַּם־אַתֶּם בְּאֶרֶץ מְגוּרֵי אֲבוֹתֵיכֶם.

(d) Write in Hebrew:

1. When he approached us, we called to our servants.
2. And he set out and crossed over as far as the river.
3. And he raised his hands heavenward and cried out in a loud voice.
4. Take (f.s.) your sons and go forth (perf.) from this place.
5. We could not bear (= carry) the affliction which he set upon us.
6. His song is pleasant and his words are good in our ears.
7. And afterward they set out each (= a man) to his land.

(e) Reading: Jacob and Rachel

וּלְלָבָן הָיוּ שְׁתֵּי בָנוֹת, שֵׁם הַגְּדוֹלָה לֵאָה וְשֵׁם הַקְּטַנָּה רָחֵל וְרָחֵל הָיְתָה יְפַת תֹּאַר וִיפַת מַרְאֶה וַיֶּאֱהַב יַעֲקֹב אֶת־רָחֵל וַיֹּאמֶר אֶל־לָבָן: אֶעֱבָדְךָ שֶׁבַע[1] שָׁנִים בְּרָחֵל[2] בִּתְּךָ הַקְּטַנָּה. וַיֹּאמֶר לָבָן: טוֹב תִּתִּי אֹתָהּ לָךְ מִתִּתִּי אֹתָהּ לְאִישׁ אַחֵר.

וַיַּעֲבֹד יַעֲקֹב בְּרָחֵל שֶׁבַע שָׁנִים אֲשֶׁר הָיוּ בְעֵינָיו כְּיָמִים אֲחָדִים[3] בְּאַהֲבָתוֹ[2] אֹתָהּ וַיֹּאמֶר יַעֲקֹב אֶל־לָבָן: הָבָה אֶת־אִשְׁתִּי כִּי מָלְאוּ יָמַי. וַיֶּאֱסֹף לָבָן אֶת־כָּל־אַנְשֵׁי הַמָּקוֹם וַיַּעַשׂ מִשְׁתֶּה וַיְהִי בָעֶרֶב וַיִּקַּח אֶת־לֵאָה בִתּוֹ הַגְּדוֹלָה וַיִּתֵּן אֹתָהּ לְיַעֲקֹב וְהוּא בָא אֵלֶיהָ בַּלָּיְלָה.

וַיְהִי כַאֲשֶׁר רָאָה יַעֲקֹב בַּבֹּקֶר כִּי לֵאָה אִתּוֹ וַיֹּאמֶר אֶל־לָבָן: מַה זֹּאת עָשִׂיתָ לִּי. הֲלֹא בְרָחֵל
עָבַדְתִּי עִמָּךְ וְלָמָּה רִמִּיתָנִי.[5] וַיֹּאמֶר לָבָן: בִּמְקוֹמֵנוּ אֵין לָתֵת הַצְּעִירָה לִפְנֵי הַבְּכִירָה.[6]
אֶתֵּן גַּם־אֶת־זֹאת בָּעֲבוֹדָה[2] אֲשֶׁר תַּעֲבֹד עִמָּדִי שֶׁבַע שָׁנִים אֲחֵרוֹת. וַיִּתֵּן לָבָן אֶת־רָחֵל לְיַעֲקֹב
לְאִשָּׁה וַיַּעֲבֹד יַעֲקֹב אֶת־לָבָן שֶׁבַע שָׁנִים אֲחֵרוֹת בְּרָחֵל.

Notes to the Reading:

1. "seven"
2. There are three idiomatic uses of בְּ in this selection:

עָבַד בְּ	to serve someone *for* a reward or compensation
בְּאַהֲבָתוֹ אֹתָהּ	*because* he loved her
בָּעֲבוֹדָה	*in exchange for* the labor

3. The pl. of אֶחָד has the sense of "several, a few"
4. "and he prepared"
5. "have you deceived me?"
6. "first-born" hence "eldest" (feminine)

Do p 187

psalm 24

whitey

לבן = white

לְבָנוֹן

LESSON 30

120. Verbs I-Yodh: Imperfect, Imperative, and Infinitive Construct.

Just as in the class of verbs I-*Nun* there are two distinct types of verbs I-*Yodh* depending on the stem vowel of the imperfect:

	Perfect	Imperfect	Imperative	Inf. Constr.	w. suff.	
ē-imperfects:	יָשַׁב	יֵשֵׁב	שֵׁב	שֶׁבֶת	שִׁבְתִּי	dwell
a-imperfects:	יָשֵׁן	יִישַׁן	[יְשַׁן]	יְשֹׁן	[יָשְׁנִי]	sleep

Verbs with *ē*-imperfects have *ē* in the preformative and have short imperative and infinitive stems. Exactly like יָשַׁב are

יָלַד	יֵלֵד	לֵד	לֶדֶת	לִדְתִּי	bear
יָרַד	יֵרֵד	רֵד	רֶדֶת	רִדְתִּי	descend

The verb יָדַע belongs to this group, even though it has an *a*-imperfect due to the final root guttural:

יָדַע	יֵדַע	דַּע	דַּעַת	דַּעְתִּי	know

The verb יָצָא has slightly different forms because it is also III-*Aleph*:

יָצָא	יֵצֵא	צֵא	צֵאת	צֵאתִי	go forth

The verb הָלַךְ is irregular in also belonging here:

הָלַךְ	יֵלֵךְ	לֵךְ	לֶכֶת	לֶכְתִּי	go

To the second group, represented by יָשֵׁן above, belong the verbs

יָרַשׁ	יִירַשׁ	רַשׁ	רֶשֶׁת	רִשְׁתִּי	inherit
יָעַץ	יִיעַץ	—	—	—	advise
יָקַץ	יִיקַץ	—	—	—	wake up
יָבֵשׁ	יִיבַשׁ	—	יְבֹשֶׁ(ת)	—	dry up

and the III-*Aleph* verb

יָרֵא	יִירָא	יְרָא	יְרֹא	—	fear

[Note: the noun יִרְאָה (fear) is normally used as the inf. construct for this verb.] The imperatives and inf. constructs of this group are poorly attested in BH but show the same mixture of the two possible types which we encountered with verbs I-*Nun*.

The verb יָכֹל has irregular forms with *û* in the preformative of the imperfect:

יוּכַל תּוּכַל תּוּכְלִי etc.

In the class of verbs I-*Yodh* and in those classes to be treated in the following lessons there is frequently a difference in the imperfect form used with waw-conversive, particularly in the 3rd pers. sing. masc. and fem., the 2nd pers. sing. masc., and the 1st pers. pl. In general the accent on these forms is retracted to an *open* preformative syllable; *ē* in the stem is replaced by *e*. A similar instance was met with יֹאמַר versus וַיֹּאמֶר. There are, however, inconsistencies:

(a) The change is regular for *ē*-imperfects other than יֵצֵא:

וַיֵּשֶׁב	וַתֵּלֶד	וַיֵּרֶד	וַיֵּלֶךְ	but	וַיֵּצֵא
וַתֵּשֶׁב		וַתֵּרֶד	וַתֵּלֶךְ		וַתֵּצֵא
וַנֵּשֶׁב		וַנֵּרֶד	וַנֵּלֶךְ		וַנֵּצֵא

(b) It is *not* found with the *a*-imperfects other than יֵדַע:

וַיִּירַשׁ	וַיִּישַׁן	וַיִּיקַץ	but	וַיֵּדַע

Several verbs have imperfects formed on the analogy of roots I-*Nun*:

יָצַר	to fashion	imperf.	יִצֹּר	(but also, irregularly, וַיִּיצֶר)
יָצַק	to pour		יִצֹּק	(but also, irregularly, וַיִּצֹק)
יָצַת	to kindle		יִצַּת	

Given below are the full paradigms of the most frequent types of the class I-*Yodh*:

	יֵשֵׁב	יֵלֵךְ	יֵצֵא	יֵדַע	יִירַשׁ
	תֵּשֵׁב	תֵּלֵךְ	תֵּצֵא	תֵּדַע	תִּירַשׁ
	תֵּשֵׁב	תֵּלֵךְ	תֵּצֵא	תֵּדַע	תִּירַשׁ
	תֵּשְׁבִי	תֵּלְכִי	תֵּצְאִי	תֵּדְעִי	תִּירְשִׁי

אֵשֵׁב	אֵלֵךְ	אֵצֵא	אֵדַע	אִירַשׁ
יֵשְׁבוּ	יֵלְכוּ	יֵצְאוּ	יֵדְעוּ	יִירְשׁוּ
תֵּשַׁבְנָה	תֵּלַכְנָה	תֵּצֶאנָה	תֵּדַעְנָה	תִּירַשְׁנָה
תֵּשְׁבוּ	תֵּלְכוּ	תֵּצְאוּ	תֵּדְעוּ	תִּירְשׁוּ
תֵּשַׁבְנָה	תֵּלַכְנָה	תֵּצֶאנָה	תֵּדַעְנָה	תִּירַשְׁנָה
נֵשֵׁב	נֵלֵךְ	נֵצֵא	נֵדַע	נִירַשׁ
שֵׁב	לֵךְ	צֵא	דַּע	רַשׁ
שְׁבִי	לְכִי	צְאִי	דְּעִי	רְשִׁי
שְׁבוּ	לְכוּ	צְאוּ	דְּעוּ	רְשׁוּ
שֵׁבְנָה	לֵכְנָה	צֶאנָה	דַּעְנָה	רַשְׁנָה

121. Vocabulary 30.

NOUNS: שָׁלוֹם *šālôm* peace, well-being; state of one's health. Note the idiom: שָׁאַל לְשָׁלוֹם לְ to inquire about the health of

עֵמֶק *ʿḗmeq* (w. suff. עִמְקִי, pl. *-îm*) valley, lowland

בַּעַל *báʿal* (pl. *-îm*) lord, master, owner, husband. Frequent in idioms as "one invested with, endowed with," as בַּעַל חֲלוֹמוֹת a dreamer. Also members (pl.) of a guild or profession, as בַּעֲלֵי הַפָּרָשִׁים professional horsemen. Also a proper name or epithet of a Canaanite deity, rarely applied to God.

ADJECTIVES: רָחוֹק *rāḥôq* distant, far; מֵרָחוֹק at a distance, from afar

קָרוֹב *qārôḇ* near, close (to: אֶל)

VERBS: קָרַב *qārab* (יִקְרַב) to be near, draw near; approach (+ אֶל, לְ, בְּ)

יָשֵׁן *yāšēn* (יִישַׁן) to sleep

שָׁאַל *šāʾal* (יִשְׁאַל) to ask, inquire, request (a thing: אֶת; a person אֶת, לְ, מִן)

עָנָה *ʿānāh* to answer (a person: אֶת); + בְּ to testify against

CONJUNCTION: טֶרֶם *ṭérem* or בְּטֶרֶם *bəṭérem* before, not yet. Usually followed by the imperfect, regardless of the tense required in English: טֶרֶם יִשְׁכַּב before he had lain down, or he not yet having lain down.

PROPER NAMES: יִשְׂרָאֵל *Yiśrāʾēl* (1) = Jacob; (2) the name of a people

יוֹסֵף *Yôsēp̄* Joseph

Exercises:

(a) Translate:

(1) רָדַ֫פְנוּ מִצְרַ֫יְמָה

(2) שֵׁב פֹּה

(3) בְּלִדְתֵּךְ בֵּן

(4) דְּעוּ כִּי הַמֶּ֫לֶךְ בָּא

(5) אַל־תִּירְאִי

(6) לֹא תוּכַל לִישֹׁן

(7) תִּירְשׁוּ אֶת־הָאָ֫רֶץ הַזֹּאת

(8) רֵד הָעִ֫ירָה

(9) שְׁבוּ בְּבֵיתְכֶם

(10) נוּכַל לָלֶ֫כֶת בַּבֹּ֫קֶר

(11) צְאוּ מֵהָעִיר

(12) יְרִשְׁתְּכֶם אַתָּה

(b) Give the Hebrew for the following orally:

1. Go forth (m. s.) today.
2. and when we knew
3. She will bear a son.
4. We shall not inherit this land.
5. He will fashion a new vessel.
6. We shall not be afraid of them.
7. and as he went forth
8. Do you know all these things?
9. Let us go down to the Negev.
10. And they went to their country.
11. Let us sit down and eat.
12. And he slept the whole night.

(c) Translate:

(1) לֹא יִישַׁן שֹׁמֵר יִשְׂרָאֵל.

(2) וַיִּקְרְבוּ הָאֲנָשִׁים אֵלָיו לִשְׁאֹל לוֹ לְשָׁלוֹם.

(3) וְהָיָה בִּקְרֹא הָעָם אֵלַי וְעָנִ֫יתִי אֹתָם.

(4) וַיְהִי בִישֹׁן הַיֶּ֫לֶד וַיַּחֲלֹם חֲלוֹם.

(5) רָחוֹק מְאֹד מֵהַמָּקוֹם הַזֶּה הָעֵ֫מֶק אֲשֶׁר אַתֶּם הֹלְכִים שָׁ֫מָּה.

(6) הָרְגוּ אֶת־בַּ֫עַל הַבַּ֫יִת וַיִּקְחוּ אֶת־כָּל־רְכֻשׁוֹ אִתָּם וַיֵּצְאוּ מֵהָעִיר.

(7) וַיִּשְׁאַל הָאִישׁ וַיֹּאמַר: מֶה עָשִׂ֫יתִי כִּי תִשְׂנָא אֹתִי.

(8) בְּשָׁלוֹם אֶשְׁכַּב וְאִישַׁן כִּי אַתָּה עִמִּי יהוה אֱלֹהִים.

(9) קְרַב אֶל־הַהֵיכָל וּשְׁמַע אֶת־דִּבְרֵי הַנָּבִיא.

(10) לָ֫מָּה לֹא עָנִיתָ כַּאֲשֶׁר שָׁאַ֫לְתִּי לְךָ לְשָׁלוֹם.

(11) לֹא תִקְרַב הָרָעָה בְּבֵיתְךָ כִּי נָתַן יהוה אֶת־מַלְאָכָיו לִשְׁמֹר אֹתְךָ וְאֶת־כָּל־דְּרָכֶ֫יךָ.

(12) מַה־תִּשְׁאַל מִמֶּ֫נִּי.

(13) לְכָדוּ אֶת־הָעִיר בְּטֶ֫רֶם יִבְרְחוּ יֹשְׁבֶ֫יהָ הַמִּדְבָּ֫רָה.

(d) Write in Hebrew:

1. Who is the husband of that beautiful woman standing near the gate?
2. They came to the city from afar to inquire after the health of the king.
3. The owner of the field came and told us to go to our (own) house(s).

4. They set out and traveled many days until they found a large and pleasant valley in which they might dwell in peace.
5. Let us hear his words so that we might know the place from which he has come.

(e) Reading: Joseph and His Brothers (1)

יָשַׁב יַעֲקֹב בְּאֶרֶץ מְגוּרֵי אָבִיו בְּאֶרֶץ כְּנָעַן. אֵלֶּה תֹּלְדוֹת יַעֲקֹב. יוֹסֵף בֶּן־שְׁבַע עֶשְׂרֵה[1] שָׁנָה הָיָה רֹעֶה אֶת־אֶחָיו בַּצֹּאן וְיִשְׂרָאֵל אָהַב אֶת־יוֹסֵף מִכָּל־בָּנָיו כִּי בֶן־זְקֻנִים הוּא לוֹ וְעָשָׂה לוֹ כְּתֹנֶת פַּסִּים.[2] רָאוּ אֶחָיו כִּי אֹתוֹ אָהַב אֲבִיהֶם מִכָּל־אֶחָיו וַיִּשְׂנְאוּ אֹתוֹ וְלֹא יָכְלוּ דַּבְּרוֹ[3] לְשָׁלוֹם.

וַיַּחֲלֹם יוֹסֵף חֲלוֹמוֹת וּבַחֲלוֹמֹתָיו יִשְׁתַּחֲווּ[4] אֶחָיו וְאָבִיו וְאִמּוֹ לְפָנָיו. וַיַּגֵּד[5] אֶת־הַחֲלוֹמוֹת לְאֶחָיו וַיִּשְׂנְאוּ אֹתוֹ עַל־חֲלוֹמֹתָיו וְעַל־דְּבָרָיו וַיַּגֵּד[5] גַּם־אֶל־אָבִיו וַיִּגְעַר בּוֹ אָבִיו וַיֹּאמֶר לוֹ: מָה הַחֲלוֹם הַזֶּה אֲשֶׁר חָלָמְתָּ. הֲבוֹא נָבוֹא[6] אֲנִי וְאִמְּךָ וְאַחֶיךָ לְהִשְׁתַּחֲוֹת[7] לְפָנֶיךָ אַרְצָה.

אֶחָיו שָׂנְאוּ אֹתוֹ וְאָבִיו שָׁמַר אֶת־הַדָּבָר.

Notes to the Reading:

1. "seventeen"
2. meaning unknown. Perhaps "a full garment with long sleeves."
3. "to speak to him"
4. "(they) would bow down"
5. "and he told"
6. "Shall we indeed come"
7. "to bow down"

LESSON 31

122. Verbs III-Hē: Imperfect, Imperative, and Infinitive Construct.

This class of verbs is quite uniform in its inflection. The imperfect ends in *-eh* except where this is replaced by an inflectional ending; the imperative ends in *-ēh*; and the inf. constr. in *-ôṯ*. Below are the paradigms of בָּנָה, which may be taken as a norm of this class, and several verbs which have other peculiarities in addition to being III-*Hē*: עָלָה, also I-guttural; הָגָה, also I-guttural but differing in the preformative vowel from עָלָה; נָטָה, also I-*Nun*; and the slightly irregular verb הָיָה.

	to build	to ascend	to meditate	to extend	to be
Imperfect:	יִבְנֶה	יַעֲלֶה	יֶהְגֶּה	יִטֶּה	יִהְיֶה
	תִּבְנֶה	תַּעֲלֶה	תֶּהְגֶּה	תִּטֶּה	תִּהְיֶה
	תִּבְנֶה	תַּעֲלֶה	תֶּהְגֶּה	תִּטֶּה	תִּהְיֶה
	תִּבְנִי	תַּעֲלִי	תֶּהְגִּי	תִּטִּי	תִּהְיִי
	אֶבְנֶה	אֶעֱלֶה	אֶהְגֶּה	אֶטֶּה	אֶהְיֶה
	יִבְנוּ	יַעֲלוּ	יֶהְגּוּ	יִטּוּ	יִהְיוּ
	תִּבְנֶ֫ינָה	תַּעֲלֶ֫ינָה	תֶּהְגֶּ֫ינָה	תִּטֶּ֫ינָה	תִּהְיֶ֫ינָה
	תִּבְנוּ	תַּעֲלוּ	תֶּהְגּוּ	תִּטּוּ	תִּהְיוּ
	תִּבְנֶ֫ינָה	תַּעֲלֶ֫ינָה	תֶּהְגֶּ֫ינָה	תִּטֶּ֫ינָה	תִּהְיֶ֫ינָה
	נִבְנֶה	נַעֲלֶה	נֶהְגֶּה	נִטֶּה	נִהְיֶה
Imperative:	בְּנֵה	עֲלֵה	הֲגֵה	נְטֵה	הֱיֵה

	בְּנִי	עֲלִי	הֲגִי	נְטִי	הֱיִי
	בְּנוּ	עֲלוּ	הֲגוּ	נְטוּ	הֱיוּ
	בְּנֶ֫ינָה	עֲלֶ֫ינָה	הֲגֶ֫ינָה	נְטֶ֫ינָה	—
Inf. Constr.	בְּנוֹת	עֲלוֹת	הֲגוֹת	נְטוֹת	הֱיוֹת

The verb חָיָה (to live) is inflected like הָיָה, except that the inf. constr. is vocalized with *ă* in the first syllable: חֲיוֹת.

The two verbs אָפָה (to bake) and אָבָה (to be willing) have imperfects יֹאפֶה and יֹאבֶה, following the I-*Aleph* patterning in conjunction with the III-*Hē*.

There is a distinct form for the jussive in the singular. It may be thought of as a shortened (or apocopated) form of the imperfect, without the final *-eh*, but the development of a secondary vowel to resolve the resulting final consonant cluster has produced inconsistencies. Here, for reference, is a list of the most important verbs III-*Hē* with their attested short forms:

	Perfect	*Imperfect*	*Jussive* 3 m. s.	3 f. s./2 m. s.	1 c. s.	1c. pl.
build	בָּנָה	יִבְנֶה	יִ֫בֶן			
despise	בָּזָה	יִבְזֶה	יִ֫בֶז	תִּ֫בֶז		
weep	בָּכָה	יִבְכֶּה	יֵ֫בְךְּ	תֵּ֫בְךְּ		
reveal	גָּלָה	יִגְלֶה	יִ֫גֶל			
be harlot	זָנָה	תִּזְנֶה		תִּ֫זֶן		
be done	כָּלָה	יִכְלֶה	יִ֫כֶל	תִּ֫כֶל		
turn	פָּנָה	יִפְנֶה	יִ֫פֶן	תֵּ֫פֶן	אֵ֫פֶן	נֵ֫פֶן
acquire	קָנָה	יִקְנֶה	יִ֫קֶן			
be many	רָבָה	יִרְבֶּה	יִ֫רֶב	תֵּ֫רֶב		
drink	שָׁתָה	יִשְׁתֶּה	יֵ֫שְׁתְּ	תֵּ֫שְׁתְּ	אֵ֫שְׁתְּ	
capture	שָׁבָה	יִשְׁבֶּה	יִשְׁבְּ			
II-*guttural*:						
pasture	רָעָה	יִרְעֶה	יֵ֫רַע			
see	רָאָה	יִרְאֶה	יֵ֫רֶא	תֵּ֫רֶא	אֵ֫רֶא	
be lost	תָּעָה	יִתְעֶה		תֵּ֫תַע		
I-*guttural*:						
answer	עָנָה	יַעֲנֶה	יַ֫עַן	תַּ֫עַן	אַ֫עַן	
ascend	עָלָה	יַעֲלֶה	יַ֫עַל	תַּ֫עַל	אַ֫עַל	נַ֫עַל
do	עָשָׂה	יַעֲשֶׂה	יַ֫עַשׂ	תַּ֫עַשׂ	אַ֫עַשׂ	נַ֫עַשׂ
conceive	הָרָה			תַּ֫הַר		
camp	חָנָה	יַחֲנֶה	יִ֫חַן			
be angry	חָרָה	יֶחֱרֶה	יִ֫חַר			
I-*Nun*:						
extend	נָטָה	יִטֶּה	יֵט	תֵּט		

Anomalous:

be	הָיָה	יִהְיֶה	יְהִי		תְּהִי	אֱהִי	נְהִי
live	חָיָה	יִחְיֶה	יְחִי				

The importance of these forms lies not so much in their use as jussives but rather in the fact that these short forms are used regularly with *waw*-conversive in the past narrative sequence:

וַיַּ֫עַשׂ and he made
וַתֵּ֫בְךְּ and she wept

The short forms of the 3rd and 2nd persons are nearly always used; in the first person there is an option between the short and normal forms:

וָאֵ֫בְךְּ or וָאֶבְכֶּה and I wept

Note the sequence form וַיַּ֫רְא (and he saw), which differs from the jussive יֵ֫רֶא. There are no cohortatives in *-āh* for verbs III-*He*. The stem of the inf. construct undergoes no changes with the addition of the pronominal suffixes:

בְּנוֹתִי my building
בְּנוֹתְךָ your building
etc.

123. Vocabulary 31.

NOUNS: בּוֹר *bôr* (pl. *-ôṯ*) pit, cistern; fig. the grave
רֵעַ *rēaʿ* (pl. *-îm*) friend, companion [the stem vowel is not changeable: pl. constr. רֵעֵי; the singular with the 3rd pers. masc. sing. suffix is רֵעֵ֫הוּ]
שִׂמְלָה *śimlāh* (pl. *-ôṯ*) outer garment, cloak
VERBS: שָׁפַךְ *šāp̄aḵ* (יִשְׁפֹּךְ) to pour, shed (blood)
תָּפַשׂ *tāp̄aś* (יִתְפֹּשׂ) to seize, grab
נָטָה *nāṭāh* (יִטֶּה) to extend; pitch (tent); turn aside (intr.)
בָּכָה *bāḵāh* (יִבְכֶּה) to weep, mourn
שָׁחַט *šāḥaṭ* (יִשְׁחַט) to slaughter (usu. of animals)
OTHER: עַתָּה *ʿattāh* (adv.) now, and so then, then
רֵיק *rêq* (adj.) empty, worthless, idle
PROPER NAMES: דּוֹתָן *Dôṯān* Dothan, a city about 13 m. north of Shechem
רְאוּבֵן *Rəʾûḇēn* Reuben, first-born son of Jacob (by Leah)

IDIOMS: (1) A plural verb followed by אִישׁ and a correlated singular suffix is to be taken distributively or reciprocally:

הָלְכוּ אִישׁ אֶל־בֵּיתוֹ Each man went to his (own) house.
וַיֹּאמְרוּ אִישׁ אֶל־רֵעֵהוּ And they said to one another.

(2) The imperative of הָלַךְ is frequently used before another imperative or cohortative in a sense difficult to translate. It is more or less an

invitation or inciting to action, like English "*Come on*, let's . . ." It may therefore be omitted often from translation.

לְכוּ וְנַהַרְגֵהוּ אֹתוֹ Come on, let's kill him.

(3) An imperative, especially of הָלַךְ and other verbs of motion, may be followed by the dative pronoun which has no translation value in English:

לֵךְ לְךָ Go! סְעוּ לָכֶם Travel!

Exercises:

(a) Translate:

(1) יִבָּנוּ עִיר חֲדָשָׁה
(2) יְהִי אוֹר
(3) וַיִּחַר לוֹ מְאֹד
(4) וַיִּכְלוּ הַמַּיִם מֵעַל פְּנֵי הָאָרֶץ
(5) וְנַעַל יְרוּשָׁלַ͏ְמָה
(6) כִּרְאוֹתִי אֹתָם
(7) נַעֲשֶׂה אֱלֹהֵי עֵץ
(8) בִּרְעוֹתָם אֶת־צֹאנָם
(9) וַיַּעַן וַיֹּאמֶר
(10) אַל־תִּשְׁתֶּה אֶת־הַמַּיִם
(11) אַל־תֵּתַע
(12) תֵּט אֶת־יָדְךָ
(13) לָמָּה תִבְכֶּה
(14) וַיְכַלּוּ לַעֲשׂוֹת אֶת־הַמְּלָאכָה
(15) וַיַּעֲלוּ הָהָרָה לִרְאוֹת אֶת־הַחַיּוֹת
(16) יִרְעֶה אֶת־עַמּוֹ כְּרֹעֶה
(17) וַנֵּשֶׁב וַנֹּאכַל וַנִּשְׁתֶּה
(18) אַל־תִּבְכֶּה עַל־הָרְשָׁעִים
(19) אֶטֶּה אֶת־יָדַי הַשָּׁמַיְמָה
(20) וַתֵּתַע הָאִשָּׁה בַּמִּדְבָּר
(21) וַיִּשְׁחֲטוּ מֵהַבָּקָר וּמֵהַצֹּאן

(b) Give the Hebrew for the following orally:

1. Don't pour the water.
2. Why are you crying?
3. You ask and he will answer.
4. before he created the earth
5. They were afraid to approach.
6. Remember the history of your people.
7. His house is close to the city.
8. I slept the whole night.
9. Her husband left her.
10. The place is too far away for us to see.

(c) Translate:

(1) וַתִּדֹּר הָאִשָּׁה נֶדֶר וַתֹּאמַר: אֶתֵּן לַיהוה אֶת־הַיֶּלֶד הַזֶּה אֲשֶׁר אֵלֵד וְהוּא יֵשֵׁב בְּהֵיכַל יהוה וְעָבַד אֹתוֹ כָּל־יְמֵי חַיָּיו.
(2) וַיֹּאמֶר הָאִישׁ: לָמָּה בָחַרְתָּ בִי וְאָנֹכִי הַצָּעִיר בְּבֵית אָבִי.
(3) וַיַּעַן אֹתוֹ יהוה לֵאמֹר: אֶהְיֶה עִמְּךָ בְּכָל־אֲשֶׁר אַתָּה עֹשֶׂה.
(4) סְבָבוּ אֹתִי שֹׂנְאַי וְעָזְבוּ אֹתִי אֹהֲבַי.
(5) לָמָּה תַעַזְבוּ אֶת־אֶרֶץ מְגוּרֵי אֲבִיכֶם וְשַׁבְתֶּם אֶל־הָאָרֶץ הַהִיא.
(6) בֹּשְׁנוּ כִּי לֹא לָקַח אֶת־הַמִּנְחָה אֲשֶׁר נָתַנּוּ לוֹ.

(7) וַיֹּאמֶר יהוה אֶל־מֹשֶׁה: נְטֵה אֶת־יָדְךָ עַל־הַשָּׁמַיִם וִיהִי חֹשֶׁךְ עַל־אֶרֶץ מִצְרָיִם וַיֵּט מֹשֶׁה אֶת־יָדוֹ עַל־הַשָּׁמַיִם וַיְהִי חֹשֶׁךְ בְּכָל־אֶרֶץ מִצְרַיִם וְלֹא רָאוּ אִישׁ אֶת־אָחִיו וְלֹא קָמוּ אִישׁ מִמְּקוֹמוֹ.

(d) Write in Hebrew:

1. The men of the city rebuked him because he had not heeded the words of the elders.
2. They are evil men because they have shed blood and sinned against the Lord.
3. And he raised his eyes and saw two men standing near the well.
4. And when she heard these words, she fell to the ground and wept.
5. You shall see and you shall know that the Lord is with us.
6. Heaven and earth are full (of) your (m. s.) glory.
7. Eat and drink for in the morning we shall go forth to battle.

(e) Reading: Joseph and his Brothers (2)

וַיֵּלְכוּ אֶחָיו לִרְעוֹת אֶת־צֹאן אֲבִיהֶם בִּשְׁכֶם וַיֹּאמֶר יִשְׂרָאֵל אֶל־יוֹסֵף: הֲלֹא אַחֶיךָ רֹעִים בִּשְׁכֶם, לְכָה וְאֶשְׁלָחֲךָ אֲלֵיהֶם, לֶךְ נָא רְאֵה אֶת־שְׁלוֹם אַחֶיךָ וְאֶת־שְׁלוֹם הַצֹּאן, וַיִּשְׁלַח אֹתוֹ מֵעֵמֶק חֶבְרוֹן וַיָּבֹא[1] שְׁכֶמָה.[2]

וַיְהִי אַחֲרֵי אֲשֶׁר לֹא מָצָא אֹתָם בִּשְׁכֶם וַיֵּלֶךְ וַיִּמְצָא אֹתָם בְּדוֹתָן וַיִּרְאוּ אֹתוֹ אֶחָיו מֵרָחוֹק וּבְטֶרֶם יִקְרַב אֲלֵיהֶם וַיֹּאמְרוּ אִישׁ אֶל־אָחִיו: בַּעַל הַחֲלוֹמוֹת בָּא וְעַתָּה לְכוּ וְנַהַרְגֵהוּ אֹתוֹ וְנַשְׁלִכֵהוּ אֹתוֹ בְּאַחַד הַבּוֹרוֹת וְאָמַרְנוּ כִּי חַיָּה רָעָה אֲכָלָתְהוּ אֹתוֹ.

וַיִּשְׁמַע רְאוּבֵן אֶת־דִּבְרֵיהֶם וַיֹּאמֶר אֲלֵיהֶם: אַל־תִּשְׁפְּכוּ דָם, וְיָד אַל־תִּשְׁלְחוּ בוֹ. וַיְהִי כַּאֲשֶׁר בָּא יוֹסֵף אֶל־אֶחָיו וַיִּתְפְּשׂוּ אֹתוֹ וַיִּקְחוּ אֶת־כֻּתָּנְתּוֹ מִמֶּנּוּ וַיַּשְׁלִיכוּ[3] אֹתוֹ הַבּוֹרָה וְהַבּוֹר הָיָה רֵיק אֵין בּוֹ מָיִם.[4]

Notes to the Reading:

1. "and he came"
2. שְׁכֶם with directive *-āh*
3. "and they threw"
4. Note the asyndetic clause beginning with אֵין.

LESSON 32

124. Hollow Verbs (II-Waw/Yodh): Imperfect, Imperative, and Infinitive Construct.

In the inflection of the perfect (§64) the lexical distinction between verbs II-*Waw* and II-*Yodh* is irrelevant. In the imperfect, however, the stem vowel reflects this distinction and is, indeed, responsible for the classification of the verbs under their respective consonantal types: verbs with *û*-imperfects are considered II-*Waw*, and those with *î*-imperfects as II-*Yodh*. Neither the *waw* nor the *yodh* has a consonantal value in the main inflections of these forms. The two basic types are

	Perfect		*Imperfect*			*Imperative*		*Inf. Construct*	
II-*Waw*	קָם	*qām*	normal	יָקוּם	*yāqûm*	קוּם	*qûm*	קוּם	*qûm*
			jussive	יָקֹם	*yāqōm*				
			converted	וַיָּ֫קָם	*wayyā́qom*				
II-*Yodh*	שָׂם	*śām*	normal	יָשִׂים	*yāśîm*	שִׂים	*śîm*	שׂוּם	*śûm*
			jussive	יָשֵׂם	*yāśēm*			שִׂים	*śîm*
			converted	וַיָּ֫שֶׂם	*wayyā́śem*				

Verbs of the second type are unstable, in that the vowel of the infinitive construct varies between *û* and *î*. Some verbs have *î* consistently, such as שִׁית (to place), while others have either vowel: לִין or לוּן (to pass the night). Because of this variation they may be listed in the lexicon under either root form.

Note that the jussive and the form used with *waw*-conversive are distinct. Remember that the jussive forms are limited to the 3rd pers. sing. masc. and fem. The distinctive converted form, with retraction of the accent to the preformative syllable, is commonly found only in these same persons, plus the 2nd pers. masc. sing.; otherwise the converted form is the same as the normal imperfect.

Imperfect:

יָקוּם	*yāqûm*	יָקֿוּמוּ	*yāqûmû*	יָשִׂים	*yāśîm*	יָשִׂ֫ימוּ	*yāśîmû*
תָּקוּם	*tāqûm*	תְּקוּמֶ֫ינָה	*təqûmẹnāh*	תָּשִׂים	*tāśîm*	תְּשִׂימֶ֫ינָה	*təśîmẹnāh*
תָּקוּם	*tāqûm*	תָּקֿוּמוּ	*tāqûmû*	תָּשִׂים	*tāśîm*	תָּשִׂ֫ימוּ	*tāśîmû*
תָּקֿוּמִי	*tāqûmî*	תְּקוּמֶ֫ינָה	*təqûmẹnāh*	תָּשִׂ֫ימִי	*tāśîmî*	תְּשִׂימֶ֫ינָה	*təśîmẹnāh*
אָקוּם	*'āqûm*	נָקוּם	*nāqûm*	אָשִׂים	*'āśîm*	נָשִׂים	*nāśîm*

Jussive:	יָקֹם	*yāqōm*	יָשֵׂם	*yāśēm*
	תָּקֹם	*tāqōm*	תָּשֵׂם	*tāśēm*
Converted:	וַיָּ֫קָם	*wayyā́qom*	וַיָּ֫שֶׂם	*wayyā́śem*
	וַתָּ֫קָם	*wattā́qom*	וַתָּ֫שֶׂם	*wattā́śem*
	וַתָּ֫קָם	*wattā́qom*	וַתָּ֫שֶׂם	*wattā́śem*
	וַתָּקֿוּמִי	*wattāqûmî*	וַתָּשִׂ֫ימִי	*wattāśîmî*
		(etc.)		(etc.)
Cohortative:	אָקֿוּמָה	*'āqûmāh*	אָשִׂ֫ימָה	*'āśîmāh*
	נָקֿוּמָה	*nāqûmāh*	נָשִׂ֫ימָה	*nāśîmāh*
Imperative:	קוּם	*qûm*	שִׂים	*śîm*
	קֿוּמִי	*qûmî*	שִׂ֫ימִי	*śîmî*
	קֿוּמוּ	*qûmû*	שִׂ֫ימוּ	*śîmû*
	קֹ֫מְנָה	*qṓmnāh*	[שֵׂ֫מְנָה	*śḗmnāh*]
Inf. Construct with Suffixes	קוּמִי	*qûmî*	שׂוּמִי	*śûmî*
	קוּמְךָ	*qûməḵā*	שׂוּמְךָ	*śûməḵā*
	קוּמֵךְ	*qûmēḵ*	שׂוּמֵךְ	*śûmēḵ*
		(etc.)		(etc.)

Remarks:

1. Imperfect fem. pl. of the form תָּקֹ֫מְנָה *tāqṓmnāh* (instead of תְּקוּמֶ֫ינָה) also occur.

2. Several verbs, mainly with gutturals or ר as the final root consonant, have *a* instead of *o* or *e* in the converted form. E.g. יָסוּר *yāsûr*, but וַיָּ֫סַר *wayyā́sar* (and he turned aside); יָנוּחַ *yānûᵃḥ*, but וַיָּ֫נַח *wayyā́naḥ* (and he rested).

The following verbs belonging to these two principal types have occurred thus far in this text:

גָּר	יָגוּר	to sojourn	מֵת	יָמוּת	to die
צָם	יָצוּם	to fast	שָׂם	יָשִׂים	to set
קָם	יָקוּם	to arise	שָׁר	יָשִׁיר	to sing
שָׁב	יָשׁוּב	to return			

A few verbs occur with *ô* as the characteristic vowel of the imperfect and related forms. The following are the most important of these:

Perfect			*Imperfect*		*Imperative*		*Inf. Construct*	
בָּא	*bā'*	normal	יָבוֹא	*yāḇô'*	בֹּא	*bō'*	בּוֹא	*bô'*
———		jussive	יָבוֹא	*yāḇô'*				
		converted	וַיָּבוֹא	*wayyāḇô'*				
בֹּשׁ	*bōš*		יֵבוֹשׁ	*yēḇôš*	בּוֹשׁ	*bôš*	בּוֹשׁ	*bôš*
אֹר	*'ōr*		[יָאוֹר	*yā'ôr*]	אוֹר	*'ôr*	אוֹר	*'ôr*

Inflection proceeds as above. The variation between *ô* and *ō* in these forms is not grammatically significant. Note that the accent is not retracted in וַיָּבוֹא.

125. Vocabulary 32.

NOUNS: בֶּ֫צַע *béṣaʻ* (w. suff. בִּצְעִי) profit, gain, advantage. Note the idiom: מַה־בֶּ֫צַע What profit is there?

סָרִיס *sārîs* (pl. irreg. סָרִיסִים) eunuch, officer.

אָדוֹן *'āḏôn* (pl. *-îm*) lord, master. Often used in the plural with singular meaning.

VERBS: שָׁת *šāṯ* (יָשִׁית) to put, place, set. A synonym of שָׂם.

רָץ *rāṣ* (יָרוּץ) to run

נָס *nās* (יָנוּס) to flee

רָדַף *rāḏap̄* (יִרְדֹּף) to pursue, chase, persecute (object with אֶת־ or אַחֲרֵי)

קָנָה *qānāh* (יִקְנֶה) to acquire, purchase, buy

OTHER: לִקְרַאת *liqra(')ṯ* (prep., with suff. לִקְרָאתִי etc.) toward, to meet, against

הִנֵּה *hinnēh* An introductory particle, customarily translated "behold," emphasizing the immediate presence of an object or a fact. In its idiomatic use with רָאָה it is best omitted from translation:
רָאָה וְהִנֵּה אֲנָשִׁים בָּאִים He saw men coming.
(or) He saw that men were coming.
But *not* "He saw, and behold men were coming."

PROPER NAMES: פַּרְעֹה *parʻōh* the title of the king of Egypt, the Pharaoh

פּוֹטִיפַר *pôṭîp̄ar* Potiphar

גִּלְעָד *gilʻāḏ* Gilead, a region east of the Jordan River

יְהוּדָה *yəhûḏāh* Judah: (1) the fourth son of Jacob, by Leah; (2) the tribe bearing his name; (3) the southern kingdom, as opposed to Israel, the northern kingdom, during the period of the divided monarchy.

יִשְׁמְעֵאלִים · *yišmə'ē(')lîm* Ishmaelites, a term applied to various little known nomadic groups several times in the OT.

Exercises:

(a) Translate:

(1) וְהָיָה בִּשְׁאֹל הָעָם אֹתוֹ וְלֹא יַעֲנֶה אֹתָם.
(2) נֹוּסוּ כִּי אֹיְבֵיכֶם רֹדְפִים אַחֲרֵיכֶם.
(3) מִי הָאִישׁ הָרָץ לִקְרָאתֵנוּ.
(4) מָכְרוּ אֶת־הַמִּקְנֶה אֲשֶׁר קָנוּ שָׁם.
(5) אֵיפֹה שַׁתָּ אֶת־כְּלֵי הַמָּיִם.
(6) וַיְהִי אִישׁ יָשָׁר בְּכָל־אֲשֶׁר עָשָׂה.
(7) וַיַּרְא וְהִנֵּה סְרִיס הַמֶּלֶךְ בָּא לִקְרָאתוֹ.
(8) וַיָּקָם וַיֵּלֶךְ עִמּוֹ הַמִּדְבָּרָה.
(9) וַיָּשֶׁת אֶת־הַסְּפָרִים לִפְנֵי אִמּוֹ.
(10) וַיְהִי בַצָּהֳרַיִם וָאֵרֶא אִישׁ בָּא לִקְרָאתִי.
(11) וָאָקוּם וָאָנוּס מִלְּפָנָיו.
(12) אֶשְׁכַּב וְיָשַׁנְתִּי פֹּה עַד־הַבֹּקֶר.
(13) בֵּיתֵנוּ קָרוֹב אֶל־הַהֵיכָל.
(14) רְדֹף אַחֲרֵיהֶם כִּי לָקְחוּ אֶת־רְכוּשֵׁנוּ.

(b) Give the Hebrew for the following orally:

1. Run to the field.
2. They will flee from their houses.
3. Who will inherit his garden?
4. Where will you buy the cattle?
5. Where did you put my money?
6. Did they chase you?
7. The king's official is very rich.
8. There is no advantage in weeping.
9. We left because of the famine.
10. You shall run and find him.
11. We fled when they burned our houses.

(c) Translate the following:

(1) יָדֵנוּ תִהְיֶה בּוֹ בְּהָרְגֵנוּ אֹתוֹ
(2) קוּמִי וְשׁוּבִי הַבַּיְתָה
(3) לֹא חָפַצְנוּ לָצוּם
(4) מַה־בֶּצַע כִּי נָגוּר פֹּה
(5) נָשִׂימָה אֶת־אָחִינוּ עַל־הַכִּסֵּא
(6) לֹא יָכֹלְתִּי לָרוּץ
(7) תֶּחְדַּל לָצוּם
(8) וַיָּגָר שָׁם
(9) וַיָּשֶׂם אֹתוֹ בְּקִבְרוֹ
(10) יָרוּץ הַיֶּלֶד אֶל־הַשָּׂדֶה
(11) הַנְּעָרִים שָׁבִים אִישׁ אֶל־בֵּיתוֹ
(12) נוּס כִּי אֹיִבְךָ בָּא
(13) חָפְצוּ לָשׁוּב וְלֹא יָכְלוּ
(14) מִי יַחְפֹּץ לָשֶׁבֶת שָׁם

(d) Write in Hebrew:

1. And in the morning his companion arose and went to the city.
2. They will slaughter our cattle and burn our vineyards.
3. It is bad to shed blood.
4. They arose and pursued him, but they could not find him.
5. And now, let us choose a king for ourselves (= us).
6. Where did you put his cloak?
7. Did you know that this vessel is empty?

(e) Reading: Joseph Is Taken to Egypt

וַיֵּשְׁבוּ אֲחֵי יוֹסֵף לֶאֱכֹל לֶ֫חֶם וַיִּשְׂאוּ עֵינֵיהֶם[1] וַיִּרְאוּ וְהִנֵּה אֹרְחַת[2] יִשְׁמְעֵאלִים בָּאָה מִגִּלְעָד וְהֵם הֹלְכִים לָרֶ֫דֶת מִצְרָ֫יְמָה.

וַיֹּ֫אמֶר יְהוּדָה אֶל־אֶחָיו לֵאמֹר: מַה־בֶּ֫צַע כִּי נַהֲרֹג אֶת־אָחִינוּ, לְכוּ וְנִמְכְּרָה אֹתוֹ לַיִּשְׁמְעֵאלִים וְיָדֵ֫נוּ אַל־תְּהִי בוֹ כִּי אָחִ֫ינוּ בְשָׂרֵ֫נוּ הוּא.

וַיִּשְׁמְעוּ אֶחָיו וַיִּמְכְּרוּ אֶת־יוֹסֵף לַיִּשְׁמְעֵאלִים וַיֵּ֫רֶד יוֹסֵף אִתָּם מִצְרָ֫יְמָה.

וַיִּ֫קֶן אֹתוֹ פּוֹטִיפַר סְרִיס פַּרְעֹה אִישׁ מִצְרִי מִיַּד הַיִּשְׁמְעֵאלִים וַיְהִי יהוה אֶת־יוֹסֵף וַיְהִי אִישׁ מַצְלִיחַ[3] בְּבֵית אֲדֹנָיו הַמִּצְרִי.

Notes to the Reading:

1. The omission of אֶת־ here and often in the readings to follow is in accord with the usage found in the text underlying the reading.
2. אֹרְחָה a caravan
3. "successful"

LESSON 33

126. Geminate Verbs: Imperfect, Imperative, and Infinitive Construct.

No single class of verbs shows as much variety in the formation of the imperfect as that of geminate verbs, i.e. whose second and third root consonants are identical. No one of these verbs occurs frequently enough to offer a complete paradigm; the following tables, therefore, represent a compilation from the available data. On historical grounds, the more original forms of the imperfect system are

	Perfect		*Imperfect*	*Imperative*	*Inf. Constr.*
ō-imperfects	סָבַב *sāḇaḇ*	normal	יָסֹב *yāsōḇ*	סֹב *sōḇ*	סֹ֫ב *sōḇ*
		jussive	יָסֹב *yāsōḇ*		
		converted	וַיָּ֫סָב *wayyā́soḇ*		
a-imperfects	קַל *qal*	normal	יֵקַל *yēqal*	——	[קֹל *qōl*]
		jussive	יֵקַל *yēqal*		
		converted	וַיֵּקַל *wayyēqal*		

In the normal inflection of these forms the original doubling of the final stem consonant shows up before any suffixed vowel. The accent, except in the case of the ending *-ẹ̄nāh*, remains on the stem:

יָסֹב *yāsōḇ*	יָסֹ֫בּוּ *yāsṓbbû*	יֵקַל *yēqal*	יֵקַ֫לּוּ *yēqállû*
תָּסֹב *tāsōḇ*	תְּסֻבֶּ֫ינָה *təsubbệnāh*	תֵּקַל *tēqal*	[תְּקַלֶּ֫ינָה *təqallệnāh*]
תָּסֹב *tāsōḇ*	תָּסֹ֫בּוּ *tāsṓbbû*	תֵּקַל *tēqal*	תֵּקַ֫לּוּ *tēqállû*

תָּסֹבִּי *tāsṓbbî*	תְּסֻבֶּינָה *təsubbênāh*	תֵּקַלִּי *tēqállî*	[תְּקַלֶּינָה *təqallênāh*]
אָסֹב *'āsōḇ*	נָסֹב *nāsōḇ*	אֵקַל *'ēqal*	נֵקַל *nēqal*

A second type of imperfect, not infrequent, follows the pattern of verbs I-*Nun* in the formation of the stem, but there are several optional forms in the inflection:

יִסֹּב *yissōḇ*	יִסֹּבּוּ *yissṓbbû* or יִסְּבוּ *yissəḇû*
תִּסֹּב *tissōḇ*	תִּסֹּבְנָה *tissṓḇnāh*
תִּסֹּב *tissōḇ*	תִּסֹּבּוּ *tissṓbbû* or תִּסְּבוּ *tissəḇû*
תִּסֹּבִּי *tissṓbbî* or תִּסְּבִי *tissəḇî*	תִּסֹּבְנָה *tissṓḇnāh*
אֶסֹּב *'essōḇ*	נִסֹּב *nissōḇ*

And similarly throughout for יִקַּל *yiqqal* etc.

The following further oddities in the inflection of the imperfect are mentioned for reference only:

(1) Assimilation to the Hollow Verb inflection is not unknown: thus, e.g., יָשׁוּד *yāšûḏ*, from the root שׁדד.

(2) Inflections like the first given above also have such alternate forms as יֵקַלוּ *yēqəlû* (with reduction) instead of יֵקַלּוּ *yēqállû*. E.g. יָזֻמוּ *yāzəmû* (they will consider) for expected יָזֹמּוּ *yāzṓmmû*.

(3) Rarely one encounters forms belonging to the paradigm of still other types, such as יֵחֵמוּ *yeḥēmû* (they will be warm, root חמם), or תִּישַׁמְנָה *tîšámnāh* (you will be devastated, root שׁמם).

The imperative and infinitive construct show similar deviations, but the following should be taken as the norm:

	Imperative	*Inf. Construct*
ō-imperfects	סֹב *sōḇ*	סֹב *sōḇ*
	סֹבִּי *sṓbbî*	סֻבִּי *subbî*
	סֹבּוּ *sṓbbû*	סֻבְּךָ *subbəḵā*
	סֹבְנָה *sṓḇnāh*	סֻבֵּךְ *subbēḵ*, etc.
a-imperfects	קַל *qal*	
	קַלִּי *qallî*	
	קַלּוּ *qallû*	
	קַלְנָה *qálnāh*	

The fem. sing. imperative also occurs with ultimate stress: גֹּזִּי *gozzî* (shear), רָנִּי *ronnî* (jubilate). Occasionally the inf. construct appears in the pattern of the regular triliteral verb: שְׁדֹד *šəḏōḏ* (to devastate), שְׁלֹל *šəlōl* (to plunder), גְּזֹז *gəzōz* (to shear).

Note the imperfects of תַּם (to be finished): יֵתַם or יִתֹּם.
רַע (to be bad): יֵרַע

127. Vocabulary 33.

NOUNS: מְאוּמָה *mə'ûmāh* (no pl.) anything; with negative: nothing

אַף *'ap̄* (w. suff. אַפִּי ; dual אַפַּיִם) nose, face, anger. Used as the subject of חָרָה ; thus חָרָה אַפּוֹ = חָרָה לוֹ. The object of the anger is expressed by the preposition בְּ .

VERBS: חָשַׂךְ *ḥāśak̲* (יַחְשֹׂךְ) to withhold, keep back for oneself

חָנַן *ḥānan* (יָחֹן) to favor, be gracious toward

שָׁמֵם *šāmēm* (יֵשֹׁם or יֵשַׁם) to be desolated (of places), to be appalled (of persons); act. part. שֹׁמֵם desolated.

דָּם *dam* (יִדֹּם) to be silent, astonished

מָדַד *mād̲ad̲* (יָמֹד) to measure

OTHER: עִבְרִי *'ib̲rî* (pl. עִבְרִים ; fem. sing. עִבְרִיָּה) Hebrew, as adj. or noun.

כִּי אִם *kî 'im* (conj.) unless, except (that); but rather

אֵיךְ *'êk̲* (interrog. adv.) how, in what manner? Also used in exclamations.

אֵיכָה *'êk̲āh* idem

Exercises:

(a) Translate:

(1) תָּחֹן אֹתוֹ וְאַל־תִּשְׁפֹּךְ אֶת־דָּמוֹ

(2) תֵּשַׁם הָעִיר וְיֹשְׁבֶיהָ יִדֹּמּוּ

(3) מִי יָכֹל לָמֹד אֶת־הַשָּׁמַיִם

(4) יֵרַע הַדָּבָר בְּעֵינָיו

(5) תַּמּוּ לַעֲבֹר אֶת־הַנָּהָר

(6) דֹּמּוּ כַּאֲשֶׁר רָאוּ אֹתָנוּ

(7) אַחַר מָדְדְךָ אֶת־הַשָּׂדֶה

(8) וַיֵּרְעוּ הַדְּבָרִים בְּעֵינַי

(9) אֵיךְ תַּעֲשֶׂה אֶת־הַמְּלָאכָה

(10) וַיִּתַּמּוּ לֶאֱכֹל

(11) וְעַתָּה חֹן אֹתִי כִּי אֲנִי עַבְדְּךָ

(12) בְּטֶרֶם תָּסֹבּוּ אֶת־הָעִיר

(13) וַתִּדֹּם הָאָרֶץ בִּנְטוֹתוֹ אֶת־יָדָיו

(14) מַדֹּתוּ אֶת־הַכֶּסֶף

(15) וַיְהִי כְּשָׁמְעוֹ אֶת־דְּבָרַי וַיִּחַר אַפּוֹ בִּי

(b) Give the Hebrew for the following orally. Use infinitival constructions where possible:

1. and when he lay down
2. and when I shall have finished building
3. and when they had become silent
4. so that he might redeem us
5. and when I measured the vessels
6. until our work is finished
7. and when they had chosen a king
8. lest he withhold his blessing from us
9. lest they smash the altar
10. when we came from east of the city
11. because we sinned against the Lord
12. after he had gone forth from the camp

(c) Write in Hebrew:

1. There was a war between the Israelites (lit. sons of Israel) and the Canaanites who were in the land at that time.
2. We will not be able to go forth unless you go forth with us.
3. Let us rejoice in his being gracious toward us and in his giving us deliverance from our enemies.
4. Where will you go and where will you dwell and what will you do?
5. After he had seized our money he ran out of the house.
6. He will give help to those who trust in him, but those who have sinned against him will perish.

(d) Reading: Joseph and Potiphar's Wife

וַיְהִי אַחַר הַדְּבָרִים הָאֵלֶּה וַתִּשָּׂא אֵשֶׁת פּוֹטִיפַר אֶת־עֵינֶיהָ[1] אֶל־יוֹסֵף כִּי הוּא הָיָה יְפֵה מַרְאֶה וַתֹּאמֶר אֵלָיו: שִׁכְבָה עִמִּי. וַיְמָאֵן[2] יוֹסֵף וַיֹּאמֶר אֵלֶיהָ: אֲדֹנִי נָתַן בְּיָדִי אֶת־כָּל־אֲשֶׁר יֵשׁ לוֹ, אֵין אִישׁ גָּדוֹל מִמֶּנִּי בַּבַּיִת הַזֶּה, וְלֹא חָשַׂךְ מִמֶּנִּי מְאוּמָה כִּי אִם אוֹתָךְ בַּאֲשֶׁר[3] אַתְּ אִשְׁתּוֹ וְאֵיךְ אֶעֱשֶׂה הָרָעָה הַגְּדוֹלָה הַזֹּאת וְחָטָאתִי לֵאלֹהִים.

וַיְהִי כְּדַבְּרָהּ[4] אֶל־יוֹסֵף יוֹם יוֹם[5] וְלֹא שָׁמַע אֵלֶיהָ לִשְׁכַּב אֶצְלָהּ לִהְיוֹת עִמָּהּ וַיְהִי כְּהַיּוֹם הַזֶּה[6] וַיָּבֹא הַבַּיְתָה לַעֲשׂוֹת מְלַאכְתּוֹ וְאֵין אִישׁ מֵאַנְשֵׁי הַבַּיִת שָׁם בַּבָּיִת וַתִּתְפֹּשׂ אֹתוֹ בְּבִגְדוֹ לֵאמֹר: שִׁכְבָה עִמִּי, וַיַּעֲזֹב בִּגְדוֹ בְּיָדָהּ וַיָּנָס וַיֵּצֵא הַחוּצָה.

וַיְהִי כִּרְאוֹתָהּ כִּי עָזַב אֶת־בִּגְדוֹ בְּיָדָהּ וַיָּנָס הַחוּצָה וַתִּקְרָא לְאַנְשֵׁי בֵיתָהּ וַתֹּאמֶר לָהֶם לֵאמֹר: רְאוּ בָּא אֵלַי הָעֶבֶד הָעִבְרִי לִשְׁכַּב עִמִּי וָאֶקְרָא בְּקוֹל גָּדוֹל וַיְהִי כְשָׁמְעוֹ אֶת־קוֹלִי וַיַּעֲזֹב בִּגְדוֹ אֶצְלִי וַיָּנָס וַיֵּצֵא הַחוּצָה.

וַיְהִי בְּבוֹא אִישָׁהּ הַבַּיְתָה וַתֹּאמֶר גַּם־אֵלָיו כַּדְּבָרִים הָאֵלֶּה וַיְהִי כְּשָׁמְעוֹ אֶת־דִּבְרֵי אִשְׁתּוֹ וַיִּחַר אַפּוֹ וַיִּקַּח אֶת־יוֹסֵף וַיִּתֵּן אֹתוֹ בַּמָּקוֹם אֲשֶׁר אֲסִירֵי הַמֶּלֶךְ שָׁם.

Notes to the Reading:

1. Obviously an amatory gesture.
2. "(he) refused"
3. "because"
4. "when she spoke"
5. Repetition of a noun to express distributive notion: every day, day after day.
6. "on a certain day." The unusual form of the preposition *kə* is due to its idiomatic usage in this phrase, where it means literally "about, approximately."

Helene Clauder

Wed 9 ✓ Mid-Term

Mon 14 ✓

Wed 16 ✓

Mon 21 ✓

Wed 23 ✓

Mon 28

Wed 30 — Final EXAM.

LESSON 34

128. The Passive Participle.

The passive participle, a verbal adjective, is formed on the pattern *ā–û* with all verbal root types except those II-*Waw/Yodh.*

Perfect	*Passive Participle*			*Infinitive Absolute*	
כָּתַב	כָּתוּב	*kāṯûḇ*	written	כָּתוֹב	*kāṯôḇ*
עָזַב	עָזוּב	*ʿāzûḇ*	abandoned	עָזוֹב	*ʿāzôḇ*
בָּחַר	בָּחוּר	*bāḥûr*	chosen	בָּחוֹר	*bāḥôr*
שָׁלַח	שָׁלוּחַ	*šālû^{a}ḥ*	sent	שָׁלוֹחַ	*šālô^{a}ḥ*
אָכַל	אָכוּל	*ʾāḵûl*	eaten	אָכוֹל	*ʾāḵôl*
נָטַע	נָטוּעַ	*nāṭû^{a}ʿ*	planted	נָטוֹעַ	*nāṭô^{a}ʿ*
נָשָׂא	נָשׂוּא	*nāśûʾ*	raised up	נָשׂוֹא	*nāśôʾ*
יָדַע	יָדוּעַ	*yāḏû^{a}ʿ*	known	יָדוֹעַ	*yāḏô^{a}ʿ*
סָבַב	סָבוּב	*sāḇûḇ*	surrounded	סָבוֹב	*sāḇôḇ*
בָּנָה	בָּנוּי	*bānûy*	built	בָּנֹה	*bānōh*
קָם	(קוּם)	(*qûm*)	——	קוֹם	*qôm*
שָׂם	(שִׂים)	(*śîm*)	placed	שׂוֹם	*śôm*

Because of semantic incompatibility the form is not usually found with verbs having stative or intransitive meanings. The generally intransitive character of verbs II-*Waw/Yodh* makes the occurrence of a passive participle in that class rare and open to question; the forms מוּל *mûl* (circumcised) and שִׂים *śîm* (placed) are often quoted as examples.

The stem forms as given above call for little comment. Note the furtive *páṯaḥ* in roots III-guttural and the final *yodh* in roots III-*Hē*.

As an adjective the participle is tenseless, but bears the connotation of completed action. In English, therefore, a relative clause with a perfect or preterite verb is often required in translation:

הָאִישׁ הַהָרוּג the slain man, the man who was slain
הַסֵּפֶר הַכָּתוּב the written book, the book which was written

The participle as a predicate adjective has the same properties as other adjectives in this position (§23). E.g.

הָאִישׁ הָרוּג The man is/was/has been slain.

gains its tense from the context in which it occurs and not from the participle itself.

The addition of a prepositional phrase to express an agent, as in "the man who was slain by his enemies," is virtually unknown in Hebrew, but like any adjective it may be in construct with a following qualifying noun:

עִיר שְׂרוּפַת אֵשׁ a city which has been burned with fire

The participle need not be in the construct state:

אִישׁ חָגוּר כְּלֵי הַמִּלְחָמָה a man girded with the weapons of war

129. The Infinitive Absolute.

The infinitive absolute, whose forms are given in the preceding paragraph, is not inflected. It is primarily an adverb whose main uses are as follows:

(1) It is placed before or after a finite verbal form to emphasize the verbal idea in some way. The English translation of this construction will vary from context to context, often requiring the use of adverbs such as "surely, certainly, indeed" or the like. E.g.

שָׁמוֹר תִּשְׁמְרוּ אֶת־מִצְוֹתַי You shall indeed observe my commandments.
אִם רָאֹה תִרְאֶה בָּעֳנִי אֲמָתֶךָ If you will indeed look upon the affliction of your maidservant . . .

The more usual position is before the verb, as above. If the verb is used intransitively the inf. absolute may follow:

שִׁמְעוּ שָׁמוֹעַ . . . וּרְאוּ רָאֹה . . . Listen carefully . . . and look carefully . . .

(2) Similar to the preceding is a sequence of two inf. absolute complementing a finite verb; the two infinitives are often antithetical in meaning:

וַיֵּלֶךְ הָלוֹךְ וְאָכוֹל And he walked along eating.
(lit.) And he walked, walking and eating

וַיֵּצֵא יָצוֹא וָשׁוֹב	And he went back and forth. (lit.) He went forth, going forth and returning.

(3) Instead of emphasizing or complementing the main verb, the inf. absolute may be used to describe action on a par with the main verb and may be viewed thus as an uninflected substitute for a finite form:

אֶת־כָּל־זֶה רָאִיתִי וְנָתוֹן אֶת־לִבִּי לְכָל־מַעֲשֶׂה...	All this have I seen and (I have) applied (lit. given) my attention (lit. heart) to every deed...

(4) The use described in (3) gives an almost independent status to the infinitive. For reasons that are quite obscure, instances occur in which the inf. absolute is used instead of a finite verb, nor is it clearly dependent on any other verb in a given clause. Note the following imperative uses:

שָׁמוֹר אֶת־כָּל־הַמִּצְוָה	Observe the entire commandment.
זָכוֹר אֶת־הַיּוֹם הַזֶּה	Remember this day.
הָלוֹךְ וְקָרָאתָ בְאָזְנֵי יְרוּשָׁלִַם	Go and cry into the ears of Jerusalem.

130. The Numbers from 3 to 10.

The numbers from three to ten have two forms: a feminine in *-āh* which is used to modify *masculine* nouns and an endingless form used to modify *feminine* nouns:

	masc. modifier				*fem. modifier*			
	absolute		*construct*		*absolute*		*construct*	
three	שְׁלֹשָׁה	*šəlōšāh*	שְׁלֹשֶׁת	*šəlṓšeṯ*	שָׁלֹשׁ	*šālōš*	שְׁלֹשׁ	*šəlōš*
four	אַרְבָּעָה	*’arbā‘āh*	אַרְבַּעַת	*’arbá‘aṯ*	אַרְבַּע	*’arba‘*	אַרְבַּע	*’arba‘*
five	חֲמִשָּׁה	*ḥămiššāh*	חֲמֵשֶׁת	*ḥămḗšeṯ*	חָמֵשׁ	*ḥāmēš*	חֲמֵשׁ	*ḥămēš*
six	שִׁשָּׁה	*šiššāh*	שֵׁשֶׁת	*šḗšeṯ*	שֵׁשׁ	*šēš*	שֵׁשׁ	*šēš*
seven	שִׁבְעָה	*šiḇ‘āh*	שִׁבְעַת	*šiḇ‘aṯ*	שֶׁבַע	*šéḇa‘*	שְׁבַע	*šéḇa‘*
eight	שְׁמֹנָה	*šəmōnāh*	שְׁמֹנַת	*šəmōnaṯ*	שְׁמֹנֶה	*šəmōneh*	שְׁמֹנֶה	*šəmōneh*
nine	תִּשְׁעָה	*tiš‘āh*	תִּשְׁעַת	*tiš‘aṯ*	תֵּשַׁע	*tḗša‘*	תְּשַׁע	*tēša‘*
ten	עֲשָׂרָה	*‘ăśārāh*	עֲשֶׂרֶת	*‘ăśéreṯ*	עֶשֶׂר	*‘éśer*	עֶשֶׂר	*‘éśer*

The absolute forms normally precede the noun, which is in the plural:

שֶׁבַע נָשִׁים	seven women	שִׁבְעָה אֲנָשִׁים	seven men
שֶׁבַע פָּרוֹת	seven cows	שִׁבְעָה יָמִים	seven days

The construct forms are used before the noun, which may be either definite or indefinite:

שְׁלֹשֶׁת אֲנָשִׁים	three men	שְׁלֹשֶׁת הָאֲנָשִׁים	the three men

Numbers may occur before collective nouns in the singular:

שִׁבְעָה בָקָר seven (head of) cattle
שִׁבְעָה לֶחֶם seven (loaves of) bread
שִׁבְעָה רֶכֶב seven (units of) chariotry

131. Vocabulary 34.

NOUNS: קֵץ *qēṣ* (no pl.) end; מִקֵּץ at the end of (usually + time word)
קָצֶה *qāṣeh* (no pl.) end, border, outskirts; מִקְצֵי at the end of (+ time or place)
פָּרָה *pārāh* (pl. *-ôṯ*) cow, heifer
שָׂפָה *śāpāh* (dual שְׂפָתַיִם ; du. constr. שִׂפְתֵי) lip, edge; language
חָכָם *ḥāḵām* (pl. *-îm*) a wise person (also used as an adjective)
יְאֹר *yəʼōr* the Nile (usually with article); river (in general)
VERBS: [יָקַץ *yāqaṣ*] (יִיקַץ) to wake up (not attested in the perfect)

Exercises:

(a) Translate:

(1) הָעָם הַנָּגוּף
(2) הַכֹּהֲנִים הַהֲרוּגִים
(3) הַכֵּלִים שְׁבוּרִים
(4) הַכֶּרֶם שָׂרוּף
(5) הָרְשָׁעִים הָאֲרוּרִים
(6) הַדָּבָר הַכָּתוּב
(7) הַמִּצְרִי הַשָּׁלוּחַ
(8) הָעֵצִים הַנְּטוּעִים
(9) הָאָסִיר אָסוּר
(10) הָעִבְרִים הַקְּרוּאִים
(11) הָעִיר הַבְּנוּיָה
(12) הַשַּׁעַר סָגוּר
(13) הַלּוּחוֹת שְׁבוּרִים
(14) הַפָּרָה הַשְּׁחוּטָה

(b) Give the Hebrew for the following orally:

1. six men (birds, vessels, women, maidservants, females)
2. three stones (images, masters)
3. five asses (horses, camels, altars)
4. eight prisoners (Canaanites, Egyptians, offerings)
5. the seven plagues, the seven cattle, the nine loaves of bread

(c) Translate:

(1) וַיֵּלֶךְ הָאִישׁ הָלוֹךְ וּבָכֹה
(2) רָאֹה רָאִיתִי אֶת־חַטַּאת עַמִּי
(3) הֲנָתוֹן תִּתֵּן לִי עֵזֶר
(4) זָכוֹר אֶת־יוֹם הַשַּׁבָּת
(5) עָשֹׂה נַעֲשֶׂה אֶת־נְדָרֵינוּ
(6) תִּשְׁמְעוּ אֶל־קוֹלִי וְשָׁמוֹר אֶת־מִצְוֹתַי
(7) שָׁבוֹת לֹא תִשְׁבְּתוּ מִמְּלַאכְתְּכֶם לִפְנֵי תֻמָּהּ
(8) הֲבוֹא נָבוֹא אֲנִי וְאִמְּךָ לְפָנֶיךָ
(9) יָצָא הָאִישׁ יָצֹא וָשׁוֹב
(10) שָׁכוֹחַ לֹא תִשְׁכְּחוּ אֶת־דִּבְרֵי חַכְמֵיכֶם כָּל־יְמֵי חַיֵּיכֶם

(d) Write in Hebrew:

1. You shall surely remember these things until the end of your life.
2. We sat down weeping on the bank of the river.
3. When we raised our voice(s), he woke up and came near so that he could hear all that we (were) saying.
4. Are you wiser than we?
5. And at the end of three years he left us and returned to his (own) land.
6. At that time there was one language in all the earth.
7. Why have you withheld your help from me?

(e) Reading: Joseph as an Interpreter of Dreams

וַיְהִי בִּהְיוֹת יוֹסֵף בְּבֵית הָאֲסִירִים וַיִּפְתֹּר[1] חֲלוֹמוֹת סָרִיסֵי פַרְעֹה אֲשֶׁר הָיוּ אִתּוֹ שָׁם וַיְהִי כַּאֲשֶׁר פָּתַר לָהֶם כֵּן הָיָה.

וַיְהִי מִקֵּץ שְׁנָתַיִם וַיַּחֲלֹם פַּרְעֹה וְהִנֵּה הוּא עֹמֵד עַל־הַיְאֹר וְהִנֵּה מִן־הַיְאֹר עֹלוֹת שֶׁבַע פָּרוֹת יְפוֹת מַרְאֶה וַתִּרְעֶינָה עַל־שְׂפַת הַיְאֹר וְהִנֵּה שֶׁבַע פָּרוֹת אֲחֵרוֹת עֹלוֹת אַחֲרֵיהֶן מִן־הַיְאֹר רָעוֹת מַרְאֶה וַתַּעֲמֹדְנָה אֵצֶל הַפָּרוֹת הַיָּפוֹת עַל־שְׂפַת הַיְאֹר וַתֹּאכַלְנָה הַפָּרוֹת רָעוֹת הַמַּרְאֶה אֶת־שֶׁבַע הַפָּרוֹת יְפוֹת הַמַּרְאֶה וַיִּיקַץ פַּרְעֹה.

וַיְהִי בַבֹּקֶר וַיִּשְׁלַח וַיִּקְרָא אֶל־כָּל־חַכְמֵי מִצְרַיִם וְלֹא יָכְלוּ לִפְתֹּר אֶת־חֲלוֹם פַּרְעֹה וַיֹּאמֶר סְרִיס פַּרְעֹה אֲשֶׁר הָיָה בְּבֵית הָאֲסִירִים אֶת־יוֹסֵף לֵאמֹר: הָיִיתִי בְּבֵית הָאֲסִירִים וְאִתִּי שָׁם נַעַר עִבְרִי וְהוּא פָּתַר לִי אֶת־חֲלוֹמִי וַיְהִי כַּאֲשֶׁר פָּתַר כֵּן הָיָה.

וַיִּשְׁלַח פַּרְעֹה וַיִּקְרָא אֶל־יוֹסֵף וַיֹּאמֶר אֵלָיו: חֲלוֹם חָלַמְתִּי וּפֹתֵר אֵין אֹתוֹ[2] וַאֲנִי שָׁמַעְתִּי עָלֶיךָ לֵאמֹר: תִּשְׁמַע[3] חֲלוֹם לִפְתֹּר אֹתוֹ.

וַיַּעַן יוֹסֵף אֶת־פַּרְעֹה לֵאמֹר: אֱלֹהִים יַעֲנֶה[4] אֶת־שְׁלוֹם פַּרְעֹה.

וַיְהִי אַחֲרֵי שָׁמְעוֹ אֶת־חֲלוֹם פַּרְעֹה וַיֹּאמֶר יוֹסֵף: אֶת־אֲשֶׁר הָאֱלֹהִים עֹשֶׂה הִגִּיד[5] לְפַרְעֹה. שֶׁבַע הַפָּרוֹת הַטּוֹבוֹת שֶׁבַע שְׁנֵי שָׂבָע[6] הֵנָּה וְשֶׁבַע הַפָּרוֹת הָרָעוֹת שֶׁבַע שְׁנֵי רָעָב הֵנָּה. הוּא הַדָּבָר אֲשֶׁר הָאֱלֹהִים עֹשֶׂה: הִנֵּה שֶׁבַע שָׁנִים בָּאוֹת, שָׂבָע[6] גָּדוֹל בְּכָל־אֶרֶץ מִצְרַיִם וְקָמוּ שֶׁבַע שְׁנֵי רָעָב אַחֲרֵיהֶן.

Notes to the Reading:

1. פָּתַר to interpret
2. אֹתוֹ goes with פֹּתֵר: "one who can interpret it"
3. תִּשְׁמַע in the sense of "understand": "You know how to interpret a dream."
4. עָנָה in the rare sense "grant"
5. "he has told"
6. "satiety, fullness"

LESSON 35

132. Clauses joined with וְ wə-.

One of the most striking features of Hebrew prose syntax is the relative rarity of subordinating conjunctions marking adverbial clauses as such. Instead, one finds almost interminable sequences of clauses connected only by a form of the conjunction *wə-* (and). A closer inspection of these sequences, however, has shown us that there is a great deal of differentiation in clause function signalled, not by variation of the conjunction, but by a variation of the word order within the clause or by a variation of the verbal form used immediately after the conjunction. Although there is some deviation from the general patterns summarized in the following discussion, the distinctions drawn here and in Lesson 55 should enable the reader to classify and understand the vast majority of sequences he will encounter.

There are two main types of clause relationships among those joined only with a form of the conjunction *wə-*:

(1) *conjunctive-sequential,* in which the second clause is temporally or logically posterior or consequent to the first, and

(2) *disjunctive*, in which the second clause may be in various relations, all non-sequential, with the first.

The major device in Hebrew for signalling the difference between conjunctive and disjunctive clauses is the type of word which stands immediately after the *wə-*:

wə- (or *wa-*) + verb is conjunctive
wə- + non-verb is disjunctive.

It follows from this definition that all non-verbal clauses (i.e. sentences with adverbial, adjectival, nominal, existential, or participial predicates) are essentially disjunctive when used as such within a narrative. Such clauses can be made part of the main sequential narrative only by being first transformed into verbal clauses with a punctual (finite) verb form. Negative clauses in which לֹא stands before the verb are disjunctive by definition.

The basic formulas of the conjunctive-sequential relationship are as follows: [Any verb describing an event as a unit and hence capable of being linked sequentially (either anterior or posterior) with other events on the time continuum will be referred to as punctual.]

(1) the narrative sequences:
- (a) punctual past tense: perfect + *wa* + (short) imperfect — § 98 above
- (b) punctual future / punctual habitual: imperfect + *wə* + perfect — § 98 above
- (c) non-verbal clause + *wə* + perfect (see below)

(2) the imperative sequences:
- (a) imperative + *wə* + perfect (§ 107 above)
- (b) imperative + *wə* + imperfect (or jussive or cohortative) (§ 107 above)

The many examples of these that have appeared in the exercises and readings should have made them familiar enough by now. A few words are necessary, however, on the sequence denoted as (1c). Because non-verbal clauses, especially those with participial predicates, may refer to the immediate future, a non-verbal clause so used may be continued with a converted perfect, in imitation of the more common type (1b):

אֲנִי נֹתֵן לְךָ אֶת־הַכֶּסֶף וְלָקַחְתָּ אֹתוֹ וְנָתַתָּ אֹתוֹ אֶל־אֲדֹנֶיךָ	I shall give you the money and you will take it and give it to your master.
אֲנַחְנוּ בָּאִים הָעִירָה וְרָאִינוּ אֶת־הַבָּתִּים הַחֲדָשִׁים הַבְּנוּיִים שָׁם	We shall come to the city and see the new houses built there.
הוּא אִישׁ טוֹב וְעָשָׂה חֶסֶד עִמָּכֶם	He is a good man and will deal properly with you.

Semantic distinctions among disjunctive clauses are difficult to define because of overlapping. The categories given below cover most uses of this construction.

(a) *Contrastive*:

וַיָּשֶׁב אֶת־שַׂר הַמַּשְׁקִים עַל־מַשְׁקֵהוּ וְאֵת שַׂר הָאֹפִים תָּלָה	He returned the chief butler to his butlership, but he hanged the chief baker. (Gen. 40:21)
וַיְהִי רָעָב בְּכָל־הָאֲרָצוֹת וּבְכָל־אֶרֶץ מִצְרַיִם הָיָה לָחֶם	There was famine in all the (other) lands, but in Egypt there was food. (Gen. 41:54)

(b) *Circumstantial,* where the disjunctive clause or clauses describe a situation or circumstance contemporary with or prior to the action of the preceding clause:

וַיִּמְצָאֵהוּ אִישׁ וְהִנֵּה תֹעֶה בַּשָּׂדֶה	And a man found him wandering lost in the field. (lit., [while] he [was] wandering lost . . .) (Gen. 37:15)
וַיָּבֹא הַבַּיְתָה לַעֲשׂוֹת מְלַאכְתּוֹ וְאֵין אִישׁ מֵאַנְשֵׁי הַבַּיִת שָׁם בַּבָּיִת	And he came home to do his work, there being none of the household present. (Gen. 39:11)

It is difficult to distinguish between circumstantial usage of such clauses and

(c) *Explanatory or parenthetical* use, where disjunctive clauses break into the main narrative to supply information relevant to or necessary for the narrative. For example, in I Sam. 1:9, between the narrative clauses "Hannah arose . . . and prayed" we find the explanatory disjunction

וְעֵלִי הַכֹּהֵן יֹשֵׁב עַל־הַכִּסֵּא עַל־מְזוּזַת הֵיכַל יהוה וְהִיא מָרַת נָפֶשׁ	(Now Eli the priest was sitting on the seat by the door post of the temple of Yahweh; and she (Hannah) was bitter of spirit)

The inserted information characterizes her mood at prayer and also explains how Eli happened to notice her. Likewise, In Gen. 29:16, the conversation between Jacob and Laban is interrupted with the clause

וּלְלָבָן שְׁתֵּי בָנוֹת...	(Now Laban had two daughters . . .)

to explain the reference to Rachel given in the next clause belonging to the main narrative: "and he (Jacob) said, 'I will serve you seven years for your youngest daughter Rachel.'" These are but two examples selected at random from the hundreds of such instances.

(d) *Terminative or Initial*, indicating either the completion of one episode or the beginning of another. The following examples are taken from the beginnings of several chapters in Genesis; the chapter divisions often correspond to initial disjunctive clauses in the Hebrew:

וְהַנָּחָשׁ הָיָה עָרוּם...	Now the serpent was more subtle . . . (3:1)
וְהָאָדָם יָדַע אֶת־חַוָּה...	Now the man knew Eve . . . (4, 1)
וְשָׂרַי אֵשֶׁת אַבְרָם לֹא יָלְדָה לוֹ...	Now Sarah, the wife of Abram, had not borne him a child . . . (16:1)
וַיהוה פָּקַד אֶת־שָׂרָה כַּאֲשֶׁר אָמָר...	Now the Lord attended Sarah as he had said . . . (21:1)

It is interesting to note that a disjunction may be preceded by a temporal clause. In this case the disjunction must be understood as applying before the clause with וַיְהִי :

וַיְהִי אַחַר הַדְּבָרִים הָאֵלֶּה וְהָאֱלֹהִים נִסָּה אֶת־אַבְרָהָם	Now after these things, God tested Abraham (22:1)

Because a new episode may always be introduced, like a new paragraph, with no conjunction at all, such as

אַחַר הַדְּבָרִים הָאֵלֶּה הָיָה דְבַר יהוה אֶל־אַבְרָם	After these things the word of the Lord came to Abram (15:1)

we not unexpectedly find a mixing of the two styles:

וַיְהִי בִּימֵי אַמְרָפֶל... עָשׂוּ מִלְחָמָה	In the days of Amraphel they made war . . . (14:1)

A third type of *wə*-clause, *conjunctive* but *non-sequential*, will be considered in a later lesson.

133. יֵשׁ and אֵין.

As predicators of existence and non-existence these two words approximate a verbal function in Hebrew, serving almost as tenseless forms of the verb "to be." It is hardly surprising, therefore, that these words are found inflected for number and gender by the addition of pronominal endings, rare in the case of יֵשׁ, but common with אֵין.

	SING.		PL.		SING.		PL.	
1c					אֵינֶנִּי	*'ênénnî*	אֵינֶנּוּ	*'ênénnû*
2m	יֶשְׁךָ	*yešḵā*	יֶשְׁכֶם	*yešḵem*	אֵינְךָ	*'ênəḵā*	אֵינְכֶם	*'ênəḵem*
2f					אֵינֵךְ	*'ênēḵ*		
3m	יֶשְׁנוֹ	*yešnô*			אֵינֶנּוּ	*'ênénnû*	אֵינָם	*'ênām*
3f					אֵינֶנָּה	*'ênénnāh*		

The rare inflected forms of יֵשׁ are found almost exclusively after the conjunction אִם (if), as in

אִם־יֶשְׁכֶם עֹשִׂים חֶסֶד If you act properly . . .

and may be regarded simply as optional replacements for the simple pronouns,

אִם־אַתֶּם עֹשִׂים חֶסֶד

The inflected forms of אֵין have a wider range of usage:

(a) Negative existential with nominal or pronominal subject:

אֵינֶנּוּ	he is not (he does not exist)
הַיֶּלֶד אֵינֶנּוּ	The boy is not (here).

Note that the inflected form is used regularly *after* a definite nominal subject. The quoted example is equivalent to אֵין הַיֶּלֶד.

(b) Negation of sentences with participial predicates (very common):

אֵינֶנִּי כֹּתֵב I am not writing.
הָאֲנָשִׁים אֵינָם יֹדְעִים The men do not know.

(c) More rarely אֵין alternates with לֹא in the negation of sentences with adjectival or adverbial predicates:

הָאִישׁ אֵינֶנּוּ בַבַּיִת The man is not in the house.
הַבְּהֵמָה אֲשֶׁר אֵינֶנָּה טְהֹרָה the animal which is not ritually pure

134. Vocabulary 35.

NOUNS: אֹכֶל *'ōḵel* (w. suff. אָכְלִי ; no pl.) food
עֶרְוָה *'erwāh* (no pl.) shame, nakedness
ADJECTIVES: נָבוֹן *nāḇôn* intelligent, discerning (cf. בִּינָה)
כֵּן *kēn* honest, true
VERBS: יטב imperf. יִיטַב ; perfect not used. To go well, used impersonally with לְ, as in יִיטַב לִי It will go well with me.
רָעֵב *rā'ēḇ* (יִרְעַב) to be hungry
חָיָה *ḥāyāh* (יִחְיֶה) to live, be alive
קָרָה *qārāh* (יִקְרֶה) to meet, encounter, befall. This verb appears also as קָרָא *qārā'* (יִקְרָא); the forms of the two types are sometimes mixed up.
OTHER: רַק *raq* (adv.) only

Note on ordinals: eighth שְׁמִינִי ; ninth תְּשִׁיעִי ; tenth עֲשִׂירִי.

Exercises:

(a) Translate:

(1) קַח אֶת־הַלֶּחֶם פֶּן־תִּרְעַב בַּדֶּרֶךְ.
(2) נַעַזְבָה אֶת־הָעִיר וְנָסְנוּ הָהָרָה לְמַעַן נִחְיֶה.
(3) וַיִּקֶר אֶת־שְׁנֵי הָאֲנָשִׁים וְהֵם עֹמְדִים עַל־שְׂפַת הַיְאֹר.
(4) תְּהִי עִם־אָחִיךְ פֶּן תִקְרָא אֹתוֹ רָעָה בְּנָסְעוֹ הֵנָּה.
(5) וַתֵּלֶךְ הָאִשָּׁה אֶל־הַהֵיכָל וְהִיא בֹכָה וַתִּשָּׂא אֶת־עֵינֶיהָ הַשָּׁמַיְמָה וַתִּדֹּר נֶדֶר לַיהוה.
(6) רָדְפוּ אַחֲרָיו וַיִּתְפְּשׂוּ אֹתוֹ וַיַּהַרְגוּ אֹתוֹ וְהוּא אֲחִי הַכֹּהֵן אֲשֶׁר בִּירוּשָׁלָםִ.
(7) לָמָּה שָׁחַטְתָּ אֶת־הַבָּקָר הַזֶּה וְהֵם אֵינָם לָךְ.
(8) יִיטַב לָעֲשִׁירִים וְהַדַּלִּים יֹאבְדוּ.
(9) קָרָה אֹתָנוּ וַאֲנַחְנוּ הֹלְכִים אֶל־הַמַּחֲנֶה וַיֹּאמֶר אֵלֵינוּ כַּדְּבָרִים הָאֵלֶּה.
(10) הָאֲנָשִׁים אֵינָם יֹדְעִים כִּי אֵינֵךְ אֲחוֹתִי.
(11) וַיָּשֶׂם אֶת־הָרָקִיעַ בֵּין־הַמַּיִם אֲשֶׁר עַל־הַשָּׁמַיִם וּבֵין הַמַּיִם אֲשֶׁר תַּחַת הַשָּׁמַיִם וְהָרָקִיעַ הוּא הַשָּׁמָיִם.
(12) אֵין אִישׁ צַדִּיק בָּעִיר רַק רְשָׁעִים.
(13) אֵין מַיִם בַּבּוֹר, רַק אֲבָנִים שָׁם.

(b) Reading: The Famine in Egypt and Canaan

וַיֹּאמֶר יוֹסֵף: וְעַתָּה יֵרֶא[1] פַרְעֹה אִישׁ נָבוֹן וְחָכָם וְיָשֵׁת אֹתוֹ עַל־אֶרֶץ מִצְרָיִם וְיִקְבֹּץ הוּא וַאֲנָשָׁיו אֶת־כָּל־אֹכֶל הַשָּׁנִים הַטּוֹבוֹת הַבָּאוֹת הָאֵלֶּה וְהָיָה הָאֹכֶל לְפִקָּדוֹן[2] לָאָרֶץ לְשֶׁבַע שְׁנֵי הָרָעָב אֲשֶׁר תִּהְיֶינָה בְּאֶרֶץ מִצְרָיִם וְלֹא תֹאבַד הָאָרֶץ בָּרָעָב.

וַיִּיטַב הַדָּבָר בְּעֵינֵי פַרְעֹה וּבְעֵינֵי כָל־עֲבָדָיו וַיֹּאמֶר פַּרְעֹה אֶל־יוֹסֵף: אֵין נָבוֹן וְחָכָם כָּמוֹךָ, אַתָּה תִּהְיֶה עַל־בֵּיתִי וְעַל־עַמִּי, רַק הַכִּסֵּא[3] אֶגְדַּל מִמֶּךָּ, וַיֹּאמֶר פַּרְעֹה אֶל־יוֹסֵף: רְאֵה נָתַתִּי אֹתְךָ עַל־כָּל־אֶרֶץ מִצְרָיִם.

וַיְהִי אַחֲרֵי שֶׁבַע הַשָּׁנִים הַטּוֹבוֹת וַיְהִי רָעָב בְּכָל־הָאֲרָצוֹת וּבְכָל־אֶרֶץ מִצְרַיִם הָיָה לֶחֶם וַתִּרְעַב כָּל־אֶרֶץ מִצְרַיִם וַיִּצְעַק הָעָם אֶל־פַּרְעֹה לַלֶּחֶם וַיֹּאמֶר פַּרְעֹה לְכָל־מִצְרַיִם: לְכוּ אֶל־יוֹסֵף, אֶת־כָּל־אֲשֶׁר יֹאמַר לָכֶם תַּעֲשׂוּ. וְהָרָעָב הָיָה עַל־כָּל־פְּנֵי הָאָרֶץ וְכָל־הָאָרֶץ בָּאוּ מִצְרַיְמָה לִקְנוֹת לֶחֶם וַיַּרְא יַעֲקֹב כִּי יֵשׁ לֶחֶם בְּמִצְרַיִם וַיֹּאמֶר יַעֲקֹב לְבָנָיו: הִנֵּה שָׁמַעְתִּי כִּי יֵשׁ לֶחֶם בְּמִצְרַיִם, רְדוּ שָׁמָּה וּקְנוּ לָנוּ מִשָּׁם וְנִחְיֶה וְלֹא נָמוּת.

Notes to the Reading:

1. in the sense "choose"
2. "storage supply"
3. Supply "in regard to" before הַכִּסֵּא.

LESSON 36

135. הִנֵּה.

The word הִנֵּה, traditionally translated as "behold," is very frequent in Hebrew prose and deserves special attention in translation. The retention of archaic expressions like "behold" even in the RSV merely points up the translators' refusal to come to grips with the meaning and syntactic functions of הִנֵּה in terms of modern English correspondents. There is, of course, some difficulty in this, but it is hoped that the following discussion will enable the reader to translate this word more accurately.

(1) The clearest and most basic use of הִנֵּה is as a predicator of existence. It differs from יֵשׁ in that it emphasizes the immediacy, the here-and-now-ness, of the situation. In this usage inflected forms are common:

	SINGULAR		PLURAL	
1c	הִנְנִי/הִנֵּנִי	*hinənî* (*hinnénnî*)	הִנְנוּ/הִנֵּנוּ	*hinənû* (*hinnénnû*)
2m	הִנְּךָ	*hinnəḵā*	הִנְּכֶם	*hinnəḵem*
2f	הִנֵּךְ	*hinnēḵ*	——	——
3m	הִנּוֹ	*hinnô*	הִנָּם	*hinnām*
3f	——	——	——	——

Examples:

הִנְנִי	Here I am. (Answer to question or address)
הִנֵּה הָאִישׁ	Here is the man.
הִנֵּה אִשְׁתְּךָ	Here is your wife.

(2) הִנֵּה may also be used to add this same nuance to sentences with adverbial, adjectival, or participial predicates. Thus, sentences such as אֲנִי בַבַּיִת become הִנְנִי בַבַּיִת I am here (now) in the house.

Examples:

הִנֵּה חָמִיךָ עֹלֶה תִמְנָתָה Your father-in-law is now on his way up to Timnah.
הִנֵּה אָבִיךָ חֹלֶה Your father is now ill.
הִנֵּה בִנְךָ בָא אֵלֶיךָ Your son is now coming to you.
הִנֵּה הָאָרֶץ לְפָנֶיךָ The land is here before you.

It may also be prefixed to verbal sentences, adding to the vividness or importance of the fact stated:

הִנֵּה אֲנָשִׁים בָּאוּ הֵנָּה Some men have just come here.

Most *hinnēh*-clauses occur in direct speech (this excludes *wəhinneh*; see below) and serve to introduce a fact upon which a following statement or command is based. It becomes important, therefore, to consider each *hinnēh*-clause together with the type of clause that follows it, i.e. whether they stand in a conjunctive or disjunctive relationship. Among the most frequent conjunctive-sequential types are:

(1) *hinnēh*-CLAUSE + IMPERATIVE. The absence of *wə-* before the imperative marks this as a rather special construction. If desired, the *hinnēh*-clause may be subordinated in English.

הִנֵּה שִׁפְחָתֵךְ בְּיָדֵךְ עֲשִׂי־לָהּ... Your handmaid is in your charge; do to her...
Or: *Since* your handmaid is etc. (Gen. 16:6)

הִנֵּה שָׁמַעְתִּי כִּי יֶשׁ־שֶׁבֶר בְּמִצְרַיִם רְדוּ־שָׁמָּה... I have heard that there are rations in Egypt; go down there and... (Gen. 42:2)

The semantic movement from one clause to the other is clear. Sometimes this can be made clear in the English by the subordination suggested; sometime the use of "so" or "therefore" in the second clause is recommended.

The imperative may be preceded by עַתָּה or וְעַתָּה:

הִנֵּה בַּעַל הַחֲלֹמוֹת... בָּא וְעַתָּה לְכוּ וְנַהַרְגֵהוּ Here comes the dreamer. Come on, now, let's kill him. (Gen. 37:19)

הִנֵּה אַתָּה זָקַנְתָּ... עַתָּה שִׂימָה־לָּנוּ מֶלֶךְ... You have grown old. So set a king over us... (I Sam. 8:5)

(2) *hinnēh*-CLAUSE + CONVERTED PERFECT. This formula is an instance of type (1c) discussed in the previous lesson.

אֲנִי הִנֵּה בְרִיתִי אִתָּךְ וְהָיִיתָ לְאַב הֲמוֹן גּוֹיִם My covenant is with you and you shall become father of a throng of nations... (Gen. 17:4)
Or: Because my covenant is (will be)...

הִנֵּה יָמִים בָּאִים וְגָדַעְתִּי אֶת־זְרֹעֲךָ	Days are coming when I shall cut off your strength . . . (I Sam. 2:31)

(3) *hinnēh*-CLAUSE + DISJUNCTIVE CLAUSE. There are several types of less frequent constructions under this heading, mostly conforming to the uses of the disjunctive relationship treated in the preceding lesson, but slightly modified by the initial *hinnēh:*

הִנֵּה בֵּרַכְתִּי אֹתוֹ... וְאֶת־בְּרִיתִי אָקִים אֶת־יִצְחָק	Although I have blessed him (i.e. Ishmael), my covenant will I establish with Isaac . . . (Gen. 17:20–21)
הִנֵּה הָאֵשׁ וְהָעֵצִים וְאַיֵּה הַשֶּׂה	Here are the fire and the wood, but where is the lamb? (Gen. 22:7)
הִנֵּה אָנֹכִי הוֹלֵךְ לָמוּת... וְלָמָּה־זֶּה לִי בְּכֹרָה	Since I am practically dead, of what use to me is a birthright? (Gen. 25:32)

In a number of instances the use of a future disjunctive clause after *hinnēh* + participle seems to require that the participial clause be rendered in a completed sense:

הִנֵּה אָנֹכִי מֵת בְּקִבְרִי... תִּקְבְּרֵנִי	When I have died, you shall bury me in my grave . . . (Gen. 50:5)
הִנֵּה אֲנַחְנוּ בָאִים... אֶת־תִּקְוַת חוּט... תִּקְשְׁרִי	When we come . . ., you shall tie the thread . . . (Jos. 2:18)

We have already noted the very frequent idiomatic use of וְהִנֵּה after רָאָה and other verbs of perception. וְהִנֵּה may also be used to introduce a circumstantial clause, sometimes without an explicit subject:

וַיָּבֹא אֶל־הָאִישׁ וְהִנֵּה עֹמֵד עַל־הַגְּמַלִּים	He came to the man while (he was) standing by the camels. (Gen. 24:30)
עוֹד שָׁאַר הַקָּטָן וְהִנֵּה רֹעֶה בַּצֹּאן	There remains yet the youngest, tending the sheep. (I Sam. 16:11)

136. נָא and הִנֵּה־נָא.

The particle נָא is frequently attached to imperatives, jussives, and cohortatives. It is traditionally known as a precative particle, translated as "please, I pray" or the like. In actual fact, however, there is little support for this rather vague rendering. The particle seems rather to denote that the command in question is a logical consequence, either of an immediately preceding statement or of the general situation in which it is uttered. As a modal particle its occurrence cannot be predicted; when it does occur, however, it would appear to show that the speaker regards his command as consequent upon his former statement or, as we have said, upon the context. It would seem natural therefore to find such a particle used in the clause following a *hinnēh* clause, because the *hinnēh* clause is precisely the kind of statement out of which an imperative emerges. This close relationship is signalled even more explicitly in Hebrew by appending **נָא** both to the *hinnēh* and to the following imperative:

הִנֵּה־נָא עֲצָרַנִי יהוה מִלֶּדֶת בֹּא־נָא אֶל־שִׁפְחָתִי	Because the Lord has prevented me from bearing a child, go to my handmaid ... (Gen. 16:2)
הִנֵּה נָא רָפָה הַיּוֹם לַעֲרוֹב לִינוּ־נָא	Since the day has drawn to a close, spend the night here. (Judges 19:9)

Otherwise *hinnēh-nā'* conforms to the categories given for *hinnēh* alone. E.g.

הִנֵּה־נָא מָצָא עַבְדְּךָ חֵן... וְאָנֹכִי לֹא אוּכַל לְהִמָּלֵט	Even though your servant has found favor..., I am nevertheless unable to escape . . . (Gen. 19:19)
הִנֵּה־נָא מוֹשַׁב הָעִיר טוֹב... וְהַמַּיִם רָעִים	Even though the site of the city is good . . ., the waters are bad . . . (II Kings 2:19)

137. עוֹד and אַיֵּה.

In verbal sentences **עוֹד** is used as a simple adverb in the sense of "again, still, yet, once more":

יָשַׁב עוֹד וַיֹּאכַל	He sat down again and ate.
וַיַּחֲלֹם עוֹד חֲלוֹם אַחֵר	And he dreamed still another dream.

But **עוֹד**, like הִנֵּה, may be inflected and used as a predicator of existence, with the nuance of "to still be, to yet be."

	SING.		PLURAL	
1c	עוֹדִי / עוֹדֶנִּי	*'ôḏî* or *'ôḏénnî*		——
2m	עוֹדְךָ	*'ôḏəḵā*		——
2f	עוֹדָךְ	*'ôḏāḵ*		——
3m	עוֹדֶנּוּ	*'ôḏénnû*	עוֹדָם	*'ôḏām*
3f	עוֹדֶנָּה	*'ôḏénnāh*		——

Examples:

עוֹדֶנּוּ שָׁם	He is still there.
אַבְרָהָם עוֹדֶנּוּ עֹמֵד לִפְנֵי יהוה	Abraham is still standing before the Lord.
עוֹדֶנִּי חַי	I am still alive.
עוֹד יוֹסֵף חַי	Joseph is still alive.
עוֹד הָעָם רַב	The people are still too many.
הַעוֹד לָכֶם אָח	Do you have yet another brother?

These examples show clearly that **עוֹד**, like **הִנֵּה**, may be extended from purely existential predication to use in other types of non-verbal sentences.

A special use of **עוֹד** and **בְּעוֹד** is found in the temporal expressions

עוֹד חָמֵשׁ שָׁנִים in yet five years, for five more years
בְּעוֹד שְׁלֹשֶׁת יָמִים in yet three days, after three more days
בְּעוֹד הַיֶּלֶד חַי while the boy was still alive
עוֹד מְעַט in just a little while, shortly, soon

Such expressions were originally non-verbal sentences, first used circumstantially:

there are still five years → there being still five years

and then incorporated as units into another clause, thus being reduced to phrase rather than clause status. בְּעוֹד would then be comparable to בְּ + the infinitive construct of הָיָה. עוֹד with a negative is translated "never again, no longer."

Occasionally אַיֵּה (where?) is found with subject suffixes similar to the preceding; attested forms are אַיֶּכָּה (2 m. s.), אַיּוֹ (3 m. s.), אַיָּם (3 m. pl.).

138. Vocabulary 36.

NOUNS: מְרַגֵּל *məraggēl* (pl. *-îm*) spy, scout
אֱמֶת *'ĕmét* (w. suff. אֲמִתִּי ; no pl.) truth
VERBS: בָּחַן *bāḥan* (יִבְחַן) to test, try, examine
OTHER: חַי *ḥay* / חֵי *ḥê* — a form of חַי (living) or חַיִּים (life) used before proper nouns in an oath: חַי אֱלֹהִים as God lives, חֵי פַרְעֹה as Pharaoh lives; cf. אִם below.
אִם *'im* (conj.) if; note the full oath formula: *ḥay/ḥê* X *'im* + imperf., where אִם has a negative force. E.g.
חֵי פַרְעֹה אִם תֵּצְאוּ מִזֶּה כִּי־אִם... As the Pharaoh lives, you shall *not* leave here unless . . .
כֻּל־ *kull-* all, every one of. Used with pronominal suffixes, in apposition: הָאֲנָשִׁים כֻּלָּם all of the men (lit. the men, all of them).

	SING.		PLURAL	
1c	——	——	כֻּלָּנוּ	*kullā́nû*
2m	כֻּלְּךָ	(*kulləkā*)	כֻּלְּכֶם	*kulləkem*
2f	כֻּלֵּךְ	*kullēk*, *-āk*	——	——
3m	כֻּלֹּה/וֹ	*kullōh*, *-ô*	כֻּלָּם	*kullām*
3f	כֻּלָּהּ	*kullāh*	——	——

Exercises:

(a) Translate:

(1) אָבִיךָ עוֹדֶנּוּ חָי.
(2) וַיֹּאמֶר הַסָּרִיס: אַיֶּכָּה אֲדֹנִי.

(3) רוּץ נָא לִקְרָאתוֹ.
(4) אֵיפֹה נוּכַל לִמְצֹא אֹכֶל וְאֵין לֶחֶם בָּעִיר.
(5) שְׁמַע נָא אֶל־קוֹלִי וְתִהְיֶה אִישׁ נָבוֹן וְחָכָם.
(6) אֵינֶנִּי נָס הָהָרָה.
(7) קְנֵה לָנוּ אֹכֶל פֶּן־נִרְעַב.
(8) הִנֵּה אִשְׁתְּךָ קַח וְלֵךְ אֶל־אַרְצְךָ.
(9) בְּנוּ עוֹד עִיר גְּדוֹלָה.
(10) הִנְנִי נֹתֵן לְךָ בִּינָה וְחָכְמָה.
(11) הִנֵּה אָחִיךָ בָּרַח מֵהָעִיר רְדֹף אַחֲרָיו.
(12) הַאֵינְךָ יֹדֵעַ כִּי זֶה יוֹם הַשַּׁבָּת.

(b) Give the Hebrew for the following orally:

1. Our mother is still here in the house.
2. Here comes your brother.
3. I am not going to go up to the city.
4. There is still a fire in the mountains.
5. The men are not eating.
6. Where are the vessels which you fashioned?
7. We are not walking.
8. On the 9th day we rode to the end of the road.
9. Are you still hungry?
10. All of us were poor.

(c) Translate:

(1) הִנֵּה־נָא אָבִיךָ מֵת שׁוּב נָא אֶל־אַרְצְךָ וְאֶל־עַמְּךָ.
(2) וַיֹּאמֶר הַמֶּלֶךְ אֶל־הַנָּבִיא: הִנֵּה־נָא דִּבְרֵי הַנְּבִיאִים הָאֲחֵרִים פֶּה אֶחָד טוֹב אֶל־הַמֶּלֶךְ יְהִיוּ נָא דְבָרֶיךָ כְּדִבְרֵיהֶם.
(3) הִנֵּה אִשְׁתְּךָ הִיא וְאֵיךְ אָמַרְתָּ כִּי אֲחוֹתְךָ הִיא.
(4) הִנֵּה הָאָרֶץ לְפָנֶיךָ שֵׁב בָּהּ בְּשָׁלוֹם.
(5) בְּעוֹד שְׁלֹשֶׁת יָמִים תֵּדַע כִּי אֱמֶת דְּבָרַי.
(6) הִנֵּה־נָא זָקַנְתִּי וְלֹא יָדַעְתִּי יוֹם מוֹתִי וְעַתָּה שְׁמַע נָא אֶל־קוֹלִי וְאֶתֵּן לְךָ בְּרָכָה.
(7) הִנֵּה־נָא הָעִיר הַזֹּאת קְרֹבָה לָנוּס שָׁמָּה אֶבְרְחָה נָא שָׁמָּה וְאֶחְיֶה.

(d) Write in Hebrew. Use *hinnēh*-clauses when possible.

1. Although our food is still plentiful (much), we cannot give you any of it.
2. Because your father has died, I shall send you to live (dwell) with your eldest (lit. great) brother.
3. Although I am here beside you, you cannot see me.
4. Now that you have come, sit down and eat with us.
5. Since we are sojourning here, let us tell them that we are rich so that it will go well with us.

6. Seeing that righteousness and truth have perished in the land, let us seek help from our God so that he will send us deliverance.
7. As the king lives, you shall not enter here before evening.

(e) Reading: Joseph Receives his Brothers in Egypt.

וַיֵּרְדוּ אֲחֵי יוֹסֵף עֲשָׂרָה לִקְנוֹת אֹכֶל מִמִּצְרַיִם וְאֶת־בִּנְיָמִין אֲחִי[1] יוֹסֵף לֹא שָׁלַח יַעֲקֹב אֶת־אֶחָיו
כִּי אָמַר פֶּן תִּקְרָאֶנּוּ[2] רָעָה וַיָּבֹאוּ בְּנֵי יִשְׂרָאֵל בְּתוֹךְ הַבָּאִים מִצְרַיְמָה כִּי הָיָה הָרָעָב בְּאֶרֶץ כְּנָעַן.
וַיָּבֹאוּ אֲחֵי יוֹסֵף וַיִּשְׁתַּחֲווּ[3] לוֹ אַפַּיִם אַרְצָה וַיַּרְא יוֹסֵף אֶת־אֶחָיו וַיַּכִּר[4] אֹתָם וְהֵם לֹא הִכִּירוּ[5]
אֹתוֹ וַיֹּאמֶר אֲלֵיהֶם קָשׁוֹת[6] לֵאמֹר: מֵאַיִן בָּאתֶם. וַיֹּאמְרוּ: מֵאֶרֶץ כְּנַעַן לִקְנוֹת אֹכֶל. וַיִּזְכֹּר יוֹסֵף
אֶת־הַחֲלוֹמוֹת אֲשֶׁר חָלַם וַיֹּאמֶר אֲלֵיהֶם: מְרַגְּלִים אַתֶּם, לִרְאוֹת אֶת־עֶרְוַת הָאָרֶץ בָּאתֶם.
וַיֹּאמְרוּ אֵלָיו: לֹא אֲדֹנִי, וַעֲבָדֶיךָ בָּאוּ לִקְנוֹת אֹכֶל, כֻּלָּנוּ בְּנֵי אִישׁ אֶחָד אֲנָחְנוּ, כֵּנִים אֲנַחְנוּ,
לֹא הָיוּ עֲבָדֶיךָ מְרַגְּלִים, וַיֹּאמֶר אֲלֵהֶם: לֹא, כִּי[7] עֶרְוַת הָאָרֶץ בָּאתֶם לִרְאוֹת.

וַיֹּאמְרוּ: שְׁנֵי עָשָׂר[8] עֲבָדֶיךָ אַחִים, אֲנַחְנוּ בְּנֵי אִישׁ אֶחָד בְּאֶרֶץ כְּנַעַן, וְהִנֵּה הַקָּטֹן אֶת־אָבִינוּ
הַיּוֹם וְהָאֶחָד אֵינֶנּוּ.

וַיֹּאמֶר יוֹסֵף: הוּא[9] אֲשֶׁר אָמַרְתִּי אֲלֵכֶם לֵאמֹר מְרַגְּלִים אַתֶּם, בְּזֹאת אֶבָּחֵן אֶתְכֶם, חֵי פַרְעֹה
אִם תֵּצְאוּ מִזֶּה כִּי־אִם בְּבוֹא אֲחִיכֶם הַקָּטֹן הֵנָּה, שִׁלְחוּ מִכֶּם אֶחָד וְיִקַּח אֶת־אֲחִיכֶם וְאַתֶּם
תֵּשְׁבוּ פֹּה וְאֶת־דִּבְרֵיכֶם אֶבְחַן הַאֱמֶת[10] אִתְּכֶם וְאִם לֹא, חֵי פַרְעֹה כִּי[11] מְרַגְּלִים אַתֶּם.

Notes to the Reading:

1. i.e. his full brother
2. = תִּקְרָא אֹתוֹ.
3. "and they bowed down"
4. "and he recognized"
5. "they did not recognize"
6. Adjectives in the fem. pl. may be used adverbially: "harshly"
7. After a negative *kî* has a strong asseverative force: "but on the contrary, you *did* come etc."
8. "twelve"
9. הוּא is the predicate (here = "so, a fact"): the אֲשֶׁר clause is the subject.
10. הֲ introduces an indirect question: "whether"
11. Note this frequent assertive use of כִּי: "As Pharaoh lives, you *are* spies."

קבוﬠ' י

when supports a vocal shewa, they sometimes omit the dagesh.

LESSON 37

maqqef

139. Derived Verbs.

All of the verbs studied in the preceding lessons belong to the conjugational
type known as Qal, or the simple conjugation, since each consists analytically
of an unaugmented root plus a stem pattern (perfect, imperfect, etc.). But
in Hebrew, as in most languages, other verbs may be constructed from these
same roots, mainly by the use of prefixal elements or by modification of the
stem patterns. There are six important types of derived verbs (often called
conjugations). Not all roots occur in all six forms, just as many roots are
not employed as verbs in the Qal although they are well attested in nouns
and adjectives. The six principal derived types are named by the Hebrew
grammarians according to the form they would assume in the 3rd per. masc.
sing. of the perfect with the root פָּעַל :

נִפְﬠַל	Niphal	Lessons 37–39
פִּﬠֵל	Piel	Lessons 40–42
פֻּﬠַל	Pual	
הִפְﬠִיל	Hiphil	Lessons 43–49
הָפְﬠַל	Hophal	
הִתְפַּﬠֵל	Hithpael	Lesson 50

140. Niphal Verbs: Meaning.

Broadly speaking, Niphal verbs, characterized by an element *n-* prefixed to
the root, are *medio-passive* in meaning. Because a theoretical discussion of

this term, by no means consistently employed in grammatical descriptions, would take us too far afield, we shall categorize these verbs on the basis of their translation value in English.

(1) *Incomplete passive:* The passive in English is a construction, not a category of verbal meaning. If a verb occurs in an active-transitive usage, such as

The students *read* the lesson,

there is a passive transformation to the corresponding

The lesson *was read* by the students.

By the incomplete passive we mean this same transformation minus the agent:

The lesson *was read*.

the use of which indicates that the speaker is not concerned with specifying the agent of the action. All Hebrew passives belong to this category; constructions with a specified agent are virtually non-existent. If the corresponding Qal verb is active-transitive, it is always possible to translate the Niphal verb as an incomplete passive:

Qal	*Niphal*	
כָּתַב אֶת־הַדָּבָר	נִכְתַּב הַדָּבָר	The word was written.
עָזַב אֶת־הָעִיר	נֶעֶזְבָה הָעִיר	The city was abandoned.
הָרַג אֶת־הָאִישׁ	נֶהֱרַג הָאִישׁ	The man was slain.

(2) *Middle.* Middle verbs in English are elusive because they pattern like active verbs and have the same form:

Active	*Middle*
He broke the window.	The window broke.
He stopped the car.	The car stopped.
He opened the door.	The door opened.

Unlike the incomplete passive construction, middle verbs are active in form, but the meaning (i.e. voice) is, in a sense, reversed: the object of the active verb has become the subject of the middle verb. Niphal verbs in Hebrew often correspond to middle verbs in English:

נִפְתַּח הַשַּׁעַר	The gate opened.
נִשְׁבַּר הַכְּלִי	The vessel broke.
נִקְבַּץ הָעָם	The people gathered.

(3) *Reflexive.* Reflexive verbs in English have an expressed object (the reflexive pronoun) which refers to the subject:

He saw himself in the water.
He washed himself.
He sold himself into slavery.

Niphal verbs often require this translation:

נִגְאַל he redeemed himself
נִמְכַּר he sold himself

(4) *Resultative*. More important than either of the two preceding categories is the Niphal verb in a resultative meaning. Essentially a stative verb, the resultative Niphal describes the state of its subject which has been produced by the verbal action named by the root:

Active		*Passive*		*Resultative*	
פָּתַח	to open	נִפְתַּח	to be opened	נִפְתַּח	to be open
שָׁבַר	to break	נִשְׁבַּר	to be broken	נִשְׁבַּר	to be broken, to be in pieces

In English the equivalent of the resultative is so often formally the same as the passive that the distinction made here is difficult to grasp. In the passive *It was broken, was* is an auxiliary verb in the unit *was-broken*; in the resultative *It was broken, was* is the verb *to be* followed by an adjective/participle. One can see this difference most clearly by applying, for example, a transformation into present real:

passive: It is being broken.
resultative: It is broken.

Very frequently the resultative-stative has the nuance of potentiality:

רָאָה – נִרְאָה :	to see	to be seen	→ to be seeable, visible → to appear
יָרֵא – נוֹרָא :	to fear	to be feared	→ to be fearful, dreadful, terrible
אָכַל – נֶאֱכַל :	to eat	to be eaten	→ to be edible
בָּחַר – נִבְחַר :	to choose	to be chosen	→ to be choice, select, acceptable
אָהַב – נֶאֱהַב :	to love	to be loved	→ to be lovely, loveable
יָשַׁב – נוֹשַׁב :	to inhabit	to be inhabited	→ to be habitable
מָצָא – נִמְצָא :	to find	to be found	→ to be extant, to exist, (cf. se trouver)

These four categories have been defined on the basis of English. In Hebrew, however, they are one: the medio-passive as expressed by the Niphal form. Only a careful study of the context will enable the reader to decide among the various possibilities.

Some Niphal verbs have no Qal counterpart:

נִלְחַם	he fought	נִסְתַּר	he hid
נִמְלַט	he escaped	נִרְדַּם	he fell fast asleep

Others would appear to be denominative, although this is a rare use of the Niphal pattern: נִבָּא (for נִנְבָּא *) to prophesy, from נָבִיא, prophet.

141. Niphal Verbs: Stems and Inflection.

The Niphal verb is derived from a triliteral root by the prefixation of *n*. In the perfect the stem has the basic form נִכְתַּב *niḵtaḇ*, which undergoes no unusual changes in inflection. The imperfect was originally of the form **yankatib,* which, with the assimilation of the *n*, became Hebrew יִכָּתֵב *yikkāṯēḇ*. The imperative and infinitive construct are based on the same stem as the imperfect, where the doubling of the first root consonant is the most striking characteristic of the type in general. The participle and infinitive absolute are based on the perfect.

Root Type	Perfect		Imperfect		Imperative	
Regular	נִכְתַּב	*niḵtaḇ*	יִכָּתֵב	*yikkāṯēḇ*	הִכָּתֵב	*hikkāṯēḇ*
III-gutt.	נִשְׁלַח	*nišlaḥ*	יִשָּׁלַח	*yiššālaḥ*	הִשָּׁלַח	*hiššālaḥ*
I-gutt.	נֶאֱמַן	*ne'ěman*	יֵאָמֵן	*yē'āmēn*	הֵאָמֵן	*hē'āmēn*

Inf. Constr.		Participle	
הִכָּתֵב	*hikkāṯēḇ*	נִכְתָּב	*niḵtāḇ*
הִשָּׁלַח	*hiššālaḥ*	נִשְׁלָח	*nišlāḥ*
הֵאָמֵן	*hē'āmēn*	נֶאֱמָן	*ne'ěmān*

Remarks:

(a) The only deviation from the regular pattern with roots III-gutt. is the replacement of *ē* with *a* in the imperfect and related forms.

(b) With roots I-gutt. (including א), the perfect usually has the pattern of נֶאֱמַן, with *e* in the preformative and *ě* after the guttural. In the imperfect and related forms the doubling of the first root consonant is replaced by a compensatory lengthening of the prefix vowel *i* to *ē*; this *ē* is unaltered in the inflection.

(c) The participle differs from the stem of the perfect only in the length of the stem vowel. As an adjective, the participle retains this vowel in inflection; e.g. the fem. נִכְתָּבָה *niḵtāḇāh*, as opposed to the verb, with reduction: נִכְתְּבָה *niḵtəḇāh*.

	Regular		III-gutt.		I-gutt.	
Perfect:	נִכְתַּב	*niḵtaḇ*	נִשְׁלַח	*nišlaḥ*	נֶאֱמַן	*ne'ěman*
	נִכְתְּבָה	*niḵtəḇāh*	נִשְׁלְחָה	*nišləḥāh*	נֶאֶמְנָה	*ne'emnāh*

	נִכְתַּ֫בְתָּ	*nik̲táḇtā*	נִשְׁלַ֫חְתָּ	*nišláḥtā*	נֶאֱמַ֫נְתָּ	*ne'ĕmántā*
	נִכְתַּ֫בְתְּ	*nik̲táḇt*	נִשְׁלַ֫חַתְּ	*nišláḥt*	נֶאֱמַ֫נְתְּ	*ne'ĕmánt*
	נִכְתַּ֫בְתִּי	*nik̲táḇtî*	נִשְׁלַ֫חְתִּי	*nišláḥtî*	נֶאֱמַ֫נְתִּי	*ne'ĕmántî*
	נִכְתְּבוּ	*nik̲təḇû*	נִשְׁלְחוּ	*nišləḥû*	נֶאֶמְנוּ	*ne'emnû*
	נִכְתַּבְתֶּם	*nik̲taḇtém*	נִשְׁלַחְתֶּם	*nišlaḥtém*	נֶאֱמַנְתֶּם	*ne'ĕmantém*
	נִכְתַּבְתֶּן	*nik̲taḇtén*	נִשְׁלַחְתֶּן	*nišlaḥtén*	נֶאֱמַנְתֶּן	*ne'ĕmantén*
	נִכְתַּ֫בְנוּ	*nik̲táḇnû*	נִשְׁלַ֫חְנוּ	*nišláḥnû*	נֶאֱמַ֫נּוּ	*ne'ĕmánnû*
IMPERFECT:	יִכָּתֵב	*yikkāṯēḇ*	יִשָּׁלַח	*yiššālaḥ*	יֵאָמֵן	*yē'āmēn*
	תִּכָּתֵב	*tikkāṯēḇ*	תִּשָּׁלַח	*tiššālaḥ*	תֵּאָמֵן	*tē'āmēn*
	תִּכָּתֵב	*tikkāṯēḇ*	תִּשָּׁלַח	*tiššālaḥ*	תֵּאָמֵן	*tē'āmēn*
	תִּכָּתְבִי	*tikkāṯəḇî*	תִּשָּׁלְחִי	*tiššāləḥî*	תֵּאָמְנִי	*tē'āmənî*
	אֶכָּתֵב	*'ekkāṯēḇ*	אֶשָּׁלַח	*'eššālaḥ*	אֵאָמֵן	*'ē'āmēn*
	יִכָּתְבוּ	*yikkāṯəḇû*	יִשָּׁלְחוּ	*yiššāləḥû*	יֵאָמְנוּ	*yē'āmənû*
	תִּכָּתַ֫בְנָה	*tikkāṯáḇnāh*	תִּשָּׁלַ֫חְנָה	*tiššāláḥnāh*	תֵּאָמַ֫נָּה	*tē'āmánnāh*
	תִּכָּתְבוּ	*tikkāṯəḇû*	תִּשָּׁלְחוּ	*tiššāləḥû*	תֵּאָמְנוּ	*tē'āmənû*
	תִּכָּתַ֫בְנָה	*tikkāṯáḇnāh*	תִּשָּׁלַ֫חְנָה	*tiššāláḥnāh*	תֵּאָמַ֫נָּה	*tē'āmánnāh*
	נִכָּתֵב	*nikkāṯēḇ*	נִשָּׁלַח	*niššālaḥ*	נֵאָמֵן	*nē'āmēn*
IMPERATIVE:	הִכָּתֵב	*hikkāṯēḇ*	הִשָּׁלַח	*hiššālaḥ*	הֵאָמֵן	*hē'āmēn*
	הִכָּתְבִי	*hikkāṯəḇî*	הִשָּׁלְחִי	*hiššāləḥî*	הֵאָמְנִי	*hē'āmənî*
	הִכָּתְבוּ	*hikkāṯəḇû*	הִשָּׁלְחוּ	*hiššāləḥû*	הֵאָמְנוּ	*hē'āmənû*
	הִכָּתַ֫בְנָה	*hikkāṯáḇnāh*	הִשָּׁלַ֫חְנָה	*hiššāláḥnāh*	הֵאָמַ֫נָּה	*hē'āmánnāh*
INF. CONSTR.	הִכָּתֵב	*hikkāṯēḇ*	הִשָּׁלַח	*hiššālaḥ*	הֵאָמֵן	*hē'āmēn*
W. SUFF.	הִכָּתְבִי	*hikkāṯəḇî*	הִשָּׁלְחִי	*hiššāləḥî*	הֵאָמְנִי	*hē'āmənî*
	הִכָּתֶבְךָ	*hikkāṯebk̲ā*	הִשָּׁלַחֲךָ	*hiššālaḥăk̲ā*	הֵאָמֶנְךָ	*hē'āmenk̲ā*
		etc.		etc.		etc.
INF. (1)	נִכְתּוֹב	*nik̲tôḇ*	נִשְׁלוֹחַ	*nišlô^{a}ḥ*	נַעֲבוֹר	*na'ăḇôr*
ABSOLUTE (2)	הִכָּתוֹב	*hikkāṯôḇ*	הִשָּׁלוֹחַ	*hiššālô^{a}ḥ*	הֵעָבוֹר	*hē'āḇôr*
PARTICIPLE:	נִכְתָּב	*nik̲tāḇ*	נִשְׁלָח	*nišlāḥ*	נֶאֱמָן	*ne'ĕmān*
	נִכְתָּבָה	*nik̲tāḇāh*	נִשְׁלָחָה	*nišlāḥāh*	נֶאֱמָנָה	*ne'ĕmānāh*
	נִכְתָּבִים	*nik̲tāḇîm*	נִשְׁלָחִים	*nišlāḥîm*	נֶאֱמָנִים	*ne'ĕmānîm*
	נִכְתָּבוֹת	*nik̲tāḇôṯ*	נִשְׁלָחוֹת	*nišlāḥôṯ*	נֶאֱמָנוֹת	*ne'ĕmānôṯ*

Remarks:

(1) The two forms of the infinitive absolute tend to pair off with the corresponding finite verb of the same general pattern:

הִשָּׁמוֹעַ יִשָּׁמַע but נִשְׁמוֹעַ נִשְׁמַע

(2) The inf. absolute of נֶאֱמַן does not occur, and since its form could be disputed (more likely to have been נֶאֱמוֹן, with *e* because of the א) we have replaced it with the better attested type of נֶעֱבַר (to be crossed).

(3) The feminine participles singular may also be of the pattern נִכְתֶּ֫בֶת, נֶאֱמֶ֫נֶת, נִשְׁלַ֫חַת.

142. Vocabulary 37.

NOUNS: נֶ֫פֶשׁ *nép̄eš* (w. suff. נַפְשִׁי etc.; pl. *-ôṯ*) soul, vital life-force; a person, living thing. With suffixes it is the equivalent of the intensive/reflexive pronoun: נַפְשִׁי myself, נַפְשְׁךָ yourself...

שַׂק *śaq* (pl. *-îm*) sack; sack-cloth (worn as a sign of mourning).

מִשְׁמָר *mišmār* (no pl.) place of confinement, jail; a guard unit.

מָלוֹן *mālôn* lodging-place, inn.

VERBS: אָשֵׁם *'āšēm* (יֶאְשַׁם) to be guilty; verbal adjective אָשֵׁם, guilty.

לָן *lān* (יָלִין) to spend the night.

נֶאֱמַן *ne'ĕman* (יֵאָמֵן) to be confirmed, verified, trustworthy.

נִשְׁאַר *niš'ar* (יִשָּׁאֵר) to be left over, remain, survive.

OTHER: לְבַד־ *ləḇadd-* w. suff.: alone, only. E.g. אֲנִי לְבַדִּי I alone, etc.

אֲבָל *'ăḇāl* (adv.) truly, indeed; however.

Note: The preposition בֵּין (between) has the following forms with pronominal suffixes:

בֵּינִי	bênî	בֵּינֵ֫ינוּ	bênênû	or	בֵּינוֹתֵ֫ינוּ	bênôṯênû (rare)
בֵּינְךָ	bênəḵā	בֵּינֵיכֶם	bênêḵem		——	
בֵּינֵךְ	bênēḵ	——	——		——	
בֵּינוֹ	bênô	בֵּינֵיהֶם	bênêhem	or	בֵּינוֹתָם	bênôṯām (rare)

Exercises:

(a) Punctuate the Niphal verbs fully and translate:

(1) נשבַּר הַכְּלִי.
(2) יֵאכל הַבָּשָׂר.
(3) נהרגו הַמְרַגְּלִים.
(4) ישמעו דִבְרֵי אֱמֶת.
(5) לֹא יכרת אִישׁ מֵעַל הַכִּסֵּא.
(6) נשמע קוֹל שִׁירָם.
(7) לֹא נחשׂך מְאוּמָה מִמְּךָ.
(8) אֵיךְ יבּחן הָעָם.
(9) אֲנַ֫חְנוּ נשארנו לְבַדֵּ֫נוּ.
(10) יֵאמן דְּבַר אֱלֹהִים.
(11) תִּזכרו כֻּלְּכֶם.
(12) אַל־יכּתב שְׁמוֹ בַּסֵּ֫פֶר.
(13) אֵ֫לֶּה שְׁמוֹת הֶעָרִים הַנִּלכּדות.
(14) וַיִּמכר יוֹסֵף בִּידֵי הַמִּצְרִים.
(15) חַי אֱלֹהִים אִם־ישפך דָּם בִּהְיוֹתִי פֹּה.
(16) יִתפשׂוּ הַבֹּרְחִים.
(17) יחֹן אֶת־הַנִּבחרים.
(18) יִדַּ֫מּוּ הַנִּשארים.
(19) הִפּתחוּ הַשְּׁעָרִים.
(20) תִּשָּׂרַ֫פְנָה הֶעָרִים הַנֶּעזבות.

(b) Write in Hebrew:

1. And when their words were heard, we knew that they were guilty.
2. As God lives, you will not see your husband until the day of his death.
3. And in the evening he entered an inn and spent the night there.
4. Now that you have been chosen as our king, give us help so that we may slay our accursed enemies before our land is captured and our cities are burned.

5. They placed the food in their sacks and set out on the road.
6. Now that he has measured the field, go to him and ask him whether (hă-) he will sell it to us.

(c) Reading: Joseph and his Brothers in Egypt.

וַיֶּאֱסֹף יוֹסֵף אֶת־אֶחָיו אֶל־מִשְׁמָר שְׁלֹשֶׁת יָמִים וַיֹּאמֶר אֲלֵיהֶם בַּיּוֹם הַשְּׁלִישִׁי: זֹאת עֲשׂוּ וִחְיוּ, אֶת־הָאֱלֹהִים אֲנִי יָרֵא, אִם־כֵּנִים אַתֶּם, אֲחִיכֶם אֶחָד יֵאָסֵר בְּבֵית מִשְׁמַרְכֶם וְאַתֶּם לְכוּ וְשׁוּבוּ אַרְצָה כְּנַעַן עִם־הָאֹכֶל אֲשֶׁר קְנִיתֶם וְאֶת־אֲחִיכֶם הַקָּטֹן תִּקְחוּ מִשָּׁם וְהוּא יָבֹא אִתְּכֶם הֵנָּה וְיֵאָמְנוּ דִבְרֵיכֶם וְלֹא תָמוּתוּ.

וַיֹּאמְרוּ אִישׁ אֶל־אָחִיו: אֲבָל אֲשֵׁמִים אֲנַחְנוּ עַל־אָחִינוּ[1] אֲשֶׁר רָאִינוּ צָרַת נַפְשׁוֹ וְלֹא שָׁמָעְנוּ, עַל־כֵּן בָּאָה אֵלֵינוּ הַצָּרָה הַזֹּאת, וַיַּעַן רְאוּבֵן אֹתָם לֵאמֹר: הֲלֹא אָמַרְתִּי אֲלֵיכֶם לֵאמֹר אַל־תֶּחֶטְאוּ בַיֶּלֶד וְלֹא שְׁמַעְתֶּם וְגַם־דָּמוֹ[2] הִנֵּה נִדְרָשׁ, וְהֵם לֹא יָדְעוּ כִּי שֹׁמֵעַ יוֹסֵף כִּי הַמֵּלִיץ[3] בֵּינוֹתָם וַיִּסֹּב[4] יוֹסֵף מֵעֲלֵיהֶם וַיֵּבְךְּ וַיָּשָׁב אֲלֵיהֶם וַיִּקַּח אֶת־שִׁמְעוֹן וַיֶּאֱסֹר אֹתוֹ לְעֵינֵיהֶם וַיִּתֵּן לָהֶם אֶת־הָאֹכֶל אֲשֶׁר בָּאוּ מִצְרַיְמָה לִקְנוֹת וַיִּתֵּן לָהֶם גַּם־צֵדָה[5] לַדָּרֶךְ וַיָּשֶׂם אֶת־הַכֶּסֶף אֲשֶׁר נָתְנוּ לוֹ בְּשַׂקֵּיהֶם וְהֵם לֹא יָדְעוּ וַיֵּלְכוּ מִשָּׁם לַעֲלוֹת אַרְצָה כְּנָעַן.

וַיְהִי בַּעֲלוֹתָם וַיָּלִינוּ בְּמָלוֹן וַיְהִי כִּפְתֹּחַ אֶחָד מֵהֶם אֶת־שַׂקּוֹ לָתֵת מֵהָאֹכֶל לַחֲמוֹרוֹ וַיַּרְא אֶת־כַּסְפּוֹ וְהִנֵּה הוּא בְּפִי שַׂקּוֹ וַיֹּאמֶר אֶל־אֶחָיו: הִנֵּה כַסְפִּי בְּשַׂקִּי, וַיִּרְאוּ וַיֶּחֶרְדוּ וַיֹּאמְרוּ אִישׁ אֶל־אָחִיו לֵאמֹר: מַה־זֹּאת עָשָׂה אֱלֹהִים לָנוּ.

וַיָּבֹאוּ אֶל־יַעֲקֹב אֲבִיהֶם אַרְצָה כְּנָעַן וַיֹּאמְרוּ לוֹ אֶת־כָּל־הַקֹּרוֹת[6] אֹתָם לֵאמֹר: אָמַר אֵלֵינוּ הָאִישׁ אֲדֹנֵי הָאָרֶץ קָשׁוֹת וַיֹּאמֶר כִּי אֲנַחְנוּ מְרַגְּלִים וְכִי בָּאנוּ לִרְאוֹת עֶרְוַת אַרְצוֹ וַנֹּאמֶר אֵלָיו: כֵּנִים אֲנַחְנוּ, לֹא הָיִינוּ מְרַגְּלִים, וַיֹּאמֶר אֵלֵינוּ הָאִישׁ אֲדֹנֵי הָאָרֶץ: בְּזֹאת אֵדַע כִּי כֵנִים אַתֶּם, אֲחִיכֶם הָאֶחָד יֵאָסֵר בְּבֵית הַמִּשְׁמָר וְאַתֶּם לְכוּ וְשַׁבְתֶּם אֶל־אַרְצְכֶם וּבוֹא יָבֹא אֲחִיכֶם הַקָּטֹן אִתְּכֶם בְּרִדְתְּכֶם עוֹד אֵלַי, וְכֵן עָשִׂינוּ וְאֶת־אָחִינוּ שִׁמְעוֹן אָסְרוּ לְעֵינֵינוּ וַיָּשִׂימוּ אֹתוֹ בְּבֵית הַמִּשְׁמָר.

וַיֹּאמֶר אֲלֵיהֶם יַעֲקֹב אֲבִיהֶם: אֹתִי שִׁכַּלְתֶּם,[7] יוֹסֵף אֵינֶנּוּ וְשִׁמְעוֹן אֵינֶנּוּ וְאֶת־בִּנְיָמִן תִּקָּחוּ, עָלַי הָיוּ כֻלָּנָה,[8] וַיֹּאמֶר רְאוּבֵן אֶל־אָבִיו לֵאמֹר: אֶת־שְׁנֵי בָנַי תָּמִית[9] אִם־לֹא יָשׁוּב בִּנְיָמִין עִמִּי אֵלֶיךָ מִמִּצְרַיִם, תְּנָה אֹתוֹ עַל־יָדִי[10] וְהוּא יָשׁוּב עִמִּי מִשָּׁם.

וַיֹּאמֶר יַעֲקֹב: לֹא יֵרֵד בְּנִי עִמָּכֶם כִּי אָחִיו מֵת וְהוּא לְבַדּוֹ נִשְׁאַר, אִם־תִּקְרָא אֹתוֹ רָעָה בַּדֶּרֶךְ אֲשֶׁר תֵּלְכוּ בָהּ וְיָרַדְתִּיו[11] בְּיָגוֹן שְׁאֹלָה.

Notes to the Reading:

1. They are referring here to their earlier treatment of Joseph.
2. Prob. to be understood as "And now, moreover, (our penalty for shedding) his blood is to be exacted." דָּם is frequently used as the equivalent of the guilt (or punishment) involved in bloodshed.
3. מֵלִיץ an interpreter
4. סָבַב in the sense "turn oneself away"
5. "provisions"
6. fem. pl. = neuter pl. "the things which befell"

7. "you have bereaved"
8. A rare form, perhaps fem. pl., "everything".
9. "you may kill"
10. "in my charge"
11. Note that the apodosis (if... *then*) is not marked except by a conjunctive-sequential construction. יָגוֹן grief.

LESSON 38

143. Niphal Verbs: Stems and Inflection (continued).

ROOT TYPE	PERFECT	IMPERFECT	IMPERATIVE	INF. CONSTRUCT
I-*Nun*	נִתַּן *nittan*	יִנָּתֵן *yinnāṯēn*	הִנָּתֵן *hinnāṯēn*	הִנָּתֵן *hinnāṯēn*
I-*Yodh*	נוֹלַד *nôlaḏ*	יִוָּלֵד *yiwwālēḏ*	הִוָּלֵד *hiwwālēḏ*	הִוָּלֵד *hiwwālēḏ*
III-*Aleph*	נִקְרָא *niqrā'*	יִקָּרֵא *yiqqārē'*	הִקָּרֵא *hiqqārē'*	הִקָּרֵא *hiqqārē'*
III-*Hē*	נִבְנָה *niḇnāh*	יִבָּנֶה *yibbāneh*	הִבָּנֵה *hibbānēh*	הִבָּנוֹת *hibbānôṯ*

Remarks:

(1) I-*Nun*. The assimilation of the first root consonant takes place in the perfect and participle: **nintan* > *nittan*. The stems and inflection are otherwise like those of the regular triliteral root. [Note: the assimilation of the stem-final *n* in the perfect of נִתַּן is proper only to this particular root; cf. the Qal perfect.]

(2) I-*Yodh*. Nearly all roots I-*Yodh* in Hebrew were originally I-*Waw*. The original *Waw* shows up clearly in the Niphal verbs. In the perfect an earlier **nawlad* (root *yld* < *wld*) appears as נוֹלַד *nôlaḏ* (he was born). In the imperfect and imperative the *n*- of the Niphal prefix is assimilated to the root -*w*- and a doubled -*ww*- results: יִוָּלֵד *yiwwālēḏ* (he will be born). Inflection is regular.

(3) III-*Aleph*. As expected, the stem vowel of the perfect is lengthened to *ā* before the quiescent א (cf. §52 etc.). Unlike the Qal perfect, however,

the stem vowel is replaced with *ē* before the 2nd and 1st person endings: e.g. *niqrḗ(')t̲ā* (you were called). The full inflection is given below.

(4) III-*Hē*. The pattern of inflection learned for the Qal will hold for most of the verbs derived from roots III-*Hē*. In the Niphal perfect, however, the stem vowel before the 2nd and 1st person suffixes is regulary *ê*, not *î*. Contrast בָּנִ֫יתִי and נִבְנֵ֫יתִי (I was built). Just as in the Qal, the jussive or short form of the imperfect loses the final vowel: יִבָּנֶה → יִבֶּן The inf. construct ends in *-ôt̲*, again like the Qal: בְּנוֹת, הִבָּנוֹת Note the participle נִבְנֶה (cf. בֹּנֶה).

PERFECT:

נִתַּן	*nittan*	נוֹלַד	*nôlad̲*	נִקְרָא	*niqrā'*	נִבְנָה	*nib̲nāh*
נִתְּנָה	*nittənāh*	נוֹלְדָה	*nôləd̲āh*	נִקְרְאָה	*niqrə'āh*	נִבְנְתָה	*nib̲nət̲āh*
נִתַּ֫תָּ	*nittáttā*	נוֹלַ֫דְתָּ	*nôlád̲tā*	נִקְרֵ֫אתָ	*niqrē(')t̲ā*	נִבְנֵ֫יתָ	*nib̲nêt̲ā*
נִתַּתְּ	*nittátt*	נוֹלַ֫דְתְּ	*nôlád̲t*	נִקְרֵאת	*niqrē(')t̲*	נִבְנֵית	*nib̲nêt̲*
נִתַּ֫תִּי	*nittáttî*	נוֹלַ֫דְתִּי	*nôlád̲tî*	נִקְרֵ֫אתִי	*niqrē(')t̲î*	נִבְנֵ֫יתִי	*nib̲nêt̲î*
נִתְּנוּ	*nittənû*	נוֹלְדוּ	*nôləd̲û*	נִקְרְאוּ	*niqrə'û*	נִבְנוּ	*nib̲nû*
נִתַּתֶּם	*nittattem*	נוֹלַדְתֶּם	*nôlad̲tém*	נִקְרֵאתֶם	*niqrē(')t̲em*	נִבְנֵיתֶם	*nib̲nêt̲em*
נִתַּתֶּן	*nittatten*	נוֹלַדְתֶּן	*nôlad̲tén*	נִקְרֵאתֶן	*niqrē(')t̲en*	נִבְנֵיתֶן	*nib̲nêt̲en*
נִתַּ֫נּוּ	*nittánnû*	נוֹלַ֫דְנוּ	*nôlád̲nû*	נִקְרֵ֫אנוּ	*niqrē(')nû*	נִבְנֵ֫ינוּ	*nib̲nênû*

IMPERFECT:

יִנָּתֵן	*yinnāt̲ēn*	יִוָּלֵד	*yiwwālēd̲*	יִקָּרֵא	*yiqqārē'*	יִבָּנֶה	*yibbāneh*
תִּנָּתֵן	*tinnāt̲ēn*	תִּוָּלֵד	*tiwwālēd̲*	תִּקָּרֵא	*tiqqārē'*	תִּבָּנֶה	*tibbāneh*
תִּנָּתֵן	*tinnāt̲ēn*	תִּוָּלֵד	*tiwwālēd̲*	תִּקָּרֵא	*tiqqārē'*	תִּבָּנֶה	*tibbāneh*
תִּנָּתְנִי	*tinnāt̲ənî*	תִּוָּלְדִי	*tiwwāləd̲î*	תִּקָּרְאִי	*tiqqārə'î*	תִּבָּנִי	*tibbānî*
אֶנָּתֵן	*'ennāt̲ēn*	אִוָּלֵד	*'iwwālēd̲*	אֶקָּרֵא	*'eqqārē'*	אֶבָּנֶה	*'ebbāneh*
יִנָּתְנוּ	*yinnāt̲ənû*	יִוָּלְדוּ	*yiwwāləd̲û*	יִקָּרְאוּ	*yiqqārə'û*	יִבָּנוּ	*yibbānû*
תִּנָּתַ֫נָּה	*tinnāt̲ánnāh*	תִּוָּלַ֫דְנָה	*tiwwālád̲nāh*	תִּקָּרֶ֫אנָה	*tiqqāré(')nāh*	תִּבָּנֶ֫ינָה	*tibbānẹnāh*
תִּנָּתְנוּ	*tinnāt̲ənû*	תִּוָּלְדוּ	*tiwwāləd̲û*	תִּקָּרְאוּ	*tiqqārə'û*	תִּבָּנוּ	*tibbānû*
תִּנָּתַ֫נָּה	*tinnāt̲ánnāh*	תִּוָּלַ֫דְנָה	*tiwwālád̲nāh*	תִּקָּרֶ֫אנָה	*tiqqāré(')nāh*	תִּבָּנֶ֫ינָה	*tibbānẹnāh*
נִנָּתֵן	*ninnāt̲ēn*	נִוָּלֵד	*niwwālēd̲*	נִקָּרֵא	*niqqārē'*	נִבָּנֶה	*nibbāneh*

IMPERATIVE:

הִנָּתֵן	*hinnāt̲ēn*	הִוָּלֵד	*hiwwālēd̲*	הִקָּרֵא	*hiqqārē'*	הִבָּנֵה	*hibbānēh*
הִנָּתְנִי	*hinnāt̲ənî,*	הִוָּלְדִי	*hiwwāləd̲î*	הִקָּרְאִי	*hiqqārə'î*	הִבָּנִי	*hibbānî*
	etc.		etc.		etc.		etc.

INF. CONSTRUCT:

הִנָּתֵן	*hinnāt̲ēn*	הִוָּלֵד	*hiwwālēd̲*	הִקָּרֵא	*hiqqārē'*	הִבָּנוֹת	*hibbānôt̲*

INF. ABSOLUTE:

נִתּוֹן	*nittôn*	[נוֹלוֹד	*nôlôd̲*]	נִקְרוֹא	*niqrô'*	הִבָּנֵה	*hibbānēh*
						נִבְנֹה	*nib̲nōh*

PARTICIPLES:

נִתָּן	*nittān*	נוֹלָד	*nôlāḏ*	נִקְרָא	*niqrā'*	נִבְנֶה	*niḇneh*
נִתָּנָה	*nittānāh*	נוֹלָדָה	*nôlāḏāh*	נִקְרָאָה	*niqrā'āh*	נִבְנָה	*niḇnāh*
נִתֶּ֫נֶת	*nitténeṯ*	נוֹלֶ֫דֶת	*nôléḏeṯ*	נִקְרֵאת	*niqrē(')ṯ*		
נִתָּנִים	*nittānîm*	נוֹלָדִים	*nôlāḏîm*	נִקְרָאִים	*niqrā'îm*	נִבְנִים	*niḇnîm*
נִתָּנוֹת	*nittānôṯ*	נוֹלָדוֹת	*nôlāḏôṯ*	נִקְרָאוֹת	*niqrā'ôṯ*	נִבְנוֹת	*niḇnôṯ*

144. Niphal Verbs: Mixed Types.

The following are a sampling of verbs whose roots combine several of the characteristics described in the preceding paragraphs. The forms are all quite predictable from the types already given and thus require no comment.

I-*Waw(Yodh)* and III-gutt.:	PERF.:	נוֹדַע	*nôḏa'*
I-*Waw(Yodh)* and III-*Aleph*:		נוֹרָא	*nôrā'*
I-gutt. and III-*Hē*:		נַעֲשָׂה	*na'ăśāh*
I-*Nun* and II-gutt. (root נחם)		נִחַם	*niḥam*

IMPERF.:	יִוָּדַע	*yiwwāḏa'*	IMPTV.:	הִוָּדַע	*hiwwāḏa'*	*be known*
	יִוָּרֵא	*yiwwārē'*		הִוָּרֵא	*hiwwārē'*	*be feared*
	יֵעָשֶׂה	*yē'āśeh*		הֵעָשֵׂה	*hē'āśēh*	*be done*
	יִנָּחֵם	*yinnāḥēm*		הִנָּחֵם	*hinnāḥēm*	*be sorry*

Note also the verb נִגַּשׁ *niggaš* (root נגשׁ). Only the perfect is a Niphal verb; in the imperfect the Qal form יִגַּשׁ is used.

145. Vocabulary 38.

NOUNS: ראשׁ *rō(')š* (pl. irreg. רָאשִׁים, see §34) head, chief, top

פֶּתַח *péṯaḥ* (w. suff. פִּתְחִי; pl. *-îm*) an opening (of tent, house, wall etc.); also used as a prep.: at the opening of

טַף *ṭap̄* (no pl.) a collective term for children; not used in construct

מְעַט *mə'aṭ* (no pl.) a little; frequent in construct: מְעַט מַ֫יִם a little water. Note מְעַט מְעַט little by little; בְּעוֹד מְעַט in a little while. Also used in a variety of idiomatic expressions with the basic meaning of slightness, smallness, unimportance.

עוֹלָם *'ôlām* (pl. *-îm*) a word referring to a long duration of time, either past or future; thus, eternity, antiquity. Note the common phrases: לְעוֹלָם, עַד־עוֹלָם forever. Frequent as the second element of a construct chain: יְמֵי עוֹלָם ancient days; בְּרִית עוֹלָם perpetual covenant.

VERBS: נוֹתַר *nôṯar* (יִוָּתֵר) to be left, remain

נִלְחַם *nilḥam* (יִלָּחֵם) to fight (+ בְּ with)

נִחַם *niḥam* (יִנָּחֵם) to be sorry, repent; to be comforted

נִגַּשׁ *niggaš* (use Qal imperf. יִגַּשׁ) to approach (+ אֶל)
נִצַּב *niṣṣab̲* (no imperf.) to station oneself, to stand; be stationed
נִפְלָא *nip̄lā'* (יִפָּלֵא) to be wonderful, marvelous.

Exercises:

(a) Point the Niphal verbs fully and translate:

(1) נגשתי וְלֹא יָכֹלְתִּי לַעֲמֹד לְפָנָיו.
(2) אֵיפֹה תָלִין הַלָּיְלָה.
(3) מִי יבחר לְרֹאשׁ הָעָם.
(4) הֵם נלחמים אֵצֶל הַקִּיר.
(5) לֹא תזכר בִּקְהַל הַצַּדִּיקִים.
(6) יֵאספו מִקְצֵי הָאָרֶץ.
(7) לֹא יותר אִישׁ מֵהַפָּרָשִׁים.
(8) קְחוּ אֶת־הַסּוּסִים הנותרים.
(9) תֵּן לִי מְעַט־לֶחֶם.
(10) מִי הָאֲנָשִׁים הנצבים שָׁם.
(11) נלקחו הָאֲנָשִׁים הַחוּצָה וַיֵּהרגו שָׁם.
(12) יֶשְׁבוּ עַל־שְׂפַת הַנָּהָר עִם־טַפָּם.
(13) אֵינֶנִּי אָשֵׁם, לֹא עָשִׂיתִי דָבָר.
(14) ויבן לוֹ בַּיִת.
(15) נחמתי עַל־הָרָעָה אֲשֶׁר עָשִׂיתִי.
(16) רָאִינוּ אֶת־מְלַאכְתּוֹ הַנִּפְלָאָה ונדם.
(17) לָמָּה יֵעשׂו הַדְּבָרִים הָאֵלֶּה.
(18) וַיְהִי אַחֲרֵי הַמִּלְחָמָה ואותר אֲנִי לְבַדִּי.
(19) ינתן לְךָ כֶּסֶף וְזָהָב.
(20) יודע שִׁמְךָ הַגָּדוֹל בְּכָל־הָאָרֶץ.
(21) ויקן שָׁם בָּקָר.
(22) וישמעו דְּבָרָיו ויאמנו.
(23) וַיְהִי מִקֵּץ אַרְבָּעָה יָמִים ותעזב הָעִיר.
(24) יקראו הַדְּבָרִים הָאֵלֶּה בְּאָזְנֵי בְּנֵיכֶם.

(b) Write in Hebrew:

1. There is a large hill between us and the camp.
2. The fruit will be taken to the house and eaten there.
3. The righteous shall be exalted (lit. raised up), but the wicked shall perish.
4. Countless men (lit. men, their number not existing) were slain near the wall.
5. Be consoled, my son; the sound of your distress has been heard and help will be given to you.
6. I was appointed (lit. stationed) to watch the women and the children.
7. A new city will be built for those who are left.

(c) Reading: Jacob and his Sons, after the First Trip to Egypt.

וְהָרָעָב כָּבֵד בָּאָרֶץ וַיְהִי כַּאֲשֶׁר כִּלָּה הָאֹכֶל אֲשֶׁר נִקְנָה בְּמִצְרַיִם וַיֹּאמֶר יַעֲקֹב אֶל־בָּנָיו: שׁוּבוּ מִצְרַיְמָה וּקְחוּ מִשָּׁם מְעַט־אֹכֶל, וַיֹּאמֶר אֵלָיו יְהוּדָה לֵאמֹר: אָמַר הָאִישׁ אֵלֵינוּ, לֹא תִרְאוּ פָּנַי בִּלְתִּי[1] אֲחִיכֶם אִתְּכֶם, אִם־יֶשְׁךָ שֹׁלֵחַ אֶת־אָחִינוּ אִתָּנוּ נֵרֵד וְנִקְנֶה לְךָ אֹכֶל וְאִם־אֵינְךָ שֹׁלֵחַ לֹא נֵרֵד כִּי אָמַר הָאִישׁ אֵלֵינוּ, לֹא תִרְאוּ פָּנַי בִּלְתִּי אֲחִיכֶם אִתְּכֶם.

וַיֹּאמֶר יִשְׂרָאֵל: לָמָה אֲמַרְתֶּם אֵלָיו כִּי עוֹד לָכֶם אָח, וַיֹּאמְרוּ: שָׁאוֹל שָׁאַל הָאִישׁ לָנוּ[2] לֵאמֹר: הַעוֹד אֲבִיכֶם חַי, הֲיֵשׁ לָכֶם אָח, וַנֹּאמֶר אֵלָיו עַל־פִּי הַדְּבָרִים הָאֵלֶּה, הֲיָדוֹעַ נֵדַע[3] כִּי יֹאמַר: אֲחִיכֶם יֵרֵד אִתְּכֶם.

וַיֹּאמֶר יְהוּדָה אֶל־יִשְׂרָאֵל אָבִיו: שִׁלְחָה הַנַּעַר אִתִּי וְנָקוּמָה וְנֵלְכָה וְנִחְיֶה וְלֹא נָמוּת גַּם־

אֲנַ֫חְנוּ גַם־אַתָּה גַּם־טַפֵּ֫נוּ, אִם־לֹא יָשׁוּב הַנַּ֫עַר אֵלֶ֫יךָ אִתִּי וְחָטָאתִי לְךָ[4] כָּל־הַיָּמִים, וַיֹּ֫אמֶר
יַעֲקֹב: אִם־כֵּן, זֹאת עֲשׂוּ, קְחוּ אִישׁ מִנְחָה, וְכֶ֫סֶף מִשְׁנֶה[5] קְחוּ, וְאֶת־אֲחִיכֶם קְחוּ וְק֫וּמוּ שׁ֫וּבוּ
אֶל־הָאִישׁ וֵאלֹהִים יִתֵּן לָכֶם רַחֲמִים[6] לִפְנֵי הָאִישׁ וְשִׁלַּח[7] לָכֶם אֶת־אֲחִיכֶם וְאֶת־בִּנְיָמִין.

Notes to the Reading:

1. בִּלְתִּי unless
2. Note לְ in the sense "about" after שָׁאַל.
3. נֵדַע and יֹאמַר are imperfects used modally: "How were we to know that he would say".
4. "I shall be accountable (lit. sin against) to you".
5. "twice the (required) money"
6. "mercy, favor"
7. "and may he release"

(d) Reading: Psalm 24:7–10.

שְׂאוּ שְׁעָרִים רָאשֵׁיכֶם
וְהִנָּשְׂאוּ פִּתְחֵי עוֹלָם
וְיָבוֹא מֶ֫לֶךְ הַכָּבוֹד:

מִי[1] זֶה מֶ֫לֶךְ הַכָּבוֹד
יהוה עִזּוּז[2] וְגִבּוֹר
יהוה גִּבּוֹר מִלְחָמָה:

שְׂאוּ שְׁעָרִים רָאשֵׁיכֶם
וּשְׂאוּ פִּתְחֵי עוֹלָם
וְיָבוֹא מֶ֫לֶךְ הַכָּבוֹד:

מִי הוּא זֶה מֶ֫לֶךְ הַכָּבוֹד
יהוה צְבָאוֹת
הוּא מֶ֫לֶךְ הַכָּבוֹד: סֶ֫לָה[3]

Notes to the Reading:

1. See §82 (end).
2. A rare word: "mighty, powerful".
3. A frequent word at the close of verses or longer sections in the Psalms. Its meaning is unknown.

LESSON 39

146. Niphal Verbs: Stems and Inflection (concluded).

Root Type		Perfect		Imperfect		Imperative	
Hollow	(כון)	נָכוֹן	*nāḵôn*	יִכּוֹן	*yikkôn*	הִכּוֹן	*hikkôn*
Geminate	(סבב)	נָסַב	*nāsaḇ*	יִסַּב	*yissaḇ*	הִסַּב	*hissaḇ*

Inf. Construct		Participle	
הִכּוֹן	*hikkôn*	נָכוֹן	*nāḵôn*
הִסֵּב	*hisseḇ*	נָסָב	*nāsāḇ*

As in the Qal, the two root types given above present the most striking deviation from the normal triliteral patterns of the preceding lessons. The retention of the stem vowel *-ô-* with the Hollow roots simplifies that paradigm, but attention must be called to the curious interchange of *ô* and *û* in pretonic syllables in the inflection of the perfect, where the stem vowel *-ô-* is added in the 1st and 2nd persons:

Perfect:	נָכוֹן	*nāḵôn*	נָכֹ֫ונוּ	*nāḵônû*
	נָכֹ֫ונָה	*nāḵônāh*		
	נְכוּנ֫וֹתָ	*nəḵûnôṯā*	נְכוּנוֹתֶם	*nəḵônôṯem*
	נְכוּנ֫וֹת	*nəḵûnôṯ*	נְכוּנוֹתֶן	*nəḵônôṯen*
	נְכוּנ֫וֹתִי	*nəḵûnôṯî*	נְכוּנ֫וֹנוּ	*nəḵûnônû*
Imperfect:	יִכּוֹן	*yikkôn*	יִכֹּ֫ונוּ	*yikkônû*
	תִּכּוֹן	*tikkôn*	[תִּכּוֹנֶ֫ינָה	*tikkônẹnāh*]

	תִּכּוֹן	*tikkôn*	תִּכֹּונוּ	*tikkônû*
	תִּכֹּונִי	*tikkônî*	[תִּכּוֹנֶינָה	*tikkônệnāh*]
	אִכּוֹן	*'ikkôn*	נִכּוֹן	*nikkôn*
IMPERATIVE:	הִכּוֹן	*hikkôn*	הִכֹּונוּ	*hikkônû*
	הִכֹּונִי	*hikkônî*		
INF. CONSTRUCT:	הִכּוֹן	*hikkôn*		
	הִכּוֹנִי	*hikkônî* etc.		
PARTICIPLE:	נָכוֹן	*nāḵôn*	נְכוֹנִים	*nəḵônîm*
	נְכוֹנָה	*nəḵônāh*	נְכוֹנוֹת	*nəḵônôṯ*

The inf. absolute may have either the form נָכוֹן *nāḵôn* or הִכּוֹן *hikkôn*.

Niphal verbs from geminate roots are quite poorly attested and in many cases one cannot be certain that the form in question is indeed a Niphal and not a Qal verb. The 3rd pers. masc. sing. of the perfect, נָסַב (from an earlier **nasabb-)* resembles a Qal verb from a root נסב. The full inflection, however, shows that this resemblance is superficial and that the doubling of the second root consonant reappears when a vowel is added to the stem. Likewise in the imperfect יִסַּב confusion with other types is possible: this form could be from a root נסב (cf. יִגַּשׁ) or it could be a Qal variant (cf. יִתַּם for the more usual יִתֹּם). Some of the alternate forms that crop up are due to analogy. For example, the original pair נָמַס – יִמַּס was altered to נָמֵס – יִמַּס probably because יִמַּס was interpreted as a stative Qal verb (like יִכְבַּד) from a root נמס:

יִכְבַּד is to כָּבֵד as יִמַּס is to נָמֵס.

This mixing of Qal and Niphal forms, together with the relative rarity of these verbs, makes it quite impossible to decide which conjugation we are dealing with. The following selection of forms is a sufficient guide to the forms that will be met:

PERFECT:	נָסַב	*nāsaḇ*	or	נָסֵב	*nāsēḇ*
	נָסַבָּה	*nāsábbāh*	or	נָסֵבָּה	*nāsébbāh*
	נְסַבּוֹתָ	*nəsabbôṯā* etc.			
	נָסַבּוּ	*nāsábbû*	or	נָסֵבּוּ	*nāsébbû*
	נְסַבּוֹתֶם	*nəsabbôṯem* etc.			
IMPERFECT:	יִסַּב	*yissab* etc.	or	יִסֹּב	*yissōḇ* etc.
	תִּסַּבִּי	*tissábbî* etc.	or	תִּסֹּבִּי	*tissóbbî* etc.
IMPERATIVE:	הִסַּב	*hissaḇ*	or	הִסֹּב	*hissōḇ*
	הִסַּבִּי	*hissábbî* etc.	or	הִסֹּבִּי	*hissóbbî* etc.
INF. CONSTR.	הִסֵּב	*hissēḇ*			
	הִסִּבִּי	*hissibbî* etc.			
PARTICIPLE:	נָסָב	*nāsāḇ*		נְסַבִּים	*nəsabbîm*
	נְסַבָּה	*nəsabbāh*		נְסַבּוֹת	*nəsabbôṯ*

147. Vocabulary 39.

NOUNS: טֶ֫בַח *ṭéḇaḥ* slaughtering

תְּחִלָּה *təḥillāh* beginning, first occasion (of some event)

צֵל *ṣēl* (w. suff. צִלִּי; pl. irreg. צְלָלִים) shade, shadow; fig., protection

יָמִין *yāmîn* the right; right hand or side (f.)

שְׂמֹאל *śəmō(')l* the left; יַד שְׂמֹאל the left hand or side (m.)

לֵב *lēḇ* (w. suff. לִבִּי; pl. *-ôṯ*) heart

VERBS: נָם *nām* (יָנוּם) to sleep

טָבַח *ṭāḇaḥ* (יִטְבַּח) to slaughter (animals for food)

רָחַץ *rāḥaṣ* (יִרְחַץ) to wash (tr. and intr.)

נָמֵס *nāmēs* (Niphal verb from root מסס; imperf. יִמַּס) to melt, dissolve

נָכוֹן *nāḵôn* (Niphal verb from root כון; imperf. יִכּוֹן) to be firm, fixed, secure, established

OTHER: יוֹמָם *yômām* (adv.) by day, in the daytime

Exercises:

(a) Translate:

(1) לֹא אִירָא לָנוּם בִּהְיוֹתְךָ אִתִּי.

(2) וַיְהִי בְּגִשְׁתֵּ֫נוּ וַנֵּ֫רֶא אֶת־רָאשֵׁי הֶהָרִים.

(3) וְנִרְאֲתָה עֶרְוָתֵךְ וּבֹ֫שְׁתֵּךְ.

(4) וְהָיָה בַבֹּ֫קֶר וְלֹא יִוָּתֵר הֶעָנָן בַּשָּׁמָ֫יִם.

(5) יִמַּס לִבָּם לִפְנֵי אֹיְבֵיהֶם.

(6) וַיְהִי בְּצֵאת הַשֶּׁ֫מֶשׁ וַיָּ֫נוּסוּ הַכּוֹכָבִים וְלֹא נִרְאוּ.

(7) תִּנָּחֲמוּ כִּי לֹא לְקַחְתֶּם אֶת־מִנְחָתִי.

(8) בְּטַח אֶל־יהוה בְּכָל־לִבְּךָ.

(9) כְּתֹב אֶת־דְּבָרַי עַל־לוּחַ לִבְּךָ.

(10) יִכּוֹן מֶ֫לֶךְ חָדָשׁ וְנָכוֹן עַל־הַכִּסֵּא.

(11) וַיְהִי בַּעֲשׂוֹתוֹ אֶת־הַמִּשְׁתֶּה וַיִּטְבַּח טֶ֫בַח גָּדוֹל.

(12) אֱלֹהִים הוּא צוּרֵ֫נוּ וְצִלֵּ֫נוּ.

(13) הֲרָחַ֫צְתָּ אֶת־אָזְנֶ֫יךָ.

(14) וַיִּשְׁכַּב בְּצֵל הָעֵץ וַיָּ֫נָם.

(15) הִנֵּה אֹיְבַי עַל־יְמִינִי וְעַל־שְׂמֹאלִי וַאֲנִי נְסַבּ֫וֹתִי.

(16) וַיִּגְּשׁוּ אֵלָיו הַמַּלְאָכִים וְהוּא יֹשֵׁב פֶּ֫תַח הַבָּ֫יִת.

(17) תִּמָּלֵא הָעִיר דָּם עַל־פִּי דְבַר הַנָּבִיא.

(18) תֵּרָאֶ֫ינָה לָכֶם נִפְלָאוֹת.

(19) אֵין מִסְפָּר לַנִּלְחָמִים.

(b) Write in Hebrew:

1. Your hearts will be broken.
2. The city will be surrounded and its inhabitants will be taken captive.
3. On the right are the tombs of their fathers.

4. Seven men were stationed over him lest he escape.
5. There was only a little food left for us.
6. We washed our hands and feet before we sat down to eat.
7. The words of his law are established for ever.
8. When I heard his words, my heart melted within me and I was not able to stand.

(c) Reading: Joseph and his Brothers: the Second Trip to Egypt.

וַיִּקְחוּ הָאֲנָשִׁים אֶת־הַמִּנְחָה הַזֹּאת וּמִשְׁנֶה[1] כֶּסֶף לָקְחוּ בְיָדָם וְאֶת־בִּנְיָמִן וַיָּקֻמוּ וַיֵּרְדוּ מִצְרַיְמָה וַיַּעַמְדוּ לִפְנֵי יוֹסֵף וַיַּרְא יוֹסֵף אִתָּם אֶת־בִּנְיָמִין וַיֹּאמֶר לַאֲשֶׁר[2] עַל־בֵּיתוֹ: הָבֵא[3] אֶת־הָאֲנָשִׁים הַבָּיְתָה וּטְבֹחַ[4] טֶבַח וְהָכֵן[5] כִּי אִתִּי יֹאכְלוּ הָאֲנָשִׁים בַּצָּהֳרָיִם.

וַיַּעַשׂ הָאִישׁ כַּאֲשֶׁר אָמַר יוֹסֵף וַיִּירְאוּ הָאֲנָשִׁים כִּי הוּבְאוּ[6] בֵּית יוֹסֵף וַיֹּאמְרוּ: עַל־דְּבַר הַכֶּסֶף הַשָּׁב בְּשַׂקֵּינוּ בַּתְּחִלָּה אֲנַחְנוּ מוּבָאִים[7] לָקַחַת אֹתָנוּ לַעֲבָדִים וְאֶת־חֲמֹרֵינוּ. וַיִּגְּשׁוּ אֶל־הָאִישׁ אֲשֶׁר עַל־בֵּית יוֹסֵף וַיֹּאמְרוּ אֵלָיו פֶּתַח הַבָּיִת: יָרוֹד יָרַדְנוּ בַתְּחִלָּה לִקְנוֹת אֹכֶל וַיְהִי כִּי בָאנוּ אֶל־הַמָּלוֹן וַנִּפְתְּחָה אֶת־שַׂקֵּינוּ וְהִנֵּה כֶסֶף אִישׁ בְּפִי שַׂקּוֹ וַנָּשֶׁב[8] אֹתוֹ בְּיָדֵנוּ. לֹא יָדַעְנוּ מִי שָׂם כַּסְפֵּנוּ בְּשַׂקֵּינוּ.

וַיֹּאמֶר הָאִישׁ אֲשֶׁר עַל־בֵּית יוֹסֵף: שָׁלוֹם לָכֶם, אַל־תִּירָאוּ. אֱלֹהֵיכֶם וֵאלֹהֵי אֲבִיכֶם נָתַן לָכֶם אֶת־הַכֶּסֶף הַהוּא. כַּסְפְּכֶם בָּא אֵלָי.

וַיּוֹצֵא[9] אֲלֵיהֶם אֶת־שִׁמְעוֹן וַיָּבֵא[10] הָאִישׁ אֶת־הָאֲנָשִׁים בֵּיתָה יוֹסֵף וַיִּתֶּן מַיִם וַיִּרְחֲצוּ רַגְלֵיהֶם וַיִּתֵּן אֹכֶל לַחֲמֹרֵיהֶם וַיֵּשְׁבוּ שָׁם עַד־בּוֹא יוֹסֵף בַּצָּהֳרָיִם כִּי שָׁמְעוּ כִּי שָׁם יֹאכְלוּ לָחֶם.

Notes to the Reading:

1. "the double amount of silver"
2. אֲשֶׁר is used substantively: "the one who".
3. "bring"
4. A rare imperative with ō instead of the normal טְבַח.
5. "and make ready"
6. "they were brought"
7. "have been brought"
8. "and we have brought it back"
9. "and he brought out"
10. "and he brought"

(d) Reading: Psalm 121 (vocalization slightly altered):

(1) אֶשָּׂא עֵינַי אֶל־הֶהָרִים מֵאַיִן יָבֹא עֶזְרִי׃
(2) עֶזְרִי מֵעִם יהוה עֹשֵׂה שָׁמַיִם וָאָרֶץ׃
(3) אַל־יִתֵּן לַמּוֹט[1] רַגְלֶךָ אַל־יָנוּם שֹׁמְרֶךָ׃
(4) הִנֵּה לֹא יָנוּם וְלֹא יִישָׁן שׁוֹמֵר יִשְׂרָאֵל׃
(5) יהוה שֹׁמְרֶךָ יהוה צִלְּךָ עַל־יַד יְמִינֶךָ׃
(6) יוֹמָם הַשֶּׁמֶשׁ לֹא יַכֶּכָּה[2] וְיָרֵחַ בַּלָּיְלָה׃
(7) יהוה יִשְׁמָרְךָ[3] מִכָּל־רָע יִשְׁמֹר אֶת־נַפְשֶׁךָ׃

(8) יהוה יִשְׁמׇר צֵאתְךָ וּבוֹאֶךָ מֵעַתָּה וְעַד־עוֹלָם׃

Notes to the Reading:

1. Inf. constr. מוֹט with לְ: to totter; note נָתַן in the sense "to allow".
2. "will not smite (strike, kill) you"
3. – יִשְׁמֹר אֹתְךָ.

LESSON 40

148. Piel Verbs: Meaning.

Piel verbs are regularly distinguished by a doubling of the second root consonant and stem patterns quite distinct from those of the Qal. Because the root of a Piel verb may not always occur as a Qal verb, it is sometimes difficult to define the meaning of a Piel form by direct comparison. Following is listed a representative collection of Piel verbs classified in regard to the meaning that may be assigned to the Piel as a derived type, i.e. secondary to some other form in the language.

a. *Factitive (transitivizing).* Perhaps the most consistent use of the Piel formation is to construct a verb with transitive active meaning from a root which appears in the Qal as an intransitive or stative verb. Such Piel verbs usually have a factitive meaning:

QAL (to be sound) → PIEL (to make sound)
QAL (to be great) → PIEL (to magnify)

Such a transformation of meaning may also be designated as causative, but we shall restrict this latter term to roots whose Qal verbs are transitive:

QAL (to learn) → PIEL (to teach, i.e. to cause to learn)

Examples:

Qal		Piel		
אָבַד	to perish	אִבַּד	*'ibbaḏ*	to destroy
קַל	to be light, trivial	קִלֵּל	*qillēl*	to curse (make light of, treat as unimportant)
קָדֵשׁ	to be holy	קִדֵּשׁ	*qiddaš*	to sanctify
שָׁלֵם	to be sound	שִׁלַּם	*šillam*	to make sound, whole; to recompense, reward
חָיָה	to live, be alive	חִיָּה	*ḥiyyāh*	to cause to live, let live
טָמֵא	to be unclean	טִמֵּא	*ṭimmē'*	to pollute
כָּלָה	to be at an end	כִּלָּה	*killāh*	to finish, complete, bring to an end
לָמַד	to learn	לִמַּד	*limmaḏ*	to teach

In some instances the Qal verb is either transitive or intransitive, while the Piel verb is specifically transitive:

מָלֵא	to be full, fill	מִלֵּא	*millē'*	to fill
בָּעַר	to burn (tr. or intr.)	בִּעֵר	*bi'ēr*	to burn (tr.)

b. *Denominative.* When the Piel verb is closer in meaning to some noun or adjective than to the Qal verb (which in most of these cases does not exist), we may say that the Piel has a denominative function:

דָּבָר	word	דִּבֶּר	*dibber*	to speak
סֵפֶר	book, record	סִפֵּר	*sippēr*	to recount, narrate, tell a story
בְּרָכָה	blessing	בֵּרַךְ	*bēraḵ*	to bless
מִצְוָה	command	צִוָּה	*ṣiwwāh*	to command
זִמְרָה	music, song	זִמֵּר	*zimmēr*	to sing, make music
שָׁלוֹשׁ	three	שִׁלֵּשׁ	*šillēš*	to divide something into three parts; to do something for a third time
קִנְאָה	jealousy	קִנֵּא	*qinnē'*	to be jealous

c. *Intensive.* In several instances the Piel denotes a pluralization of the action named in the Qal. This may take on the nuance of an intensive, but the intensive force is difficult to discern in most occurrences. Many of the so-called intensive Piels seem more to be stylistic variants of the Qal verb (most likely denominative in origin) used in poetry, probably for variation rather than intensification.

d. *Unclassified.* In addition to the three preceding categories there are many Piel verbs whose origin is not clear. Some of these verbs could doubtlessly be placed in the above classifications if we had more data on the related Qal or nominal forms.

פִּזַּר *pizzar* to scatter	בִּקֵּשׁ *biqqēš* to seek
גֵּרֵשׁ *gērēš* to drive away	מִהַר *mihar* to hurry, hasten

Awareness of the factitive-denominative-intensive function of the Piel, together with familiarity with a given root, will certainly assist the learner in mastering these new verbs, but because he will not be able to predict unerringly the meaning of a new Piel verb, they will all be listed in the vocabularies of the following lessons.

149. Piel Verbs: Stems and Inflection.

ROOT TYPE	PERFECT	IMPERFECT	IMPERATIVE
Regular	גִּדֵּל *giddēl*	יְגַדֵּל *yəgaddēl*	גַּדֵּל *gaddēl*
III-gutt.	שִׁלַּח *šillaḥ*	יְשַׁלַּח *yəšallaḥ*	שַׁלַּח *šallaḥ*
II-gutt.	בִּעֵר *bi'ēr*	יְבַעֵר *yəḇa'ēr*	בַּעֵר *ba'ēr*
	מֵאֵן *mē'ēn*	יְמָאֵן *yəmā'ēn*	מָאֵן *mā'ēn*

INF. CONSTRUCT	PARTICIPLE
גַּדֵּל *gaddēl*	מְגַדֵּל *məḡaddēl*
שַׁלַּח *šallaḥ*	מְשַׁלֵּחַ *məšallēᵃḥ*
בַּעֵר *ba'ēr*	מְבַעֵר *məḇa'ēr*
מָאֵן *mā'ēn*	מְמָאֵן *məmā'ēn*

Remarks:

1. There are essentially only two stems, the perfect and the imperfect. As elsewhere, the imperative and inf. construct are predictable from the imperfect. The participle also resembles the imperfect, but with the prefix מְ *mə-*.

2. Piel verbs from roots III-gutt. deviate only in having *a* as the second stem vowel throughout, except in the participle.

3. Even in non-guttural verbs the stem vowel *a* instead of *ē* is found in the perfect; thus *giddēl* or *giddal*. The choice would appear to be optional. There are a few verbs, notably דִּבֶּר *dibber* (to speak) and כִּפֶּר *kipper* (to atone for), which have *e* instead of *ē* or *a* in the 3rd masc. sing. of the perfect.

4. Piel verbs from roots II-gutt. (including ר) fall into two classes:

(a) those with virtual doubling of the guttural in question (see בִּעֵר above); the vocalization is the same as that of the regular verb; (b) those with compensatory lengthening of the vowel before the guttural ($i \rightarrow$ *ē*, $a \rightarrow$ *ā*; see מֵאֵן above). Before ר compensatory lengthening is the rule. The other gutturals may be treated in either way, as will be indicated in the vocabularies.

PERFECT:

גִּדֵּל *giddēl*	שִׁלַּח *šillaḥ*	בִּעֵר *bi'ēr*	מֵאֵן *mē'ēn*
גִּדְּלָה *giddəlāh*	שִׁלְּחָה *šilləḥāh*	בִּעֲרָה *bi'ărāh*	מֵאֲנָה *mē'ănāh*

גִּדַּ֫לְתָּ	*giddáltā*	שִׁלַּ֫חְתָּ	*šilláḥtā*	בִּעַ֫רְתָּ	*bi‘ártā*	מֵאַ֫נְתָּ	*mē’ántā*
גִּדַּלְתְּ	*giddált*	שִׁלַּחַתְּ	*šilláḥt*	בִּעַרְתְּ	*bi‘árt*	מֵאַנְתְּ	*mē’ánt*
גִּדַּ֫לְתִּי	*giddáltî*	שִׁלַּ֫חְתִּי	*šilláḥtî*	בִּעַ֫רְתִּי	*bi‘ártî*	מֵאַ֫נְתִּי	*mē’ántî*
גִּדְּלוּ	*giddəlû*	שִׁלְּחוּ	*silləḥû*	בִּעֲרוּ	*bi‘ărû*	מֵאֲנוּ	*mē’ănû*
גִּדַּלְתֶּם	*giddaltém*	שִׁלַּחְתֶּם	*šillaḥtém*	בִּעַרְתֶּם	*bi‘artém*	מֵאַנְתֶּם	*mē’antém*
גִּדַּלְתֶּן	*giddaltén*	שִׁלַּחְתֶּן	*šillaḥtén*	בִּעַרְתֶּן	*bi‘artén*	מֵאַנְתֶּן	*mē’antén*
גִּדַּ֫לְנוּ	*giddálnû*	שִׁלַּ֫חְנוּ	*šilláḥnû*	בִּעַ֫רְנוּ	*bi‘árnû*	מֵאַ֫נּוּ	*mē’ánnû*

IMPERFECT:

יְגַדֵּל	*yəḡaddēl*	יְשַׁלַּח	*yəšallaḥ*	יְבַעֵר	*yəḇa‘ēr*	יְמָאֵן	*yəmā’ēn*
תְּגַדֵּל	*təḡaddēl*	תְּשַׁלַּח	*təšallaḥ*	תְּבַעֵר	*təḇa‘ēr*	תְּמָאֵן	*təmā’ēn*
תְּגַדֵּל	*təḡaddēl*	תְּשַׁלַּח	*təšallaḥ*	תְּבַעֵר	*təḇa‘ēr*	תְּמָאֵן	*təmā’ēn*
תְּגַדְּלִי	*təḡaddəlî*	תְּשַׁלְּחִי	*təšalləḥî*	תְּבַעֲרִי	*təḇa‘ărî*	תְּמָאֲנִי	*təmā’ănî*
אֲגַדֵּל	*’ăḡaddēl*	אֲשַׁלַּח	*’ăšallaḥ*	אֲבַעֵר	*’ăḇa‘ēr*	אֲמָאֵן	*’ămā’ēn*
יְגַדְּלוּ	*yəḡaddəlû*	יְשַׁלְּחוּ	*yəšalləḥû*	יְבַעֲרוּ	*yəḇa‘ărû*	יְמָאֲנוּ	*yəmā’ănû*
תְּגַדֵּ֫לְנָה	*təḡaddḗlnāh*	תְּשַׁלַּ֫חְנָה	*təšalláḥnāh*	תְּבַעֵ֫רְנָה	*təḇa‘ḗrnāh*	תְּמָאֵ֫נָּה	*təmā’ḗnnāh*
תְּגַדְּלוּ	*təḡaddəlû*	תְּשַׁלְּחוּ	*təšalləḥû*	תְּבַעֲרוּ	*təḇa‘ărû*	תְּמָאֲנוּ	*təmā’ănû*
תְּגַדֵּ֫לְנָה	*təḡaddḗlnāh*	תְּשַׁלַּ֫חְנָה	*təšalláḥnāh*	תְּבַעֵ֫רְנָה	*təḇa‘ḗrnāh*	תְּמָאֵ֫נָּה	*təmā’ḗnnāh*
נְגַדֵּל	*nəḡaddēl*	נְשַׁלַּח	*nəšallaḥ*	נְבַעֵר	*nəḇa‘ēr*	נְמָאֵן	*nəmā’ēn*

IMPERATIVE:

גַּדֵּל	*gaddēl*	שַׁלַּח	*šallaḥ*	בַּעֵר	*ba‘ēr*	מָאֵן	*mā’ēn*
גַּדְּלִי	*gaddəlî*	שַׁלְּחִי	*šalləḥî*	בַּעֲרִי	*ba‘ărî*	מָאֲנִי	*mā’ănî*
גַּדְּלוּ	*gaddəlû*	שַׁלְּחוּ	*šalləḥû*	בַּעֲרוּ	*ba‘ărû*	מָאֲנוּ	*mā’ănû*
גַּדֵּ֫לְנָה	*gaddḗlnāh*	שַׁלַּ֫חְנָה	*šalláḥnāh*	בַּעֵ֫רְנָה	*ba‘ḗrnāh*	מָאֵ֫נָּה	*mā’ḗnnāh*

INFINITIVE CONSTRUCT:

גַּדֵּל	*gaddēl*	שַׁלַּח	*šallaḥ*	בַּעֵר	*ba‘ēr*	מָאֵן	*mā’ēn*
גַּדְּלִי	*gaddəlî*	שַׁלְּחִי	*šalləḥî*	בַּעֲרִי	*ba‘ărî*	מָאֲנִי	*mā’ănî*
גַּדֶּלְךָ	*gaddelḵā*	שַׁלַּחֲךָ	*šallaḥăḵā*	בַּעֶרְךָ	*ba‘erḵā*	מָאֶנְךָ	*mā’enḵā*
גַּדְּלֵךְ	*gaddəlēḵ* etc.	שַׁלְּחֵךְ	*šalləḥēḵ* etc.	בַּעֲרֵךְ	*ba‘ărēḵ* etc.	מָאֲנֵךְ	*mā’ănēḵ*

INFINITIVE ABSOLUTE:

גַּדּוֹל	*gaddôl*	שַׁלּוֹחַ	*šallô^{a}ḥ*	בַּעוֹר	*ba’ôr*	מָאוֹן	*mā’ôn*

PARTICIPLE:

מְגַדֵּל	*məḡaddēl*	מְשַׁלֵּחַ	*məšallē^{a}ḥ*	מְבַעֵר	*məḇa‘ēr*	מְמָאֵן	*məmā’ēn*
מְגַדְּלָה	*məḡaddəlāh*	מְשַׁלְּחָה	*məšalləḥāh*	מְבַעֲרָה	*məḇa‘ărāh*	מְמָאֲנָה	*məmā’ănāh*
מְגַדְּלִים	*məḡaddəlîm*	מְשַׁלְּחִים	*məšalləḥîm*	מְבַעֲרִים	*məba‘ărîm*	מְמָאֲנִים	*məmā’ănîm*
מְגַדְּלוֹת	*məḡaddəlôṯ*	מְשַׁלְּחוֹת	*məšalləḥôṯ*	מְבַעֲרוֹת	*məḇa‘ărôṯ*	מְמָאֲנוֹת	*məmā’ănôṯ*

Remarks:

(1) After a *waw*-conversive the prefix *yə-* of the imperfect loses its vowel and the *y* is not doubled:

וַיְמָאֵן *way-mā-'ēn* (not: *way-yə-mā-'ēn*) and he refused

(2) The characteristic doubling of the middle radical is given up sometimes when it is followed by the vowel *ə*:

בִּקֵּשׁ	*biqqēš*	he sought	but	בִּקְשׁוּ	*biqšû*	they sought
יְבַקֵּשׁ	*yəḇaqqēš*	he will seek	but	יְבַקְשׁוּ	*yəḇaqšû*	they will seek

This loss of doubling never occurs with the consonants ב ג ד כ פ ת. Otherwise no clear rule can be formulated.

(3) The forms listed above and in the next lesson for the infinitive absolute are rather rare. More frequently the Piel infinitive construct is used as the infinitive absolute.

150. Vocabulary 40.

VERBS:	קִדֵּשׁ	*qiddēš*		to sanctify (cf. קָדוֹשׁ)
	בָּעַר	*bā'ar*	(יִבְעַר)	to burn (tr. or intr.)
	בִּעֵר	*bi'ēr*	(יְבַעֵר)	to burn (tr.), consume, remove completely
	דִּבֶּר	*dibber*	(יְדַבֵּר)	to speak, talk (cf. דָּבָר)
	בֵּרֵךְ	*bērēḵ*	(יְבָרֵךְ)	to bless (cf. בְּרָכָה) [Note וַיְבָ֫רֶךְ]
	בִּקֵּשׁ	*biqqēš*	(יְבַקֵּשׁ)	to seek
	שִׁלַּח	*šillaḥ*	(יְשַׁלַּח)	to expel, send forth, let go
	גֵּרֵשׁ	*gērēš*	(יְגָרֵשׁ)	to drive away [Note וַיְגָ֫רֶשׁ]
	נִאֵץ	*ni'ēṣ*	(יְנַאֵץ)	to spurn
	מֵאֵן	*mē'ēn*	(יְמָאֵן)	to refuse
	שֵׁרֵת	*šērēṯ*	(יְשָׁרֵת)	to serve, administer [Note וַיְשָׁ֫רֶת]
OTHER:	אוֹ	*'ô*	(conj.)	or

Note the idiom: כְּ...כְּ. Translation may vary with the context, but the implication is that the two items involved are in some way equal. E.g.

כָּמוֹךָ כְּפַרְעֹה You are the equal of the Pharaoh.

כָּמוֹךָ כָּמוֹנִי You and I are equal, are in the same predicament.

Exercises:

(a) Translate:

(1) וַיְגָ֫רֶשׁ אֶת־הָאֲנָשִׁים פַּעֲמַ֫יִם וְלֹא שָׁבוּ.

(2) נִאַ֫צְתָּ אֶת־בְּרִיתִי וְאֶת־תּוֹרוֹתַי מֵאַ֫נְתָּ לִשְׁמֹר.

(3) וַיְשָׁ֫רֶת הַיֶּ֫לֶד בְּהֵיכַל יהוה.

(4) וַיְבָ֫רֶךְ אֹתוֹ כִּי הוּא מָצָא חֵן בְּעֵינָיו.

(5) יְבַקְשׁוּ אֶת־הָאֲשֵׁמִים וְשִׁלְּחוּ אֹתָם מִן־הָעִיר.
(6) אֲנִי לְבַדִּי אוּכַל לְבָרֶךְ אֹתְךָ.
(7) תִּשְׁמֹר אֶת־דְּבָרַי בְּלִבְּךָ.
(8) מֵאֲנוּ לֶאֱכֹל אֶת־הַבְּהֵמוֹת הַטְּבוּחוֹת.
(9) אֶת־מִי אַתְּ תְּבַקְשִׁי.
(10) וַיְדַבְּרוּ אֵלָיו כַּדְּבָרִים הָאֵלֶּה.
(11) קוֹל שִׂמְחָה יִשָּׁמַע בָּאָרֶץ.
(12) וַיְקַדֵּשׁ אֶת־הָאֲנָשִׁים לִפְנֵי בוֹאָם בֵּית יהוה.
(13) אֲמָאֵן לִרְדֹּף אַחֲרֵיהֶם.
(14) וַיְדַבֵּר אֵלַי עַל־הַמָּלוֹן אֲשֶׁר לָן בּוֹ הַלַּיְלָה.
(15) לֹא תֹאכַל אֶת־הַבָּשָׂר אֲשֶׁר בּוֹ נֶפֶשׁ חַיָּה.
(16) מֵאֲנָה לִרְחֹץ אֶת־הַבְּגָדִים.
(17) וַיְהִי כְנוּמוֹ וַיְבַקְשׁוּ אֹתוֹ וַיַּהַרְגוּ אֹתוֹ.
(18) בַּיּוֹם הַהוּא יִמַּסּוּ הֶהָרִים וְהָיוּ כְמַּיִם.
(19) תְּקַדֵּשׁ אֶת־הַנִּשְׁאָרִים כִּי נֶאֱמָנִים הֵם בְּעֵינַי.

(b) Give the Hebrew for the following orally:

1. Drive them away.
2. Do not spurn his words.
3. Why do you refuse to speak?
4. Are you looking for me?
5. Bless me.
6. I have sanctified you.
7. He did not want to serve.
8. They expelled us.
9. Let us bless them.
10. We sought them.

(c) Write in Hebrew:

1. They took the vessels with which they served and gave them to the priest.
2. The Pharaoh became angry and expelled them from his presence (lit. from before him).
3. He refused to sanctify them, for he knew that they were not honest men.
4. He sought his brothers there, for he did not know that they had travelled eastward.
5. You shall completely-remove the evil from your midst.
6. We drove the guilty men out of the congregation.
7. We could not refuse to spend the night there.

(d) Reading: Joseph and his Brothers: the Final Test.

After meeting with Joseph and obtaining the release of Simon through Benjamin's presence with them, the sons of Jacob set out again for Canaan with the provisions they had obtained in Egypt. Joseph had had a silver goblet planted in Benjamin's sack, and as soon as the brothers had begun the return journey, he sent his men after them to examine their baggage, find the goblet and accuse them of theft and treachery. Joseph then expressed his willingness to allow all the brothers except Benjamin to return home, but Judah stands up to this final test and delivers the following plea: (Gen. 44:18–26, vocalization slightly altered).

(18) וַיִּגַּשׁ אֵלָיו יְהוּדָה וַיֹּאמֶר בִּי[1] אֲדֹנִי, יְדַבֶּר־נָא עַבְדְּךָ דָבָר בְּאָזְנֵי אֲדֹנִי, וְאַל־יִחַר אַפְּךָ
בְּעַבְדֶּךָ כִּי כָמוֹךָ כְּפַרְעֹה.

(19) אֲדֹנִי שָׁאַל אֶת־עֲבָדָיו לֵאמֹר הֲיֵשׁ לָכֶם אָב אוֹ אָח.

(20) וַנֹּאמֶר אֶל־אֲדֹנִי יֵשׁ לָנוּ אָב זָקֵן וְיֶלֶד זְקוּנִים קָטָן וְאָחִיו מֵת וַיִּוָּתֵר הוּא לְבַדּוֹ לְאִמּוֹ
וְאָבִיו אֲהֵבוֹ.[2]

(21) וַתֹּאמֶר אֶל־עֲבָדֶיךָ הוֹרִידֻהוּ[3] אֵלַי וְאָשִׂימָה עֵינִי עָלָיו.

(22) וַנֹּאמֶר אֶל־אֲדֹנִי לֹא יוּכַל הַנַּעַר לַעֲזֹב אֶת־אָבִיו וְעָזַב[4] אֶת־אָבִיו וָמֵת.

(23) וַתֹּאמֶר אֶל־עֲבָדֶיךָ אִם לֹא יֵרֵד אֲחִיכֶם הַקָּטֹן אִתְּכֶם לֹא תוֹסִיפוּן[5] לִרְאוֹת פָּנָי.

(24) וַיְהִי כִּי עָלִינוּ אֶל־עַבְדְּךָ אָבִי וַנַּגֶּד[6] לוֹ אֵת־דִּבְרֵי אֲדֹנִי.

(25) וַיֹּאמֶר אָבִינוּ שֻׁבוּ שִׁבְרוּ[7] לָנוּ מְעַט־אֹכֶל.

(26) וַנֹּאמֶר לֹא נוּכַל לָרֶדֶת, אִם יֵשׁ אָחִינוּ הַקָּטֹן אִתָּנוּ וְיָרַדְנוּ[8] כִּי לֹא נוּכַל לִרְאוֹת פְּנֵי
הָאִישׁ וְאָחִינוּ הַקָּטֹן אֵינֶנּוּ אִתָּנוּ.

Notes to the Reading:

1. A rare particle of entreaty: "Please, I beg you".
2. = אָהַב אֹתוֹ
3. "bring him down"
4. וְעָזַב ... וָמֵת a conditional sequence: "if he abandon... he would die".
5. "you will not (see) again"
6. "we told him"
7. "obtain (as rations or provisions)"
8. Note the apodosis after the אם clause.

LESSON 41

151. Piel Verbs: Stems and Inflection (concluded).

Root Type	Perfect	Imperfect	Imperative
III-*Aleph*	מִלֵּא *millē'*	יְמַלֵּא *yəmallē'*	מַלֵּא *mallē'*
III-*Hē*	עִנָּה *'innāh*	יְעַנֶּה *yə'anneh*	עַנֵּה *'annēh*
Geminate	הִלֵּל *hillēl*	יְהַלֵּל *yəhallēl*	הַלֵּל *hallēl*

Inf. Construct	Participle
מַלֵּא *mallē'*	מְמַלֵּא *məmallē'*
עַנּוֹת *'annôṯ*	מְעַנֶּה *mə'anneh*
הַלֵּל *hallēl*	מְהַלֵּל *məhallēl*

Remarks: So far as the stems are concerned, only verbs from roots III-*Hē* require special attention. The forms of these verbs conform to the patterns encountered in the Niphal and Qal: the perfect ends in *-āh,* the imperfect in *-eh,* the imperative in *-ēh,* and the infinitive construct in *-ôṯ*. In the inflection of these forms the only unpredictable feature is the prevalence of *-î-* over *-ê-* in the perfect, but *-ê-* is found in the first person singular as well: thus both עִנִּיתִי and עִנֵּיתִי

Perfect:	מִלֵּא/מִלָּא *millē'/millā'*	עִנָּה *'innāh*	הִלֵּל *hillēl*
	מִלְּאָה *millə'āh*	עִנְּתָה *'innəṯāh*	הִלְלָה *hiləlāh*
	מִלֵּאתָ *millḗ(')ṯā*	עִנִּיתָ *'innîṯā*	הִלַּלְתָּ *hillálta*
	מִלֵּאת *millḗ(')ṯ*	עִנִּית *'innîṯ*	הִלַּלְתְּ *hillált*
	מִלֵּאתִי *millḗ(')ṯî*	עִנִּיתִי/עִנֵּיתִי *'innîṯî/'innêṯî*	הִלַּלְתִּי *hilláltî*
	מִלְּאוּ *millə'û*	עִנּוּ *'innû*	הִלְלוּ *hiləlû*

	מִלֵּאתֶם	*millē(’)ṯem*	עִנִּיתֶם	*‘innîṯem*	הִלַּלְתֶּם	*hillaltém*
	מִלֵּאתֶן	*millē(’)ṯen*	עִנִּיתֶן	*‘innîṯen*	הִלַּלְתֶּן	*hillaltén*
	מִלֵּאנוּ	*millḗ(’)nû*	עִנִּינוּ	*‘innînû*	הִלַּלְנוּ	*hillálnû*
IMPERFECT:	יְמַלֵּא	*yəmallē’*	יְעַנֶּה	*yə‘anneh*	יְהַלֵּל	*yəhallēl*
	תְּמַלֵּא	*təmallē’*	תְּעַנֶּה	*tə‘anneh*	תְּהַלֵּל	*təhallēl*
	תְּמַלֵּא	*təmallē’*	תְּעַנֶּה	*tə‘anneh*	תְּהַלֵּל	*təhallēl*
	תְּמַלְּאִי	*təmallə’î*	תְּעַנִּי	*tə‘annî*	תְּהַלְלִי	*təhaləlî*
	אֲמַלֵּא	*’ămallē’*	אֲעַנֶּה	*’ă‘anneh*	אֲהַלֵּל	*’ăhallēl*
	יְמַלְּאוּ	*yəmallə’û*	יְעַנּוּ	*yə‘annû*	יְהַלְלוּ	*yəhaləlû*
	תְּמַלֶּאנָה	*təmallé(’)nāh*	תְּעַנֶּינָה	*tə‘annênāh*	תְּהַלֵּלְנָה	*təhallḗlnah*
	תְּמַלְּאוּ	*təmallə’û*	תְּעַנּוּ	*tə‘annû*	תְּהַלְלוּ	*təhaləlû*
	תְּמַלֶּאנָה	*təmallé(’)nāh*	תְּעַנֶּינָה	*tə‘annênāh*	תְּהַלֵּלְנָה	*təhallḗlnāh*
	נְמַלֵּא	*nəmallē’*	נְעַנֶּה	*nə‘anneh*	נְהַלֵּל	*nəhallēl*
IMPERATIVE:	מַלֵּא	*mallē’*	עַנֵּה	*‘annēh*	הַלֵּל	*hallēl*
	מַלְּאִי	*mallə’î*	עַנִּי	*‘annî*	הַלְלִי	*haləlî*
	מַלְּאוּ	*mallə’û*	עַנּוּ	*‘annû*	הַלְלוּ	*haləlû*
	מַלֶּאנָה	*mallé(’)nāh*	עַנֶּינָה	*‘annênāh*	הַלֵּלְנָה	*hallḗlnāh*
INF. CONSTR.:	מַלֵּא	*mallē’*	עַנּוֹת	*‘annôṯ*	הַלֵּל	*hallēl*
	מַלְּאִי	*mallə’î* etc.	עַנּוֹתִי	*‘annôṯî* etc.	הַלְלִי	*halləlî* etc.
INF. ABS.:	מַלֹּא	*mallō’*	עַנֹּה	*‘annōh*	הַלֹּל	*hallōl*
			עַנֵּה	*‘annēh*		
PARTICIPLE:	מְמַלֵּא	*məmallē’*	מְעַנֶּה	*mə‘anneh*	מְהַלֵּל	*məhallel*
	מְמַלְּאָה	*məmallə’āh*	מְעַנָּה	*mə‘annāh*	מְהַלְּלָה	*məhalləlāh*
	מְמַלֵּאת	*məmallē(’)ṯ*			מְהַלֶּלֶת	*məhalléleṯ*
	מְמַלְּאִים	*məmallə’îm*	מְעַנִּים	*mə‘annîm*	מְהַלְּלִים	*məhalləlîm*
	מְמַלְּאוֹת	*məmallə’ôṯ*	מְעַנּוֹת	*mə‘annôṯ*	מְהַלְּלוֹת	*məhalləlôṯ*

Piel verbs from roots I-*Yodh*, I-*Nun*, I-guttural are in no way irregular. Piel verbs from Hollow roots are very rare.

152. Pausal Forms.

The text of the Hebrew Bible is divided into short groups of clauses known as verses. Each verse is usually subdivided into two parts, often of unequal length, the first of which is closed by the accent sign known as *’aṯnaḥ* (˄) and the second by a sign similar to metheg called *sillûq* (ˌ), followed by *sôp̄ pāsûq* (:), marking the end of the verse. Each half of the verse is then subdivided into as many parts as the syntax demands, with each accentual unit receiving an accent mark. The accents fall into two main groups, conjunctive and disjunctive, the former being used when a word is closely bound syntactically with the following word and the latter elsewhere. The use of the various accents is very complex and will not be taken up in this book.

In the text of the reading selections we shall employ only *sillûq* (+ *sôp̄ pāsûq*). Clause divisions that are likely to cause difficulty will be marked by commas, but it should be noted that the comma does not appear in the original text.

Words standing at the end of the major verse divisions, and thus especially with *'aṯnaḥ* and *sillûq*, are said to be in pause because of the break in the recitation of the text at these points. Such words may have a vocalization slightly different from that of the normal context form. The following changes are the most frequent:

(a) *a* → *ā*: כָּתָב (he wrote) for כָּתַב

(b) *e* → *ā* in some segholate nouns: קָ֫בֶר (grave) for קֶ֫בֶר

(c) If a word ends in the sequence -*əCv́* the accent is usually retracted and the *ə* is replaced by the full vowel it corresponds to elsewhere in the paradigm:

כָּתְבָ֫ה	→	כָּתָ֫בָה	she wrote
כָּבְדָה	→	כָּבֵ֫דָה	it (f.) was heavy

The *ə* of the second person masc. sing. suffix -*əḵā* is regularly replaced by *e*:

מַלְכְּךָ	→	מַלְכֶּ֫ךָ	your king
סוּסְךָ	→	סוּסֶ֫ךָ	your horse
שֹׁמֶרְךָ	→	שֹׁמְרֶ֫ךָ	your keeper (note the change in the word structure)

But the pausal forms of לְךָ and בְּךָ are לָךְ and בָּךְ, both of which are the same as the corresponding feminine form. Other prepositions have a similar change.

Because of printing difficulties, the pausal accents within a verse do not appear in the biblical texts accompanying the following lessons. Pausal forms, however, have been retained. The reader should be on the alert for their occurrence.

153. Vocabulary 41.

VERBS: צִוָּה *ṣiwwāh* (יְצַוֶּה juss. יְצַו) to command; charge; appoint. Examples:

וַיְצַו שֹׁפְטִים עֲלֵיהֶם	and he appointed judges over them
וַיְצַו אֶת־הָאֲנָשִׁים לָלֶ֫כֶת	and he commanded the men to go
וַיְצַו אֹתָם לֵאמֹר...	and he commanded them, saying...
וַיְצַו אֹתָם בְּיַד מַלְאָכוֹ	and he handed them over to the charge of his messenger

הִלֵּל *hillēl* (יְהַלֵּל) to praise. Note הַלְלוּיָהּ Halelujah. Praise Yah(weh).

כִּסָּה *kissāh* (יְכַסֶּה juss. יְכַס) to cover, overwhelm

עִנָּה *'innāh* (יְעַנֶּה juss. יְעַן) to oppress (cf. עָנִי)

סִפֵּר *sippēr* (יְסַפֵּר) to tell, narrate (cf. סֵ֫פֶר)

קִלֵּל *qillēl* (יְקַלֵּל) to curse

עָרַב *'ārab* (יַעֲרֹב) to stand as pledge for
קָשַׁר *qāšar* (יִקְשֹׁר) to bind (*'et* + something + *'al* [to] + something); to band together, conspire (*'al*: against)

NOUNS: שֵׂיבָה *śêbāh* grey hair, old age
שְׁאֹל *šə'ōl* Sheol, Hell, the residence of the dead

OTHER: אַךְ *'ak* (adv.) surely, doubtlessly; but, however, only
עַד־הֵנָּה *'ad-hēnnāh* (adv.) until now

Exercises:

(a) Translate

(1) וַיְצַו אֹתָם לָתֵת מְעַט אֹכֶל לְטַפָּם.
(2) לָכְדוּ אֶת־רְכוּשׁ הַכְּנַעֲנִי וַיְבַעֲרוּ אֹתוֹ.
(3) שָׁמְעָה הָאָמָה קוֹל וַתִּפֹּל אַרְצָה וַתְּכַס אֶת־פָּנֶיהָ בְּיָדֶיהָ.
(4) וַיְצַו אֶת־הַנִּצָּבִים וַיִּגְּשׁוּ אֵלָיו.
(5) לֹא מֵאֵן לַעֲרֹב אֶת־הַיֶּלֶד וְלֹא מֵאֵן לִגְאֹל אֹתוֹ.
(6) שִׁלַּח אֹתָם מֵאַרְצוֹ כִּי קָשְׁרוּ עָלָיו לַהֲרֹג אֹתוֹ וְלִבְחֹר אִישׁ אַחֵר לְרֹאשׁ הָעָם.
(7) וַיִּזְבַּח הַמֶּלֶךְ הָרָשָׁע אֶת־בִּתּוֹ הַקְּטַנָּה עַל־הַמִּזְבֵּחַ.
(8) וַיְסַפְּרוּ לוֹ אֶת־הַקֹּרוֹת אֹתָם בַּדֶּרֶךְ.
(9) עַד־הֵנָּה לֹא רָאִיתִי אֶת־יְשׁוּעַת עַמִּי.
(10) לָמָּה תַּחְפֹּץ לְעַנּוֹת אֹתִי.
(11) אֲהַלְלָה אֹתְךָ מֵעַתָּה וְעַד־עוֹלָם.
(12) וַיְכַס אֶת־פָּנָיו בְּיָדָיו וַיֵּבְךְּ.
(13) אַל־תְּקַלְלוּ אֶת־הַנֹּתְנִים לָכֶם עֵזֶר.
(14) וָאֶבְרַח כִּי בִקְשׁוּ אֹתִי לַהֲרֹג אֹתִי.
(15) זְכֹר נָא אֶת־הַבֹּטְחִים בְּךָ וְאַל־תְּנַאֵץ אֶת־דִּבְרֵיהֶם.
(16) וַיְצַו אֶת־בְּנוֹ בְּיַד הַנּוֹתָרִים כִּי הָיָה לָמוּת.

(b) Write in Hebrew:

1. He tied his donkey to a tree, lay down under the tree, and slept.
2. Let us curse them and the place from which they came.
3. I will stand as surety for you and your sons.
4. He will praise the Lord all the days of his life until he goes down to Sheol with grey hair.
5. It is not good to oppress the poor and not to give them food.
6. Darkness shall cover the earth on that day.
7. He drove us away from the well and we were not able to find water in an(y) other place.

(c) Reading: Judah's Plea to Joseph (concluded) Gen. 44:27–34.

(27) וַיֹּאמֶר עַבְדְּךָ אָבִי אֵלֵינוּ אַתֶּם יְדַעְתֶּם כִּי שְׁנַיִם יָלְדָה לִּי אִשְׁתִּי׃
(28) וַיֵּצֵא הָאֶחָד מֵאִתִּי וָאֹמַר אַךְ טָרֹף טֹרָף[1] וְלֹא רְאִיתִיו[2] עַד־הֵנָּה׃
(29) וּלְקַחְתֶּם גַּם־אֶת־זֶה מֵעִם פָּנַי וְקָרָהוּ[3] אָסוֹן[4] וְהוֹרַדְתֶּם[5] אֶת־שֵׂיבָתִי בְּרָעָה שְׁאֹלָה׃

(30) וְעַתָּה כְּבֹאִי אֶל־עַבְדְּךָ אָבִי וְהַנַּעַר אֵינֶנּוּ אִתָּנוּ וְנַפְשׁוֹ קְשׁוּרָה בְנַפְשׁוֹ׃

(31) וְהָיָה כִּרְאוֹתוֹ כִּי אֵין הַנַּעַר וָמֵת וְהוֹרִידוּ[6] עֲבָדֶיךָ אֶת־שֵׂיבַת עַבְדְּךָ אָבִינוּ בְּיָגוֹן[7] שְׁאֹלָה׃

(32) כִּי עַבְדְּךָ עָרַב אֶת־הַנַּעַר מֵעִם אָבִי לֵאמֹר אִם־לֹא אֲבִיאֶנּוּ[8] אֵלֶיךָ וְחָטָאתִי[9] לְאָבִי
כָּל־הַיָּמִים׃

(33) וְעַתָּה יֵשֶׁב נָא עַבְדְּךָ תַּחַת הַנַּעַר עֶבֶד לַאדֹנִי וְהַנַּעַר יַעַל עִם־אֶחָיו׃

(34) כִּי־אֵיךְ אֶעֱלֶה אֶל־אָבִי וְהַנַּעַר אֵינֶנּוּ אִתִּי פֶּן[10] אֶרְאֶה בָרָע אֲשֶׁר יִמְצָא אֶת־אָבִי׃

Notes to the Reading:

1. "he has surely been torn to pieces (by some wild animal)"
2. = רָאִיתִי אֹתוֹ
3. = קָרָה אֹתוֹ
4. "an accident"
5. "you will send down"
6. "and (we) will have sent down"
7. "sorrow"
8. "I shall bring him"
9. cf. note 8 p. 199
10. פֶּן here = "except that"

Joseph, unable to continue his deception, revealed himself to his brothers, whom he forgave of their past crime against him. He caused Jacob and his entire family to be brought down to Egypt and settled them in the rich pasture land of the Nile Delta. Jacob died and was taken back to Canaan for burial in accordance with his wishes; Joseph was embalmed upon his death and his body placed in a sarcophagus for eventual burial in Canaan. After the death of Joseph there is a break in the traditional history until the story of Moses and a pharaoh "who knew not Joseph".

LESSON 42

154. The Pual.

Corresponding to every Piel verb there is a passive counterpart known as the Pual, characterized, like the Piel, by a doubling of the middle root consonant. The pattern of vowels is more or less consistent throughout, with *u* in the first stem syllable and *a* (when not reduced) in the second.

Piel	Pual		
גִּדֵּל	גֻּדַּל	*guddal*	he was magnified
בִּקֵּשׁ	בֻּקַּשׁ	*buqqaš*	he was sought
הִלֵּל	הֻלַּל	*hullal*	he was praised

Pual forms are relatively infrequent, being most often encountered in the participle, which functions as a passive to that of the Piel:

מְבָרֵךְ	מְבֹרָךְ	*məḇōrāḵ*	being (having been) blessed
מְבַקֵּשׁ	מְבֻקָּשׁ	*məḇuqqāš*	being (having been) sought

Attested stem forms are as follows:

Root Type	Perfect	Imperfect	Imperative	Inf. Construct	Participle
Regular	גֻּדַּל *guddal*	יְגֻדַּל *yəḡuddal*	—	—	מְגֻדָּל *məḡuddā*
II-guttural	בֹּרַךְ *bōraḵ*	יְבֹרַךְ *yəḇōraḵ*	—	—	מְבֹרָךְ *məḇōrāḵ*
III-*Aleph*	מֻלָּא *mullā'*	יְמֻלָּא *yəmullā'*	—	—	מְמֻלָּא *məmullā'*
III-*Hē*	עֻנָּה *‘unnāh*	יְעֻנֶּה *yə‘unneh*	—	עֻנּוֹת *‘unnôṯ*	מְעֻנֶּה *mə‘unneh*

Remarks: With roots II-guttural virtual doubling is also attested, as in נֻחַם *nuḥam* (he was comforted) corresponding to the Piel verb נִחַם *niḥam* (to comfort); the more common form בֹּרַךְ shows compensatory lengthening of *u* to *ō*.

The lengthening of the final stem vowel in מֻלָּא should be an expected phenomenon by now, as should the conformity of the stem endings of verbs from roots III-*Hē* to those of the other verb types (Qal, Niphal, and Piel).

PERFECT:

גֻּדַּל	*guddal*	בֹּרַךְ	*bōrak̲*	מֻלָּא	עֻנָּה
גֻּדְּלָה	*guddəlāh*	בֹּרְכָה	*bōrək̲āh*	מֻלְּאָה	עֻנְּתָה
גֻּדַּלְתָּ	*guddáltā*	בֹּרַכְתָּ	*bōrák̲tā*	מֻלֵּאתָ	עֻנֵּיתָ
גֻּדַּלְתְּ	*guddált*	בֹּרַכְתְּ	*bōrak̲t*	מֻלֵּאת	עֻנֵּית
גֻּדַּלְתִּי	*guddáltî*	בֹּרַכְתִּי	*bōrák̲tî*	מֻלֵּאתִי	עֻנֵּיתִי
גֻּדְּלוּ	*guddəlû*	בֹּרְכוּ	*bōrək̲û*	מֻלְּאוּ	עֻנּוּ
גֻּדַּלְתֶּם	*guddaltem*	בֹּרַכְתֶּם	*bōrak̲tem*	מֻלֵּאתֶם	עֻנֵּיתֶם
גֻּדַּלְתֶּן	*guddalten*	בֹּרַכְתֶּן	*bōrak̲ten*	מֻלֵּאתֶן	עֻנֵּיתֶן
גֻּדַּלְנוּ	*guddálnû*	בֹּרַכְנוּ	*bōrák̲nû*	מֻלֵּאנוּ	עֻנֵּינוּ

IMPERFECT:

יְגֻדַּל	*yəḡuddal*	יְבֹרַךְ	*yəḇōrak̲*	יְמֻלָּא	יְעֻנֶּה
תְּגֻדַּל	*təḡuddal*	תְּבֹרַךְ	*təḇōrak̲*	תְּמֻלָּא	תְּעֻנֶּה
תְּגֻדַּל	*təḡuddal*	תְּבֹרַךְ	*təḇōrak̲*	תְּמֻלָּא	תְּעֻנֶּה
תְּגֻדְּלִי	*təḡuddəlî*	תְּבֹרְכִי	*təḇōrək̲î*	תְּמֻלְּאִי	תְּעֻנִּי
אֲגֻדַּל	*'ăḡuddal*	אֲבֹרַךְ	*'ăḇōrak̲*	אֲמֻלָּא	אֲעֻנֶּה
יְגֻדְּלוּ	*yəḡuddəlû*	יְבֹרְכוּ	*yəḇōrək̲û*	יְמֻלְּאוּ	יְעֻנּוּ
תְּגֻדַּלְנָה	*təḡuddálnāh*	תְּבֹרַכְנָה	*təḇōrák̲nāh*	תְּמֻלֶּאנָה	תְּעֻנֶּינָה
תְּגֻדְּלוּ	*təḡuddəlû*	תְּבֹרְכוּ	*təḇōrək̲û*	תְּמֻלְּאוּ	תְּעֻנּוּ
תְּגֻדַּלְנָה	*təḡuddálnāh*	תְּבֹרַכְנָה	*təḇōrák̲nāh*	תְּמֻלֶּאנָה	תְּעֻנֶּינָה
נְגֻדַּל	*nəḡuddal*	נְבֹרַךְ	*nəḇōrak̲*	נְמֻלָּא	נְעֻנֶּה

PARTICIPLE:

מְגֻדָּל	*məḡuddāl*	מְבֹרָךְ	*məḇōrāk̲*	מְמֻלָּא	מְעֻנֶּה
מְגֻדָּלָה	*məḡuddālāh*	מְבֹרָכָה	*məḇōrāk̲āh*	מְמֻלָּאָה	מְעֻנָּה
מְגֻדֶּלֶת	*məḡuddélet̲*	מְבֹרֶכֶת	*məḇōrék̲et̲*	מְמֻלָּאִים	מְעֻנִּים
מְגֻדָּלִים	*məḡuddālîm*	מְבֹרָכִים	*məḇōrāk̲îm*	מְמֻלָּאוֹת	מְעֻנּוֹת
מְגֻדָּלוֹת	*məḡuddālôt̲*	מְבֹרָכוֹת	*məḇōrāk̲ôt̲*		

Note: One occasionally finds *o* for *u* in the first stem syllable; e.g. כָּסּוּ *kossû* (they were covered).

The passive represented by the Pual has no expressed agent:

סֻפַּר לוֹ הַדָּבָר The matter was related to him.

Because this corresponds semantically to an active verb with an indefinite subject (somebody, one, they), it may be followed ("ungrammatically") by an object with אֶת־:

סֻפַּר לוֹ אֶת־הַדָּבָר One recounted the matter to him.

A second construction peculiar to passive verbs is that in which a preposition is omitted before a specifying noun.

כֻּסּוּ הֶהָרִים צִלָּהּ The mountains were covered with a shadow.

This probably has its origin in the following mixture of constructions:

(a) A verb like מָלֵא in its intransitive sense (to be full) regularly has a specifying noun without a preposition:

מָלֵא הַכְּלִי מַיִם The vessel is full of water.

This is an old construction in Semitic and may be termed "historically correct".

(b) The corresponding transitive usage of מָלֵא employs the same construction:

מָלֵא אֶת־הַכְּלִי מַיִם He filled the vessel with water.

(c) The Piel verb מִלֵּא being a transitive form only is used in two ways, first as a normal verb without reference to the above,

מִלֵּא אֶת־הַכְּלִי בְּמַיִם He filled the vessel with water.

or, as the equivalent of מָלֵא:

מִלֵּא אֶת־הַכְּלִי מַיִם He filled the vessel with water.

(d) The Pual verb מֻלָּא may be regarded as a transformation of either of the two constructions given in (c):

מֻלָּא הַכְּלִי בְּמַיִם The vessel was filled with water.
מֻלָּא הַכְּלִי מַיִם

155. Proclisis, Retraction of Stress, and Conjunctive Daghesh.

There are several orthographic features of the Masoretic Text which, because of their frequency, must be noted at this point.

a. *Proclisis.* As was mentioned in our discussion of pause (§ 152), certain types of words stand in a syntactically conjunctive relationship.

Any word in this category may be made proclitic to the one that follows if the accentual pattern of the verse so demands. Proclisis is marked with *maqqēp̄* and is more or less the rule for the monosyllabic prepositions and particles אֶל־, עַל־, עַד־, עִם־, מִן־, אִם־, פֶּן־ and אַל־ (negative), though instances may be cited where these words are accentually distinct. Examples of other types of words in proclisis are:

לֹא־יָסוּר	he will not depart	נִמְצָא־חֵן	we shall find favor
אֲשֶׁר־נָתַן־לִי	which he gave to me	קְנֵה־אֹתָנוּ	buy us
כִּי־יָשִׁית	that he was placing	יֵשְׁבוּ־נָא	let them dwell now

The only important vowel changes before *maqqēp̄* are $ē \rightarrow e$ and $ō \rightarrow o$ in the final syllable of many words:

יִתֶּן־לִי he will give to me
שְׁמָר־נָא observe now

b. *Retraction of Stress (nəsîḡāh* or *nāsôḡ ʾāḥôr).* There is a tendency, by no means consistently applied, to avoid two stressed syllables in succession, such as

תֹּאכַל לֶ֫חֶם you will eat bread.

Instead, one may find either proclisis תֹּאכַל־לֶ֫חֶם in which the stress of the first word is surrendered completely, or retraction of the stress, in which the stress of the first word is moved back to the next full vowel (not *ə*):

תֹּ֫אכַל לֶ֫חֶם your will eat bread
וַיִּ֫הְיוּ שָׁם and they were there

c. *Conjunctive Daghesh.* When a word ending in an unstressed *-ā(h)* or *-eh* is followed by one beginning with a stressed syllable, a daghesh may be placed in the first consonant of the second word:

הָיִ֫יתָ לָּ֫נוּ you were for us

The absence of stress on the final *-ā(h)* or *-eh* of the first word may be

(1) normal, as in the preceding example;
(2) due to retraction, as in יֵ֫עָשֶׂה לּוֹ it was done for him;
(3) due to proclisis, as in הָבָה־לָּ֫נוּ give to us.

The phonetic value of this daghesh is not certain.

156. Vocabulary 42.

VERBS:	זָעַק	*zāʿaq*	(יִזְעַק)	a synonym (and doublet) of צָעַק to cry out
	סָר	*sār*	(יָסוּר)	to turn aside (from a given course), to depart, go away (all intransitive).
	חִלֵּל	*ḥillēl*	(יְחַלֵּל)	to defile, pollute, dishonor

כִּפֶּר *kipper* (יְכַפֵּר) to atone for, make atonement
נִחַם *niḥam* (יְנַחֵם) to comfort, console (cf. נִחַם Niphal)
שִׂמַּח *śimmaḥ* (יְשַׂמַּח) to gladden, cause to rejoice (cf. שָׂמַח, שִׂמְחָה)

NOUNS: חֹתֵן *ḥōṯēn* father-in-law
לֶהָבָה *lehāḇāh* (constr. לַהֶ֫בֶת or לַבַּת; pl. *-ôṯ*) flame
נַ֫עַל *náʿal* (pl. *-îm*) shoe, sandal (f.)
קֹ֫דֶשׁ *qṓḏeš* (pl. *-îm*) holiness, sacredness
עָוֺן *ʿāwōn* (pl. *-ôṯ*) guilt, iniquity; punishment

OTHER: מַדּוּעַ *maddûaʿ* (interrog. adv.) why? for what reason?
הֲלֹם *hălōm* (adv.) hither (a less frequent synonym of הֵ֫נָּה)

PROPER NAMES: מֹשֶׁה *Mōšeh* Moses
מִדְיָן *Miḏyān* Midian, a land in northwestern Arabia.
יִתְרוֹ *Yiṯrô* Jethro, the father-in-law of Moses
חֹרֵב *Ḥōrēḇ* Mt. Horeb, an alternate name for Mt. Sinai, the location of which is disputed.

Exercises:

(a) Translate:

(1) מַדּוּעַ חִלַּ֫לְתָּ אֶת־מְקוֹם קָדְשִׁי.
(2) וַיַּ֫עַשׂ מֹשֶׁה כַּאֲשֶׁר צִוָּה.
(3) טוֹב־לִי כִּי־עֻנֵּ֫יתִי לְמַ֫עַן אֶזְכֹּר אֶת־תּוֹרָתְךָ.
(4) כִּי אֲשֶׁר־לֹא סֻפַּר לָהֶם יִרְאוּ וַאֲשֶׁר לֹא שָׁמְעוּ יֵדְעוּ.
(5) מְבֹרָכָיו יִירְשׁוּ אֶת־הָאָ֫רֶץ וּמְקֻלָּלָיו יִכָּרֵ֫תוּ.
(6) שַׂמַּח נֶ֫פֶשׁ עַבְדֶּךָ כִּי אֵלֶ֫יךָ אֲדֹנָי נַפְשִׁי אֶשָּׂא.
(7) אִישׁ־אֹהֵב חָכְמָה יְשַׂמַּח אָבִיו.
(8) כְּאִישׁ אֲשֶׁר אִמּוֹ תְּנַחֵם אֹתוֹ כֵּן אָנֹכִי אֲנַחֵם אֶתְכֶם וּבִירוּשָׁלַ֫ם תְּנֻחָ֫מוּ:
(9) גָּדוֹל יהוה וּמְהֻלָּל מְאֹד בְּעִיר אֱלֹהֵ֫ינוּ הַר קָדְשׁוֹ.
(10) וַיִּפֹּל דָּוִד וְהַזְּקֵנִים מְכֻסִּים בַּשַּׂקִּים עַל־פְּנֵיהֶם.
(11) נִרְאָה אֵלַי בַּחֲלוֹם אַחֵר אַחֲרֵי הֵרָאוֹתוֹ אֵלַי בַּתְּחִלָּה.
(12) קָשֹׁר קָשַׁ֫רְתִּי עַל־אֲדֹנִי וָאֶהֱרֹג אֹתוֹ.
(13) וַיֹּ֫אמֶר קַ֫יִן אֶל־יהוה גָּדוֹל עֲוֺנִי מִנְּשֹׂא. הִנֵּה גֵּרַ֫שְׁתָּ אֹתִי מֵעַל פְּנֵי הָאֲדָמָה.
(14) אַל־תָּסוּר עַל־יָמִין אוֹ עַל־שְׂמֹאל.
(15) אֲכַסֶּה צִלְּךָ.
(16) בֻּקְּשׁוּ הָאֲתוֹנוֹת וְלֹא נִמְצְאוּ.
(17) עַד־הֵ֫נָּה צַמְתִּי עַל־דְּבַר עֲוֺנִי הַגָּדוֹל לְמַ֫עַן יְכֻפַּר.

(b) Write in Hebrew:

1. Because of the righteous (ones) I shall not send a flame of fire upon the city to consume it and its inhabitants.
2. Where did you put your shoes?
3. His father-in-law was an Egyptian priest.

4. If you touch the vessels in the temple you will pollute them.
5. They turned off the road and stayed (= dwelt) in an inn until morning.
6. She used to come to the river every day with her sister to wash clothes, and when the clothes had been washed, she would return to the city.
7. Why did you not receive the men who had been driven out of the city?

(c) Reading: Moses and the Burning Bush (Ex. 2:23–3:6)

(23) וַיְהִי בַיָּמִים הָרַבִּים הָהֵם וַיָּמָת מֶלֶךְ מִצְרַיִם וַיֵּאָנְחוּ[1] בְנֵי־יִשְׂרָאֵל מִן־הָעֲבוֹדָה וַיִּזְעָקוּ וַתַּעַל שַׁוְעָתָם[2] אֶל־הָאֱלֹהִים מִן־הָעֲבֹדָה:

(24) וַיִּשְׁמַע אֱלֹהִים אֶת־נַאֲקָתָם[3] וַיִּזְכֹּר אֱלֹהִים אֶת־בְּרִיתוֹ אֶת־אַבְרָהָם אֶת־יִצְחָק וְאֶת־יַעֲקֹב:

(25) וַיַּרְא אֱלֹהִים אֶת־בְּנֵי־יִשְׂרָאֵל וַיֵּדַע אֱלֹהִים:

(1) וּמֹשֶׁה הָיָה רֹעֶה אֶת־צֹאן יִתְרוֹ חֹתְנוֹ כֹּהֵן מִדְיָן וַיִּנְהַג[4] אֶת־הַצֹּאן אַחַר[5] הַמִּדְבָּר וַיָּבֹא אֶל־הַר הָאֱלֹהִים חֹרֵבָה:

(2) וַיֵּרָא מַלְאַךְ יהוה אֵלָיו בְּלַבַּת־אֵשׁ מִתּוֹךְ הַסְּנֶה[6] וַיַּרְא וְהִנֵּה הַסְּנֶה בֹּעֵר בָּאֵשׁ וְהַסְּנֶה אֵינֶנּוּ אֻכָּל:[7]

(3) וַיֹּאמֶר מֹשֶׁה אָסֻרָה־נָּא וְאֶרְאֶה אֶת־הַמַּרְאֶה הַגָּדֹל הַזֶּה מַדּוּעַ לֹא־יִבְעַר הַסְּנֶה:

(4) וַיַּרְא יהוה כִּי סָר לִרְאוֹת וַיִּקְרָא אֵלָיו אֱלֹהִים מִתּוֹךְ הַסְּנֶה וַיֹּאמֶר מֹשֶׁה מֹשֶׁה וַיֹּאמֶר הִנֵּנִי:

(5) וַיֹּאמֶר אַל־תִּקְרַב הֲלֹם שַׁל[8] נְעָלֶיךָ מֵעַל רַגְלֶיךָ כִּי הַמָּקוֹם אֲשֶׁר אַתָּה עוֹמֵד עָלָיו אַדְמַת־קֹדֶשׁ הוּא:

(6) וַיֹּאמֶר אָנֹכִי אֱלֹהֵי אָבִיךָ אֱלֹהֵי אַבְרָהָם אֱלֹהֵי יִצְחָק וֵאלֹהֵי יַעֲקֹב וַיַּסְתֵּר[9] מֹשֶׁה פָּנָיו כִּי יָרֵא מֵהַבִּיט[10] אֶל־הָאֱלֹהִים:

Notes to the Reading:

1. **אנח** Niphal: "to sigh"
2. שַׁוְעָה a cry
3. נְאָקָה a cry
4. נָהַג Qal: "to lead, drive"
5. In the sense: "to the edge of"
6. סְנֶה a bush
7. An irregular passive adjective: "consumed"
8. "Remove"
9. "and he hid"
10. "to look"

LESSON 43

157. Hiphil Verbs: Meaning.

Hiphil verbs are, for the most part, causatives of the corresponding Qal. The distinctive mark of this conjugational type is a prefixed *h-*, but because this is not present in the imperfect and the participle, one must rely also on vowel patterns to identify these forms and to distinguish them from the Qal. The meanings that can be assigned to the Hiphil may be grouped as follows:

a. *Causative*. From roots whose Qal verbs are transitive, the causative may be doubly transitive, i.e. with an object of the "causing" and an object of the verbal idea expressed by the root:

הִשְׁמִיעַ	he caused (someone) to hear (something)
הִשְׁמִיעַ אֶת־הָאִישׁ אֶת־דִּבְרֵי הַמֶּלֶךְ	he caused the man to hear the words of the king

More commonly, however, there is only one object. If the second object is omitted, the verbal idea is intransitive:

הִשְׁמִיעַ אֶת־הָאִישׁ he caused the man to hear

It is better to seek a more idiomatic translation value in English, one that contains the force of the causative but requires no further object: "He informed (or notified) the man". If the first object is omitted, the verbal notion becomes passive in English:

הִשְׁמִיעַ אֶת־דִּבְרֵי הַמֶּלֶךְ he caused the words of the king to be heard.

Here again, a more suitable translation can usually be found: "He announced (or made public) the words of the king".

A further example with הֶרְאָה (to cause to see):

כַּאֲשֶׁר הֶרְאָה אֹתְךָ בָּהָר	as he showed you on the mountain (no second object)
יַרְאֶה אֶת־כְּבוֹדוֹ	he will reveal his glory (no first object)

From roots whose Qal verbs are intransitive, Hiphil verbs are simply transitive. To this group belong the extremely frequent causatives from verbs of motion:

עָבַר	הֶעֱבִיר	to bring (take, lead, send) across
יָצָא	הוֹצִיא	to bring (take, lead, send) out
יָרַד	הוֹרִיד	to bring (take, lead, send) down
עָלָה	הֶעֱלָה	to bring (take, lead, send) up
שָׁב	הֵשִׁיב	to bring (take, lead, send) back
בָּא	הֵבִיא	to bring (take, lead, send) in, to, into

From roots stative in the Qal, Hiphil verbs often partially overlap with the Piel:

כִּבֵּד	to honor; (rarely) make heavy	הִכְבִּיד	to make heavy; (rarely) honor
קִדֵּשׁ	to sanctify, consecrate	הִקְדִּישׁ	to sanctify, consecrate
גִּדֵּל	to cause to grow; rear; magnify	הִגְדִּיל	*idem* + to do great things

b. *Permissive*. This is closely related to the causative meaning and can be decided only from context: E.g.

הֶרְאָה אֹתִי אֱלֹהִים גַּם־אֶת־זַרְעֶךָ God has allowed me to see your children too.

c. *Stative* (or *intransitive*). A rather unusual use of the Hiphil is the formation of stative verbs from roots that are also stative in the Qal:

QAL		HIPHIL	
——		הִלְבִּין	to be white
קָרֵב	to be near	הִקְרִיב	to be near, about to (do something)
רָחַק	to be distant	הִרְחִיק	to move or go to a distance

A subgroup of this type consists of verbs describing action or behavior:

יטב	to be good	הֵיטִיב	to do well, get along well
רַע	to be wicked	הֵרַע	to act wickedly

These do constitute a translation problem since nearly all of them have a transitive causative meaning as well:

הִלְבִּין	to make white	הִרְחִיק	to remove, put away
הִקְרִיב	to bring near, presént	הֵיטִיב	to make (something) good

The causative value is the more frequent one.

d. *Denominative.* Like the Piel, the Hiphil is used to form verbs from roots attested (in a specialized meaning) in nouns:

אֹזֶן ear — הֶאֱזִין to give ear, to listen
עֶרֶב evening — הֶעֱרִיב to do something in the evening.

e. *Unclassified:* Many verbs of the Hiphil type cannot be placed in the preceding classification. As in the Piel, this is due mainly to our ignorance of the sources in the language from which they were derived. E.g.

הִשְׁקָה to water, give to drink (used as causative of שָׁתָה)
הִשְׁכִּים to do something early in the day
הִשְׁלִיךְ to throw, cast away
הִשְׁמִיד to annihilate, destroy

158. Hiphil Verbs: Stems and Inflection.

Root Type	Perfect	Imperfect	Jussive
Regular	הִשְׁמִיד *hišmîd*	יַשְׁמִיד *yašmîd*	יַשְׁמֵד *yašmēd*
I-*Nun*	הִגִּיד *higgîd*	יַגִּיד *yaggîd*	יַגֵּד *yaggēd*
I-Guttural	הֶעֱמִיד *he'ĕmîd*	יַעֲמִיד *ya'ămîd*	יַעֲמֵד *ya'ămēd*
Imperative	**Inf. Construct**	**Infinitive Absol.**	**Participle**
הַשְׁמֵד *hašmēd*	הַשְׁמִיד *hašmîd*	הַשְׁמֵד *hašmēd*	מַשְׁמִיד *mašmîd*
הַגֵּד *haggēd*	הַגִּיד *haggîd*	הַגֵּד *haggēd*	מַגִּיד *maggîd*
הַעֲמֵד *ha'ămēd*	הַעֲמִיד *ha'ămîd*	הַעֲמֵד *ha'ămēd*	מַעֲמִיד *ma'ămîd*

Remarks:

(a) The basic stem of the perfect has prefixed *hi-* and a long stem vowel *î*; this is replaced with *a* in inflection (see paradigm below). With roots I-*Nun*, the familiar assimilation takes place: **hingîd* > *higgîd*. With roots I-guttural (including א) the prefix is *he-*, with a secondary vowel after the guttural.

(b) In the imperfect only the vowel pattern identifies the form as a Hiphil verb. Note again the secondary vowel with roots I-guttural. The short imperfect (jussive) has *ē* as the stem vowel.

(c) The *h*-prefix appears also in the imperative and the infinitives, which have different stem vowels. The participle, like that of the Piel/Pual system, has prefixed *m-*.

Perfect: ✓ הִשְׁמִיד *hišmîd* — הִשְׁמִידוּ *hišmîdû*
הִשְׁמִידָה *hišmîdāh*

	הִשְׁמַ֫דְתָּ	*hišmáḏtā*	הִשְׁמַדְתֶּם	*hišmaḏtem*
	הִשְׁמַ֫דְתְּ	*hišmáḏt*	הִשְׁמַדְתֶּן	*hišmaḏten*
	הִשְׁמַ֫דְתִּי	*hišmáḏtî*	הִשְׁמַ֫דְנוּ	*hišmáḏnû*
IMPERFECT:	יַשְׁמִיד	*yašmîḏ*	יַשְׁמִ֫ידוּ	*yašmîḏû*
	תַּשְׁמִיד	*tašmîḏ*	תַּשְׁמֵ֫דְנָה	*tašmḗḏnāh*
	תַּשְׁמִיד	*tašmîḏ*	תַּשְׁמִ֫ידוּ	*tašmîḏû*
	תַּשְׁמִ֫ידִי	*tašmîḏî*	תַּשְׁמֵ֫דְנָה	*tašmḗḏnāh*
	אַשְׁמִיד	*'ašmîḏ*	נַשְׁמִיד	*našmîḏ*
JUSSIVE:	יַשְׁמֵד	*yašmēḏ*	וַיַּ֫שְׁמֵד	*wayyašmēḏ*
	תַּשְׁמֵד	*tašmēḏ*	וַתַּשְׁמֵד	*wattašmēḏ*
COHORTATIVE:	אַשְׁמִ֫ידָה	*'ašmîḏāh*	נַשְׁמִ֫ידָה	*našmîḏāh*
IMPERATIVE:	הַשְׁמֵד	*hašmēḏ*	הַשְׁמִ֫ידוּ	*hašmîḏû*
	הַשְׁמִ֫ידִי	*hašmîḏî*	הַשְׁמֵ֫דְנָה	*hašmḗḏnāh*
INFINITIVE CONSTRUCT:	הַשְׁמִיד	*hašmîḏ*		
	הַשְׁמִידִי	*hašmîḏî*		
	הַשְׁמִידְךָ	*hašmîḏəḵā* etc.		
INFINITIVE ABSOLUTE:	הַשְׁמֵד	*hašmēḏ*		
PARTICIPLE	מַשְׁמִיד	*mašmîḏ*	מַשְׁמִידִים	*mašmîḏîm*
	מַשְׁמִ֫ידָה	*mašmîḏāh*	מַשְׁמִידוֹת	*mašmîḏôṯ*

The paradigms of הִגִּיד and הֶעֱמִיד are the same as the preceding. In learning the paradigm of the Hiphil, the reader should note the vowel replacements (perfect: *î* → *a*; imperfect: *î* → *ē*) and the fact that the stem vowel *ē* does not occur in open syllables, while *î* occurs in all open stem syllables and in all final syllables except that of the jussive, the imperative, and the infinitive absolute.

One peculiarity should be mentioned in connection with the perfect of הֶאֱמִין and other Hiphil verbs from roots I-guttural: when used in a future sequence, the converted form, with the customary shift of stress, has *a* in the preformative syllable:

וְהַאֲמַנְתָּ֫ and you will believe
וְהַאֲמַנְתִּ֫י and I shall believe

A very rare alternate form for הֶאֱמִין is הַאֲמִין.

159. Vocabulary 43.

The following Hiphil verbs are derived from roots which have already occurred in this text. Note the meanings which are not completely predictable.

הֶאֱבִיד to destroy, kill (אָבַד)
הֶאֱמִין to believe, trust (נֶאֱמַן)
הִגְדִּיל to magnify, make great (גָּדַל)
הֶעֱבִיר to lead (bring) across
הֶעֱמִיד to station, set up, appoint
הִקְרִיב to bring near, present

הִזְכִּיר to cause to remember or be remembered; to remind; to mention
הֶחֱזִיק to seize, lay hold of (חָזַק)
הִגִּישׁ to bring near (נִגַּשׁ)
הִצִּיב to station, set up (נִצַּב)

VERBS:	הִבִּיט	*hibbîṭ*	(root נבט)	to look (at: אֶל, עַל); to look at (+dir.obj.)
	הִגִּיד	*higgîḏ*	(root נגד)	to tell (something) (to: לְ)
	הִצִּיל	*hiṣṣîl*	(root נצל)	to rescue, deliver
	הִשִּׂיג	*hiśśîḡ*	(root נשׂג)	to reach, attain, overtake
	הִסְתִּיר	*histîr*	(root סתר)	to hide, conceal (trans.)
	נִקְרָה	*niqrāh*	(imperf. יִקָּרֶה)	to meet, encounter (+ אֶל, עַל, בְּ)
	נִקְרָא	*niqrā'*	(imperf. יִקָּרֵא)	

NOUNS:	חָלָב	*ḥālāḇ*	(constr. irreg. חֲלֵב; no pl.)	milk
	דְּבַשׁ	*dəḇaš*	honey	
	זֵכֶר	*zēḵer*	(w. suff. זִכְרִי; no pl.)	remembrance, memorial
	אוֹת	*'ôṯ*	(pl. *-ôṯ*)	sign, omen
	דּוֹר	*dôr*	(pl. *-îm* or *-ôṯ*)	generation, corresponding period of time

ADJECTIVE: רָחָב *rāḥāḇ* broad, wide

Note: Hiphil verbs from roots whose Qal is unknown or little used often have a corresponding Niphal; in addition to נֶאֱמַן, נִצַּב, and נִגַּשׁ note

נִצַּל *niṣṣal* to be rescued   נִסְתַּר *nistar* to hide (oneself)

Exercises:

(a) Translate:

(1) וַיָּ֫סַר מֹשֶׁה לְהַבִּיט אֶל־לַהֶ֫בֶת הָאֵשׁ.
(2) תָּבוֹא וְהַאֲבַדְתָּ֫ אֹתָם מִתַּ֫חַת הַשָּׁמָ֫יִם.
(3) מַדּוּעַ אֵינְכֶם מַאֲמִינִים בַּיהוה אֱלֹהֵיכֶם.
(4) וַיַּגִּ֫ידוּ לוֹ אֶת־כָּל־הַדְּבָרִים אֲשֶׁר שָׁמְעוּ בַּלָּ֫יְלָה.
(5) וַיְהִי כְּהַשִּׂיגֻ֫נוּ אֹתָם וַיִּזְעֲקוּ בְּקוֹל גָּדוֹל וַיַּסְתִּ֫ירוּ אֶת־פְּנֵיהֶם.
(6) וְהָיָה בְּהַזְכִּירָם אֶת־שִׁירֵי אֲבִיהֶם וּבָכוּ.
(7) הֶעֱבִיר אֹתָם אֶת־הַנָּהָר וַיַּקְרֵב אֹתָם הָעִ֫ירָה.
(8) הֶחֱזִ֫יקָה אֶת־בִּגְדוֹ וְהוּא נָס הַחֽוּצָה.
(9) אַגְדִּיל אֶת־שִׁמְךָ הַקָּדוֹשׁ יוֹמָם וָלַ֫יְלָה וְלֹא אֶשְׁכַּח אֶת־מִצְוֹתֶ֫יךָ.
(10) אֵי־מִזֶּה אַתְּ תָּבֹ֫אִי הֲלֹם וְאֶת־מִי אַתְּ מְבַקֶּ֫שֶׁת פֹּה.
(11) אַל־תַּקְרִ֫יבוּ אֶת־הַבְּהֵמָה פֶּן־תְּחַלְּלוּ אֶת־הַמָּקוֹם הַזֶּה.
(12) וַתַּסְתֵּר אֶת־הָאֲנָשִׁים פֶּן־יִמָּֽצְאוּ וְנֶהֶרְגוּ.
(13) הִזְכִּיר אֹתָ֫נוּ אֶת־הָאוֹתוֹת אֲשֶׁר שָׁלַח אֵלֵ֫ינוּ.
(14) יַגְדִּיל אֶת־שֵׁם הַמַּאֲמִין בּוֹ.
(15) הַגֶּד־לוֹ כִּי־סָֽבְבוּ אֹתָ֫נוּ אֹיְבֵ֫ינוּ וְכִי אֵין מַצִּיל אֹתָ֫נוּ בְּצָרָתֵ֫נוּ.
(16) אָרוּר אַתָּה עַל־דְּבַר עֲוֹנְךָ הַגָּדוֹל הַזֶּה.
(17) תְּנִי אֶת־הֶחָלָב אֶל־גְּבִרְתֵּךְ לְמַ֫עַן תִּשְׁתֶּה.

(b) Write in Hebrew:

1. The maidservant hid near the well.
2. Overtake him and tell him that we are returning to our city.
3. We were not able to rescue them.
4. Look at the mountains and tell me what you see there.
5. He will station his men by the road.
6. The man who meets you will tell you where I have hidden.
7. Why have you come to destroy us?
8. He hid the money so that no one could find it.

(c) Reading: Moses and the Burning Bush (concl.); Ex. 3:7–15.

(7) וַיֹּאמֶר יהוה רָאֹה רָאִיתִי אֶת־עֳנִי עַמִּי אֲשֶׁר בְּמִצְרָיִם וְאֶת־צַעֲקָתָם[1] שָׁמַעְתִּי מִפְּנֵי נֹגְשָׂיו[2]
כִּי יָדַעְתִּי אֶת־מַכְאֹבָיו:[3]
(8) וָאֵרֵד לְהַצִּילוֹ[4] מִיַּד מִצְרַיִם וּלְהַעֲלֹתוֹ[5] מִן־הָאָרֶץ הַהִוא אֶל־אֶרֶץ טוֹבָה וּרְחָבָה אֶל־אֶרֶץ
זָבַת[6] חָלָב וּדְבָשׁ אֶל־מְקוֹם הַכְּנַעֲנִי וְהַחִתִּי[7] וְהָאֱמֹרִי וְהַפְּרִזִּי וְהַחִוִּי וְהַיְבוּסִי:
(9) וְעַתָּה הִנֵּה צַעֲקַת בְּנֵי־יִשְׂרָאֵל בָּאָה אֵלָי וְגַם־רָאִיתִי אֶת־הַלַּחַץ[8] אֲשֶׁר מִצְרַיִם לֹחֲצִים
אֹתָם:
(10) וְעַתָּה לְכָה וְאֶשְׁלָחֲךָ[9] אֶל־פַּרְעֹה וְהוֹצֵא[10] אֶת־עַמִּי בְנֵי יִשְׂרָאֵל מִמִּצְרָיִם:
(11) וַיֹּאמֶר מֹשֶׁה אֶל־הָאֱלֹהִים מִי אָנֹכִי כִּי אֵלֵךְ אֶל־פַּרְעֹה וְכִי אוֹצִיא[11] אֶת־בְּנֵי יִשְׂרָאֵל
מִמִּצְרָיִם:
(12) וַיֹּאמֶר כִּי־אֶהְיֶה עִמָּךְ וְזֶה־לְּךָ הָאוֹת כִּי אָנֹכִי שְׁלַחְתִּיךָ[12] בְּהוֹצִיאֲךָ[13] אֶת־הָעָם מִמִּצְרַיִם
תַּעַבְדוּן אֶת־הָאֱלֹהִים עַל הָהָר הַזֶּה:
(13) וַיֹּאמֶר מֹשֶׁה אֶל־הָאֱלֹהִים הִנֵּה אָנֹכִי בָא אֶל־בְּנֵי יִשְׂרָאֵל וְאָמַרְתִּי לָהֶם אֱלֹהֵי אֲבוֹתֵיכֶם
שְׁלָחַנִי[14] אֲלֵיכֶם וְאָמְרוּ־לִי מַה־שְּׁמוֹ מָה אֹמַר אֲלֵהֶם:
(14) וַיֹּאמֶר אֱלֹהִים אֶל־מֹשֶׁה אֶהְיֶה אֲשֶׁר אֶהְיֶה[15] וַיֹּאמֶר כֹּה תֹאמַר לִבְנֵי יִשְׂרָאֵל אֶהְיֶה
שְׁלָחַנִי אֲלֵיכֶם:
(15) וַיֹּאמֶר עוֹד אֱלֹהִים אֶל־מֹשֶׁה כֹּה־תֹאמַר אֶל־בְּנֵי יִשְׂרָאֵל יהוה אֱלֹהֵי אֲבֹתֵיכֶם אֱלֹהֵי
אַבְרָהָם אֱלֹהֵי יִצְחָק וֵאלֹהֵי יַעֲקֹב שְׁלָחַנִי[14] אֲלֵיכֶם זֶה־שְּׁמִי לְעֹלָם וְזֶה זִכְרִי לְדֹר דֹּר:[16]

Notes to the Reading:

1. צְעָקָה cry
2. נָגַשׂ to drive, oppress
3. מַכְאֹב pain
4. The suffix *-ô* is an object pronoun.
5. "to lead him (them) up"
6. זָב to flow
7. The Hittites, the Amorites, the Perizzites, the Hivites, and the Jebusites; names of peoples occupying Palestine at that time.
8. לַ֫חַץ oppression; לָחַץ to oppress
9. = וְאֶשְׁלַח אֹתְךָ
10. "and bring forth"

11. "I should bring forth"
12. = שָׁלַֽחְתִּי אֹתְךָ
13. inf. construct of הוֹצִיא to bring forth
14. = שָׁלַח אֹתִי
15. A cryptic phrase, not fully understood.
16. "forever;" an idiomatic use of repetition for durational expression.

LESSON 44

160. Hiphil Verbs: Stems and Inflection (cont.).

Root Type	Perfect	Imperfect	Jussive	Imperative	Inf. Constr.	Participle
III-guttural	הִשְׁמִיעַ	יַשְׁמִיעַ	יַשְׁמַע	הַשְׁמַע	הַשְׁמִיעַ	מַשְׁמִיעַ
III-*Aleph*	הִמְצִיא	יַמְצִיא	יַמְצֵא	הַמְצֵא	הַמְצִיא	מַמְצִיא

Remarks: A guttural (other than א) in third root position affects only those forms which have *ē* in the final stem syllable of the corresponding non-guttural type. In the imperfect (fem. pl.), jussive, and imperative this is replaced by *a*. The paradigm is otherwise like that of הִשְׁמִיד except for the furtive *paṯaḥ* with the final guttural: הִשְׁמִיעַ, יַשְׁמִיעַ.

Imperfect	Jussive	Imperative
יַשְׁמִיעַ	יַשְׁמַע	הַשְׁמַע
תַּשְׁמִיעַ	תַּשְׁמַע	הַשְׁמִ֫יעִי
...	...	הַשְׁמִ֫יעוּ
תַּשְׁמַ֫עְנָה	...	הַשְׁמַ֫עְנָה

Hiphil verbs from roots III-*Aleph* have *ē(')* in the perfect before endings beginning with a consonant: הִמְצֵ֫אתָ (just like the Niphal נִמְצֵ֫אתָ, Piel מִלֵּ֫אתָ, and the Pual מֻלֵּ֫אתָ). All other forms are the same as those of הִשְׁמִיד except for the fem. pl. of the imperfect, where we find the usual *-é(')nāh:* תַּמְצֶ֫אנָה

Perfect	Imperfect	Imperative
הִמְצִיא	יַמְצִיא	הַמְצֵא
הִמְצִיאָה	...	הַמְצִיאִי
הִמְצֵאתָ	תַּמְצֶאנָה	הַמְצִיאוּ
...	...	הַמְצֶאנָה

The verb הֶחֱטִיא combines the features of verbs I-guttural and III-*Aleph*.

161. More on the Numbers.

(a) The tens. Apart from *twenty,* which is expressed by the plural form of *ten,* namely עֶשְׂרִים, the tens are the plurals of the corresponding units:

שְׁלֹשִׁים	thirty	שִׁבְעִים	seventy
אַרְבָּעִים	forty	שְׁמֹנִים	eighty
חֲמִשִּׁים	fifty	תִּשְׁעִים	ninety
שִׁשִּׁים	sixty		

They may be used with either a singular noun (the more common usage) or a plural noun:

שְׁלֹשִׁים אִישׁ or שְׁלֹשִׁים אֲנָשִׁים thirty men.

They may also be used as ordinals: בִּשְׁנַת אַרְבָּעִים in the fortieth year.

(b) Fractions are poorly attested. The expression for *half* (חֲצִי) is unrelated to the number two. A *fourth* is רֶבַע or רֹבַע; a *fifth* is חֹמֶשׁ.

(c) In addition to the regular series of ordinals (רִאשׁוֹן, שֵׁנִי, שְׁלִישִׁי, etc.) there is a second type attested only by שִׁלֵּשׁ (third) and רִבֵּעַ (fourth). To judge from their limited use, they are more substantival than adjectival: "that which pertains to the third," etc.

(d) Adverbial multiplicatives are usually expressed with פַּעַם (once), פַּעֲמַיִם (twice), שָׁלוֹשׁ פְּעָמִים (three times), etc., but also attested are the forms שִׁבְעָתַיִם (sevenfold), אַרְבַּעְתַּיִם (fourfold).

(e) Most of the units have corresponding verbs (usually Piel) which have rather wide-ranging meanings: "to do something x-times; to divide into x-parts; to do something for an x time." Thus,

שָׁנָה to repeat, do again
שִׁלֵּשׁ to divide into three parts
רָבַע to be square; [רִבַּע] to make square, and similarly for the others.

162. Vocabulary 44.

VERBS: הִשְׁמִיעַ to cause to hear; to tell, to proclaim.
הִמְצִיא to cause to find; to present (= cause to be found).

הֶחֱטִיא to cause to sin, to lead into sin
הִצְלִ֫יחַ to make prosperous; to be prosperous
הִשְׁלִיךְ to throw
הִשְׁמִיד to destroy
הֶאֱרִיךְ to lengthen (tr.); to be long (intr.)
זָבַח (יִזְבַּח) to sacrifice
גָּנַב (יִגְנֹב) to steal
רָצַח (יִרְצַח) to kill (with or without intent or premeditation)

NOUNS: מַטֶּה (pl. *-ôṯ*) staff, rod; tribe
כַּף (w. suff. כַּפִּי; dual כַּפַּ֫יִם; pl. *-ôṯ*) palm or hollow of hand; sole

OTHER: הֵן (adv.) a synonym of הִנֵּה; if

Exercises:

(a) Translate:

(1) יַשְׁמִ֫ידוּ אֶת־שַׁעֲרֵי עִירֵ֫נוּ.
(2) וַיַּצְלַח יהוה אֶת־יוֹסֵף.
(3) צִוִּ֫יתִי אֹתוֹ לְהַחֲזִיק אֶת־הַצְּלָמִים וּלְהַשְׁמִיד אֹתָם.
(4) הִשְׁלִ֫יכוּ אֶת־אֲחִיהֶם בַּבּוֹר.
(5) גָּדוֹל עֲוֹנֵ֫נוּ כִּי הֶחֱטִ֫אנוּ אֹתוֹ.
(6) יַאֲרֵךְ יהוה אֶת־יְמֵי חַיֶּ֫יךָ.
(7) הַשְׁמִ֫יעוּ אֶת־כָּל־הָעָם אֶת־דְּבָרַי.
(8) יְבֹרַךְ הַמַּאֲמִין בּוֹ וְהַמְקַלֵּל אֹתוֹ יֹאבַד.
(9) אַצִּיל אֶת־הָעָם הַמְעֻנֶּה הַזֶּה.
(10) אַל־תַּחֲטִיא אֶת־רֵעֲךָ.
(11) לָ֫מָּה תִסָּתֵר מִמֶּ֫נִּי.
(12) לֹא תְעַנּוּ אֶת־הַדַּלִּים.
(13) מִי גָנַב אֶת־הַלּוּחוֹת.
(14) הִשְׁלִיךְ אֶת־הַדָּג בַּיָּם.
(15) בֹּ֫אוּ וְהַלְלוּ אֶת־יהוה אֱלֹהֵיכֶם.
(16) נַשִּׂ֫יגָה־נָּא אֹתוֹ לִפְנֵי הִקָּרְאוֹ עַל־מַחֲנֵה אֹיְבֵ֫ינוּ.
(17) קָרַע אֶת־בְּגָדָיו וַיְכַס אֶת־רֹאשׁוֹ בַּשַּׂקִּים.
(18) זֶה אוֹת אַהֲבָתִי.
(19) קָם עַל־רֵעֵ֫הוּ וַיִּרְצַח אֹתוֹ.
(20) אַל־תִּזְבְּחוּ אֶת־עוֹף הַשָּׁמַ֫יִם.

(b) Give the Hebrew for the following orally:

1. 50 fish
2. 20 tablets
3. 30 stones
4. 40 days and 40 nights
5. 50 honest men
6. 90 garments
7. half of the milk.

(c) Write in Hebrew:

1. And when he had proclaimed the commandments of the Lord, he departed from their midst.
2. And when they destroy this city, you will be slain with the remaining inhabitants.
3. And when they told him about the enemies' army, his heart melted within him and he fled from before them.
4. Now that the Lord has made you prosperous, leave your place and come with us to be our king.
5. It is bad to steal and kill in this manner.

(d) Reading: Exodus 3:16–4:5.

(16) לֵךְ וְאָסַפְתָּ אֶת־זִקְנֵי יִשְׂרָאֵל וְאָמַרְתָּ אֲלֵהֶם יהוה אֱלֹהֵי אֲבֹתֵיכֶם נִרְאָה אֵלַי אֱלֹהֵי
אַבְרָהָם יִצְחָק וְיַעֲקֹב לֵאמֹר פָּקֹד פָּקַדְתִּי אֶתְכֶם וְאֶת־הֶעָשׂוּי לָכֶם בְּמִצְרָיִם׃
(17) וָאֹמַר אַעֲלֶה[1] אֶתְכֶם מֵעֳנִי מִצְרַיִם אֶל־אֶרֶץ הַכְּנַעֲנִי וְהַחִתִּי[2] וְהָאֱמֹרִי וְהַפְּרִזִּי וְהַחִוִּי
וְהַיְבוּסִי אֶל־אֶרֶץ זָבַת[3] חָלָב וּדְבָשׁ׃
(18) וְשָׁמְעוּ לְקֹלֶךָ וּבָאתָ אַתָּה וְזִקְנֵי יִשְׂרָאֵל אֶל־מֶלֶךְ מִצְרַיִם וַאֲמַרְתֶּם אֵלָיו יהוה אֱלֹהֵי
הָעִבְרִיִּים נִקְרָה עָלֵינוּ וְעַתָּה נֵלְכָה־נָּא דֶּרֶךְ[4] שְׁלֹשֶׁת יָמִים בַּמִּדְבָּר וְנִזְבְּחָה לַיהוה אֱלֹהֵינוּ׃
(19) וַאֲנִי יָדַעְתִּי כִּי לֹא־יִתֵּן אֶתְכֶם מֶלֶךְ מִצְרַיִם לַהֲלֹךְ[5] וְלֹא בְּיָד חֲזָקָה׃[6]
(20) וְשָׁלַחְתִּי אֶת־יָדִי וְהִכֵּיתִי[7] אֶת־מִצְרַיִם בְּכֹל נִפְלְאֹתַי אֲשֶׁר אֶעֱשֶׂה בְּקִרְבּוֹ וְאַחֲרֵי־כֵן
יְשַׁלַּח אֶתְכֶם׃
(21) וְנָתַתִּי אֶת־חֵן הָעָם־הַזֶּה בְּעֵינֵי מִצְרָיִם וְהָיָה כִּי תֵלֵכוּן לֹא תֵלְכוּ רֵיקָם׃[8]
(22) וְשָׁאֲלָה אִשָּׁה מִשְּׁכֶנְתָּהּ[9] וּמִגָּרַת בֵּיתָהּ כְּלֵי־כֶסֶף וּכְלֵי זָהָב וּשְׂמָלֹת וְשַׂמְתֶּם עַל־בְּנֵיכֶם
וְעַל־בְּנֹתֵיכֶם וְנִצַּלְתֶּם[10] אֶת־מִצְרָיִם׃
(1) וַיַּעַן מֹשֶׁה וַיֹּאמֶר וְהֵן לֹא־יַאֲמִינוּ לִי וְלֹא יִשְׁמְעוּ בְּקֹלִי כִּי יֹאמְרוּ לֹא־נִרְאָה אֵלֶיךָ יהוה׃
(2) וַיֹּאמֶר אֵלָיו יהוה מַזֶּה[11] בְיָדֶךָ וַיֹּאמֶר מַטֶּה׃
(3) וַיֹּאמֶר הַשְׁלִיכֵהוּ[12] אַרְצָה וַיַּשְׁלִכֵהוּ[13] אַרְצָה וַיְהִי לְנָחָשׁ וַיָּנָס מֹשֶׁה מִפָּנָיו׃
(4) וַיֹּאמֶר יהוה אֶל־מֹשֶׁה שְׁלַח יָדְךָ וֶאֱחֹז בִּזְנָבוֹ[14] וַיִּשְׁלַח יָדוֹ וַיַּחֲזֶק בּוֹ וַיְהִי לְמַטֶּה בְּכַפּוֹ׃
(5) לְמַעַן[15] יַאֲמִינוּ כִּי־נִרְאָה אֵלֶיךָ יהוה אֱלֹהֵי אֲבֹתָם אֱלֹהֵי אַבְרָהָם אֱלֹהֵי יִצְחָק וֵאלֹהֵי יַעֲקֹב

Notes to the Reading:

1. "I shall lead (you) up"
2. The Hittites, the Amorites, the Perizzites, the Hivites, and the Jebusites.
3. זוּב to flow
4. "a journey (of three days)"
5. לַהֲלֹךְ a "regular" inf. construct of הָלַךְ
6. "except by a show of strength"
7. "and I shall smite"
8. רֵיקָם empty (adv.)
9. "from her neighbor;" fem. form of שָׁכֵן
10. נִצֵּל (Piel): to plunder, take spoil from
11. = מַה זֶּה
12. = הַשְׁלֵךְ אֹתוֹ
13. = וַיַּשְׁלֵךְ אֹתוֹ
14. זָנָב tail
15. The purpose clause fits only loosely with the preceding verses.

LESSON 45

163. Hiphil Verbs: Stems and Inflection.

With roots I-*Yodh* (originally I-*Waw*) the Hiphil verb has the same contraction to *ô* that was found in the Niphal.

Perfect	Imperfect	Jussive	Imperative	Inf. Construct	Participle
הוֹרִיד	יוֹרִיד	יוֹרֵד וַיּ֫וֹרֶד	הוֹרֵד	הוֹרִיד	מוֹרִיד (to lead down)

The inflection is perfectly regular; the syllable with *ô* is unchanged throughout, and the final stem syllable undergoes the changes given in the paradigm of הִשְׁמִיד Because the preformative syllable is open, the accent of the converted imperfect is regularly retracted, with *ē* → *e*: וַיּ֫וֹלֶד.

The following verbs combine several inflectional peculiarities:

(a) I-*Yodh* and III-guttural:

הוֹדִיעַ	יוֹדִיעַ	וַיּ֫וֹדַע / יוֹדַע	הוֹדַע	הוֹדִיעַ	מוֹדִיעַ	(cause to know)
הוֹשִׁיעַ	יוֹשִׁיעַ	וַיּ֫וֹשַׁע / יוֹשַׁע	הוֹשַׁע	הוֹשִׁיעַ	מוֹשִׁיעַ	(deliver, save)
הוֹכִיחַ	יוֹכִיחַ	וַיּ֫וֹכַח / יוֹכַח	הוֹכַח	הוֹכִיחַ	מוֹכִיחַ	(reprove)

(b) I-*Yodh* and III-*Aleph*:

הוֹצִיא	יוֹצִיא	וַיּ֫וֹצֵא / יוֹצֵא	הוֹצֵא	הוֹצִיא	מוֹצִיא	(bring forth)

The Hiphil verb corresponding to Qal הָלַךְ is הוֹלִיךְ, as though from a root ילך.

The few verbs in Hebrew which are from roots originally I-*Yodh* have the Hiphil form הֵיטִיב (to treat well; root יטב). The *ê* is not reducible and the inflection is regular throughout.

164. The Numbers from 11–19.

The 'teens are formed by placing the unit before the word for ten, which has special forms differing from those already learned:

	Masculine Modifier	*Feminine Modifier*
eleven	אַחַד עָשָׂר	אַחַת עֶשְׂרֵה
	עַשְׁתֵּי עָשָׂר	עַשְׁתֵּי עֶשְׂרֵה
twelve	שְׁנֵים עָשָׂר	שְׁתֵּים עֶשְׂרֵה
	שְׁנֵי עָשָׂר	שְׁתֵּי עֶשְׂרֵה
thirteen	שְׁלֹשָׁה עָשָׂר	שְׁלֹשׁ עֶשְׂרֵה
fourteen	אַרְבָּעָה עָשָׂר	אַרְבַּע עֶשְׂרֵה
fifteen	חֲמִשָּׁה עָשָׂר	חֲמֵשׁ עֶשְׂרֵה
sixteen	שִׁשָּׁה עָשָׂר	שֵׁשׁ עֶשְׂרֵה
seventeen	שִׁבְעָה עָשָׂר	שְׁבַע עֶשְׂרֵה
eighteen	שְׁמֹנָה עָשָׂר	שְׁמֹנֶה עֶשְׂרֵה
nineteen	תִּשְׁעָה עָשָׂר	תְּשַׁע עֶשְׂרֵה

As with the tens (§161a), both singular and plural nouns occur with the numbers from 11 to 19. Nouns frequently itemized, such as אִישׁ, שָׁנָה, יוֹם, נֶפֶשׁ (in the sense of "person"), and שֵׁבֶט (tribe) are usually singular:

חֲמִשָּׁה עָשָׂר אִישׁ fifteen men
חֲמֵשׁ עֶשְׂרֵה נֶפֶשׁ 15 persons (rem.: נֶפֶשׁ is fem.)

With other nouns the plural is regularly used.

165. Vocabulary 45.

VERBS: הוֹשִׁיב to cause to dwell; to settle (someone in a place) (cf. יָשַׁב)
הוֹרִיד to bring (lead, take) down (cf. יָרַד)
הוֹלִיד to beget, engender (cf. יָלַד)
הוֹדִיעַ to cause to know; to teach (someone); to declare or proclaim (something) (cf. יָדַע)
הוֹצִיא to bring (lead, take) out (cf. יָצָא)
הוֹלִיךְ to cause to go; to lead (cf. הָלַךְ)
הוֹסִיף to do again; to continue doing something. Two constructions are frequent:

הוֹסִיף לָצוּם he fasted again, continued to fast
הוֹסִיף וַיָּצָם he fasted again, continued to fast

In the second construction the verbs are simply coordinated

in Hebrew. The verb may also have the meaning "to add" but the actual translation value depends on the context:

וְהוֹסַפְתִּי עַל־יָמֶיךָ חֲמֵשׁ עֶשְׂרֵה שָׁנָה	I shall add to your days fifteen years
הוֹסַפְתָּ חָכְמָה... אֶל־הַשְּׁמוּעָה אֲשֶׁר שָׁמַעְתִּי	You are wiser than you are reputed to be. (lit.: You have added wisdom to the report I have heard.)

Note also the common phrase (exclamatory, asseverative):

כֹּה יַעֲשֶׂה לִּי יהוה וְכֹה יוֹסִיף	May God do thus for me, and even more so (if such-and-such is/is-not true).

	הוֹשִׁיעַ	to save, deliver
	הוֹכִיחַ	to reprove; to decide
	קִנֵּא	to be jealous (אֶת־ or בְּ + person); to be zealous (לְ: for)
NOUNS:	פֶּסֶל	(pl. irreg. פְּסִילִים) idol, image
	אֵל	(pl. *-îm*) god; God (w. or without article)
	שָׁוְא	emptiness, vanity; לַשָּׁוְא in vain, for nothing
	גֵּר	(pl. *-îm*) sojourner, resident alien
	שׁוֹר	a head of cattle (a singular corresponding to the collective בָּקָר)
OTHER:	מִמַּעַל	(adv.) above; + לְ (=prep.)
	מִתַּחַת	(adv.) below; + לְ (=prep.)

Exercises:

(a) Translate:

(1) אֶת־הָרְשָׁעִים הוֹשִׁיב בְּחֹשֶׁךְ וְאֶת־הַצַּדִּיקִים הוֹלִיךְ בְּאוֹר פָּנָיו.
(2) הוֹלִיךְ אֹתִי בְּדַרְכֵי עָנִי וְלֹא שָׁמַע לְקוֹלִי בְּקָרְאִי אֵלָיו.
(3) לֹא אוֹסִיף עוֹד לַעֲשׂוֹת חֶסֶד עִמָּכֶם.
(4) וַיּוֹדַע אֹתִי אֶת־הָאֹתוֹת וְאֶת־הַנִּפְלָאוֹת אֲשֶׁר יֵעָשׂוּ בַּיָּמִים הָהֵם.
(5) אֱלֹהִים הוּא הַמּוֹצִיא אֹתָנוּ מֵאֶרֶץ מְעַנֵּינוּ.
(6) וַיּוֹלֶד בֵּן לִזְקוּנָיו וְהַיֶּלֶד שִׂמַּח אֶת־לֵב אָבִיו עַד־קֵץ יָמָיו.
(7) וַיּוֹרֶד אֶת־אָבִיו וְאֶת־אֶחָיו מִצְרַיְמָה.
(8) הוֹשִׁיעָה אֹתָנוּ יהוה וּפָקְדָה אֹתָנוּ כַּאֲשֶׁר דִּבַּרְתָּ.
(9) לֹא אוֹכִיחַ אֶתְכֶם עַל־חַטַּאת בְּנֵיכֶם.
(10) הַגֶּשׁ־נָא אֶת־סְפָרַי וְאֶקְרְאָה אֵלֶיךָ אֶת־הַדְּבָרִים אֲשֶׁר בָּם.
(11) וְעָשִׂיתָ נָּא עִמָּדִי חֶסֶד וְהִזְכַּרְתָּ אֹתִי אֶל־פַּרְעֹה וְהוֹצֵאתָ אֹתִי מִבֵּית הָאֲסִירִים הַזֶּה.
(12) לַשָּׁוְא דִּבַּרְתִּי אֲלֵיכֶם כִּי לֹא שְׁמַעְתֶּם אֶת־דְּבָרַי.
(13) אַל־תִּתֵּן אֶת־הַגֵּרִים לָבוֹא הַהֵיכָל כִּי מְקוֹם קֹדֶשׁ הוּא.
(14) וַיִּבְחַר שְׁלֹשָׁה עָשָׂר אִישׁ וַיַּקְרֵב אֹתָם אֶל־הָעִיר.
(15) וַיְקַנְאוּ אֹתוֹ אֶחָיו כִּי אֲבִיהֶם אָהַב אֹתוֹ מִכָּל־אֶחָיו.
(16) לֹא תוֹסִיפוּ לִתְעוֹת כִּי אוֹדִיעַ לָכֶם אֶת־הַדֶּרֶךְ.
(17) לֹא יָכֹלְנוּ לְנַחֵם אֹתָהּ אַחֲרֵי מוֹת אִישָׁהּ.

(b) Write in Hebrew:

1. He begot seventeen sons during his lifetime.
2. They settled the people in twelve small cities near the great river.
3. We defiled their holy place and brought out the fifteen large stones that they had set up there.
4. When he saw the flame of the fire, he ran out of the house without his clothes and shoes (= circum. clause: "and his clothes and shoes [were] not with him").
5. Now that my days on earth are finished, I charge these eighteen persons to you so that you may be a help and a comforter to them.
6. And after that he left the house of his father-in-law and set forth with this people as a sojourner in their midst.

(c) Reading: The Ten Commandments (Ex. 20:1–14):

(1) וַיְדַבֵּר אֱלֹהִים אֵת כָּל־הַדְּבָרִים הָאֵלֶּה לֵאמֹר׃
(2) אָנֹכִי יהוה אֱלֹהֶיךָ אֲשֶׁר הוֹצֵאתִיךָ[1] מֵאֶרֶץ מִצְרַיִם מִבֵּית עֲבָדִים׃[2]
(3) לֹא יִהְיֶה־לְךָ אֱלֹהִים אֲחֵרִים עַל־פָּנָיַ׃
(4) לֹא תַעֲשֶׂה־לְךָ פֶסֶל וְכָל־תְּמוּנָה[3] אֲשֶׁר בַּשָּׁמַיִם מִמַּעַל וַאֲשֶׁר בָּאָרֶץ מִתָּחַת וַאֲשֶׁר בַּמַּיִם
מִתַּחַת לָאָרֶץ׃
(5) לֹא־תִשְׁתַּחֲוֶה[4] לָהֶם וְלֹא תָעָבְדֵם[5] כִּי אָנֹכִי יהוה אֱלֹהֶיךָ אֵל קַנָּא[6] פֹּקֵד עֲוֺן אָבֹת עַל־
בָּנִים עַל־שִׁלֵּשִׁים[7] וְעַל־רִבֵּעִים לְשֹׂנְאָי׃
(6) וְעֹשֶׂה חֶסֶד לַאֲלָפִים[8] לְאֹהֲבַי וּלְשֹׁמְרֵי מִצְוֺתָי׃
(7) לֹא תִשָּׂא[9] אֶת־שֵׁם־יהוה אֱלֹהֶיךָ לַשָּׁוְא כִּי לֹא יְנַקֶּה יהוה אֵת אֲשֶׁר־יִשָּׂא אֶת־שְׁמוֹ לַשָּׁוְא׃
(8) זָכוֹר אֶת־יוֹם הַשַּׁבָּת לְקַדְּשׁוֹ׃[10]
(9) שֵׁשֶׁת יָמִים תַּעֲבֹד וְעָשִׂיתָ כָּל־מְלַאכְתֶּךָ׃
(10) וְיוֹם הַשְּׁבִיעִי שַׁבָּת לַיהוה אֱלֹהֶיךָ לֹא־תַעֲשֶׂה כָל־מְלָאכָה אַתָּה וּבִנְךָ־וּבִתֶּךָ עַבְדְּךָ
וַאֲמָתְךָ וּבְהֶמְתֶּךָ וְגֵרְךָ אֲשֶׁר בִּשְׁעָרֶיךָ׃
(11) כִּי שֵׁשֶׁת־יָמִים עָשָׂה יהוה אֶת־הַשָּׁמַיִם וְאֶת־הָאָרֶץ אֶת־הַיָּם וְאֶת־כָּל־אֲשֶׁר־בָּם וַיָּנַח[11]
בַּיּוֹם הַשְּׁבִיעִי עַל־כֵּן בֵּרַךְ יהוה אֶת־יוֹם הַשַּׁבָּת וַיְקַדְּשֵׁהוּ׃[12]
(12) כַּבֵּד אֶת־אָבִיךָ וְאֶת־אִמֶּךָ לְמַעַן יַאֲרִכוּן יָמֶיךָ עַל־הָאֲדָמָה אֲשֶׁר יהוה אֱלֹהֶיךָ נֹתֵן לָךְ׃
(13) לֹא תִרְצָח׃ לֹא תִנְאָף׃[13] לֹא תִגְנֹב׃ לֹא־תַעֲנֶה[14] בְרֵעֲךָ עֵד[15] שָׁקֶר׃
(14) לֹא תַחְמֹד[16] בֵּית רֵעֶךָ לֹא־תַחְמֹד אֵשֶׁת רֵעֶךָ וְעַבְדּוֹ וַאֲמָתוֹ וְשׁוֹרוֹ וַחֲמֹרוֹ וְכֹל אֲשֶׁר לְרֵעֶךָ׃

Notes to the Reading:

1. = הוֹצֵאתִי אֹתְךָ
2. A plural noun used as an abstract: "bondage"
3. תְּמוּנָה "likeness"
4. "You shall (not) bow down"
5. = תַעֲבֹד אֹתָם
6. קַנָּא (adj.) "jealous"
7. See § 161c.
8. אֶלֶף "thousand"
9. נָשָׂא here = "to utter" (prob. in an oath); נִקָּה to absolve, regard as innocent
10. The suffix is objective.
11. "And he rested"
12. = וַיְקַדֵּשׁ אֹתוֹ

13. נָאַף "to commit adultery"
14. עָנָה בְּ "to testify against; to bring as testimony against"
15. עֵד "witness, testimony" שֶׁקֶר "falsehood"
16. חָמַד "to desire, covet"

LESSON 46

166. Hiphil Verbs: Stems and Inflection (cont.).

The stems of Hiphil verbs from roots III-*Hē* are as follows:

Root Type	Perfect	Imperfect	Jussive	Imperative	Inf.Construct	Participle
III-*Hē*	הִרְבָּה	יַרְבֶּה	יֶ֫רֶב	הַרְבֵּה	הַרְבּוֹת	מַרְבֶּה
Also I-gutt.	הֶעֱלָה	יַעֲלֶה	יַ֫עַל	הַעֲלֵה	הַעֲלוֹת	מַעֲלֶה
Also I-*Yodh*	הוֹרָה	יוֹרֶה	יוֹר	הוֹרֵה	הוֹרוֹת	מוֹרֶה
Also I-*Nun*	הִכָּה	יַכֶּה	יַךְ	הַכֵּה	הַכּוֹת	מַכֶּה

Remarks: Note that the otherwise characteristic long vowel *î* of Hiphil verbs is not present in these forms. The stem endings and their inflection are virtually the same as that learned for all other verbs from roots III-*Hē* (cf. בָּנָה, נִבְנָה, עִנָּה); only the beginning of the form marks it clearly as a Hiphil verb.

The inflection is given below only in abbreviated form because of the similarities to other verbs already mentioned. Note that in the perfect the stem vowel before the suffixes beginning with a consonant is either *ê* or *î*:

PERFECT: הִרְבָּה	IMPERFECT: יַרְבֶּה	IMPERATIVE: הַרְבֵּה
הִרְבְּתָה	. . .	הַרְבִּי
הִרְבֵּ֫יתָ }	תַּרְבִּי	הַרְבּוּ
הִרְבִּ֫יתָ }	. . .	הַרְבֶּ֫ינָה
etc.	תַּרְבֶּ֫ינָה	
	etc.	

INFINITIVE CONSTRUCT: הַרְבּוֹת, הַרְבּוֹתִי, הַרְבּוֹתְךָ, etc.
INFINITIVE ABSOLUTE: הַרְבֵּה
PARTICIPLE: מַרְבֶּה מַרְבָּה מַרְבִּים מַרְבּוֹת

The verbs הֶעֱלָה, הוֹרָה, and הִכָּה illustrate various combinations of root types. Their inflection is like that of הִרְבָּה.

The jussive forms, like those of the Qal verbs from roots III-*Hē*, show the loss of the final stem vowel *(-eh)* and the resultant secondary vowel: *yarbeh* > **yarb* > *yéreḇ*. Hiphil verbs, then, are distinguished from Qal verbs only by having *é* and not *í* or *ḗ* in the first syllable of the jussive (and converted) form:

QAL:	וַיִּבֶן	and he built	וַתִּרֶב	and it (f.) grew numerous
HIPHIL:	וַיֶּבֶן	and he caused to build	וַתֶּרֶב	and it (f.) caused to grow numerous

When the root is I-guttural as well, there is no distinction:

וַיַּעַל QAL: and he went up or HIPHIL: and he led up

Note that in the jussive form of הִכָּה (root נכה) the expected **yakk* (< *yakkeh*) becomes יַךְ *yaḵ* by the regular loss of doubling at the end of a word. Compare the Qal verb יִטֶּה (he will extend), jussive יֵט.

Occasionally *e* is found instead of *i* in the preformative of the perfect:

הֶרְאָה to cause to see
הֶגְלָה to lead into exile

The infinitive absolute הַרְבֵּה (from הִרְבָּה to increase, cause to be numerous) is commonly used as an adverb "very, much," sometimes with an added מְאֹד:

וַתֵּבְךְּ הַרְבֵּה מְאֹד and she wept very much

167. The Numbers from 21–99.

Because the tens are not inflected for gender, the combination of these with the units (21, 22, etc.) is not unduly complicated. The unit may precede or follow the ten, but agrees in gender with the modified noun, which is usually in the singular.

עֶשְׂרִים וְאֶחָד אִישׁ	or	אֶחָד וְעֶשְׂרִים אִישׁ	21 men
שְׁלֹשִׁים וּשְׁנַיִם אִישׁ	or	שְׁנַיִם וּשְׁלֹשִׁים אִישׁ	32 men
		אַרְבָּעִים וְשָׁלוֹשׁ אִשָּׁה	43 women
		חֲמִשִּׁים וְשֵׁשׁ נֶפֶשׁ	56 persons

If the counted item is placed before the numeral it may be in the plural:

אֲנָשִׁים שְׁלֹשִׁים וְאֶחָד 31 men

168. Vocabulary 46.

VERBS:
הֶרְאָה to cause to see; to show (cf. רָאָה)
הִכָּה to strike, smite, kill (root נכה)
הוֹדָה to give thanks. In the imperfect the *h* is sometimes anomalously retained: יְהוֹדֶה = יוֹדֶה. (root ידה)
הִשְׁקָה to give water to, to cause to drink; used as the causative of שָׁתָה.
הוֹרָה to shoot (arrows); to direct, teach (root ירה)
הֶעֱלָה to lead (take, bring) up (cf. עָלָה)
גָּלָה (יִגְלֶה) to uncover, reveal; to go into exile; גָּלָה אֶת־אָזְנִי he informed me.
הֶגְלָה to carry away into exile
לָמַד (יִלְמַד) to learn
לִמֵּד (יְלַמֵּד) to teach
רָבָה (יִרְבֶּה) to be(come) numerous; to be great
הִרְבָּה to increase (tr.); make numerous

NOUNS:
חֹק (w. suff. חֻקִּי; pl. *-îm*) statute
חֻקָּה (pl. *-ôṯ*) statute
מִשְׁפָּט (pl. *-îm*) judgement; court decision
לֵבָב (pl. *-ôṯ*) a synonym of לֵב heart.

Exercises:

(a) For each of the following jussive and converted forms first give the corresponding normal imperfect and then the perfect. Translate. E.g. הִרְבָּה ← יַרְבֶּה ← יֶ֫רֶב

(1) וַיֹּ֫ושֶׁב	(6) יֵ֫תַע	(11) יַשֵּׂג
(2) יָקֵר	(7) יֶ֫גֶל	(12) יְעַן
(3) וַיֹּ֫ודַע	(8) יֶ֫כֶל	(13) יוֹר
(4) יֵ֫שֶׁק	(9) יַ֫עַן	(14) וַיֹּ֫וסֶף
(5) יַ֫עַל	(10) וַיֹּ֫ושַׁע	(15) יַךְ

(b) Translate:

(1) וַיַּךְ אֶת־הַמִּצְרִי וַיַּהֲרֹג אֹתוֹ וַיִּקְבֹּר אֹתוֹ פֶּן־יִמָּצֵא.
(2) הוֹדוּ לוֹ, בָּרְכוּ אֶת־שְׁמוֹ, כִּי טוֹב יהוה, לְעוֹלָם חַסְדּוֹ.
(3) בֹּ֫אוּ אֶל־הָעַ֫יִן לְמַ֫עַן הַשְׁקוֹת אֶת־צֹאנָם.
(4) וְהוֹרֵיתִי אֶתְכֶם אֶת־הַדֶּ֫רֶךְ הַטּוֹב וְהַיָּשָׁר.
(5) וְאַתָּה תַעֲלֶה אֶת־עַמִּי אַ֫רְצָה כְּנַ֫עַן.
(6) וַיהוה גָּלָה אֶת־אֹ֫זֶן הַנָּבִיא יוֹם אֶחָד לִפְנֵי בוֹא הַמֶּ֫לֶךְ.
(7) יוֹדוּ שִׁמְךָ כִּי קָדוֹשׁ אַתָּה.
(8) גָּלָה כְבוֹד יִשְׂרָאֵל.
(9) לַמֵּד אֹתִי אֶת־חֻקֶּ֫יךָ וְאֶהְיֶה לְאִישׁ צַדִּיק.
(10) מַדּוּעַ הִכֵּ֫יתָ אֶת־הַגֵּר לַהֲרֹג אֹתוֹ.

(11) לְכוּ וְנַהַרְגָה אֹתָם פֶּן־יִרְבּוּ וְנִלְחֲמוּ בָּנוּ.
(12) נָס הָעָם מִן־הַמִּלְחָמָה וְגַם־הַרְבֵּה נָפַל מִן־הָעָם.
(13) וַיְצַו אֹתָנוּ לַעֲשׂוֹת אֶת־כָּל־הַחֻקִּים הָאֵלֶּה.
(14) שָׁלַח אֶת־הָאִישׁ לִפְנֵיהֶם לְהוֹרוֹת אֹתָם אֶת־הַדָּרֶךְ.
(15) יִשְׁמְעוּ וְלָמְדוּ לְיִרְאָה אֶת־יהוה.
(16) אַרְבֶּה אֹתְךָ עַל־פְּנֵי הָאָרֶץ וְהָיִיתָ לְעַם גָּדוֹל וְחָזָק.
(17) וְקִרְעוּ לְבַבְכֶם וְאַל־בִּגְדֵיכֶם וְשׁוּבוּ אֶל־יהוה אֱלֹהֵיכֶם.
(18) יהוה אֲשֶׁר עָשָׂה אֶת־מֹשֶׁה וַאֲשֶׁר הֶעֱלָה אֶת־אֲבֹתֵיכֶם מֵאֶרֶץ מִצְרָיִם.
(19) וַיֶּגֶל אֶת־יֹשְׁבֵי יְרוּשָׁלַםִ אֶל־אֶרֶץ רְחוֹקָה.

(c) Write in Hebrew:

1. I shall give thanks to the Lord.
2. They led us into exile.
3. Teach me so that I may know your (m. s.) many wonders.
4. Deliver us from the hands of our enemies.
5. When he hears about this matter, he will be jealous.
6. You have served them in vain, for they will not give you help.
7. The Lord will reprove his people.

(d) Reading: Deuteronomy 6:1–9.

(1) וְזֹאת הַמִּצְוָה הַחֻקִּים וְהַמִּשְׁפָּטִים אֲשֶׁר צִוָּה יהוה אֱלֹהֵיכֶם לְלַמֵּד אֶתְכֶם לַעֲשׂוֹת בָּאָרֶץ
אֲשֶׁר אַתֶּם עֹבְרִים שָׁמָּה לְרִשְׁתָּהּ:[1]
(2) לְמַעַן תִּירָא אֶת־יהוה אֱלֹהֶיךָ לִשְׁמֹר אֶת־כָּל־חֻקֹּתָיו וּמִצְוֹתָיו אֲשֶׁר אָנֹכִי מְצַוֶּךָ[2] אַתָּה
וּבִנְךָ וּבֶן־בִּנְךָ כֹּל יְמֵי חַיֶּיךָ וּלְמַעַן יַאֲרִכֻן יָמֶיךָ:
(3) וְשָׁמַעְתָּ יִשְׂרָאֵל וְשָׁמַרְתָּ לַעֲשׂוֹת אֲשֶׁר יִיטַב לְךָ וַאֲשֶׁר[3] תִּרְבּוּן מְאֹד כַּאֲשֶׁר דִּבֶּר יהוה אֱלֹהֵי
אֲבֹתֶיךָ לָךְ אֶרֶץ[4] זָבַת חָלָב וּדְבָשׁ:
(4) שְׁמַע יִשְׂרָאֵל יהוה אֱלֹהֵינוּ יהוה אֶחָד:
(5) וְאָהַבְתָּ אֵת יהוה אֱלֹהֶיךָ בְּכָל־לְבָבְךָ וּבְכָל־נַפְשְׁךָ וּבְכָל־מְאֹדֶךָ:[5]
(6) וְהָיוּ הַדְּבָרִים הָאֵלֶּה אֲשֶׁר אָנֹכִי מְצַוְּךָ[2] הַיּוֹם עַל־לְבָבֶךָ:
(7) וְשִׁנַּנְתָּם[6] לְבָנֶיךָ וְדִבַּרְתָּ בָּם בְּשִׁבְתְּךָ בְּבֵיתֶךָ וּבְלֶכְתְּךָ בַדֶּרֶךְ וּבְשָׁכְבְּךָ וּבְקוּמֶךָ:
(8) וּקְשַׁרְתָּם[7] לְאוֹת עַל יָדֶךָ וְהָיוּ לְטֹטָפֹת[8] בֵּין עֵינֶיךָ:
(9) וּכְתַבְתָּם עַל־מְזֻזוֹת[9] בֵּיתֶךָ וּבִשְׁעָרֶיךָ:

Notes to the Reading:

1. The suffix is objective.
2. = מְצַוֶּה אֹתְךָ
3. Both אֲשֶׁר 's are used as compound relatives: "that which... and that (by) which..."
4. The phrase "a land flowing..." is rather loosely attached to what precedes it.
5. מְאֹד is a noun here: "strength".
6. "You shall teach them"
7. = וְקָשַׁרְתָּ אֹתָם
8. "bands, frontlet-bands"
9. מְזוּזָה "door-post"

LESSON 47

169. Hiphil Verbs: Stems and Inflection (cont.).

The Qal distinction between roots II-*Waw* (יָקוּם) and roots II-*Yodh* (יָשִׂים) is not maintained in the Hiphil verbs derived from these same roots. The forms given for הֵקִים (from the root of קָם) are standard.

Root Type	Perfect	Imperfect	Jussive	Imperative	Inf. Constr.	Participle
Hollow (II-Waw/Yodh)	הֵקִים	יָקִים	יָקֵם	הָקֵם	הָקִים	מֵקִים
Also III-gutt.	הֵנִיחַ	יָנִיחַ	יָנַח	הָנַח	הָנִיחַ	מֵנִיחַ
Also III-*Aleph*	הֵבִיא	יָבִיא	יָבֵא	הָבֵא	הָבִיא	מֵבִיא

Note that the participle has the same preformative vowel as the perfect. This stands in contrast to all other Hiphil verbs studied up to this point. The presence of a guttural (other than א) in final root position has the same effect it has in הִשְׁמִיעַ. For הֵבִיא compare הִמְצִיא.

In the inflection of the perfect there are two distinct paradigms, one with the linking vowel *-ô-* and one without:

I		II	
הֵקִים	הֵקִימוּ	הֵקִים	הֵקִימוּ
הֵקִימָה		הֵקִימָה	
הֲקִימוֹתָ	הֲקִימוֹתֶם	הֵקַמְתָּ	הֲקֵמְתֶּם
הֲקִימוֹת	הֲקִימוֹתֶן	הֵקַמְתְּ	הֲקֵמְתֶּן
הֲקִימוֹתִי	הֲקִימוֹנוּ	הֵקַמְתִּי	הֵקַמְנוּ

Paradigm I is by far the more frequent.

The very common verb הֵבִיא (to bring; root בוא) is usually inflected according to paradigm II: הֵבִיא, הֵבִ֫יאָה, הֵבֵ֫אתָ, etc.

The imperfect and the remaining forms follow a single inflectional pattern; note the retraction of stress and the vowel replacement in the converted imperfect:

IMPERFECT:		JUSSIVE:		IMPERATIVE:
יָקִים	יָקִ֫ימוּ	יָקֵם	וַיָּ֫קָם	הָקֵם
תָּקִים	תְּקִימֶ֫ינָה	תָּקֵם	וַתָּ֫קָם	הָקִ֫ימִי
תָּקִים	תָּקִ֫ימוּ			הָקִ֫ימוּ
תָּקִ֫ימִי	תְּקִימֶ֫ינָה			——
אָקִים	נָקִים			

INF. CONSTRUCT: הָקִים, הֲקִימִ֫י, הֲקִימְךָ, etc.
INF. ABSOLUTE: הָקֵם
PARTICIPLE: מֵקִים, מְקִימָה, מְקִימִים, מְקִימוֹת

170. An Idiomatic Use of הָלַךְ.

In the example:

(a) וַיֵּ֫לֶךְ הָלוֹךְ וְאָכוֹל   And he walked along eating.

the inf. absolute הָלוֹךְ is used in accordance with the construction studied in §129 and may be taken as modifying or supplementing the main verb of the clause, with which it is cognate. But in

(b) וַיָּשֻׁ֫בוּ הַמַּ֫יִם הָלוֹךְ וָשׁוֹב   And the waters receded *gradually* (Gen. 8:3)

the idiomatic use of הָלוֹךְ is clear, since a literal translation is impossible. More explicitly, if the first of two infinitives absolute in the construction instanced above is הָלוֹךְ, there is a nuance of continuous or gradual action.

Closely related to this is a parallel use of the participle הֹלֵךְ; the basic idiom is:

subject + הֹלֵךְ + { a second participle / an adjective }

(c) הַיָּם הֹלֵךְ וְסֹעֵר   The sea (was) growing more and more tempestuous.

(d) דָּוִד הֹלֵךְ וְגָדוֹל   David was growing more and more important.

Now, in transforming a participial clause into a verbal one, the usual result is (for past tense):

הָאִישׁ הֹלֵךְ →	וַיֵּ֫לֶךְ הָאִישׁ
The man is going.	The man went.

This same transformation was applied to the idiom cited in (c) and (d):

(e) וַיֵּלֶךְ הַיָּם הָלוֹךְ וְסָעֵר The sea grew more and more tempestuous.

(f) וַיֵּלֶךְ דָּוִד הָלוֹךְ וְגָדוֹל David grew more and more important.

The verb הָלַךְ is taken as the main verb and is repeated, now as an infinitive absolute in the manner of (b) above to express the idea of continuity. But although (e) and (f) correspond to (b) in construction, their meaning can be gained only from a knowledge of the idiom in (c) and (d): "the sea grew..." and *not* "the sea went..."; "David grew (or became)..." and *not* "David went...".

As a further example take the sentence:

(g) וַתֵּלֶךְ יַד בְּנֵי־יִשְׂרָאֵל הָלוֹךְ וְקָשָׁה עַל־מֶלֶךְ כְּנָעַן (cf. Judges 4:24)

Assuming a basic idiomatic construction:

*(g) יַד בְּנֵי־יִשְׂרָאֵל הֹלֶכֶת וְקָשָׁה עַל־מֶלֶךְ כְּנָעַן

the obvious translation (and the correct one) of (g) is "The strength of the Israelites grew more and more severe against the king of Canaan."

These constructions, though not too frequent, are troublesome unless understood properly.

171. Vocabulary 47.

VERBS: זָנָה (יִזְנֶה) to be a prostitute; to act wantonly. זֹנָה a prostitute.

מִהַר (יְמַהֵר) to hurry; the inf. abs. מַהֵר is used as an adverb: quickly.

עָרַךְ (יַעֲרֹךְ) to arrange, set in order; draw up (in battle array).

הֶחֱרִים (יַחֲרִים) to destroy, exterminate (often as a religious act of banning).

הֵכִין (יָכִין) to make ready, prepare; establish (cf. נָכוֹן).

הֵבִין (יָבִין) to perceive, consider, understand; to cause to understand (cf. בִּינָה).

הֵסִיר (יָסִיר) to remove, take away, turn away (tr.) (cf. סָר).

נָח (יָנוּחַ) to rest; to settle down. There are two Hiphil verbs related to this Qal verb: (1) הֵנִיחַ (יָנִיחַ) to cause to rest, set at rest; (2) הִנִּיחַ (יַנִּיחַ) to set down, deposit, leave alone.

רָם (יָרוּם) to be high, lofty; הֵרִים (יָרִים) to lift up, lift off.

הֵשִׁיב (יָשִׁיב) to bring (lead, take) back (cf. שָׁב)

הֵבִיא (יָבִיא) to bring (cf. בָּא)

NOUNS: גָּג (w. suff. גַּגִּי; pl. *ôṯ*) roof

PROPER NAMES: יְהוֹשֻׁעַ בִּן־נוּן Joshua, the son of Nun.

יְרִחוֹ Jericho, an important city at the lower end of the Jordan valley.

שִׁטִּים an unidentified site across the Jordan from Jericho, where the Israelites camped before crossing the river.

רָחָב Rahab, a prostitute in Jericho.

סִיחֹן Síhon, a king of Heshbon (east of the Jordan) whom, together with Og, king of Bashan, the Israelites defeated in their passage to Canaan.

עוֹג Og (see Síhon above).

Exercises:

(a) Translate:

(1) הָבֵא אֹתוֹ הֵנָּה.
(2) הַנַּח אֹתוֹ שָׁם.
(3) הָסִירוּ אֹתוֹ מֵעַל הַשֻּׁלְחָן.
(4) הָכִינוּ לִי מְעַט לֶאֱכֹל.
(5) הַנִּיחוּ אֶת־סְפָרַי פֹּה.
(6) הָשֵׁב אֹתָם אֵלַי.
(7) הָנַח לָנוּ.
(8) הָרִימוּ אֶת־הָאֲבָנִים.
(9) הָבִיאִי אֵלֵינוּ מַיִם וְלֶחֶם.
(10) מַהֲרוּ כִּי הֵמָּה רֹדְפִים אַחֲרֵינוּ.

(b) Negate each of the imperative sentences in (a): Ex. אַל־תָּבִיא (תָּבֵא) אֹתוֹ הֵנָּה

(c) Translate:

(1) הֵבֵאתִי אֶת־מִנְחָתִי.
(2) הֵסִירוּ אֶת־פְּנֵיהֶם.
(3) הֲכִינוֹתִי אֶת־הַבַּיִת לָכֶם.
(4) הִנַּחְנוּ אֶת־הַזָּהָב אֵצֶל הַכֵּלִים.
(5) הֵבִין אֶת־דִּבְרֵי הַחֻקִּים.
(6) הֲרִימוֹתִי אֶת־קוֹלִי וָאֵבְךְּ.
(7) הֵשִׁיב אֹתָנוּ אֶל־אַרְצֵנוּ.
(8) הֶחֱרִימוּ אֶת־עָרֵי הָאֹיְבִים.
(9) עָרַכְנוּ אֶת־הָאֲבָנִים עַל־שְׂפַת הַנָּהָר.
(10) מִהֲרָה לִקְרָאתִי.

(d) Convert each of the sentences in (c) to a sequential form: Ex.וָאָבִיא אֶת־מִנְחָתִי.

(e) Translate:

(1) יהוה בַּשָּׁמַיִם הֵכִין כִּסְאוֹ.
(2) וְגַם אֶל־שֹׁפְטֵיהֶם לֹא שָׁמֵעוּ כִּי זָנוּ אַחֲרֵי אֱלֹהִים אֲחֵרִים.
(3) אֵיפֹה הִנַּחְתָּ אֶת־כְּלֵי הַמִּזְבֵּחַ.
(4) יִרְאֶה הָעָם בְּעֵינָיו וּבְאָזְנָיו יִשְׁמַע וּלְבָבוֹ יָבִין וְשָׁב אֵלַי.
(5) וַיְהִי כַּהֲרִימוֹ אֶת־מַטֵּהוּ וַיִּדֹּם הָעָם.
(6) מַדּוּעַ לֹא תָשִׁיב אֹתָנוּ אֶל־עִירֵנוּ וְאֶל־עַמֵּנוּ.
(7) סוּרוּ מִדֶּרֶךְ הָרְשָׁעִים וְשִׁמְרוּ אֶת־תּוֹרוֹתַי אֶת־חֻקּוֹתַי וְאֶת־מִצְוֹתַי לַעֲשׂוֹת אוֹתָן כָּל־יְמֵי חַיֵּיכֶם.
(8) אָז תָּבִין צֶדֶק וּמִשְׁפָּט כִּי תָבוֹא חָכְמָה בְלִבְּךָ וְהָיִיתָ לְאִישׁ יָשָׁר.
(9) לֹא הֵבִינוּ אֶת־עֲצָתִי וְלֹא שָׁמְעוּ בְּקוֹלִי.
(10) יַעַן אֲשֶׁר הֲרִימוֹתִי אֹתְךָ מִתּוֹךְ הָעָם וָאֶתֵּן אֹתְךָ רֹאשׁ עַל־עַמִּי וְלֹא הָיִיתָ כְּעַבְדִּי דָוִד אֲשֶׁר שָׁמַר אֶת־מִצְוֹתַי וַאֲשֶׁר הָלַךְ אַחֲרַי בְּכָל־לְבָבוֹ לַעֲשׂוֹת רַק הַיָּשָׁר בְּעֵינָי, וַתַּעַשׂ הָרַע בְּעֵינַי וְאוֹתִי הִשְׁלַכְתָּ אַחֲרֶיךָ הִנְנִי מֵבִיא רָעָה עַל־בֵּיתְךָ וּבִעַרְתִּי אַחֲרֶיךָ עַד־תֻּמְּךָ.

(f) Translate into Hebrew:

1. He will give rest to his people when he has settled them in the new city.
2. I brought them to the place I had prepared for them and left them there.
3. Where did the men prepare the camp?
4. I shall go with you and give you rest.
5. Do not raise your voice lest they hear and come and slay us.
6. As he led us into exile, thus will he bring us back.
7. He will teach us many new songs so that we may give thanks to the Lord.

(g) Reading: Rahab and the Spies (Joshua 2:1–11).

(1) וַיִּשְׁלַח יְהוֹשֻׁעַ בִּן־נוּן מִן־הַשִּׁטִּים שְׁנַיִם אֲנָשִׁים מְרַגְּלִים חֶרֶשׁ[1] לֵאמֹר לְכוּ רְאוּ אֶת־
הָאָרֶץ וְאֶת־יְרִיחוֹ וַיֵּלְכוּ וַיָּבֹאוּ בֵּית אִשָּׁה זוֹנָה וּשְׁמָהּ רָחָב וַיִּשְׁכְּבוּ־שָׁמָּה׃
(2) וַיֵּאָמַר לְמֶלֶךְ יְרִיחוֹ לֵאמֹר הִנֵּה אֲנָשִׁים בָּאוּ הֵנָּה הַלַּיְלָה מִבְּנֵי יִשְׂרָאֵל לַחְפֹּר[2] אֶת־הָאָרֶץ׃
(3) וַיִּשְׁלַח מֶלֶךְ יְרִיחוֹ אֶל־רָחָב לֵאמֹר הוֹצִיאִי הָאֲנָשִׁים הַבָּאִים אֵלַיִךְ אֲשֶׁר־בָּאוּ לְבֵיתֵךְ
כִּי לַחְפֹּר אֶת־כָּל־הָאָרֶץ בָּאוּ׃
(4) וַתִּקַּח הָאִשָּׁה אֶת־שְׁנֵי הָאֲנָשִׁים וַתִּצְפְּנוֹ[3] וַתֹּאמֶר כֵּן בָּאוּ אֵלַי הָאֲנָשִׁים וְלֹא יָדַעְתִּי
מֵאַיִן הֵמָּה׃
(5) וַיְהִי הַשַּׁעַר לִסְגּוֹר בַּחֹשֶׁךְ וְהָאֲנָשִׁים יָצָאוּ לֹא יָדַעְתִּי אָנָה הָלְכוּ הָאֲנָשִׁים רִדְפוּ מַהֵר
אַחֲרֵיהֶם כִּי תַשִּׂיגוּם׃[4]
(6) וְהִיא הֶעֱלָתַם[5] הַגָּגָה וַתִּטְמְנֵם[6] בְּפִשְׁתֵּי הָעֵץ[7] הָעֲרֻכוֹת לָהּ עַל־הַגָּג׃
(7) וְהָאֲנָשִׁים רָדְפוּ אַחֲרֵיהֶם דֶּרֶךְ[8] הַיַּרְדֵּן עַל הַמַּעְבְּרוֹת[9] וְהַשַּׁעַר סָגָרוּ אַחֲרֵי כַּאֲשֶׁר יָצְאוּ
הָרֹדְפִים אַחֲרֵיהֶם׃
(8) וְהֵמָּה טֶרֶם יִשְׁכָּבוּן וְהִיא עָלְתָה עֲלֵיהֶם עַל־הַגָּג׃
(9) וַתֹּאמֶר אֶל־הָאֲנָשִׁים יָדַעְתִּי כִּי־נָתַן יהוה לָכֶם אֶת־הָאָרֶץ וְכִי נָפְלָה אֵימַתְכֶם עָלֵינוּ
וְכִי נָמֹגוּ[10] כָּל־יֹשְׁבֵי הָאָרֶץ מִפְּנֵיכֶם׃
(10) כִּי שָׁמַעְנוּ אֵת[11] אֲשֶׁר־הוֹבִישׁ[12] יהוה אֶת־מֵי יַם־סוּף[13] מִפְּנֵיכֶם בְּצֵאתְכֶם מִמִּצְרָיִם וַאֲשֶׁר[14]
עֲשִׂיתֶם לִשְׁנֵי מַלְכֵי הָאֱמֹרִי[15] אֲשֶׁר בְּעֵבֶר[16] הַיַּרְדֵּן לְסִיחֹן וּלְעוֹג אֲשֶׁר הֶחֱרַמְתֶּם אוֹתָם׃
(11) וַנִּשְׁמַע וַיִּמַּס לְבָבֵנוּ וְלֹא קָמָה עוֹד רוּחַ בְּאִישׁ מִפְּנֵיכֶם כִּי יהוה אֱלֹהֵיכֶם הוּא אֱלֹהִים
בַּשָּׁמַיִם מִמַּעַל וְעַל־הָאָרֶץ מִתָּחַת׃

(to be continued)

Notes to the Reading:

1. A difficult word, probably meaning "secretly"
2. חָפַר to dig, search out, explore
3. "and she hid them" (צָפַן to hide)
4. תַּשִּׂיגוּ אֹתָם = תַּשִּׂיגוּם
5. הֶעֱלְתָה אֹתָם = הֶעֱלָתַם
6. "and she hid them" (טָמַן to hide)
7. "stalks of flax" lit. "flax (פִּשְׁתִּים) of the tree". Note that פִּשְׁתִּים is feminine
8. Often used thus without a preposition in the meaning "by way of"

9. "as far as the fords" (sing. מַעְבָּרָה)
10. "(they) have melted away"
11. אֵת marks the אֲשֶׁר clause as the object of שָׁמַעְנוּ.
12. הוֹבִישׁ to dry up (root יבשׁ cf. יַבָּשָׁה)
13. יַם־סוּף The Red Sea; lit. "sea of reeds"
14. "that which"
15. Amorite
16. עֵבֶר the other side

LESSON 48

172. Hiphil Verbs: Stems and Inflection (concluded).

Hiphil verbs from geminate roots have the following stems:

Root Type	Perfect	Imperfect	Converted Impf.	Imperative	Inf. Constr.
Geminate Also II/III-gutt.	הֵסֵב הֵרַע	יָסֵב יָרַע	וַיָּ֫סֶב וַיָּרַע	הָסֵב הָרַע	הָסֵב הָרַע

Inf. Abs.	Participle
הָסֵב הָרֵעַ	מֵסֵב מֵרַע

Note the general (but not consistent) replacement of *ē* by *a* in the final stem syllable before a guttural. In inflection the *ē* appears before the guttural whenever the non-guttural counterpart has *i*:

PERFECT

הֵסֵב	הֵסַ֫בּוּ	הֵרַע	הֵרַ֫עוּ
הֵסַ֫בָּה		הֵרַ֫עָה	
הֲסִבּ֫וֹתָ	הֲסִבּוֹתֶם	הֲרֵע֫וֹתָ	הֲרֵעוֹתֶם
הֲסִבּ֫וֹת	הֲסִבּוֹתֶן	הֲרֵעוֹת	הֲרֵעוֹתֶן
הֲסִבּ֫וֹתִי	הֲסִבּ֫וֹנוּ	הֲרֵע֫וֹתִי	הֲרֵע֫וֹנוּ

IMPERFECT

יָסֵב	יָסֵבּוּ	יָרַע	יָרֵעוּ
תָּסֵב	תְּסִבֶּינָה	תָּרַע	תְּרֵעֶינָה
תָּסֵב	תָּסֵבּוּ	תָּרַע	תָּרֵעוּ
תָּסֵבִּי	תְּסִבֶּינָה	תָּרֵעִי	תְּרֵעֶינָה
אָסֵב	נָסֵב	אָרַע	נָרַע

IMPERATIVE

הָסֵב	הָסֵבּוּ	הָרַע	הָרֵעוּ
הָסֵבִּי	(הֲסִבֶּינָה)	הָרֵעִי	(הֲרֵעֶינָה)

INF. CONSTRUCT

הָסֵב	הָרַע
הֲסִבִּי	הֲרֵעִי
הֲסִבְּךָ	הֲרֵעֲךָ

PARTICIPLE

מֵסֵב	מְסִבִּים	מֵרַע	מְרֵעִים
מְסִבָּה	מְסִבּוֹת	מְרֵעָה	מְרֵעוֹת

Deviant forms are attested, most frequently those showing a doubling of the first root consonant, such as יַסֵּב (for יָסֵב). Compare the similar confusion in Qal verbs from these same roots (§126).

173. Verbal Hendiadys and Related Idioms.

In the construction

וַיָּשָׁב וַיֵּבְךְּ and he wept again

the two verbs are simply coordinated, both having the form as required by the narrative sequence in which they occur, but in meaning the first serves to qualify the second and is best translated adverbially in English. The verbs most commonly used in this way in Hebrew are:

- שָׁב to do something again
- הוֹסִיף to do something again
- הוֹאִיל to do something willingly, voluntarily; to be content to do; the imperative is virtually equivalent to "please"
- מִהַר to do something quickly
- הִשְׁכִּים to do something early in the day
- הִרְבָּה to do something much or a lot

Examples:

וַיֹּסֶף אַבְרָהָם וַיִּקַּח אִשָּׁה (Gen. 25:1) And Abraham took another wife.

לוּ הוֹאַלְנוּ וַנֵּשֶׁב בְּעֵבֶר הַיַּרְדֵּן (Joshua 7:7) Would that we had been content to dwell on the other side of the Jordan.

וַיָּשָׁב וַיָּלֶן שָׁם (Judges 19:7) And he again spent the night there.

וּמִהַרְתֶּם וְהוֹרַדְתֶּם אֶת־אָבִי הֵנָּה (Gen. 45:13) And you shall quickly bring my father down here.

וְהִשְׁכַּמְתֶּם וַהֲלַכְתֶּם לְדַרְכְּכֶם (Gen. 19:2) And early in the morning you will go on your way.

The two verbs may have no conjunction between them. This construction, termed asyndetic, is common with imperative, rare with narrative forms:

אָשׁוּבָה אֶרְעֶה צֹאנְךָ (Gen. 30:31) I will again tend your sheep.

שׁוּב שְׁכַב (I Sam. 3:5) Lie down again.

אוֹסִיף אֲבַקְשֶׁנּוּ עוֹד (Prov. 23:35) I will again search for him.

כִּי הוֹאִיל הָלַךְ אַחֲרֵי־צָו (Hosea 5:11) For he has willingly gone after filth.

הוֹאֵל קַח כִּכָּרָיִם (II Kings 5:23) Be content to take two talents.

מָה רְאִיתֶם עָשִׂיתִי מַהֲרוּ עֲשׂוּ כָמוֹנִי (Judges 9:48) What you have seen me do quickly do likewise.

Most of these same verbs may also occur with a following complementary infinitive usually with לְ:

כִּי יָשׁוּב יהוה לָשׂוּשׂ עָלֶיךָ (Deut. 30:9) For the Lord will again rejoice over you.

וַיּוֹאֶל מֹשֶׁה לָשֶׁבֶת אֶת־הָאִישׁ (Ex. 2:21) And Moses was content to stay with the man.

וַיְמַהֵר לַעֲשׂוֹת אֹתוֹ (Gen. 18:7) And he quickly prepared it.

מַהֲרוּ לָלֶכֶת (II Sam. 15:14) Go quickly.

The two verbs may function together in complementary usage after another verb:

לֹא יוּכַל... לָשׁוּב לְקַחְתָּהּ (Deut. 24:4) He will not be able to take her back again.

Rarely more than one may appear before the main verb:

וַיְמַהֲרוּ וַיַּשְׁכִּימוּ וַיֵּצְאוּ (Joshua 8:14) And early in the morning they went forth quickly...

The verbs קָם and הָלַךְ, especially the former, are employed in a similar construction where a literal translation is awkward or impossible. וַיָּקָם so used seems to do little more than give a slight emphasis to the fact that some activity is about to begin, corresponding to English "then, thereupon;" the imperative often corresponds to "come, come now, so." E.g.

קוּם־נָא שְׁבָה (Gen. 27:19) Come now and sit... (hardly "arise and sit...").

קוּם עֲשֵׂה־לָנוּ אֱלֹהִים (Ex. 32:1) Come, make for us a god who...

174. Vocabulary 48.

VERBS: הֵרַע (root רעע) to injure, hurt (dir. obj. or with לְ/בְּ); to act wickedly, badly.

הֵסֵב (root סבב) to turn, turn away, turn around (all trans.); to cause to go around.

הֵחֵל (root חלל) to begin (usually followed by a complementary inf.).

הֵפֵר (root פרר) to break, vitiate, annul.

הִשְׁכִּים to do something early in the day (see §173).

הוֹאִיל to be willing or content to do something (see §173).

נִשְׁבַּע (Niphal) to swear (an oath); to promise (something) by an oath.

הִשְׁבִּיעַ (Hiphil) to cause to take an oath.

חִיָּה (Piel) to let live, to revive, restore to life.

הֶחֱיָה (Hiphil) idem (not used in the imperfect).

פָּגַע (יִפְגַּע) to meet, encounter (with dir. obj. or בְּ).

NOUNS: שְׁבוּעָה (pl. -*ôṯ*) oath

חוֹמָה (pl. -*ôṯ*) wall of a city.

דֶּלֶת (w. suff. דַּלְתִּי; dual דְּלָתַיִם; pl. דְּלָתוֹת) door (of house or room).

PREPOSITIONS: בְּעַד through. The translation of this preposition varies widely. After verbs of prayer or entreaty it has the meaning "for, on behalf of." Note its use with verbs of closing:

וַיִּסְגְּרוּ בַּעֲדָם and they shut themselves in

סָגַר יהוה בְּעַד רַחְמָהּ the Lord had closed up her womb

It also has the sense of "around, surrounding" as in

וְאַתָּה מָגֵן בַּעֲדִי You are a shield surrounding me.

עַל־יַד beside, in the company of, to the side of.

Exercises:

(a) Translate:

(1) הֲפֵרוֹתִי אֶת־מִצְוָתוֹ.

(2) לֹא נָתַן אֹתוֹ יהוה לְהָרַע עִמָּדִי.

(3) וַיַּעַשׂ הַמֶּלֶךְ הָרַע בְּעֵינֵי יהוה וַיָּרַע מִכֹּל אֲשֶׁר לְפָנָיו.

(4) הֵחֵלּוּ לִבְכּוֹת וְלִקְרֹעַ אֶת־בִּגְדֵיהֶם.

(5) וַתָּחֶל לִזְנוֹת וּלְהָרַע.

(6) וַיָּפֶר אֶת־בְּרִיתוֹ עִמִּי.

(7) יָחֵלּוּ לְהָבִין בְּדַבְּרִי אֲלֵיהֶם.

(8) יֵרָעוּ דִבְרֵיהֶם כִּי יָרֵעוּ.

(9) הַחִלּוֹנוּ לַעֲרֹךְ מִלְחָמָה.

(10) וַיָּסֶב אֶת־עֵינָיו מֵהַמַּרְאֶה.

(b) Translate into Hebrew using the constructions treated in §173.

1. and we shall bring again.
2. they were content to rest.
3. I arranged it quickly.
4. and early in the day he removed them.
5. and he struck him again.
6. and he prepared again.
7. and they quickly brought it.
8. be content to bring them back.

(c) Translate:

(1) וַיַּשְׁכֵּם וַיַּעֲמֹד עַל־יַד דֶּרֶךְ הַשַּׁעַר.
(2) וַיִּשְׁלַח הַמֶּלֶךְ לֵאמֹר לֵךְ פְּגַע בּוֹ וְהִכִּיתָ אֹתוֹ וְיָמוֹת.
(3) וְהָאִישׁ מִהַר וַיָּבֹא וַיַּגֵּד אֶת־הַדְּבָרִים לַכֹּהֵן.
(4) וְהָיָה בְּסֹבֵּנוּ אֶת־הָעִיר וְנָפְלָה חוֹמָתָהּ.
(5) הִרְבָּה לַעֲשׂוֹת הָרַע בְּעֵינֵי יהוה.
(6) וַיָּבֹאוּ הַבַּיִת וַיִּסְגְּרוּ אֶת־הַדֶּלֶת בַּעֲדָם.
(7) וַיַּשְׁכֵּם דָּוִד הוּא וַאֲנָשָׁיו לָלֶכֶת בַּבֹּקֶר לָשׁוּב אֶל־הָאָרֶץ הַהִיא.
(8) בַּיּוֹם הַהוּא יְחַיֶּה אֶת־הַמֵּתִים וְלֹא יִהְיֶה עוֹד הַמָּוֶת.
(9) מַהֲרוּ לָלֶכֶת פֶּן־יְמַהֵר וְהִשִּׂיג אֹתָנוּ.
(10) הֲלֹא נִשְׁבַּעְתִּי לָכֶם כִּי אֱלֹהִים אִתְּכֶם. לָמָּה לֹא הֶאֱמַנְתֶּם אֶת־דִּבְרֵי שְׁבוּעָתִי.
(11) הוֹאַלְתָּ לְבָרֵךְ אֶת־בֵּית עַבְדְּךָ לִהְיוֹת לְעוֹלָם.
(12) וַתַּשְׁבַּע אֹתָם כִּי לֹא יִרְצְחוּ אֹתָהּ וְאֶת־בֵּית אָבִיהָ.

(d) Reading: Joshua 2:12–24. Rahab and the Spies (concluded).

(12) וְעַתָּה הִשָּׁבְעוּ־נָא לִי בַּיהוה כִּי־עָשִׂיתִי עִמָּכֶם חָסֶד וַעֲשִׂיתֶם גַּם־אַתֶּם עִם־בֵּית אָבִי חֶסֶד
וּנְתַתֶּם לִי אוֹת אֱמֶת:
(13) וְהַחֲיִתֶם אֶת־אָבִי וְאֶת־אִמִּי וְאֶת־אַחַי וְאֶת־אַחְיוֹתַי[1] וְאֵת כָּל־אֲשֶׁר לָהֶם וְהִצַּלְתֶּם אֶת־
נַפְשֹׁתֵינוּ מִמָּוֶת:
(14) וַיֹּאמְרוּ לָהּ הָאֲנָשִׁים נַפְשֵׁנוּ תַחְתֵּיכֶם לָמוּת[2] אִם לֹא תַגִּידוּ אֶת־דְּבָרֵנוּ זֶה[3] וְהָיָה בְּתֵת־
יהוה לָנוּ אֶת־הָאָרֶץ וְעָשִׂינוּ עִמָּךְ חֶסֶד וֶאֱמֶת:
(15) וַתּוֹרִדֵם[4] בַּחֶבֶל[5] בְּעַד הַחַלּוֹן[6] כִּי בֵיתָהּ בְּקִיר הַחוֹמָה וּבַחוֹמָה הִיא יוֹשָׁבֶת:
(16) וַתֹּאמֶר לָהֶם הָהָרָה לֵּכוּ פֶּן־יִפְגְּעוּ בָכֶם הָרֹדְפִים וְנַחְבֵּתֶם[7] שָׁמָּה שְׁלֹשֶׁת יָמִים עַד שׁוֹב[8]
הָרֹדְפִים וְאַחַר[9] תֵּלְכוּ לְדַרְכְּכֶם:
(17) וַיֹּאמְרוּ אֵלֶיהָ הָאֲנָשִׁים נְקִיִּם[10] אֲנַחְנוּ מִשְּׁבֻעָתֵךְ הַזֶּה אֲשֶׁר הִשְׁבַּעְתָּנוּ:
(18) הִנֵּה אֲנַחְנוּ בָאִים בָּאָרֶץ אֶת־תִּקְוַת חוּט הַשָּׁנִי הַזֶּה[11] תִּקְשְׁרִי בַּחַלּוֹן אֲשֶׁר הוֹרַדְתֵּנוּ[12] בוֹ
וְאֶת־אָבִיךְ וְאֶת־אִמֵּךְ וְאֶת־אַחַיִךְ וְאֵת כָּל־בֵּית אָבִיךְ תַּאַסְפִי אֵלַיִךְ הַבָּיְתָה:
(19) וְהָיָה כֹּל אֲשֶׁר־יֵצֵא מִדַּלְתֵי בֵיתֵךְ הַחוּצָה דָּמוֹ בְרֹאשׁוֹ וַאֲנַחְנוּ נְקִיִּם וְכֹל אֲשֶׁר יִהְיֶה
אִתָּךְ בַּבַּיִת דָּמוֹ בְרֹאשֵׁנוּ אִם־יָד תִּהְיֶה־בּוֹ:
(20) וְאִם־תַּגִּידִי אֶת־דְּבָרֵנוּ זֶה וְהָיִינוּ נְקִיִּם מִשְּׁבֻעָתֵךְ אֲשֶׁר הִשְׁבַּעְתָּנוּ:[13]
(21) וַתֹּאמֶר כְּדִבְרֵיכֶם כֶּן־הוּא וַתְּשַׁלְּחֵם[14] וַיֵּלֵכוּ וַתִּקְשֹׁר אֶת־תִּקְוַת הַשָּׁנִי בַּחַלּוֹן:

(22) וַיֵּלְכוּ וַיָּבֹאוּ הָהָרָה וַיֵּשְׁבוּ שָׁם שְׁלֹשֶׁת יָמִים עַד־שָׁבוּ הָרֹדְפִים וַיְבַקְשׁוּ הָרֹדְפִים בְּכָל־
הַדֶּרֶךְ וְלֹא מָצָאוּ׃
(23) וַיָּשֻׁבוּ שְׁנֵי הָאֲנָשִׁים וַיֵּרְדוּ מֵהָהָר וַיַּעַבְרוּ וַיָּבֹאוּ אֶל־יְהוֹשֻׁעַ בִּן־נוּן וַיְסַפְּרוּ־לוֹ אֵת כָּל־
הַמֹּצְאוֹת[15] אוֹתָם׃
(24) וַיֹּאמְרוּ אֶל־יְהוֹשֻׁעַ כִּי־נָתַן יהוה בְּיָדֵנוּ אֶת־כָּל־הָאָרֶץ וְגַם־נָמֹגוּ[16] כָּל־יֹשְׁבֵי הָאָרֶץ
מִפָּנֵינוּ׃

Notes to the reading:

1. "my sisters"
2. "our lives in exchange for yours"
3. Note the absence of the article on זֶה.
4. וַתֹּורֶד אֹתָם = וַתּוֹרִדֵם
5. חֶבֶל a rope
6. חַלּוֹן a window
7. נַחְבֵּאתֶם = נַחְבֵּתֶם from נֶחְבָּא to hide (oneself)
8. שָׁב alternate inf. construct for שׁוּב
9. Take adverbially as "afterwards".
10. נָקִי innocent, guiltless. Verse 17 seems to be displaced; see vs. 20 below.
11. "this line of scarlet thread"
12. הוֹרַדְתְּ אֹתָנוּ = הוֹרַדְתֵּנוּ
13. הִשְׁבַּעְתְּ אֹתָנוּ = הִשְׁבַּעְתָּנוּ
14. וַתְּשַׁלַּח אֹתָם = וַתְּשַׁלְּחֵם
15. in the sense "befall"
16. "they have melted away"

LESSON 49

175. The Hophal.

As in the Piel-Pual relationship, there is for each Hiphil verb a passive counterpart of the type called Hophal. The form is characterized by an *u*-vowel in the first stem syllable and *a* in the second. The exact nature of the first vowel depends on the root type, as is seen from the following synopsis:

Root Type	Hiphil Verb	Hophal		
	Perfect	Perfect	Imperfect	Participle
Regular	הִשְׁמִיד	הָשְׁמַד	יָשְׁמַד	מָשְׁמָד
I-gutt.	הֶעֱמִיד	הָעֳמַד	יָעֳמַד	מָעֳמָד
I-*Nun*	הִגִּיד	הֻגַּד	יֻגַּד	מֻגָּד
III-*Aleph*	הִמְצִיא	הָמְצָא	יָמְצָא	מָמְצָא
I-*Yodh/Waw*	הוֹרִיד	הוּרַד	יוּרַד	מוּרָד
III-*Hē*	הִבְנָה	הָבְנָה	יָבְנֶה	מָבְנֶה
Hollow	הֵקִים	הוּקַם	יוּקַם	מוּקָם
Geminate	הֵסֵב	הוּסַב	יוּסַב	מוּסָב

The following samples of their inflection will suffice for the remainder:

PERFECT

הָשְׁמַד	הָעֳמַד		הָבְנָה	הוּקַם
הָשְׁמְדָה	הָעָמְדָה	(*hoʻom-*)	הָבְנְתָה	הוּקְמָה
הָשְׁמַדְתָּ...	הָעֳמַדְתָּ...		הָבְנֵיתָ...	הוּקַמְתָּ...

IMPERFECT

...יָשְׁמַד	יָעֳמַד	יָבְנֶה	יוּקַם
...תָּשְׁמְדִי	תָּעָמְדִי *(to'om-)*	תָּבְנִי	תּוּקְמִי
...תָּשְׁמַדְנָה	תָּעֳמַדְנָה	תָּבְנֶינָה	תּוּקַמְנָה

PARTICIPLE

מָשְׁמָד	מָעֳמָד	מָבְנֶה	מוּקָם
מָשְׁמָדָה / מָשְׁמֶדֶת	מָעֳמָדָה / מָעֳמֶדֶת	מָבְנָה	מוּקָמָה / מוּקֶמֶת
מָשְׁמָדִים	מָעֳמָדִים	מָבְנִים	מוּקָמִים
מָשְׁמָדוֹת	מָעֳמָדוֹת	מָבְנוֹת	מוּקָמוֹת

As the passive of the Hiphil, the Hophal offers no problems in translation when the Hiphil is a simply transitive verb:

הִשְׁמִיד	he destroyed	הָשְׁמַד	he was destroyed
הִשְׁלִיךְ	he threw	הָשְׁלַךְ	he was thrown
הוֹרִיד	he brought down	הוּרַד	he was brought down

But when the Hiphil verb is capable of a double object construction, it is the causative portion of the meaning which is rendered passive in the Hophal:

הֶרְאָה אֶת־הָאִישׁ אֶת־הָאוֹר He showed the man the light. (lit. he *caused the man* to see the light).

הָרְאָה הָאִישׁ אֶת־הָאוֹר The man was shown the light. (lit. *the man was caused* to see the light).

הֶעֱבִיר אֶת־הָעָם אֶת־הַנָּהָר He brought the people across the river.

הָעֳבַר הָעָם אֶת־הַנָּהָר The people were brought across the river.

Or, when one of the two possible objects is omitted (cf. §157a):

הֶעֱבִיר אֶת־הָעָם He led the people across.

הָעֳבַר הָעָם The people were led across.

הֶרְאָה אֶת־הָאוֹר He showed the light. (lit. he *caused the light* to be seen)

הָרְאָה הָאוֹר The light was shown. (lit. *the light was caused* to be seen).

Note, too, the impersonal construction with the retention of אֶת (cf. §154 end):

הֻגַּד לוֹ אֶת־הַדְּבָרִים He was told the words.

176. Vocabulary 49.

VERBS:	מָשַׁל	(יִמְשֹׁל)	to rule, have dominion over (obj. with בְּ)
	יָשַׁר	(יִישַׁר)	to be pleasing, agreeable
	קָצַף	(יִקְצֹף)	to be(come) angry (עַל against)
	שָׁכַן	(יִשְׁכֹּן)	to settle down, dwell
	חָזַק	(יֶחֱזַק)	to become strong, firm, hard
	הָגָה	(יֶהְגֶּה)	to mutter, roar, moan, sigh; to meditate, imagine

NOUNS: אַרְיֵה (no pl.) } lion
אֲרִי (pl. אֲרָיוֹת) } lion
עֵת (w. suff. עִתִּי; pl. *-îm* or *-ôṯ*) time, appointed time (f.).
גְּדִי (pl. גְּדָיִים; constr. גְּדָיֵי) kid
עֵדָה (no pl.) congregation, assembly
בָּחוּר (pl. irreg. בַּחוּרִים) young man

OTHER: עָרֵל (adj.) uncircumcised; (fig.) inept, deficient
עַל־כֵּן (adv.) therefore

PROPER NAMES: שִׁמְשׁוֹן Samson
תִּמְנָתָה Timnah (or Timnathah), a town held by the Philistines; exact location unknown
פְּלִשְׁתִּים The Philistines

Exercises:

(a) Transform each of the following sentences into the passive, replacing the Hiphil verb with the Hophal according to the example:

הֵבִיא אֶת־הָאִישׁ he brought the man → הוּבָא הָאִישׁ the man was brought

(1) הֵסִיר אֶת־הַכְּלִי מֵעַל הַמִּזְבֵּחַ.
(2) וַיַּכּוּ אֶת־הָאֲנָשִׁים.
(3) הוֹשִׁיב אֶת־הָעָם שָׁם.
(4) הוֹרִידָה אֶת־הָאֲנָשִׁים מִן־הַגָּג.
(5) הוֹצִיא אֶת־הָרְשָׁעִים חוּצָה.
(6) הֶעֱלָה אֶת־הַפָּרָה עַל־הַמִּזְבֵּחַ.
(7) הִגִּיד לוֹ אֶת־דִּבְרֵי הַסָּרִיס.
(8) הִשְׁלִיךְ אֶת־הָאִישׁ מֵעַל הַחוֹמָה.
(9) הֶרְאֵיתִי אֶתְכֶם נִפְלָאוֹת רַבּוֹת.
(10) וַיָּבֵא אֹתוֹ אֶל־הַהֵיכָל.

(b) Translate:

(1) הֻצַּלְנוּ
(2) הָעָמְדוּ
(3) הֻגְּשָׁה
(4) הָאִישׁ הַמּוּבָא
(5) הָעָם הַמָּגְלֶה
(6) הוּסַרְתִּי
(7) יוּכְלוּ
(8) הָעָם הַמּוּשָׁב
(9) הָעָבְדוּ
(10) הָאֲנָשִׁים הַמֻּכִּים
(11) יוּסְרוּ
(12) הַבְּרִית הַמּוּפָרָה

(c) Translate:

(1) הֲמָשֹׁל תִּמְשֹׁל בָּנוּ.
(2) אֶתֵּן אֹתָהּ לַאֲשֶׁר יָשַׁר בְּעֵינַי.
(3) וַיְהִי כִּרְאוֹתוֹ אֶת־הָאֲנָשִׁים וַיִּקְצֹף עֲלֵיהֶם.
(4) חָזַק הָרָעָב בְּכָל־הָאָרֶץ בָּעֵת הַהִיא.
(5) כַּאֲרִי אֶרְדֹּף אַחֲרֵי שֹׂנְאַי וַעֲלֵיהֶם אֶהְגֶּה כַּאֲשֶׁר יֶהְגֶּה אַרְיֵה.
(6) וַיִּישַׁר הַדָּבָר בְּעֵינֵי הַמֶּלֶךְ.
(7) חִזְקוּ וְאַל־תִּירְאוּ כִּי אֲנִי אִתְּכֶם.
(8) וּבְתוֹרַת יהוה יֶהְגֶּה יוֹמָם וָלָיְלָה.
(9) אַל־תִּקְצֹף עָלַי אָבִי כִּי לֹא חָטָאתִי לָךְ.
(10) מָשַׁל יוֹסֵף בְּכָל־אֶרֶץ מִצְרָיִם.
(11) וַיֶּחֱזַק לֵב פַּרְעֹה וַיְמָאֵן לְשַׁלַּח אֶת־הָעִבְרִיִּים.
(12) עַל־כֵּן לֹא יָקוּמוּ רְשָׁעִים בַּעֲדַת צַדִּיקִים.

(13) וְכֵן דִּבֶּר מֹשֶׁה אֶל־כָּל־עֲדַת יִשְׂרָאֵל.
(14) וַיִּטְבַּח אֶת־הַגְּדִי וַיָּשֶׂם אֹתוֹ מִנְחָה עַל־הַמִּזְבֵּחַ.

(d) Write in Hebrew:

1. The statute was annulled.
2. The work was begun but not finished.
3. He was made to swear that he would return early on the fourth day.
4. He fell from the wall and died.
5. He was taken outside the city and there was put to death (lit. was caused to die).
6. She stood beside the door until they had departed.

(e) Reading: Judges 14 : 1–10. Samson and the Riddle.

(1) וַיֵּרֶד שִׁמְשׁוֹן תִּמְנָתָה וַיַּרְא אִשָּׁה בְּתִמְנָתָה מִבְּנוֹת פְּלִשְׁתִּים׃
(2) וַיַּעַל וַיַּגֵּד לְאָבִיו וּלְאִמּוֹ וַיֹּאמֶר אִשָּׁה רָאִיתִי בְתִמְנָתָה מִבְּנוֹת פְּלִשְׁתִּים וְעַתָּה קְחוּ אוֹתָהּ
לִי לְאִשָּׁה׃
(3) וַיֹּאמֶר לוֹ אָבִיו וְאִמּוֹ הַאֵין בִּבְנוֹת אַחֶיךָ וּבְכָל־עַמִּי אִשָּׁה כִּי אַתָּה הוֹלֵךְ לָקַחַת אִשָּׁה
מִפְּלִשְׁתִּים הָעֲרֵלִים וַיֹּאמֶר שִׁמְשׁוֹן אֶל־אָבִיו אוֹתָהּ קַח־לִי כִּי־הִיא יָשְׁרָה בְעֵינָי׃
(4) וְאָבִיו וְאִמּוֹ לֹא יָדְעוּ כִּי מֵיהוה הִיא[1] כִּי־תֹאֲנָה[2] הוּא־מְבַקֵּשׁ מִפְּלִשְׁתִּים וּבָעֵת הַהִיא
פְּלִשְׁתִּים מֹשְׁלִים בְּיִשְׂרָאֵל׃
(5) וַיֵּרֶד שִׁמְשׁוֹן וְאָבִיו וְאִמּוֹ תִּמְנָתָה וַיָּבֹאוּ עַד־כַּרְמֵי תִמְנָתָה וְהִנֵּה כְּפִיר[3] אֲרָיוֹת שֹׁאֵג[4]
לִקְרָאתוֹ׃
(6) וַתִּצְלַח[5] עָלָיו רוּחַ יהוה וַיְשַׁסְּעֵהוּ[6] כְּשַׁסַּע הַגְּדִי וּמְאוּמָה אֵין בְּיָדוֹ וְלֹא הִגִּיד לְאָבִיו
וּלְאִמּוֹ אֵת אֲשֶׁר עָשָׂה׃
(7) וַיֵּרֶד וַיְדַבֵּר לָאִשָּׁה וַתִּישַׁר בְּעֵינֵי שִׁמְשׁוֹן׃
(8) וַיָּשָׁב מִיָּמִים לְקַחְתָּהּ[7] וַיָּסַר לִרְאוֹת אֵת מַפֶּלֶת[8] הָאַרְיֵה וְהִנֵּה עֲדַת דְּבֹרִים[9] בִּגְוִיַּת[10]
הָאַרְיֵה וּדְבָשׁ׃
(9) וַיִּרְדֵּהוּ[11] אֶל־כַּפָּיו וַיֵּלֶךְ הָלוֹךְ וְאָכֹל וַיֵּלֶךְ אֶל־אָבִיו וְאֶל־אִמּוֹ וַיִּתֵּן לָהֶם וַיֹּאכֵלוּ וְלֹא
הִגִּיד לָהֶם כִּי מִגְּוִיַּת הָאַרְיֵה רָדָה[12] הַדְּבָשׁ׃
(10) וַיֵּרֶד אָבִיהוּ אֶל־הָאִשָּׁה וַיַּעַשׂ שָׁם שִׁמְשׁוֹן מִשְׁתֶּה כִּי כֵּן יַעֲשׂוּ הַבַּחוּרִים׃

(to be concluded)

Notes to the Reading:

1. "that it (i.e. the situation) was the Lord's doing"
2. תֹּאֲנָה opportunity (for a quarrel)
3. כְּפִיר a young lion
4. שָׁאַג to roar
5. צָלַח to rush
6. שָׁסַע to rend, tear apart; "and he tore it apart"
7. The suffix is objective: "to take her"
8. מַפֶּלֶת carcass
9. דְּבוֹרָה (pl. *-îm*) bee(s)

10. גְּוִיָּה body
11. "and he scraped it"
12. "he had scraped"

LESSON 50

177. The Hithpael.

Relatively infrequent, Hithpael verbs are distinguished by the prefixal element *(h)iṯ-* and the doubling of the second root consonant.

Root Type	Perfect	Imperfect	Imperative	Inf. Construct	Participle
Regular	הִתְגַּדֵּל	יִתְגַּדֵּל	הִתְגַּדֵּל	הִתְגַּדֵּל	מִתְגַּדֵּל
III-*Hē*	הִתְגַּלָּה	יִתְגַּלֶּה	הִתְגַּלֵּה	הִתְגַּלּוֹת	מִתְגַּלֶּה
Geminate	הִתְפַּלֵּל	יִתְפַּלֵּל	הִתְפַּלֵּל	הִתְפַּלֵּל	מִתְפַּלֵּל

In regard to formation the following points should be noted:

(a) With roots beginning with a sibilant (צ שׂ שׁ ז ס) there is regularly a metathesis of this consonant and the ת of the prefix: **hiṯšammēr* > הִשְׁתַּמֵּר. A further assimilation takes place, wherein *-*zt*- > -*zd*-, as in **hiṯzakkēr* > **hiztakkēr* > הִזְדַּכֵּר; and *-*ṣt*- > -*ṣṭ*- as in **hiṯṣaddēq* > **hiṣtaddēq* > הִצְטַדֵּק. Other assimilations occur sporadically, as in הִנַּבֵּא for more regular הִתְנַבֵּא.

(b) With geminate roots the doubling of the middle root consonant is often given up, as in the Piel verb, when preceding a *ə*: הִתְחַנְנוּ for הִתְחַנְּנוּ.

(c) Roots II-gutt, show either compensatory lengthening or virtual doubling, as in the Piel. E.g. הִתְרָאָה but הִתְנַחֵם.

(d) The final stem syllable may have *a* instead of *ē*. This is normal before gutturals, optional elsewhere: הִתְוַדַּע, הִתְאַנַּף.

(e) With roots I-Waw/Yodh the original ו is sometimes preserved, as in הִתְוַכַּח (to argue) and הִתְוַדַּע (to make oneself known): contrast הִתְיַלֵּד (to declare or claim a pedigree) and הִתְיָעֵץ (to conspire against), both with י.

(f) Hollow roots seldom occur as Hithpael verbs.

(g) Vestiges of a closely related verb type without the doubling of the second root consonant occur sporadically, especially in the verb הִתְפָּקֵד (note the long *ā* and single ק).

Inflection is as follows:

PERFECT

הִתְגַּדֵּל	הִתְגַּדְּלוּ	הִתְגַּלָּה	הִתְגַּלּוּ	הִתְפַּלֵּל	הִתְפַּלְלוּ
הִתְגַּדְּלָה		הִתְגַּלְּתָה		הִתְפַּלְלָה	
הִתְגַּדַּלְתָּ	הִתְגַּדַּלְתֶּם	הִתְגַּלִּיתָ	הִתְגַּלִּיתֶם	הִתְפַּלַּלְתָּ	הִתְפַּלַּלְתֶּם
הִתְגַּדַּלְתְּ	הִתְגַּדַּלְתֶּן	הִתְגַּלִּית	הִתְגַּלִּיתֶן	הִתְפַּלַּלְתְּ	הִתְפַּלַּלְתֶּן
הִתְגַּדַּלְתִּי	הִתְגַּדַּלְנוּ	הִתְגַּלֵּיתִי	הִתְגַּלִּינוּ	הִתְפַּלַּלְתִּי	הִתְפַּלַּלְנוּ

IMPERFECT

יִתְגַּדֵּל	יִתְגַּדְּלוּ	יִתְגַּלֶּה	יִתְגַּלּוּ	יִתְפַּלֵּל	יִתְפַּלְלוּ
תִּתְגַּדֵּל	תִּתְגַּדֵּלְנָה	תִּתְגַּלֶּה	תִּתְגַּלֶּינָה	תִּתְפַּלֵּל	תִּתְפַּלֵּלְנָה
תִּתְגַּדֵּל	תִּתְגַּדְּלוּ	תִּתְגַּלֶּה	תִּתְגַּלּוּ	תִּתְפַּלֵּל	תִּתְפַּלְלוּ
תִּתְגַּדְּלִי	תִּתְגַּדֵּלְנָה	תִּתְגַּלִּי	תִּתְגַּלֶּינָה	תִּתְפַּלְלִי	תִּתְפַּלֵּלְנָה
אֶתְגַּדֵּל	נִתְגַּדֵּל	אֶתְגַּלֶּה	נִתְגַּלֶּה	אֶתְפַּלֵּל	נִתְפַּלֵּל

IMPERATIVE

הִתְגַּדֵּל	הִתְגַּדְּלוּ	הִתְגַּלֵּה	הִתְגַּלּוּ	הִתְפַּלֵּל	הִתְפַּלְלוּ
הִתְגַּדְּלִי	הִתְגַּדֵּלְנָה	הִתְגַּלִּי	הִתְגַּלֶּינָה	הִתְפַּלְלִי	הִתְפַּלֵּלְנָה

INF. CONSTRUCT

הִתְגַּדֵּל	הִתְגַּלּוֹת	הִתְפַּלֵּל

PARTICIPLE

מִתְגַּדֵּל	מִתְגַּדְּלִים	מִתְגַּלֶּה	מִתְגַּלִּים	מִתְפַּלֵּל	מִתְפַּלְלִים
מִתְגַּדְּלָה	מִתְגַּדְּלוֹת	מִתְגַּלָּה	מִתְגַּלּוֹת	מִתְפַּלְלָה	מִתְפַּלְלוֹת
מִתְגַּדֶּלֶת				מִתְפַּלֶּלֶת	

Hithpael verbs are intransitive and often have a reflexive or reciprocal meaning in relation to their active counterparts of the Qal, Piel, or Hiphil type from the same root. The following is a representative list:

(a) Reflexive: הִתְקַדֵּשׁ to sanctify oneself (cf. קִדֵּשׁ; הִקְדִּישׁ)
הִתְגַּדֵּל to magnify oneself (cf. גִּדֵּל; הִגְדִּיל)
הִתְחַבֵּא to hide oneself

(b) Reciprocal: הִתְרָאָה to see one another (cf. רָאָה)
הִדַּבֵּר to converse (cf. דִּבֶּר)

(c) Indirect reflexive (i.e. to do something for one's self, for one's own benefit or to one's own detriment):
הִתְחַנֵּן to implore favor (cf. חָנַן)
הִתְפַּלֵּל to pray (see below)
הִצְטַיֵּד to supply oneself with provisions (cf. צַיִד provision)

(d) Iterative: הִתְהַלֵּךְ to walk back and forth; to go continually

(e) Denominative: הִתְנַבֵּא to prophesy (cf. נָבִיא)
הִתְאַנַּף to become angry (cf. אַף; root אנף)

Classification is often difficult, owing to the lack of data. The verb הִתְפַּלֵּל (to pray) offers a good example. One's first inclination is to regard it as denominative from תְּפִלָּה (prayer), to which it is most closely related in form and meaning. This is too simple an approach, however, since nouns of the type תְּפִלָּה (with prefixed *t*-) are often associated with Hithpael verbs in Hebrew and would appear to be derived from them and not vice versa. There is no Qal verb פָּלַל but there are several poorly attested nouns, such as פָּלִיל (referee, judge, arbiter), which suggest that there was a root verb (Qal) at one time in the meaning "to arbitrate, mediate" or the like. The Piel verb פִּלֵּל (to mediate, act as an arbiter for) is a denominative from פָּלִיל. The Hithpael verb, then, would have the force of a causative/indirect-reflexive: "to cause a mediation (by seeking or asking) for oneself." It would thus belong to the same category as הִתְחַנֵּן. It is obviously necessary to learn the exact nuance of a Hithpael verb as part of vocabulary acquisition.

178. Vocabulary 50.

VERBS:	הִתְפַּלֵּל	to pray
	הִתְחַנֵּן	to seek or implore favor
	הִתְחַבֵּא	to hide oneself
	נֶחְבָּא	(יֵחָבֵא) to hide oneself
	הִתְהַלֵּךְ	to walk back and forth; to go continually or constantly
	הִתְנַבֵּא	to prophesy
	נִבָּא	(יִנָּבֵא) to prophesy
	חָרַשׁ	(יַחֲרֹשׁ) to plow; to engrave
	פָּרַשׂ	(יִפְרֹשׂ) to spread out (trans.)
	סָפַר	(יִסְפֹּר) to count
NOUNS:	מַאֲכָל	(no pl.) food
	מָשִׁיחַ	one who has been anointed, the Messiah
	עֹז	(w. suff. עֻזִּי or עָזִּי) strength, might

תְּפִלָּה (pl. *-ôṯ*) prayer
עֵגֶל (w. suff. עֶגְלִי; pl. *-îm*) calf
עֶגְלָה (pl. *-ôṯ*) heifer
OTHER: עַז (adj.) strong, mighty (see §22)
לוּלֵי (conj.) unless, if not
כֹּה (adv.) thus (generally referring to what follows)
PROPER NAMES: אַשְׁקְלוֹן Ashkelon, an important Philistine city on the coast, about 12 miles north of Gaza.

Exercises:

(a) Translate:

(1) לָמָה הִתְחַבֵּאתֶם מִמֶּנִּי
(2) הִתְחַנֵּן אֵלַי וְחַנּוֹתִי אֹתְךָ
(3) הַבַּחוּרִים הַמִּתְהַלְּכִים בְּרַגְלָיו
(4) וַיָּחֶל לְהִתְנַבֵּא
(5) הִתְפַּלַּלְתִּי אֵלָיו וְלֹא שָׁמַע
(6) וַיִּתְחַבְּאוּ כִּי יָרְאוּ מְאֹד
(7) הֲתִתְפַּלֵּל בַּעֲדִי
(8) מִי הַמִּתְנַבְּאִים
(9) נִשְׁמְעָה תְפִלָּתֵךְ
(10) אִנָּבֵא עַל־בֵּיתְךָ
(11) הֵחָבְאִי

(b) Translate:

(1) אֲבָל אֲשֵׁמִים אֲנַחְנוּ עַל־אָחִינוּ אֲשֶׁר רָאִינוּ צָרַת נַפְשׁוֹ בְּהִתְחַנְנוֹ אֵלֵינוּ וְלֹא שָׁמָעְנוּ.
(2) וַיַּגֵּד לְדָוִד לֵאמֹר מְבַקֵּשׁ אָבִי לְהָמִית אֹתְךָ וְעַתָּה הִשָּׁמֵר נָא בַבֹּקֶר וְנֶחְבֵּאתָ.
(3) וַהֲקִימֹותִי לִי כֹּהֵן נֶאֱמָן, כַּאֲשֶׁר בִּלְבָבִי וּבְנַפְשִׁי יַעֲשֶׂה, וּבָנִיתִי לוֹ בַּיִת נֶאֱמָן וְהִתְהַלֵּךְ לְפָנֵי מְשִׁיחִי כָּל־הַיָּמִים.
(4) חַטַּאת יְהוּדָה חֲרוּשָׁה עַל־לוּחַ לִבָּם.
(5) וַיִּפְרְשׂוּ אֶת־שִׂמְלוֹתֵיהֶם עַל־הָאָרֶץ וַיֵּשְׁבוּ עֲלֵיהֶן.
(6) וַיּוֹצֵא יהוה אֶת־אַבְרָם הַחוּצָה וַיֹּאמֶר הַבֶּט־נָא הַשָּׁמַיְמָה וּסְפֹר הַכּוֹכָבִים, אִם תּוּכַל לִסְפֹּר אֹתָם, וַיֹּאמֶר לוֹ כֹּה יִהְיֶה זַרְעֶךָ.
(7) וַיֵּט מֹשֶׁה אֶת־יָדוֹ עַל־הַיָּם וַיּוֹלֶךְ יהוה אֶת־הַיָּם בְּרוּחַ עַזָּה כָּל־הַלַּיְלָה וַיָּשֶׂם אֶת־הַיָּם לַיַּבָּשָׁה.
(8) וַיִּפְרֹשׂ אֶת־כַּפָּיו אֶל־הַשָּׁמַיִם וַיִּתְפַּלֵּל.
(9) וַיִּשְׁמְעוּ אֶת־קוֹל יהוה אֱלֹהִים מִתְהַלֵּךְ בַּגָּן וַיִּתְחַבְּאוּ הָאָדָם וְאִשְׁתּוֹ מִפְּנֵי יהוה אֱלֹהִים בְּתוֹךְ עֵץ הַגָּן.
(10) וָאֶתְחַנַּן אֶל־יהוה בָּעֵת הַהִוא לֵאמֹר אֲדֹנָי יֱהוִה אַתָּה הַחִלּוֹתָ לְהַרְאוֹת אֶת־עַבְדְּךָ אֶת־גָּדְלְךָ וְאֶת־יָדְךָ הַחֲזָקָה כִּי מִי אֵל בַּשָּׁמַיִם וּבָאָרֶץ אֲשֶׁר יַעֲשֶׂה כַּאֲשֶׁר אַתָּה עֹשֶׂה.

(c) Write in Hebrew:

1. The lion was slain and his carcass (מַפֶּלֶת) was cast to the side of the road.
2. They searched all that evening but were not able to find the lost kid.
3. There was at that time no king ruling over Israel.
4. We were content to settle down there.
5. Be strong, therefore, and do not flee from your enemies.

6. The congregation will be destroyed.
7. There was no one prophesying in the land in those days.

(d) Reading: Judges 14:11–20. Samson and the Riddle.

(11) וַיְהִי כִּרְאוֹתָם אוֹתוֹ וַיִּקְחוּ שְׁלֹשִׁים מֵרֵעִים[1] וַיִּהְיוּ אִתּוֹ׃

(12) וַיֹּאמֶר לָהֶם שִׁמְשׁוֹן אָחוּדָה־נָּא[2] לָכֶם חִידָה[3] אִם־הַגֵּד תַּגִּידוּ אוֹתָהּ לִי שִׁבְעַת[4] יְמֵי
הַמִּשְׁתֶּה וּמְצָאתֶם וְנָתַתִּי לָכֶם שְׁלֹשִׁים סְדִינִים[5] וּשְׁלֹשִׁים חֲלִפֹת[6] בְּגָדִים׃

(13) וְאִם־לֹא תוּכְלוּ לְהַגִּיד לִי וּנְתַתֶּם לִי שְׁלֹשִׁים סְדִינִים וּשְׁלֹשִׁים חֲלִיפוֹת בְּגָדִים וַיֹּאמְרוּ לוֹ
חוּדָה חִידָתְךָ וְנִשְׁמָעֶנָּה׃[7]

(14) וַיֹּאמֶר לָהֶם מֵהָאֹכֵל יָצָא מַאֲכָל וּמֵעַז יָצָא מָתוֹק[8] וְלֹא יָכְלוּ לְהַגִּיד הַחִידָה שְׁלֹשֶׁת יָמִים׃

(15) וַיְהִי בַּיּוֹם הַשְּׁבִיעִי וַיֹּאמְרוּ לְאֵשֶׁת שִׁמְשׁוֹן פַּתִּי[9] אֶת־אִישֵׁךְ וְיַגֶּד־לָנוּ אֶת־הַחִידָה פֶּן־נִשְׂרֹף
אוֹתָךְ וְאֶת־בֵּית אָבִיךְ בָּאֵשׁ הַלְיָרְשֵׁנוּ[10] קְרָאתֶם לָנוּ הֲלֹא׃[11]

(16) וַתֵּבְךְּ אֵשֶׁת שִׁמְשׁוֹן עָלָיו וַתֹּאמֶר רַק שְׂנֵאתַנִי[12] וְלֹא אֲהַבְתָּנִי[13] הַחִידָה חַדְתָּ לִבְנֵי עַמִּי
וְלִי לֹא הִגַּדְתָּה וַיֹּאמֶר לָהּ הִנֵּה לְאָבִי וּלְאִמִּי לֹא הִגַּדְתִּי וְלָךְ אַגִּיד׃

(17) וַתֵּבְךְּ עָלָיו שִׁבְעַת הַיָּמִים אֲשֶׁר־הָיָה לָהֶם הַמִּשְׁתֶּה וַיְהִי בַּיּוֹם הַשְּׁבִיעִי וַיַּגֶּד־לָהּ כִּי
הֱצִיקַתְהוּ[14] וַתַּגֵּד הַחִידָה לִבְנֵי עַמָּהּ׃

(18) וַיֹּאמְרוּ לוֹ אַנְשֵׁי הָעִיר בַּיּוֹם הַשְּׁבִיעִי בְּטֶרֶם יָבֹא הַחַרְסָה[15] מַה־מָּתוֹק מִדְּבַשׁ וּמֶה עַז
מֵאֲרִי וַיֹּאמֶר לָהֶם לוּלֵא חֲרַשְׁתֶּם בְּעֶגְלָתִי לֹא מְצָאתֶם חִידָתִי׃

(19) וַתִּצְלַח[16] עָלָיו רוּחַ יהוה וַיֵּרֶד אַשְׁקְלוֹן וַיַּךְ מֵהֶם שְׁלֹשִׁים אִישׁ וַיִּקַּח אֶת־חֲלִיצוֹתָם[17]
וַיִּתֵּן הַחֲלִיפוֹת לְמַגִּידֵי הַחִידָה וַיִּחַר אַפּוֹ וַיַּעַל בֵּית אָבִיהוּ׃

(20) וַתְּהִי אֵשֶׁת שִׁמְשׁוֹן לְמֵרֵעֵהוּ אֲשֶׁר רֵעָה[18] לוֹ׃

Notes to the Reading:

1. מֵרֵעַ companion
2. חָד (יָחוּד) to propound a riddle
3. חִידָה a riddle
4. Notice the temporal expression without a preposition: "*during* the seven days..."
5. סָדִין a linen garment
6. חֲלִיפָה a change (of clothing)
7. וְנִשְׁמָעֶנָּה = וְנִשְׁמַע אֹתָהּ
8. מָתוֹק sweet
9. פִּתָּה to lure, entice, beguile
10. הַלְיָרְשֵׁנוּ = הֲ + לְ + יָרַשׁ + suff. 1st pers. pl.: "have (you summoned us) in order to dispossess us?"
11. הֲלֹא probably a mistake for הֲלֹם, but it may be taken literally as an emphatically placed interrogative: "You've summoned us... haven't you?"
12. שְׂנֵאתַנִי = שָׂנֵאתָ אֹתִי
13. אֲהַבְתָּנִי = אָהַבְתָּ אֹתִי
14. הֱצִיקַתְהוּ "she harrassed (הֵצִיק) him"
15. An uncertain expression; probably "before the sun had set"
16. צָלַח to rush
17. חֲלִיצָה armor
18. רֵעָה to be a companion to, to be "best man"

LESSON 51

179. The Qal Passive.

There are several forms, taken by the Masoretes as Pual or Hophal, which must rather be viewed as survivors of an obsolete passive of the Qal.

PERFECT	IMPERFECT	
לֻקַּח	יֻקַּח	to be taken
יֻלַּד	—	to be born
—	יֻתַּן	to be given

Isolated participial forms also occur: אֻכָּל (eaten,consumed), יִלּוֹד (born).

That these verbs are not true Pual or Hophal types is suggested (1) by the absence of a corresponding Piel or Hiphil active verb with the appropriate meaning, (2) by the absence of a מ -preformative on the few remaining participial forms, (3) by the irregular assimilation of the ל in יֻקַּח, a special feature of the Qal not found elsewhere, and (4) by the asymmetry of a Pual perfect and a Hophal imperfect. It is quite likely that a number of other Pual and Hophal verbs belong here, but assignment on the basis of meaning alone is precarious.

180. Polel, Polal, and Hithpolel.

In place of Piel, Pual, and Hithpael verbs from Hollow roots there is a derived system of verbs characterized by the reduplication of the final root consonant and *ô* in the first stem syllable:

	POLEL (active)	POLAL (passive)	HITHPOLEL (reflexive)
Perfect	קוֹמֵם	קוֹמַם	הִתְקוֹמֵם
Imperfect	יְקוֹמֵם	יְקוֹמַם	יִתְקוֹמֵם
Inf. Constr.	קוֹמֵם	——	——
Participle	מְקוֹמֵם	מְקוֹמָם	מִתְקוֹמֵם

Typical verbs are קוֹמֵם (to raise up), מוֹתֵת (to slay, kill), רוֹמֵם (to raise), כּוֹנֵן (to establish), and עוֹרֵר (to arouse) from the roots קום, מות, רום, כון, and עור respectively. All verbs of this type are rare.

In the inflection of the perfect the distinction between the Polel and Polal is obscured:

POLEL	POLAL
קוֹמֵם	קוֹמַם
קוֹמְמָה	קוֹמְמָה
...קוֹמַמְתָּ	...קוֹמַמְתָּ

Similar forms occur from geminate roots, as חוֹנֵן (to favor; root חנן) and סוֹבֵב (to encompass; root סבב).

181. Other Verb Types.

Biblical Hebrew has a number of verb types not belonging to those already treated. Most of these are so infrequent that a complete paradigm cannot be constructed for them. Given below, with the traditional name of the type, are a few examples.

POEL: similar to the Polel of the preceding paragraph but formed from regular triliteral roots. E.g. שֹׁרֵשׁ (imperf. יְשֹׁרֵשׁ; part. מְשֹׁרֵשׁ) to take root, a denominative from the noun שֹׁרֶשׁ (root). Contrast the Piel verb שֵׁרֵשׁ (to root up, destroy the roots of).

PALAL: presumably from triliteral roots with reduplication of the final root consonant E.g. שַׁאֲנַן (to be at rest); אֻמְלַל (to be weary).

PILPEL: perhaps traceable to reduplicated biconsonantal (i.e. Hollow) roots. E.g. כִּלְכֵּל (imperf. יְכַלְכֵּל; inf. constr. כַּלְכֵּל; part. מְכַלְכֵּל) to sustain, support; גִּלְגֵּל (to roll).

The relatively frequent verb הִשְׁתַּחֲוָה formerly taken as a Hithpalel form of a root שחה is now known to be a Hishtaphel (i.e. prefix [*h*]*išt-*, root חוה). The attested forms of this verb are given below and should be learned. Its inflection is like that of other verbs from roots III-*Hē*.

PERF:	3 m.s. הִשְׁתַּחֲוָה		IMPERF:	3 m.s. יִשְׁתַּחֲוֶה		IMPERATIVE:	2 f.s. הִשְׁתַּחֲוִי
	2 m.s. הִשְׁתַּחֲוִיתָ			3 m.pl. יִשְׁתַּחֲווּ			2 m.pl. הִשְׁתַּחֲווּ .

3 m.pl. הִשְׁתַּחֲווּ 2 f.pl. תִּשְׁתַּחֲוֶין
INF. CONSTRUCT: הִשְׁתַּחֲוֹת JUSSIVE: יִשְׁתַּחוּ PARTICIPLE: מִשְׁתַּחֲוֶה

182. Final Remarks on the Numbers.

The numbers above 99 employ the following words:

		CONSTR.	DUAL	PL.	CONSTR.
hundred	מֵאָה	מְאַת	מָאתַיִם	מֵאוֹת	מְאוֹת
thousand	אֶלֶף	אֶלֶף	אַלְפַּיִם	אֲלָפִים	אַלְפֵי
ten thousand	רִבּוֹ רְבָבָה		רִבֹּתַיִם	רִבֹּאוֹת	

Because the gender of מֵאָה is fem., modifiers have the masculine form:

שְׁלֹשׁ מֵאוֹת 300 אַרְבַּע מֵאוֹת 400

Whereas אֶלֶף is masculine:

שְׁלֹשֶׁת אֲלָפִים 3000 אַרְבַּעַת אֲלָפִים 4000

There is a great deal of variety in the order and syntax of the higher numbers, but the following points will apply in most instances:

(a) מֵאָה is usually followed by a singular noun:

מֵאָה שָׁנָה 100 years מֵאָה כֶּסֶף 100 pieces of silver
מֵאָה רֶכֶב 100 chariots

The number may be in the construct:

מְאַת שָׁנָה 100 years מְאַת כִּכָּר 100 talents

(b) מָאתַיִם, אֶלֶף, אַלְפַּיִם are also followed by the singular noun, but plurals are attested:

מָאתַיִם שָׁנָה 200 years אֶלֶף אִישׁ 1000 men
מָאתַיִם כֶּסֶף 200 pieces of silver אֶלֶף פְּעָמִים 1000 times
אַלְפַּיִם אִישׁ 2000 men
אַלְפַּיִם סוּסִים 2000 horses

(c) Compound numbers usually begin with the highest unit: x-thousand, y-hundred, and z. Only the final element (z) is affected by the gender of the noun being modified and will conform to the patterns already discussed (§§ 130, 161).

Note first the construction with אֶלֶף:

שְׁלֹשֶׁת אֲלָפִים 3000 עֶשְׂרִים וַחֲמִשָּׁה אֶלֶף 25000
שְׁלֹשֶׁת עָשָׂר אֶלֶף 13000 מְאַת אֶלֶף 100000
עֶשְׂרִים אֶלֶף 20000 מָאתַיִם אֶלֶף 200000

Following is a selection of compound numbers illustrating normal usage. Study them and be sure their construction is clear.

103	מֵאָה (וּ)שְׁלֹשָׁה
113	מֵאָה (וּ)שְׁלֹשֶׁת עָשָׂר
123	מֵאָה (וְ)עֶשְׂרִים וּשְׁלֹשָׁה
203	מָאתַיִם (וּ)שְׁלֹשָׁה
303	שְׁלֹשׁ מֵאוֹת (וּ)שְׁלֹשָׁה
1003	אֶלֶף (וּ)שְׁלֹשָׁה
1103	אֶלֶף (וּ)מֵאָה (וּ)שְׁלֹשָׁה
1203	אֶלֶף (וּ)מָאתַיִם (וּ)שְׁלֹשָׁה
3203	שְׁלֹשֶׁת אֲלָפִים (וּ)מָאתַיִם (וּ)שְׁלֹשָׁה
13000	שְׁלֹשֶׁת עָשָׂר אֶלֶף
23000	עֶשְׂרִים וּשְׁלֹשֶׁת אֶלֶף
100000	מְאַת אֶלֶף
103000	מֵאָה וּשְׁלֹשֶׁת אֶלֶף
113000	מֵאָה (וּ)שְׁלֹשֶׁת עָשָׂר אֶלֶף
300000	שְׁלֹשׁ מֵאוֹת אֶלֶף
303000	שְׁלֹשׁ מֵאוֹת (וּ)שְׁלֹשֶׁת אֶלֶף
303333	שְׁלֹשׁ מֵאוֹת (וּ)שְׁלֹשֶׁת אֶלֶף (וּ)שְׁלֹשׁ מֵאוֹת (וּ)שְׁלֹשִׁים וּשְׁלֹשָׁה

The words for ten-thousand are seldom used.

183. Vocabulary 51.

VERBS:
- מוֹתֵת to slay, kill (§ 180)
- כּוֹנֵן to set up, establish (§ 180)
- עוֹרֵר to arouse, stir up (§ 180)
- רוֹמֵם to raise up, exalt (§ 180)
- הִשְׁתַּחֲוָה to bow down (§ 181)
- הִתְיַצֵּב to take one's stand, station oneself
- שָׁפַט (יִשְׁפֹּט) to judge
- כִּחֵד (יְכַחֵד) to hide, conceal
- פָּרַץ (יִפְרֹץ) to break down, breach (a wall); to burst out suddenly (בְּ upon); to increase precipitously (in numbers, wealth etc.)

NOUNS:
- אֲרוֹן (w. art. הָאָרוֹן) the Ark of the temple, containing the tablets of the Law
- זֶבַח (w. suff. זִבְחִי; pl. *-îm*) sacrifice
- מֵאָה hundred (see § 182)
- אֶלֶף thousand (see § 182)

ADVERB:
- לָכֵן therefore (usually introduces a divine judgement or declaration)

PROPER NAMES:
- עֵלִי Eli, the priest of the Lord at Shiloh to whom Samuel was entrusted.

Exercises:

(a) Give the Hebrew for the following numbers:

1. 3554	6. 7325	11. 100000
2. 1238	7. 5899	12. 220000
3. 9671	8. 2107	13. 460000
4. 8442	9. 4960	14. 587963
5. 7683	10. 10349	15. 666666

(b) Analyze and translate the following verbs:

(1) מוֹתַתְנוּ
(2) תִּתְכּוֹנְנִי
(3) תְּעוֹרֵר
(4) הִתְיַצְּבִי
(5) מְכֹנְנִים
(6) רוֹמַמְתָּ
(7) יִתְמוֹתְתוּ
(8) וַיִּשְׁתַּחוּ
(9) הִתְעוֹרַרְתֶּם
(10) מוֹתַתִּי
(11) הִתְרוֹמַמְתִּי
(12) הִשְׁתַּחֲווּ

(c) Translate:

(1) פָּרַץ יהוה אֶת־אֹיְבַי לְפָנַי.
(2) מִי אֲנִי כִּי אֶשְׁפֹּט אֶת־עַמְּךָ הַזֶּה.
(3) וְעוֹרַרְתִּי אֶת־אֲנָשַׁי עַל־אֹיְבַי.
(4) לֹא כִחַדְתִּי חַסְדְּךָ וַאֲמִתְּךָ מֵהָעֵדָה הַזֹּאת.
(5) וַיִּפְרְצוּ בְּחוֹמַת יְרוּשָׁלַםִ.
(6) וְאֵין מִתְעוֹרֵר לִקְרֹא בְּשִׁמְךָ.
(7) יִשָּׁפְטוּ וְהָשְׁמְדוּ מֵעַל הָאָרֶץ.
(8) וַיִּפְרֹץ הָאִישׁ מְאֹד מְאֹד.
(9) הַגֶּד־נָא לִי מֶה עָשִׂיתָ וְאַל־תְּכַחֵד מִמֶּנִּי.
(10) בָּעֵת הַהִיא יֻקַּח אֲרוֹן הַבְּרִית מִקִּרְבֵּנוּ.
(11) אָסְפָה שִׁבְעִים אִישׁ מִזִּקְנֵי יִשְׂרָאֵל וְלָקַחְתָּ אֹתָם וְהִתְיַצְּבוּ שָׁם עִמְּךָ.
(12) וַיִּזְבַּח יַעֲקֹב זֶבַח שָׁם.
(13) וַיֹּאמֶר אֵלָיו דָּוִד דָּמְךָ עַל־רֹאשְׁךָ כִּי פִּיךָ עָנָה בְךָ לֵאמֹר אָנֹכִי מוֹתַתִּי אֶת־מְשִׁיחַ יהוה.
(14) לֹא עַל־זְבָחֶיךָ אוֹכִיחַ אֹתָךְ.
(15) כּוֹנֵן יהוה אֶת־הָאָרֶץ עַל־הַנְּהָרוֹת אֲשֶׁר תַּחְתֶּיהָ.
(16) וַתֻּקַּח הָאִשָּׁה בֵּית פַּרְעֹה.

(d) Write in Hebrew:

1. He was a just and righteous man and walked continually in the way of the Lord.
2. He will heed your prayer when you pray to him.
3. When they begin to prophesy in my name, do not listen to their words for they are evil men, going the way of the wicked.
4. They approached him and bowed down to the ground, for they feared him greatly.
5. This people will increase precipitously and prevail against us.

6. Our salvation is in his strength; he will not abandon us if we implore favor from (lit. to) him.

(e) Reading: Samuel and Eli (I Sam. 3:1–18).

(1) וְהַנַּעַר שְׁמוּאֵל מְשָׁרֵת אֶת־יהוה לִפְנֵי עֵלִי[1] וּדְבַר יהוה הָיָה יָקָר בַּיָּמִים הָהֵם אֵין חָזוֹן נִפְרָץ׃[2]

(2) וַיְהִי בַּיּוֹם הַהוּא וְעֵלִי שֹׁכֵב בִּמְקוֹמוֹ וְעֵינָיו הֵחֵלּוּ כֵהוֹת[3] לֹא יוּכַל לִרְאוֹת׃

(3) וְנֵר[4] אֱלֹהִים טֶרֶם יִכְבֶּה[5] וּשְׁמוּאֵל שֹׁכֵב בְּהֵיכַל יהוה אֲשֶׁר־שָׁם אֲרוֹן אֱלֹהִים׃

(4) וַיִּקְרָא יהוה אֶל־שְׁמוּאֵל וַיֹּאמֶר הִנֵּנִי׃

(5) וַיָּרָץ אֶל־עֵלִי וַיֹּאמֶר הִנְנִי כִּי־קָרָאתָ לִּי וַיֹּאמֶר לֹא קָרָאתִי שׁוּב שְׁכָב וַיֵּלֶךְ וַיִּשְׁכָּב׃

(6) וַיֹּסֶף יהוה קְרֹא עוֹד שְׁמוּאֵל וַיָּקָם שְׁמוּאֵל וַיֵּלֶךְ אֶל־עֵלִי וַיֹּאמֶר הִנְנִי כִּי קָרָאתָ לִי וַיֹּאמֶר לֹא קָרָאתִי בְנִי שׁוּב שְׁכָב׃

(7) וּשְׁמוּאֵל טֶרֶם יָדַע אֶת־יהוה וְטֶרֶם יִגָּלֶה אֵלָיו דְּבַר יהוה׃

(8) וַיֹּסֶף יהוה קְרֹא־שְׁמוּאֵל בַּשְּׁלִשִׁית וַיָּקָם וַיֵּלֶךְ אֶל־עֵלִי וַיֹּאמֶר הִנְנִי כִּי קָרָאתָ לִי וַיָּבֶן עֵלִי כִּי יהוה קֹרֵא לַנָּעַר׃

(9) וַיֹּאמֶר עֵלִי לִשְׁמוּאֵל לֵךְ שְׁכָב וְהָיָה אִם־יִקְרָא אֵלֶיךָ וְאָמַרְתָּ דַּבֵּר יהוה כִּי שֹׁמֵעַ עַבְדֶּךָ וַיֵּלֶךְ שְׁמוּאֵל וַיִּשְׁכַּב בִּמְקוֹמוֹ׃

(10) וַיָּבֹא יהוה וַיִּתְיַצַּב וַיִּקְרָא כְפַעַם־בְּפַעַם[7] שְׁמוּאֵל שְׁמוּאֵל וַיֹּאמֶר שְׁמוּאֵל דַּבֵּר כִּי שֹׁמֵעַ עַבְדֶּךָ׃

(11) וַיֹּאמֶר יהוה אֶל־שְׁמוּאֵל הִנֵּה אָנֹכִי עֹשֶׂה דָבָר בְּיִשְׂרָאֵל אֲשֶׁר כָּל־שֹׁמְעוֹ תְּצִלֶּינָה[8] שְׁתֵּי אָזְנָיו׃

(12) בַּיּוֹם הַהוּא אָקִים אֶל־עֵלִי אֵת כָּל־אֲשֶׁר דִּבַּרְתִּי אֶל־בֵּיתוֹ הָחֵל וְכַלֵּה׃[9]

(13) וְהִגַּדְתִּי לוֹ כִּי־שֹׁפֵט אֲנִי אֶת־בֵּיתוֹ עַד־עוֹלָם בַּעֲוֹן[10] אֲשֶׁר־יָדַע כִּי מְקַלְלִים לָהֶם[11] בָּנָיו וְלֹא כִהָה[12] בָּם׃

(14) וְלָכֵן נִשְׁבַּעְתִּי לְבֵית עֵלִי אִם־יִתְכַּפֵּר[13] עֲוֹן בֵּית־עֵלִי בְּזֶבַח וּבְמִנְחָה עַד־עוֹלָם׃

(15) וַיִּשְׁכַּב שְׁמוּאֵל עַד־הַבֹּקֶר וַיִּפְתַּח אֶת־דַּלְתוֹת בֵּית יהוה וּשְׁמוּאֵל יָרֵא מֵהַגִּיד אֶת־הַמַּרְאָה[14] אֶל־עֵלִי׃

(16) וַיִּקְרָא עֵלִי אֶת־שְׁמוּאֵל וַיֹּאמֶר שְׁמוּאֵל בְּנִי וַיֹּאמֶר הִנֵּנִי׃

(17) וַיֹּאמֶר מָה הַדָּבָר אֲשֶׁר דִּבֶּר אֵלֶיךָ אַל־נָא תְכַחֵד מִמֶּנִּי כֹּה[15] יַעֲשֶׂה־לְּךָ אֱלֹהִים וְכֹה יוֹסִיף אִם־תְּכַחֵד מִמֶּנִּי דָּבָר מִכָּל־הַדָּבָר אֲשֶׁר־דִּבֶּר אֵלֶיךָ׃

(18) וַיַּגֶּד־לוֹ שְׁמוּאֵל אֶת־כָּל־הַדְּבָרִים וְלֹא כִחֵד מִמֶּנּוּ וַיֹּאמַר יהוה הוּא הַטּוֹב בְּעֵינָיו יַעֲשֶׂה׃

Notes to the Reading:

1. Note the series of disjunctive clauses giving the setting and explaining the circumstances of the narrative to follow.
2. חָזוֹן נִפְרָץ a frequent vision. Note the asyndetic אֵין clause: "there being no frequent vision."
3. כֵּהֶה weak (of the eyes)
4. נֵר light, lamp
5. כָּבָה to be extinguished, to go out (of a fire or light)
6. שְׁלִישִׁית fem. of the ordinal used adverbially: "for the third time."
7. An idiom: "as (he had) at the other times."
8. צָלַל to tingle. The form תְּצִלֶּינָה

is unusual; it looks like a Hiphil verb but is generally taken as a Qal.

9. Normal use of inf. absolutes (see § 129); translate: "from start to finish."

10. עֲוֹן is in construct with אֲשֶׁר and hence with the whole following clause: "for the iniquity of (the fact that) he knew."

11. לָהֶם is reflexive here: "they were bringing a curse upon themselves."

12. כִּהָה to rebuke

13. אִם after a verb of swearing has a negative force: "I swear... that the iniquity... will not be expiated..."

14. מַרְאָה a vision

15. Cf. remarks under הוֹסִיף in § 165.

LESSON 52

184. The Verb with Object Suffixes.

A pronominal direct object may be suffixed directly to a verb rather than to the object marker אֶת (אֹתִי etc.):

רָאִ֫יתִי אֹתוֹ	–	רְאִיתִ֫יהוּ	I saw him.
הָרַג אֹתָהּ	–	הֲרָגָהּ	He killed her.

There is no difference in meaning between the two constructions, though there do appear to be stylistic preferences.

As with the noun, the major problem is to accommodate the proper form of the suffix to the proper form of the verbal stem. The following table shows the object suffixes as they appear after various types of stems:

	A. Post-consonantal, stressed		B. Post-vocalic, unstressed		C. Post-consonantal, unstressed	
1 c. s.	־ַ֫נִי	*-ánî*	־נִי	*-nî*	־נִי	*-nî*
2 m. s.	־ְךָ	*–(ə)kā*	־ךָ	*–kā*	־ךָ	*–kā*
2 f. s.	־ֵךְ	*–ēk*	־ךְ	*–k*	־ֶךְ	*–ek*
3 m. s.	־וֹ/־ָ֫הוּ	*–ô* or *–ā́hû*	־הוּ/־ו	*–hû* or *–w*	־הוּ/־וּ	*–hû* or *–:û*
3 f. s.	־ָהּ	*–āh*	־הָ	*–hā*	־ָהּ	*–:āh*
1 c. pl.	־ָ֫נוּ	*–ā́nû*	־נוּ	*–nû*	־נוּ	*–nû*
3 m. pl.	־ָם	*–ām*	־ם	*–m*	־ַם	*–am*
3 f. pl.	־ָן	*–ān*	־ן	*–n*	־ַן	*–an*

The use of object suffixes for the 2nd pers. pl. is so infrequent that we have omitted them from our table; they were presumably of the forms *–kem* and *–ken* after all types of stems.

185. Object Suffixes on the Perfect: 3rd pers. masc. sing.

	שְׁמָרַ֫נִי	he observed me
	שְׁמָרְךָ	he observed you (m.s.)
	שְׁמָרֵךְ	he observed you (f.s.)
שְׁמָרָ֫הוּ or	שְׁמָרוֹ	he observed him
	שְׁמָרָהּ	he observed her
	שְׁמָרָ֫נוּ	he observed us
	שְׁמָרָם	he observed them (m.)
	שְׁמָרָן	he observed them (f.)

The suffixes used are those given in column A of the preceding table. Because the suffixes are stressed, the propretonic vowel of the verbal stem is reduced to *ə*. In Piel verbs, however, where the propretonic syllable is closed or at least unchangeable, it is the pretonic vowel that is reduced: בִּקְשַׁ֫נִי he sought me. A further difference with Piel verbs is the change of *ē* to *e* before the suffix of the 2nd pers. masc. sing.: בִּקֶּשְׁךָ he sought you. The following list includes all of the main types of Qal, Piel, and Hiphil verbs as they appear before the suffixes:

QAL	שָׁמַר	שְׁמָרַ֫נִי	שְׁמָרְךָ	שְׁמָרֵךְ	etc.
	עָזַב	עֲזָבַ֫נִי	עֲזָבְךָ		
	שָׁלַח	שְׁלָחַ֫נִי	שְׁלָחֲךָ		
	מָצָא	מְצָאַ֫נִי	מְצָאֲךָ		
	בָּנָה	בָּנַ֫נִי	בָּנְךָ		
	שָׂם	שָׂמַ֫נִי	שָׂמְךָ		
	סָבַב	סְבָבַ֫נִי	סְבָבְךָ		
	חָנַן	חַנַּ֫נִי	חַנְּךָ		
PIEL	בִּקֵּשׁ	בִּקְשַׁ֫נִי	בִּקֶּשְׁךָ		
	שִׁלַּח	שִׁלְּחַ֫נִי	שִׁלַּחֲךָ		
	בֵּרַךְ	בֵּרְכַ֫נִי	בֵּרַכְךָ		
	עִנָּה	עִנַּ֫נִי	עִנְּךָ		
HIPHIL	הִשְׁמִיד	הִשְׁמִידַ֫נִי	הִשְׁמִידְךָ		
	הִשְׁמִיעַ	הִשְׁמִיעַ֫נִי	הִשְׁמִיעֲךָ		
	הִמְצִיא	הִמְצִיאַ֫נִי	הִמְצִיאֲךָ		
	הֶעֱמִיד	הֶעֱמִידַ֫נִי	הֶעֱמִידְךָ		
	הֶעֱלָה	הֶעֱלַ֫נִי	הֶעֶלְךָ		
	הוֹרִיד	הוֹרִידַ֫נִי	הוֹרִידְךָ		
	הֵשִׁיב	הֱשִׁיבַ֫נִי	הֱשִׁיבְךָ		
	הֵסֵב	הֲסִבַּ֫נִי	הֲסִבְּךָ		

Remarks:

(1) Verbs from roots III-*Hē*, regardless of the conjugational type, have a shortened form before the suffix: בָּנָה → בָּנ– עִנָּה → עִנּ– הִגְלָה → הִגְל– .

(2) A variation between *ĕ* and *ă* is found in the reduced syllable of verbs like הֵשִׁיב; thus either הֲשִׁיבַנִי or הֱשִׁיבַנִי.

186. Object Suffixes on the Perfect: 2nd pers. masc. sing.

שְׁמַרְתַּנִי	you observed me	שְׁמַרְתָּנוּ	you observed us
שְׁמַרְתּוֹ / שְׁמַרְתָּהוּ	you observed him	שְׁמַרְתָּם	you observed them (m.)
שְׁמַרְתָּהּ	you observed her	שְׁמַרְתָּן	you observed them (f.)

The endings are exactly the same as those of the 3rd pers. masc. sing. verb; it is convenient, therefore, to describe the stem change as שָׁמַרְתָּ → שְׁמַרְתְּ (note the propretonic reduction) and to specify the suffixes of Column A above. Thus

QAL	שָׁמַרְתָּ	שְׁמַרְתַּנִי	שְׁמַרְתּוֹ	etc.
	עָזַבְתָּ	עֲזַבְתַּנִי	עֲזַבְתּוֹ	
	שָׁלַחְתָּ	שְׁלַחְתַּנִי	שְׁלַחְתּוֹ	
	מָצָאתָ	מְצָאתַנִי	מְצָאתוֹ	
	בָּנִיתָ	בְּנִיתַנִי	בְּנִיתוֹ	
	שַׂמְתָּ	שַׂמְתַּנִי	שַׂמְתּוֹ	
	סַבּוֹתָ	סַבּוֹתַנִי	סַבּוֹתוֹ	
PIEL	בִּקַּשְׁתָּ	בִּקַּשְׁתַּנִי	בִּקַּשְׁתּוֹ	
	שִׁלַּחְתָּ	שִׁלַּחְתַּנִי	שִׁלַּחְתּוֹ	
	בֵּרַכְתָּ	בֵּרַכְתַּנִי	בֵּרַכְתּוֹ	
	עִנִּיתָ	עִנִּיתַנִי	עִנִּיתוֹ	
HIPHIL	הִשְׁמַדְתָּ	הִשְׁמַדְתַּנִי	הִשְׁמַדְתּוֹ	
	הִשְׁמַעְתָּ	הִשְׁמַעְתַּנִי	הִשְׁמַעְתּוֹ	
	הִמְצֵאתָ	הִמְצֵאתַנִי	הִמְצֵאתוֹ	
	הֶעֱמַדְתָּ	הֶעֱמַדְתַּנִי	הֶעֱמַדְתּוֹ	
	הִרְאִיתָ	הִרְאִיתַנִי	הִרְאִיתוֹ	
	הֲשִׁיבוֹתָ	הֲשִׁיבוֹתַנִי	הֲשִׁיבוֹתוֹ	
	הֲסִבּוֹתָ	הֲסִבּוֹתַנִי	הֲסִבּוֹתוֹ	
	הֲפֵרוֹתָ	הֲפֵרוֹתַנִי	הֲפֵרוֹתוֹ	

Remarks:

Only the Hiphil verbs from roots I-gutt. require comment. We noted at the end of §158 that the converted perfect וְהַאֲמַנְתָּ has *a–ă* instead of the usual *e–ĕ*, as in הֶאֱמַנְתָּ. This same substitution is made where pronominal suffixes are added to the converted forms; thus:

הֶעֱמַדְתִּיךָ I stationed you → וְהַעֲמַדְתִּיךָ and I shall station you

It is interesting to note that the stress is the same in both of these forms, and that the substitution is morphologically rather than phonologically determined. There are, moreover, a few instances where this replacement is not made.

187. Vocabulary 52.

VERBS: מָאַס (יִמְאַס) to refuse, despise, reject
מָלַךְ (יִמְלֹךְ) to rule (עַל / בְּ over); to be/become king
קָצַר (יִקְצֹר) to reap, harvest
בָּלַע (יִבְלַע) to swallow
סָלַח (יִסְלַח) to pardon, forgive (+ לְ with person or thing)
מָרַד (יִמְרֹד) to rebel (עַל / בְּ against)
כָּשַׁל (יִכְשֹׁל) to stumble, totter
הֵעִיד (יָעִיד) to warn (בְּ)

NOUNS: מַעֲשֶׂה (pl. *-îm*) deed, act, work
זַ֫יִת (pl. *-îm*) olive-tree, olive
שַׂר (pl. *-îm*) chief, officer
קָצִיר (no pl.) harvest, crop; time of harvest
גּוֹי (pl. *-îm*) people, nation; sometimes synonymous with עַם in referring to Israel, but more often used for non-Israelites.

PROPER NAMES: רָמָה Ramah, a town in the hill-country of Ephraim; home of Samuel.

Exercises:

(a) Transform the following according to the example and translate:

Ex. הֲרָגַ֫נִי → הָרַג אֹתִי he killed me

(1) זְכַרְתָּם	(6) שְׁבַרְתּוֹ	(11) שְׁכַחְתַּ֫נִי
(2) שְׁפָטָ֫נוּ	(7) קְבַצְתָּן	(12) עֲזַבְתָּ֫הוּ
(3) לְכַדְתַּ֫נִי	(8) מְכָרֶ֫ךְ	(13) אֲסָרֶ֫ךְ
(4) סְגָרוֹ	(9) גְּנָבָהּ	(14) בְּרָאָם
(5) תְּפַשְׂתָּהּ	(10) גְּאָלֵךְ	(15) מְאָסָ֫הוּ

(b) Transform the following according to the example and translate:

Ex. הָרַג אֹתִי → הֲרָגַ֫נִי

(1) אָחַז אֹתָהּ	(6) קָצַר אֹתוֹ	(11) שָׁתָה אֹתוֹ
(2) נָגַ֫פְתָּ אֹתוֹ	(7) שָׂם אֹתָךְ	(12) בָּזָה אֹתִי
(3) נָשָׂא אֹתָ֫נוּ	(8) שָׁלַ֫חְתָּ אֹתִי	(13) רָאִ֫יתָ אֹתָן
(4) נָתַ֫תָּ אֹתָ֫נוּ	(9) בָּנִ֫יתָ אֹתוֹ	(14) עִנִּ֫יתָ אֹתוֹ
(5) יָצַר אֹתָם	(10) קָנָה אֹתָהּ	(15) סָבַב אֹתָ֫נוּ

(c) Translate the following. Replace the nominal object with the appropriate pronoun, suffixed to the verb.

Ex. הִלֵּל אֶת־הַנָּבִיא → הִלְּלוֹ he praised him

(1) קִדֵּשׁ אֶת־הַשַּׂר	(6) עִנָּה אֶת־הַדַּלִּים	(11) הֶעֱבִיר אֶת־הָעָם
(2) גֵּרַשׁ אֶת־הַגּוֹיִם	(7) צִוָּה אֶת־שָׂרָיו	(12) הִגִּישׁ אֶת־הַלֶּ֫חֶם
(3) בֵּרַךְ אֶת־הַקָּצִיר	(8) כִּחֵד אֶת־הַמַּעֲשֶׂה	(13) הוֹרִיד אֶת־הַמְרַגְּלִים
(4) שִׁלַּח אֶת־הַמַּלְאָךְ	(9) הִזְכִּיר אֶת־שְׁמוֹ	(14) הֶרְאָה אֶת־אוֹתוֹ
(5) נִאֵץ אֶת־הָאָדוֹן	(10) הִקְרִיב אֶת־מִנְחָתוֹ	(15) הֶחֱיָה אֶת־הַמֶּ֫לֶךְ

(d) Transform the verbs of Exercise (c) to the 2nd pers. masc. sing. and add the object suffix of the 1st pers. pl. E.g. קִדֵּשׁ → קִדַּ֫שְׁתָּ → קִדַּשְׁתָּ֫נוּ

(e) Give the Hebrew for the following orally; use object suffixes when possible.

1. And he will gladden us.
2. And he will comfort them.
3. And you (m.s.) will cause them to swear.
4. And he will bring you back.
5. And you will take me up.
6. And he will strike him.
7. And you will save her.
8. And he will throw them.
9. And he will warn them.
10. And you will plant it.

(f) Write in Hebrew:

1. And when they rebelled against him, he became very angry and sent his men that they might put them to death.
2. But when they came to the city, they saw that the people had fled and had abandoned their houses, their property, their crops, and everything that belonged to them.
3. When the people saw the deeds that their chiefs had done, they rebelled against them and slew them.
4. Why should (=shall) I bow down before these idols of wood and stone? There is no breath of life in them, nor can they act in my behalf when I pray to them and call in their name.

(g) Reading: I Samuel 8:4-22. The Evils of Kingship:

(4) וַיִּתְקַבְּצוּ כֹּל זִקְנֵי יִשְׂרָאֵל וַיָּבֹ֫אוּ אֶל־שְׁמוּאֵל הָרָמָֽתָה׃
(5) וַיֹּאמְרוּ אֵלָיו הִנֵּה אַתָּה זָקַ֫נְתָּ וּבָנֶ֫יךָ לֹא הָלְכוּ בִּדְרָכֶ֫יךָ עַתָּה שִׂימָה־לָּ֫נוּ מֶ֫לֶךְ לְשָׁפְטֵ֫נוּ
כְּכָל־הַגּוֹיִֽם׃
(6) וַיֵּ֫רַע הַדָּבָר בְּעֵינֵי שְׁמוּאֵל כַּאֲשֶׁר אָֽמְרוּ תְּנָה־לָּ֫נוּ מֶ֫לֶךְ לְשָׁפְטֵ֫נוּ וַיִּתְפַּלֵּל שְׁמוּאֵל אֶל־
יהוָֽה׃
(7) וַיֹּ֫אמֶר יהוה אֶל־שְׁמוּאֵל שְׁמַע בְּקוֹל הָעָם לְכֹל אֲשֶׁר־יֹאמְרוּ אֵלֶ֫יךָ כִּי לֹא אֹתְךָ מָאָ֫סוּ
כִּי־אֹתִי מָֽאֲסוּ מִמְּלֹךְ עֲלֵיהֶֽם׃

(8) כְּכָל־הַמַּעֲשִׂים אֲשֶׁר־עָשׂוּ מִיּוֹם הַעֲלֹתִי אֹתָם מִמִּצְרַיִם וְעַד־הַיּוֹם הַזֶּה וַיַּעַזְבֻנִי[2] וַיַּעַבְדוּ אֱלֹהִים אֲחֵרִים כֵּן הֵמָּה עֹשִׂים גַּם־לָךְ׃

(9) וְעַתָּה שְׁמַע בְּקוֹלָם אַךְ[3] כִּי־הָעֵד תָּעִיד בָּהֶם וְהִגַּדְתָּ לָהֶם מִשְׁפַּט הַמֶּלֶךְ אֲשֶׁר יִמְלֹךְ עֲלֵיהֶם׃

(10) וַיֹּאמֶר שְׁמוּאֵל אֵת כָּל־דִּבְרֵי יהוה אֶל־הָעָם הַשֹּׁאֲלִים מֵאִתּוֹ מֶלֶךְ׃

(11) וַיֹּאמֶר זֶה יִהְיֶה מִשְׁפַּט הַמֶּלֶךְ אֲשֶׁר יִמְלֹךְ עֲלֵיכֶם אֶת־בְּנֵיכֶם יִקָּח וְשָׂם לוֹ בְּמֶרְכַּבְתּוֹ וּבְפָרָשָׁיו וְרָצוּ לִפְנֵי מֶרְכַּבְתּוֹ׃

(12) וְלָשׂוּם[4] לוֹ שָׂרֵי אֲלָפִים וְשָׂרֵי חֲמִשִּׁים וְלַחֲרֹשׁ חֲרִישׁוֹ[5] וְלִקְצֹר קְצִירוֹ וְלַעֲשׂוֹת כְּלֵי־מִלְחַמְתּוֹ וּכְלֵי רִכְבּוֹ׃[6]

(13) וְאֶת־בְּנוֹתֵיכֶם יִקָּח לְרַקָּחוֹת[7] וּלְטַבָּחוֹת וּלְאֹפוֹת׃

(14) וְאֶת־שְׂדוֹתֵיכֶם וְאֶת־כַּרְמֵיכֶם וְזֵיתֵיכֶם הַטּוֹבִים יִקָּח וְנָתַן לַעֲבָדָיו׃

(15) וְזַרְעֵיכֶם וְכַרְמֵיכֶם יַעְשֹׂר[8] וְנָתַן לְסָרִיסָיו וְלַעֲבָדָיו׃

(16) וְאֶת־עַבְדֵיכֶם וְאֶת־שִׁפְחוֹתֵיכֶם וְאֶת־בַּחוּרֵיכֶם הַטּוֹבִים וְאֶת־חֲמוֹרֵיכֶם יִקָּח וְעָשָׂה לִמְלַאכְתּוֹ׃

(17) צֹאנְכֶם יַעְשֹׂר וְאַתֶּם תִּהְיוּ־לוֹ לַעֲבָדִים׃

(18) וּזְעַקְתֶּם בַּיּוֹם הַהוּא מִלִּפְנֵי מַלְכְּכֶם אֲשֶׁר בְּחַרְתֶּם לָכֶם וְלֹא־יַעֲנֶה יהוה אֶתְכֶם בַּיּוֹם הַהוּא׃

(19) וַיְמָאֲנוּ הָעָם לִשְׁמֹעַ בְּקוֹל שְׁמוּאֵל וַיֹּאמְרוּ לֹּא כִּי אִם־מֶלֶךְ יִהְיֶה עָלֵינוּ׃

(20) וְהָיִינוּ גַם־אֲנַחְנוּ כְּכָל־הַגּוֹיִם וּשְׁפָטָנוּ מַלְכֵּנוּ וְיָצָא לְפָנֵינוּ וְנִלְחַם אֶת־מִלְחֲמֹתֵנוּ׃

(21) וַיִּשְׁמַע שְׁמוּאֵל אֵת כָּל־דִּבְרֵי הָעָם וַיְדַבְּרֵם[9] בְּאָזְנֵי יהוה׃

(22) וַיֹּאמֶר יהוה אֶל־שְׁמוּאֵל שְׁמַע בְּקוֹלָם וְהִמְלַכְתָּ לָהֶם מֶלֶךְ וַיֹּאמֶר שְׁמוּאֵל אֶל־אַנְשֵׁי יִשְׂרָאֵל לְכוּ אִישׁ לְעִירוֹ׃

Notes to the Reading:

1. The suffix is objective: "to judge us"
2. וַיַּעַזְבֻנִי = וַיַּעַזְבוּ אֹתִי
3. אַךְ כִּי but, however
4. The infinitives can be taken gerundially, continuing the preceding sentence: "appointing (them) for him (self) as..."
5. חָרִישׁ land to be plowed
6. רֶכֶב chariotry
7. רַקָּחָה perfumer; טַבָּחָה cook; אֹפָה baker (all feminine)
8. עָשַׂר to tithe, exact a tenth of
9. וַיְדַבְּרֵם = וַיְדַבֵּר אֹתָם

LESSON 53

188. Object Suffixes on the Perfect: 3rd pers. fem. sing.

The feminine ending *-āh* is replaced by *-āt* or *-at* before the pronominal suffixes, which have the forms given in Column C, §184:

שְׁמָרַתְנִי	she observed me	שְׁמָרַתְנוּ	she observed us
שְׁמָרַתְךָ	she observed you (m.s.)		
שְׁמָרָתֶךְ	she observed you (f.s.)		
שְׁמָרַתְהוּ / שְׁמָרַתּוּ	she observed him	שְׁמָרָתַם	she observed them (m.)
שְׁמָרַתָּה	she observed her		

Peculiar features of this paradigm are (1) the restoration of the full vowel *ā* in pretonic positions, (2) the assimilation of *-at* + *hû* and *-at* + *hā* to *-áttû* and *-áttāh* respectively. A survey of extant forms:

QAL	שָֽׁמְרָה	שְׁמָרַתְנִי	שְׁמָרַתְךָ
	עָֽזְבָה	עֲזָבַתְנִי	עֲזָבַתְךָ
	שָֽׁלְחָה	שְׁלָחַתְנִי	שְׁלָחַתְךָ
	רָֽאֲתָה	רָאַתְנִי	רָאַתְךָ
PIEL	בִּקְשָׁה	בִּקְשַׁתְנִי	בִּקְשַׁתְךָ
	עִנְּתָה	עִנַּתְנִי	עִנַּתְךָ
HIPHIL	הִשְׁמִידָה	הִשְׁמִידַתְנִי	הִשְׁמִידַתְךָ
	הֶרְאֲתָה	הֶרְאַתְנִי	הֶרְאַתְךָ
	הֶעֱלְתָה	הֶעֱלַתְנִי	הֶעֱלַתְךָ
	הֵשִׁיבָה	הֲשִׁיבַתְנִי	הֲשִׁיבַתְךָ

189. Object Suffixes on the Remaining Forms of the Perfect.

These offer no new problems, other than the alterations in the form of the subject suffix:

(a) The 2nd pers. fem. sing. ending *-t* → *-tî-*

(b) The 2nd pers. masc. (and fem.?) pl. ending *-tem* → *-tû-*

All the remaining stems, then, end in a vowel, to which are added the suffixes of Column B, §184. Here is a representative sampling (cf. also the Exercises):

שְׁמַרְתִּינִי	you (f.s.) observed me
שְׁמַרְתִּים	you (f.s.) observed them
שְׁמַרְתִּיךָ	I observed you (m.s.)
שְׁמַרְתִּיךְ	I observed you (f.s.)
שְׁמַרְתִּים	I observed them (m.)
שְׁמָרוּנִי	they observed me
שְׁמָרוּךְ	they observed you (f.s.)
שְׁמָרוּהוּ	they observed him
שְׁמָרוּם	they observed them
שְׁמַרְתּוּנִי	you (pl.) observed me
שְׁמַרְתּוּהוּ	you (pl.) observed him
שְׁמַרְנוּךָ	we observed you (m.s.)
שְׁמַרְנוּהוּ	we observed him

Note again (1) the shift of stress and resultant propretonic reduction; (2) the restoration of the full vowel in שְׁמָרוּהוּ etc.; (3) the possibility of confusion between the 2nd pers. fem. sing. and the 1st pers. com. sing. with *-tî-*.

QAL	שָׁמַרְתִּי	שְׁמַרְתִּיהוּ	שָׁמְרוּ	שְׁמָרוּהוּ
	עָזַבְתִּי	עֲזַבְתִּיהוּ	עָזְבוּ	עֲזָבוּהוּ
	מָצָאתִי	מְצָאתִיהוּ	מָצְאוּ	מְצָאוּהוּ
	רָאִיתִי	רְאִיתִיהוּ	רָאוּ	רָאוּהוּ
PIEL	בִּקַּשְׁתִּי	בִּקַּשְׁתִּיהוּ	בִּקְשׁוּ	בִּקְשׁוּהוּ
	עִנִּיתִי	עִנִּיתִיהוּ	עִנּוּ	עִנּוּהוּ
	בֵּרַכְתִּי	בֵּרַכְתִּיהוּ	בֵּרְכוּ	בֵּרְכוּהוּ
HIPHIL	הִשְׁמַדְתִּי	הִשְׁמַדְתִּיהוּ	הִשְׁמִידוּ	הִשְׁמִידוּהוּ
	הֶעֱלִיתִי	הֶעֱלִיתִיהוּ	הֶעֱלוּ	הֶעֱלוּהוּ
	הֲשִׁיבוֹתִי	הֲשִׁיבוֹתִיהוּ	הֵשִׁיבוּ	הֲשִׁיבוּהוּ

190. A Group of Irregular Qal Verbs.

There are several Qal verbs which have *ē* or *i* in second stem syllable before the pronominal suffixes. Two of these יָרַשׁ and שָׁאַל have unusual forms even in the 2nd pers. pl. of the non-suffixal paradigm: שְׁאֶלְתֶּם you asked; יְרִשְׁתֶּם

you inherited. Below, for reference, are the anomalous forms of the four important verbs of this type. Regular forms also occur in some instances.

אָהֵב or אָהַב	to love	3 m.s.	אֲהֵבְךָ	אֲהֵבוֹ	אֲהֵבָהּ
		3 f.s.	אֲהֵבָתֶךָ	אֲהֵבַתְהוּ	
		3 m.pl.	אֲהֵבוּךָ	אֲהֵבוּנִי	
יָלַד	to bear	2 f.s.	יְלִדְתִּנִי		
		1 c.s.	יְלִדְתִּיךָ	יְלִדְתִּיהוּ	
יָרַשׁ	to inherit	2 m.s.	יְרִשְׁתָּהּ	יְרִשְׁתָּם	
		3 m.pl.	יְרֵשׁוּךָ	יְרֵשׁוּהוּ	
		2 m.pl.	יְרִשְׁתֶּם		
שָׁאַל	to ask	3 m.s.	שְׁאֵלְךָ		
		1 c.s.	שְׁאִלְתִּיו	שְׁאִלְתִּיהוּ	
		3 m.pl.	שְׁאֵלוּנוּ		
		2 m.pl.	שְׁאֶלְתֶּם		

191. Vocabulary 53.

VERBS: חָמַל (יַחְמֹל) to spare (+ inf.: to spare oneself the trouble/expense of doing something); to pity (+ עַל)
שִׁלֵּם (יְשַׁלֵּם) to restore, make good, recompense
מָשַׁח (יִמְשַׁח) to anoint
בָּזָה (יִבְזֶה) to despise
בָּקַע (יִבְקַע) to split
עָזַר (יַעֲזֹר) to help
רָפָא (יִרְפָּא) to cure, heal; P רִפֵּא idem.

NOUNS: כֶּבֶשׂ (pl. *-îm*) lamb (male)
כִּבְשָׂה (pl. *-ôt*) lamb (female)
חֵיק bosom
חֶרֶב (w. suff. חַרְבִּי; pl. *-ôt*) sword (f.)

OTHER: יַחְדָּו / יַחַד (adv.) together, all together
עֵקֶב אֲשֶׁר / כִּי (conj.) because
נֶגֶד (prep.) before, in front of; w. suff. נֶגְדִּי etc. Also לְנֶגֶד
אֶפֶס a rare syn. of אַיִן "non-existence"; אֶפֶס כִּי (conj.) except that, save that

PROPER NAMES: נָתָן Nathan, the prophet
אוּרִיָּה Uriah
חִתִּי Hittite (adj.)

Exercises:

(a) Transform the following according to the example and translate.

עָזְרוּ אֹתִי → עֲזָרוּנִי they helped me

(1) גֵּרְשׁוּם
(2) מְכַרְנוּם
(3) אֲחָזוּנִי
(4) זְכַרְתִּיךְ
(5) קְצַרְתּוּהוּ
(6) שְׁתִיתִיהוּ
(7) קִדְּשׁוּנִי
(8) לְכַדְתִּים
(9) גְּנַבְנוּהוּ
(10) נְגַפְתִּינִי
(11) בֵּרְכוּךְ
(12) הֶעֱבִירוּם
(13) הִזְכַּרְתּוּנִי
(14) סְגַרְתִּיהוּ
(15) גְּאַלְנוּךְ

(b) Transform the following according to the example and translate.

רְאִיתִיהוּ → רָאִיתִי אֹתוֹ I saw him

(1) תְּפַשְׂתִּי אֹתָן
(2) שִׁלְּחָה אֹתָנוּ
(3) עִנִּינוּ אֹתָם
(4) מָשַׁחְנוּ אֹתוֹ
(5) שַׁמְנוּ אֹתָם
(6) נִאֲצוּ אֹתוֹ
(7) צִוִּינוּ אֹתָם
(8) הִרְאוּ אֹתִי
(9) הוֹרִידָה אֹתָם
(10) בָּנִיתִי אֹתָהּ
(11) עֲנִתָה אֹתָם
(12) שְׁכָחוּ אֹתָךְ
(13) בָּזִינוּ אֹתוֹ
(14) הִגַּשְׁתִּי אֹתָהּ
(15) בְּזָתָה אֹתִי

(c) Translate the following. Replace the object with the appropriate pronoun suffixed to the verb.

(1) עָזְבוּ אֶת־אֱלֹהֵיהֶם
(2) שָׁבַרְתִּי אֶת־הַחֶרֶב
(3) רָאִיתָ אֶת־עֶגְלֵיהֶם
(4) עִנּוּ אֶת־הָעָם
(5) אָסְרוּ אֶת־הַבַּחוּרִים
(6) מָאֲסוּ אֶת־דְּבָרַי
(7) עָזַרְנוּ אֶת־הַדַּלִּים
(8) לָקְחוּ אֶת־קְצִירֵנוּ
(9) הוֹשַׁעְנוּ אֶת־הַשָּׂרִים
(10) נְטַעְתֶּם כְּרָמִים
(11) בָּקְעוּ אֶת־הָעֵצִים
(12) נִחֲמוּ אֶת־הָאֲנָשִׁים
(13) קִבַּצְתִּי אֶת־הַכְּבָשִׂים
(14) הֶעֱלִיתָ אֶת־הַיְלָדִים
(15) שִׁלֵּם אֶת־הַכֶּסֶף

(d) Write in Hebrew:

1. We shall continue to meet him.
2. They began to approach the city in the evening, before the gate had been closed.
3. At that time there was no place for us to settle in, so we continued travelling.
4. Even in this congregation there are unrighteous men who do not heed the word of the Lord and who take pleasure in nullifying his statutes.
5. Prophesy now to the people, for evil days are coming and they will not be able to hide themselves from the terror which is about to fall upon them.
6. Bow down before the one who has made you and give thanks to the one who has delivered you from your distress.

(e) Reading: II Samuel 12:1-15a

(1) וַיִּשְׁלַח יהוה אֶת־נָתָן אֶל־דָּוִד וַיָּבֹא אֵלָיו וַיֹּאמֶר לוֹ שְׁנֵי אֲנָשִׁים הָיוּ בְּעִיר אֶחָת[1] אֶחָד
עָשִׁיר וְאֶחָד רָאשׁ:[2]

(2) לְעָשִׁיר הָיָה צֹאן וּבָקָר הַרְבֵּה מְאֹד׃
(3) וְלָרָשׁ אֵין־כֹּל כִּי אִם־כִּבְשָׂה אַחַת קְטַנָּה אֲשֶׁר קָנָה וַיְחַיֶּהָ[3] וַתִּגְדַּל עִמּוֹ וְעִם־בָּנָיו יַחְדָּו
מִפִּתּוֹ[4] תֹאכַל וּמִכֹּסוֹ[5] תִשְׁתֶּה וּבְחֵיקוֹ תִשְׁכָּב וַתְּהִי־לוֹ כְּבַת׃
(4) וַיָּבֹא הֵלֶךְ[6] לְאִישׁ הֶעָשִׁיר[7] וַיַּחְמֹל לָקַחַת מִצֹּאנוֹ וּמִבְּקָרוֹ לַעֲשׂוֹת לָאֹרֵחַ הַבָּא לוֹ וַיִּקַּח
אֶת־כִּבְשַׂת הָאִישׁ הָרָאשׁ וַיַּעֲשֶׂהָ[8] לָאִישׁ הַבָּא אֵלָיו׃
(5) וַיִּחַר־אַף דָּוִד בָּאִישׁ מְאֹד וַיֹּאמֶר אֶל־נָתָן חַי יהוה כִּי בֶן־מָוֶת[9] הָאִישׁ הָעֹשֶׂה זֹאת׃
(6) וְאֶת־הַכִּבְשָׂה יְשַׁלֵּם אַרְבַּעְתָּיִם[10] עֵקֶב אֲשֶׁר עָשָׂה אֶת־הַדָּבָר הַזֶּה וְעַל אֲשֶׁר לֹא־חָמָל׃
(7) וַיֹּאמֶר נָתָן אֶל־דָּוִד אַתָּה הָאִישׁ כֹּה אָמַר יהוה אֱלֹהֵי יִשְׂרָאֵל אָנֹכִי מְשַׁחְתִּיךָ לְמֶלֶךְ
עַל־יִשְׂרָאֵל וְאָנֹכִי הִצַּלְתִּיךָ מִיַּד שָׁאוּל׃
(8) וָאֶתְּנָה לְךָ אֶת־בֵּית אֲדֹנֶיךָ וְאֶת־נְשֵׁי אֲדֹנֶיךָ בְּחֵיקֶךָ וָאֶתְּנָה לְךָ אֶת־בֵּית יִשְׂרָאֵל וִיהוּדָה
וְאִם מְעָט וְאֹסִפָה לְּךָ כָּהֵנָּה וְכָהֵנָּה׃[11]
(9) מַדּוּעַ בָּזִיתָ אֶת־דְּבַר יהוה לַעֲשׂוֹת הָרַע בְּעֵינַי אֵת אוּרִיָּה הַחִתִּי הִכִּיתָ בַחֶרֶב וְאֶת־אִשְׁתּוֹ
לָקַחְתָּ לְּךָ לְאִשָּׁה וְאֹתוֹ הָרַגְתָּ בְּחֶרֶב בְּנֵי עַמּוֹן׃[12]
(10) וְעַתָּה לֹא־תָסוּר חֶרֶב מִבֵּיתְךָ עַד־עוֹלָם עֵקֶב כִּי בְזִתָנִי וַתִּקַּח אֶת־אֵשֶׁת אוּרִיָּה הַחִתִּי
לִהְיוֹת לְךָ לְאִשָּׁה׃
(11) כֹּה אָמַר יהוה הִנְנִי מֵקִים עָלֶיךָ רָעָה מִבֵּיתֶךָ וְלָקַחְתִּי אֶת־נָשֶׁיךָ לְעֵינֶיךָ וְנָתַתִּי לְרֵעֶיךָ
וְשָׁכַב עִם־נָשֶׁיךָ לְעֵינֵי הַשֶּׁמֶשׁ הַזֹּאת׃
(12) כִּי אַתָּה עָשִׂיתָ בַסָּתֶר[13] וַאֲנִי אֶעֱשֶׂה אֶת־הַדָּבָר הַזֶּה נֶגֶד כָּל־יִשְׂרָאֵל וְנֶגֶד הַשָּׁמֶשׁ׃
(13) וַיֹּאמֶר דָּוִד אֶל־נָתָן חָטָאתִי לַיהוה וַיֹּאמֶר נָתָן אֶל־דָּוִד גַּם־יהוה הֶעֱבִיר חַטָּאתְךָ לֹא
תָמוּת׃
(14) אֶפֶס כִּי־נִאֵץ נִאַצְתָּ אֶת־אֹיְבֵי[14] יהוה בַּדָּבָר הַזֶּה גַּם הַבֵּן הַיִּלּוֹד[15] לְךָ מוֹת יָמוּת׃
(15) וַיֵּלֶךְ נָתָן אֶל־בֵּיתוֹ׃

Notes to the reading:

1. אֶחָת pausal form of אַחַת
2. רָאשׁ (or רָשׁ) poor (adj.)
3. וַיְחַיֶּהָ = יְחַיֶּה אֹתָהּ
4. פַּת morsel
5. כּוֹס or כֹּס cup
6. הֵלֶךְ traveller
7. Note the construction לְאִישׁ הֶעָשִׁיר to the rich man, where the noun is in construct with the definite adjective.
8. וַיַּעֲשֶׂהָ = וַיַּעַשׂ אֹתָהּ
9. "deserving of/sentenced to death"
10. Note § 161 (d)
11. "and if (that were) too little, I would add unto you (i.e. increase your wealth and prestige) so much more"
12. בְּנֵי עַמּוֹן the Ammonites
13. בְּסָתֶר secretly; סֵתֶר secret
14. אֹיְבֵי may have been inserted at an early date to prevent the verb נִאֵץ from having יהוה as its direct object. The word must be ignored in translation. נִאֵץ = inf. abs. (irreg.).
15. יִלּוֹד a rare type of verbal adjective: "born"

LESSON 54

192. Object Suffixes on the Imperfect.

When the form of the imperfect ends in a consonant, the suffix *-ē-* or *-en-* is added before the object pronoun; thus *yišmōr* + *ē*/*en* + *nî* → *yišmərḗnî*/*yišmərénnî* (he will observe me). Because of various contractions, however, it is simpler to learn the suffixed elements as a unit:

	(1)		(2)	
1 c.s.	ֶ֫נִּי	*–énnî*	ֵ֫נִי	*–ḗnî*
2 m.s.	ֶ֫ךָּ	*–ékkā*	——	——
2 f.s.	——	——	ֵךְ	*–ḗḵ*
3 m.s.	ֶ֫נּוּ	*–énnû*	ֵ֫הוּ	*–ḗhû*
3 f.s.	ֶ֫נָּה	*–énnāh*	ֶ֫הָ	*–ḗhā*
1 c.pl.	ֶ֫נּוּ	*–énnû*	ֵ֫נוּ	*–ḗnû*
3 m.pl.	——	——	ֵם	*–ḗm*
3 f.pl.	——	——	ֵן	*–ḗn*

Neither paradigm is complete in itself. Forms of either column may be used, with no difference in meaning.

Excluding for the moment the imperfects of verbs from roots III-*Hē,* we may distinguish those whose stem vowel is reducible (as in יִשְׁמֹר, יִשְׁמְרוּ), which includes most Qal and Piel verbs, and those whose stem vowel is not reducible, mainly Qal verbs from Hollow Roots and Hiphil verbs. When the stem vowel is *ō* or *ē,* the same reduction takes place as in the main paradigm:

cf. יִשְׁמְרוּ (they will observe) and יִשְׁמְרֵ֫נִי (he will observe me); יִתְּנוּ (they will give) and יִתְּנֵ֫נִי (he will give me). But when the stem vowel is *-a-*, this is not reduced but lengthened to *ā* before the accented syllable of the suffix. Contrast יִשְׁמַע and יִשְׁמְעוּ with יִשְׁמָעֵ֫נִי (he will hear me). Read carefully through the representative forms given below to be sure that this point is clear.

The imperfect plural forms in *-û* (e.g. יִשְׁמְרוּ, תִּשְׁמְרוּ) take the suffixes given in Column B, §184. But even in these forms the *a* vowel of the stem is restored. Contrast

יִשְׁמְרוּ יִשְׁמְר֫וּנִי יִשְׁמְעוּ יִשְׁמָע֫וּנִי.

QAL	יִשְׁמֹר	יִשְׁמְרֵ֫נִי	יִשְׁמְרוּ	יִשְׁמְר֫וּנִי
	יִלְמַד	יִלְמָדֵ֫הוּ	יִלְמְדוּ	יִלְמָד֫וּהוּ
	יִשְׁמַע	יִשְׁמָעֵ֫נִי	יִשְׁמְעוּ	יִשְׁמָע֫וּנִי
	יַעֲזֹב	יַעַזְבֵ֫נִי	יַעַזְבוּ	יַעַזְב֫וּנִי
	יִמְצָא	יִמְצָאֵ֫נִי	יִמְצְאוּ	יִמְצָא֫וּנִי
	יֹאכַל	יֹאכְלֵ֫הוּ	יֹאכְלוּ	יֹאכְל֫וּהוּ
	תֵּלֵד	תֵּלְדֵ֫הוּ	—	—
	יֵדַע	יֵדָעֵ֫הוּ	יֵדְעוּ	יֵדָע֫וּהוּ
	יָשִׂים	יְשִׂימֵ֫הוּ	יָשִׂימוּ	יְשִׂימ֫וּהוּ
	יָסֹב	יְסֻבֵּ֫הוּ	יָסֹבּוּ	יְסֻבּ֫וּהוּ
	יִתֵּן	יִתְּנֵ֫נִי	יִתְּנוּ	יִתְּנ֫וּנִי
PIEL	יְבַקֵּשׁ	יְבַקְשֵׁ֫נִי	יְבַקְשׁוּ	יְבַקְשׁ֫וּנִי
	יְשַׁלַּח	יְשַׁלְּחֵ֫נִי	יְשַׁלְּחוּ	יְשַׁלְּח֫וּנִי
	יְבָרֵךְ	יְבָרְכֵ֫נִי	יְבָרְכוּ	יְבָרְכ֫וּנִי
HIPHIL	יַשְׁמִיד	יַשְׁמִידֵ֫הוּ	יַשְׁמִ֫ידוּ	יַשְׁמִיד֫וּהוּ
	יַמְצִיא	יַמְצִיאֵ֫הוּ	יַמְצִ֫יאוּ	יַמְצִיא֫וּהוּ
	יוֹרִיד	יוֹרִידֵ֫הוּ	יוֹרִ֫ידוּ	יוֹרִיד֫וּהוּ
	יָקִים	יְקִימֵ֫הוּ	יָקִ֫ימוּ	יְקִימ֫וּהוּ
	יָסֵב	יְסִבֵּ֫הוּ	יָסֵ֫בּוּ	יְסִבּ֫וּהוּ

The distinction between short (jussive, "converted") and normal imperfects is not retained before pronominal suffixes.

וַיַּשְׁמֵד אֹתוֹ → וַיַּשְׁמִידֵ֫הוּ and he destroyed him

Note that the *-a-* in the final stem syllable of the Piel imperfects such as יְשַׁלַּח does not conform to the rule given above and is reduced: יְשַׁלְּחֵ֫הוּ. Note also יֹאכְלֵ֫הוּ.

The object suffix *-ḵā* (you, m.s.) may be added directly to the imperfect stem, in which $\bar{o} \rightarrow o$ and $\bar{e} \rightarrow e$; *a* remains *a*; *î* remains *î*.

יִשְׁמֹר אֹתְךָ → יִשְׁמָרְךָ֫

יִתֵּן אֹתְךָ → יִתֶּנְךָ֫

יְבַקֵּשׁ אֹתְךָ → יְבַקֶּשְׁךָ֫

יְשַׁלַּח אֹתְךָ → יְשַׁלַּחֲךָ (but note Qal יִשְׁלָחֲךָ)
יַשְׁמִיד אֹתְךָ → יַשְׁמִידְךָ

Verbs from roots III-*Hē* drop the final *-eh* before the suffixes:

QAL	יִבְנֶה / יִבֶן	יִבְנֵהוּ	יִבְנְךָ	יִבְנֶךָּ
PIEL	יְצַוֶּה / יְצַו	יְצַוֵּהוּ	יְצַוְּךָ	יְצַוֶּךָּ
HIPHIL	יַרְאֶה	יַרְאֵהוּ	יַרְאֲךָ	יַרְאֶךָּ
	יַעֲלֶה	יַעֲלֵהוּ	יַעַלְךָ	יַעֲלֶךָּ

193. Object Suffixes on the Imperative.

The suffixes used are the same as those found with the imperfect. The general similarity with the imperfect is such that no new principles are involved in the attachment of the suffixes. The following examples should suffice:

QAL	שְׁמֹר	שָׁמְרֵנִי	שִׁמְרוּ	שִׁמְרוּנִי
	תֵּן	תְּנֵנִי	תְּנוּ	תְּנוּנִי
	שְׁמַע	שָׁמְעֵנִי	שִׁמְעוּ	שָׁמְעוּנִי
	מְצָא	מְצָאֵנִי	מִצְאוּ	מְצָאוּנִי
	בְּנֵה	בְּנֵהוּ	בְּנוּ	בְּנוּהוּ
	שִׂים	שִׂימֵהוּ	שִׂימוּ	שִׂימוּהוּ
	סֹב	סְבֵּהוּ	סֹבּוּ	סְבּוּהוּ
PIEL	בַּקֵּשׁ	בַּקְּשֵׁהוּ	בַּקְּשׁוּ	בַּקְּשׁוּהוּ
	שַׁלַּח	שַׁלְּחֵהוּ	שַׁלְּחוּ	שַׁלְּחוּהוּ
HIPHIL	הַשְׁמֵד	הַשְׁמִידֵהוּ	הַשְׁמִידוּ	הַשְׁמִידוּהוּ
	הַרְבֵּה	הַרְבֵּהוּ	הַרְבּוּ	הַרְבּוּהוּ
	הַעֲלֵה	הַעֲלֵהוּ	הַעֲלוּ	הַעֲלוּהוּ

194. Object Suffixes on the Infinitive Construct.

Because of the ambivalence of the infinitive with regard to voice, the subject suffixes learned in §115 may have an object value in translation. E.g. "he sought my killing" may refer to "my killing someone else" or "my being killed." In the first person singular the ambiguity may be resolved by employing *-ênî* as object versus *-î* as subject: הָרְגִי versus הָרְגֵנִי In the third person singular masculine it is possible to use *-ô* as opposed to *-êhû* in this same way. In general, however, it is necessary to translate the infinitive plus pronominal suffix as the context demands. This is analogous, of course, to the situation when a noun follows: הֲרֹג אִישׁ "killing a man" (objective) or "a man's killing (someone)" (subjective).

195. Vocabulary 54.

VERBS: הִטָּה (יַטֶּה) to turn aside, incline, thrust aside (all transitive)
פָּנָה (יִפְנֶה) to turn toward, turn (both trans. and intrans.)
נָטַשׁ (יִטֹּשׁ) to leave, forsake, abandon
חָשַׁב (יַחְשֹׁב) to think, devise, reckon, impute

NOUNS: תְּחִנָּה (pl. *-ôṯ*) supplication
צְדָקָה (pl. *-ôṯ*) righteousness, righteous act
מָטָר (pl. *-ôṯ*) rain
נַחֲלָה (pl. *-ôṯ*) property, possession, inheritance, portion
זְרוֹעַ (pl. *-îm*/*-ôṯ*) arm; (fig.) strength (usually fem.)
יִרְאָה fear; used also as the infinitive construct of יָרֵא (constr. יִרְאַת)

OTHER: נָכְרִי (adj.) foreign, strange; fem. נָכְרִיָּה
אָמְנָם / אֻמְנָם (adv.) truly, indeed

Exercises:

(a) Transform according to the example and translate.

Ex. תִּשְׁמֹר אֹתָם → תִּשְׁמְרֵם you shall observe them

(1) יַטֶּה אֹתָם
(2) יִמְאֲסוּ אֹתוֹ
(3) שַׁלֵּם אֹתָהּ
(4) אַל־תִּטֹּשׁ אֹתִי
(5) עֲזֹר אֹתָנוּ
(6) רְפָא אֹתָם
(7) מִשְׁחוּ אֹתוֹ
(8) יְכַחֵד אֹתָם
(9) תְּנַחֲמוּ אֹתָנוּ
(10) תִּמְצָא אֹתִי
(11) הַטֵּה אֹתוֹ
(12) גָּרֵשׁ אֹתָם
(13) אַל־תְּקַלֵּל אֹתָהּ
(14) שָׁרֵת אֹתוֹ
(15) אַל־תִּבְזֶה אֹתִי

(b) Transform according to the example and translate.

Ex. שְׁמָרוּהוּ → שִׁמְרוּ אֹתוֹ observe him

(1) הֲעִידֵם
(2) יַאֲרִיכֵם
(3) הוֹרִידֵהוּ
(4) יוֹלִיכְךָ
(5) יְבַקְעֵם
(6) יַחְשְׁבוּנִי
(7) יַגְדִּילֵם
(8) וַיּוֹרֵהוּ
(9) וַיַּשִּׂיגֵנוּ
(10) הַאֲבִידֵם
(11) שְׁלָחוּנִי
(12) וַיַּכֵּנִי
(13) הַצְלִיחֵנִי
(14) וַיַּשְׁמִיעֵם
(15) יִטְּשׁוּךָ

(c) Translate the following. Replace the nominal object with the appropriate pronoun, suffixed to the verb. E.g. הֲרֹג אֶת־הָאִישׁ → הָרְגֵהוּ

(1) יִתֵּן לָנוּ מָטָר
(2) שְׁמַע אֶת־תְּחִנָּתִי
(3) הָשֵׁב אֶת־הַנָּכְרִי
(4) נִאֵץ אֶת־הָרְשָׁעִים
(5) הַשְׁמַע אֶת־הַגּוֹיִם
(6) הַסְתֵּר אֶת־הַכֶּסֶף
(7) הָמֵת אֶת־שָׂרֵיהֶם
(8) בַּעֵר אֶת־עָרֵיהֶם
(9) אַל־תִּזְבַּח אֶת־הַכֶּבֶשׂ
(10) יַשְׁלִיךְ אֶת־חַרְבּוֹ אַרְצָה
(11) תֵּן לִי אֶת־נַחֲלָתִי
(12) הַזְכֵּר אֶת־שְׁמוֹ

(13) הַזְכִּירוּ אֶת־מַעֲשֵׂיהֶם
(14) הָבֵא אֶת־הָאָרוֹן
(15) נְטַע אֶת־הַזֵּיתִים

(d) Write in Hebrew.

1. Let my supplication come before thee, O Lord.
2. He will continue to give rain upon the earth.
3. Who is that strange man the elders are speaking with?
4. Fear of him fell upon them and their hearts melted within them.
5. I shall walk in truth and righteousness all the days of my life.
6. The fear of the Lord is the beginning of wisdom.
7. Even the strong will fall before him.
8. Because you have slain his anointed one, you also shall die.
9. Have pity on the poor, for there is no other to help them.
10. I will not heed your prayers and your supplications.

LESSON 55

196. Conditional Sentences.

Any two clauses, the first of which states a real or hypothetical condition, and the second of which states a real or hypothetical consequence thereof, may be taken as a conditional sentence. Because conditional sentences entail a logical and (usually) temporal sequence, they form a natural subgroup related to the narrative sequences. Conditional sentences in Hebrew may be virtually unmarked; the translation of certain sets of clauses in a regular future narrative sequence often requires a conditional sentence in English:

וְעָזַב אֶת־אָבִיו וָמֵת	and if he leaves his father, he (i.e. his father) will die (Gen. 44 : 22)
וְשָׁמַע שָׁאוּל וַהֲרָגָנִי	and if Saul hears (about it), he will kill me (I Sam. 16 : 2)

Many such occurrences are ambiguous, since a non-conditional translation can also be found. In a series of three or more clauses, it is only a matter of the translator's judgement where to end the protasis and begin the apodosis. In poetic, aphoristic, or legal styles an otherwise unmarked participial protasis is not infrequent:

וּמַכֵּה אָבִיו וְאִמּוֹ מוֹת יוּמָת	and if a man slays his father or his mother, he shall be put to death (Ex. 21 : 15)
וְגֹנֵב אִישׁ וּמְכָרוֹ וְנִמְצָא בְיָדוֹ מוֹת יוּמָת	and if a man kidnaps a man and sells

him, or (if) he is found in his hand,
he shall be put to death (Ex. 21:16)

These may also be translated non-conditionally as "Anyone who slays... shall be put to death" etc.

Conditional sentences marked by a special conjunction "if" are of two types: (1) those introduced by אִם, הֵן, or כִּי, which are real, fulfilled, or fulfillable and (2) those introduced by לוּ (neg. לוּלֵי), which are unreal, contrary-to-fact, unfulfillable.

Type (1). The protasis (the "if"-clause) may have a perfect, imperfect, or participial predicate. It is difficult to maintain these distinctions in translation. The perfect sometimes has the value of the English perfect or (perhaps over-correctly) of the future-perfect, but more often takes on the value of the Hebrew imperfect in its general present-future function. Thus, although one may make a valid distinction between

אִם מָצָאתִי חֵן...	if I have found favor...
אִם אֶמְצָא חֵן...	if I find favor (in the future)...

that same distinction becomes artificial if applied, e.g., to

אִם עָבַרְתָּ אִתִּי וְהָיִתָ עָלַי לְמַשָּׂא	If you cross over with me, you will be a burden to me (II Sam. 15:33)
אִם־יַעַבְרוּ... אִתְּכֶם... וּנְתַתֶּם לָהֶם...	If they cross over with you, you shall give them... (Num. 32:29).

Both protases refer to future events as conditions. It is always possible to justify the use of the perfect in the protasis as representing a completed action of accomplished state in the mind of the speaker. It is difficult within Hebrew itself to predict the choice between the perfect and the imperfect in the construction with the same meaning. Whatever the original distinction was, it has become obscured in Hebrew of the biblical period, so that both verbs will have, in general, the same range of translation values.

The apodosis corresponds closely to a clause in a present-future sequence:

wə + perfect (converted)
wə (optional) + non-verb + imperfect (disjunctive pattern)
wə + non-verbal clause
imperative

None of these offers any special problems in translation. The following examples illustrate the more frequent combinations of the possible clause types:

וְאִם־יָשַׁבְנוּ פֹה וָמַתְנוּ	And if we stay here, we shall die (II Kings 7:4)
אִם לֹא הֲבִיאֹתִיו אֵלֶיךָ... וְחָטָאתִי לְךָ	If I do not bring him back to you...

	I shall be accountable to you (Gen. 43:9)
אִם שָׁכַחְנוּ שֵׁם אֱלֹהֵינוּ וַנִּפְרֹשׂ כַּפֵּינוּ לְאֵל זָר הֲלֹא אֱלֹהִים יַחֲקָר־זֹאת	If we forget the name of our God and extend our hands to a foreign god, will not God find this out? (Ps. 44:21)
וְהָיָה אִם־לֹא חָפַצְתָּ בָּהּ וְשִׁלַּחְתָּהּ	And if you are not pleased with her, you shall send her forth (Deut. 21:14)
וְאִם־יִהְיוּ חֲטָאֵיכֶם כַּשָּׁנִים כַּשֶּׁלֶג יַלְבִּינוּ	Even if your sins are as scarlet, they shall become as white as snow (Is. 1:18)
וְהָיָה אִם־אִישׁ יָבֹא וּשְׁאֵלֵךְ... וְאָמַרְתְּ	And if a man comes and asks you... you shall say... (Judges 4:20)

A clause introduced by the particles הֵן, כִּי and אֲשֶׁר (cf. §70) may also be equivalent to the protasis of a conditional sentence.

It was pointed out in a previous lesson (cf. §138) that אִם has a negative translation value as part of an oath formula. The expression אִם לֹא has thus a positive value in the same context.

חַי־אָנִי... אִם־לֹא כַּאֲשֶׁר דִּבַּרְתֶּם בְּאָזְנָי כֵּן אֶעֱשֶׂה לָכֶם	As I live, I shall do to you as you have spoken into my ears (or: as you have confided in me) (Num. 14:28)
וַיִּשָּׁבַע מֹשֶׁה... לֵאמֹר אִם־לֹא הָאָרֶץ... לְךָ תִהְיֶה לְנַחֲלָה	And Moses swore saying: "The land .....will be an inheritance for you... (Joshua 14:9)

Type (2). Contrary-to-fact conditional sentences introduced by לוּ are too infrequent to allow a meaningful analysis. Here are some typical examples:

לוּ יֶשׁ־חֶרֶב בְּיָדִי כִּי עַתָּה הֲרַגְתִּיךְ	If there were a sword in my hand, I would surely now kill you (Num. 22:29)
לוּ חָכְמוּ יַשְׂכִּילוּ זֹאת	If they were wise, they would understand this (Deut. 32:29)
לוּ הַחֲיִתֶם אוֹתָם לֹא הָרַגְתִּי אֶתְכֶם	If you had let them live, I would not kill you (Judges 8:19)
לוּ חָפֵץ יהוה לַהֲמִיתֵנוּ לֹא־לָקַח מִיָּדֵנוּ עֹלָה	If the Lord had wanted to kill us, he would not have received an offering from us (Judges 13:23)
לוּלֵי אֱלֹהֵי אָבִי... הָיָה לִי כִּי־עַתָּה רֵיקָם שִׁלַּחְתָּנִי	If the God of my father had not been on my side, you would have sent me away empty (Gen. 31:42)

The particle לוּ may also be used in the sense "would that" without a following apodosis:

וְלוּ הוֹאַלְנוּ וַנֵּשֶׁב בְּעֵבֶר הַיַּרְדֵּן	Would that we had been content to dwell on the other side of the Jordan (Joshua 7:7)

197. Concluding Remarks on Clause Sequences.

The syntax of Biblical Hebrew presents difficult and often insoluble problems. Given the unknown numbers of sources, writers, and editors that have had a hand in the formation of the text, together with the grammatical schools of the later traditionalists, we can never be sure how much reliance (grammatically speaking) we may place in the textus receptus and, consequently, how refined our analysis can be before becoming meaningless. The narrative sequences presented in this grammar are a good case in point. To maintain that these are the sole devices pertinent to the syntax of *wə*-clauses would be false in the face of the many obvious exceptions. But because most sequences can be reduced to these patterns there is certainly some value in regarding them as standard. The evolution of Hebrew toward the post-biblical type replaced most of the older converting sequences by simpler non-converting ones. Thus, a formal tendency directly opposed to an earlier one must have been a work in the latest redactions of the text before it achieved its fixed form. Certainly some of the inconsistencies in verbal usage and clause syntax are to be attributed to this influence.

(**a**) Further remarks on the present-future narrative sequence (1b–c). This sequence, characterized by a continuing series of converted perfects, may be led off by a variety of clause types; we have already mentioned leading clauses with verbal (imperfect) and non-verbal predicates. The verb הָיָה in a leading clause requires special consideration. By virtue of its double meaning "be/become" it may be used to describe a non-punctual past tense situation (e.g. "there was a famine in the land"). If a narrative sequence begins with a clause containing the verb הָיָה (or וַיְהִי), the real nature of the sequence is not clear until we reach a continuing verb. Contrast

הָיָה רָעָב בָּאָרֶץ וְיָרַד מִצְרַיְמָה...	There was a famine in the land and he used to go down to Egypt... (habitual)
הָיָה רָעָב בָּאָרֶץ וַיֵּרֶד מִצְרַיְמָה...	There was a famine in the land and he went down to Egypt (specific; punctual)

The leading clause of the present-future sequence may thus be redefined as comprising the formal subtypes:

(a) imperfect
(b) non-verbal clause (including those with participial predicates)
(c) conditional clauses, with perfect or imperfect finite verb in a present-future meaning
(d) the verb הָיָה in a non-punctual sense

all continued by *wə* + (converted) perfect.

(b) Conjunctive, non-converting sequences:
(1) perfect + *wə* + perfect (unconverted)
(2) imperfect + *wə* + imperfect (unconverted)
(3) imperative + *wə* + imperative

The third of these sequences has already been mentioned (§107) and is included here only because of its formal similarity. Sequences (1) and (2), however, are new and because they are by no means uncommon deserve some comment. They seldom occur in punctual narrative and are used mainly where there is a simple listing of clauses without an explicit expression of logical or temporal consecution; they may thus be defined as conjunctive but non-consecutive. But when they *are* used in a consecutive series it is usually to continue a disjunctive clause rather than in the main narrative. For example, suppose that in the main narrative a person has been mentioned about whom the writer wishes to supply additional information. Such information is usually introduced by a disjunctive formula (verb not first). It is often the case that this explanatory disjunction will continue for several clauses before the writer returns to the main narrative; it is in this type of sub-sequence that (1) and (2) are frequently met in a consecutive sense. Note, for example, I Sam. 23:20, concerning a certain Benayahu:

וְהוּא יָרַד וְהִכָּה אֶת־הָאֲרִי	and he is the one who went down and killed the lion...

Another use of sequences (1) and (2) above is an analog of the imperative + *wə* + cohortative sequence, in which the second clause is best translated as a purpose or result clause (cf. §107). Thus corresponding to a hypothetical (but normal) sequence of the type (1b):

הַרְחֵב לָ֫נוּ וְנִפְרֶה בָאָ֫רֶץ	Make room for us, so that we may be fruitful in the land

we have the statement of fact in Gen. 26:22:

כִּי־עַתָּה הִרְחִיב יהוה לָ֫נוּ וּפָרִ֫ינוּ בָאָ֫רֶץ	....for now the Lord has made room for us to be fruitful in the land.

(c) Finally, note the unusual sequence occurring in each of the three passages outlined below as illustrations. We are dealing in each case with a punctual, habitual sequence. Circumstantial information about action which is prior to the clause that will follow is introduced by *wa* + imperfect (converted), best rendered "and when he had done so-and-so..." Such clauses are conjunctive by definition, but because of their formal departure from the sequence in which they occur, they clearly mark an anticipatory temporal subordination.

Illustrative Passages

I Sam. 17:34–5. In this passage David describes his prowess as a shepherd. The sequence begins with the ambiguous verb הָיָה and is uniformly with converted perfects (1b), with the exception of וַיָּקָם which belongs to the peculiar type mentioned in the preceding paragraph. [In this and the following passages only the leading elements of each clause are given. Clauses irrelevant to the discussion at hand are omitted. Indentation indicates subordination or disjunction. The reader should compare our outlines with the original text.]

רֹעֶה הָיָה עַבְדְּךָ	I (your servant) was a shepherd...	Note ambiguous *hāyāh*.
וּבָא הָאֲרִי	and (whenever) a lion would come	
וְנָשָׂא	and take	
וְיָצָאתִי	I would go out	
וְהִכִּתִיו	and strike	
וְהִצַּלְתִּי	and rescue	
וַיָּקָם	and when he attacked me	Anticipatory subordination
וְהֶחֱזַקְתִּי	I would grab him	Resumption of main sequence.
וְהִכִּתִיו	and beat him	
וַהֲמִיתִּיו	and kill him	

Job 1:1–5:

אִישׁ הָיָה	There was a man	Beginning of the main narrative; note ambiguous *hāyāh*.
וְהָיָה הָאִישׁ הַהוּא	and that man was	Continuation with *wəhāyāh* marks the sequence as type 1b (habitual).
וַיִּוָּלְדוּ	and when there was born to him	Anticipatory subordination, continued by two consecutive clauses.
וַיְהִי	and his herds had reached (the extent of)	
וַיְהִי	and he had become great	
וְהָלְכוּ	his sons used to go	Resumption of main narrative
וְעָשׂוּ	and make	

וְשָׁלְחוּ	and send	
וְקָרְאוּ	and call	
וַיְהִי כִּי הִקִּיפוּ	and when the feast days had run their course	Another anticipatory subordination marked by *wa* + imperf. (converted), complicated by a temporal clause insertion with *kî*.
וַיִּשְׁלַח	and he had sent	
וַיְקַדְּשֵׁם	and had sanctified them	
וְהִשְׁכִּים	he would get up early	Resumption of main narrative.
וְהֶעֱלָה	and send up offerings	
כִּי אָמַר אִיּוֹב	for Job said	Simple subordination with *kî*.
אוּלַי חָטְאוּ	perhaps they have sinned	Quotation, beginning a secondary sequence (type 3a).
וּבֵרְכוּ	and "blessed"	
כָּכָה יַעֲשֶׂה	thus he used to do	Disjunction marking the end of the general introduction to the narrative.

Note the correct reversion to the imperfect in the final disjunction.

I Sam. 1:1–7.

וַיְהִי אִישׁ אֶחָד	(and) there was a certain man	Beginning of main sequence, followed by four disjunctive non-verbal clauses (omitted here).
וַיְהִי לִפְנִנָּה	(and) Peninah had children	Continuation of main sequence, still with the ambiguous *wayhî*.
וְעָלָה הָאִישׁ הַהוּא	(and) that man used to go up	Continuation of main sequence, now clearly habitual, with the converted perfect.
וַיְהִי הַיּוֹם וַיִּזְבַּח	and when, on a given day he had sacrificed	Anticipatory subordination, doubled here with a temporal clause.
וְנָתַן	he would give	Continuation of main sequence.
וּלְחַנָּה יִתֵּן	but to Hannah he would give	Disjunction for contrast. Note the correct reversion to the imperfect.
וְכִעֲסַתָּה צָרָתָהּ	and her rival would vex	Main narrative.
וְכֵן יַעֲשֶׂה	and thus he would do	End of main sequence, as marked by the disjunction.

At this point in the narrative the writer turns to the specific occasion of Hannah's encounter with Eli and employs the regular past-punctual sequence, beginning with the *wayyṓmer* of vs. 8.

198. Vocabulary 55.

VERBS:	כִּלְכֵּל (יְכַלְכֵּל)	to contain, sustain, support
	שָׁבָה (יִשְׁבֶּה)	to lead into exile; N. passive
	רִחֵם (יְרַחֵם)	to be compassionate toward
	הִבְדִּיל (יַבְדִּיל)	to divide, make a separation between
	כִּלָּה (יְכַלֶּה)	to complete, bring to an end; + inf.: to finish doing
	כָּרַע (יִכְרַע)	to bow down
	אָנַף (יֶאֱנַף)	to become angry
	פָּשַׁע (יִפְשַׁע)	to rebel, transgress (בְּ: against)
NOUNS:	רִנָּה	(no pl.) a cry of joy (less commonly, of supplication)
	בַּרְזֶל	(no pl.) iron
	פֶּשַׁע	(w. suff. פִּשְׁעִי; pl. *-îm*) transgression, sin
	מְנוּחָה	(pl. *-ôṯ*) rest, resting-place
ADJ:	בָּרוּךְ	blessed
PROPER NAME:	שְׁלֹמֹה	Solomon

Reading: I Kings 8:22–30; 44–58: Solomon's Prayer.

(22) וַיַּעֲמֹד שְׁלֹמֹה לִפְנֵי מִזְבַּח יהוה נֶגֶד כָּל־קְהַל יִשְׂרָאֵל וַיִּפְרֹשׂ כַּפָּיו הַשָּׁמָיִם׃[1]
(23) וַיֹּאמַר יהוה אֱלֹהֵי יִשְׂרָאֵל אֵין־כָּמוֹךָ אֱלֹהִים בַּשָּׁמַיִם מִמַּעַל וְעַל־הָאָרֶץ מִתָּחַת שֹׁמֵר
הַבְּרִית וְהַחֶסֶד לַעֲבָדֶיךָ הַהֹלְכִים לְפָנֶיךָ בְּכָל־לִבָּם׃
(24) אֲשֶׁר שָׁמַרְתָּ לְעַבְדְּךָ דָּוִד אָבִי אֵת אֲשֶׁר־דִּבַּרְתָּ לוֹ וַתְּדַבֵּר בְּפִיךָ וּבְיָדְךָ מִלֵּאתָ כַּיּוֹם הַזֶּה׃
(25) וְעַתָּה יהוה אֱלֹהֵי יִשְׂרָאֵל שְׁמֹר לְעַבְדְּךָ דָוִד אָבִי אֵת אֲשֶׁר דִּבַּרְתָּ לּוֹ לֵאמֹר לֹא־יִכָּרֵת
לְךָ אִישׁ מִלְּפָנַי יֹשֵׁב עַל־כִּסֵּא יִשְׂרָאֵל רַק אִם־יִשְׁמְרוּ בָנֶיךָ אֶת־דַּרְכָּם לָלֶכֶת לְפָנַי
כַּאֲשֶׁר הָלַכְתָּ לְפָנָי׃
(26) וְעַתָּה אֱלֹהֵי יִשְׂרָאֵל יֵאָמֶן נָא דְּבָרְיךָ[2] אֲשֶׁר דִּבַּרְתָּ לְעַבְדְּךָ דָּוִד אָבִי׃
(27) כִּי הַאֻמְנָם יֵשֵׁב אֱלֹהִים עַל־הָאָרֶץ הִנֵּה[3] הַשָּׁמַיִם וּשְׁמֵי הַשָּׁמַיִם לֹא יְכַלְכְּלוּךָ אַף כִּי־
הַבַּיִת הַזֶּה אֲשֶׁר בָּנִיתִי׃
(28) וּפָנִיתָ[4] אֶל־תְּפִלַּת עַבְדְּךָ וְאֶל־תְּחִנָּתוֹ יהוה אֱלֹהָי לִשְׁמֹעַ אֶל־הָרִנָּה וְאֶל־הַתְּפִלָּה אֲשֶׁר
עַבְדְּךָ מִתְפַּלֵּל לְפָנֶיךָ הַיּוֹם׃
(29) לִהְיוֹת עֵינֶךָ[5] פְתֻחוֹת אֶל־הַבַּיִת הַזֶּה לַיְלָה וָיוֹם אֶל־הַמָּקוֹם אֲשֶׁר אָמַרְתָּ יִהְיֶה שְׁמִי
שָׁם לִשְׁמֹעַ אֶל־הַתְּפִלָּה אֲשֶׁר יִתְפַּלֵּל עַבְדְּךָ אֶל־הַמָּקוֹם הַזֶּה׃
(30) וְשָׁמַעְתָּ אֶל־תְּחִנַּת עַבְדְּךָ וְעַמְּךָ יִשְׂרָאֵל אֲשֶׁר יִתְפַּלְלוּ אֶל־הַמָּקוֹם הַזֶּה וְאַתָּה תִּשְׁמַע
אֶל־מְקוֹם שִׁבְתְּךָ אֶל־הַשָּׁמַיִם וְשָׁמַעְתָּ וְסָלָחְתָּ׃
(44) כִּי־יֵצֵא עַמְּךָ לַמִּלְחָמָה עַל־אֹיְבוֹ בַּדֶּרֶךְ אֲשֶׁר תִּשְׁלָחֵם וְהִתְפַּלְלוּ אֶל־יהוה דֶּרֶךְ[6] הָעִיר
אֲשֶׁר בָּחַרְתָּ בָּהּ וְהַבַּיִת אֲשֶׁר־בָּנִתִי לִשְׁמֶךָ׃
(45) וְשָׁמַעְתָּ הַשָּׁמַיִם אֶת־תְּפִלָּתָם וְאֶת־תְּחִנָּתָם וְעָשִׂיתָ מִשְׁפָּטָם׃
(46) כִּי יֶחֶטְאוּ־לָךְ כִּי אֵין אָדָם אֲשֶׁר לֹא־יֶחֱטָא וְאָנַפְתָּ בָם וּנְתַתָּם לִפְנֵי אוֹיֵב וְשָׁבוּם שֹׁבֵיהֶם
אֶל־אֶרֶץ הָאוֹיֵב רְחוֹקָה אוֹ קְרוֹבָה׃
(47) וְהֵשִׁיבוּ[7] אֶל־לִבָּם בָּאָרֶץ אֲשֶׁר נִשְׁבּוּ־שָׁם וְשָׁבוּ וְהִתְחַנְּנוּ אֵלֶיךָ בְּאֶרֶץ שֹׁבֵיהֶם לֵאמֹר
חָטָאנוּ וְהֶעֱוִינוּ[8] רָשָׁעְנוּ׃[9]
(48) וְשָׁבוּ אֵלֶיךָ בְּכָל־לְבָבָם וּבְכָל־נַפְשָׁם בְּאֶרֶץ אֹיְבֵיהֶם אֲשֶׁר־שָׁבוּ אֹתָם וְהִתְפַּלְלוּ אֵלֶיךָ
דֶּרֶךְ אַרְצָם אֲשֶׁר נָתַתָּה לַאֲבוֹתָם הָעִיר אֲשֶׁר בָּחַרְתָּ וְהַבַּיִת אֲשֶׁר־בָּנִיתִי לִשְׁמֶךָ׃

(49) וְשָׁמַעְתָּ הַשָּׁמַיִם מְכוֹן[10] שִׁבְתְּךָ אֶת־תְּפִלָּתָם וְאֶת־תְּחִנָּתָם וְעָשִׂיתָ מִשְׁפָּטָם׃

(50) וְסָלַחְתָּ לְעַמְּךָ אֲשֶׁר חָטְאוּ־לָךְ וּלְכָל־פִּשְׁעֵיהֶם אֲשֶׁר פָּשְׁעוּ־בָךְ וּנְתַתָּם לְרַחֲמִים[11] לִפְנֵי
שֹׁבֵיהֶם וְרִחֲמוּם׃

(51) כִּי־עַמְּךָ וְנַחֲלָתְךָ הֵם אֲשֶׁר הוֹצֵאתָ מִמִּצְרַיִם מִתּוֹךְ כּוּר[12] הַבַּרְזֶל׃

(52) לִהְיוֹת עֵינֶיךָ פְּתֻחֹת אֶל־תְּחִנַּת עַבְדְּךָ וְאֶל־תְּחִנַּת עַמְּךָ יִשְׂרָאֵל לִשְׁמֹעַ אֲלֵיהֶם בְּכֹל
קָרְאָם אֵלֶיךָ׃

(53) כִּי־אַתָּה הִבְדַּלְתָּם לְךָ לְנַחֲלָה מִכֹּל עַמֵּי הָאָרֶץ כַּאֲשֶׁר דִּבַּרְתָּ בְּיַד מֹשֶׁה עַבְדֶּךָ בְּהוֹצִיאֲךָ
אֶת־אֲבֹתֵינוּ מִמִּצְרַיִם אֲדֹנָי יְהוִה׃

(54) וַיְהִי כְּכַלּוֹת שְׁלֹמֹה לְהִתְפַּלֵּל אֶל־יהוה אֵת כָּל־הַתְּפִלָּה וְהַתְּחִנָּה הַזֹּאת קָם[13] מִלִּפְנֵי
מִזְבַּח יהוה מִכְּרֹעַ עַל־בִּרְכָּיו[14] וְכַפָּיו פְּרֻשׂוֹת הַשָּׁמָיִם׃

(55) וַיַּעֲמֹד וַיְבָרֶךְ אֵת כָּל־קְהַל יִשְׂרָאֵל קוֹל[15] גָּדוֹל לֵאמֹר׃

(56) בָּרוּךְ יהוה אֲשֶׁר נָתַן מְנוּחָה לְעַמּוֹ יִשְׂרָאֵל כְּכֹל אֲשֶׁר דִּבֵּר לֹא־נָפַל דָּבָר אֶחָד מִכֹּל
דְּבָרוֹ הַטּוֹב אֲשֶׁר דִּבֶּר בְּיַד מֹשֶׁה עַבְדּוֹ׃

(57) יְהִי יהוה אֱלֹהֵינוּ עִמָּנוּ כַּאֲשֶׁר הָיָה עִם־אֲבֹתֵינוּ אַל־יַעַזְבֵנוּ וְאַל־יִטְּשֵׁנוּ׃

(58) לְהַטּוֹת לְבָבֵנוּ אֵלָיו לָלֶכֶת בְּכָל־דְּרָכָיו וְלִשְׁמֹר מִצְוֹתָיו וְחֻקָּיו וּמִשְׁפָּטָיו אֲשֶׁר צִוָּה
אֶת־אֲבֹתֵינוּ׃

Notes to the Reading:

1. Note הַשָּׁמַיִם in the sense "heavenward" and "in heaven" throughout this passage.
2. The plural form in the consonantal text is pointed as a singular.
3. The הִנֵּה should be correlated with the אַף כִּי: "Since even the heavens and the heavens' heavens cannot contain you, how much less this house which I have built."
4. וּפָנִיתָ continues the sequence of vs. 26.
5. Defectively spelled עֵינֶךָ in the original text.
6. Here in the sense "toward".
7. Idiomatic: "if they lay it to heart, consider it".
8. הֶעֱוָה to sin
9. רָשַׁע to act wickedly
10. מָקוֹם = מָכוֹן
11. Idiomatic: "and you make them an object of compassion".
12. כּוּר a furnace
13. The form קָם instead of וַיָּקָם marks this as the first main verb of a new sequence. Compare the discussion at the end of §132.
14. בִּרְכַּיִם (dual) knees
15. Adverbially: "in a loud voice".

Appendix A

A CLASSIFIED LIST OF NOUNS

The following list contains all the nouns appearing in this book, classified according to the vocalic pattern of the absolute singular. Nouns of a given pattern are included under a single number; differences in the inflected form, such as construct or plural, account for the further subdivisions. The principal forms are arranged as follows:

absolute singular	construct singular	singular with 1 pers. sing. suff.	absolute plural	construct plural

Other forms with pronominal suffixes are listed under the appropriate stem.

When an entry presents a virtually unique type, parentheses indicate a conjectured, but securely based form. E.g., (יַמִּי) "my sea" is not attested, but the form is reasonably certain because יַמָּהּ "her sea" is attested. The same suffixal forms are given for each noun for the sake of consistency.

Square brackets enclose conjectures which are probable, but not as firmly established as those just mentioned.

Dual forms may be found in §92.

I. Monosyllabic nouns with a normally changeable (reducible) long vowel or *a* (plural §34; constr. sing. §§73, 75; constr. plur. §§78–79; w. suff. §§85, 88, 96):

1a.	יָד	יַד יֶדְכֶם	יָדִי יָדֶךָ	יָדוֹת	יְדוֹת (יְדוֹתַי)	hand (f.)
1b.	דָּם	דַּם דִּמְכֶם	דָּמִי דָּמְךָ	דָּמִים (דָּמַי)	דְּמֵי (דְּמֵיכֶם)	blood
1c.	אָב	אֲבִי אֲבִיכֶם	אָבִי אָבִ֫יךָ	אָבוֹת	אֲבוֹת אֲבוֹתַי	father
1d.	אָח	אֲחִי אֲחִיכֶם	אָחִי אָחִ֫יךָ	אַחִים אַחַי אֶחָיו	אֲחֵי אֲחֵיכֶם	brother
1e.	יָם יָ֫מָּה	יַם / יָם	(יַמִּי)	יַמִּים	—	sea
2a.	עַם	עַם עַמְּכֶם	עַמִּי עַמְּךָ	עַמִּים עַמַּי	עַמֵּי / עַמְמֵי עַמֵּיכֶם	people

Also:	אַף nose		חַיִּים lifetime		כַּף palm
	גַּן *(ôṯ)* garden		חַג *(îm)* festival		עַז mighty (adj.)
	דַּל poor (adj.)		טַף children		רַב numerous (adj.)
	חַי alive (adj.)		Note: With def. art.: הֶחָג הַגָּן הָעָם		

2b.	שַׂר	שַׂר שַׂרְכֶם	שָׂרִי שָׂרְךָ	שָׂרִים שָׂרַי	שָׂרֵי שָׂרֵיכֶם	chief

Also:	מַר bitter (adj.)	צַר *(îm)* adversary
	פַּר *(îm)* steer (הַפָּר)	רַע evil (adj.); wickedness (noun)

2c.	הַר הָ֫רָה הָהָר	הַר הַרְכֶם	הַרְרִי / הֲרָרִי הַרְרָם	הָרִים הָרַי הֲרָרֶ֫יהָ	הָרֵי / הַרְרֵי	mountain
2d.	צַד	צַד (צִדְּכֶם)	(צִדִּי) צִדְּךָ	צִדִּים (צִדַּי)	צִדֵּי צִדֵּיכֶם	side
3a.	עֵץ	עֵץ (עֶצְכֶם)	(עֵצִי) עֵצְךָ	עֵצִים (עֵצַי)	עֲצֵי (עֲצֵיכֶם)	tree
3b.	גֵּר	גֵּר גֵּרְכֶם	גֵּרִי גֵּרְךָ	גֵּרִים גֵּרַי	גֵּרֵי גֵּרֵיכֶם	sojourner

Also: אֵל *(îm)* god מֵת *(îm)* dead person
מֵעִים inward parts רֵעַ *(îm)* companion

3c.	בֵּן	בֵּן/ בֶּן־ (בִּנְכֶם)	בְּנִי בִּנְךָ	בָּנִים בָּנַי	בְּנֵי בְּנֵיכֶם	son
3d.	שֵׁם	שֵׁם/ שֶׁם־ שִׁמְכֶם	שְׁמִי שִׁמְךָ	שֵׁמוֹת	שְׁמוֹת (שְׁמוֹתַי)	name
3e.	חֵץ	חֵץ (חֶצְכֶם)	חִצִּי חִצְּךָ חִצְּכֶם	חִצִּים חִצַּי	חִצֵּי חִצֵּיכֶם	arrow

Also: אֵם *(ôṯ)* mother חֵן grace קֵץ end
אֵשׁ fire לֵב *(ôṯ)* heart שֵׁן (du.) teeth

3f.	צֵל	צֵל	צִלִּי	צְלָלִים	צִלְלֵי	shadow
3g.	חֵטְא	(חֵטְא)	(חֶטְאִי)	חֲטָאִים חֲטָאַי	חֲטָאֵי חֲטָאֵיכֶם	sin

II. Monosyllabic nouns with a normally unchangeable long vowel (plural §34; constr. sing. §73; constr. plur. §§78–79; w. suff. §85):

4a.	שִׁיר	שִׁיר שִׁירְכֶם	שִׁירִי שִׁירְךָ	שִׁירִים שִׁירַי	שִׁירֵי שִׁירֵיכֶם	song

Also: קִיר *(ôṯ)* wall רִיב *(îm, ôṯ)* quarrel

4b.	עִיר	עִיר (עִירְכֶם)	עִירִי עִירְךָ	עָרִים עָרַי	עָרֵי עָרֵיכֶם	city
4c.	אִישׁ	אִישׁ (אִישְׁכֶם)	אִישִׁי (אִישְׁךָ)	אֲנָשִׁים אֲנָשַׁי	אַנְשֵׁי (אַנְשֵׁיכֶם)	man
5a.	קוֹל	קוֹל קוֹלְכֶם	קוֹלִי קוֹלְךָ	קוֹלוֹת	קוֹלוֹת קוֹלוֹתַי	voice

אוֹר *(îm)* light דּוֹר *(ôṯ)* generation עוֹף fowl
אוֹת *(ôṯ)* sign הוֹד splendor עוֹר *(ôṯ)* hide
בּוֹר *(ôṯ)* cistern טוֹב good (adj.) צֹאן small cattle
גּוֹי *(îm)* people כֹּחַ power שׁוֹר *(îm)* head of cattle

Note: The once attested plural שְׁוָרִים represents a rare alternative in nouns of this type.

5b.	יוֹם	יוֹם	(יוֹמִי)	יָמִים	יְמֵי	day
		(יוֹמְכֶם)	יוֹמְךָ	יָמַי	יְמֵיכֶם	
5c.	רֹאשׁ	רֹאשׁ	רֹאשִׁי	רָאשִׁים	רָאשֵׁי	head
		רֹאשְׁכֶם	רֹאשְׁךָ	(רָאשַׁי)	רָאשֵׁיכֶם	
5d.	עֹז	עֹז / עָז־	עֻזִּי / עָזִּי	[עֻזִּים]	[עֻזֵּי]	might
		עֻזְּכֶם	עֻזְּךָ / עָזְּךָ			

Also: תֹּם / integrity רֹב multitude

5e.	חֹק	חֹק / חָק־	חֻקִּי	חֻקִּים	חֻקֵּי / חֻקְּקֵי	statute
		חָקְכֶם	חָקְךָ			
6.	סוּס	סוּס	סוּסִי	סוּסִים	סוּסֵי	horse
		סוּסְכֶם	סוּסְךָ	סוּסַי	סוּסֵיכֶם	

Also: לוּחַ (*ôṯ*) tablet צוּר (*îm*) rock רוּחַ (*ôṯ*) wind, spirit

III. Dissyllabic nouns with penultimate stress (the Segholates) and related rarer types (plur. §§19, 50; constr. sing. §§73, 75; constr. plur. 99; w. suff. §§99, 104).

7a.	מֶ֫לֶךְ	מֶ֫לֶךְ	מַלְכִּי	מְלָכִים	מַלְכֵי	king
			מַלְכְּךָ	מְלָכַי	מַלְכֵיכֶם	
			מַלְכְּכֶם			

Also:

אֶ֫בֶן	(*îm*) stone	חֶ֫סֶד	(*îm*) kindness	עֶ֫בֶד	(*îm*) servant
אֶ֫לֶף	(*îm*) thousand	חֶ֫רֶב	(*ôṯ*) sword	עֶ֫צֶם	(*îm/ôṯ*) bone
אֶ֫רֶז	(*îm*) cedar	יֶ֫לֶד	(*îm*) boy	עֶ֫רֶב	evening
אֶ֫רֶץ	(*ôṯ*) earth	כֶּ֫סֶף	(*îm*) silver	צֶ֫לֶם	(*îm*) image
גֶּ֫בֶר	(*îm*) man	כֶּ֫רֶם	(*îm*) vineyard	קֶ֫רֶן	(*îm/ôṯ*) horn
גֶּ֫פֶן	(*îm*) vine	לֶ֫חֶם	bread	רֶ֫גֶל	(du.; pl. *îm*) foot
דֶּ֫רֶךְ	(*îm*) way	נֶ֫פֶשׁ	(*ôṯ*) soul	שֶׁ֫מֶן	(*îm*) oil

7b.	חֶ֫דֶר	חֶ֫דֶר / חֲדַר	(חֶדְרִי)	חֲדָרִים	חַדְרֵי	room
			(חֶדְרְךָ)	(חֲדָרַי)	(חַדְרֵיכֶם)	
			(חֶדְרְכֶם)			

Similarly: הֶ֫בֶל *(îm)* vanity

7c.	קֶ֫בֶר	קֶ֫בֶר	קִבְרִי קִבְרְךָ קִבְרְכֶם	קְבָרִים קְבָרַי	קִבְרֵי קִבְרֵיכֶם	grave

Also: גֶּ֫שֶׁם *(îm)* rain פֶּ֫סֶל idol שֶׁ֫מֶשׁ *(ôṯ)* sun
יֶ֫תֶר remainder צֶ֫דֶק righteousness שֶׁ֫קֶל *(îm)* shekel
כֶּ֫בֶשׂ *(îm)* lamb קֶ֫רֶב midst שֶׁ֫קֶר *(îm)* deception
נֶ֫דֶר *(îm)* vow רֶ֫כֶב chariotry
פֶּ֫גֶר *(îm)* corpse שֶׁ֫בֶר *(îm)* breaking

8a.	זֶ֫רַע	זֶ֫רַע	זַרְעִי זַרְעֲךָ זַרְעֲכֶם	סְלָעִים	(סַלְעֵי)	seed rock

The following may belong here or to the next type (8b); evidence insufficient.

פֶּ֫סַח *(îm)* Passover יֶ֫רַח *(îm)* month בֶּ֫טַח trust

8b.	זֶ֫בַח	זֶ֫בַח	זִבְחִי זִבְחֲךָ זִבְחֲכֶם	זְבָחִים זְבָחַי	זִבְחֵי זִבְחֵיכֶם	sacrifice

Also: נֶ֫גַע *(îm)* stroke פֶּ֫שַׁע *(îm)* transgression פֶּ֫תַח *(îm)* opening

9.	נַ֫עַר	נַ֫עַר	נַעֲרִי נַעַרְךָ נַעַרְכֶם	נְעָרִים נְעָרַי	נַעֲרֵי נַעֲרֵיכֶם	young man

Also: בַּ֫עַל *(îm)* master פַּ֫חַד (פַּחְדְּךָ) *(îm)* dread
יַ֫עַר *(îm)* woods שַׁ֫עַר *(îm)* gate
נַ֫חַל *(îm)* wadi

10a.	סֵ֫פֶר	סֵ֫פֶר	סִפְרִי סִפְרְךָ סִפְרְכֶם	סְפָרִים סְפָרַי	סִפְרֵי סִפְרֵיכֶם	book

Also: עֵ֫מֶק *(îm)* valley שֵׁ֫בֶט *(îm)* rod

10b.	עֵ֫דֶר	עֵ֫דֶר	עֶדְרִי עֶדְרְךָ עֶדְרְכֶם	עֲדָרִים עֲדָרַי	עֶדְרֵי עֶדְרֵיכֶם	flock

Also: חֵ֫לֶב *(îm)* fat, חֵ֫לֶק *(îm)* share, עֵ֫גֶל *(îm)* calf, עֵ֫זֶר help, עֵ֫שֶׂב herbage

11.	קֹ֫דֶשׁ	קֹ֫דֶשׁ	קָדְשִׁי קָדְשְׁךָ קָדְשְׁכֶם	קָדָשִׁים / קֳדָשִׁים קָדָשַׁי / קֳדָשַׁי	קָדְשֵׁי קָדְשֵׁיכֶם	holiness

Also: אֹ֫הֶל *(îm)* tent, גֹּ֫רֶן *(ôṯ)* threshing floor, עֹ֫רֶף neck, אֹ֫זֶן (du.) ear, חֹ֫דֶשׁ *(îm)* month, צָהֳרַ֫יִם noon, אֹ֫כֶל food, חֹ֫שֶׁךְ darkness, שֹׁ֫רֶשׁ *(îm)* root, בֹּ֫קֶר morning, מָתְנַ֫יִם loins

The plural forms of אֹ֫הֶל (tent) show some irregularities:

אֹהָלִים בָּאֳהָלִים	אֹהָלַי אֹהָלֶ֫יךָ אָהֳלֵיכֶם

12a.	אֹ֫רַח	אֹ֫רַח	אָרְחִי אָרְחֲךָ אָרְחֲכֶם	אֲרָחוֹת	אָרְחוֹת (אָרְחוֹתֵיכֶם)	way
12b.	רֹ֫חַב	רֹ֫חַב	רָחְבִּי רָחְבְּךָ רָחְבְּכֶם	—	—	breadth

Also: תֹּ֫אַר (w. suff. תָּאֳרוֹ or תֹּאֲרוֹ) form

13a.	עַ֫יִן	עֵין	עֵינִי עֵינְךָ עֵינְכֶם	עֲיָנוֹת	עֵינוֹת	eye spring

Also: חַ֫יִל *(îm)* strength, יַ֫יִן wine

13b.	זַ֫יִת	זֵית	זֵיתִי זֵיתְךָ (זֵיתְכֶם)	זֵיתִים (זֵיתַי)	זֵיתֵי זֵיתֵיכֶם	olive-tree

Also: אַ֫יִל *(îm)* ram

13c.	בַּ֫יִת	בֵּית בֵּיתְכֶם	בֵּיתִי בֵּיתְךָ	בָּתִּים (בָּתַּי)	בָּתֵּי בָּתֵּיכֶם	house
14.	גַּ֫יְ(א)	גֵּי(א)	—	גֵּאָיוֹת	(גֵּיאוֹת)	valley
15.	מָ֫וֶת	מוֹת מוֹתְכֶם	מוֹתִי מוֹתְךָ	—	—	death

Also: אָ֫וֶן trouble תָּ֫וֶךְ midst

16. שָׁוְא not inflected — nothingness

IV. Dissyllabic nouns with a sometimes changeable *ə* in the first syllable and a changeable vowel in the second.

17.	שְׁכֶם	שְׁכֶם	שִׁכְמִי (שִׁכְמְךָ)	—	—	shoulder
18.	דְּבַשׁ	—	דִּבְשִׁי	—	—	honey
19.	שְׁאָר	שְׁאָר	—	—	—	remainder
20.	בְּאֵר	בְּאֵר	(בְּאֵרִי)	בְּאֵרוֹת	בְּאֵרוֹת	well
	זְאֵב	זְאֵב	(זְאֵבִי)	זְאֵבִים	זְאֵבֵי	wolf

V. Dissyllabic nouns with an unchangeable *ə* in the first syllable and an unchangeable long vowel in the second (plural §19; constr. sing. §73; constr. plur. §§78, 79; with suffixes §85).

22.	בְּכוֹר	בְּכוֹר בְּכוֹרְכֶם	בְּכוֹרִי בְּכוֹרְךָ	בְּכוֹרִים בְּכוֹרַי	בְּכוֹרֵי בְּכוֹרֵיכֶם	first-born

Also: אֱלוֹהַּ *(îm)* god, God; חֲלוֹם *(ôt)* dream; רְחוֹב *(ôṯ)* street;
אֲרוֹן (הָאָרוֹן) ark; חֲמוֹר *(îm)* ass; שְׂמֹאל left-hand;
זְרוֹעַ *(ôṯ, îm)* arm; יְאֹר Nile

23.	גְּבוּל	גְּבוּל	גְּבוּלִי	גְּבוּלִים	גְּבוּלֵי	boundary

Also: לְבוּשׁ clothing כְּרוּב *(îm)* cherub נְאוּם declaration
רְכוּשׁ property

24.	מְעִיל	(מְעִיל)	(מְעִילִי)	מְעִילִים	(מְעִילֵי)	robe

VI. Dissyllabic nouns with normally changeable vowels in both syllables (plural §19; constr. sing. §§73, 75; constr. plur. §§78, 79; with suffixes §85).

25a.	דָּבָר	דְּבַר	דְּבָרִי	דְּבָרִים	דִּבְרֵי	word
		דְּבַרְכֶם	דְּבָרְךָ	דְּבָרַי	דִּבְרֵיכֶם	

Also: בָּקָר large cattle יָקָר precious (adj.) רָשָׁע evil (adj.)
בָּשָׂר flesh יָשָׁר just (adj.) שָׁלָל booty
חָזָק strong (adj.) מָטָר *(ôṯ)* rain

25b.	הָדָר	הֲדַר	הֲדָרִי	הֲדָרִים	הַדְרֵי	splendor
		הֲדַרְכֶם	הֲדָרְךָ	הֲדָרַי	הַדְרֵיכֶם	

Also: אָדָם man (-kind) חָלָל slain (adj.) קָהָל *(îm)* assembly
זָהָב gold נָהָר *(ôṯ)* river רָעָב hunger
חָדָשׁ new (adj.) עָנָן *(îm)* cloud
חָכָם wise (adj.) עָפָר *(ôṯ)* dust

25c.	פָּרָשׁ	(פָּרַשׁ)	(פָּרָשִׁי)	פָּרָשִׁים	(פָּֽרָשֵׁי)	horseman
		(פָּרַשְׁכֶם)	(פָּרָשְׁךָ)	פָּרָשַׁי	(פָּֽרָשֵׁיכֶם)	

Also: חָרָשׁ *(îm)* engraver

25d.	גָּמָל	גְּמַל	(גְּמַלִּי)	גְּמַלִּים	גְּמַלֵּי	camel
			(גְּמַלְּךָ)	(גְּמַלַּי)	(גְּמַלֵּיכֶם)	
25e.	חָלָב	חֲלֵב	חֲלָבִי	—	—	milk
			חֲלָבֵךְ			
26a.	זָקֵן	זְקַן	זְקֵנִי	זְקֵנִים	זִקְנֵי / (זְקֵנֵי)	elder
		זְקַנְכֶם	זְקֵנְךָ	זְקֵנַי	זִקְנֵיכֶם	

Also: כָּבֵד heavy (adj.) שָׁלֵם complete (adj.)

שָׂמֵחַ glad (adj.)

שָׁכֵן *(îm)* neighbor

26b.	חָצֵר	חֲצַר	חֲצֵרִי	חֲצֵרוֹת	חַצְרוֹת	courtyard

Also: עָרֵל uncircumcised (adj.)

26c.	כָּתֵף	כֶּ֫תֶף	כְּתֵפִי	כְּתֵפוֹת	כִּתְפוֹת	shoulder

Also: יָרֵחַ moon יָרֵךְ (du.) thigh עָרֵל uncircumcised (adj.)

26d.	מָלֵא	מְלֵא	(מְלֵאִי)	מְלֵאִים	(מְלֵאֵי)	full (adj.)

Also: צָמֵא thirsty (adj.) טָמֵא unclean (adj.)

26e.	מָגֵן	מָגֵן	מָגִנִּי	מָגִנִּים	מָגִנֵּי	shield
			(מָגִנְּךָ)	(מָגִנַּי)	(מָגִנֵּיכֶם)	

27a.	לֵבָב	לְבַב	לְבָבִי	לְבָבוֹת	(לִבְבוֹת)	heart
		לְבַבְכֶם	לְבָבְךָ			

Alsc עֵנָב *(îm)* grapes שֵׂעָר hair

27b.	צֵלָע	צֵ֫לַע צֶ֫לַע	(צַלְעִי)	צְלָעִים	צַלְעוֹת	rib

VII. Dissyllabic nouns with a normally changeable long vowel in the first syllable and an unchangeable long vowel in the second (plural §19; constr. sing. §73; constr. plur. §§78–79; with suffixes §85).

28a.	נָגִיד	נְגִיד	נְגִידִי	נְגִידִים	נְגִידֵי	leader
		נְגִידְכֶם	נְגִידְךָ	נְגִידַי	נְגִידֵיכֶם	

Also: יָמִין right hand נָשִׂיא *(îm)* prince

מָשִׁיחַ *(îm)* anointed one עָשִׁיר rich (adj.)

נָדִיב noble (adj.) פָּלִיט *(îm)* fugitive

פָּקִיד *(îm)* deputy קָצִיר harvest

צָעִיר small (adj.) שָׂעִיר *(îm)* he-goat

28b.	סָרִיס	סְרִיס	(סְרִיסִי)	סָרִיסִים	סָרִיסֵי / סְרִיסֵי	eunuch

29a.	מָקוֹם	מְקוֹם	מְקוֹמִי	מְקוֹמוֹת	מְקוֹמוֹת	place
		מְקוֹמְכֶם	מְקוֹמְךָ		מְקוֹמוֹתֵיכֶם	

Also:	אָדוֹן *(îm)* lord	לָשׁוֹן *(ôṯ)* tongue
	גָּאוֹן majesty	עָוֹן *(ôṯ)* guilt
	הָמוֹן roar	צָפוֹן north
	כָּבוֹד glory	שָׁלוֹם *(îm)* welfare

29b.	מָעוֹז	מָעוֹז	מָֽעֻזִּי	מָֽעֻזִּים	(מָֽעֻזֵּי)	refuge
30a.	כָּתוּב	כְּתוּב כְּתוּבְכֶם	כְּתוּבִי כְּתוּבְךָ	כְּתוּבִים כְּתוּבַי	כְּתוּבֵי כְּתוּבֵיכֶם	written (adj.)

Here belong all Qal passive participles.

30b.	בָּחוּר	—	—	בַּחוּרִים	בַּחוּרֵי	young man
30c.	שָׁבוּעַ	שְׁבוּעַ	—	שָֽׁבוּעוֹת	שְׁבוּעוֹת שָֽׁבוּעוֹתֵיכֶם	week

VIII. Dissyllabic nouns ending in -*î* (§112).

31a.	כְּלִי	כְּלִי	(כְּלְיִי) כֶּלְיְךָ	כֵּלִים	כְּלֵי כְּלֵיכֶם	vessel
	פְּרִי	פְּרִי פִּרְיהֶם	פִּרְיִי פֶּרְיְךָ פֶּרְיְכֶם	—	—	fruit
	שְׁבִי	שְׁבִי שְׁבִיכֶם	(שִׁבְיִי) שֶׁבְיְךָ שִׁבְיָם	—	—	captivity
31b.	חֲצִי	חֲצִי	(חֶצְיִי) (חֶצְיְךָ) חֶצְיוֹ	—	—	half
	אֲרִי	—	—	אֲרָיוֹת / אֲרָיִים	—	lion

(Cf. also אַרְיֵה below)

31c.	חֳלִי	—	(חָלְיִי)	חֳלָיִים	—	sickness
	עֳנִי	עֳנִי	עָנְיִי (עָנְיְךָ) עָנְיָם	—	—	affliction

32.	נָקִי	נְקִי	נְקִיִּי	נְקִיִּם	נְקִיֵּי	innocent (adj.)

A subtype of 28a nearly always written defectively.

IX. Dissyllabic nouns with an unchangeable first syllable (closed or with an unchangeable long vowel) and a changeable vowel *(ā ē a)* in the second syllable (plural §25, constr. sing. §73, constr. plur. §§78–79, w. suff. §85):

33.	מוֹשָׁב	מוֹשַׁב	מוֹשָׁבִי	מוֹשָׁבִים	מוֹשְׁבֵי	dwelling place
		מוֹשַׁבְכֶם	מוֹשָׁבְךָ	מוֹשָׁבַי	מוֹשְׁבֵיכֶם	

Also: גּוֹרָל *(ôṯ)* lot נוֹרָא dreadful (adj.) שׁוֹפָר *(ôṯ)* shofar

כּוֹכָב *(îm)* star עוֹלָם *(îm)* eternity

34.	הֵיכָל	הֵיכַל	הֵיכָלִי	(הֵיכָלִים)	הֵיכְלֵי	palace
				הֵיכָלוֹת		

Also: תֵּימָן south (no pl.)

35.	אֹיֵב	אֹיֵב	אֹיְבִי	אֹיְבִים	אֹיְבֵי	enemy
			אֹיִבְךָ	אֹיְבַי	אֹיְבֵיכֶם	
			אֹיִבְכֶם			

Also: חֹתֵן father-in-law מוֹעֵד *(îm)* appointed time

כֹּהֵן *(îm)* priest סֹפֵר *(îm)* scribe

36.	חֵרֵשׁ	—	—	חֵרְשִׁים	—	deaf (adj.)
37.	מִשְׁפָּט	מִשְׁפַּט	מִשְׁפָּטִי	מִשְׁפָּטִים	מִשְׁפְּטֵי	judgment

Also: מִגְדָּל *(îm, ôṯ)* tower מִזְרָח east מִשְׁכָּן *(ôṯ)* tabernacle

מִגְרָשׁ *(îm)* pasture מִסְפָּר *(îm)* number

מִדְבָּר wilderness מִקְדָּשׁ *(îm)* sanctuary

38.	גַּנָּב	גַּנַּב	גַּנָּבִי	גַּנָּבִים	גַּנְּבֵי	thief

Also: מַאֲכָל food מַעֲלָל *(îm)* deed צַוָּאר *(îm)* neck

מַלְאָךְ *(îm)* messenger מַשָּׂא oracle שַׁבָּת *(ôṯ)* Sabbath

Note the irregular presuffixal form of שַׁבָּת: שַׁבַּתּוֹ (his Sabbath).

39.	אֶצְבַּע	אֶצְבַּע	(אֶצְבָּעִי)	אֶצְבָּעוֹת	אֶצְבְּעוֹת	finger

40.	שֻׁלְחָן	שֻׁלְחַן	שֻׁלְחָנִי	שֻׁלְחָנוֹת	שֻׁלְחֲנוֹת	table
41a.	עִוֵּר	—	—	עִוְרִים	—	blind

Also: פִּסֵּחַ (adj.) lame

41b.	כִּסֵּא	כִּסֵּא	כִּסְאִי כִּסְאֲךָ	כִּסְאוֹת	(כִּסְאוֹת)	throne
41c.	מִזְבֵּחַ	מִזְבַּח	מִזְבְּחִי	מִזְבְּחוֹת	מִזְבְּחוֹת	altar

X. Dissyllabic nouns with two unchangeable syllables (§50).

42.	אֶבְיוֹן	אֶבְיוֹן	(אֶבְיוֹנִי)	אֶבְיוֹנִים	אֶבְיוֹנֵי	poor (adj.)

Also: עֶלְיוֹן high, lofty

43.	גִּבּוֹר	גִּבּוֹר	(גִּבּוֹרִי)	גִּבּוֹרִים	גִּבּוֹרֵי	warrior

Also: מִזְמוֹר *(îm)* psalm

44.	תַּחְתּוֹן	—	—	תַּחְתּוֹנִים	—	lower (adj.)

Also: אַחֲרוֹן latter (adj.)

45.	תִּיכוֹן	—	—	תִּיכוֹנִים	—	inner (adj.)

Also: רִאשׁוֹן first (adj.)

46.	צַדִּיק	צַדִּיק	(צַדִּיקִי)	צַדִּיקִים	צַדִּיקֵי	righteous person
47.	עַמּוּד	עַמּוּד	(עַמּוּדִי)	עַמּוּדִים	עַמּוּדֵי	pillar

XI. Nouns ending in *-eh* and *-ēh* (§88, §116).

48a.	פֶּה	פִּי	פִּי פִּ֫יךָ (פִּיכֶם)	—	—	mouth
48b.	שֶׂה	שֵׂה	שֵׂיו שֵׂ֫יֵהוּ	—	—	sheep/goat
49.	שָׂדֶה	שְׂדֵה	שָׂדִי שָׂדְךָ	שָׂדוֹת	שְׂדוֹת	field

Also: יָפֶה (adj.) beautiful קָצֶה end

קָנֶה *(îm, ô̱t)* reed קָשֶׁה (adj.) hard, harsh

50.	מִקְנֶה	מִקְנֵה	מִקְנַי/מִקְנִי מִקְנֵ֫יהוּ/מִקְנָיו	(מִקְנִים)	(מִקְנֵי)	property

Also: מִשְׁתֶּה banquet

51.	מַחֲנֶה	מַחֲנֵה	מַחֲנִי/מַחֲנִי מַחֲנֵ֫הוּ	מַחֲנוֹת	מַחֲנוֹת	camp

Also: מַטֶּה *(ô̱t)* staff מַעֲשֶׂה *(îm)* deed מַרְאֶה appearance

52.	אַרְיֵה	—	—	—	—	lion

XII. Feminine nouns in *-āh* (plural §53; constr. sing. §76; constr. pl. §§78, 79; with suffixes § 85).

53a.	שָׁנָה	שְׁנַת	(שְׁנָתִי)	שָׁנִים	שְׁנֵי/שְׁנוֹת	year
53b.	צָרָה	צָרַת	צָרָתִי	צָרוֹת	צָרוֹת	distress

Also: פָּרָה *(ô̱t)* heifer

רָעָה *(ô̱t)* evil

Likewise participles of Qal verbs from hollow roots, like קָם, שָׂם etc.

53c.	בָּמָה	—	—	בָּמוֹת	בָּמֳתֵי בָּמוֹתֵי	sacred high place
53d.	שָׂפָה	שְׂפַת	(שְׂפָתִי)	— שְׂפָתַ֫יִם	— שִׂפְתֵי	lip
53e.	אָמָה	(אֲמַת)	אֲמָתִי	אֲמָהוֹת	אַמְהוֹת	maidservant
54.	עֵצָה	עֲצַת	עֲצָתִי	עֵצוֹת	עֲצוֹת	counsel

Also: חֵמָה rage עֵדָה congregation

מֵאָה *(ô̱t)* hundred פֵּאָה corner

55.	עוֹלָה	עוֹלַת	עוֹלָתִי	עוֹלוֹת	עוֹלוֹת	burnt-offering

Also: חוֹמָה *(ô̱t)* wall טוֹבָה welfare תּוֹרָה *(ô̱t)* law, Law

56.	בִּינָה	בִּינַת	בִּינָתִי	—	—	understanding
57.	אַמָּה	(אַמַּת)	(אַמָּתִי)	אַמּוֹת	(אַמּוֹת)	cubit

Also: חַיָּה *(ôṯ)* wild beast

58a.	פִּנָּה	פִּנַּת	(פִּנָּתִי)	פִּנּוֹת	פִּנּוֹת	corner

Also: מִדָּה *(ôṯ)* measure

58b.	אִשָּׁה	אֵשֶׁת	אִשְׁתִּי	נָשִׁים	נְשֵׁי	woman
59.	חֻקָּה	חֻקַּת	חֻקָּתִי	חֻקּוֹת	חֻקּוֹת	statute
60a.	מַלְכָּה	מַלְכַּת	מַלְכָּתִי	מְלָכוֹת	מַלְכוֹת	queen
60b.	נַחֲלָה	נַחֲלַת	נַחֲלָתִי	נְחָלוֹת	נַחֲלוֹת	portion

Also: אַהֲבָה love　　נַעֲרָה *(ôṯ)* girl

61a.	גִּבְעָה	גִּבְעַת	גִּבְעָתִי	גְּבָעוֹת	גִּבְעוֹת	hill

Also: יִרְאָה fear　　שִׂמְחָה *(ôṯ)* joy　　שִׁפְחָה *(ôṯ)* maidservant
מִנְחָה *(ôṯ)* gift　　שִׂמְלָה *(ôṯ)* cloak

61b.	מִצְוָה	מִצְוַת	מִצְוָתִי	מִצְוֹת	מִצְוֹת	commandment
62.	חֶרְפָּה	חֶרְפַּת	חֶרְפָּתִי	חֲרָפוֹת	חֶרְפּוֹת	reproach

Also: עֶגְלָה *(ôṯ)* heifer　　עֶרְוָה nakedness

63.	חָכְמָה	חָכְמַת	חָכְמָתִי	חָכְמוֹת	(חָכְמוֹת)	wisdom
64a.	בְּרָכָה	בִּרְכַּת	בִּרְכָתִי	בְּרָכוֹת	בִּרְכוֹת	blessing

Also: צְדָקָה *(ôṯ)* righteousness　　רְבָבָה myriad
קְלָלָה curse　　שְׁמָמָה desolation

64b.	אֲדָמָה	אַדְמַת	אַדְמָתִי	עֲרָבוֹת	עַרְבוֹת	land/ steppe
64c.	מְעָרָה	מְעָרַת	—	מְעָרוֹת	מְעָרוֹת	cave

64d.	מְלָאכָה	מְלֶאכֶת	מְלַאכְתִּי	(מַלְאֲכוֹת)	מַלְאָכוֹת	task
65a.	נְבֵלָה	נִבְלַת	נִבְלָתִי נִבְלָתְךָ נִבְלָתוֹ	——	(נְבֵלוֹת)	corpse
65b.	שְׁאֵלָה	——	שְׁאֵלָתִי שֶׁאֱלָתִי	——	——	request
65c.	בְּהֵמָה	בֶּהֱמַת	(בְּהֶמְתִּי) בְּהֶמְתְּךָ	בְּהֵמוֹת	בַּהֲמוֹת	beast
65d.	בְּרֵכָה	בְּרֵכַת	——	בְּרֵכוֹת	——	pond

Also fem. adj. and stative participles of the type כְּבֵדָה.

66.	עֲבוֹדָה	עֲבוֹדַת	עֲבוֹדָתִי	——	——	work
67.	תְּבוּאָה	תְּבוּאַת	תְּבוּאָתִי	תְּבוּאוֹת	תְּבוּאוֹת	product

Also: בְּתוּלָה *(ôṯ)* maiden יְשׁוּעָה deliverance תְּבוּנָה understanding

68.	תְּפִלָּה	תְּפִלַּת תְּפִלַּתְכֶם	תְּפִלָּתִי תְּפִלָּתְךָ	תְּפִלּוֹת	תְּפִלּוֹת	prayer

Also: מְגִלָּה *(ôṯ)* scroll תְּהִלָּה praise תְּחִנָּה supplication
מְסִלָּה *(ôṯ)* highway תְּחִלָּה beginning

69.	אֲחֻזָּה	אֲחֻזַּת	אֲחֻזָּתִי	——	——	possession
70.	מַמְלָכָה	מַמְלֶכֶת	מַמְלַכְתִּי	מַמְלָכוֹת	מַמְלְכוֹת	kingdom

Also: אַלְמָנָה *(ôṯ)* widow

71.	מֶרְכָּבָה	מִרְכֶּבֶת	(מֶרְכַּבְתִּי)	מַרְכָּבוֹת	מַרְכְּבוֹת	chariot
72.	מִשְׁפָּחָה	מִשְׁפַּחַת	מִשְׁפַּחְתִּי	מִשְׁפָּחוֹת	מִשְׁפְּחוֹת	family

Also: מִלְחָמָה (מִלְחֶמֶת) war

73.	תּוֹעֵבָה	תּוֹעֲבַת	——	תּוֹעֵבוֹת	תּוֹעֲבוֹת	abomination
	——	——	——	(תּוֹלֵדוֹת)	תּוֹלְדוֹת	history

XIII. Feminine Nouns in *-t* (plural §62; with suffixes §111).

74.	בַּת	בַּת	בִּתִּי	בָּנוֹת	בְּנוֹת	daughter
75.	עֵת	עֵת	עִתּוֹ	עִתִּים עִתּוֹת	(עִתֵּי) (עִתּוֹת)	time
76.	אֱמֶת	——	אֲמִתְּךָ	——	——	truth
77.	דֶּלֶת	דֶּלֶת	(דַּלְתִּי)	דְּלָתוֹת	דַּלְתוֹת	door

Also: קֶשֶׁת bow

78.	דַּעַת	דַּעַת	דַּעְתִּי	——	——	knowledge
79.	נְחֹשֶׁת	נְחֹשֶׁת	נְחָשְׁתִּי	——	——	bronze (fetter)
80.	(מוֹלֶדֶת)	מוֹלֶדֶת	מוֹלַדְתִּי	——	——	kindred
81.	מִשְׁמֶרֶת	מִשְׁמֶרֶת	מִשְׁמַרְתִּי	מִשְׁמָרוֹת	מִשְׁמְרוֹת	office

Also: תִּפְאֶרֶת beauty

82.	חַטָּאת	חַטַּאת	חַטָּאתִי	חַטָּאוֹת	חַטאוֹת	sin
83a.	חֲנִית	(חֲנִית)	(חֲנִיתִי)	חֲנִיתִים	(חֲנִיתֵי)	spear

Also probably the following (insufficient attestation):

בְּרִית pact   אַחֲרִית close   שְׁבִית captivity

83b.	מִצְרִית	(מִצְרִית)	מִצְרִיתִי	מִצְרִיּוֹת	(מִצְרִיּוֹת)	Egyptian (fem.adj)

Also the many other fem. adj. ending in *-îṯ*, such as שְׁלִשִׁית third,

for which we have not made separate classifications.

84.	עֵדוּת	——	——	——	עֵדְוֹת	testimony
85.	מַלְכוּת	מַלְכוּת	מַלְכוּתִי	מַלְכֻיוֹת	——	kingdom
86.	אָחוֹת	אֲחוֹת	אֲחוֹתִי	(אֲחָיוֹת)	(אַחְיוֹת)	sister

XIV. Masculine nouns in *-āh*.

87.	לַ֫יְלָה	——	——	לֵילוֹת	לֵילוֹת	night
88.	פֶּחָה	פַּחַת	(פֶּחָתִי)	פַּחֲוֹת/פַּחוֹת	פַּחֲוֹת/פַּחוֹת	governor

Appendix B

QAL VERBS: THE PRINCIPAL PARTS ACCORDING TO ROOT TYPES

The following is a classified list of all the Qal verbs appearing in this grammar. Under the heading "imperfect" are included: (1) the normal imperfect, (2) the jussive (if it differs from the preceding), and (3) the converted imperfect. Under "imperative": (1) the 2nd pers. masc. sing., (2) the 2nd pers. fem. sing., and (3) the "emphatic" form of the 2nd pers. masc. sing. in *-āh*. Under "inf. constr.": (1) the free (unbound) form of the infinitive construct, and (2) the inf. construct with the suffix of the 1st person singular. Under "other": (1) the active participle, (2) the passive participle, and (3) the infinitive absolute, in that order. The numbers in parentheses refer to the paragraphs of the grammar where the full paradigms of the form in question may be found. Minor deviations from the given type are indicated in parentheses.

1. Triliteral roots with no phonetic peculiarities (called Regular or Sound).

	Perfect	*Imperfect*	*Imperative*	*Inf. Construct*	*Other*
1a.	כָּתַב (43)	יִכְתֹּב (90)	כְּתֹב (102)	כְּתֹב (114)	כֹּתֵב (26)
		וַיִּכְתֹּב	כִּתְבִי	כָּתְבִי	כָּתוּב (128)
			כָּתְבָה		כָּתוֹב

גָּנַב	to steal	פָּרַץ	to break out
דָּרַךְ	to tread	פָּרַשׂ	to spread

דָּרַשׁ to seek, inquire
זָכַר to remember
כָּרַת to cut
כָּשַׁל to stumble
כָּתַב to write
לָכַד to capture
מָכַר to sell
מָלַךְ to rule
מָרַד to rebel
מָשַׁךְ to drag
מָשַׁל to rule
סָגַר to close
סָפַר to count
פָּקַד to attend to

קָבַץ to gather
קָבַר to bury
קָצַף to become angry
קָצַר to harvest
קָשַׁר to bind together
רָדַף to pursue
שָׂרַף to burn
שָׁבַר to break
שָׁבַת to cease, rest
שָׁכַן to dwell
שָׁמַר to observe
שָׁפַט to judge
שָׁפַךְ to pour
תָּפַשׂ to catch hold of

	Perfect	*Imperfect*	*Imperative*	*Inf. Construct*	*Other*
1b.	לָמַד (43)	יִלְמַד (94)	לְמַד (102)	לְמֹד (114)	לֹמֵד (26)
		וַיִּלְמַד	לִמְדִי	לָמְדִי }	לָמוּד (128)
			לָמְדָה }	לִמְדִי }	לָמוֹד
			לִמְדָה }		

לָמַד to learn
רָכַב to ride

שָׁכַב to lie down

	Perfect	*Imperfect*	*Imperative*	*Inf. Construct*	*Other*
1c.	קָרַב (43)	יִקְרַב (94)	קְרַב (102)	קְרֹב (114)	———
		וַיִּקְרַב	קִרְבִי	קָרְבִי	———
			קָרְבָה		קָרוֹב

גָּדַל to be big
לָבַשׁ to dress

קָרַב to approach

	Perfect	*Imperfect*	*Imperative*	*Inf. Construct*	*Other*
1d.	כָּבֵד (87)	יִכְבַּד (94)	כְּבַד (102)	כְּבֹד } (114)	———
		וַיִּכְבַּד	כִּבְדִי	כְּבַד }	———
				כָּבְדִי	כָּבוֹד

זָקֵן to be old
טָהֵר to be pure
כָּבֵד to be heavy

רָעֵב to be hungry
שָׁפֵל to be low

	Perfect	*Imperfect*	*Imperative*	*Inf. Construct*	*Other*
1e.	קָטֹן	יִקְטַן (94)	(קְטַן)	(קְטֹן) (87)	———
		וַיִּקְטַן			———
					קָטוֹן

(to be small)

2. Roots II/III-guttural; II/III-*Aleph*

	Perfect	*Imperfect*	*Imperative*	*Inf. Construct*	*Other*
2a.	בָּחַר (48)	יִבְחַר (94) וַיִּבְחַר	בְּחַר (102) בַּחֲרִי	בְּחֹר (114) בָּחֳרִי	בֹּחֵר (35) בָּחוּר (128) בָּחוֹר

בָּחַר	to choose	פָּעַל	to do
בָּחַן	to test	צָחַק	to laugh
בָּעַר	to burn	צָעַק	to cry out
גָּאַל	to redeem	רָחַץ	to wash
גָּעַר	to rebuke	שָׂחַק	to laugh
זָעַק	to cry out	שָׁאַל	to ask
מָאַס	to reject	שָׁחַט	to slaughter

	Perfect	*Imperfect*	*Imperative*	*Inf. Construct*	*Other*
2b.	שָׁמַע (48)	יִשְׁמַע (94) וַיִּשְׁמַע	שְׁמַע (102) שִׁמְעִי שָׁמְעָה / שִׁמְעָה	שְׁמֹעַ (114) שָׁמְעִי / שִׁמְעִי	שֹׁמֵעַ (35) שָׁמוּעַ (128) שָׁמוֹעַ

בָּטַח	to trust	פָּשַׁע	to rebel, err
בָּלַע	to swallow	פָּתַח	to open
בָּקַע	to split	קָרַע	to tear
בָּרַח	to flee	רָצַח	to kill
זָבַח	to sacrifice	שָׂבַע	to be sated
כָּרַע	to bow down	שָׂמַח	to rejoice
מָשַׁח	to anoint	שָׁכַח	to forget
סָלַח	to pardon	שָׁלַח	to send
פָּגַע	to meet	תָּקַע	to thrust, blow
שָׁמַע	to hear		

	Perfect	*Imperfect*	*Imperative*	*Inf. Construct*	*Other*
2c.	מָצָא (52)	יִמְצָא (95) וַיִּמְצָא	מְצָא (102) מִצְאִי מָצְאָה	מְצֹא (114) מָצְאִי	מֹצֵא (35) מָצוּא (128) מָצוֹא (128)

בָּרָא	to create	קָרָא	to call
מָצָא	to find	רָפָא	to heal

	Perfect	*Imperfect*	*Imperative*	*Inf. Construct*	*Other*
2d.	מָלֵא (87)	יִמְלָא (95) וַיִּמְלָא	מְלָא (102) מִלְאִי	מְלֹא (114)	— — מָלוֹא (128)

מָלֵא	to be full	שָׂנֵא	to hate

3. Roots I-guttural (not I-*Aleph*)

	Perfect	*Imperfect*	*Imperative*	*Inf. Construct*	*Other*
3a.	עָמַד (48)	יַעֲמֹד (103) וַיַּעֲמֹד	עֲמֹד (103) עִמְדִי עָמְדָה	עֲמֹד (114) עָמְדִי	עֹמֵד (26) עָמוּד (128) עָמוֹד (128)

הָפַךְ to overturn
הָרַג to kill
הָרַס to break down (tr.) (also יֶהֱרַס)
חָגַר to gird (יַחְגֹּר)
חָלַם to dream
חָמַל to spare
חָקַר to explore (also יַחְקֹר)
חָרַשׁ to plow
חָשַׁב to reckon (יַחְשֹׁב)

חָשַׂךְ to withhold (יַחְשֹׂךְ)
עָבַד to serve
עָבַר to cross
עָזַב to abandon
עָזַר to help (also יַעְזֹר)
עָמַד to stand
עָרַב to give as pledge
עָרַךְ to arrange

	Perfect	*Imperfect*	*Imperative*	*Inf. Construct*	*Other*
3b.	חָזַק (48)	יֶחֱזַק (103) וַיֶּחֱזַק	חֲזַק (103) חִזְקִי	חֲזֹק (114) חָזְקִי	— — חָזוֹק (128)

הָדַר to honor (יֶהְדַּר)
חָדַל to cease (יֶחְדַּל)

חָזַק to be strong

	Perfect	*Imperfect*	*Imperative*	*Inf. Construct*	*Other*
3c.	חָטָא (52)	יֶחֱטָא (103) וַיֶּחֱטָא	— —	חֲטֹא (114) חָטְאִי	חֹטֵא (35) —

(to sin)

	Perfect	*Imperfect*
3d.	חָפֵץ (48)	יַחְפֹּץ (103)

(to take pleasure in)

4. Roots I-*Aleph*

	Perfect	*Imperfect*	*Imperative*	*Inf. Construct*	*Other*
4a.	אָסַר (48)	יֶאֱסֹר (108) וַיֶּאֱסֹר	אֱסֹר (108) אִסְרִי אָסְרָה	אֱסֹר (114) אָסְרִי	אֹסֵר (26) אָסוּר (128) אָסוֹר (128)

אָסַף to collect, gather

אָסַר to bind, take captive

	Perfect	*Imperfect*	*Imperative*	*Inf. Construct*	*Other*
4b.	אָכַל (48)	יֹאכַל (108) וַיֹּאכַל	אֱכֹל (108) אִכְלִי אָכְלָה	אֱכֹל (114) אָכְלִי	אֹכֵל (26) אָכוּל (128) אָכוֹל (128)

אָבַד to perish
אָחַז to seize (יֶאֱחֹז or יֹאחֵז)
אָכַל to eat
אָמַר to say (וַיֹּ֫אמֶר)

	Perfect	*Imperfect*	*Imperative*	*Inf. Construct*	*Other*
4c.	אָהַב (48)	יֶאֱהַב (108)	אֱהַב (108)	אַהֲבָה (114)	אֹהֵב (35)
	אָהֵב	יֹאהַב	——	אַהֲבָתִי	אָהוּב (128)

אָהַב to love
אָשֵׁם (יֶאְשַׁם) to be guilty

5. Roots I-*Nun*

	Perfect	*Imperfect*	*Imperative*	*Inf. Construct*	*Other*
5a.	נָפַל (43)	יִפֹּל (118)	נְפֹל (118)	נְפֹל (118)	נֹפֵל (26)
		וַיִּפֹּל	נִפְלִי	נָפְלִי	(נָפוּל) (128)
			נִפְלָה		נָפוֹל (128)

נָגַף to strike
נָדַר to vow
נָטַשׁ to forsake
נָפַל to fall
נָצַר to guard

	Perfect	*Imperfect*	*Imperative*	*Inf. Construct*	*Other*
5b.	נָגַע (43)	יִגַּע (118)	גַּע (118)	גַּ֫עַת (118)	נֹגֵעַ (35)
		וַיִּגַּע	גְּעִי	גַּעְתִּי	נָגוּעַ (128)
			גְּעָה	נְגֹעַ	נָגוֹעַ (128)
				נָגְעִי	

נָגַע to touch
נָטַע to plant
נָסַע to set out

	Perfect	*Imperfect*	*Imperative*	*Inf. Construct*	*Other*
5c.	נָשָׂא (52)	יִשָּׂא (118)	שָׂא (118)	שְׂאֵת (118)	נֹשֵׂא (35)
		וַיִּשָּׂא	שְׂאִי	שְׂאֵתִי	נָשׂוּא (128)
			שְׂאָה		נָשׂוֹא (128)

(to raise up)

	Perfect	*Imperfect*	*Imperative*	*Inf. Construct*	*Other*
5d.	נָתַן (49)	יִתֵּן (118)	תֵּן (118)	תֵּת (118)	נֹתֵן (26)
		וַיִּתֵּן	תְּנִי	תִּתִּי	נָתוּן (128)
			תְּנָה		נָתוֹן (128)

(to give)

	Perfect	*Imperfect*	*Imperative*	*Inf. Construct*	*Other*
5e.	לָקַח (48)	יִקַּח (118)	קַח (118)	קַ֫חַת (118)	לֹקֵחַ (35)
		וַיִּקַּח	קְחִי	קַחְתִּי	לָקוּחַ (128)
			קְחָה		לָקוֹחַ (128)

(to take)

6. Roots I-*Yodh*

	Perfect	*Imperfect*	*Imperative*	*Inf. Construct*	*Other*
6a.	יָשַׁב (43)	יֵשֵׁב (120)	שֵׁב (120)	שֶׁבֶת (120)	יֹשֵׁב (26)
		וַיֵּשֶׁב	שְׁבִי	שִׁבְתִּי	
			שְׁבָה		יָשׁוּב (128)

יָרַד to go down
יָלַד to bear (a child)
יָשַׁב to dwell

6b.	יָדַע (48)	יֵדַע (120)	דַּע (120)	דַּעַת (120)	יֹדֵעַ (35)
		וַיֵּדַע	דְּעִי	דַּעְתִּי	יָדוּעַ (128)
			דְּעָה		יָדוֹעַ (128)

(to know)

6c.	יָצָא (52)	יֵצֵא (120)	צֵא (120)	צֵאת (120)	יֹצֵא (35)
		וַיֵּצֵא	צְאִי	צֵאתִי	
			צְאָה		יָצוֹא (128)

(to go forth)

6d.	יָרַשׁ (43)	יִירַשׁ (120)	רֵשׁ (120)	רֶשֶׁת (120)	יֹרֵשׁ (26)
		וַיִּירַשׁ		רִשְׁתִּי	יָרוּשׁ (128)
					יָרוֹשׁ (128)

יָשַׁר to be upright
יָעַץ to advise
יָרַשׁ to inherit

6e.	יָשֵׁן (87)	יִישַׁן (120)	—	יְשֹׁן (120)	

(to sleep)

6f.	יָרֵא (87)	יִירָא (120)	יְרָא (102)		

(to fear)

6g.	יָצַר (43)	יִצַּר/ (118)	—	—	יֹצֵר (26)
		יִצֹּר			
		וַיִּיצֶר/וַיִּצֶר			

(to fashion)

6h.	יָצַק (43)	יִצֹּק (118)	יְצֹק/צַק (118)	צֶקֶת (120)	
		וַיִּצֶק			

(to pour)

	Perfect	*Imperfect*	*Imperative*	*Inf. Construct*	*Other*
6i.	יָכֹל (87)	יוּכַל (120)	—	יְכֹ֫לֶת	
(to be able)					
6j.	הָלַךְ (48)	יֵלֵךְ (120)	לֵךְ (120)	לֶ֫כֶת (120)	הֹלֵךְ (26)
		וַיֵּ֫לֶךְ	לְכִי	לֶכְתִּי	
			לְכָה		הָלוֹךְ (128)
(to go, walk)					

7. Hollow Roots (II-*Waw*/*Yodh*)

7a.	קָם (64)	יָקוּם (124)	קוּם (124)	קוּם (124)	קָם (64)
		יָקֹם	ק֫וּמִי	קוּמִי	—
		וַיָּ֫קָם	ק֫וּמָה		קוּם (128)

גָּר to sojourn
מָל to circumcise
נָח to rest (וַיָּ֫נַח)
נָם to sleep
נָס to flee
סָר to turn aside (וַיָּ֫סַר)
עָר to arouse oneself

פָּץ to be scattered
צָם to fast
צָר to besiege (וַיָּ֫צַר)
קָם to arise
רָם to be high
רָץ to run
שָׁב to return

7b.	שָׂם (64)	יָשִׂים (124)	שִׂים (124)	שׂוּם/שִׂים (124)	שָׂם (64)
		יָשֵׂם	שִׂ֫ימִי	שׂוּמִי	שִׂים (128)
		וַיָּ֫שֶׂם	שִׂ֫ימָה		שׂוּם (128)

גָּל to rejoice
דָּן to judge
לָן to spend the night

שָׂם to put, place
שָׁר to sing
שָׁת to set, place

7c.	מֵת (87)	יָמוּת (124)	מוּת (124)	מוּת (124)	מֵת (87)
		יָמֹת			—
(to die)		וַיָּ֫מָת			מוֹת (128)
7d.	בֹּשׁ (87)	יֵבֹשׁ (124)	בֹּשׁ (124)		
(to be ashamed)					
7e.	בָּא (64)	יָבֹא (124)	בֹּא (124)	בֹּא (124)	בָּא (64)
		וַיָּבֹא	בֹּ֫אִי	בֹּאִי	
			בֹּ֫אָה		בֹּא (128)
(to come)					

8. Roots III-*Hē*

	Perfect	*Imperfect*	*Imperative*	*Inf. Construct*	*Other*
8a.	בָּנָה (57)	יִבְנֶה (122)	בְּנֵה (122)	בְּנוֹת (122)	בֹּנֶה (41)
		יִ֫בֶן	בְּנִי	בְּנוֹתִי	בָּנוּי (128)
		וַיִּ֫בֶן			בָּנֹה (128)

בָּזָה	to despise	קָנָה	to acquire
בָּכָה	to weep (וַיֵּבְךְּ)	קָרָה	to meet
בָּנָה	to build	רָאָה	to see (וַיַּרְא)
גָּלָה	to reveal; go into exile	רָבָה	to be many
זָנָה	to be a harlot	רָעָה	to pasture (וַיִּ֫רַע)
כָּלָה	to be done, finished	שָׁבָה	to take captive
פָּדָה	to ransom	שָׁתָה	to drink (וַיֵּ֫שְׁתְּ)
פָּנָה	to turn toward	תָּלָה	to hang
		תָּעָה	to wander lost

	Perfect	*Imperfect*	*Imperative*	*Inf. Construct*	*Other*
8b.	עָלָה (57)	יַעֲלֶה (122)	עֲלֵה (122)	עֲלוֹת (122)	עֹלֶה (41)
		יַ֫עַל	עֲלִי	עֲלוֹתִי	
		וַיַּ֫עַל			עָלֹה (128)

הָרָה	to conceive	עָנָה	to answer
חָנָה	to camp	עָשָׂה	to do, make
עָלָה	to ascend, go up		

	Perfect	*Imperfect*	*Imperative*	*Inf. Construct*	*Other*
8c.	חָזָה (57)	יֶחֱזֶה (122)	חֲזֵה (122)	חֲזוֹת (122)	חֹזֶה (41)
		יִ֫חַז	חֲזִי	חֲזוֹתִי	חָזוּי (128)
		וַיִּ֫חַז			חָזֹה (128)

הָגָה	to mutter, meditate	חָזָה	to see
הָמָה	to roar	חָרָה	to be angry

	Perfect	*Imperfect*	*Imperative*	*Inf. Construct*	*Other*
8d.	הָיָה (57)	יִהְיֶה (122)	הֱיֵה (122)	הֱיוֹת (122)	
		יְהִי	הֱיִי	הֱיוֹתִי	
		וַיְהִי		לִהְיוֹת	

הָיָה	to be	חָיָה	to live

	Perfect	*Imperfect*	*Imperative*	*Inf. Construct*	*Other*
8e.	אָבָה (57)	יֹאבֶה (122)			
		יֹאב			

אָבָה	to be willing	אָפָה	to bake

	Perfect	*Imperfect*	*Imperative*	*Inf. Construct*	*Other*
8f.	נָטָה (57)	יִטֶּה (122)	נְטֵה (122)	נְטוֹת (122)	נֹטֶה (41)
		יֵט			נָטוּי (128)
		וַיֵּט			

(to stretch forth)

9. Geminate Roots (a sampling of major types only; for details see §126).

	Perfect	*Imperfect*	*Imperative*	*Inf. Construct*	*Other*
9a.	סָבַב (68)	יָסֹב/יִסֹּב (126)	סֹב (126)	סֹב (126)	סֹבֵב (26)
		וַיָּ֫סָב	סֹ֫בִּי	סֻבִּי	סָבוּב (128)
					סָבוֹב (128)

(to surround, go around)

9b.	אָרַר (68)	יָאֹר (126)	אֹר (126)	———	אָרוּר (128)

(to curse)

9c.	תַּם (87)	יֵתַם (126)	———	תֻּמִּי תֹּם (126)

רַע to be bad   תַּם to be finished, completed
קַל to be light, contemptible

Appendix C

THE DERIVED CONJUGATIONS: A SYNOPSIS*

	Niphal	Piel	Pual	Hiphil	Hophal	Hithpael
1. Sound Triliteral Roots	(141)	(149)	(154)	(158)	(175)	(178)
Perfect	נִכְתַּב	כִּתֵּב	כֻּתַּב	הִכְתִּיב	הָכְתַּב	הִתְכַּתֵּב
Imperfect	יִכָּתֵב	יְכַתֵּב	יְכֻתַּב	יַכְתִּיב	יָכְתַּב	יִתְכַּתֵּב
Jussive	יִכָּתֵב	יְכַתֵּב	יְכֻתַּב	יַכְתֵּב	יָכְתַּב	יִתְכַּתֵּב
Imperative	הִכָּתֵב	כַּתֵּב	——	הַכְתֵּב	——	הִתְכַּתֵּב
Inf. Construct	הִכָּתֵב	כַּתֵּב	——	הַכְתִּיב	——	הִתְכַּתֵּב
Inf. Absolute	נִכְתֹּב	כַּתֹּב	כֻּתֹּב	הַכְתֵּב	הָכְתֵּב	הִתְכַּתֵּב
Participle	נִכְתָּב	מְכַתֵּב	מְכֻתָּב	מַכְתִּיב	מָכְתָּב	מִתְכַּתֵּב
2. Roots I-guttural (excluding I-*Aleph*)	(141)	(149)	(154)	(158)	(175)	(178)
Perfect	נֶעֱמַד	עִמֵּד	עֻמַּד	הֶעֱמִיד	הָעֳמַד	הִתְעַמֵּד
Imperfect	יֵעָמֵד	יְעַמֵּד	יְעֻמַּד	יַעֲמִיד	יָעֳמַד	יִתְעַמֵּד
Jussive	יֵעָמֵד	יְעַמֵּד	יְעֻמַּד	יַעֲמֵד	יָעֳמַד	יִתְעַמֵּד
Imperative	הֵעָמֵד	עַמֵּד	——	הַעֲמֵד	——	הִתְעַמֵּד
Inf. Construct	הֵעָמֵד	עַמֵּד	——	הַעֲמִיד	——	הִתְעַמֵּד
Inf. Absolute	נַעֲמֹד	עַמֹּד	עֻמֹּד	הַעֲמֵד	הָעֳמֵד	הִתְעַמֵּד
Participle	נֶעֱמָד	מְעַמֵּד	מְעֻמָּד	מַעֲמִיד	מָעֳמָד	מִתְעַמֵּד

* The same root is used to illustrate all the conjugations of a given root type, regardless of whether it is attested in that particular form or not. References are to paragraphs in the body of the grammar where the complete paradigms may be found.

	Niphal	Piel	Pual	Hiphil	Hophal	Hithpael
3. Roots II-guttural	(141)	(149)	(154)	(158)	(175)	(178)
Perfect	נִבְרַךְ	בֵּרַךְ	בֹּרַךְ	הִבְרִיךְ	הָבְרַךְ	הִתְבָּרֵךְ
Imperfect	יִבָּרֵךְ	יְבָרֵךְ	יְבֹרַךְ	יַבְרִיךְ	יָבְרַךְ	יִתְבָּרֵךְ
Jussive	יִבָּרֵךְ	יְבָרֵךְ	יְבֹרַךְ	יַבְרֵךְ	יָבְרַךְ	יִתְבָּרֵךְ
Imperative	הִבָּרֵךְ	בָּרֵךְ	——	הַבְרֵךְ	——	הִתְבָּרֵךְ
Inf. Construct	הִבָּרֵךְ	בָּרֵךְ	——	הַבְרִיךְ	——	הִתְבָּרֵךְ
Inf. Absolute	נִבְרֹךְ	בָּרֵךְ	——	הַבְרֵךְ	הָבְרֵךְ	הִתְבָּרֵךְ
Participle	נִבְרָךְ	מְבָרֵךְ	מְבֹרָךְ	מַבְרִיךְ	מָבְרָךְ	מִתְבָּרֵךְ
4. Roots III-guttural (excluding III-*Aleph*)	(141)	(149)	(154)	(160)	(175)	(178)
Perfect	נִשְׁמַע	שִׁמַּע	שֻׁמַּע	הִשְׁמִיעַ	הָשְׁמַע	הִשְׁתַּמַּע
Imperfect	יִשָּׁמַע	יְשַׁמַּע	יְשֻׁמַּע	יַשְׁמִיעַ	יָשְׁמַע	יִשְׁתַּמַּע
Jussive	יִשָּׁמַע	יְשַׁמַּע	יְשֻׁמַּע	יַשְׁמַע	יָשְׁמַע	יִשְׁתַּמַּע
Imperative	הִשָּׁמַע	שַׁמַּע	——	הַשְׁמַע	——	הִשְׁתַּמַּע
Inf. Construct	הִשָּׁמַע	שַׁמַּע	——	הַשְׁמִיעַ	——	הִשְׁתַּמַּע
Inf. Absolute	נִשְׁמוֹעַ	שַׁמֵּעַ	——	הַשְׁמֵעַ	הָשְׁמֵעַ	——
Participle	נִשְׁמָע	מְשַׁמֵּעַ	מְשֻׁמָּע	מַשְׁמִיעַ	מָשְׁמָע	מִשְׁתַּמֵּעַ
5. Roots III-*Aleph*	(143)	(151)	(154)	(160)	(175)	(178)
Perfect	נִמְצָא	מִצֵּא	מֻצָּא	הִמְצִיא	הָמְצָא	הִתְמַצֵּא
Imperfect	יִמָּצֵא	יְמַצֵּא	יְמֻצָּא	יַמְצִיא	יָמְצָא	יִתְמַצֵּא
Jussive	יִמָּצֵא	יְמַצֵּא	יְמֻצָּא	יַמְצֵא	יָמְצָא	יִתְמַצֵּא
Imperative	הִמָּצֵא	מַצֵּא	——	הַמְצֵא	——	הִתְמַצֵּא
Inf. Construct	הִמָּצֵא	מַצֵּא	——	הַמְצִיא	——	הִתְמַצֵּא
Inf. Absolute	נִמְצֹא	מַצֹּא	——	הַמְצֵא	——	——
Participle	נִמְצָא	מְמַצֵּא	מְמֻצָּא	מַמְצִיא	מָמְצָא	מִתְמַצֵּא
6. Roots I-*Nun*	(143)	(149)	(154)	(158)	(175)	(178)
Perfect	נִפַּל	נִפֵּל	נֻפַּל	הִפִּיל	הֻפַּל	הִתְנַפֵּל
Imperfect	יִנָּפֵל	יְנַפֵּל	יְנֻפַּל	יַפִּיל	יֻפַּל	יִתְנַפֵּל
Jussive	יִנָּפֵל	יְנַפֵּל	יְנֻפַּל	יַפֵּל	יֻפַּל	יִתְנַפֵּל
Imperative	הִנָּפֵל	נַפֵּל	——	הַפֵּל	——	הִתְנַפֵּל
Inf. Construct	הִנָּפֵל	נַפֵּל	——	הַפִּיל	הֻפַּל	הִתְנַפֵּל
Inf. Absolute	נִפֹּל	נַפֹּל	——	הַפֵּל	הֻפֵּל	הִתְנַפֵּל
Participle	נִפָּל	מְנַפֵּל	מְנֻפָּל	מַפִּיל	מֻפָּל	מִתְנַפֵּל
7. Roots I-*Waw/Yodh*	(143)	(149)	(154)	(163)	(175)	(178)
Perfect	נוֹשָׁב	יִשֵּׁב	יֻשַּׁב	הוֹשִׁיב	הוּשַׁב	הִתְיַשֵּׁב
Imperfect	יִוָּשֵׁב	יְיַשֵּׁב	יְיֻשַּׁב	יוֹשִׁיב	יוּשַׁב	יִתְיַשֵּׁב
Jussive	יִוָּשֵׁב	יְיַשֵּׁב	יְיֻשַּׁב	יוֹשֵׁב	יוּשַׁב	יִתְיַשֵּׁב

	Niphal	Piel	Pual	Hiphil	Hophal	Hithpael
Imperative	הִוָּשֵׁב	יַשֵּׁב	——	הוֹשֵׁב	——	הִתְיַשֵּׁב
Inf. Construct	הִוָּשֵׁב	יַשֵּׁב	——	הוֹשִׁיב	הוּשַׁב	הִתְיַשֵּׁב
Inf. Absolute	——	יַשֹּׁב	——	הוֹשֵׁב	——	הִתְיַשֵּׁב
Participle	נוֹשָׁב	מְיַשֵּׁב	מְיֻשָּׁב	מוֹשִׁיב	מוּשָׁב	מִתְיַשֵּׁב
8. Roots II-*Waw/Yodh* (Hollow)	(146)			(169)	(175)	
Perfect	נָקוֹם	——	——	הֵקִים	הוּקַם	——
Imperfect	יִקּוֹם	——	——	יָקִים	יוּקַם	——
Jussive	יִקּוֹם	——	——	יָקֵם	יוּקַם	——
Imperative	הִקּוֹם	——	——	הָקֵם	——	——
Inf. Construct	הִקּוֹם	——	——	הָקִים	הוּקַם	——
Inf. Absolute	נָקוֹם	——	——	הָקֵם	——	——
Participle	נָקוֹם	——	——	מֵקִים	מוּקָם	——
9. Roots III-*Hē*	(143)	(151)	(154)	(166)	(175)	(178)
Perfect	נִבְנָה	בִּנָּה	בֻּנָּה	הִבְנָה	הָבְנָה	הִתְבַּנָּה
Imperfect	יִבָּנֶה	יְבַנֶּה	יְבֻנֶּה	יַבְנֶה	יָבְנֶה	יִתְבַּנֶּה
Jussive	יִבָּן	יְבַן	——	יֶ֫בֶן	——	יִתְבַּן
Imperative	הִבָּנֵה	בַּנֵּה	——	הַבְנֵה	——	הִתְבַּנֵּה
Inf. Construct	הִבָּנוֹת	בַּנּוֹת	בֻּנּוֹת	הַבְנוֹת	——	הִתְבַּנּוֹת
Inf. Absolute	נִבְנֹה	בַּנֹּה	——	הַבְנֵה	הָבְנֵה	——
Participle	נִבְנֶה	מְבַנֶּה	מְבֻנֶּה	מַבְנֶה	מָבְנֶה	מִתְבַּנֶּה
10. Geminate Roots	(146)	(151)	(154)	(172)	(175)	(178)
Perfect	נָסַב	סִבֵּב	סֻבַּב	הֵסֵב	הוּסַב	הִסְתַּבֵּב
Imperfect	יִסַּב	יְסַבֵּב	יְסֻבַּב	יָסֵב	יוּסַב	יִסְתַּבֵּב
Jussive	יִסַּב	יְסַבֵּב	יְסֻבַּב	יָסֵב	יוּסַב	יִסְתַּבֵּב
Imperative	הִסַּב	סַבֵּב	——	הָסֵב	——	הִסְתַּבֵּב
Inf. Construct	הִסֵּב	סַבֵּב	——	הָסֵב	——	הִסְתַּבֵּב
Inf. Absolute	הִסּוֹב	——	——	הָסֵב	——	הִסְתַּבֵּב
Participle	נָסָב	מְסַבֵּב	מְסֻבָּב	מֵסֵב	מוּסָב	מִסְתַּבֵּב

Appendix D

CHRONOLOGICAL TABLE

Patriarchal Period, as reflected in the traditional accounts of Genesis	c. 1900–1500 B.C.
The Exodus	c. 1280
The Conquest of Canaan	c. 1250–1200
The Period of the Judges	c. 1200–1020
Reign of Saul	c. 1020–1000
Reign of David	c. 1000–961
Reign of Solomon	c. 961–922
Division into the Kingdoms of Judah and Israel	922
Fall of Samaria (cap. of Israel) to Assyria	722
Fall of Jerusalem (cap. of Judah) to Babylon	587/6
The Babylonian Exile	587–538
Post-Exilic Period (Persian domination)	538–332
Beginning of Greek Rule (with Alexander)	332

Appendix E

BRIEF BIBLIOGRAPHY

DICTIONARIES

F. BROWN, S. R. DRIVER, C. A. BRIGGS: *Hebrew and English Lexicon of the Old Testament.* Oxford, 1907 (corrected impression, 1952).

W. GESENIUS, F. BUHL: *Hebräisches und aramäisches Handwörterbuch über das Alte Testament.* 17th edition, Berlin, 1915.

K. FEYERABEND: *Langenscheidt's Pocket Hebrew Dictionary to the Old Testament.* 13th edition, New York, 1961.

GRAMMARS

W. GESENIUS, E. KAUTZSCH, A. E. COWLEY: *Hebrew Grammar.* Oxford, 1910.

G. BERGSTRÄSSER: *Hebräische Grammatik,* Leipzig, 1918. Reissued in Hildesheim, 1962.

TEXT AND VERSIONS

B. J. ROBERTS: *The Old Testament Text and Versions.* Cardiff, 1951.

F. M. CROSS: *The Ancient Library of Qumran.* New York, 1958.

Biblia Hebraica, ed. by R. Kittel and others. 3rd edition, Stuttgart, 1937.

HISTORY AND ARCHAEOLOGY

W. F. ALBRIGHT: *Archaeology and the Religion of Israel.* Baltimore, 1946.

J. BRIGHT: *A History of Israel.* Philadelphia, 1959.

R. DE VAUX: *Ancient Israel, Its Life and Institutions.* New York, 1961.

HEBREW-ENGLISH GLOSSARY

Verbs are listed according to the root. Conjugational types are abbreviated as follows:

Q	qal	H	hiphil
N	niphal	Ho	hophal
P	piel	Ht	hithpael
Pu	pual	Po	polel

All other words are listed alphabetically as they appear.
References of the types A1c and B3c refer to the Appendices A and B respectively.
All other references are to paragraphs in the grammar.

א

אָב (-*ô<u>t</u>*) father, ancestor (A1c)
אָבַד (יֹאבַד) to perish, be destroyed (B4b); H הֶאֱבִיד to destroy, kill
אָבָה (יֹאבֶה) to be willing (B8e)
אֲבָל truly, indeed; however
אֶבֶן (îm) stone (f.) A7a
אַבְרָהָם Abraham
אַבְרָם Abram = Abraham
אָדָם Adam; man; mankind (80)
אֲדָמָה earth, ground, soil (A64b)
אָדוֹן (îm) lord, master (A29a)
אָהַב (יֶאֱהַב) to love (B4c)
אַהֲבָה love (A60b)
אוֹ or
אוֹר (îm) light (A5a)
אוּרִיָּה Uriah
אוֹת (ô<u>t</u>) sign, omen (A5a)
אָז then, at that time
אֹזֶן (du. אָזְנַיִם) ear (f.) A11
אָח (אַחִים) brother (A1d)

אֶחָד one (m.)
אָחוֹת sister (f.) A86
אָחַז (יֹאחֵז) to seize, grasp, take hold of (108, B4b)
אַחֵר (אֲחֵרִים) other; fem. אַחֶרֶת, pl. אֲחֵרוֹת
אַחַר after (prep.); afterwards
אַחֲרֵי after (prep.); + אֲשֶׁר after (conj.); + כֵּן afterwards
אַחַת one (f.)
אֵי־מִזֶּה from what place, from which?
אֹיֵב (îm) enemy (A35)
אַיֵּה where?
אֵיךְ/אֵיכָה how? in what manner?
אֵימָה dread, terror (cf. A55, 56)
אַיִן there is not, are not
אֵיפֹה where?
אִישׁ (אֲנָשִׁים) man, husband (A4c)
אַךְ surely, doubtlessly; but, however
אָכַל (יֹאכַל) to eat (B4b)
אֹכֶל food (A11)
אֶל to, toward
אֵל (îm) god; God (A3b)
אֵלֶּה these; 40
אֱלֹהִים gods; God (59; cf. A22)
אֶלֶף (îm) thousand (181; A7a)
אִם if
אֵם (אִמּוֹת) mother (f.) A3e
אָמָה (אֲמָהוֹת) maidservant, fem. slave (A54e)
(אמן) N. נֶאֱמַן to be confirmed, verified, trustworthy; H. הֶאֱמִין to believe, trust
אָמְנָם surely, indeed
אָמַר (יֹאמַר) to say (B4b)
אֱמֶת truth (A76)
אָנָה whither?
אֲנַחְנוּ we (81)
אֲנִי I (81)
אָנֹכִי I (81)
אָסִיר (îm) prisoner (A28a)
אָסַף (יֶאֱסֹף) to gather (B4a)
אָסַר (יֶאֱסֹר) to bind, take prisoner (B4a)
אַף (du. אַפַּיִם) nose, face; anger (A2a)
אֶפֶס + כִּי except that, save that (conj.)
אֵצֶל near, beside, by (A10b)
אַרְבַּע four (f.)
אַרְבָּעָה four (m.)
אַרְבָּעִים forty
אֲרוֹן ark (of the covenant); w. art. הָאָרוֹן (A22)
אָרוּר accursed (A30a)
אֲרִי (אֲרָיוֹת) lion (cf. A31b)
אַרְיֵה lion (A52)
(ארך) H. הֶאֱרִיךְ to be long; to lengthen
אָרַר (יָאוֹר) to curse (B9b)
אֶרֶץ (ôṯ) earth, land (f.) A7a
אֵשׁ fire (f.) A3e
אִשָּׁה (נָשִׁים) woman, wife (A58b)
אָשֵׁם (יֶאְשַׁם) to be guilty; (adj.) guilty
אַשְׁקְלוֹן Ashkelon
אֲשֶׁר who, which, that (rel. pron.); that, since, because (conj.)
אֵת/אֶת־ dir. obj. marker
אֵת/אֶת־ with, together with
אַתְּ you (f.s.) 81
אַתָּה you (m.s.) 81
אָתוֹן (ôṯ) she-ass, donkey (f.) A29a
אַתֶּם you (m.pl.) 81
אֶתְמוֹל yesterday
אַתֶּן you (f.pl.) 81
אַתֵּנָה you (f.pl.) 81

ב

בְּ in, with (instrumental); (+ inf.) when, while

בְּאֵר (ôṯ) well, pit (A20a)
בֶּ֫גֶד (îm) garment (A7c)
(בדד) לְבַד־ alone, only; 142
בְּהֵמָה (ôṯ) beast, animal; 80 (A65c)
(בוא) בָּא (יָבוֹא) to come, enter (B7e); H. to bring
(בין) H. הֵבִין to perceive, consider, understand; to make understand
בּוֹר (ôṯ) pit, cistern (A5a)
(בושׁ) בֹּשׁ (יֵבוֹשׁ) to be ashamed (B7d)
בָּזָה (יִבְזֶה) to despise (B8a)
בָּחוּר (îm) young man (A30b)
בָּחַן (יִבְחַן) to test, try, examine (B2a)
בָּחַר (יִבְחַר) to choose (obj. with בְּ) B2a
בָּטַח (יִבְטַח) to trust, rely (B2a)
בֵּין between; 47
בִּינָה understanding, perceptiveness (A56)
בַּ֫יִת (בָּתִּים) house (A13c)
בָּכָה (יִבְכֶּה) to weep, mourn (B8a)
בָּלַע (יִבְלַע) to swallow (B2b)
בִּלְתִּי not (negates infinitive; 115)
בֵּן (בָּנִים) son (A3c)
בָּנָה (יִבְנֶה) to build (B8a); H. caus., N. pass.
בַּעֲבוּר for the sake of, because of
בְּעַד through; around; on behalf of; 174
בְּעֵינֵי in the eyes of, in the opinion of
בַּ֫עַל (îm) lord, master, husband, owner; 121 (A9)
בָּעַר (יִבְעַר) to burn (tr. and intr.) B2a; P. to burn (tr.), consume completely
בֶּ֫צַע profit, advantage; מַה־בֶּ֫צַע what profit is there? (A8b)
בָּקַע (יִבְקַע) to split (B2b)
בֹּ֫קֶר morning (A11)
בָּקָר (large) cattle (coll.)
(בקשׁ) P. בִּקֵּשׁ to seek
בָּרָא (יִבְרָא) to create (B2c); N. pass.
בְּרִית covenant, treaty (A83)
בָּרַח (יִבְרַח) to flee (B2b)
(ברך) P. בֵּרַךְ to bless
בְּרָכָה (ôṯ) blessing (A64a)
בָּשָׂר flesh, meat; כָּל־בָּשָׂר mankind (A25a)
בַּת (בָּנוֹת) daughter (A74)

ג

גָּאַל (יִגְאַל) to redeem (B2a); N. pass.
גִּבּוֹר (îm) warrior, hero; + חַ֫יִל idem (A43)
גִּבְעָה (ôṯ) hill (A61a)
גְּבֶ֫רֶת mistress, lady (cf. A81)
גָּדוֹל big, great (A29a)
גָּדַל (יִגְדַּל) to be(come) great, big; to grow up (B1c); H. to magnify, make great
גְּדִי (גְּדָיִים) kid (A31a)
(גור) גָּר (יָגוּר) to sojourn, dwell (B7a)
(גיל) גָּל (יָגִיל) to rejoice (B7b)
גָּלָה (יִגְלֶה) to reveal, uncover; go into exile (B8a); N. pass.; H. to carry away into exile
גִּלְעָד Gilead
גַּם also, too, even
גָּמָל (גְּמַלִּים) camel (A25d)
גַּן (גַּנּוֹת) garden; הַגָּן, §21 (A2a)
גָּנַב (יִגְנֹב) to steal (B1a)
גָּעַר (יִגְעַר) to rebuke (B2a)

גֵּר (îm) sojourner, resident alien (A3b)

(גרשׁ) P. גֵּרֵשׁ to drive away

ד

דָּבָר (îm) word, thing, matter, affair; עַל־דְּבַר because of, for the sake of

(דבר) P. דִּבֶּר to speak, talk

דְּבַשׁ honey (A18)

דָּג (îm) fish (cf. A1a, 1b)

דָּגָה fish (coll.) A53a

דָּוִד David

דּוֹר (îm, ôṯ) generation (A5a)

דּוֹתָן Dothan

(דין) דָּן (יָדִין) to judge (B7b)

דַּל poor; §22 (A2a)

דֶּלֶת (du. דְּלָתַיִם; pl. ôṯ) door (A77)

דָּם (îm) blood (A1b)

(דמם) דַּם (יִדֹּם) to be silent, astonished (B9a, c)

דֶּרֶךְ (îm, ôṯ) road, way (m. or f.) A7a

דָּרַשׁ (יִדְרֹשׁ) to inquire, seek, require (B2a)

ה

הַ הָ הֶ the def. art.; §14, 18, 21

הֲ הַ interrog. marker

הַב (defective verb) give! come! let's...! 119

הֶבֶל Abel

הָגָה (יֶהְגֶּה) to mutter, moan, roar; meditate, imagine (B8c)

הוּא he; that

הִוא = היא; see 87

הִיא she, it; that

הָיָה (יִהְיֶה) to be, become (B8d)

הֵיכָל (îm) palace, temple (A34)

הָלַךְ (יֵלֵךְ) to go, walk; H. הוֹלִיךְ to cause to go, lead; Ht. to walk back and forth, to go continually (B6j)

(הלל) P. הִלֵּל to praise; הַלְלוּיָהּ Halelujah, Praise Yah(weh)

הֲלֹם hither

הֵם they; those

הֵן if

הִנֵּה see §135–6

הֵ֫נָּה they (f.); those (f.)

הֵ֫נָּה hither, to this place, here

הַר (הָרִים) mountain (A2c)

הָרַג (יַהֲרֹג) to slay, kill; N. pass. (B3a)

הָרָה (יַהֲרֶה) to become pregnant, conceive (B8b)

ו

וְ and; 17

ז

זֹאת this (f.); 40

זָבַח (יִזְבַּח) to sacrifice (B2b)

זֶ֫בַח (îm) sacrifice (A8b)

זֶה this (m.); 40

זָהָב gold (A25a)

זַ֫יִת (îm) olive, olive-tree (A13b)

זָכַר (יִזְכֹּר) to remember; N. pass.; H. to mention, cause to remember (B1a)

זֵ֫כֶר remembrance, memorial (A10a)

זָכָר (îm) male (A25a)

זָנָה (יִזְנֶה) to be(come) a prostitute, harlot; זֹנָה a harlot (B8a)

זָעַק (יִזְעַק) = צָעַק to cry out (in distress) B2a

זָקֵן (יִזְקַן) to be(come) old; (adj.) old (B1d)

זָקֵן (îm) old man, elder (of city) A26a
זְקוּנִים (pl.) old age (cf. A23, 30a)
זְרוֹעַ (îm, ôṯ) arm; fig. strength (A22)
זֶרַע seed, offspring, progeny (A8a)

ח

(חבא) N. נֶחְבָּא to hide (intr.); Ht. הִתְחַבֵּא to hide (intr.)
חָדַל (יֶחְדַּל) to cease, stop; 117 (B3b)
חָדָשׁ new (A25b)
חַוָּה Eve
(חוה) Hišt. הִשְׁתַּחֲוָה to bow down, humble oneself
חוֹמָה (ôṯ) city-wall (A55)
חוּץ outside; הַחוּצָה, חוּצָה (to the) outside; מִחוּץ לְ outside (prep.)
חָזַק (יֶחֱזַק) to be(come) strong, firm, hard; (adj.) idem (B3b)
חָטָא (יֶחֱטָא) to sin (לְ against); H. to lead into sin (B3c)
חַטָּאת (חַטָּאוֹת) sin (A82)
חַי living, alive; as-lives (in oath), 138 (A2a)
חָיָה (יִחְיֶה) to live, be alive (B8d); P. חִיָּה to let live, revive, restore to life; H. הֶחֱיָה, same as P.
חַיָּה (ôṯ) animal, living thing (A57)
חַיִל (חֲיָלִים) army; strength; גִּבּוֹר חַיִל warrior (A13a)
חַיִּים life, lifetime (cf. A2a)
חֵיק bosom (cf. A3b)
חָכָם wise; wise man (A25b)
חָכְמָה wisdom (A63)
חָלָב milk (cf. A25b)
חֲלוֹם (ôṯ) dream (A22)
(חלל) H. הֵחֵל to begin
(חלל) P. חִלֵּל to defile, pollute, dishonor
חָלַם (יַחֲלֹם) to dream (B3a)
חֲמוֹר (îm) he-ass, donkey (A22)
חֲמִישִׁי fifth
חָמַל (יַחְמֹל) to spare (B3a)
חָמֵשׁ five (f.)
חֲמִשָּׁה five (m.)
חֲמִשִּׁים fifty
חֵן grace, favor (A3e)
חָנַן (יָחוֹן) to favor, be gracious toward (B9a); Ht. הִתְחַנֵּן to seek or implore favor
חֶסֶד (îm) kindness, mercy, proper conduct
חָפֵץ (יַחְפֹּץ) to take delight in; to desire (B3d)
חֲצִי half (A31b)
חֹק (îm) statute (A5d)
חֻקָּה (ôṯ) statute (A59)
חֶרֶב (ôṯ) sword (f.) A7a
חֹרֵב (Mt.) Horeb
חָרָה (יֶחֱרֶה) to become enraged, angry (B8c); used impersonally with לְ or with אַף
(חרם) H. הֶחֱרִים to destroy, exterminate (often as a religious act)
חָרַשׁ (יַחֲרֹשׁ) to plow; engrave (B3a)
חָשַׂךְ (יַחְשֹׂךְ) to withhold, keep back for oneself (B3a)
חָשַׁב (יַחְשֹׁב) to think, devise, reckon, impute (B3a)
חֹשֶׁךְ darkness
חִתִּי Hittite
חֹתֵן father-in-law (A35)

ט

טָבַח (יִטְבַּח) to slaughter (B2b)
טֶבַח a slaughtering (A8b)

טוֹב good (A5a)
טַף children (coll.) A2a
טֶרֶם before, not yet; בְּטֶרֶם idem; 121

י

(יאל) H. הוֹאִיל to be willing, content (173)
יְאֹר The Nile; river
יַבָּשָׁה dry ground (cf. A70)
יָד (du. áyim; pl. ôṯ) hand, side (f.) A1a
(ידה) H. הוֹדָה to give thanks
יָדַע (יֵדַע) to know (B6b); H. to make known, teach, declare
יְהוּדָה Judah
יהוה Yahweh, "Jehovah," the Lord (59)
יוֹם (pl. יָמִים) day; כַּיּוֹם ,הַיּוֹם today (A5b)
יוֹמָם by day, in the daytime
יוֹסֵף Joseph
יַחַד together
יַחְדָּו together
(יטב) יִיטַב to go well with (לְ) B6d
(יכח) H. הוֹכִיחַ to reprove; to decide
יָכֹל (יוּכַל) to be able; to prevail against (לְ) B6i
יָלַד (יֵלֵד) to bear (a child); N. pass.; H. to beget, engender (B6a)
יֶלֶד (pl. îm) boy (A7a)
יָם (pl. יַמִּים) sea; יָמָּה seaward, westward (A1e)
יָמִין the right hand (f.) A28a
(יסף) H. הוֹסִיף to add; to do something again; to continue doing something
יָפֶה beautiful,handsome(A49)

יַעַן because (+ inf.); יַעַן אֲשֶׁר because
יַעֲקֹב Jacob
יָצָא (יֵצֵא) to go out, to go forth (B6c); H. caus.
(יצב) Ht. הִתְיַצֵּב to take one's stand, to station oneself
יָצַר (יִיצֶר) to form, fashion (B6g)
(יקץ) יִיקַץ to wake up (B6d)
יָקָר precious (A25a)
יָרֵא (יִירָא) to be afraid (of: מִפְּנֵי ,מִן) B6f.; N. to be dreadful, terrible
יִרְאָה fear (A61a)
יָרַד (יֵרֵד) to go down, descend (B6a); H. caus.
יְרוּשָׁלַםִ Jerusalem
(ירה) H. הוֹרָה to shoot (arrows); to direct, teach
יָרֵחַ the moon
יָרַשׁ (יִירַשׁ) to inherit (B6d); to dispossess
יִשְׂרָאֵל Israel
יֵשׁ there is, are
יָשַׁב (יֵשֵׁב) to sit, dwell (B6a); H. caus.
יְשׁוּעָה (pl. ôṯ) salvation, deliverance (A67)
יִשְׁמְעֵאלִים Ishmaelites
יָשֵׁן (יִישַׁן) to sleep (B6e)
(ישע) H. הוֹשִׁיעַ to save, deliver
יָשַׁר (יִישַׁר) to be pleasant, agreeable (B6d)
יָשָׁר just, upright (A25a)
(יתר) N. נוֹתַר to be left, remain
יִתְרוֹ Jethro

כ

כְּ like, as; (+ inf.) when, as
כַּאֲשֶׁר as, according as
כָּבֵד (יִכְבַּד) to be (come) heavy,

important, serious; (adj.) idem (B1d)

כָּבוֹד glory, honor (A29a)

כֶּ֫בֶשׂ (îm) lamb (m.) A7c

כִּבְשָׂה (ôṯ) lamb (f.) A61a

כֹּה thus, as follows

כֹּהֵן (îm) priest (A35)

כּוֹכָב (îm) star (A33)

(כון) N. נָכוֹן to be firm, fixed, established; H. הֵכִין to prepare, establish; Po. כּוֹנֵן to set up, establish

(כחד) P. כִּחֵד to hide, conceal

כִּי because, since; for; that; כִּי אִם unless, except that, but rather

כַּיּוֹם today, this day

כֹּל/כָּל־ all, each, every; presufixal כֻּל־ 138; כָּל־אֲשֶׁר everything which (cf. A5d)

כָּלָה (יִכְלֶה) to be depleted, finished, at an end (B8a); P. to finish, bring to an end

כְּלִי (îm) vessel, utensil (A31a)

כֵּן thus, so; עַל־כֵּן therefore; לָכֵן therefore

כֵּן honest, true (A3b)

כְּנַ֫עַן Canaan

כְּנַעֲנִי Canaanite

כִּסֵּא (ôṯ) throne (A41b)

(כסה) P. כִּסָּה to cover, overwhelm

כֶּ֫סֶף silver, money (A7a)

כַּף (du. כַּפַּ֫יִם; pl. ôṯ) palm or hollow of hand, sole of foot (A2a)

(כפר) P. כִּפֶּר to atone for, make atonement

כֶּ֫רֶם (îm) vineyard (A7a)

כָּרַת (יִכְרֹת) to cut (B1a); כָּרַת בְּרִית to make a treaty

כַּשְׂדִּים Chaldaeans

כָּשַׁל (יִכְשֹׁל) to stumble (B1a)

כָּתַב (יִכְתֹּב) to write (B1a)

כְּתֹ֫נֶת or כֻּתֹּ֫נֶת (ôṯ) tunic (A79)

ל

לְ to, for

לֹא not, no

לֵאמֹר "saying" (used to mark a direct quote)

לֵב (ôṯ) heart (A3e)

לֵבָב (ôṯ) heart (A27a)

לְבַד־ see (בדד)

לָבָן Laban

לֶהָבָה (ôṯ) flame (cf. A71)

לוּחַ (ôṯ) tablet (A6)

לוֹט Lot

לוּלֵא/לוּלֵי unless, if not

לֶ֫חֶם bread, food (A7a)

(לחם) N. נִלְחַם to fight

לַ֫יְלָה night; at night (A87)

(לין) לָן (יָלִין) to spend the night (B7b)

לָכַד (יִלְכֹּד) to capture (B1a)

לָכֵן therefore

לָמַד (יִלְמַד) to learn (B1b); P. לִמַּד to teach

לָ֫מָּה why? (לָמָה before ח ה ע) 74

לְמַ֫עַן so that, in order that

לִפְנֵי before, in front of, in the presence of

לָקַח (יִקַּח) to take (B5e); N. pass.

לִקְרַאת toward, against, to meet (125)

מ

מְאֹד very, much

מֵאָה (ôṯ) hundred; 181

מֵאַ֫יִן from where?

מַאֲכָל food (A38)

מְאוּ֫מָה anything; w. neg. nothing (A67)

(מאן) P. מֵאֵן to refuse

מָאַס (יִמְאַס) to refuse, despise (B2a)
מְגוּרִים (pl.) sojourning, residence (A30a)
מַגֵּפָה (ôṯ) plague, stroke (cf. A73)
מִדְבָּר wilderness (A37)
מָדַד (יָמֹד) to measure (B9a)
מַדּוּעַ why?
מִדְיָן Midian
מַה what?
(מהר) P. מִהַר to hurry; מַהֵר quickly
מָוֶת death (A15)
(מות) מֵת (יָמוּת) to die (B7c); H. הֵמִית to kill; Po. מוֹתֵת to kill
(מול) מָל (יָמוּל) to circumcise (B7a)
מִזְבֵּחַ (ôṯ) altar (A41c)
מַחֲנֶה (ôṯ) camp (A51)
מַטֶּה (ôṯ) staff, rod; tribe (A51)
מָטָר rain (A25a)
מִי who?
מַיִם (pl.) water
מָכַר (יִמְכֹּר) to sell (B1a)
מָלֵא (יִמְלָא) to be full, filled (B2d); (adj.) idem; P. מִלֵּא to fill
מַלְאָךְ (îm) messenger, angel (A38)
מְלָאכָה occupation, work (A64d)
מָלוֹן lodging place (A29a)
מִלְחָמָה (ôṯ) battle, war (A72)
מֶלֶךְ (îm) king, ruler (A7a)
מָלַךְ (יִמְלֹךְ) to rule, be(come) king (B1a)
מִמַּעַל above (adv.); (+ לְ) above (prep.)
מִן from; some of
מִנְחָה (ôṯ) offering (A61a)
(מסס) N. נָמֵס to melt
מִסְפָּר number; אֵין מִסְפָּר לְ is/are innumerable; אַנְשֵׁי מִסְפָּר a few men (A37)
מְעַט a little; מְעַט מְעַט little by little; עוֹד מְעַט in a little while
מַעֲשֶׂה (îm) deed, act, work (A51)
מָצָא (יִמְצָא) to find (B2c); N. נִמְצָא to be extant; H. הִמְצִיא to present
מִצְוָה (ôṯ) commandment (A61b)
מִצְרִי Egyptian; fem. מִצְרִית
מִצְרַיִם Egypt; מִצְרַיְמָה toward Egypt
מָקוֹם (ôṯ) place (A29a)
מִקְנֶה cattle, property (A50)
מַרְאֶה appearance (A51)
מְרַגֵּל (îm) spy, scout (P. participle)
מָרַד (יִמְרֹד) to rebel (B1a)
מֶרְכָּבָה (ôṯ) chariot (A71)
מֹשֶׁה Moses
מָשַׁח (יִמְשַׁח) to anoint (B2b)
מָשַׁל (יִמְשֹׁל) to rule, have dominion (over: בְּ) B1a
מִשָּׁם from there; thence
מִשְׁמָר place of confinement, jail (A37)
מִשְׁפָּט (îm) judgement, court decision; manner (A37)
מִשְׁתֶּה banquet (A50)

נ

נָא particle used after imperative, jussive, or cohortative; 102, 105
(נאץ) P. נִאֵץ to spurn
(נבא) N. נִבָּא, Ht. הִתְנַבֵּא to prophesy
נָבוֹן intelligent, discerning (A29a)
(נבט) H. הִבִּיט to look at (אֶל, עַל)
נָבִיא (îm) prophet (A28a)

נֶגֶב the Negev, הַ(נֶּגְבָּה) toward the Negev, Southward

נֶגֶד before, in front of (cf. A7b)

(נגד) H. הִגִּיד to tell

נָגַע (יִגַּע) to touch, strike (B5b)

נָגַף (יִגֹּף) to strike, smite (B5a)

(נגשׁ) N. נִגַּשׁ (יִגַּשׁ) to approach; H. הִגִּישׁ to bring near

נֶדֶר or נֵדֶר (îm) vow (A7c, 10a)

נָדַר (יִדֹּר) to vow (B5a)

נָהָר (ôṯ) river (A25b)

(נוח) נָח (יָנוּחַ) to rest, settle down (B7a); H. הֵנִיחַ to set at rest; H. הִנִּיחַ to set down, deposit, leave alone

(נום) נָם (יָנוּם) to sleep (B7a)

(נוס) נָס (יָנוּס) to flee (B7a)

נַחֲלָה property, possession, inheritance, portion (A60b)

(נחם) N. נִחַם (יִנָּחֵם) to be sorry, repent, be comforted; P. נִחַם (יְנַחֵם) to comfort, console

נֶחְמָד pleasant (A39)

נָחָשׁ (îm) snake (A25b)

נָטָה (יִטֶּה) to extend; pitch (tent); turn aside (intr.) B8f.; H. הִטָּה to turn or thrust aside, to incline (tr.)

נָטַע (יִטַּע) to plant (B5b)

נָטַשׁ (יִטֹּשׁ) to leave, forsake, abandon (B5a)

(נכה) H. הִכָּה to strike, smite, slay

נָכְרִי foreign, strange

נָסַע (יִסַּע) to set out, travel, journey (B5b)

נַעַל (îm) shoe, sandal (f.) A9

נַעַר (îm) young man, attendant (A9)

נָפַל (יִפֹּל) to fall (B5a); H. הִפִּיל caus.

נֶפֶשׁ (ôṯ) soul, person, living thing; life; (+ pron. suff.) self (A7a)

(נצב) N. נִצַּב to station oneself, stand; H. הִצִּיב to station, set up

(נצל) N. נִצַּל to be rescued, saved; H. הִצִּיל to deliver, rescue

נְקֵבָה female (A65a)

נָשָׂא (יִשָּׂא) to raise, lift up (B5c); N נִשָּׂא pass.

(נשׂג) H. הִשִּׂיג to reach, attain, overtake

נָתַן (יִתֵּן) to give, set, put, allow (B5d)

נָתָן Nathan

ס

סָבַב (יָסֹב) to surround, go around (B9a); H. הֵסֵב to turn away, to turn around (tr.), cause to go around

סָגַר (יִסְגֹּר) to close (B1a)

סוּס (îm) horse (A6)

(סור) סָר (יָסוּר) to turn aside (intr.), to depart (B7a); H. הֵסִיר to remove, take away, turn away

סָלַח (יִסְלַח) to pardon (B2b)

סֵפֶר (îm) book, writing (A10a)

סָפַר (יִסְפֹּר) to count (B1a); P. סִפֵּר to tell, narrate

סָרִיס (סָרִיסִים) eunuch, officer (A28b)

(סתר) N. נִסְתַּר to hide (intr.); H. הִסְתִּיר to hide (tr.)

ע

עֶבֶד (îm) servant, slave (A7a)

עָבַד (יַעֲבֹד) to work, serve, till (ground) B3a
עֲבוֹדָה work, task, servitude (A66)
עָבַר (יַעֲבֹר) to cross; to transgress (B3a); H. הֶעֱבִיר caus.
עִבְרִי Hebrew; fem. עִבְרִיָּה
עֵגֶל (îm) calf (m.) A10b
עֶגְלָה (ôṯ) heifer (A62)
עַד to, as far as, by; (+ inf.) until; עַד־אֲשֶׁר until; עַד־הֵנָּה until now; עַד־עוֹלָם forever
עֵדָה congregation, assembly (A54)
עֵדֶר (îm) flock, herd (A10b)
עוֹד again, still, yet
(עוד) H. הֵעִיד to warn, protest
עוֹלָם (îm) eternity; עַד־עוֹלָם, לְעוֹלָם, forever (A33)
עָוֹן (ôṯ) guilt, iniquity, punishment (A29a)
עוֹף birds, fowl (coll.) A5a
(עור) Po. עוֹרֵר to arouse, stir up
עַז strong, mighty (A2a)
עֹז strength (A5e)
עָזַב (יַעֲזֹב) to abandon (B3a)
עָזַר (יַעֲזֹר) to help (B3a)
עֵזֶר help, assistance (A10b)
עַיִן (du. עֵינַיִם) eye; spring, well (f.) A13a
עִיר (עָרִים) city (f.) A4b
עַל on, upon, over, against, concerning; עַל־דְּבַר for the sake of, because of; עַל־יַד beside, in the company of, to the side of; עַל־כֵּן therefore; עַל־פְּנֵי on the surface of, up against
עָלָה (יַעֲלֶה) to ascend, go up (B8b); H. הֶעֱלָה caus.
עֵלִי Eli
עִם with, together with
עַם (îm) people, nation (A2a)
עָמַד (יַעֲמֹד) to stand (B3a); H. הֶעֱמִיד to station, set up, appoint
עֵמֶק (îm) valley, lowland (A10a)
עָנָה (יַעֲנֶה) to answer (B8b); P. עִנָּה to oppress
עֳנִי affliction (A32a)
עָנָן (îm) cloud (A25b)
עֵץ (îm) tree, wood (A3a)
עֵצָה counsel, advice (A54)
עֵקֶב + אֲשֶׁר/כִּי because
עֶרֶב evening
עָרַב (יַעֲרֹב) to stand as pledge for (B3a)
עֶרְוָה shame, nakedness (A62)
עָרַךְ (יַעֲרֹךְ) to arrange, set in order; draw up (in battle array) B3a
עָרֵל uncircumcised; (fig.) deficient, inept
עֵשֶׂב grass, herbage (coll.) A10b
עָשָׂה (יַעֲשֶׂה) to do, make, act, bring about (B8b)
עֲשִׂירִי tenth; fem. עֲשִׂירִית
עֶשֶׂר ten (f.)
עָשָׂר -teen (m.)
עֲשָׂרָה ten (m.)
עֶשְׂרֵה -teen (f.)
עֶשְׂרִים twenty
עָשִׁיר rich (A28a)
עֵת (îm, ôṯ) time (f.) A75
עַתָּה now, then, (and) so then

פ

פָּגַע (יִפְגַּע) to meet, encounter (בְּ/אֶת־) B2b
פָּדָה (יִפְדֶּה) to ransom (B8a)
פֶּה mouth; עַל־פִּי, כְּפִי according to; כְּפִי אֲשֶׁר

according as; פֶּה אֶחָד unanimous, in agreement (A48a)

פֹּה here

פּוֹטִיפַר Potiphar

(פלא) N. נִפְלָא to be wonderful, marvelous

(פלל) Ht. הִתְפַּלֵּל to pray

פְּלִשְׁתִּים the Philistines

פֶּן lest, so that not

פָּנָה (יִפְנֶה) to turn (toward) (tr. & intr.) B8a

פָּנִים (pl.) face; לִפְנֵי before, in the presence of; מִפְּנֵי, מִלִּפְנֵי from before; עַל־פְּנֵי on the surface of, up against. 100, 101 (A89)

פֶּסֶל (פְּסִילִים) idol, image (A7c/28a)

פַּעַם (îm) time; פַּעֲמַיִם twice (A9)

פָּקַד (יִפְקֹד) to keep one's promise to; to pay attention to; to visit; to appoint; to pass in review (B1a)

פָּרָה (ôṯ) cow, heifer (A53b)

פְּרִי fruit (A31a)

פַּרְעֹה Pharaoh

פָּרַץ (יִפְרֹץ) to break down, breach, burst (out) B1a

(פרר) H. הֵפֵר to annul, cancel

פָּרַשׂ (יִפְרֹשׂ) to spread (out) (tr.) B1a

פָּרָשׁ (פָּרָשִׁים) horseman (A25c)

פָּתַח (יִפְתַּח) to open (B2b)

פֶּתַח (îm) opening (A8b)

צ

צֹאן small cattle (sheep and goats) cf. A5c

צָבָא (ôṯ) army, host (A25e)

צַדִּיק righteous (A46)

צֶדֶק righteousness (A7c)

צְדָקָה (ôṯ) righteousness, righteous act (A64a)

צָהֳרַיִם noon (cf. A12b)

(צוה) P. צִוָּה to command, charge, appoint 153

(צום) צָם (יָצוּם) to fast (B7a)

(צור) צָר (יָצוּר) to besiege, confine (B7a)

צוּר (îm) rock, cliff; (fig.) support, defense (A6)

צֵל (צְלָלִים) shade, shadow, protection (A3f)

(צלח) H. הִצְלִיחַ to make prosperous; to be prosperous

צֶלֶם (îm) image, likeness (A7a)

צֵלָע (îm, ôṯ) rib, side (A27b)

צָעִיר small, young (A28a)

צָעַק (יִצְעַק) to cry out (in distress) B2a

צָרָה (ôṯ) distress, trouble (A53b)

ק

קָבַץ (יִקְבֹּץ) to gather; Ht. to gather (intr.)

קֶבֶר (îm) grave, sepulchre (A7c)

קָבַר (יִקְבֹּר) to bury, inter (B1a)

קָדוֹשׁ holy

קֶדֶם east; קֵדְמָה eastward; מִקֶּדֶם לְ to the east of (cf. A7b)

קֹדֶשׁ (îm) holiness (A11)

(קדשׁ) P. קִדֵּשׁ to sanctify

קָהָל assembly, congregation (A25b)

קוֹל (ôṯ) voice, sound (A5a)

(קום) קָם (יָקוּם) to arise (B7a); H. הֵקִים to establish, set up

קָטָן small, little, unimportant; also קָטֹן (cf. A25d)

קַיִן Cain

קִיר (ôṯ) wall (A4a)

(קלל) קַל (יֵקַל) to be light, of little importance (B9c); P. קִלֵּל to curse

(קנא) P. קִנֵּא to be jealous (of: בְּ/אֶת); to be zealous (for: לְ)

קָנָה (יִקְנֶה) to acquire, purchase (B8a)

קֵץ end; מִקֵּץ at the end of (A3e)

קָצֶה end, border; מִקְצֵי at the end of (A49)

קָצִיר harvest, crop; time of harvest (A28a)

קָצַף (יִקְצֹף) to be(come) angry (against: עַל) B1a

קָצַר (יִקְצֹר) to reap, harvest (B1a)

קָרָא (יִקְרָא) to call, name, summon, declare, read; (+ אֶל) to call unto; (+ לְ) to summon (B2c)

קָרָא (יִקְרָא) a common variant of קָרָה

קָרַב (יִקְרַב) to be near, draw near, approach (B1c); H. הִקְרִיב to bring near, present

קֶרֶב midst, interior; בְּקֶרֶב in, within, inside of (A7c)

קָרָה (יִקְרֶה) to meet, encounter, befall (person usually object) B8a; N. נִקְרָה idem (person usually subject; object with עַל/אֶל/בְּ)

קָרוֹב near, close (to: אֶל) A29a

קָרַע (יִקְרַע) to rend, tear (B2b)

קָשֶׁה difficult, hard, harsh (A49)

קָשַׁר (יִקְשֹׁר) to bind; to band together, conspire (B1a)

ר

רָאָה (יִרְאֶה) to see (B8a); N. נִרְאָה to appear; H. הֶרְאָה to show

רְאוּבֵן Reuben

רֹאשׁ (רָאשִׁים) head, top, chief

רִאשׁוֹן first (A45)

רַב much, many, numerous (A2a)

רָבָה (יִרְבֶּה) to be(come) numerous, great (B8a); H. הִרְבָּה to make numerous, great; to do (something) much

רְבִיעִי fourth; fem. רְבִיעִית

רֶגֶל (du. רַגְלַיִם) foot (f.); בְּרַגְלֵי in the following of, belonging to (A7a)

רָדַף (יִרְדֹּף) to pursue, chase, persecute (+ אַחֲרֵי) B1a

רוּחַ (ôṯ) spirit, wind, soul

(רום) רָם (יָרוּם) to be high, lofty (B7a); H. הֵרִים to lift up, off; Po. רוֹמֵם to raise up

(רוץ) רָץ (יָרוּץ) to run (B7a)

רָחָב broad, wide (A25b)

רָחוֹק distant, far; מֵרָחוֹק at a distance, from afar; of old (A29a)

רָחֵל Rachel

רָחַץ (יִרְחַץ) to wash (B2a)

רֵיק empty, worthless, idle (cf. A3b)

רָכַב (יִרְכַּב) to ride (B1b)

רְכוּשׁ (moveable) property (A23)

רֶמֶשׂ creeping things (coll.)

רֵעַ (îm) friend, companion (A3b)

רַע evil, bad, wicked (A2b)

רָעָב famine (A25b)
רָעֵב (יִרְעַב) to be(come) hungry (B2a); (adj.) idem (A26)
רֹעֶה (îm) shepherd (Qal part. act.)
רָעָה (יִרְעֶה) to tend flocks, shepherd (B8a)
(רעע) רַע (יֵרַע) to be bad, wicked (B9d); H. הֵרַע to injure, to act wickedly
רָפָא (יִרְפָּא) to heal, cure (B2c)
רָצַח (יִרְצַח) to kill (B2b)
רַק only
רָקִיעַ firmament (A28a)
רָשָׁע evil, bad, criminal (A25a)

שׂ

שָׂדֶה (ôṯ) field (A49)
(שׂים) שָׂם (יָשִׂים) to put, place; to make (x) into (y) B7b
שֵׂיבָה old age, grey hair (cf. A56)
שְׂמֹאל left (hand); north (cf. A22)
שָׂמַח (יִשְׂמַח) to rejoice (B2b); P. שִׂמַּח to gladden
שִׂמְחָה (ôṯ) joy (A61a)
שִׂמְלָה (ôṯ) cloak, outer garment (A61a)
שָׂנֵא (יִשְׂנָא) to hate (B2d)
שָׂפָה (du. שְׂפָתַיִם) lip; language; edge (A53d)
שַׂק (îm) sack (-cloth) A2a
שַׂר (îm) chief, leader (A2b)
שָׂרַף (יִשְׂרֹף) to burn (tr.) B1a; N. to burn (intr.)

שׁ

שָׁאַל (יִשְׁאַל) to ask, inquire, request (B2a)
שְׁאֹל Sheol
(שׁאר) N. נִשְׁאַר to be left over, remain, survive
שָׁבָה (יִשְׁבֶּה) to take captive (B8a)
שְׁבוּעָה (ôṯ) oath (A67)
שְׁבִיעִי seventh; fem. שְׁבִיעִית
(שׁבע) N. נִשְׁבַּע to swear; H. הִשְׁבִּיעַ to cause to swear
שֶׁבַע seven (f.)
שִׁבְעָה seven (m.)
שִׁבְעִים seventy
שָׁבַר (יִשְׁבֹּר) to break, smash (B1a)
שָׁבַת (יִשְׁבֹּת) to cease, rest (B1a)
שַׁבָּת (שַׁבָּתוֹת) sabbath (f.) cf. A82
שָׁוְא emptiness, vanity; לַשָּׁוְא in vain (A16)
(שׁוב) שָׁב (יָשׁוּב) to return, go/come back (B7a); H. הֵשִׁיב to bring back
שׁוֹר (îm) a head of cattle (A5a [note])
שָׁחַט (יִשְׁחַט) to slaughter (an animal) B2a
שִׁיר (îm) song (A4a)
(שׁיר) שָׁר (יָשִׁיר) to sing (B7b)
(שׁית) שָׁת (יָשִׁית) to put, place, set (B7b)
שָׁכַב (יִשְׁכַּב) to lie down (B1b)
שָׁכַח (יִשְׁכַּח) to forget (B2b)
שְׁכֶם Shechem
(שׁכם) H. הִשְׁכִּים to do something early in the day 173
שָׁכַן (יִשְׁכֹּן) to settle down, dwell (B1a)
שָׁלוֹם peace, well-being, health; שָׁאַל לְשָׁלוֹם לְ to ask about someone (A29a)
שְׁלִישִׁי third; fem. שְׁלִישִׁית
שָׁלַח (יִשְׁלַח) to send (B2b); P. שִׁלַּח to expel, send forth, let go
שֻׁלְחָן (ôṯ) table (A40)
(שׁלך) H. הִשְׁלִיךְ to throw
(שׁלם) P. שִׁלֵּם to restore, make good, recompense
שָׁלֹשׁ three (f.)
שְׁלֹשָׁה three (m.)

שְׁלשִׁים thirty
שֵׁם (ôṯ) name (A3d)
שָׁם there, in that place; שָׁמָּה thither, to that place
(שמד) H. הִשְׁמִיד to destroy
שְׁמוּאֵל Samuel
שָׁמַיִם heaven(s)
שְׁמִינִי eighth; fem. שְׁמִינִית
שָׁמֵם (יֵשַׁם) to be desolated, appalled (B9c); (adj.) idem
שְׁמֹנֶה eight (f.)
שְׁמֹנָה eight (m.)
שְׁמֹנִים eighty
שָׁמַע (יִשְׁמַע) to hear; heed, listen to (לְ/בְּ; + לְקוֹל) B2b; N. pass.; H. הִשְׁמִיעַ to tell, declare, proclaim
שָׁמַר (יִשְׁמֹר) to watch, keep, observe (B1a)
שֶׁמֶשׁ sun (A7c)
שִׁמְשׁוֹן Samson
שָׁנָה (îm) year (A53a)
שֵׁנִי second; fem. שֵׁנִית
שְׁנַיִם two (m.)
שַׁעַר (îm) gate (A9)
שִׁפְחָה (ôṯ) maidservant, fem. slave (A61a)
שָׁפַט (יִשְׁפֹּט) to judge (B1a)
שֹׁפֵט (îm) judge (A35)
שָׁפַךְ (יִשְׁפֹּךְ) to pour, shed (blood) B1a
שָׁפֵל (יִשְׁפַּל) to be(come) low (B1d); H. הִשְׁפִּיל to lay low, abase
(שקה) H. הִשְׁקָה to give water to, cause to drink
(שרת) P. שֵׁרֵת to serve, administer
שֵׁשׁ six (f.)
שִׁשָּׁה six (m.)
שִׁשִּׁי sixth
שִׁשִּׁים sixty
שָׁתָה (יִשְׁתֶּה) to drink
שְׁתַּיִם two (f.)

ת

תֹּאַר form, appearance (A12b)
תָּוֶךְ midst; בְּתוֹךְ in the midst of; מִתּוֹךְ from the midst of (A15a)
תּוֹלְדוֹת (pl.) history, genealogy (A73)
תּוֹרָה (ôṯ) law, Law (A55)
תְּחִלָּה beginning, first occasion (A68)
תְּחִנָּה (ôṯ) supplication (A68)
תַּחַת under; instead of; מִתַּחַת beneath (adv.), (+ לְ) idem (prep.)
תָּלָה (יִתְלֶה) to hang (B8a)
תְּמוֹל yesterday
(תמם) תַּם (יִתַּם) to be finished, at an end; to finish (doing something) B9c
תִּמְנָתָה Timnah, Timnathah
תָּעָה (יִתְעֶה) to wander lost (B8a)
תְּפִלָּה (ôṯ) prayer (A68)
תָּפַשׂ (יִתְפֹּשׂ) to seize, grab (B1a)
תְּשִׁיעִי ninth; fem. תְּשִׁיעִית
תֵּשַׁע nine (f.)
תִּשְׁעָה nine (m.)
תִּשְׁעִים ninety

ENGLISH-HEBREW GLOSSARY

A

a: (see §14)
abandon, to: נָטַשׁ, עָזַב
abase, to: הִשְׁפִּיל
Abel: הֶבֶל
able, to be: יָכֹל

above (prep.): עַל; (adv.) מִמַּעַל
Abraham: אַבְרָהָם
according as: כַּאֲשֶׁר
according to: כְּפִי, עַל־פִּי, לְפִי, כְּ
accursed: אָרוּר
acquire, to: קָנָה
act, to: עָשָׂה; to – – wickedly: הֵרַע
act: מַעֲשֶׂה
Adam: אָדָם
add, to: הוֹסִיף
administer, to: שֵׁרֵת
advantage: בֶּצַע
advice: עֵצָה
afar; from – –: מֵרָחוֹק
affair: דָּבָר
affliction: עֳנִי, צָרָה
afraid: יָרֵא; to be – –: יָרֵא
after (prep.): אַחַר, אַחֲרֵי
(conj.): אַחֲרֵי אֲשֶׁר
afterwards: אַחֲרֵי־כֵן, אַחַר
again: עוֹד; to do – –: שָׁב, הוֹסִיף
against: עַל
agreeable; to be – –: יָשַׁר
alive: חַי; to be – –: חָיָה
all: כָּל־, כֹּל
alone: לְבַד־
also: גַּם
altar: מִזְבֵּחַ
although: see §§135–136
and: וְ
angel: מַלְאָךְ
anger: אַף
angry, to be(come): חָרָה; he became – –: קָצַף; חָרָה לוֹ
animal: בְּהֵמָה, חַיָּה
annul, to: הֵפֵר
anoint, to: מָשַׁח
answer, to: עָנָה
another: אַחֵר
anything: מְאוּמָה; anything + adj.: כֹּל + adj.
appalled, to be: שָׁמֵם
appear, to: נִרְאָה
appearance: מַרְאֶה
appoint, to: שָׂם, צִוָּה, פָּקַד
appointed, to be: נִצַּב
approach, to: הִקְרִיב, קָרַב, נִגַּשׁ
arise, to: קָם
ark: אֲרוֹן
arm: זְרוֹעַ
army: צָבָא, חַיִל
around: בְּעַד
arouse, to: עוֹרֵר
arrange, to: עָרַךְ
as: כְּ + inf., כַּאֲשֶׁר; as X lives: חַי
ascend, to: עָלָה
ashamed, to be(come): בּשׁ
ask, to: שָׁאַל
ass: (m) חֲמוֹר; (f) אָתוֹן
assembly: עֵדָה, קָהָל
assistance: עֵזֶר
astonished, to be(come): דַּם
atone for, to: כִּפֶּר
attain, to: הִשִּׂיג
attend to, to: פָּקַד

B

bad: רָשָׁע, רַע
bad, to be: רַע
band together, to: קָשַׁר
bank: שָׂפָה
banquet: מִשְׁתֶּה
battle: מִלְחָמָה
be, to: הָיָה
bear (child), to: יָלַד
bear witness, to: הֵעִיד
beast: חַיָּה, בְּהֵמָה
beautiful: יָפֶה
because: כִּי, יַעַן + inf., יַעַן אֲשֶׁר, עֵקֶב כִּי/אֲשֶׁר
because of: עַל־דְּבַר, בַּעֲבוּר
become, to: הָיָה (+ לְ)
befall, to: נִקְרָא, קָרָא, קָרָה
before (prep.) נֶגֶד, לִפְנֵי; (conj.) לִפְנֵי + inf., (בְּ)טֶרֶם

beget, to: הוֹלִיד
begin, to: הֵחֵל
beginning: תְּחִלָּה
behalf; on – – of: בְּעַד
believe, to: הֶאֱמִין
belong, to: use אֲשֶׁר לְ (§72) or (§93) בְּרַגְלֵי
below: (prep.) תַּחַת; (adv.) מִתַּחַת
beside: עַל־יַד, אֵצֶל
besiege, to: צָר
better: comparative of "good"
between: בֵּין
big: גָּדוֹל
big, to be(come): גָּדַל
bind, to: קָשַׁר
birds: עוֹף
bless, to: בֵּרַךְ
blessing: בְּרָכָה
blood: דָּם
book: סֵפֶר
border: קָצֶה
bosom: חֵיק
bow down, to: הִשְׁתַּחֲוָה
boy: נַעַר, יֶלֶד
bread: לֶחֶם
break, to: הֵפֵר, שָׁבַר
break down, to: פָּרַץ
bring, to: הִקְרִיב, הֵבִיא
bring about, to: עָשָׂה
bring across, to: הֶעֱבִיר
bring back, to: הֵשִׁיב
bring down, to: הוֹרִיד
bring near, to: הִגִּישׁ, הִקְרִיב
bring out, to: הוֹצִיא
bring up, to: הֶעֱלָה; (= rear): גִּדֵּל
broad: רָחָב
brother: אָח
build, to: בָּנָה
burn, to: (intr.) בָּעַר, שָׂרַף (tr.) בִּעֵר, שָׂרַף
burst out, to: פָּרַץ
bury, to: קָבַר
but: אֲבָל, אַךְ, וְ
but rather: כִּי־אִם
by (= near, at): אֵצֶל

C

Cain: קַיִן
calf: עֵגֶל, עֶגְלָה
call, to: קָרָא
camel: גָּמָל
camp: מַחֲנֶה
can: יָכֹל
Canaan: כְּנַעַן
captive, to take: שָׁבָה, לָכַד
capture, to: לָכַד
cattle: (large) בָּקָר; (small) צֹאן; a head of – –: שׁוֹר; (as property): מִקְנֶה
cease, to: חָדַל, שָׁבַת
chariot: מֶרְכָּבָה
chase, to: רָדַף
chief: שַׂר, רֹאשׁ
children: בָּנִים, טַף
choose, to: בָּחַר
circumcise, to: מָל
cistern: בּוֹר
city: עִיר
cliff: צוּר
cloak: שִׂמְלָה
close (adj.): קָרוֹב; to be – –: קָרַב
close, to: סָגַר
cloud: עָנָן
come, to: בָּא; see also "to go"
come back, to: שָׁב
come to an end, to: תַּם, כָּלָה
comfort, to: נִחַם be – – ed: נִחַם;
commandment: מִצְוָה
command, to: צִוָּה
commit (a sin), to: חָטָא
companion: רֵעַ
conceal, to: הִסְתִּיר, כִּחֵד
conceive, to: הָרָה
concerning: עַל
confine, to: צָר

confirmed, to be: נֶאֱמַן
congregation: עֵדָה, קָהָל
consider, to: חָשַׁב
console, to: נִחַם be – – ed: נִחַם;
conspire, to: קָשַׁר
consume, to: אָכַל; be – –ed: בָּעַר, נֶאֱכַל
content, to be: הוֹאִיל
continue (doing something), to: הוֹסִיף
counsel: עֵצָה
count, to: סָפַר
countless: = without number
covenant: בְּרִית
cover, to: כִּסָּה
cow: פָּרָה
create, to: בָּרָא
creeping things: רֶמֶשׂ
criminal (adj.): רָשָׁע
crop: קָצִיר
cross, to: עָבַר
cry (= weep), to: בָּכָה
cry out, to: זָעַק, צָעַק
cure, to: רָפָא
curse, to: אָרַר
cut, to: כָּרַת

D

darkness: חֹשֶׁךְ
daughter: בַּת
David: דָּוִד
day: יוֹם; by – –: יוֹמָם
daytime; in the – –: יוֹמָם
dead: מֵת
death: מָוֶת
deed: מַעֲשֶׂה
defence: צוּר
defile, to: חִלֵּל
decide, to: הוֹכִיחַ
declare, to: הוֹדִיעַ, קָרָא
deliver, to: הוֹשִׁיעַ
deliverance: יְשׁוּעָה
depart, to: סָר
depleted, to be(come): כָּלָה
deposit, to: הִנִּיחַ
descend, to: יָרַד
descendants: זֶרַע
desert: מִדְבָּר
desire, to: חָפֵץ
desolated, to be(come): שָׁמֵם
despise, to: בָּזָה, מָאַס
destroy, to: הֶאֱבִיד, הִשְׁמִיד, הֶחֱרִים
destroyed, to be: אָבַד
die, to: מֵת
difficult: קָשֶׁה
discerning: נָבוֹן
dishonor, to: חִלֵּל
distance; at a – –: מֵרָחוֹק
distant: רָחוֹק
distress: עֳנִי, צָרָה
do, to: עָשָׂה; to – – early in the day: הִשְׁכִּים
do again, to: שָׁב, הוֹסִיף
donkey: (m) חֲמוֹר; (f) אָתוֹן
door: דֶּלֶת
draw near, to: נִגַּשׁ, קָרַב
draw up (for battle), to: עָרַךְ
dread: אֵימָה
dream: חֲלוֹם to – –: חָלַם
drink, to: שָׁתָה; cause to – –: הִשְׁקָה
drive away, to: גֵּרֵשׁ
dry ground: יַבָּשָׁה
dwell, to: שָׁכַן, גָּר, יָשַׁב; cause to – –: הוֹשִׁיב

E

each: כֹּל, אִישׁ (see §123)
ear: אֹזֶן
earth: אֲדָמָה, אֶרֶץ
east: קֶדֶם; to the – – of: מִקֶּדֶם לְ
eat, to: אָכַל
edge: שָׂפָה
Egypt: מִצְרַיִם; Egyptian: מִצְרִי
eight: שְׁמֹנָה, שְׁמֹנֶה
eighty: שְׁמֹנִים

Eli: עֵלִי
elder: זָקֵן; (= older) use: גָּדוֹל
emptiness: שָׁוְא
empty: רֵיק
encounter, to: נִקְרָא ,נִקְרָה ,קָרָא ,קָרָה
end: קָצֶה ,קֵץ; at the – – of: מִקְצֵי ,מִקֵּץ;
to be at an – –: כָּלָה ,תַּם
enemy: אֹיֵב
engender, to: הוֹלִיד
enter, to: בָּא
entire: כֹּל
establish, to: הֵכִין; be – – ed: נָכוֹן
eternity: עוֹלָם
Eve: חַוָּה
even (adv.): גַּם
evening: עֶרֶב
every: כֹּל; everything (which): כֹּל אֲשֶׁר (§66)
evil (adj.): רָשָׁע ,רַע
evil (noun): רָעָה ,רַע
evil, to be(come): רַע
exalt, to: רוֹמֵם ,הֵרִים ,נָשָׂא
except (that): אֶפֶס כִּי ,כִּי־אִם
expel, to: שִׁלַּח
extend, to: שָׁלַח ,נָטָה.
exterminate, to: הֶחֱרִים ,בִּעֵר
eye: עַיִן; in the – – s of: בְּעֵינֵי

F

face: פָּנִים
fall, to: נָפַל
famine: רָעָב
far: רָחוֹק; as – – as: עַד
fashion, to: יָצַר
fast, to: צָם
father: אָב
father-in-law: חֹתֵן
favor: חֵן; to seek – –: הִתְחַנֵּן
fear: יִרְאָה
female: נְקֵבָה
few: מִסְפָּר (§86); אֲחָדִים (pl. of אֶחָד)
field: שָׂדֶה
fifth: חֲמִישִׁי
fifty: חֲמִשִּׁים
fight, to: נִלְחַם
filled = to be full
find, to: מָצָא
finish, to: כִּלָּה
finished, to be: תַּם ,כָּלָה
fire: אֵשׁ
firm: חָזָק; to be(come) – –: נָכוֹן ,חָזַק
firmament: רָקִיעַ
first: רִאשׁוֹן
fish: דָּגָה ,דָּג
five: חֲמִשָּׁה ,חָמֵשׁ
flame: לֶהָבָה
flee, to: נָס ,בָּרַח
flesh: בָּשָׂר
flock: עֵדֶר
following; in the – – of: בְּרַגְלֵי
food: לֶחֶם
foot: רֶגֶל
for: (prep.) לְ ,בְּעַד; (conj.): כִּי
foreign: נָכְרִי
forever: עַד־עוֹלָם ,לְעוֹלָם
forget, to: שָׁכַח
form: תֹּאַר
form, to: יָצַר
forsake, to: נָטַשׁ ,עָזַב
forty: אַרְבָּעִים
four: אַרְבָּעָה ,אַרְבַּע
fourth: רְבִיעִי
fowl: עוֹף
friend: רֵעַ
from: מִן
front; in – – of: נֶגֶד ,לִפְנֵי
fruit: פְּרִי
full: מָלֵא; to be(come)– –: מָלֵא

G

gain: בֶּצַע
garden: גַּן
garment: בֶּגֶד
gate: שַׁעַר

gather, to קָבַץ
genealogy: תּוֹלְדוֹת
generation: דּוֹר
give, to: נָתַן
give birth to, to: יָלַד
gladden, to: שִׂמַּח
glory: כָּבוֹד
go, to: הָלַךְ; to cause to – –: הוֹלִיךְ; to – – continuously: הִתְהַלֵּךְ
go around, to סָבַב
go back, to: שָׁב
go down, to: יָרַד
go forth, to: יָצָא
go up, to: עָלָה
go well with, to: יִיטַב
god: אֵל
God: אֵל, אֱלֹהִים
gold: זָהָב
good: טוֹב; to make – – (as compensation): שִׁלֵּם
grab, to: תָּפַשׂ
grace: חֵן
gracious; to be – – toward: חָנַן
grasp, to: אָחַז, הֶחֱזִיק
grass: עֵשֶׂב
grave: קֶבֶר
great: גָּדוֹל; to become – –: גָּדַל; to make – –: הִגְדִּיל
grey hair: שֵׂיבָה
ground: אֲדָמָה; dry – –: יַבָּשָׁה; onto the – –: אַרְצָה
grow fond of, to: (מָצָא חֵן בְּעֵינֵי)
grow up, to: גָּדַל
guard, to: שָׁמַר, נָצַר
guilt: עָוֹן
guilty, to be: אָשֵׁם

H

half: חֲצִי
hand: יָד
handsome: יָפֶה
hang, to: תָּלָה
hard: חָזָק; (= difficult): קָשֶׁה
harsh: קָשֶׁה
harvest, to: קָצַר
harvest: קָצִיר
hate, to: שָׂנֵא
he: הוּא
head: רֹאשׁ
heal, to: רָפָא
health: שָׁלוֹם
hear, to: שָׁמַע
heart: לֵב, לֵבָב
heaven(s): שָׁמַיִם
heavy: כָּבֵד; to be – –: כָּבֵד
Hebrew: עִבְרִי
heed, to: שָׁמַע (+ בְּ/לְ; בְּ/לְקוֹל
heifer: פָּרָה, עֶגְלָה
help, to: עָזַר
help: עֵזֶר
herbage: עֵשֶׂב
herd: עֵדֶר
here: פֹּה see also §135
hide, to: (tr.) כִּחֵד, הִסְתִּיר; (intr.) נִסְתַּר, נֶחְבָּא, הִתְחַבֵּא
high, to be: רָם
hill: גִּבְעָה
history: תּוֹלְדוֹת
hither: הֲלֹם, הֵנָּה
Hittite: חִתִּי
holiness: קֹדֶשׁ
honest: כֵּן
honey: דְּבַשׁ
honor: כָּבוֹד
horse: סוּס
horseman: פָּרָשׁ
host: צָבָא
house: בַּיִת
how?: אֵיכָה
however: אַךְ, אֲבָל
hundred: מֵאָה
hunger: רָעָב
hungry, to be: רָעֵב
hurry, to: מִהַר
hurt, to: הֵרַע
husband: אִישׁ

I

I: אָנֹכִי ,אֲנִי
idle: רֵיק
idol: פֶּסֶל ,צֶלֶם
if: הֵן ,אִם; if not: לוּלֵי ,לוּלֵא
image: צֶלֶם
important: כָּבֵד
in: בְּ
indeed: אָמְנָם ,אֲבָל
inherit, to: יָרַשׁ
inheritance: נַחֲלָה
iniquity: עָוֹן
injure, to: הֵרַע
inn: מָלוֹן
innumerable: אֵין מִסְפָּר לְ
inquire, to: שָׁאַל ,דָּרַשׁ
inside: בְּקֶרֶב ,בְּתוֹךְ
instead of: תַּחַת
intelligent: נָבוֹן
Israel: יִשְׂרָאֵל
is (see "to be")
it: הִיא ,הוּא

J

Jacob: יַעֲקֹב
jail: מִשְׁמָר
jealous, to be: קִנֵּא
Jerusalem: יְרוּשָׁלַםִ
Joseph: יוֹסֵף
journey, to: נָסַע
joy: שִׂמְחָה
Judah: יְהוּדָה
judge, to: שָׁפַט; judge: שֹׁפֵט
just: יָשָׁר

K

kid: גְּדִי
kill, to: מוֹתֵת ,הֶאֱבִיד ,רָצַח ,הָרַג
king: מֶלֶךְ; to be(come) – –: מָלַךְ
know, to: יָדַע

L

lamb: כִּבְשָׂה ,כֶּבֶשׂ
land: אֲדָמָה ,אֶרֶץ
language: שָׂפָה
law (Law) תּוֹרָה
lead, to: הוֹלִיךְ
lead across, to: הֶעֱבִיר
lead into sin, to: הֶחֱטִיא
leave, to: נָטַשׁ ,עָזַב
leave alone, to: הִנִּיחַ
left, to be: נוֹתַר ,נִשְׁאַר
left hand: שְׂמֹאל
left over, to be: נוֹתַר
lengthen, to: (tr.) הֶאֱרִיךְ
lest: פֶּן
lie down, to: שָׁכַב
life: נֶפֶשׁ ,חַיִּים
lifetime: חַיִּים
lift up, to: הֵרִים ,נָשָׂא
light: אוֹר
like (prep.): כְּ
likeness: צֶלֶם
lion: אַרְיֵה ,אֲרִי
lip: שָׂפָה
listen to, to (see "obey")
little: קָטָן ,קָטֹן; a little: מְעַט; in a little while: עוֹד מְעַט; little by little מְעַט מְעַט
live, to: חָיָה ,יָשַׁב; to let – –: חִיָּה
living (adj.): חַי
lodging-place: מָלוֹן
lofty, to be: רָם
long, to be: הֶאֱרִיךְ
look at, to: הִבִּיט
lord: בַּעַל ,אָדוֹן
Lord: יהוה
Lot: לוֹט
love: אַהֲבָה
love, to: אָהַב
low, to be(come): שָׁפֵל; to lay – –: הִשְׁפִּיל

M

magnify, to: הִגְדִּיל
maidservant: אָמָה, שִׁפְחָה
make, to: עָשָׂה; to – – a treaty: כָּרַת בְּרִית
male: זָכָר
man: אִישׁ, אָדָם; young – –: נַעַר, בָּחוּר
old – –: זָקֵן
mankind: אָדָם, כָּל־בָּשָׂר
manner; in this – –: כֵּן, כֹּה
many: רַב
marvelous, to be: נִפְלָא
master: בַּעַל, אָדֹן
matter: דָּבָר
measure, to: מָדַד
meat: בָּשָׂר
meditate, to: הָגָה
meet, to: קָרָא, קָרָה; see also לִקְרַאת (§ 125); פָּגַע
melt, to: נָמֵס
mention, to: הִזְכִּיר
memorial: זֵכֶר
messenger: מַלְאָךְ
midst; in the – – of: בְּתוֹךְ; from the – – of: מִתּוֹךְ
might: עֹז, זְרוֹעַ
mighty: עַז
milk: חָלָב
mistress: גְּבֶרֶת
money: כֶּסֶף
month: חֹדֶשׁ
moon: יָרֵחַ
morning: בֹּקֶר
Moses: מֹשֶׁה
mother: אֵם
mountain: הַר
mourn, to: בָּכָה
mouth: פֶּה
much: (adj.) רַב; (adv.) מְאֹד, הַרְבֵּה

N

name: שֵׁם
name, to: קָרָא
narrate, to: סִפֵּר, הִגִּיד
Nathan: נָתָן
nation: עַם
near: (prep.) אֵצֶל; (adj.) קָרוֹב
near, to be: קָרֵב
Negev: נֶגֶב
new: חָדָשׁ
night: לַיְלָה
Nile, the: יְאֹר
nine: תֵּשַׁע, תִּשְׁעָה
ninety: תִּשְׁעִים
none = no one, not one (cf. §65 end); use negative with verb or predicate
noon: צָהֳרַיִם
north: צָפֹן, שְׂמֹאל
nose: אַף
not: לֹא; there is – –: אֵין
not yet: (בְּ)טֶרֶם
now: עַתָּה; see also §135
number: מִסְפָּר
numerous: רַב

O

oath: שְׁבוּעָה
obey, to: שָׁמַע בְּ/לְקוֹל
observe, to: שָׁמַר
occupation: מְלָאכָה
offering: מִנְחָה
officer: שַׂר, סָרִיס
offspring: זֶרַע
olive (-tree): זַיִת
old: זָקֵן; old man: idem
old age: זְקוּנִים, שֵׂיבָה
omen: אוֹת
on: עַל, בְּ
one: אֶחָד, אַחַת
only: רַק, לְבַד־
open, to: פָּתַח
opening: פֶּתַח
opinion; in the – – of: בְּעֵינֵי
oppress, to: עִנָּה

or: אוֹ
order; in – – that: לְמַעַן
other: אַחֵר
outside: (הַ)חוּצָה, חוּץ; outside of: מִחוּץ לְ
overtake, to: הִשִּׂיג
overwhelm, to. כִּסָּה
own, to: (use idiom for possession with לְ)
owner: בַּעַל

P

palace: הֵיכָל
palm: כַּף
pardon, to: סָלַח
peace: שָׁלוֹם
people: עַם, גּוֹי
perceive, to: הֵבִין
perceptiveness: בִּינָה
perform, to: עָשָׂה
perish, to: אָבַד
permitted, it is not – –: אֵין לְ (+ inf.)
persecute, to: רָדַף
person: נֶפֶשׁ, אִישׁ
Pharaoh: פַּרְעֹה
Philistines: פְּלִשְׁתִּים
pit: בּוֹר
pitch (tent), to: נָטָה
place: מָקוֹם
place, to: נָתַן, שָׂם, שָׁת, הֶעֱמִיד, הִצִּיב
plague, to: נָגַף
plague: מַגֵּפָה
plant, to: נָטַע
pleasant: נֶחְמָד
pleased with, to be: x was pleased with y = y found favor in the eyes of x
pleasing, to be: יָשַׁר
pledge; to stand as – – for: עָרַב
plow, to: חָרַשׁ
portion: נַחֲלָה
pollute, to: חִלֵּל
poor: דַּל
pour, to: שָׁפַךְ
praise, to: הִלֵּל
pray, to: הִתְפַּלֵּל
prayer: תְּפִלָּה
precious: יָקָר
pregnant, to become: הָרָה
prepare, to: הֵכִין
presence; in the – – of: לִפְנֵי, נֶגֶד
present, to: הֵבִיא, הִקְרִיב, הִמְצִיא
prevail, to: יָכֹל
priest: כֹּהֵן
prisoner: אָסִיר
proclaim, to: קָרָא, הוֹדִיעַ
profit: בֶּצַע
progeny: זֶרַע
property: רְכוּשׁ, מִקְנֶה, נַחֲלָה
prophesy, to: נִבָּא, הִתְנַבֵּא
prophet: נָבִיא
prosperous, to make: הִצְלִיחַ; to be – –: הִצְלִיחַ
prostitute; to be(come) a – –: זָנָה
prostitute: זֹנָה
protection: צוּר
protest, to: הֵעִיד
punishment: עָוֹן
purchase, to: קָנָה
pursue, to: רָדַף
put, to: שָׂם, שָׁת
put forth, to: שָׁלַח

Q

quickly: מַהֵר

R

rain: מָטָר
raise, to: נָשָׂא, הֵרִים, רוֹמֵם; (= to rear) גִּדֵּל
ransom, to: פָּדָה
read, to: קָרָא
ready; to make – –: הֵכִין

reap, to: קָצַר
rebel, to: מָרַד
rebuke, to: גָּעַר
reckon, to: חָשַׁב
recompense, to: שִׁלֵּם
redeem, to: גָּאַל
refuse, to: מֵאֵן, מָאַס
rejoice, to: שָׂמַח; cause to – –: שִׂמַּח
remain, to: (= stay) יָשַׁב; (= be left over): נִשְׁאַר, נוֹתַר
remember, to: זָכַר
remembrance: זֵכֶר
remind, to: הִזְכִּיר
remove, to: הֵסִיר
remove completely, to: בִּעֵר
rend, to: קָרַע
repent, to: נִחַם
reprove, to: הוֹכִיחַ
request, to: שָׁאַל, דָּרַשׁ
require, to: דָּרַשׁ
rescue, to הִצִּיל; to be – – ed: נִצַּל
residence: מְגוּרִים
rest, to: נָח, שָׁבַת; cause to – –: הֵנִיחַ
restore, to: שִׁלֵּם
return, to: שָׁב
revive, to: הֶחֱיָה, חִיָּה
rib: צֵלָע
rich: עָשִׁיר
ride, to: רָכַב
right hand: יָמִין
righteous: צַדִּיק
righteousness: צְדָקָה, צֶ֫דֶק
river: נָהָר
road: דֶּ֫רֶךְ
rock: צוּר
rod: מַטֶּה
roof: גָּג
rule, to: מָלַךְ, מָשַׁל
run, to: רָץ

S

Sabbath: שַׁבָּת

sack: שַׂק; sack-cloth: idem
sacrifice, to: זָבַח
sacrifice: זֶ֫בַח
sake; for the – – of: עַל־דְּבַר, בַּעֲבוּר
salvation: יְשׁוּעָה
Samuel: שְׁמוּאֵל
sanctify, to: הִקְדִּישׁ, קִדֵּשׁ
sandal: נַ֫עַל
save, to: הִצִּיל, הוֹשִׁיעַ
say, to: דִּבֶּר, אָמַר
sea: יָם; seaward: יָ֫מָּה
second: שֵׁנִי
secure, to be: נָכוֹן
see, to: רָאָה
seed: זֶ֫רַע
seek, to: דָּרַשׁ, בִּקֵּשׁ
seize, to: הֶחֱזִיק, אָחַז
self: נֶ֫פֶשׁ (+ suffix)
sell, to: מָכַר
send, to: שָׁלַח
send forth, to: שִׁלַּח
servant: עֶ֫בֶד
serve, to: עָבַד
serious: כָּבֵד; to be – –: כָּבֵד
serpent: נָחָשׁ
servitude: עֲבוֹדָה
set, to: שָׁת, שָׂם, נָתַן
set at rest, to: הֵנִיחַ
set down, to הִנִּיחַ
set in order, to: עָרַךְ
set out, to: נָסַע
set up, to: הִצִּיב, הֶעֱמִיד
settle, to: (tr.) הוֹשִׁיב
settle down, to: שָׁכַן, נָח
seven: שִׁבְעָה, שֶׁ֫בַע
seventh: שְׁבִיעִי
seventy: שִׁבְעִים
shade: צֵל
shadow: צֵל
shame: עֶרְוָה
she: הִיא
Shechem: שְׁכֶם
shed (blood), to: שָׁפַךְ

shepherd: רֹעֶה; to – –: רָעָה
Sheol: שְׁאֹל
shoe: נַעַל
side: יָד; at/to the – – of: עַל־יַד
sign: אוֹת
silent, to be: דַּם
silver: כֶּסֶף
since: see §135; (= because): כִּי
sinful: רַע, רָשָׁע
sing, to: שָׁר
sin: חַטָּאת
sin, to: חָטָא; cause to – –: הֶחֱטִיא
sister: אָחוֹת
sit, to: יָשַׁב
six: שֵׁשׁ, שִׁשָּׁה
sixth: שִׁשִּׁי
sixty: שִׁשִּׁים
sky: שָׁמַיִם
slaughter, to: טָבַח, שָׁחַט
slaughtering: טֶבַח
slave: (m) עֶבֶד; (f) אָמָה, שִׁפְחָה
slay, to: הָרַג, רָצַח, מוֹתֵת
sleep, to: יָשֵׁן, נָם
small: קָטֹן, קָטָן, צָעִיר
smash, to: שָׁבַר
snake: נָחָשׁ
so that: לְמַעַן + imperf. or inf.; so that...not: פֶּן
soil: אֲדָמָה
sojourn, to: גָּר
sojourner: גֵּר
sojourning: מְגוּרִים
sole: כַּף
some (of): מִן
son: בֵּן
song: שִׁיר
sorry, to be: נִחַם
soul: נֶפֶשׁ, רוּחַ
sound: קוֹל
south: יָמִין
spare, to: חָמַל
speak, to: דִּבֶּר
spend the night, to: לָן
split, to: בָּקַע
spread (out), to: פָּרַשׂ
spring: עַיִן, בְּאֵר
spurn, to: מָאַס, נִאֵץ
spy: מְרַגֵּל
staff: מַטֶּה
stand, to: עָמַד, נִצַּב; to take one's– –: הִתְיַצֵּב
star: כּוֹכָב
station, to: הֶעֱמִיד, הִצִּיב; to – – oneself: הִתְיַצֵּב, נִצַּב; to be – – ed. נִצַּב
steal, to: גָּנַב
still (adv.): עוֹד
stone: אֶבֶן
stop, to: שָׁבַת, חָדַל
strange: נָכְרִי
strength: עֹז, חַיִל
strike, to: הִכָּה
stroke: נֶגַע
strong: חָזָק, עַז to be(come) – –: חָזַק
stumble, to: כָּשַׁל
surround, to: סָבַב
summon, to: קָרָא לְ
sun: שֶׁמֶשׁ
supplication: תְּחִנָּה
support (fig.): צוּר
surely: אֲבָל, אָמְנָם
surety: (see pledge)
surface; on the – – of: עַל־פְּנֵי
survive, to: נִשְׁאַר, נוֹתַר
swallow, to: בָּלַע
swear, to: נִשְׁבַּע; to make – –: הִשְׁבִּיעַ
sword: חֶרֶב

T

table: שֻׁלְחָן
tablet: לוּחַ
talk, to: דִּבֶּר
task: מְלָאכָה, עֲבוֹדָה
take, to: לָקַח
take across, to: הֶעֱבִיר
take away, to: הֵסִיר

take captive, to: שָׁבָה, לָכַד
take hold of, to: תָּפַשׂ, אָחַז
take prisoner, to: אָסַר, לָכַד
take pleasure in, to: חָפֵץ
teach, to: לִמֵּד
tear, to: קָרַע
tell, to: הִגִּיד
temple: הֵיכָל
ten: עֲשָׂרָה, עֶשֶׂר
tend (flocks), to: רָעָה
terror: אֵימָה
test, to: בָּחַן
that (conj.): כִּי
that (rel.): אֲשֶׁר
the: see §§14, 18, 21
then (at that time): אָז
then (and – –): וְ; (and) so then: וְעַתָּה
thence: מִשָּׁם
there: שָׁם
therein = "in it" or "in them"
there is/are: יֵשׁ
there is/are not: אֵין
therefore: לָכֵן, עַל־כֵּן
thing: מְאוּמָה, דָּבָר
think, to: חָשַׁב
third: שְׁלִישִׁי
three: שְׁלֹשָׁה, שָׁלֹשׁ
thirty: שְׁלֹשִׁים
thousand: אֶלֶף
throne: כִּסֵּא
through: בְּעַד
throw, to: הִשְׁלִיךְ
thrust aside, to: הִטָּה
thus: כֹּה, כֵּן
till, to: עָבַד, חָרַשׁ
time: עֵת, פַּעַם
time; at that – –: אָז
to: אֶל, לְ
today: כַּיּוֹם, הַיּוֹם
together: יַחְדָּו, יַחַד
together with: אֵת, עִם
too (= also): גַּם
too: see § 31

top: רֹאשׁ
touch, to: נָגַע
toward: עַד, לִקְרַאת, אֶל
travel, to: נָסַע
transgress, to: עָבַר
treaty: בְּרִית
tree: עֵץ
tribe: מַטֶּה
trouble: צָרָה, עֳנִי
true: כֵּן
truly: אָמְנָם, אֲבָל
trust, to: בָּטַח, הֶאֱמִין
trustworthy, to be: נֶאֱמַן
truth: אֱמֶת
tunic: כְּתֹנֶת, כֻּתֹּנֶת
turn around, to: סָבַב
turn aside, to: סָר, נָטָה; (tr.) הִטָּה
turn away, to: (tr.) הֵסֵב, הֵסִיר
turn toward, to: פָּנָה
two: שְׁתַּיִם, שְׁנַיִם
twice: פַּעֲמַיִם

U

unanimous: פֶּה אֶחָד
uncircumcised: עָרֵל
under: תַּחַת
understand, to: הֵבִין
understanding: בִּינָה
unimportant: קָטֹן
unless: לוּלֵא, כִּי אִם
until: עַד
until now: עַד־הֵנָּה
up against: עַל־פְּנֵי
up to: עַד
upon: עַל
upright: יָשָׁר
utensil: כְּלִי

V

vain; in – –: לַשָּׁוְא

valley: עֵמֶק
vanity: שָׁוְא
verified, to be: נֶאֱמַן
very: הַרְבֵּה ,מְאֹד
vessel: כְּלִי
vineyard: כֶּרֶם
visit, to: פָּקַד
voice: קוֹל
vow: נֶדֶר
vow, to: נָדַר

W

wake up, to: יִיקַץ
walk, to: הָלַךְ; to – – back & forth: הִתְהַלֵּךְ
wall: קִיר
wander about lost, to: תָּעָה
want to, to: אָבָה ,חָפֵץ
war: מִלְחָמָה
warn, to: הֵעִיד
warrior: גִּבּוֹר
wash, to: רָחַץ
watch, to: נָצַר ,שָׁמַר
water: מַיִם
we: אֲנַחְנוּ
weep, to: בָּכָה
well: בּוֹר ,בְּאֵר
west: יָם westward: יָמָּה
when: כְּ/בְּ + inf.
whence: מֵאַיִן
where?: אֵיפֹה ,אַיֵּה
which: אֲשֶׁר
while: כְּ/בְּ + inf.
whither: אָנָה
who?: מִי
who (rel.): אֲשֶׁר
whole: כֹּל
why?: מַדּוּעַ ,לָמָה ,לָמָּה
wicked: רָשָׁע ,רַע
wide: רָחָב
wife: אִשָּׁה
wilderness: מִדְבָּר
willing, to be: הוֹאִיל ,אָבָה
wisdom: חָכְמָה
wise: חָכָם
with: אֵת ,עִם ,בְּ
withhold, to: חָשַׂךְ
without; use אַיִן
write, to: כָּתַב
woman: אִשָּׁה
wonderful, to be: נִפְלָא
wood: עֵץ
word: דָּבָר
work: מַעֲשֶׂה ,עֲבוֹדָה ,מְלָאכָה; עָשָׂה ,עָבַד
worse: (comp. of "bad")
worthless: רֵיק

Y

year: שָׁנָה
yesterday: אֶתְמוֹל
yet: עוֹד
you: אַתֵּנָה ,אַתֶּן ,אַתֶּם ,אַתְּ ,אַתָּה
young: צָעִיר; – – man: בָּחוּר ,נַעַר

Z

zealous, to be: קִנֵּא

INDEX

References are to the numbered paragraphs.
For the location of verb forms and paradigms see the table at the end of the Index.